LOST

FROM OUR LANDSCAPE

Threatened species of the Northern Territory

Edited by John Woinarski, Chris Pavey, Raelee Kerrigan, Ian Cowie and Simon Ward

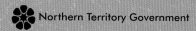

Northern Territory Government

First published in 2007 by the Northern Territory Department of
Natural Resources, Environment and The Arts

National Library of Australia
Cataloguing-in-Publication data:

Lost from our landscape: threatened species
of the Northern Territory.

Bibliography.
Includes index.
ISBN 9781920772468 (pbk.).

1. Endangered species - Northern Territory I. Woinarski,
J. C. Z. (John Casimir Zichy), 1955- . II. Northern
Territory. Dept. of Natural Resources, Environment and
The Arts.

333.9522099429

Requests and inquiries concerning reproduction and rights should
be addressed to:
Department of Natural Resources,
Environment and The Arts
PO Box 496
Palmerston
Northern Territory 0831
Australia

Cover image:
Central Australian desert (near Uluru), Peter Jarver Gallery.

Inset:
Yellow-snouted gecko, Ted Johansen.

Design:
Xpressive, Darwin, Northern Territory

Printing:
Northern Territory Government Printing Office

TABLE OF CONTENTS

ACKNOWLEDGEMENTS

This is a collaborative work, involving many researchers from the Northern Territory Department of Natural Resources, Environment and The Arts and others.

For advice and written contributions, we thank David Albrecht, Martin Armstrong, Kerry Beggs, Tony Bowland, Michael Braby, Kym Brennan, Ray Chatto, Jeff Cole, Dale Dixon, Angus Duguid, Alaric Fisher, Paul Horner, Vince Kessner, Helen Larson, Peter Latz, Milton Lewis, Dave Liddle, Damian Milne, Catherine Nano, Carol Palmer, Helen Puckey, Andrew Schubert, Neil Smit, Simon Stirrat, Rob Taylor, Colin Wilson and Marc Ziembicki.

For permission to use photographs or other illustrations, we thank AIMS, David Albrecht, P. Alderslade, Martin Armstrong, Neil Armstrong, Michael Barritt, Kerry Beggs, Michael Braby, Kym Brennan, Peter Canty, Graeme Chapman, Ray Chatto, Sue Churchill, Laurie Corbett, D. Coughran, Mark Cowan, CSIRO Publishing, Alex Dudley, Alaric Fisher, Ron Firth, Don Franklin, Andrew Gibbons, Roger Jaensch, Ted Johansen, David Jones, Kay Kessing, Helen Larson, Bill Lavarack, D.P. Lewis, Milton Lewis, David Liddle, Jenni Low Choy, Steve McAlpin, Greg Miles, Damian Milne, Ian Morris, B. Mullins, Museum and Art Gallery of the Northern Territory, Museum Victoria, National Library of Australia, P. & M. Nicholas, Monica Osterkamp Madsen, Christopher Palmer, Stirling Peverell, Richard Pillans, Queensland Environmental Protection Agency, P. Rasmussen, Tony Robinson, Kym Schwartskopff, A. Small, C. Spencer, Tom Tarrant, Steve Taylor, Dave Watts and Lochman Transparencies, Sean Webster, Babs and Bert Wells, Western Australian Museum, Richard Willan, Alan Withers and Marc Ziembicki. In a few cases, we were unable to identify original photographers of images held in our corporate collection: in such cases, we apologise for not specifically acknowledging the photographer. Copies of paintings of the lesser bilby and short-tailed hopping-mouse are reproduced by permission of Oxford University Press and Mr Frank Knight (illustrator) from *A Field Guide to Mammals of Australia*, 2nd edition, 2004, Menkhorst and Knight © Oxford University Press, www.oup.com.au.

Felicity Watt collated the maps and illustrations, and Craig Hempel, Phil Hickey and Jane Edwards prepared the final distributional maps.

Kerryn Bastin guided this work through publication with admirable care, tact and interest. We also thank Simon Love for his skill and patience with design.

The information presented here is based on studies, research and observations by many people, including scientific research staff and the general public. Rob Taylor provided a major contribution to the collation of the first collection of the dossiers included here. The administrative support of Dr Greg Leach and Dr David Ritchie has provided the sustenance necessary to this work.

PREFACE

The Northern Territory has a unique and pristine environment. With our natural and beautiful lands, it is no wonder that so many people are drawn to our part of the world. Native plants and animals adorn much of our surrounds, but not all is as it seems.

Many of the plants and animals that were once a feature of our landscape have become extinct. Many others are also threatened. It is up to all Territorians to ensure these plant and animal species don't disappear. The time to act is now.

The Northern Territory Government is committed to maintaining the remaining threatened plant and animal species and has produced this book identifying these threatened species. This book offers Territorians the chance to learn more about our threatened plants and animals, to better understand the problems they face, and to recognise there are environmental limits to what we do.

The plight of some threatened Territory species is quite well known. The Gouldian finch and bilby are high profile species, with broad public appeal and sympathy. But this book shows that threatened species – tiny, large, obscure or charismatic – come in all shapes and sizes. Around 200 species that are faring poorly are listed here. The problems are extensive and generic. We must stop the rot.

Each threatened species tells a story. Each provides some insight into the workings of the environment, and the flaws and disruptions that now change the smooth workings of that environment.

Each provides a lesson that we can learn should we wish to truly achieve sustainability in our livelihood.

I care for the species listed here. They are part of my country, and your country too. The Northern Territory Government is committed to maintaining the essence and health of the lands and seas we share with them. We must ensure development does not come with unwanted or unreasonable environmental cost. These are species that belong to all of us and are not simply a government responsibility. I urge you to use this book to enter the worlds of the species listed here; to see, respect and understand their lives and problems; and to help them. They have just as much right to be here as we do.

MARION SCRYMGOUR
Minister for Parks and Wildlife

INTRODUCTION

The Northern Territory is one of the most undeveloped areas in the world. Its natural environments are vast and its population is small. Its wildlife and landscapes continue to be a major drawcard for tourists and a source of pride and wonderment for locals. Many plant and animal species that have disappeared or declined from their former ranges in more developed areas of southern Australia remain common in the Northern Territory.

Given these features, it comes as a surprise to many that the Northern Territory does face some major conservation challenges. One of these challenges is to protect plant and animal species that are in decline and/or have very small populations and/or are restricted to very small areas.

These species are part of our heritage, part of the unique Territory environment; and our society has a responsibility for sharing this land with them. In some cases, these species are also important in the lifestyle and spiritual beliefs of Indigenous Territorians. In some cases, the decline of these species provides a warning to us, that there are things awry in our environment or its management.

This book provides information about the Northern Territory's threatened species. We want Territorians and visitors to learn about these species and the problems that they face, to help in efforts to maintain and foster these species,

and to share information about them. We also want future generations to have the opportunity to see them.

WHAT IS A THREATENED SPECIES?

Throughout the world, government conservation agencies maintain lists of plant and animal species that they recognise as threatened. Most of these lists relate to internationally accepted guidelines and criteria for listing, and particularly to those of the International Union for the Conservation of Nature (IUCN). These criteria rate and categorise the likelihood of a species becoming extinct.

Two listings are relevant to the Northern Territory, one maintained by the Australian Government (under the *Environment Protection and Biodiversity Conservation Act 1999*: the EPBC Act) and the other by the Northern Territory Government (under the *Territory Parks and Wildlife Conservation Act 2000*). The listings are similar, but there are also many inconsistencies.

The Australian listing is based on the national status of the species and this categorisation applies uniformly across all states and territories within the species' range. This listing includes the categories of Extinct, Extinct in the Wild, Critically Endangered, Endangered, Vulnerable and Conservation Dependent.

Allocation to these categories is based on an adapted version of IUCN criteria (Table I on page 10). The process of listing comprises nomination (by the public or any interested

party), assessment by an independent expert body (the Threatened Species Scientific Committee: TSSC), public comment, recommendation by the TSSC, and approval by the Australian Minister for the Environment and Water Resources. The EPBC Act also allows listing of threatened ecological communities. However, at the time of writing (April 2007), no such listed threatened ecological communities exist in the Northern Territory.

The Northern Territory listing is based directly on the application of the IUCN version 3.1 criteria (Table II on page 11), and includes the categories Extinct, Extinct in the Wild, Critically Endangered, Endangered, Vulnerable, Near Threatened, Least Concern and Data Deficient. The process of listing comprises comprehensive assessment of all Territory biota (at least for the species for which there is adequate information available) by experts within the Department of Natural Resources, Environment and The Arts (NRETA), public comment, recommendation by NRETA (with additional advice where appropriate from external experts), and consent by the Administrator of the Northern Territory. The list is comprehensively reviewed at approximately five year intervals. The *Territory Parks and Wildlife Conservation Act* does not provide for listing of threatened ecological communities.

Note that the term **threatened** is conventionally used to apply to species in any of the categories Critically Endangered, Endangered and Vulnerable.

Lists of threatened species change with time, and some species may be included as threatened on the Australian list but not the Northern Territory list, and vice-versa. This inconsistency can be frustrating and confusing. Changes over time may reflect:

- deteriorating conservation outlook;
- improving conservation outlook;
- the availability of additional information;
- taxonomic change; or
- misapplication of criteria at initial assessment.

Discrepancies between Australian and Northern Territory listings may be because:

- of minor differences in the criteria (and their application) used in assessments;
- of differences in the amount of information available at the time of assessments;
- species may be declining or restricted in their Australian range outside the Territory, but be more secure in the Territory (an example is the olive ridley turtle); or
- species may be declining or restricted in the Territory but more secure in their broader Australian range beyond the Territory (an example is the emu).

Because lists of threatened species change, the information presented in this book may become less current with time. Continually updated lists of threatened species can be found on the websites of the Department of Environment and Water Resources (for nationally-listed species: www.environment.gov.au/biodiversity/threatened)

and the Department of Natural Resources Environment and The Arts (for Northern Territory-listed species: www.nt.gov.au/threatenedspecies).

Beyond the two main threatened species listings considered in this book, there are other lists of threatened and significant plant and animal species. The most notable of these are the world wide lists collated by the IUCN (the "Red List": www.iucnredlist.org); lists of wildlife species for which international trade is banned or tightly regulated (the Convention on the International Trade in Endangered Species ("CITES"): www.cites.org/eng/disc/species); and bilateral and other agreements for the protection of migratory species (notably the Japan-Australia Migratory Bird Agreement (JAMBA); the China-Australia Migratory Bird Agreement (CAMBA); and the Convention on the Conservation of Migratory Species of Wild Animals ("Bonn Convention")).

Some of the species listed as threatened under these other lists occur in the Territory, but are not recognised as threatened under either Australian or Territory legislation. One such example is the dugong (*Dugong dugon*), listed as Vulnerable on the IUCN Red List, but not considered threatened at the national or Territory level. In part, this is because the dugong also occurs in 47 other countries, and the IUCN listing must consider its status across this much broader range. In part, the disparity in listing also reflects some differences in qualification criteria and recency

of assessment. For species such as the dugong, the Territory offers a conservation opportunity of international significance, for the Territory has one of the largest and most secure populations of this otherwise generally declining species. We still have what other countries have lost.

WHY ARE SPECIES THREATENED?

Ecological systems do not remain constant. They change according to climate variation, to the advent of newly-colonising species, and to the way the land is managed. The collection of plants and animals that we see in the Northern Territory today is different to what was here a million years ago, ten thousand years ago or even one hundred years ago. Some species, such as cycads, have existed here for millions of years. Others, such as dingoes, have a far more recent history. Scattered collections of bones are all that remains of some of the most impressive animals that ever lived in the Territory, like mihirungs, the giant flightless birds that would have dwarfed emus; crocodiles and goannas far larger than the largest crocodile alive now; and diprotodons, marsupial herbivores the size of a small car.

Aboriginal rock art, and mummified carcasses, show that humans shared this land with thylacines and Tasmanian devils. These probably became extinct in the Northern Territory sometime in the last 10 000 years. Indeed, many of the largest and most distinctive species in our fauna disappeared between about 10 000 and 40 000 years ago.

The cause of such prehistoric losses is uncertain and contested, indeed effectively unprovable. The most recent review and assessment (Johnson C. (2006) *Australia's mammal extinctions: a 50,000-year history.* (Cambridge University Press)) concludes that the most likely cause was over-hunting by people. But others have suggested that the most potent cause was environmental change, itself driven by a changed climate and/or the imposition of Aboriginal fire regimes.

The extent of change to our environments and their plant and animal communities increased dramatically with European settlement of Australia. Europeans brought foxes and cats, efficient predators against which many of our native mammals, and some ground-dwelling birds such as the night parrot, proved highly susceptible. A very wide range of herbivorous mammals, including cattle, water buffalo, rabbits, camels, horses, donkeys, sheep and goats, were introduced, or found their own way, across much of Australia. Their grazing pressure diminished some preferred or sensitive plants (and the native animals that may have been linked to them), altered the composition of vegetation communities and changed the timing and patterning of seed, fruit and leaf availability to which many native herbivores had adapted. Other exotic animals brought to Australia are now affecting Northern Territory wildlife directly or through their impacts on the environment, including species like the cane toad, mosquito

fish, European honeybee, many ants and several exotic pigeons and doves.

European settlers also brought a vast range of foreign plants to the Northern Territory, sometimes accidentally, often on purpose. The introduction of many of these was designed to change the natural landscapes, to make it more suitable for livestock, or for ornament. Some of these plants, such as mission grass, gamba grass, buffel grass, para grass, mimosa and athel pine, have spread rapidly and altered ecological systems to such an extent that they now threaten some native plant and animal species. Some continue to be deliberately spread into native vegetation.

European settlers, and their plants and animals, have also brought a range of parasites and diseases. At least some of these have probably affected some of the Northern Territory's native plants and animals, but there is little information available to assess the extent and severity of any such impacts.

Either deliberately or by default (through breakdown of traditional Aboriginal management), European settlement of the Territory also led to broad-scale and major changes in fire regimes. Over tens of thousands of years of relatively consistent imposition of Aboriginal fire regimes, many Territory environments and species had developed an equilibrium maintained by characteristics of that regime. Once the pattern of burning was

interrupted and changed, that environmental patterning became unstable. In any environmental change, there will be some species that will benefit and others that will be disadvantaged. If species are so disadvantaged over much of their range, they will decline and perhaps face extinction. It is such species that we consider in this book.

WHY WORRY ABOUT THREATENED SPECIES?

Some of the species listed here, such as tiny snails, obscure plants and nondescript lizards, have little public appeal. Why should our society concern itself with them?

This question is a philosophical and moral one, as much as it is a scientific or legal one; and there are a range of answers:

(1) We should consider threatened species because they have an intrinsic right to exist.

(2) We should consider threatened species because unselfishness is a mark of a civilised and moral society. Our role as a dominant species on Earth should come with some responsibility for the welfare of less dominant species.

(3) We should ensure that species do not decline, because we cannot pretend to be living sustainably if our actions (or inactions) result in the decline of other species or the loss of biodiversity.

(4) We should consider threatened species because many have particular real or potential utility to us, and many of them enrich our lives. Some perform irreplaceable ecological services; some may have potential pharmaceutical or other utility; some may have particular significance for Indigenous culture and being; some are simply beautiful adornments to our environment.

(5) We should consider threatened species because their decline marks a flaw in our environmental management. They offer an insight, a guide to better ways of looking after our lands and seas.

(6) We should consider threatened species because there are legal and regulatory obligations to do so. This is so not only in conservation reserves, but in lands of all tenures.

(7) We should consider threatened species because one of the Territory's few unique assets is its largely natural landscapes. Should we besmirch that asset, our lands will be less enticing to tourists and our environments diminished for locals.

(8) We should consider threatened species because we have some moral obligations to pass on to our descendants as much as possible of the environmental legacy we have been bequeathed. These species have existed for hundreds of thousands or millions of years. It should not be in our watch that they die out.

WHAT DOES IT MEAN IF I HAVE A THREATENED SPECIES ON MY LAND?

To many landholders, it is a privilege to have threatened species sharing their property. To others, it is an unwanted burden. To some extent, the occurrence of threatened species on a property may suggest the property is being well managed. But in other cases, the management of the property may itself be a contributing factor in the threatened status of the species.

There are moral, social and legal grounds to consider threatened species within the planning and management of any landholding. In general, the community has a stake and interest in protecting the natural world; it would be an unreasonably selfish act for a single landholder to cause the extinction of a species that happened to occur only on his or her land.

Both the *Environment Protection and Biodiversity Conservation Act* and the *Territory Parks and Wildlife Conservation Act* contain provisions for the explicit protection of threatened species. The EPBC Act regulates against any actions that may have a significant detrimental impact on any listed threatened species. The *Territory Parks and Wildlife Conservation Act* allows for the declaration of areas of essential habitat for threatened species on lands of any tenure. A range of other Acts also directly or indirectly govern the management of threatened species and the lands on which they occur: for example, the *Pastoral Land Act* includes the object of providing

for "*the prevention or minimisation of degradation of or other damage to the land and its indigenous plant and animal life*".

Landholders, community groups, and other bodies can get support for management actions that benefit threatened species on their lands or in areas of their interest, through competitive funding from a range of sources, including the Envirofund of the Natural Heritage Trust (www.nht.gov.au/envirofund), the Northern Territory's EnvironmeNT grant scheme (www.environmentgrants.nt.gov.au), and grants from the Threatened Species Network administered by WWF (wwf.org.au/ourwork/species/tsngrants).

WHERE, WHAT AND HOW MANY?

This report lists 203 threatened plant and animal taxa (refer to Table IV on pages 14-20), comprising:

- 72 plants (about 1.7% of the Northern Territory's known native plant species);
- 35 invertebrates;
- 10 fish (about 1.3% of the Northern Territory's known fish fauna);
- 1 frog (2% of the Northern Territory's frog species);
- 17 reptiles (about 7% of the Northern Territory's reptile species);
- 23 birds (5.5% of the Northern Territory's bird species); and
- 45 mammals (about 30% of the Northern Territory's native mammal species).

These species occur in all land tenures, and in all regions. Some are largely restricted to in and around our few built-up areas, others are in the most remote areas. Some occur only on pastoral lands, some only on Aboriginal lands. The regions with the most threatened species include the sandstone plateau of western Arnhem Land, the Tiwi Islands and the MacDonnell Ranges.

Some threatened species (notably including some land snails and plants) have extremely restricted distributions - in some cases, less than a few hectares. Other threatened species (such as emus and bustards) remain widespread.

Many threatened species are represented in the Northern Territory's national parks and conservation reserves (refer to Table III on page 13), giving them some protection against potentially threatening factors. Some national parks are particularly important for individual threatened species, or groups of species. Kakadu National Park has the largest number of threatened species, other national parks with relatively many threatened species include West MacDonnells, Garig Gunak Barlu, Finke Gorge, Nitmiluk and Gregory. However, 82 species, which is about 44% of the non-extinct threatened species, are not in any national park or conservation reserve.

WHAT ARE WE DOING ABOUT THREATENED SPECIES?

Threatened species need help and there are many ways that people can help.

It is very important to generate public awareness about threatened species. This book is one way of achieving that. It should provide landholders, natural resource managers, developers, and others interested in the Northern Territory's environments with an accessible digest of information about these species, the problems they face, and how we can help to improve their outlook.

More information about the Northern Territory's threatened species is also available from the Threatened Species Network (wwf.org.au/ourwork/species/tsn), and from the relevant Territory and national agencies (the Department of Natural Resources, Environment and The Arts, and the Department of the Environment and Water Resources, respectively).

There has been a great deal of research into some threatened species, such as the Gouldian finch, mala and bilby over many years, and this has contributed to a large knowledge base that has allowed for the confident development of management recommendations and implementation. But these cases are exceptions. For most threatened species, there is limited information available.

The information vacuum means that our management responses are inevitably blunt and perhaps misguided. Knowledge about threatened species is fundamental to improving their outlook. Such knowledge may not come easily or quickly. Often, threatened species are hard to research - they may be difficult to locate

and study; the factors that affect them may not be readily identified; these factors may interact in complex and composite ways; and it may take many years to understand their response to an array of possible management impositions.

To build up the knowledge base required to manage threatened species with appropriate expertise, research programs need to:
- better describe their distribution and habitat preferences, through broad-ranging and targeted survey;
- better describe their responses to a range of possible threatening factors and management actions;
- better estimate their population size and life history attributes;
- collate all other relevant available information, such as from indigenous ecological knowledge; and
- integrate this information, through mathematical modeling or other appropriate tools, in order to optimise management responses.

We need to keep track of the trends in population size and distribution of individual threatened species so that we can assess the success of management responses, and to continually critically review priorities for remedial action. Monitoring programs are being conducted for some of the Northern Territory's threatened species, but have not been implemented for others. Some species are far easier to monitor than others. For example, it is a relatively simple exercise to make annual counts of the number of all mature and immature palms present at Palm Valley in Finke Gorge National Park, but a far more challenging and expensive task to monitor the abundance of more mobile and less visible species, such as the Butler's dunnart, humpback whale or atlas moth.

Where information is adequate, recovery plans have been developed for many Northern Territory threatened species. These provide a structured set of priorities for management responses, and serve as a basis for funded management actions. These recovery plans are approved by the Commowealth's Minister for the Environment and Water Resources and are available at the website (www.environment.gov.au/biodiversity/threatened/recovery). Recovery plans are being prepared for many other threatened species.

In some cases, there are such apparently insurmountable risks to threatened species in the wild that some individuals have been transferred to captive breeding populations as insurance against catastrophic loss of wild populations. These populations are held in the George Brown Darwin Botanic Gardens, the Territory Wildlife Park and the Alice Springs Desert Park. These populations are important for safeguarding the future of the species and to provide invaluable insight into the biology of the species, and allow for future translocations.

But threatened species will have a future only when wild populations can be sustained. Generally this will mean when the management of fire, exotic animals and/or exotic plants is improved. The species that are now threatened mostly prospered in an age before we introduced so many foreign plants and animals, and when fire regimes were different to what they are now. Across most of the Territory, the enhanced control of exotic plants and animals, and improvements in fire regimes, will benefit most threatened species, and biodiversity more generally. In some cases, especially for highly localised plants and animals, the management of fire or exotic species may need to be highly specific and intensively applied.

As well as these landscape-wide threats, some threatened species occur in areas subjected to, or proposed for, more intensive development. To avoid significant detrimental impacts from such development, it is critical that possible consequences for threatened species are adequately considered in development applications, and that the fate of any affected threatened species is adequately monitored following any development approval.

Threatened species are a major consideration in current environmental impact assessment legislation and regulations.

Threatened species also occur in areas subject to more extensive exploitation, such as on pastoral lands, in Northern Territory fisheries and on lands devoted to military training. The consequences to threatened species of management practices used by these industries are to some degree regulated through impact assessment and reporting on sustainability.

The chances of protecting threatened species will be improved through strategic collaboration between relevant research and management agencies, industry groups, landholders and an informed and interested public. The protection of threatened species cannot be, and should not be, the sole responsibility of particular government agencies; it is something to which we can all contribute.

GETTING TO SPECIES BEFORE THEY BECOME THREATENED

Threatened species are like the Accident and Emergency section in a health system. They may demand the most attention and most immediate response. But there are many other parts of the system that need to be considered, and often may produce the most cost-effective results. Over the longer term, biodiversity will fare better if we can protect the species before their status deteriorates so much that they qualify as threatened. The sustenance of threatened species may be a very costly, long-term and difficult process. It is usually far easier and cheaper to manage and conserve species while they remain unthreatened.

To prevent more species becoming threatened, our lands and waters need to be managed sustainably and with care and expertise. We are fortunate in inheriting a land that is fundamentally whole and natural.

But as the Northern Territory's population and industry expands, our impact on our natural systems is likely to become more and more pronounced.

ORGANISATION OF THIS BOOK

The bulk of this book comprises individual information dossiers for every threatened species known from the Northern Territory. These are arranged in the order: plants (by alphabetical order of scientific names), invertebrates other than insects (by alphabetical order of scientific names), then insects, fish, frogs, reptiles, birds and mammals (each by taxonomic order).

For each species, we list the current (2007) conservation status under national (EPBC Act) and Northern Territory legislation; a brief description (in some cases, including a reference to where a more comprehensive description may be available); an illustration (where possible); information on the distribution (in the Northern Territory and in some cases, beyond); a distributional map (for the Northern Territory component of its distribution only: note that in some cases, this may not exactly match the written description of distribution, for example, where we do not hold precise records in our distributional data base); the Northern Territory conservation reserves from which the species has been reported; some information on ecology; the rationale for the conservation status assigned to the species; the factors that may be threatening the species; and brief notes on the research and management priorities for the species.

Some of the terms used in the information dossiers presented in this book have specialised and obscure meanings. Wherever possible, we have attempted to write these accounts as accessibly as possible, but in some cases, technical terms have been unavoidable. To help avoid confusion, we present a glossary of terms on page 268.

NAMES

Most plants and animals listed in this book have well established scientific names. These comprise a generic name (with its first letter capitalised) followed by a specific name (uncapitalised), for example *Conilurus penicillatus*. In some cases, there may be well defined variation within a species, almost always related to separate geographic populations. These distinctions may be recognised at subspecific level, and labelled with a third name, for example *Trichosurus vulpecula arnhemensis* refers to the form of brush-tailed possum occurring in the Top End, whereas *Trichosurus vulpecula vulpecula* refers to the form of brush-tailed possum occurring in central Australia (and also occurring in south-eastern and eastern Australia). The different subspecies may have very different conservation outlooks and status.

In some cases, a species may have been recognised by appropriate authorities but not yet officially named. In such cases, the species is temporarily described by association with a particular numbered scientific specimen, with a descriptor usually referring to the collection location or notable feature. An example is the plant *Eremophila* sp. Rainbow Valley, where Rainbow Valley is the location from which the first specimen was collected.

Scientific names are not always constant. With taxonomic review, they may change. What we once thought was a single species may prove to be a collection of two or more related species. What we once thought was a distinct species may prove to be just part of another species. The Darwin palm *Ptychosperma bleeseri* is one such case. Until recent taxonomic scrutiny it was thought to be a distinct species restricted to the Northern Territory, however, it is now thought to be so closely related to another palm that grows in Queensland and New Guinea, that the two species have been combined (as *Ptychosperma macarthurii*). Wherever possible, we have described recent taxonomic changes so that it is possible to relate current names to other recent synonyms.

While most vertebrates listed here have common names, this is generally not the case for plants and some invertebrate groups.

INFORMATION AVAILABILITY

For many species, we know very little about the total population size, the limits of geographic range, and the rate of change of populations, so allocation to threatened categories will always be based on estimates and best judgements. In some cases, the information is simply too meagre to allow an assessment to be made with any confidence. In the Northern Territory lists, these species are coded as Data Deficient. With more information available, at least some of these species may be found to be threatened. A listing of Data Deficient species is provided in Appendix A.

Some Northern Territory species have not been evaluated against threatened criteria. These include all fungi, many invertebrates, some plants, and some vagrants, which are species occurring in the Territory infrequently and irregularly. We don't have a comprehensive catalogue of names of Territory invertebrate species yet, let alone information from which to assess their status, and our knowledge base for marine species is generally less than for terrestrial species.

In the dossiers included here, we have used best available information and judgement to suggest what the most likely threats are, but in many cases far more detailed experimental investigation will be required before we can be certain about how different factors affect these threatened species.

WHAT IF I HAVE INFORMATION ON THREATENED SPECIES?

Increasing our knowledge on threatened species will allow for more precise determination of status, more accurate assessment of threats, and better prioritisation of management. We therefore encourage anyone with information on threatened species to contact the Department of Natural Resources, Environment and The Arts offices:

Darwin

PO Box 496, Palmerston,
Northern Territory, 0831
08 8995 5000

Alice Springs

PO Box 1120, Alice Springs,
Northern Territory, 0871
08 8951 8250

Katherine

PO Box 344, Katherine,
Northern Territory, 0851
08 8973 8888

Those interested in volunteering for, and collaborating in, research work and management of threatened species may also contact the:

Volunteer Coordinator

Parks and Wildlife Service
PO Box 496, Palmerston,
Northern Territory, 0831
08 8999 4555
volunteer.nreta@nt.gov.au

The Threatened Species Network may also help provide opportunities to work with or protect threatened species. Contacts are:

TSN Coordinator (northern region)
GPO Box 1268, Darwin,
Northern Territory, 0801
08 8941 7554

TSN Coordinator (southern region)
PO Box 2796, Alice Springs,
Northern Territory, 0871
08 8952 1541

TABLE I.

Qualification criteria for categorisation of threatened species in Australia under the EPBC Act; these criteria are loosely based on IUCN criteria. Note that the full description of the criteria is given for critically endangered (CR) status. For endangered (EN) and vulnerable (VU) status, only the variation from the CR description is given, with this variation marked by bolding and highlighting. Note that only one criterion needs to be met to qualify for listing.

CR	EN	VU
1. It has undergone, is suspected to have undergone or is likely to undergo in the near future a **very severe** reduction in numbers	severe	substantial
2. Its geographic distribution is precarious for the survival of the species and is **very restricted.**	restricted	limited
3. The estimated total number of mature individuals is **very low**; and	low	limited
(a) evidence suggests that the number will continue to decline at a **very high rate;** or (b) the number is likely to continue to decline and its geographic distribution is precarious for its survival.	high	substantial
4. The estimated total number of mature individuals is **extremely low**	very low	low
5. The probability of its extinction in the wild is **at least 50% in the immediate future**	20% in the near future	10% in the medium term future

TABLE II.

Qualification criteria for categorisation of threatened species under Northern Territory legislation (IUCN criteria version 3.1). Note that the full description of the criteria is given for critically endangered (CR) status. For endangered (EN) and vulnerable (VU) status, only the variation from the CR description is given, with this variation marked by bolding and highlighting. Note that only one criterion needs to be met to qualify for listing.

	CR	EN	VU
A. Reduction in population size based on any of the following:	1. An observed, inferred or suspected population size reduction of **more than 90%** over the last 10 years or three generations, whichever is the longer, where the causes of the reduction are clearly reversible AND understood AND ceased, based on (and specifying) any of the following: (a) direct observation; (b) an index of abundance appropriate to the taxon; (c) a decline in area of occupancy, extent of occurrence and/or quality of habitat; (d) actual or potential levels of exploitation; (e) the effects of introduced taxa, hybridization, pathogens, pollutants, competitors or parasites.	70%	50%
	2. An observed, estimated, inferred or suspected population size reduction of **more than 80%** over the last 10 years or three generations, whichever is the longer, where the reduction or its causes may not have ceased OR may not be understood OR may not be reversible, based on (and specifying) any of (a) to (e) under A1.	50%	30%
	3. A population size reduction of **more than 80%**, projected or suspected to be met within the next 10 years or three generations, whichever is the longer (up to a maximum of 100 years), based on (and specifying) any of (b) to (e) under A1.	50%	30%
	4. An observed, estimated, inferred or suspected population size reduction of **more than 80%** over any 10 year or three generation period, whichever is longer (up to a maximum of 100 years in the future), where the time period must include both the past and the future, and where the reduction or its causes may not have ceased OR may not be understood OR may not be reversible, based on (and specifying) any of (a) to (e) under A1.	50%	30%
B. Geographic range in the form of either B1 (extent of occurrence) OR B2 (area of occupancy) OR both:	1. Extent of occurrence estimated to be **less than 100 km²**, and estimates indicating at least two of a-c: a. Severely fragmented or known to exist at **only a single location.** b. Continuing decline, observed, inferred or projected, in any of the following: (i) extent of occurrence; (ii) area of occupancy; (iii) area, extent and/or quality of habitat; (iv) number of locations or subpopulations; (v) number of mature individuals.	5000 km² no more than five locations	20 000 km² no more than 10 locations

TABLE II. *cont...*

	CR	EN	VU

B. Geographic range in the form of either B1 (extent of occurrence) OR B2 (area of occupancy) OR both:	1. cont...
	  c. Extreme fluctuations in any of the following:
	    (i) extent of occurrence;
	    (ii) area of occupancy;
	    (iii) number of locations or subpopulations;
	    (iv) number of mature individuals.		

	2. Area of occupancy estimated to be **less than 10 km²**, and estimates indicating at least two of a-c:
	  a. Severely fragmented or known to exist at **only a single location.**
	  b. Continuing decline, observed, inferred or projected, in any of the following:
	    (i) extent of occurrence;
	    (ii) area of occupancy;
	    (iii) area, extent and/or quality of habitat;
	    (iv) number of locations or subpopulations;
	    (v) number of mature individuals.
	  c. Extreme fluctuations in any of the following:
	    (i) extent of occurrence;
	    (ii) area of occupancy;
	    (iii) number of locations or subpopulations;
	    (iv) number of mature individuals.
		500 km²
		
		no more than five locations
			2000 km²
			
			no more than 10 locations

C. Population size estimated to number **fewer than 250** mature individuals and either:		2500	10 000
	1. An estimated continuing decline of at least **25% within three years or one generation,** whichever is longer (up to a maximum of 100 years in the future); OR	20% within five years or two generations	10% within 10 years or three generations

	2. A continuing decline, observed, projected or inferred, in numbers of mature individuals AND at least one of the following (a-b):
	  a. Population structure in the form of one of the following:
	    (i) no subpopulation estimated to contain more than **50** mature individuals, OR
	    (ii) **at least 90%** of mature individuals in one subpopulation;
	  b. Extreme fluctuation in number of mature individuals.
		250
		95%
			1000
			all

D. Population size estimated to number fewer than **50** mature individuals		250	1000*
E. Quantitative analysis showing the probability of extinction in the wild is at least **50% within 10 years or three generations**, whichever is the longer (up to a maximum of 100 years)		20% within 20 years or five generations	10% within 100 years

* or (for VU only): 2. *Population with a very restricted area of occupancy (typically less than 20 km²) or number of locations (typically five or fewer) such that it is prone to the effects of human activities or stochastic events within a very short time period in an uncertain future, and is thus capable of becoming Critically Endangered or even Extinct in a very short time period.*

TABLE III.

(a) The occurrence of threatened species on Northern Territory national parks and conservation reserves. Note that this table lists the number of national parks from which each threatened species has been recorded (e.g. 35 plant species are known from no conservation reserves, 29 plant species are known from one conservation reserve only). EX = extinct

NUMBER OF RESERVES	TAXONOMIC GROUP						
	PLANTS	INVERTEBRATES	FISH	FROGS	REPTILES	BIRDS	MAMMALS
0	35	12	3	1	4	10	11
1	29	18	6	0	3	2	10
2	4	4	1	0	3	2	6
3	2	0	0	0	1	2	1
4	0	1	0	0	4	1	0
5+	2	0	0	0	2	5	2
TOTAL	**72**	**35**	**10**	**1**	**17**	**22** (+1EX)	**30** (+15 EX)

(b) National Parks and conservation reserves with the largest numbers of threatened species in the Northern Territory.

Abbreviations: P=plant; I=invertebrate; FI=fish; FR=frog; R=reptile; B=bird; M=mammal.

RESERVE NAME	NUMBER OF THREATENED SPECIES							
	P	I	FI	FR	R	B	M	TOTAL
Kakadu	9	0	4	0	10	9	8	**40**
West MacDonnell	7	11	1	0	1	3	4	**27**
Garig Gunak Barlu	2	2	1	0	8	4	4	**21**
Nitmiluk	3	0	0	0	2	8	1	**14**
Gregory	3	2	1	0	2	6	0	**14**
Finke Gorge	5	5	1	0	1	0	1	**13**
Litchfield	2	0	0	0	2	4	3	**11**
Mary River	3	0	0	0	3	4	1	**11**
Watarrka	3	1	0	0	1	2	2	**9**
Uluru – Kata Tjuta	1	0	0	0	1	3	3	**8**

TABLE IV.

Listing of all Northern Territory plant and animal taxa that are recognised as threatened at national (EPBC Act) or Northern Territory level. Conservation status codes: EX extinct; EX(W) extinct in the wild; CR critically endangered; EN endangered; VU vulnerable; DD data deficient; NT near threatened; LC least concern; NE not evaluated. Note that species are arranged in taxonomic order. Note that recent taxonomic changes render the conservation status applied nationally to the mulgaras uncertain.

GENUS	SPECIES	SUBSPECIES (VARIETY)	FAMILY	COMMON NAME	NORTHERN TERRITORY STATUS	EPBCA STATUS
PLANTS						
Angiopteris	evecta		Marattiaceae		VU	
Cephalomanes	obscurum		Hymenophyllaceae		EN	
Gleichenia	sp. Victoria River		Gleicheniaceae		VU	
Sticherus	flabellatus	compactus	Gleicheniaceae		VU	
Adiantum	capillus-veneris		Adiantaceae	Venus-hair fern, Maidenhair fern, Avenca	VU	
Cycas	armstrongii		Cycadaceae		VU	
Macrozamia	macdonnellii		Zamiaceae	MacDonnell Ranges Cycad	NT	VU
Mitrella	sp. Melville Island		Annonaceae		VU	VU
Xylopia	sp. Melville Island		Annonaceae		EN	EN
Cryptocarya	hypospodia		Lauraceae		EN	
Endiandra	limnophila		Lauraceae		VU	
Hernandia	nymphaeifolia		Hernandiaceae		VU	
Garcinia	warrenii		Clusiaceae		EN	
Elaeocarpus	miegei		Elaeocarpaceae		CR	
Schoutenia	ovata		Tiliaceae		VU	
Helicteres	sp. Glenluckie Creek		Sterculiaceae		EN	EN
Hibiscus	brennanii		Malvaceae		VU	VU
Hibiscus	cravenii		Malvaceae		VU	VU
Mukia	sp. Tobermorey Station		Cucurbitaceae		VU	
Acacia	latzii		Mimosaceae	Tjilpi Wattle, Latz's Wattle	VU	VU
Acacia	peuce		Mimosaceae	Waddy-Wood	EN	VU
Acacia	pickardii		Mimosaceae	Bird's Nest Wattle	VU	VU
Acacia	praetermissa		Mimosaceae		VU	VU
Acacia	undoolyana		Mimosaceae	Sickle-leaf Wattle , Undoolya Wattle	VU	VU
Acacia	sp. Graveside Gorge		Mimosaceae		CR	CR
Pternandra	coerulescens		Melastomaceae		VU	
Lithomyrtus	linariifolia		Myrtaceae		VU	
Thryptomene	hexandra		Myrtaceae	Palm Valley Myrtle	VU	VU
Dendromyza	reinwardtiana		Santalaceae		VU	

TABLE IV. *cont...*

GENUS	SPECIES	SUBSPECIES (VARIETY)	FAMILY	COMMON NAME	NORTHERN TERRITORY STATUS	EPBCA STATUS
PLANTS...						
Santalum	*acuminatum*		Santalaceae	Quandong	VU	
Ricinocarpos	*gloria-medii*		Euphorbiaceae	Glory of the Centre	VU	VU
Sauropus	*filicinus*		Euphorbiaceae		DD	VU
Toechima	sp. East Alligator		Sapindaceae		EN	EN
Boronia	*quadrilata*		Rutaceae		VU	VU
Boronia	*viridiflora*		Rutaceae		VU	VU
Actinotus	*schwarzii*		Apiaceae	Desert Flannel Flower	VU	VU
Platysace	*saxatilis*		Apiaceae		VU	
Hoya	*australis*	*oramicola*	Asclepiadaceae		VU	VU
Solanum	*carduiforme*		Solanaceae		DD	VU
Ipomoea	sp. Stirling		Convolvulaceae	Giant Sweet Potato	VU	VU
Wrixonia	*schultzii*		Lamiaceae		VU	VU
Eremophila	sp. Rainbow Valley		Myoporaceae	Rainbow Vallley Fuschia Bush	VU	VU
Utricularia	*dunstaniae*		Lentibulariaceae		VU	
Utricularia	*singeriana*		Lentibulariaceae		VU	
Goodenia	*quadrifida*		Goodeniaceae		DD	VU
Tarennoidea	*wallichii*		Rubiaceae		EN	
Minuria	*tridens*		Asteraceae		VU	VU
Olearia	*macdonnellensis*		Asteraceae		VU	VU
Arenga	*australasica*		Areacaceae	Australian Arenga Palm	DD	VU
Livistona	*mariae*	*mariae*	Arecaceae	Palm Valley Palm, Red Cabbage Palm	VU	VU
Ptychosperma	*macarthurii*		Arecaceae	Darwin Palm	EN	EN
Freycinetia	*excelsa*		Pandanaceae		VU	
Freycinetia	*percostata*		Pandanaceae		VU	
Typhonium	*jonesii*		Araceae		EN	EN
Typhonium	*mirabile*		Araceae		EN	EN
Typhonium	*taylori*		Araceae		EN	EN
Baumea	*arthophylla*		Cyperaceae		EN	
Bolboschoenus	*caldwellii*		Cyperaceae	Marsh Club-rush	EN	
Eleocharis	*papillosa*		Cyperaceae	Dwarf Desert Spike-rush	VU	VU
Eleocharis	*retroflexa*		Cyperaceae		DD	VU
Mapania	*macrocephala*		Cyperaceae		VU	
Ectrosia	*blakei*		Poaceae		DD	VU

TABLE IV. *cont...*

GENUS	SPECIES	SUBSPECIES (VARIETY)	FAMILY	COMMON NAME	NORTHERN TERRITORY STATUS	EPBCA STATUS
PLANTS...						
Triodia	*fitzgeraldii*		Poaceae		VU	
Monochoria	*hastata*		Pontederiaceae		VU	
Burmannia	sp. Bathurst Island		Burmanniaceae		EN	EN
Calochilus	*caeruleus*		Orchidaceae		VU	
Habenaria	*rumphii*		Orchidaceae		EN	
Luisia	*teretifolia*		Orchidaceae		VU	
Malaxis	*latifolia*		Orchidaceae		VU	
Malaxis	*marsupichila*		Orchidaceae		VU	
Thrixspermum	*congestum*		Orchidaceae		VU	
Zeuxine	*oblonga*		Orchidaceae		VU	
INVERTEBRATES						
Pillomena	*aemula*		Charopidae		VU	
Bothriembryon	*spenceri*		Bulimulidae	Spencer's Land Snail	VU	
Amphidromus	*cognatus*		Camaenidae	Cognate Land Snail	VU	
Basedowena	*squamulosa*		Camaenidae		VU	
Dirutrachia	*sublevata*		Camaenidae		VU	
Divellomelon	*hillieri*		Camaenidae		VU	
Granulomelon	*arcigerens*		Camaenidae	West MacDonnell's Land Snail	VU	
Granulomelon	*gilleni*		Camaenidae	Gillen Ceek Land Snail	VU	
Granulomelon	*grandituberculatum*		Camaenidae		VU	
Mesodontrachia	*desmonda*		Camaenidae	Desmond's Land Snail	EN	
Mesodontrachia	*fitzroyana*		Camaenidae	Fitzroy Land Snail	CR	EN
Ordtrachia	*australis*		Camaenidae		EN	
Ordtrachia	*septentrionalis*		Camaenidae		EN	
Prototrachia	*sedula*		Camaenidae		VU	
Semotrachia	*caupona*		Camaenidae		VU	
Semotrachia	*elleryi*		Camaenidae	Ellery Gorge Land Snail	VU	
Semotrachia	*emilia*		Camaenidae	Emile's Land Snail	VU	
Semotrachia	*esau*		Camaenidae		VU	
Semotrachia	*euzyga*		Camaenidae		EN	EN
Semotrachia	*filixiana*		Camaenidae		VU	
Semotrachia	*huckittana*		Camaenidae		VU	
Semotrachia	*illarana*		Camaenidae		VU	

TABLE IV. *cont...*

GENUS	SPECIES	SUBSPECIES (VARIETY)	FAMILY	COMMON NAME	NORTHERN TERRITORY STATUS	EPBCA STATUS
INVERTEBRATES...						
Semotrachia	*jessieana*		Camaenidae		VU	
Semotrachia	*jinkana*		Camaenidae		VU	
Semotrachia	*rossana*		Camaenidae		VU	
Semotrachia	*runutjirbana*		Camaenidae	Runutjirbana Land Snail	VU	
Semotrachia	*winneckeana*		Camaenidae	Winnecke Land Snail	VU	
Setobaudinia	*victoriana*		Camaenidae	Victoria's Land Snail	VU	
Sinumelon	*bednalli*		Camaenidae	Bednall's Land Snail	CR	EN
Vidumelon	*wattii*		Camaenidae	Watt's Land Snail	VU	
Trochomorpha	*melvillensis*		Trochomorphidae		VU	
Attacus	*wardi*		Saturniidae	Atlas Moth	EN	
Croitana	*aestiva*		Hesperiidae	Desert Sand-Skipper	EN	EN
Euploea	*alacathoe*	*enastri*	Nymphalidae	Gove Crow	EN	EN
Ogyris	*iphis*	*doddi*	Lycaenidae	Dodd's Azure	EN	
FISH						
Rhincodon	*typus*		Rhincodontidae	Whale Shark	DD	VU
Carcharius	*taurus*		Carcharhinidae	Grey Nurse Shark	DD	CR
Glyphis	sp.A		Carcharhinidae	Speartooth Shark, Bizant River Shark	VU	CR
Glyphis	sp.C		Carcharhinidae	Northern River Shark	EN	EN
Pristis	*clavata*		Pristidae	Dwarf Sawfish	VU	
Pristis	*microdon*		Pristidae	Freshwater Sawfish	VU	VU
Pristis	*zijsron*		Pristidae	Green Sawfish	VU	
Pingalla	*lorentzi*		Terapontidae	Lorentz Grunter	VU	
Scortum	*neili*		Terapontidae	Angalarri Grunter	VU	
Chlamydogobius	*japalpa*		Gobiidae	Finke Goby	VU	
FROGS						
Uperoleia	*daviesae*		Myobatrachidae	Howard River Toadlet	VU	
REPTILES						
Caretta	*caretta*		Cheloniidae	Loggerhead Turtle	EN	EN
Chelonia	*mydas*		Cheloniidae	Green Turtle	LC	VU
Eretmochelys	*imbricata*		Cheloniidae	Hawksbill Turtle	DD	VU
Lepidochelys	*olivacea*		Cheloniidae	Olive Ridley, Pacific Ridley	DD	EN
Natator	*depressus*		Cheloniidae	Flatback Turtle	DD	VU
Dermochelys	*coriacea*		Dermochelyidae	Leatherback Turtle	VU	VU

TABLE IV. *cont...*

GENUS	SPECIES	SUBSPECIES (VARIETY)	FAMILY	COMMON NAME	NORTHERN TERRITORY STATUS	EPBCA STATUS
REPTILES...						
Elseya	lavarackorum		Chelidae	Gulf Snapping Turtle	LC	EN
Diplodactylus	occultus		Gekkonidae	Yellow-snouted Gecko	VU	EN
Ophidiocephalus	taeniatus		Pygopodidae	Bronzeback, Bronzeback Snake-lizard	DD	VU
Varanus	mertensi		Varanidae	Mertens Water Monitor	VU	
Varanus	panoptes		Varanidae	Yellow-spotted Monitor, Northern Sand Goanna, Floodplain Monitor	VU	
Cryptoblepharus	sp. New Year and Oxley Islands		Scincidae		EN	
Ctenotus	rimacola	camptris	Scincidae	VRD Blacksoil Ctenotus	VU	
Egernia	kintorei		Scincidae	Great Desert Skink, Tjakura	VU	VU
Egernia	obiri		Scincidae	Arnhem Land Egernia	EN	EN
Egernia	slateri		Scincidae	Slater's Skink	EN	EN
Morelia	oenpelliensis		Boidae	Oenpelli Python	VU	
BIRDS						
Dromaius	novaehollandiae		Casuariidae	Emu	VU	
Leipoa	ocellata		Megapodiidae	Malleefowl	CR	VU
Fregata	andrewsi		Fregatidae	Christmas Frigatebird, Christmas Island Frigatebird	NE	VU
Erythrotriorchis	radiatus		Accipitridae	Red Goshawk	VU	VU
Ardeotis	australis		Otididae	Australian Bustard	VU	
Pedionomus	torquatus		Pedionomidae	Plains-wanderer	DD	VU
Rostratula	australis		Rostratulidae	Australian Painted Snipe	VU	VU
Geophaps	smithii	smithii	Columbidae	Partridge Pigeon (eastern subspecies)	VU	VU
Polytelis	alexandrae		Psittacidae	Princess Parrot	VU	VU
Pezoporus	occidentalis		Psittacidae	Night Parrot	CR	EN
Tyto	novaehollandiae	melvillensis	Tytonidae	Masked Owl (Tiwi subspecies)	EN	EN
Tyto	novaehollandiae	kimberli	Tytonidae	Masked Owl (north Australian mainland subspecies)	VU	VU
Malurus	coronatus	coronatus	Maluridae	Purple-crowned Fairy-wren (western subspecies)	VU	VU
Amytornis	woodwardi		Maluridae	White-throated Grasswren	VU	
Amytornis	dorotheae		Maluridae	Carpentarian Grasswren	EN	
Amytornis	textilis	modestus	Maluridae	Thick-billed Grasswren (eastern subspecies)	EN	VU
Acanthiza	iredalei	iredalei	Pardalotidae	Slender-billed Thornbill (western subspecies)	EX	VU
Epthianura	crocea	tunneyi	Meliphagidae	Yellow Chat (Alligator River subspecies)	EN	VU
Melanodryas	cucullata	melvillensis	Petroicidae	Hooded Robin (Tiwi subspecies)	EN	EN
Drymodes	superciliaris	colcloughi	Petroicidae	Northern Scrub-robin	DD	EX

TABLE IV. *cont...*

GENUS	SPECIES	SUBSPECIES (VARIETY)	FAMILY	COMMON NAME	NORTHERN TERRITORY STATUS	EPBCA STATUS
BIRDS...						
Falcunculus	*frontatus*	*whitei*	Pachycephalidae	Northern (crested) Shrike-tit	VU	VU
Strepera	*versicolor*	*plumbea*	Artamidae	Grey Currawong (western subspecies)	CR	
Erythrura	*gouldiae*		Passeridae	Gouldian Finch	EN	EN
MAMMALS						
Dasycercus	*blythi*		Dasyuridae	Brush-tailed Mulgara, Mulgara	VU	[EN]
Dasycercus	*cristicauda*		Dasyuridae	Crest-tailed Mulgara, Ampurta	VU	[VU]
Dasyuroides	*byrnei*		Dasyuridae	Kowari	DD	VU
Dasyurus	*geoffroii*		Dasyuridae	Western Quoll, Chuditch	EX	VU
Dasyurus	*hallucatus*		Dasyuridae	Northern Quoll	CR	EN
Phascogale	*calura*		Dasyuridae	Red-tailed Phascogale	EX	EN
Phascogale	*tapoatafa*	*pirata*	Dasyuridae	Northern Brush-tailed Phascogale	VU	
Pseudantechinus	*mimulus*		Dasyuridae	Carpentarian Antechinus	EN	VU
Sminthopsis	*butleri*		Dasyuridae	Butler's Dunnart	VU	VU
Sminthopsis	*longicaudata*		Dasyuridae	Long-tailed Dunnart	VU	
Sminthopsis	*psammophila*		Dasyuridae	Sandhill Dunnart	DD	EN
Myrmecobius	*fasciatus*		Myrmecobiidae	Numbat	EX	VU
Chaeropus	*ecaudatus*		Peramelidae	Pig-footed Bandicoot	EX	EX
Isoodon	*auratus*		Peramelidae	Golden Bandicoot	EN	VU
Perameles	*eremiana*		Peramelidae	Desert Bandicoot	EX	EX
Macrotis	*lagotis*		Thylacomyidae	Greater Bilby, Bilby	VU	VU
Macrotis	*leucura*		Thylacomyidae	Lesser Bilby	EX	EX
Notoryctes	*typhlops*		Notoryctidae	Southern Marsupial Mole, Itjaritjari	VU	EN
Bettongia	*lesueur*	*graii*	Potoroidae	Burrowing Bettong, Boodie (inland subspecies)	EX	EX
Bettongia	*penicillata*		Potoroidae	Brush-tailed Bettong, Woylie	EX	
Lagorchestes	*asomatus*		Macropodidae	Central Hare-wallaby	EX	EX
Lagorchestes	*hirsutus*	central mainland form	Macropodidae	Mala, Rufous Hare-wallaby	EX(W)	EN
Onychogalea	*lunata*		Macropodidae	Crescent Nailtail Wallaby	EX	EX
Petrogale	*lateralis*		Macropodidae	Black-footed Rock-wallaby	NT	VU
Trichosurus	*vulpecula*	*vulpecula*	Phalangeridae	Common Brushtail Possum	EN	
Saccolaimus	*saccolaimus*		Emballonuridae	Bare-rumped Sheathtail Bat	DD	CR
Hipposideros	*inornata*		Hipposideridae	Arnhem Leaf-nosed Bat	VU	
Conilurus	*penicillatus*		Muridae	Brush-tailed Rabbit-rat	VU	

TABLE IV. *cont...*

GENUS	SPECIES	SUBSPECIES (VARIETY)	FAMILY	COMMON NAME	NORTHERN TERRITORY STATUS	EPBCA STATUS
MAMMALS...						
Leporillus	*apicalis*		Muridae	Lesser Stick-nest Rat	EX	EX
Mesembriomys	*macrurus*		Muridae	Golden-backed Tree-rat	CR	VU
Notomys	*amplus*		Muridae	Short-tailed Hopping-mouse	EX	EX
Notomys	*aquilo*		Muridae	Northern Hopping-mouse	VU	VU
Notomys	*cervinus*		Muridae	Fawn Hopping-mouse	EN	VU
Notomys	*fuscus*		Muridae	Dusky Hopping-mouse	EN	VU
Notomys	*longicaudatus*		Muridae	Long-tailed Hopping-mouse	EX	EX
Pseudomys	*australis*		Muridae	Plains Rat	EN	VU
Pseudomys	*fieldi*		Muridae	Shark Bay Mouse, Alice Springs Mouse	EX	VU
Rattus	*sordidus*		Muridae	Canefield Rat	VU	
Xeromys	*myoides*		Muridae	False Water-rat, Water Mouse	DD	VU
Zyzomys	*maini*		Muridae	Arnhem Rock-rat	VU	VU
Zyzomys	*palatalis*		Muridae	Carpentarian Rock-rat	CR	EN
Zyzomys	*pedunculatus*		Muridae	Central Rock-rat	EN	EN
Balaenoptera	*borealis*		Balaenopteridae	Sei Whale	DD	VU
Balaenoptera	*musculus*		Balaenopteridae	Blue Whale	DD	EN
Megaptera	*novaeangliae*		Balaenopteridae	Humpback Whale	DD	VU

PLANTS ⊢————

Tjilpi wattle,
Latz's wattle
Acacia latzii

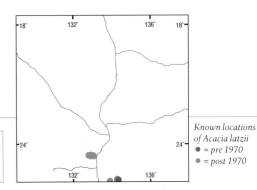

Known locations of Acacia latzii
● = pre 1970
● = post 1970

CONSERVATION STATUS
AUSTRALIA: **VULNERABLE**
NORTHERN TERRITORY: **VULNERABLE**

DESCRIPTION

Acacia latzii is a small tree or shrub to 4 m high with thick rough bark. The flowers are in globular heads, and the pods are linear.

Flowering: April–October; December–January
Fruiting: May–November

DISTRIBUTION

Acacia latzii is known from the Beddome Range (Umbeara, New Crown and Tieyon pastoral leases) and the Bacon Range (Henbury pastoral lease) (White *et al.* 2000). Flora surveys in 2001, as part of the Finke bioregion survey (Neave *et al.* 2004), located outlying stands in both areas. The northern and western limits of this species' range occur within the Northern Territory. The species is also known from, but rare in, South Australia.

Conservation reserves where reported: None

ECOLOGY

Acacia latzii occurs on low hills, typically mesas or buttes, characterised by skeletal soils and occasional steep gullies. It also occurs along small, rocky watercourses associated with hill foot slopes, especially in the Bacon Range. It often grows in pure stands.

CONSERVATION ASSESSMENT

The species is considered **Vulnerable** (under criteria B2ab(v); D2) due to:

- a restricted area of occupancy estimated to be less than 20 km^2;
- fragmented population known from fewer than 10 subpopulations; and
- an inferred population reduction.

The population of *A. latzii* is skewed towards the oldest age classes. There is no evidence of recent recruitment within known stands.

THREATENING PROCESSES

Potential threats include inappropriate fire regimes, trampling and grazing of seedlings by cattle, browsing by rabbits and invasion by buffel grass along creek lines.

CONSERVATION OBJECTIVES AND MANAGEMENT

A national recovery plan for threatened arid zone acacias, including this species, has been prepared (Nano *et al.* 2005). Recovery actions identified for *A. latzii* in the Northern Territory include to:

- carry out targeted surveys for additional populations;
- establish formal protection for significant populations;
- carry out population and habitat monitoring at selected sites;
- implement management strategies for key threatening processes as required;
- undertake research on fire, seed and reproductive biology;
- collect and store seeds from all populations in recognised seed-banks;
- assess genetic population structure; and
- engage Indigenous ecologists to provide input into the recovery process.

Compiled by: Raelee Kerrigan, David Albrecht, Catherine Nano, Chris Pavey [April 2006] / **References:** Nano, C., Harris, M., and Pavey, C. R. (2006). *Recovery plan for threatened Acacias and Ricinocarpos gloria-medii in central Australia, 2006-2011.* (NT Department of Natural Resources Environment and the Arts, Alice Springs.) / Neave, H., Nano, C., Pavey, C., Moyses, M., Clifford, B., Cole, J., Harris, M., and Albrecht, D. (2004). *A resource assessment towards a conservation strategy for the Finke bioregion, NT.* (Department of Infrastructure Planning and Environment, Alice Springs.) / White, M., Albrecht, D., Duguid, A., Latz, P., and Hamilton, M. (2000). *Plant species and sites of botanical significance in the southern bioregions of the Northern Territory. Volume 1: significant vascular plants.* A report to the Australian Heritage Commission. (Arid Lands Environment Centre, Alice Springs.)

Waddy-wood
Acacia peuce

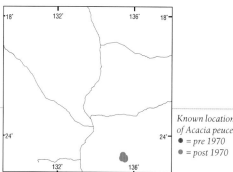

Known locations of Acacia peuce
● = pre 1970
● = post 1970

CONSERVATION STATUS
AUSTRALIA: **VULNERABLE**
NORTHERN TERRITORY: **ENDANGERED**

DESCRIPTION

Acacia peuce is usually an erect tree able to reach heights of up to 18 m. The foliage can be variable: very small seedlings are grass-like and smell strongly; the foliage of immature plants comprises rigid, sharply-pointed and outwardly-directed phyllodes; and that of taller, mature plants is relatively soft and weeping. Johnson (2006) argued that this variable growth habit was a legacy of defensive adaptations to (now extinct) browsing megafauna. The pale yellow flowers are solitary and often inconspicuous, and the pods are large (up to 5 x 20 cm) and flattened. The bark is grey-brown and fibrous, and the timber is very dense with dark red heart-wood. Under laboratory conditions, *A. peuce* germinates readily after most seed-coat treatments (Pryor 1967).

Flowering and the consequent seed set may correlate with large rainfall events.

Flowering: October–March
Fruiting: December–June

DISTRIBUTION

With northerly migration of the Simpson Desert dune fields and the consequent expansion of unsuitable habitat from the south, waddy-wood has retracted to three disjunct populations on the fringes of the Simpson Desert (Deveson 1980; Chuk 1982). Two populations in the east, 300 km apart, occur at Boulia and Birdsville in Queensland.

The third and smallest population is 400 km west in the Mac Clark Conservation Reserve, 230 km south east of Alice Springs (Schabort 2000).

While all three populations are restricted in area, the Northern Territory population is the smallest with a geographic range of around 20 km and area occupied about 10 km². The locations of stands within the known Northern Territory population have been mapped but not accurately georeferenced.

Conservation reserves where reported:
Mac Clark Conservation Reserve

ECOLOGY

Acacia peuce is slow growing and is estimated to live for 500 years or longer. Germination and seedling establishment in *A. peuce* are periodic phenomena that culminate over short periods within cycles of above average rainfall.

It occurs on stony flats or gibber, alluvial flats or low rocky rises.

CONSERVATION ASSESSMENT

In the Northern Territory the species has been classified as **Endangered** (under criteria B1ab(iv,v)+2ab(iv,v)) due to:
• area of occupancy less than 500 km² ;
• extent of occurrence less than 5000 km²;
• reduction in population size over the last 10 years through a decline in area of occupancy and quality of habitat;

• severe fragmentation and decline of subpopulations; and
• a continuing decline of mature individuals.

THREATENING PROCESSES

Fire, cattle impact (through grazing, trampling and rubbing), and lightning strikes are causes of recent deaths.

CONSERVATION OBJECTIVES AND MANAGEMENT

All stands of *Acacia peuce* in Mac Clark Conservation Reserve and adjoining Andado pastoral lease have recently been fenced to protect them from feral and native herbivores.

A national recovery plan for threatened arid zone acacias, including this species, has been prepared (Nano *et al.* 2006). Recovery actions identified for *A. peuce* in the Northern Territory include to:
• carry out population and habitat monitoring to assess trends in population size and assess the impacts of threatening processes;
• implement management strategies for key threatening processes as required;
• undertake research on fire, seed and reproductive biology;
• collect and store seeds from all populations in recognized seed-banks;
• assess genetic population structure; and
• engage Indigenous ecologists to provide input into the recovery process.

Compiled by Tony Bowland, Raelee Kerrigan, Catherine Nano, Chris Pavey [April 2006] / **References:** Chuk, M. (1982). *The status and ecology of Acacia peuce in the Northern Territory.* Technical Report No.2. (Conservation Commission of the Northern Territory, Alice Springs.) / Deveson, E. (1980). *An inventory of Acacia peuce (F.Muell.) stands in Central Australia: Biogeography and ecology.* M.Sc. Thesis. (Australian National University, Canberra.) / Johnson, C. (2006). *Australia's mammal extinctions: a 50,000 year history.* (Cambridge University Press, Cambridge.) / Nano, C., Harris, M., and Pavey, C. R. (2006). *Recovery plan for threatened Acacias and Ricinocarpos gloria-medii in central Australia, 2006-2011.* (NT Department of Natural Resources Environment and the Arts, Alice Springs.) / Pryor, L.D. (1967). *Acacia peuce: a tree for arid areas. Unisylvia* 21, 28-30. / Schabort, I. (2000). *Preliminary analysis of the monitoring of Acacia peuce at Andado - 1979 to 1996.* Unpublished report. 17 pp.

Image courtesy of Connie Spencer

Birds nest wattle
Acacia pickardii

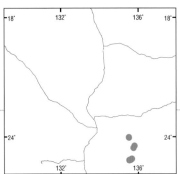

*Known locations
of Acacia pickardii*
● = *pre 1970*
● = *post 1970*

DESCRIPTION

Acacia pickardii is a shrub or small tree 3 to 5 m high. The stipules are spinose and the inflorescence globular. It is distinguished within the *A. victoriae* group by its sharp cylindrical foliage (phyllodes).

Galls commonly grow on the leaves of this species and can be confused as fruit by inexperienced observers.

Flowering: August–November
Fruiting: Very rare and the species is thought to reproduce mainly by root suckering

DISTRIBUTION

In the Northern Territory, it is known from two small, and one larger, populations on the edge of the Simpson Desert (White *et al.* 2000; Maslin 2001). One of these is near, but outside, the Mac Clark Reserve. In South Australia, the species is known from three locations; two in the vicinity of Mt Gason and the third north of Lake Etamunbanie (Pandie Pandie pastoral lease). The western and northern limit of this species' known range occurs within the Northern Territory.

Conservation reserves where reported: None

ECOLOGY

Acacia pickardii typically grows on gibber-covered sand plains and stony rises and low hills, including mesas and tablelands, and adjacent flats. The species usually forms a low woodland or low open woodland with an understorey dominated by either open chenopod shrubland or open grassland. Galls are common on the species and are produced by thrips.

CONSERVATION ASSESSMENT

This species appears to be extremely rare in the Northern Territory. The taxon is **Vulnerable** (under criteria C2a(i); D1+2) due to:
• only several hundred individuals known from only three localities in the Northern Territory;
• no populations greater than 2 km² in extent;
• the total population fewer than 10 000 mature individuals, with no subpopulation containing more than 1000 mature individuals; and
• a decline in the number of mature individuals is inferred due to poor recruitment.

Seedlings have not been observed. Seed set is extremely poor.

THREATENING PROCESSES

Grazing pressure from rabbits may be affecting recruitment (Davies 1995). The species does not occupy all suitable habitats in the region and it is possible that fire may have played a role in fragmenting its distribution. However, surrounding fuel loads are typically very low. Disturbance by cattle is another potential threat.

CONSERVATION OBJECTIVES AND MANAGEMENT

A national recovery plan for threatened arid zone acacias, including this species, has been prepared (Nano *et al.* 2006). Recovery actions identified for *A. pickardii* in the Northern Territory include to:
• carry out targeted surveys for additional populations;
• establish formal protection for significant populations;
• carry out population and habitat monitoring at selected sites;
• implement management strategies for key threatening processes as required;
• undertake research on fire, seed and reproductive biology;
• collect and store seeds from all populations in recognised seed-banks;
• assess genetic population structure; and
• engage Indigenous ecologists to provide input into the recovery process.

Compiled by Raelee Kerrigan, David Albrecht, Catherine Nano, Chris Pavey [April 2006] / **References:** Davies, R.P.J. (1995). *Threatened Plant Species Management in the Arid Pastoral Zone of South Australia.* (Pastoral Management Branch, Department of Environment and Natural Resources, Adelaide.) / Maslin, B.R. (2001). *Acacia pickardii. In: Flora of Australia Volume 11A, Mimosaceae, Acacia part 1.* (eds A.E. Orchard and A.J.G. Wilson), p. 383. (ABRS/CSIRO Publishing, Melbourne.) / Nano, C., Harris, M., and Pavey, C. R. (2006). *Recovery plan for threatened Acacias and Ricinocarpos gloria-medii in central Australia, 2006-2011.* (NT Department of Natural Resources Environment and the Arts, Alice Springs.) / White, M., Albrecht, D., Duguid, A., Latz, P., and Hamilton, M. (2000). *Plant species and sites of botanical significance in the southern bioregions of the Northern Territory. Volume 1: significant vascular plants.* A report to the Australian Heritage Commission. (Arid Lands Environment Centre, Alice Springs.)

Image courtesy of Kym Brennan

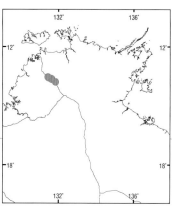

Known locations of Acacia praetermissa
● = pre 1970
● = post 1970

Acacia praetermissa

CONSERVATION STATUS
AUSTRALIA: **VULNERABLE**
NORTHERN TERRITORY: **VULNERABLE**

DESCRIPTION

Acacia praetermissa is a shrub, often multi-stemmed, with stems 50 cm to around 2 m high arising from rootstock. The foliage is bluish and narrow. The flowers are in rod-like spikes on simple axillary stalks, mostly two per axil. This species can be confused with *Acacia oligoneura* and requires careful identification. The flower spikes are bright yellow.

Flowering: January–September
Fruiting: January, March, July–October

DISTRIBUTION

A Northern Territory endemic, this species has been collected from two general roadside localities, near Emerald Springs and Hayes Creek (Dunlop *et al.* 1995). (Note that the map presents three localities, but it is likely that one of these is a result of inaccurate georeferencing).

The extent of occurrence of this species is not easily determined from a minimum convex polygon as the known populations are distributed linearly along the highway for approximately 52 km and less than 1 km in width.

Conservation reserves where reported: None

ECOLOGY

This species usually grows on hillsides in lateritic skeletal soil in eucalypt woodland (Tindale and Kodela 2001).

CONSERVATION ASSESSMENT

Further survey is required to record the area of occupancy and size of these populations; however, collections do indicate that this species is restricted in distribution and abundance. Anecdotal evidence from collectors' notes indicates approximately 30 individuals in a 1 ha search of the population 2 km north of Emerald Springs while between 100 to 250 individuals were estimated in a second population 1 km south of Hayes Creek.

While no extensive targeted searches have been conducted for this species, considerable survey has been conducted in the area, suggesting that existing records reflect this species' restricted distribution and abundance.

This species qualifies as **Vulnerable** (under criteria D1+2) based on:
• restricted distribution and population size estimated to be fewer than 1000 mature individuals; and
• area of occupancy estimated to be less than 20 km².

THREATENING PROCESSES

Areas adjacent to the Stuart Highway are frequently burnt. Collections indicate that the species can re-sprout from a perennial root-base, but the longer term impact of frequent fire on the longevity of adults and on their ability to re-sprout is unknown. No seedling recruitment has been observed in the field during recent collections despite evidence of seed pods. This suggests limited seedling recruitment from which, over time, a potential population decline could be inferred. Although the populations of existing adults appear stable, the long term viability of these populations is unknown and their location, restricted distribution and relatively low numbers make them susceptible to stochastic events such as road widening.

CONSERVATION OBJECTIVES AND MANAGEMENT

Further research is required to establish the extent of the populations, the impact of fire and the likelihood of other threatening processes such as potential clearing for road works. Such research should be associated with a specific monitoring program. Reservation may be required.

Compiled by Raelee Kerrigan, Ian Cowie [April 2006] / **References:** Dunlop, C.R., Leach, G.J., and Cowie, I.D. (1995). *Flora of the Darwin Region. Vol 2.* (Conservation Commission of the Northern Territory, Darwin.) / Tindale, M.D., and Kodela, P.G. (2001). *Acacia praetermissa.* In: *Flora of Australia* Volume 11B, *Mimosaceae, Acacia part 2.* (eds A.E. Orchard and A.J.G. Wilson) pp. 252-253. (ABRS/CSIRO Publishing, Melbourne.)

Sickle-leaf wattle,
Undoolya wattle
Acacia undoolyana

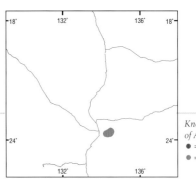

*Known locations
of Acacia undoolyana*
● = *pre 1970*
● = *post 1970*

CONSERVATION STATUS
AUSTRALIA: **VULNERABLE**
NORTHERN TERRITORY: **VULNERABLE**

DESCRIPTION

Acacia undoolyana is a small tree to 11 m high, but rarely exceeding 8 m. It is slow growing and long lived. The leaves (phyllodes) are strongly curved and silvery when fresh. The flowers are in dense rod-like spikes, and the pods are linear.

Flowering: June–September
Fruiting: August–October

DISTRIBUTION

Endemic to a small part of the East MacDonnell Ranges (White *et al.* 2000), *Acacia undoolyana* is among the better surveyed rare plants, being comprehensively surveyed and mapped by Pitts *et al.* (1995). Additional distribution information has since been collected in association with fire management by the Parks and Wildlife Service, from 1997 to 2000. The extent of the confirmed occurrence (minimum convex polygon) is 195 km², and the estimated area of occupancy based on the extent of suitable land units is 16 km², within which the distribution is patchy (Duguid and Schunke 1998).

Conservation reserves where reported:
N'Dhala Gorge Nature Park

ECOLOGY

This species is found predominantly on steep south-facing slopes and gullies of rocky sandstone or quartzite ranges with skeletal acid soils.

However, it also occurs on ridges, plateaus, gently north-facing aspects and on alluvial flats. In most situations it grows in association with spinifex (various *Triodia* species) and often occurs as small patches or groves with relatively low density of spinifex in the understorey. These groves are separated by vegetation with higher densities of spinifex and other shrubs and mallees, which are possibly more fire tolerant. It can form a more continuous open shrubland and rarely a low open woodland.

The species is typically dominant within patches but can occasionally co-occur with mulga (*Acacia aneura*) and cypress pine (*Callitris glaucophylla*). Hill mulga (*Acacia macdonnelliensis*) is only present on one of the various hill ranges and geologies where *A. undoolyana* occurs.

The presence of this species is highly correlated with the presence of bare, outcropping rock. Most of the taller and presumably older 'stands' of *Acacia undoolyana* grow in areas with high proportions of bare, exposed bedrock, including south-facing slopes and gullies. These areas are considered to be naturally fire-protected. Only the most intense wildfires can burn into these sites.

In nursery conditions it reproduces well from the hard coated seeds, which appear to have long-lasting viability. However, seed production is sporadic and probably linked to extreme wet periods. The requirements for successful *in situ* seedling establishment are not well known. There

has been minimal seed production during monitoring of an accessible population over the past seven years. Following very high rainfall in early 2000, there was surprisingly little seed production at several sites visited the following spring (J. Barnetson *pers. comm.*). More extensive seed production was reported in the late 1980s and cultivated trees regularly produce seed under irrigation.

This species has been regarded as fire-sensitive because of the relatively low proportion of large trees, and the small, patchy distribution. However, it readily re-sprouts from basal and lateral roots after fires (Angus Duguid, unpublished data). Many existing mature plants have been observed to have originated from lateral roots indicating there may be a substantial degree of asexual reproduction in some patches or populations.

CONSERVATION ASSESSMENT

This species qualifies as **Vulnerable** (under criteria B1ab(v)+2ab(v)), based on:
• restricted area of occupancy of less than 2000 km²;
• extent of occurrence less than 20 000 km²;
• occurrence in fewer than 10 known localities; and
• a continuing and inferred decline due to an increase in fire frequency (Soos *et al.* 1987; Latz 1992; Pitts *et al.* 1995).

There is circumstantial evidence for the recent decline of *A. undoolyana* particularly as a structural dominant.

continued.../

THREATENING PROCESSES

Decline is inferred due to an increase in fire frequency (Soos *et al.* 1987; Latz 1992; Pitts *et al.* 1995).

Widespread infestations of the introduced buffel grass (*Cenchrus ciliaris*) may detrimentally affect this species, particularly by increasing fire frequency and intensity in adjacent alluvial land systems, such that fires can more readily spread into *Acacia undoolyana* stands.

CONSERVATION OBJECTIVES AND MANAGEMENT

Strategic fire management has been carried out at a number of locations to minimise the risk of severe wildfire entering stands from surrounding highly flammable spinifex-dominated plant communities (Duguid 1999). However, many of the fire breaks created from 1987 to 2000 proved ineffective in ameliorating the effect of a large wildfire in 2002.

A national recovery plan for threatened arid zone acacias, including this species, has been prepared (Nano *et al.* 2006). Recovery actions identified for *A. undoolyana* include to:

• carry out population and habitat monitoring of the population at N'Dhala Gorge Nature Park and at an additional off-reserve site;
• implement management strategies for key threatening processes as required;
• undertake research on fire, seed and reproductive biology;
• collect and store seeds from all populations in recognised seed-banks; and
• engage Indigenous ecologists to provide input into the recovery process.

Compiled by Raelee Kerrigan, David Albrecht, Catherine Nano, Chris Pavey, Angus Duguid [June 2006] / **References:** Duguid, A. (1999). *Protecting Acacia undoolyana from Wildfires: an Example of Off Park Conservation from Central Australia*. Proceedings of Australian Bushfire Conference, Bushfire 99, Albury, Australia 7-9 July 1999. / Duguid, A., and Schunke, D. (1998). *Final Report on Project 290 Acacia undoolyana (Undoolyana Wattle) Species Recovery Plan.* (Parks and Wildlife Commission of the Northern Territory, Alice Springs.) / Latz, P.K. (1992). Conservation research statement: *Acacia undoolyana Leach.* ANPWS Endangered Species programme Project proposal, March 1992. (Conservation Commission of the Northern Territory, Alice Springs.) / Nano, C., Harris, M., and Pavey, C. R. (2006). *Recovery plan for threatened Acacias and Ricinocarpos gloria-medii in central Australia, 2006-2011.* (NT Department of Natural Resources Environment and the Arts, Alice Springs.) / Pitts, B., Schunke, D., and Parsons, D. (1995). *Species recovery plan for Acacia undoolyana – recovery action 2.4: GIS analysis.* (Parks and Wildlife Commission of the Northern Territory, Alice Springs.) / Soos, A. Latz, P.K., and Kube, P.D. (1987). *Occurrence of two rare plant populations in the eastern MacDonnell Ranges.* Technical Memorandum 87/11. (Conservation Commission of the Northern Territory, Alice Springs.) / White, M., Albrecht, D., Duguid, A., Latz, P., and Hamilton, M. (2000). *Plant species and sites of botanical significance in the southern bioregions of the Northern Territory. Volume 1: significant vascular plants.* A report to the Australian Heritage Commission. (Arid Lands Environment Centre, Alice Springs.)

Images courtesy of Kym Brennan

Acacia sp. Graveside Gorge

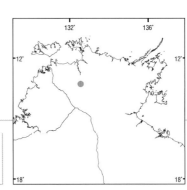

*Known locations
of Acacia sp.
Graveside Gorge*
● = *pre 1970*
● = *post 1970*

CONSERVATION STATUS
AUSTRALIA: **CRITICALLY ENDANGERED**
NORTHERN TERRITORY: **CRITICALLY ENDANGERED**

DESCRIPTION

Acacia sp. Graveside Gorge is a very distinctive, grey-green shrub immediately obvious in the field although with similar foliage to *Drummondita calida*. The leaves (phyllodes) are narrow and needle like, 10 to 15 mm long, hairy and arranged in whorls around the stem. The inflorescence is globular and the pods short. It is closely related to *A. hippuroides*, a Kimberley (Western Australia) species.

DISTRIBUTION

Apparently endemic to the Northern Territory, it is known from recent (post 2004) collections from Graveside Gorge, Kakadu National Park. An additional collection from the Park, dating from 1981, lacks a georeference.

Conservation reserves where reported:
Kakadu National Park

ECOLOGY

Very little is known about the ecology of this species, although evidence suggests it is an obligate seeder. Collection notes record it growing on west to south-west facing rocky sandstone slopes and ledges at the tops of sheer cliff lines.

CONSERVATION ASSESSMENT

In 2004, only a single adult plant was found at Graveside Gorge although there were also about 30 dead stems, which were burnt the previous season, and 20 small seedlings (around 10 cm tall) within 20 m. No other plants of this species were seen in the area (Kerrigan 2004).

Follow up surveys were undertaken in 2005 and 2006. On the first, the death of the single adult plant of 2004 and the presence of more seedlings was noted. Following maturation of seedlings and the discovery of new plants, in 2006 this population stood at around 150 individuals with many flowering and fruiting. Also during this survey a second, more extensive population of some 700 to 800 plants was located in a similar aspect 1 km north-east of the first. It also comprised many flowering and fruiting plants.

Although the Arnhem Land and Kakadu escarpment is remote and difficult to access, this species is considered adequately surveyed as a relatively high proportion of herbarium collections come from the Arnhem Land/Kakadu area. The quarter degree grid cell where this taxon was found has 1530 plant records.

From our scant current knowledge, this species qualifies as **Critically Endangered** (under criterion B [1a+c(iv) and 2a+c(iv)]) based on having:
- an extent of occurrence estimated to be less than 100 km^2; and
- a known area of occupancy of less than 10 km^2, in just two isolated populations where the number of mature plants undergoes extreme fluctuations.

Given the highly distinctive nature of this species and the intensive recent and historical survey effort in the Kakadu area, the current data are believed to reflect the very restricted distribution of this species.

THREATENING PROCESSES

Acacia sp. Graveside Gorge appears to be an obligate seeder currently exposed to unfavourable fire regimes. Russell-Smith *et al.* (1998, 2002) suggested that in some cases current fire regimes are detrimentally affecting obligate seeders in sandstone heath communities and inappropriate fire regimes are a potential threat to this species.

Unfortunately the generation time for this species has not been assessed and the potential for frequent fire events to kill individuals before reproductive maturity has not been evaluated. Similarly, seed bank stores, seed longevity and germination and establishment requirements are unknown. With such small, restricted populations, the species is vulnerable to stochastic events and inappropriate fire regimes.

While a fire in one year may reduce the threat of another fire at a site for one or more years afterwards, there is little doubt that any series of fires that repeatedly destroyed successive generations of seedlings before they matured and set seed would pose a serious threat, especially if the species does not have a resilient or persistent seed bank.

CONSERVATION OBJECTIVES AND MANAGEMENT

Further survey in the Graveside Gorge area is required to locate extra populations.
Regular monitoring in the short term to establish the persistence of seedlings and time taken to reproductive maturity is recommended. Research into the role of fire and other ecological processes in the distribution and abundance of the species is required. Collection of propagation material and translocation to botanic gardens may safeguard the species from stochastic events.

Compiled by Raelee Kerrigan, Ian Cowie, Kym Brennan [March 2006] / **References:** Kerrigan, R. (2004). *Kakadu Threatened Flora Report. Volume 2. Results of a threatened flora survey 2004.* (NT Department of Infrastructure Planning and Environment, Darwin.) / Russell-Smith, J., Ryan, P.G., Klessa, D., Waight, G., and Harwood, R.K. (1998). Fire regimes, fire-sensitive vegetation and fire management of the sandstone Arnhem Plateau, monsoonal northern Australia. *Journal of Applied Ecology* 35, 829-846. / Russell-Smith, J., Ryan, P.G., and Cheal, D.C. (2002). Fire regimes and the conservation of sandstone heath in monsoonal northern Australia: frequency, interval, patchiness. *Biological Conservation* 104, 91-107.

Desert flannel flower
Actinotus schwarzii

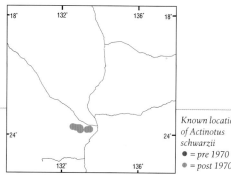

*Known locations
of Actinotus
schwarzii*
● = *pre 1970*
● = *post 1970*

DESCRIPTION

The desert flannel flower is an erect perennial shrub to 60 cm tall with soft dense tomentum. The leaves are dissected; the flowers are large, showy and daisy-like, forming a dense head to 2.5 cm diameter. The fruit are covered with silky hairs to 3 mm long.

Flowering: July, October–January
Fruiting: December

DISTRIBUTION

This species is endemic to the Chewings and Heavitree Ranges in the West MacDonnell Ranges. It is known from only approximately six locations, each highly restricted in size (White *et al.* 2000). It is also purported to occur in the Petermann Ranges (Central Ranges bioregion). The latitudinal range of this species from current records is 19 km and its longitudinal range is 90 km.

Conservation reserves where reported:
West MacDonnell National Park

ECOLOGY

The desert flannel flower occurs exclusively in sheltered gorges and on steep south-facing precipices.

CONSERVATION ASSESSMENT

This species qualifies as **Vulnerable** (under criteria D1+2) based on:
• number of mature individuals estimated to be fewer than 1000; and
• a very restricted area of occupancy estimated to be less than 20 km².

This is an attractive and naturally 'rare' species. Most populations occur within the West MacDonnell National Park. Accurate estimates of the total population are difficult due to the rugged and often inaccessible habitat. Little is known of the population structure and dynamics, and reproductive biology of this species.

THREATENING PROCESSES

Given the limited number of populations and their relatively small size, the species is potentially threatened by stochastic events such as wildfire or disease. Seed collecting and flower picking are potential threats, particularly at more accessible locations.

CONSERVATION OBJECTIVES AND MANAGEMENT

A recovery plan for this species is being prepared (C. Nano *pers. comm.*). The possible occurrence in the Petermann Ranges needs to be investigated. Focused studies should include a systematic assessment of factors that may threaten the species. Known populations should be monitored.

Compiled by Raelee Kerrigan, David Albrecht [February 2007] / **References:** White, M., Albrecht, D., Duguid, A., Latz, P., and Hamilton, M. (2000). *Plant species and sites of botanical significance in the southern bioregions of the Northern Territory. Volume 1: significant vascular plants.* A report to the Australian Heritage Commission. (Arid Lands Environment Centre, Alice Springs.)

Image courtesy of Martin Armstrong

Venus-hair fern,
Maidenhair fern, Avenca
Adiantum capillus-veneris

CONSERVATION STATUS
AUSTRALIA: **NOT LISTED**
NORTHERN TERRITORY: **VULNERABLE**

*Known locations
of Adiantum
capillus-veneris*
● = pre 1970
● = post 1970

DESCRIPTION

This species is a rock-dwelling fern. Its fronds/leaves are tufted, to 36 cm long. The delicate and membranous leaf blade is 2 to 3 pinnate, triangular 5 to 20 cm long and 4 to 15 cm wide. There are 1 to 10 spore clusters (sori) along margins.

DISTRIBUTION

The Venus-hair fern occurs in all Australian states and territories except Tasmania and the Australian Capital Territory, but is not common anywhere (Bostock 1998). It also occurs in moist forests across much of the world, including the Amazon, southern Europe and the United States. In the Northern Territory, it has a disjunct distribution occurring at Jasper Gorge (where last collected in 1974) and Mount Wilson Creek in or near Gregory National Park and at one location (Hugh Gorge) in the West MacDonnell Ranges (Short *et al.* 2003).

Conservation reserves where reported:
Gregory National Park, West MacDonnell National Park

ECOLOGY

In Australia, this species usually grows on limestone or sandstone rock, or on alkaline soils. At the Chewings Range (Hugh Gorge) it grows in quartzite rock crevices in deep sheltered gorges where the root zone is fed by permanent streams or seepage (White *et al.* 2000).

CONSERVATION ASSESSMENT

With fewer then 50 individuals known from the West MacDonnell locality and no indication of abundance in the Jasper Gorge locality, the population size and distribution of this species is difficult to estimate. The precautionary principle and consideration of the survey effort in likely habitat were taken into account in estimating these parameters. In the Northern Territory, this species qualifies as **Vulnerable** (under criteria D1+2), based on:
- its highly restricted distribution, with an estimated area of occupancy of less than 20 km^2; and
- a small population size of fewer than 1000 individuals.

THREATENING PROCESSES

The populations are probably secure in the short term, barring unforeseen events such as the cessation of spring waters or disease. In the longer term, populations may be threatened by global climate change.

CONSERVATION OBJECTIVES AND MANAGEMENT

The Northern Territory distribution of this species is not necessarily relictual and it could conceivably be a vagrant that has 'recently' dispersed to these locations via wind blown spore. The populations are probably secure in the short term. Searches are recommended to attempt to relocate the Jasper Gorge population, and to monitor all populations.

Compiled by Raelee Kerrigan, David Albrecht [April 2006] / **References:** Bostock, P.D. (1998). Adiantaceae. *Flora of Australia* 48, 248-286. / Short, P., Dixon, D., and Osterkamp Madsen, M. (2003). A review of ferns and fern allies of the Northern Territory. *The Beagle* 19, 7-80. / White, M., Albrecht, D., Duguid, A., Latz, P., and Hamilton, M. (2000). *Plant species and sites of botanical significance in the southern bioregions of the Northern Territory. Volume 1: significant vascular plants.* A report to the Australian Heritage Commission. (Arid Lands Environment Centre, Alice Springs.)

Images courtesy of Martin Armstrong & P.Rasmussen

Angiopteris evecta

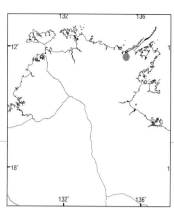

Known locations of Angiopteris evecta
● = pre 1970
● = post 1970

CONSERVATION STATUS
AUSTRALIA: **NOT LISTED**
NORTHERN TERRITORY: **VULNERABLE**

DESCRIPTION

Angiopteris evecta is a distinctive large ground-dwelling fern. The leaf blade is 2 pinnate, deltoid to 3.2 m long and 2.5 m wide. The spore clusters (sori) are submarginal. The trunk is less than 90 cm tall (Short *et al.* 2003).

DISTRIBUTION

In Australia it occurs in the Northern Territory, eastern Queensland and north-eastern New South Wales. It also occurs throughout the Palaeotropics (Camus 1998). In the Northern Territory, it is recorded from only one locality in north-eastern Arnhem Land (Short *et al.* 2003).

Conservation reserves where reported: None

ECOLOGY

This species grows in monsoon rainforest at perennial springs in narrow sandstone gorges.

CONSERVATION ASSESSMENT

No indication of abundance was given with the collected specimen. Given the size of the species and restricted habitat, it is unlikely that more than 250 individuals exist at the one locality. As such this species could qualify for Endangered based on Criterion D.

There is some data deficiency associated with this species as no species-specific surveys have been undertaken. Although the Rainforest Atlas data (Russell-Smith 1991; Liddle *et al.* 1994) generally reflect the restricted distribution and abundance of this species, it is probable that more populations exist in the vicinity and as such the species is listed as **Vulnerable** (under criteria D1+2).

THREATENING PROCESSES

This species is known from only one population, and as such is susceptible to exposure to fire, or stochastic events that may affect hydrology. At present it is known from a spring rainforest in a sandstone gorge and it is difficult to identify any imminent threats. Accessibility of the locality to feral animals such as pigs is unknown.

CONSERVATION OBJECTIVES AND MANAGEMENT

Further research is required to establish the extent of populations and to monitor population dynamics. Propagation of material and translocation to George Brown Darwin Botanic Gardens is recommended.

Compiled by Raelee Kerrigan, Ian Cowie [April 2006] / **References:** Camus, J.M. (1998). Marattiaceae. *Flora of Australia* 48, 109-112. / Liddle, D.T., Russell-Smith, J., Brock, J., Leach, G.J., and Connors, G.T. (1994). *Atlas of the vascular rainforest plants of the Northern Territory.* Flora of Australia Supplementary Series no. 3. (Australian Biological Resources Study, Canberra.) / Russell-Smith, J. (1991). Classification, species richness, and environmental relations of monsoon rain forest in northern Australia. *Journal of Vegetation Science* 2, 259-278. / Short, P., Dixon, D., and Osterkamp Madsen, M. (2003). A review of ferns and fern allies of the Northern Territory. *The Beagle* 19, 7-80.

Image courtesy of Kym Brennan

Australian arenga palm
Arenga australasica

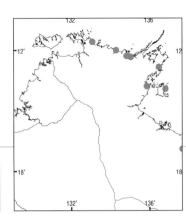

Known locations of Arenga australasica
● = pre 1970
● = post 1970

CONSERVATION STATUS
AUSTRALIA: **VULNERABLE**
NORTHERN TERRITORY: **DATA DEFICIENT**

DESCRIPTION

Arenga australasica is a clumping palm to 16 m tall. The leaves are pinnate, to 5 m long, leaflets to 60 cm long, irregularly rounded and erose at apex. The inflorescence forms a raceme of spikes. The flowers are about 6 mm long; the fruit is pink, fleshy, globular, about 15 mm diameter. *Arenga microphylla* is closely related to this species and was previously confused with it.

DISTRIBUTION

In the Northern Territory, it is known with certainty from eight widely scattered localities between Murgenella and Wollogorang Station near the Queensland border. These include Murgenella, Ramingining, Maningrida, and Groote Eylandt. Most of the range of the species lies in Arnhem Land.

Note that previous reported distributions for this species in the Northern Territory (e.g. Liddle *et al.* 1984) include what is now considered to be two species, *A. australasica* and *A. microcarpa*.

Conservation reserves where reported: None

ECOLOGY

It usually occurs as a minor component of monsoon rainforest associated with coastal dunes but sometimes in sandstone gorges. It grows on sandy substrates with a good moisture supply at sites with some fire protection. The ecology and distribution of *A. australasica* overlaps with the apparently more common *A. microcarpa* and the two can be locally sympatric.

CONSERVATION ASSESSMENT

In the Northern Territory, this species is coded as **Data Deficient** based on:
• data are considered inadequate for assessment; and
• it is known from eight localities, none of which are believed to be under threat.

There is little abundance information available for this species and it is considered not adequately surveyed. Label data from one collection estimated that population at more than 500 individuals, while others are of few individuals. Assessments of distribution and abundance are hampered by taxonomic uncertainty surrounding data collected during previous surveys. Forty-five records are known from plant survey data bases, but for the most part these lack voucher specimens and cannot be accurately ascribed to a species. If *A. australasica* and *A. microcarpa* are represented in survey records at the same ratio as in herbarium collections (1:2), then 15 of the survey records would represent *A. australasica*.

Based on herbarium records, the extent of occurrence is estimated at 28 000 km².

THREATENING PROCESSES

None are known. It is likely that seasonal drought, fire and competition with other species interact to limit the area of occupancy. Fire and feral animals, such as pigs and buffalo, may affect some populations.

CONSERVATION OBJECTIVES AND MANAGEMENT

Further field work and collecting is needed to establish the identity of the many survey records. Surveys of population size, area of occupancy and threats are also needed at a number of places across its range.

Compiled by Ian Cowie, Raelee Kerrigan [April 2006] / **References:** Liddle, D.T., Russell-Smith, J., Brock, J., Leach, G.J., and Connors, G.T. (1994). *Atlas of the vascular rainforest plants of the Northern Territory*. Flora of Australia Supplementary Series No. 3. (ABRS, Canberra.)

Image courtesy of Martin Armstrong

Baumea arthrophylla

CONSERVATION STATUS
AUSTRALIA: **NOT LISTED**
NORTHERN TERRITORY: **ENDANGERED**

*Known location
of Baumea
arthrophylla*
● = *pre 1970*
● = *post 1970*

DESCRIPTION

This species is a perennial sedge to 2 m high.
The inflorescence is narrow, interrupted and
10 to 30 cm long. The leaves are round in
cross-section, septate and pith-filled.

Flowering and Fruiting: October–November

DISTRIBUTION

This sedge is widely distributed in sub-tropical and
temperate areas of the continent. In the Northern
Territory, it is exceptionally rare; known only from
a single population, consisting of only a few plants,
in Watarrka National Park (White *et al.* 2000).
The closest occurrence outside the Northern
Territory of this species is at Dalhousie Springs in
South Australia.

Conservation reserves where reported:
Watarrka National Park

ECOLOGY

This species occurs in a seepage area amongst
rocks in a sandstone gorge. It is unclear whether
this species is a relict of wetter climatic periods
or a more recent immigrant.

CONSERVATION ASSESSMENT

This species qualifies as **Endangered** in the
Northern Territory (under criterion D), based on:
• restricted distribution, with area of occupancy
  estimated to be less than 20 km²; and
• a small population size estimated to be fewer
  than 250 mature individuals.

THREATENING PROCESSES

With such a small population size and restricted
distribution in the Northern Territory, this species
is vulnerable to stochastic events. The drying
out of the drainage line and wildfires are
potential threats.

CONSERVATION OBJECTIVES
AND MANAGEMENT

Protection from intense fires is required.
A monitoring program should be established.

Compiled by Raelee Kerrigan, David Albrecht [April 2006] / **References:** White, M., Albrecht, D., Duguid, A., Latz, P., and Hamilton, M. (2000). *Plant species and sites of botanical significance in the southern bioregions of the Northern Territory. Volume 1: significant vascular plants.* A report to the Australian Heritage Commission. (Arid Lands Environment Centre, Alice Springs.)

Image courtesy of Martin Armstrong

Marsh club-rush
Bolboschoenus caldwellii

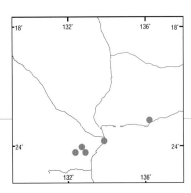

Known locations
of *Bolboschoenus
caldwellii*
● = pre 1970
● = post 1970

CONSERVATION STATUS
AUSTRALIA: **NOT LISTED**
NORTHERN TERRITORY: **ENDANGERED**

DESCRIPTION
This species is a rhizomatous perennial sedge. Its stems are acutely 3-angled; its inflorescence is compound, umbel-like with 1 to 3 erect or spreading rays. The spikelets are golden or red-brown.

Flowering: January, May, June, September
Fruiting: January, March, April, June, September, October

DISTRIBUTION
This sedge occurs in all Australian states and New Zealand. It is very rare in the Northern Territory, with the only records comprising one site within Finke Gorge National Park, two sites south of Finke Gorge, a bore overflow on Jervois Station and a sewerage outflow at Ilparpa Swamp (near Alice Springs) (White *et al.* 2000). The Finke Gorge National Park population is now presumed extinct.

Conservation reserves where reported:
Finke Gorge National Park (although it may be locally extinct there).

ECOLOGY
It occurs in damp soils adjacent to permanent or semi permanent water.

CONSERVATION ASSESSMENT
The Northern Territory population of this species qualifies as Critically Endangered based on the population size estimated to be fewer than 50 mature individuals. However, numbers of individuals of clonal species are difficult to estimate.

Considering that suitable habitat for this species occurs in the Dulcie Ranges and more populations may exist there, it is listed as **Endangered** (under criterion D).

The populations on Jervois Station and at Ilparpa Swamp are presumably the result of propagules transported by birds. Both are considered unnatural and ephemeral populations expected to disappear as the artificial conditions change in the near future.

THREATENING PROCESSES
Competition from couch grass (*Cynodon dactylon*) is an established threat for this species. The impact of stock through habitat degradation has yet to be determined.

CONSERVATION OBJECTIVES AND MANAGEMENT
Suitable habitat for this species occurs in the Dulcie Ranges and future fieldwork in this area should include searches for this species.

Known populations should be monitored; and their response to putative threats and management responses assessed.

Compiled by Raelee Kerrigan, David Albrecht [April 2006] / **References:** White, M., Albrecht, D., Duguid, A., Latz, P., and Hamilton, M. (2000). *Plant species and sites of botanical significance in the southern bioregions of the Northern Territory. Volume 1: significant vascular plants.* A report to the Australian Heritage Commission. (Arid Lands Environment Centre, Alice Springs.)

Images courtesy of Kym Brennan

Boronia quadrilata

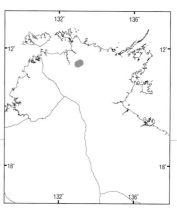

Known locations
of Boronia
quadrilata
● = pre 1970
● = post 1970

CONSERVATION STATUS
AUSTRALIA: **VULNERABLE**
NORTHERN TERRITORY: **VULNERABLE**

DESCRIPTION

Boronia quadrilata is an erect slender shrub or bushy multi-stemmed shrub, 1.5 to 3 m tall. The stems are distinctly 4-angled with small wings undulating longitudinally along the stem. *Boronia quadrilata* is very distinctive, with bright green new growth becoming blue/green and waxy with age.

DISTRIBUTION

This species is endemic to the Northern Territory, where it is known only from the type locality at upper Magela Creek on the Arnhem Land plateau to the east of Kakadu National Park.

Conservation reserves where reported: None

ECOLOGY

Very little is known about the ecology of this species. Plants grow in pockets of sand amongst sandstone outcrops, in crevices amongst dissected sandstone and on rocky scree slopes. The species is absent from flatter sandstone country and from massive sandstone outcrops. The dominant vegetation in this country is characteristic of much of the region, that is *Corymbia arnhemensis* open woodland to shrubland with *Triodia microstachya* and a variable shrub layer.

Boronia quadrilata was observed to re-sprout after fire with strong and vigorous new growth in a 2003 survey. The majority of re-sprouting individuals were flowering/fruiting in this population. Unburnt individuals were large and spindly with foliage only present distally on stem.

CONSERVATION ASSESSMENT

This species is known from only one locality, where it was collected in 1991 and revisited in 2003 and 2004. Due to inaccurate locational data, previous search efforts had failed to relocate this species.

Re-survey in 2004 extended the known range of the species by about 1 km, giving a combined area of occupancy of 23 ha, when data from the 2003 survey are included. The total extent of occurrence after the two surveys was estimated at 94 ha. The combined population estimates from the two surveys comprise more than 2644 plants. The total extent of the population is still not known as potentially suitable habitat to the south and south west of the known population remains to be surveyed. However, given the extensive survey effort (10 300 points in a 1 degree grid cell) in this area, current data are believed to largely reflect the very restricted distribution of this species.

A permanent monitoring plot established in March 2003 was reassessed in August 2004. There had been an increase of 24 individuals in the plot since March 2003, primarily in the juvenile class. The most plausible interpretation of the data was that some of the 2003 juveniles had moved into the adult class while others have remained as juveniles, with significant recruitment of juveniles over the 2003–04 wet season. This indicates a maximum growth rate for seedlings in excess of 50 cm in their first year, with the data suggesting that some plants may reach (limited) reproductive maturity in their second year (Cowie 2005).

It has a status of **Vulnerable** (under criteria D2 and B1 biii,2 biii) based on:
- an area of occupancy much less than 20 km²;
- a projected decline in quality of habitat.

THREATENING PROCESSES

Although individuals have been observed to respond vigorously to fire, the impact of frequent burning on the fate of individuals and their perennial root stocks is unknown. The extremely restricted distribution of this species suggests the population is at best static and not recruiting. Although sporadic/random recruitment events may be enough to maintain this population, this species is in a fire prone habitat and the factors behind its restricted distribution and abundance are not clear.

CONSERVATION OBJECTIVES AND MANAGEMENT

A recovery plan for this species was implemented from 2006 (Liddle and Gibbons 2006). Actions described in that plan, and currently being implemented, include to:
- conduct further searches and establish a monitoring program;
- develop and implement a fire management program;
- involve landholders and the broader community; and
- where appropriate, develop an *ex-situ* population.

Compiled by Raelee Kerrigan, Ian Cowie [April 2006] / **References:** Cowie, I.D. (2005). Kakadu *Threatened Flora Report (Vol 3.). Results of a threatened flora survey.* Unpublished report to Parks Australian North (NT Department of Infrastructure Planning and Environment, Darwin.) / Duretto, M.F. (1999). Systematics of *Boronia* section *Valvatae sensu lato* (Rutaceae). *Muelleria* 12, 1-132. / Kerrigan, R. (2003). *Kakadu Threatened Flora Report. Results of a threatened flora survey 2003.* (NT Department of Infrastructure Planning and Environment, Darwin.) / Liddle, D.T., and Gibbons, A. (2006). *Recovery plan for Boronia quadrilata and Boronia viridiflora in the Northern Territory of Australia, 2006 to 2010.* (NT Department of Natural Resources Environment and the Arts, Darwin.)

Image courtesy of Kym Brennan

Boronia viridiflora

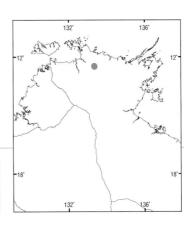

Known locations of Boronia viridiflora
● = pre 1970
● = post 1970

CONSERVATION STATUS
AUSTRALIA: **VULNERABLE**
NORTHERN TERRITORY: **VULNERABLE**

DESCRIPTION
Boronia viridiflora is a shrub, growing perpendicular or slightly upwards from vertical rock faces. Its stems are 1.5 to 2 m long, and 4-angled. Its leaves are simple, elliptic to oblanceolate, red tipped. *Boronia viridiflora* differs from *B. quadrilata* by its horizontal habit, smaller, oblanceolate, sub-sessile leaves and smaller flowers and fruits.

Flowering and Fruiting: April, June

DISTRIBUTION
This species is endemic to the Northern Territory, where it is known from two populations south of Nabarlek in Arnhem Land.

Conservation reserves where reported: None

ECOLOGY
Boronia viridiflora grows from vertical surfaces of cliffs or boulders on the sandstone plateau.

CONSERVATION ASSESSMENT
The population is estimated at approximately 700 mature individuals (K. Brennan *pers. comm.*). This species thus qualifies as **Vulnerable** (under criteria D1+2) as:
• the estimated number of mature individuals is fewer than 1000; and
• the species has a restricted distribution estimated to be less than 20 km².

THREATENING PROCESSES
With a small population of restricted distribution, this species is susceptible to stochastic events. The habitat it occurs in suggests an intolerance of fire and thus an expansion of the population into areas exposed to fire is unlikely. Its recruitment potential is likely to be low given the availability of suitable sites and probability of successful dispersal to these sites.

CONSERVATION OBJECTIVES AND MANAGEMENT
A recovery plan for this species has been implemented from 2006 (Liddle and Gibbons 2006). Actions described in that plan, and currently being implemented, include to:
• conduct further searches and establish a monitoring program;
• develop and implement a fire management program;
• involve landholders and the broader community; and
• where appropriate, develop an *ex-situ* population.

Compiled by Raelee Kerrigan, Ian Cowie [April 2006] / **References:** Duretto, M.F. (1999). Systematics of *Boronia* section *Valvatae sensu lato* (Rutaceae). *Muelleria* 12, 1-132. / Liddle, D.T., and Gibbons, A. (2006). *Recovery plan for Boronia quadrilata and Boronia viridiflora in the Northern Territory of Australia, 2006 to 2010.* (NT Department of Natural Resources Environment and the Arts, Darwin.)

Image courtesy of Kym Brennan

Burmannia sp. Bathurst Island

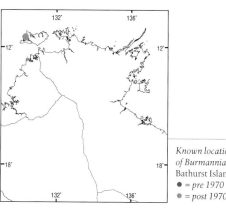

Known locations of Burmannia sp. Bathurst Island.
● = *pre 1970*
● = *post 1970*

CONSERVATION STATUS
AUSTRALIA: **ENDANGERED**
NORTHERN TERRITORY: **ENDANGERED**

DESCRIPTION

This species is a herbaceous leafless saprophyte to 12 cm tall with an annual above-ground inflorescence/infructescence which may last for up to several weeks under appropriate conditions. Most of the plant, including the stem and fruit, is translucent white; however the flower (which is only open for a short time) has a yellow corolla. It has a small perennial underground corm from which flowers are believed to emerge annually. However it is possible that an individual corm may produce more than one inflorescence in a single season.

This species is as yet undescribed, but is closely related to the Asian species *B. bifaria* (Jonker 1954).

Flowering and Fruiting: This cryptic species is only visible when in flower or fruit. It has been recorded in previous surveys in July and November. However both Fensham (1993) and recent work during the 2006–07 wet season suggest that it undergoes a mass flowering event in December and then continues to emerge in cohorts over coming weeks. Surveys during the dry season have only ever recorded a few individuals (Kym Brennan *pers. comm.*).

DISTRIBUTION

This species is known only from five spring-fed rainforest patches in the north of Bathurst Island in the Northern Territory.

Conservation reserves where reported: None

ECOLOGY

Very little is known of the ecology of this plant. It is recorded from wet spring-fed rainforests, growing out of damp peat in raised areas.

Burmannia seems to have a disturbance requirement (probably through seasonal flooding). While the species may be able to persist in areas lightly disturbed by pigs, individual plants have been recorded in areas of pig rooting only where the plants were protected within a network of sizeable tree roots (Fensham 1993). The saprophytic habit requires soil organic material and this species may be unable to establish on mineral soil (Fensham 1993).

CONSERVATION ASSESSMENT

This species was recorded from two subpopulations in 1991 with a total population estimated between 500 to 2000 individuals in a 40 ha area (Fensham 1993). None were detected in the area in the next searches, from 1998–2000. Only one population of six individuals was recorded in 2001. Searches and surveys in 2006 re-located these two populations and discovered three new ones nearby (D. Liddle *pers. obs.*).

This species qualifies as **Endangered** (under criteria B1ab(iii)+2ab(iii); C2b) based on:
• an extent of occurrence estimated to be less than 5000 km²;
• an area of occupancy estimated to be less than 500 km²;

• extreme fluctuations in number of locations and subpopulations; and
• an inferred continuing decline due to extensive and frequent pig disturbance.

THREATENING PROCESSES

Feral pigs are likely to dig up *Burmannia* plants to eat their small tubers, and the general rooting and disturbance by pigs in these wet rainforests may also detrimentally affect this plant.

CONSERVATION OBJECTIVES AND MANAGEMENT

A recovery plan for this species, and other threatened plants on the Tiwi Islands, is due to be released in 2007, but many actions in its draft are currently being implemented through a collaborative project involving Tiwi rangers and scientists from the Department of Natural Resources, Environment and The Arts, with funding from the Natural Heritage Trust.

Research on the impact of pig disturbance, the environmental requirements of the species and the dynamics of the population are underway. This monitoring program was established in 2006, and should be maintained. It has included the fencing of some areas of habitat to afford protection from pigs which was recommended as urgent by Fensham (1993).

Compiled by Raelee Kerrigan, Ian Cowie, David Liddle, Louis Elliott [April 2007] / **References:** Fensham, R.J. (1993). The impact of pig rooting on populations of *Burmannia* sp., a rare rainforest herb on Bathurst Island. *Proceedings of the Royal Society of Queensland* 103, 5-12. / Jonker, F.P. (1954). Burmanniaceae. *Flora Malesiana* 4, 13-26.

Calochilus caeruleus

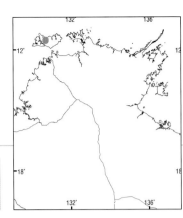

Known locations of Calochilus caeruleus
● = pre 1970
● = post 1970

CONSERVATION STATUS
AUSTRALIA: **NOT LISTED**
NORTHERN TERRITORY: **VULNERABLE**

DESCRIPTION

Calochilus caeruleus is an erect terrestrial orchid, dying back to an underground tuber each dry season. The leaf (to 40 cm x 8 mm) is shallowly 3-cornered in cross section and fleshy. The flower stem (to 80 cm tall) is slender, wiry and bears four to eight flowers. The flowers are greenish with red-brown markings and red labellum hairs. A closely-related species, *C. caesius,* has recently been described from the Northern Territory mainland (Yarrawonga Swamp) (Jones and Clements 2004).

Flowering: December–January
Fruiting: January

DISTRIBUTION

This species occurs in tropical Queensland, the Northern Territory, Western Australia and New Guinea. In the Northern Territory, it is known from only two collections (in 1975 and 1992) on Melville Island. These are likely to be from the same population.

Conservation reserves where reported: None

ECOLOGY

The species grows in swamps and seasonally inundated flats in open forest, wet heathland and *Melaleuca* woodland. The flower stem emerges before the leaves and these are not fully developed until after the seeds are shed. Each flower lasts about one day and usually only one or two open on an inflorescence at once.

CONSERVATION ASSESSMENT

This species is classified as **Vulnerable** (under criteria D1+2) based on:

- a population size estimated to be fewer than 1000; and
- a restricted area of occupancy estimated to be less than 20 km^2.

Current data supports a category of Endangered, though it has been downgraded due to the probable negative collection bias associated with this species. The flowering period is short and occurs during the early wet season when preferred habitat is difficult to access.

The classification of data deficient is unwarranted because of the considerable survey effort on Melville and Bathurst Island during the wet season in 2000–2001 (Woinarski *et al.* 2003).

THREATENING PROCESSES

With a very restricted distribution and small population this species is susceptible to stochastic events. As a terrestrial orchid, threatening processes would include weed infestation, changes in hydrology and impact of fire. The presence and impact of these processes are as yet unknown.

CONSERVATION OBJECTIVES AND MANAGEMENT

A recovery plan for this species, and other threatened plants on the Tiwi Islands, is due to be released in 2007, but many actions in its draft are currently being implemented.

Further specific surveys are required to determine the status and management requirements of the population. Non-targeted surveys undertaken in 2007 did not encounter the plant.

Compiled by Raelee Kerrigan, Ian Cowie, Louis Elliott [April 2007] / **References:** Jones, D. L. (1988). *Native Orchids of Australia.* (Reed, Sydney.) / Jones, D.L., and Clements, M.A. (2004). Miscellaneous new species, new genera, reinstated genera and new combinations in Australian Orchidaceae. *The Orchadian, Scientific Supplement* 14(8): iv-v. / Woinarski, J., Brennan, K., Cowie, I., Kerrigan, R., and Hempel, C. (2003). *Biodiversity conservation on the Tiwi Islands, Northern Territory. Part 1. Plants and environments.* 144 pp. (Department of Infrastructure Planning and Environment, Darwin.)

Images courtesy of Jenni Low Choy & Kym Brennan

Cephalomanes obscurum

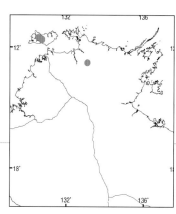

Known locations of Cephalomanes obscurum
● = *pre 1970*
● = *post 1970*

CONSERVATION STATUS
AUSTRALIA: **NOT LISTED**
NORTHERN TERRITORY: **ENDANGERED**

DESCRIPTION

Cephalomanes obscurum is a terrestrial fern, erect to 20 cm tall. The leaf blade is 3-pinnate to 3-pinnate-pinnatifid, 5 to 15 cm long, and 2 to 9 cm wide. Clusters of spores (sori) are erect, borne on short lobes in the axils of tertiary segments.

DISTRIBUTION

This species occurs from north-eastern Queensland to north-eastern New South Wales. It also occurs in Sri Lanka, southern India to Taiwan, Malesia, Solomon Island and possibly Vanuatu. In the Northern Territory, it has been collected from Tarracumbie Falls on Melville Island, and Magela Creek in Arnhem Land (Short *et al*. 2003).

Conservation reserves where reported: None

ECOLOGY

Across its range beyond the Northern Territory, this species grows in damp gullies, along creek banks or under rock ledges, in tropical and subtropical rainforest, and in the splash zones of permanent waterfalls.

It has been recorded as a common coloniser, growing in dense patches, with young plants (sporelings) appearing in disturbed sites.

CONSERVATION ASSESSMENT

This taxon qualifies for **Endangered** (under criterion D) based on the number of mature individuals in the total population estimated to be fewer than 250.

The Magela Creek population, collected in 1984, consisted of four individuals. The Tarracumbie population, first collected in 1975, then in 2000 and 2006, consists of approximately 150 individuals. A possible second population nearby on Melville Island has not been recollected since 1994. No further populations have been located, despite substantial survey effort on the Tiwi Islands since 2000 (Woinarski *et al*. 2003) and the implementation of a Tiwi Islands Threatened Species Recovery Plan in 2006–07.

THREATENING PROCESSES

With a small population size this species is susceptible to stochastic events. Changes to hydrology and infestation from exotic weeds have the potential to threaten known populations but at present they are not imminent threats.

CONSERVATION OBJECTIVES AND MANAGEMENT

A recovery plan for this species, and other threatened plants on the Tiwi Islands, is due to be released in 2007, but many actions in its draft are currently being implemented through a collaborative project involving Tiwi rangers and scientists from the Department of Natural Resources, Environment and The Arts, with funding from the Natural Heritage Trust. A monitoring program for the Melville Island population was established in 2006.

Compiled by Raelee Kerrigan, Ian Cowie, Louis Elliott [April 2007] / **References:** Bostock, P.D., and Spokes, M.T. (1998). Hymenophyllaceae. *Flora of Australia* 48, 116-147. (ABRS, Canberra.) Liddle, D.T., Russell-Smith, J., Brock, J., Leach, G.J., and Connors, G.T. (1994) *Atlas of the vascular rainforest plants of the Northern Territory*. Flora of Australia Supplementary Series No. 3, (ABRS, Canberra.) Short, P., Dixon, D., and Osterkamp Madsen, M. (2003). A review of ferns and fern allies of the Northern Territory. *The Beagle* 19, 7-80. / Woinarski, J., Brennan, K., Cowie, I., Kerrigan, R., and Hempel, C. (2003). *Biodiversity conservation on the Tiwi Islands, Northern Territory. Part 1. Plants and environments.* 144 pp. (Department of Infrastructure Planning and Environment, Darwin.)

Image courtesy of Martin Armstrong

Cryptocarya hypospodia

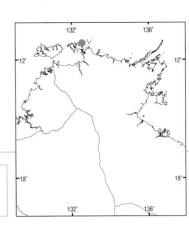

Known location of Cryptocarya hypospodia
● = pre 1970
● = post 1970

CONSERVATION STATUS
AUSTRALIA: **NOT LISTED**
NORTHERN TERRITORY: **ENDANGERED**

DESCRIPTION
Cryptocarya hypospodia is a tree to 30 m tall, with bark usually nondescript, emitting an odour, often described as peppery. The leaf undersurface is green or slightly bluish (glaucous), clothed in short, straight and tortuous white or pale brown appressed hairs when young but eventually becoming glabrous. The flowers are pale brown, cream or green, unpleasantly perfumed. The floral tube is 1 to 1.8 mm x 1.3 to 1.5 mm. The fruit is black when ripe, globular 13 to 18 mm x 12 to 17 mm.

Fruiting: May

DISTRIBUTION
This species is known from eastern Australia and New Guinea. In the Northern Territory, it has been collected only from Croker Island, in 1987.

Conservation reserves where reported: None

ECOLOGY
In Queensland, it occurs in rainforests of various types, particularly gallery forests on soils derived from a variety of rock types. It ranges in altitude from sea level to 900 m (Hyland 1989).

CONSERVATION ASSESSMENT
In the Northern Territory, this species is classified as **Endangered** (under criterion D) based on a presumed population of fewer than 250 mature individuals of this tree. This species is potentially a vagrant taxon and may not be reproducing in the area and hence would not warrant inclusion on a regional list. However, using the precautionary principle we have treated it as a local species as we are unable to establish if it is a remnant or a recent coloniser. No additional populations have been identified despite recent substantial survey effort on the Tiwi Islands and Cobourg Peninsula.

THREATENING PROCESSES
Stochastic events such as cyclones and impact of feral animals such as pigs are potential threats.

CONSERVATION OBJECTIVES AND MANAGEMENT
Further research is required to establish the status of this population and the extent of its distribution. A monitoring program should be established.

Compiled by Raelee Kerrigan, Ian Cowie [April 2006] / **References:** Hyland, B.P.M. (1989). Lauraceae in Australia. *Australian Systematic Botany* 2, 135-367.

Image courtesy of David Liddle

Cycas armstrongii

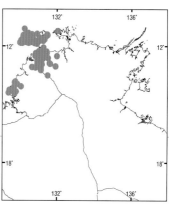

Known locations of Cycas armstrongii
● = *pre 1970*
● = *post 1970*

CONSERVATION STATUS
AUSTRALIA: **NOT LISTED**
NORTHERN TERRITORY: **VULNERABLE**

DESCRIPTION

Cycas armstrongii is a medium-sized cycad up to 6 m tall with a slender trunk 6 to 12 cm in diameter. Branching occurs along with occasional offsets and basal suckers. Leaves form an obliquely erect to spreading crown. Each has 160 to 300 leaflets attached to the rachis at about 70° with a prominent midrib above.

DISTRIBUTION

This species is endemic to the Northern Territory. It is known from Gunn Point to Hayes Creek, west to within 50 km of the coast and east to the Wildman River catchment, and its also occurs on the Tiwi Islands and Cobourg Peninsula.

Conservation reserves where reported:
Berry Springs Nature Park, Blackmore River Conservation Reserve, Casuarina Coastal Reserve, Djukbinj National Park, Garig Gunak Barlu National Park, Holmes Jungle Nature Park, Howard Springs Nature Park, Howard Springs Hunting Reserve, Kakadu National Park, Litchfield National Park, Manton Dam Recreation Area.

ECOLOGY

It occurs mainly in open grassy woodland on yellow and red earths, limited in the area by drainage.

CONSERVATION ASSESSMENT

This species is locally abundant, but has less than 1% of its population included in conservation reserves. Applying the precautionary principle, this species qualifies as **Vulnerable** (under criteria A4ce) based on a predicted reduction in population size over a 100 year period (i.e. less than three generations) of more than 30%, commencing a decade ago (Liddle 2004).

THREATENING PROCESSES

Land clearing due to the expansion of Darwin, rural residential living, horticulture, agriculture and forestry is a major threat to the species. Available habitat in and around Darwin and the Litchfield Shire has been reduced and further land clearing is expected as Darwin expands. In particular, prime cycad habitat with deep loamy soil has been identified as land suitable for horticulture and agriculture. Substantial areas of prime habitat on the Tiwi Islands will be cleared for forestry.

In areas not subject to clearing, there is a major threat from the combined impact of introduced grasses and fire whereby increased fuel loads lead to increased mortality of adult stems and subsequent population decline (Liddle 2004). Mortality in excess of 50% of adult stems per fire event has been recorded when subject to fuel loads of 20 tonnes per hectare. While adult stem mortality is substantial with these high intensity fire events, many plants re-sprout from the base.

Despite this capacity to re-sprout, a frequency of intense fire in excess of around one in five years is predicted to result in long-term population decline. Fires commonly occur more frequently than one in five years throughout the range of *Cycas armstrongii* and the occurrence of intense fire is set to increase as exotic grasses spread rapidly across the landscape (Kean and Price 2003). The exotic pasture species, gamba grass (*Andropogon gayanus*), supports fuel loads up to 20 tonnes per hectare (Barrow 1995), and the exotic perennial mission grass (*Pennisetum polystachyon*), supports fuel loads up to 27 tonnes per hectare (Panton 1993), both far higher than the fuel loads of native grasses. These exotic species have the potential to extend over the full range of *C. armstrongii*. Fire also reduces seed viability in *C. armstrongii* (Liddle 2004).

CONSERVATION OBJECTIVES AND MANAGEMENT

A management program for this species, and other cycads, has been established (Anon 1997).

Reservation of high quality habitat, control of exotic grasses and fire management are priority management requirements. Promotion of the value of cycad habitat through the economic returns gained by the sustainable use of this species may assist conservation of the species. A monitoring program for this species has been established, and should be maintained.

Compiled by Raelee Kerrigan, Ian Cowie, Dave Liddle [May 2006] / **References:** Anon. (1997). *A Management Program for Cycads in the Northern Territory of Australia.* (Parks and Wildlife Commission of the Northern Territory, Darwin.) / Barrow, P. (1995). *The Ecology and Management of Gamba Grass (Andropogon gayanus Kunth.).* Final Report to the Australian Nature Conservation Agency. (NT Department of Primary Industry and Fisheries, Darwin.) / Kean, L., and. Price, O. (2003). The extent of Mission grasses and Gamba Grass in the Darwin region of Australia's Northern Territory. *Pacific Conservation Biology* 8, 281-290. / Liddle, D.T. (2004). *The ecology of Cycas armstrongii and management of fire in Australia's tropical savannas.* PhD, thesis (Charles Darwin University, Darwin.) / Panton, W.J. (1993). Changes in Post World War II distribution and status of monsoon rainforests in the Darwin area. *Australian Geographer* 24, 50-59.

Image courtesy of David Liddle

Dendromyza reinwardtiana

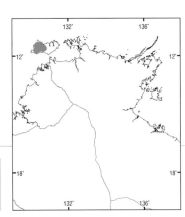

Known locations of Dendromyza reinwardtiana
● = *pre 1970*
● = *post 1970*

CONSERVATION STATUS
AUSTRALIA: **NOT LISTED**
NORTHERN TERRITORY: **VULNERABLE**

DESCRIPTION

This species is a parasitic vine or scrambling shrub. The leaves are alternate, elliptic to obovate, 20 to 100 mm long, with 3 to 9 longitudinal primary veins. It has separate male and female flowers. The fruit is pink, ovoid, and 6 to 8 mm long.

Fruiting: January, September, November

DISTRIBUTION

It occurs from Sumatra and Luzon to New Guinea. In Australia, it is known from Cape York Peninsula and the Northern Territory. In the Northern Territory, it was previously known from three sites from Bathurst Island and four sites from Melville Island (Woinarski *et al.* 2003). Recent survey in 2006 has increased that number to eight sites from Bathurst island and 13 sites from Melville Island.

Conservation reserves where reported: None

ECOLOGY

It is found in perennial wet rainforest, where it is usually hosted by *Calophyllum soulattri*. It has been recorded on a number of other species including *Syzygium eucalyptoides* subsp. *bleeseri* (Dunlop *et al.* 1995) and *Melicope elleryana*.

CONSERVATION ASSESSMENT

This species is classified as **Vulnerable** (under criteria D1+2) based on:
• a population size estimated at fewer than 1000 individuals; and
• a restricted area of occupancy (estimated to be less than 20 km²).

THREATENING PROCESSES

With a small population size and restricted distribution, this species is susceptible to stochastic events. As an epiphyte, loss of habitat via cyclonic events is a potential threat. Changes to hydrology are also a possible threat, although not imminent. Wet riparian rainforests are more susceptible to fire following a reduction in water availability.

CONSERVATION OBJECTIVES AND MANAGEMENT

A recovery plan for this species, and other threatened plants on the Tiwi Islands, is due to be released in 2007, but many actions in its draft are currently being implemented through a collaborative project involving Tiwi rangers and scientists from the Department of Natural Resources, Environment and The Arts, with funding from the Natural Heritage Trust.

Research is required to establish the status of populations of this species and the extent of its distribution. It is difficult to prescribe recovery actions without knowledge on the dynamics of the population or the associated threats. Management of fire in surrounding savanna is required to ensure that fires do not burn into the rainforests. A monitoring program should be established. Collection of propagation material and translocation to botanic gardens may be required.

Compiled by Raelee Kerrigan, Ian Cowie, Louis Elliott [April 2007] / **References:** Dunlop, C.R., Leach, G.J., and Cowie, I.D. (1995). *Flora of the Darwin Region Vol 2.* (Conservation Commission of the Northern Territory, Darwin.) / Woinarski, J., Brennan, K., Cowie, I., Kerrigan, R., and Hempel, C. (2003). *Biodiversity conservation on the Tiwi Islands, Northern Territory. Part 1. Plants and environments.* 144 pp. (Department of Infrastructure Planning and Environment, Darwin.)

Image courtesy of Ian Cowie

Ectrosia blakei

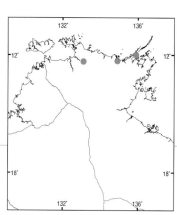

*Known locations
of Ectrosia blakei*
● = *pre 1970*
● = *post 1970*

DESCRIPTION

Ectrosia blakei is a weak-stemmed, annual grass to 45 cm tall. The inflorescences are lax and open. The spikelets are spreading and have 9 to 12 florets arranged in two rows, 12 to 16 mm long (excluding awns) and 2 to 3 mm wide. The lemmas are 5 to 7 mm long, with the upper ones long-awned (Nightingale and Weiller 2005).

With *E. danesii, E. laxa* and *E. schultzii* var. *annua, E. blakei* forms a species complex with poorly defined limits between taxa in the Northern Territory. These species can be difficult to tell apart.

Flowering and fruiting: April–July

DISTRIBUTION

This species is endemic to Australia, occurring in Queensland and the Northern Territory. In the Northern Territory, it is known only from four widely separated localities in Arnhem Land. These are near Oenpelli, near Ramingining, near Goyder River and on Elcho Island.

Conservation reserves where reported: None

ECOLOGY

This species occurs on laterite, white sand or sandy loam soils, in woodlands dominated by *Eucalyptus tetrodonta, E. tectifica* or *Melaleuca nervosa*. In some instances, the species has been recorded on seasonally poorly drained areas.

CONSERVATION ASSESSMENT

This species is listed as Vulnerable under Federal legislation.

In the Northern Territory, this species is coded as **Data Deficient** based on:
• data are considered inadequate for assessment; and
• known from four populations, none of which are believed to be under threat.

There is little information available about abundance in populations of this species, and it is considered not adequately surveyed. The species was abundant (many thousands) in the vicinity of Galiwinku (Elcho Island), when collected there in 1992, and near Ramingining in 2001. No information on abundance is available for the other populations. At the optimal time of year for detection, which is late wet season and early dry season, sites are difficult to access by ground transport. This, and the remoteness of the area, lead to a negative collection bias. No data on area of occupancy are available. The known extent of occurrence is estimated at approximately 12 000 km².

THREATENING PROCESSES

None are known. Parts of the Northern Territory where this species occurs are relatively remote and among the least affected by European settlement. Fire during the main May to June fertile period may be a threat. Much of the area where it occurs frequently receives rain until well into May and traditional burning in at least some parts of that area does not begin until the end of July.

CONSERVATION OBJECTIVES AND MANAGEMENT

This species complex is in need of further field survey, collecting and taxonomic assessment to determine species limits. Further targeted surveys of appropriate habitat at an appropriate time of year are needed to gather distribution and abundance data and assess possible threats.

Compiled by Ian Cowie, Raelee Kerrigan, John Woinarski [May 2006] / **References:** Nightingale, M.E., and Weiller, C.M. (2005). *Ectrosia. Flora of Australia* 44B, 426-439.

Image courtesy of David Liddle

Elaeocarpus miegei

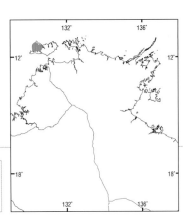

Known locations
of *Elaeocarpus
miegei*
● = *pre 1970*
● = *post 1970*

CONSERVATION STATUS
AUSTRALIA: **NOT LISTED**
NORTHERN TERRITORY: **CRITICALLY ENDANGERED**

DESCRIPTION

Elaeocarpus miegei is a tall tree, to 35 m.
Like other *Elaeocarpus* spp., the leaves are clustered
toward the end of their branches and older leaves
may turn a distinct autumnal red both in
the canopy and on the ground. It is occasionally
reported to have buttresses. In Papua New Guinea,
it is reported to be a variable species (Coode 1981).
It is distinguished from the more common
Elaeocarpus arnhemicus (a much smaller tree) by
longer petals (3 to 3.5 mm in *E. arnhemicus* and
5 mm long in *E. miegei*), and leaf shape (elliptic
acute and usually acuminate in *E. arnhemicus*,
obovate and obtuse in *E. miegei*). It is similarly
distinguished from *E. culminicola* and
E. angustifolius on leaf shape, petiole length
and form, and more distinctly, on the spacing
of teeth on the blade margin (*E. miegei* has
1 to 3 teeth per 2 cm).

Fruiting: November

DISTRIBUTION

The only Australian occurrences of this tall
rainforest tree are on the Tiwi Islands. Beyond
Australia, it is also known from New Guinea,
Malesia and the Solomon Islands. On the
Tiwi Islands, it has been recorded from six wet
rainforest patches (in at least some of which it is
known from only a single tree). Only one specimen
is lodged at the Northern Territory Herbarium in
Darwin. Recent survey in 2006 has relocated only
one population on Melville Island. Several records
occur at a rainforest that was severely affected by
cyclone in 2005 and no individuals have as yet been
re-located there.

Conservation reserves where reported: None

ECOLOGY

This species grows in permanently moist soils in
wet rainforest patches.

CONSERVATION ASSESSMENT

Without detailed knowledge of abundance, it
is very difficult to assign a conservation status
category. Given the survey effort applied to
this species, its habitat on the Tiwi Islands, the
non-cryptic nature of the species, and use of the
precautionary principle, a status of **Critically
Endangered** (under criterion D) is warranted
based on an assumed number of mature
individuals of fewer than 50.

THREATENING PROCESSES

Potential threats include cyclonic events, feral
animal activity (which may affect recruitment),
changes to hydrology, possibly due to more
intensive land-use near rainforest patches, and the
subsequent threat from fire.

CONSERVATION OBJECTIVES
AND MANAGEMENT

A recovery plan for this species, and other
threatened plants on the Tiwi Islands, is due
to be released in 2007, but many actions in its
draft are currently being implemented through
a collaborative project involving Tiwi rangers
and scientists from the Department of Natural
Resources, Environment and The Arts, with
funding from the Natural Heritage Trust.

Further research into the status and extent of the
population is required. A monitoring program is
being established.

Compiled by Raelee Kerrigan, Ian Cowie, Louis Elliott [April 2007] / **References:** Coode, M.J.E. (1981). Elaeocarpaceae. In *Handbooks of the Flora of Papua New Guinea: Volume II.* (ed. E.E. Henty.) (Melbourne University Press, Melbourne.) / Woinarski, J., Brennan, K., Cowie, I., Kerrigan, R., and Hempel, C. (2003). *Biodiversity conservation on the Tiwi Islands, Northern Territory. Part 1. Plants and environments.* 144 pp. (Department of Infrastructure Planning and Environment, Darwin.)

Dwarf desert spike-rush
Eleocharis papillosa

CONSERVATION STATUS
AUSTRALIA: **VULNERABLE**
NORTHERN TERRITORY: **VULNERABLE**

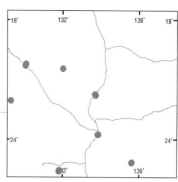

Known locations of Eleocharis papillosa
● = pre 1970
● = post 1970

DESCRIPTION
The dwarf desert spike-rush is a small, erect perennial sedge, typically less than 10 cm high. The above-ground parts grow in response to inundation, subsequently dying back to underground parts which consist of roots, rhizomes and tuberoids.
The leaf sheaths are purplish at base.

Flowering and fruiting: recorded throughout the year.

DISTRIBUTION
The dwarf desert spike-rush is endemic to the Northern Territory. It is known from just eight locations, ranging from the northern Tanami Desert to the southern parts of the Finke bioregion and the edge of the Simpson Desert (White *et al.* 2000). Most locations are remote and repeated collections have been made at only three of them. The latitudinal range of the species is 600 km and the longitudinal range is 560 km.

Conservation reserves where reported: None

ECOLOGY
All records are from temporary wetlands - predominantly freshwater and semi-saline swamps - but one record is from the edge of a temporary riverine waterhole.

Growth, seeding and germination are presumed to occur in response to temporary inundation. Seed set has not been observed at Ilparpa Swamp which is the most frequently visited location. Cultivated greenhouse plants from Ilparpa, with constant water conditions, have also 'failed' to set seed.

However, some herbarium specimens from other locations do have seed, indicating that sexual reproduction may occur in some populations. The abundance of above-ground shoots may vary between different inundation events. On occasions it can be difficult to determine whether a population consists of many individuals or few individuals that are extensively rhizomatous. The species has been locally abundant (estimated at up to approximately 1000 plants, D.Albrecht and P.Latz *pers. obs.*) at some times at some sites. However, the actual number of genetically different individuals may be substantially fewer in some populations where asexual reproduction is significant.

During dry times, populations persist as soil-stored seed or soil-stored root tuberoids and/or rhizomes. Plants with constant water conditions (at the Alice Springs Desert Park nursery) exhibit an annual die-off of the above-ground shoots. It is not known what controls this die-off but age, season and cold are all possible factors. These plants subsequently re-sprout. Informal trials indicate that re-sprouting can occur from the tuberoids after they have been stored in dry conditions (Tim Collins *pers. comm.*).

It is recorded as growing both in the open and under shrubs, which may provide protection from trampling by stock at some sites.

CONSERVATION ASSESSMENT
Eleocharis papillosa appears to be genuinely rare. Due to its small size and the intermittent presence of surface shoots it is likely that it is under collected

and that additional populations do exist. However, an extensive survey of wetlands in 2000 and 2001, in apparently ideal conditions, found only one new population (Duguid *et al.* 2002). The population at Ilparpa Swamp and one from the Burt Plain bioregion are being encroached upon by the exotic couch grass (*Cynodon dactylon*) such that they are highly likely to be eliminated. Recent searches (from 2000–04) at Ilparpa Swamp, following two particularly wet summers, failed to find the species.

It is rated as **Vulnerable** (under criteria B2ab(iii,iv)) due to:
- the small area of occupancy (less than 2000 km²);
- the severely fragmented distribution;
- the small number of known locations (fewer than 10); and
- a continuing, projected decline in the area, extent and quality of habitat and number of subpopulations.

THREATENING PROCESSES
Invasion by couch grass (*Cynodon dactylon*) is the main threat at two populations. Changed hydrological conditions may affect some subpopulations. Trampling by stock occurs at some sites, but any long term effect has not been quantified.

CONSERVATION OBJECTIVES AND MANAGEMENT
Known populations require monitoring as does the spread of couch grass. The feasibility of controlling couch grass in swamp environments needs to be investigated.

Compiled by Angus Duguid, Raelee Kerrigan, David Albrecht [June 2006] / **References:** Duguid, A., Barnetson, J., Clifford, B., Pavey, C., Albrecht, D., Risler, J., and McNellie, M. (2002). *Wetlands in the arid Northern Territory.* A report to Environment Australia on the inventory and significance of wetlands in the arid Northern Territory. (Parks and Wildlife Commission of the Northern Territory, Alice Springs.) / White, M., Albrecht, D., Duguid, A., Latz, P., and Hamilton, M. (2000). *Plant species and sites of botanical significance in the southern bioregions of the Northern Territory. Volume 1: significant vascular plants.* Report to the Australian Heritage Commission. (Arid Lands Environment Centre, Alice Springs.)

Image courtesy of Ian Cowie

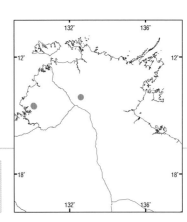

*Known locations
of Eleocharis
retroflexa*
● = pre 1970
● = post 1970

Eleocharis retroflexa

CONSERVATION STATUS
AUSTRALIA: **VULNERABLE**
NORTHERN TERRITORY: **DATA DEFICIENT**

DESCRIPTION
Eleocharis retroflexa is a small, cryptic grass-like sedge to 10 cm tall. The stems are mostly submerged, and 4-angled. The leaves are reduced to a sheath. The flower heads are 2 to 3.5 mm long, 1 to 2 mm diameter. The nut is white, approximately 0.7 mm long, pitted (Cowie *et al.* 2000).

Flowering and fruiting: April–May

DISTRIBUTION
This species is pantropical in distribution, and in Australia occurs in Queensland and the Northern Territory. In the Northern Territory, it is known only from two swamps on the Wingate Mountains plateau (Daly River/Port Keats Aboriginal Land Trust) and from a swamp on the sandstone plateau in Nitmiluk National Park.

Conservation reserves where reported:
Nitmiluk National Park

ECOLOGY
This species has been reported growing in shallow water on the margins of seasonal swamps. The substrates were laterite or clay loam. Associated species included *Melaleuca viridiflora, Eucalyptus phoenicea, Corymbia oocarpa, Capillipedium parviflorum, Sorghum plumosum* and *Heteropogon triticeus*, all common species.

CONSERVATION ASSESSMENT
This species is listed as Vulnerable under Federal legislation.

In the Northern Territory, this species is coded as **Data Deficient** based on:
• data are considered inadequate for assessment; and
• known from three populations, none of which are believed to be under threat.

No abundance data are available for this species and it is considered not adequately surveyed. Although there has been considerable recent botanical survey effort in Nitmiluk National Park, the species is inconspicuous. Also, *E. retroflexa* appears to have a relatively short flowering and fruiting period, outside of which it would be very difficult to identify. There has been little botanical collecting and only one short general botanical survey in the remote Wingate Mountains since European settlement. All of the sites where it is known could be accessed only by helicopter at the time it was collected.

THREATENING PROCESSES
No threats are known. Parts of the Northern Territory where this species occurs are among the most remote and least affected by European settlement. Fire during the April to May fertile period could potentially be a threat. It is possible that high densities of feral stock may affect the species, but there is no information available to demonstrate such threat.

CONSERVATION OBJECTIVES AND MANAGEMENT
Further targeted surveys of appropriate habitat at an appropriate time of year are needed to gather distribution and abundance data and assess threats.

Compiled by Ian Cowie, Raelee Kerrigan [April 2006] / **References:** Cowie, I.D., Short, P.S., and Osterkamp Madsen, M. (2000). *Floodplain Flora: A flora of the coastal floodplains of the Northern Territory, Australia.* Flora of Australia Supplementary Series 10. (ABRS, Canberra.)

Image courtesy of David Liddle

Endiandra limnophila

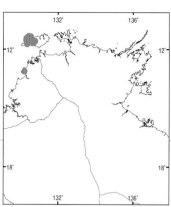

Known locations
of Endiandra
limnophila
● = pre 1970
● = post 1970

CONSERVATION STATUS
AUSTRALIA: **NOT LISTED**
NORTHERN TERRITORY: **VULNERABLE**

DESCRIPTION
Endiandra limnophila is a tree to 20 m tall and
30 cm diameter at breast height, but usually
smaller. Its leaves are somewhat bluish (glaucous)
below, with domatia present. The flowers are pale
green to cream, turning brown with age, perfumed
or odourless. The fruits are black and glaucous,
28 to 38 mm x 14 to 15 mm.

Flowering: December

DISTRIBUTION
This species is an Australian endemic, known
from the far north of Cape York Peninsula and the
Northern Territory. In the Northern Territory, it is
known from the Tiwi Islands and Channel Point.
It was recorded in the Rainforest Atlas (Liddle *et al.*
1994) at approximately 22 localities.

Conservation reserves where reported: None

ECOLOGY
This species grows in well-developed rainforest.
It is normally found on swampy or wet situations
along creek margins.

CONSERVATION ASSESSMENT
Although recorded from a relatively large number
of sites, there have usually been no more than
five or six individuals observed at any one locality.

Extensive survey of the Tiwi Islands in 2000–02
yielded no further populations of this species
(Woinarski *et al.* 2003). This species is classified
as **Vulnerable** (under criteria D1+2) based on:
• an area of occupancy, although difficult to
determine, estimated to be less than 20 km²;
and
• a population size estimated at fewer than
1000 individuals.

THREATENING PROCESSES
A small population and restricted distribution
makes this species susceptible to stochastic events.
Known localities on Bathurst Island have high
pig populations that may affect recruitment.
Only being known from very wet, peat-like
rainforests, this species would easily be affected
by changes in hydrology. However, such changes
are not anticipated.

CONSERVATION OBJECTIVES
AND MANAGEMENT
A recovery plan for this species, and other
threatened plants on the Tiwi Islands, is due
to be released in 2007, but many actions in its
draft are currently being implemented through
a collaborative project involving Tiwi rangers
and scientists from the Department of Natural
Resources, Environment and The Arts, with
funding from the Natural Heritage Trust.

Research is required to establish population size,
the extent of its distribution and the impact of feral
animals. Fencing is not practical for these areas. A
monitoring program should be established for at
least some populations.

Compiled by Raelee Kerrigan, Ian Cowie [April 2006] / **References:** Hyland, B.P.M., and Whiffin, T. (1993). *Australian Tropical Rain Forest Trees*. An interactive system Volume 2. (CSIRO Publications,
Melbourne.) / Liddle, D.T., Russell-Smith, J., Brock, J., Leach, G.J., and Connors, G.T. (1994). *Atlas of the vascular rainforest plants of the Northern Territory*. Flora of Australia Supplementary Series No. 3,
(Australian Biological Resources Study, Canberra.) / Woinarski, J., Brennan, K., Cowie, I., Kerrigan, R., and Hempel, C. (2003). *Biodiversity conservation on the Tiwi Islands, Northern Territory. Part 1.
Plants and environments*. 144 pp. (Department of Infrastructure Planning and Environment, Darwin.)

Rainbow Valley fuschia bush
Eremophila sp. Rainbow Valley

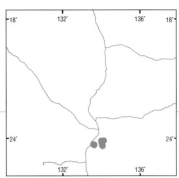

Known locations of Eremophila sp. Rainbow Valley
● = *pre 1970*
● = *post 1970*

CONSERVATION STATUS
AUSTRALIA: **VULNERABLE**
NORTHERN TERRITORY: **VULNERABLE**

DESCRIPTION

Eremophila sp. Rainbow Valley is a prostrate perennial shrub. The flower (corolla) is purple with white in the throat, upper lip 2-lobed, lower lip 3-lobed; occasionally white corolla. The fruits are 1 cm in diameter.

Flowering and Fruiting: January–April, August–November

Note that some documents refer to this species as *Eremophila prostrata* which is an unpublished name from a preliminary manuscript by Robert Chinock (D. Albrecht *pers. comm.*).

DISTRIBUTION

Eremophila sp. Rainbow Valley is endemic to the Northern Territory, with a latitudinal range of 25 km and longitudinal range of 61 km. It is presently known from seven populations: two from the Mt. Ooraminna area, four from between Deep Well and Mt Ooramina and another from the Rainbow Valley area (Eldridge 1996; White *et al.* 2000). The total area occupied by the species is less than 50 ha.

Five of the seven populations are small and have fewer then 50 individuals recorded. Until 2002, the largest known population was to the east of Mt Ooraminna. Many hundreds of plants were present at this site in 1998. In 2002, very large numbers of seedlings were observed to have recruited in an area burnt during fire management activities in and adjacent to Rainbow

Valley Conservation Reserve (Jason Barnetson *pers. comm.*). This population numbered tens of thousands of individuals at its peak (A. Duguid *pers. obs.*).

Conservation reserves where reported:
Rainbow Valley Conservation Reserve

ECOLOGY

Knowledge about the ecology and distribution of this species was summarised in a report by Eldridge (1996). It inhabits sandplains and the lower slopes of low sand dunes, supporting spinifex (*Triodia basedowii*) with a varied overstorey including shrubs of *Grevillea*, *Hakea* and *Acacia*, and desert oak trees (*Allocasuarina decaisneana*). Known populations occur in the vicinity of low rocky ranges and probably receive additional 'run-on' of rainwater from adjacent areas.

An experiment conducted at Rainbow Valley Conservation Reserve has confirmed that germination is stimulated by environmental perturbations including fire and road grading (A. Duguid, unpublished data). Eldridge (1996) also documented a germination event triggered by local flooding (sheet flow of water) across an inter-dune area.

Eldridge (1996) reported that the species can re-sprout and subsequent work confirms this with basal re-sprouting occurring after burning and short term drought. It is not know how long individuals can survive as dormant roots before

rains allow them to re-sprout. From limited data it can be estimated that plants are not very long-lived, in the order of two to 10 years.

CONSERVATION ASSESSMENT

This species qualifies as **Vulnerable** (under criteria B1+2; a and c.iv) based on:
- a small extent of occurrence and small area of occupancy (estimated to be less than 20 km²);
- small number of locations; and
- extreme fluctuations in population size.

THREATENING PROCESSES

With a restricted area of occupancy and population size, this species is vulnerable to stochastic events.

CONSERVATION OBJECTIVES AND MANAGEMENT

Given that several new populations have been found in recent years during opportunistic survey work, further focused survey is required to establish an accurate picture of the distribution of the species. The relationship between disturbance and recruitment also requires further research. Appropriate use of fire to increase the diversity of successional states in the spinifex sandplains occupied by this species could increase and stabilise population numbers.

A monitoring program should be maintained for at least representative populations.

Compiled by Raelee Kerrigan, David Albrecht, Angus Duguid [June 2006] / **References:** Eldridge, S.R. (1996). *A Preliminary Survey of the Distribution, Status and Basic Ecology of Eremophila (prostrata).* Report to the Australian Heritage Commission NEGP programme, National Threatened Species Network. / White, M., Albrecht, D., Duguid, A., Latz, P., and Hamilton, M. (2000). *Plant species and sites of botanical significance in the southern bioregions of the Northern Territory. Volume 1: significant vascular plants.* A report to the Australian Heritage Commission. (Arid Lands Environment Centre, Alice Springs.)

Image courtesy of A. Small (GHD)

Freycinetia excelsa

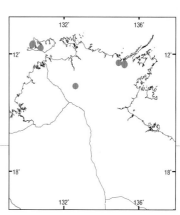

Known locations of Freycinetia excelsa
● = pre 1970
● = post 1970

DESCRIPTION

Freycinetia excelsa is a small woody climber with stems of 7 to 8 mm in diameter. The leaf auricles each have a rounded apex and no distinct lobe. The bracts are orange to red. The male spikes are yellow to cream-brown, and the fruit strawberry-red (Stone 1982).

This species has not been collected while reproductive in the Northern Territory and some taxonomic uncertainty exists regarding the threatened species *F. excelsa* and *F. percostata*. For example, both species are recorded from a single location on the Tiwi Islands, where it seems likely that only one species is present at that site.

Fruiting: February

DISTRIBUTION

This species is known from Australia and New Guinea. In the Northern Territory, it has been recorded from seven localities from Bathurst Island to the Arafura Swamp.

Conservation reserves where reported:
Kakadu National Park

ECOLOGY

It occurs in wet lowland rainforest and spring-fed rainforests in sandstone gullies (Woinarski *et al.* 2003).

CONSERVATION ASSESSMENT

This species is recorded from only seven localities across the Top End. The species qualifies as **Vulnerable** (under criteria D1+2) based on:

• the total number of individuals is estimated to be fewer than 1000; and

• a restricted area of occupancy estimated to be less than 20 km².

THREATENING PROCESSES

The impact of feral animals on this species is unknown but pigs in large numbers are likely to affect recruitment either through disturbance or browsing. Populations on the Tiwi Islands could be susceptible to severe cyclonic events. This species has not been collected while reproductive, despite re-survey throughout the year (K. Brennan *pers. comm.*). Changes to hydrology, although none are foreseen, are likely to affect this species.

One population is located at Glyde Point, in an area proposed as industrial estate and is consequently at risk.

CONSERVATION OBJECTIVES AND MANAGEMENT

A recovery plan for this species, and other threatened plants on the Tiwi Islands, is due to be released in 2007, but many actions in its draft are currently being implemented through a collaborative project involving Tiwi rangers and scientists from the Department of Natural Resources, Environment and The Arts, with funding from the Natural Heritage Trust.

Research and further surveys are required to establish the status of these populations, the distribution of the species and the impact of feral animals. Conservation of the Glyde Point population is recommended. A monitoring program should be established for at least some populations.

Given that there are ambiguous records of *F. excelsa* and *F. percostata*, targeted surveys should be made for this species at known locations when flowering is likely to be taking place, and further research is required into the taxonomic status of the two species on the Tiwi Islands.

Compiled by Raelee Kerrigan, Ian Cowie, Louis Elliott [April 2007] / **References:** Stone, B.C. (1982). The Australian species of *Freycinetia* (Pandanaceae). *Brunonia* 5, 79-94. / Woinarski, J., Brennan, K., Cowie, I., Kerrigan, R., and Hempel, C. (2003). *Biodiversity conservation on the Tiwi Islands, Northern Territory. Part 1. Plants and environments.* 144 pp. (Department of Infrastructure Planning and Environment, Darwin.)

Freycinetia percostata

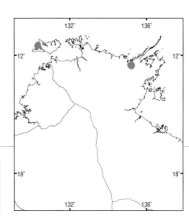

*Known locations
of Freycinetia
percostata*
● = pre 1970
● = post 1970

CONSERVATION STATUS
AUSTRALIA: **NOT LISTED**
NORTHERN TERRITORY: **VULNERABLE**

DESCRIPTION

Freycinetia percostata is a moderately large woody climber, with stems to 2 cm diameter. The leaf auricles each have a distinct apical deltoid lobe, with margins distinctly ciliate-spinulose.
The spathe is yellow-orange to salmon pink.
The male spikes are pale to orange-brown.
The broken fruit is crimson. Some taxonomic uncertainty exists regarding the threatened species *F. excelsa* and *F. percostata*.

Fruiting: November

DISTRIBUTION

This species is known from Australia, New Guinea and the Solomon Islands (Stone 1982).
In the Northern Territory, it has been recorded from localities on Bathurst Island and the Arafura Swamp.

Conservation reserves where reported: None

ECOLOGY

It occurs in wet lowland rainforest and spring-fed rainforests in sandstone gullies (Woinarski *et al.* 2003).

CONSERVATION ASSESSMENT

In the Northern Territory, this species is known only from two wet rainforest patches of restricted area. The species is considered **Vulnerable** (under criteria D1+2) based on:
• the total number of individuals estimated to be fewer than 1000; and
• a restricted area of occupancy estimated to be less than 20 km².

THREATENING PROCESSES

The impact of feral animals on this species is unknown but pigs in large numbers are likely to affect recruitment either through disturbance or grazing. Populations on the Tiwi Islands, although inland, would be susceptible to severe cyclonic events. Any changes to hydrology may affect this species.

CONSERVATION OBJECTIVES AND MANAGEMENT

A recovery plan for this species, and other threatened plants on the Tiwi Islands, is due to be released in 2007, but many actions in its draft are currently being implemented through a collaborative project involving Tiwi rangers and scientists from the Department of Natural Resources, Environment and The Arts, with funding from the Natural Heritage Trust.

Research and further surveys are required to establish the status of these populations, the distribution of the species and the impact of feral animals. Fencing to keep out feral animals would not be practical. A monitoring program should be established.

Given that there are ambiguous records of *F. excelsa* and *F. percostata,* targeted surveys should be made for this species at known locations when flowering is likely to be taking place, and further research is required into the taxonomic status of the two species on the Tiwi Islands.

Compiled by Raelee Kerrigan, Ian Cowie, Louis Elliott [April 2007] / **References:** Stone, B.C. (1982). The Australian species of *Freycinetia* (Pandanaceae). *Brunonia* 5, 79-94.
Woinarski, J., Brennan, K., Cowie, I., Kerrigan, R., and Hempel, C. (2003). *Biodiversity conservation on the Tiwi Islands, Northern Territory. Part 1. Plants and environments.* 144 pp. (Department of Infrastructure Planning and Environment, Darwin.)

Garcinia warrenii

CONSERVATION STATUS
AUSTRALIA: **NOT LISTED**
NORTHERN TERRITORY: **ENDANGERED**

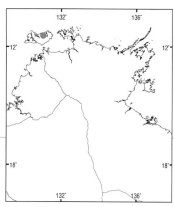

*Known locations
of Garcinia
warrenii*
● = *pre 1970*
● = *post 1970*

DESCRIPTION

Garcinia warrenii is a tree to 8 m. The leaves are simple and opposite. The foot of the petiole has extensions or gland-like stipules that run along the stem axis. The leaf venation is distinctly parallel. Broken petioles and twigs produce a yellow exudate.

Flowering: August

DISTRIBUTION

In the Northern Territory, this species is known only from a small hill surrounded by mangroves in the Jessie River on Melville Island. It is also found on Cape York Peninsula and in New Guinea.

Conservation reserves where reported: None

ECOLOGY

Little is known about the ecology of this species in the Northern Territory. In Queensland, it is usually found in well-developed rainforest but also along watercourses in the open (Hyland and Whiffin 1993).

CONSERVATION ASSESSMENT

The species has been classified as **Endangered** (under criterion D) based on:
• a small population (estimated at fewer than 250 mature individuals); and
• a very restricted distribution.

This population occurs in a remote estuary on Melville Island and appears healthy, with a number of saplings present.

THREATENING PROCESSES

A cyclonic event is the only imaginable threat as the community is surrounded by an extensive mangrove system and is unlikely to be affected by weeds, feral animals, clearing or development.

CONSERVATION OBJECTIVES AND MANAGEMENT

A recovery plan for this species, and other threatened plants on the Tiwi Islands, is due to be released in 2007.

Collection of propagation material and translocation to a botanic gardens would seem the only action available to protect the species from a cyclonic event. Although similar habitats in the area were well surveyed, further survey may yield more populations.

Compiled by Raelee Kerrigan, Ian Cowie [April 2006] / **References:** Hyland, B.P.M., and Whiffin, T. (1993). *Australian Tropical Rain Forest Trees. An interactive system Volume 2.* (CSIRO, Melbourne.) / Woinarski, J., Brennan, K., Cowie, I., Kerrigan, R., and Hempel, C. (2003). *Biodiversity conservation on the Tiwi Islands, Northern Territory. Part 1. Plants and environments.* 144 pp. (Department of Infrastructure Planning and Environment, Darwin.)

Image courtesy of Kym Brennan

Gleichenia sp. Victoria River

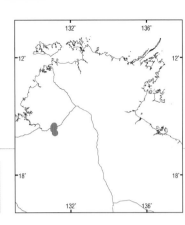

Known locations of Gleichenia sp. Victoria River
● = *pre 1970*
● = *post 1970*

CONSERVATION STATUS
AUSTRALIA: **NOT LISTED**
NORTHERN TERRITORY: **VULNERABLE**

DESCRIPTION

This undescribed taxon is a pendulous or erect fern to 50 cm. The leaves (fronds) of 1 to 3 tiers of branches, are 9 to 200 cm long. The leaf stalk (stipe) is 10 to 55 cm long. The pinnules are oblong to triangular 1 to 2.5 mm long, 1 to 2 mm wide. The spores are in clusters (sori) of 2 to 4 sporangia.

This taxon is very similar to *Gleichenia dicarpa* (known in the Northern Territory only from Twin Falls) and is distinguished by having larger ultimate frond segments and in the number of sporangia per sorus (Short *et al.* 2003).

Fertile plant: May

DISTRIBUTION

This taxon is apparently endemic to the Northern Territory. It has been recorded only from the Victoria River Gorge.

Conservation reserves where reported:
Gregory National Park

ECOLOGY

This species is found growing in seepage areas at the base of sandstone scarps or rock overhangs (Chinnock and Bell 1998). One collection was reported as regrowing after fire damage.

CONSERVATION ASSESSMENT

Until recent records, this taxon was known only from a collection by Ferdinand Mueller from the upper Victoria River during the 1855-56 North Australian Expedition (Short *et al.* 2003).

Substantial survey in Gregory National Park yielded only four small populations of this taxon, however, extensive areas of potential habitat remain unsurveyed. Under the precautionary principle, this taxon qualifies as **Vulnerable** (under criteria D1+2) based on:
• a population size estimated to be fewer than 1000 individuals; and
• a restricted area of occupancy estimated to be less than 20 km².

At present all known populations are found in a conservation reserve.

THREATENING PROCESSES

This species is susceptible to stochastic events. Rock slides and changes to hydrology are a potential threat.

CONSERVATION OBJECTIVES AND MANAGEMENT

Research and further survey is required to establish population size and the extent of its distribution. A monitoring program should be established for at least one population.

Compiled by Raelee Kerrigan, Ian Cowie [April 2006] / **References:** Chinnock, R.J., and Bell, G.H. (1998). Gleicheniaceae. *Flora of Australia* 48, 148-161. / Short, P., Dixon, D., and Osterkamp Madsen, M. (2003). A review of the ferns and fern allies of the Northern Territory. *The Beagle* 19, 7-80.

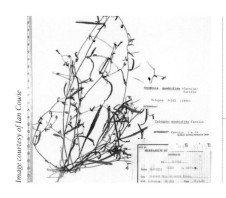

Image courtesy of Ian Cowie

Goodenia quadrifida

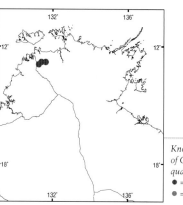

Known locations
of Goodenia
quadrifida
● = pre 1970
● = post 1970

CONSERVATION STATUS
AUSTRALIA: **VULNERABLE**
NORTHERN TERRITORY: **DATA DEFICIENT**

DESCRIPTION

Goodenia quadrifida is a slender annual herb with weak stems to 30 cm long. Short glandular tipped hairs are present throughout. The leaves are alternate, narrow, 15 to 75 mm long, 1 to 5 mm wide, often with two basal lobes. The flowers are purple-brown with a yellow throat. The style is 4-armed. Seeds are rough. It is closely related to *G. purpurea* and apparently differs only by the 4-armed style (Cowie *et al.* 2000).

Flowering and fruiting: March–May

DISTRIBUTION

This species is endemic to the Northern Territory, occurring at three places near Darwin. It is known from the Marrakai Crossing area on the Adelaide River and Hardies Creek, a tributary of the Mary River (Cowie *et al.* 2000).

Conservation reserves where reported:
Mary River National Park (although imprecision in collection locality information means that the tenure on which this population occurs may need confirmation).

ECOLOGY

Collection notes indicate that plants in one population grow in grassland. It occurs on the upper parts of estuarine floodplains, on poorly drained grey clays or silty soils.

CONSERVATION ASSESSMENT

In the Northern Territory, this species is coded as **Data Deficient** because available data are considered inadequate for assessment.

Assessment of conservation status is hampered by taxonomic uncertainty surrounding the species. *Goodenia quadrifida* is closely related to, and possibly conspecific with, the much more widespread *G. purpurea*. There is also a negative collection bias due to difficult access to the habitat during the wet season. The species has not been collected since 1968 and no data on population size or area of occupancy are available. The extent of occurrence is estimated at 170 km^2.

THREATENING PROCESSES

Parts of the Adelaide River where the species was recorded have been invaded by the introduced shrub *Mimosa pigra* for more than 25 years. This species converts wetlands dominated by herbaceous vegetation into shrublands with a consequent loss of biodiversity.

While little is known of threatening processes in the Hardies Creek population, the area has been managed as a national park for many years. At the time the Hardies Creek collection was made, most similar habitat in the region was heavily grazed by feral buffalo.

CONSERVATION OBJECTIVES AND MANAGEMENT

Further research is required to:
• confirm that *G. quadrifida* is specifically distinct from *G. purpurea*;
• confirm the location of previously identified populations;
• provide an estimate of population size;
• establish a monitoring program;
• assess possible threats; and
• attempt to locate additional populations.

Compiled by Ian Cowie, Raelee Kerrigan [April 2006] / **References:** Cowie, I.D., Short, P.S., and Osterkamp Madsen, M. (2000). *Floodplain Flora: A flora of the coastal floodplains of the Northern Territory, Australia*. Flora of Australia Supplementary Series 10. (ABRS, Canberra.)

Image courtesy of Bill Lavarack

Habenaria rumphii

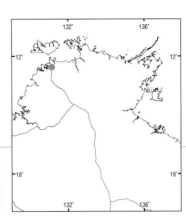

Known locations of Habenaria rumphii
● = *pre 1970*
● = *post 1970*

CONSERVATION STATUS
AUSTRALIA: **NOT LISTED**
NORTHERN TERRITORY: **ENDANGERED**

DESCRIPTION

Habenaria rumphii is a terrestrial orchid with leaves 14 cm x 20 mm. The flower stem grows to 50 cm tall, is thin and wiry and bears up to 30 or more white flowers about 10 mm across. It is easily recognised by its scattered rosette of stiffly spreading leaves, the densely congested inflorescence and the obliquely erect labellum with the long mid-lobe and short pointed lateral lobes. This species was previously known as *H. holtzei*.

Flowering and Fruiting: February

DISTRIBUTION

This species is known from across much of south-east Asia, including Indochina and Indonesia. In Australia, it is restricted to the northern parts of Queensland and the Northern Territory (Jones 1988). The only Northern Territory record is from the upper Howard River at Humpty Doo.

Conservation reserves where reported: None

ECOLOGY

This species occurs in open forest and woodland growing amongst grass. It is reported to be prominent in low lying sites that are partially inundated during the wet season. In the Northern Territory, this species has been collected from a sandplain adjacent to a spring-fed rainforest.

CONSERVATION ASSESSMENT

This species has been collected only once in the Northern Territory (1989) and is still known from only one locality despite considerable survey in the area during the wet season in 2000 and 2001.

Based on extent of occurrence and area of occupancy, this species qualifies for Critically Endangered. However, as a terrestrial geophyte with ephemeral above-ground parts, there is an element of data deficiency and as such it is listed as **Endangered** (under criteria B1ab(iii)+2ab(iii);D).

Declines in the extent and area of occurrence as well as the quality of habitat of this species are projected for the future based on the threatening processes listed below.

THREATENING PROCESSES

Sand-mining in the area is a current and continuing threat both directly through clearing of individuals and indirectly through changes to hydrology in the area. The impacts of increases in exotic weeds, changes to the fire regime, and disturbance by feral animals (especially pigs) are yet to be assessed. The area is also extensively subdivided for rural residential allotments. As the grid references differed from the locality description, threats to this species were assessed on the written locality.

CONSERVATION OBJECTIVES AND MANAGEMENT

Further survey is required to relocate this species and establish its susceptibility to the threatening processes in the area. Recovery actions such as monitoring, fire management, weed and feral animal control and habitat reservation may need to be implemented.

Compiled by Raelee Kerrigan, Ian Cowie [April 2006] / **References:** Jones, D. L. (1988). *Native Orchids of Australia.* (Reed, Sydney.)

Helicteres sp. Glenluckie Creek

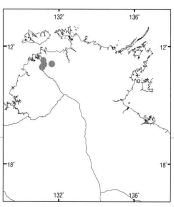

Known locations of Helicteres sp. Glenluckie Creek
● = *pre 1970*
● = *post 1970*

CONSERVATION STATUS
AUSTRALIA: **ENDANGERED**
NORTHERN TERRITORY: **ENDANGERED**

DESCRIPTION

Helicteres sp. Glenluckie Creek is an undescribed, erect multi-stemmed shrub to 40 cm becoming more lax with age. The aerial parts of the plant are annual, with perennial root stock. The flowers are pink-purple. The fruits are green and woolly-hairy.

Flowering: January, September, November
Fruiting: January, March, October –November

DISTRIBUTION

The species is endemic to the Northern Territory. It has been recorded from three populations; near Mt Bundy, near Batchelor and Lake Bennett. The known extent of occurrence of this species is 915 km².

Conservation reserves where reported:
Mary River National Park

ECOLOGY

This species occurs in woodlands dominated by *Eucalyptus tectifica* or *E. miniata,* on sandy loam soils on rocky siltstone slopes or granite.

No individuals were identified as juveniles in recent surveys of this species, however many individuals were observed to resprout from a perennial root stock, often vigorously after fire.

CONSERVATION ASSESSMENT

Survey of populations at the Glenluckie Creek and particularly Lake Bennett localities in 2002 indicated that populations are localised but may be abundant where found. A total of 407 individuals were counted in quadrats from both populations and preliminary population estimates indicate a population size in the 100 000s with an area of occupancy of approximately 10 ha.

There is limited population statistics for the Mt Bundy locality with 700 individuals recorded from three subpopulations in 4 ha.

While it is possible that extensive targeted searches may uncover additional populations of this species there is a high degree of confidence in the current distribution data.

This taxon is classified as **Endangered** (under criteria B1ab(iii,iv,v)+2ab(iii,iv,v)) based on:
• extent of occurrence estimated to be less than 5000 km²;
• area of occupancy estimated to be less than 500 km²;
• known to exist at no more than five locations; and
• a projected decline in extent of occurrence, area of occupancy and quality of habitat.

THREATENING PROCESSES

Two populations of this species are vulnerable to potential clearing for subdivision (NTG 2000), maintenance of railway easement or road maintenance. Both populations may be susceptible to invasion from perennial weedy grasses such as gamba grass (*Andropogon gayanus*) and mission grass (*Pennisetum polystachion*). These grasses are likely to smother individuals and alter fire intensity and frequency and potentially affect recruitment. Gamba grass supports fuel loads up to 20 tonnes per hectare (Barrow 1995) and mission grass supports fuel loads up to 27 tonnes per hectare (Panton 1993).

Kean and Price (2003) reported that 80% of rural blocks in the Humpty Doo area contain mission grasses. Mission grasses are known to invade undisturbed bushland, however they are prevalent on disturbed land and along roadsides. While there is some evidence to suggest that soil disturbance favours the establishment of mission grass (Cowie and Werner 1988), the high prevalence on freehold land may also reflect the dense road network and high levels of vehicle movement (Kean and Price 2003).

Therefore, any further clearing activities in or around the populations of *Helicteres* sp. Glenluckie Creek may either directly affect population numbers by active removal of plants, or more indirectly through competition with invading exotic species or via altered fire regimes as a result of invasion by exotic plant species.

CONSERVATION OBJECTIVES AND MANAGEMENT

Research priorities are to:
• provide a more detailed assessment of its distribution, habitat requirements and population size; and
• provide an assessment of the factors limiting distribution, and/or threats to its survival.

Further survey may yield additional populations. If clearing becomes imminent, habitat protection on private lands and state lands may need to be negotiated. A monitoring program should be established at some representative populations.

Compiled by Raelee Kerrigan, Ian Cowie [April 2006] / **References:** Barrow, P. (1995). *The Ecology and Management of Gamba Grass (Andropogon gayanus Kunth.)* Final Report to the Australian Nature Conservation Agency. (Northern Territory Department of Primary Industry and Fisheries, Darwin.) / Cowie, I.D., and Werner, P.A. (1988). *Weeds in Kakadu National Park – a survey of alien plants – Phase II.* (CSIRO Division of Wildlife and Rangelands Research, Tropical Ecosystems Research Centre, Darwin.) / Kean, L., and. Price, O. (2003). The extent of Mission grasses and Gamba Grass in the Darwin region of Australia's Northern Territory. *Pacific Conservation Biology* 8, 281-290. / Northern Territory Government (2000). *Coomalie planning concepts and land use objectives 2003.* (Northern Territory Department of Infrastructure, Planning and Environment, Darwin.) / Panton, W.J. (1993). Changes in Post World War II distribution and status of monsoon rainforests in the Darwin area. *Australian Geographer* 24, 50-59.

Image courtesy of Kym Brennan

Hernandia nymphaeifolia

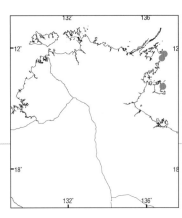

*Known locations
of Hernandia
nymphaeifolia*
● = *pre 1970*
● = *post 1970*

DESCRIPTION

Hernandia nymphaeifolia is a shrub or tree 5 to 22 m high. The leaves are peltately attached, narrowly or broadly ovate or subcircular. The 5 to 9 veins are palmate. The flowers are greenish or white, fragrant, with male and female separate. The fruit is fleshy, waxy white or reddish.

Flowering: March
Fruiting: June–July

DISTRIBUTION

This species occurs throughout the tropics (Duyfjes 1996). In the Northern Territory, it is known only from Groote Eylandt and Port Bradshaw in north-east Arnhem Land.

Conservation reserves where reported: None

ECOLOGY

This species occurs exclusively in coastal areas, along the sea shore in littoral forest and in coastal swamps.

CONSERVATION ASSESSMENT

This species was difficult to code. The number of plants present in forests where it was collected indicates the species is reproducing in the region and therefore does not qualify as a vagrant or visitor. The species satisfies the criteria for Endangered based on number of individuals estimated to be fewer than 250. However, as a coastal species with potential for immigration it is listed as **Vulnerable** (under criteria D1+2).

THREATENING PROCESSES

The species is susceptible to stochastic events such as cyclones.

CONSERVATION OBJECTIVES
AND MANAGEMENT

Further survey work in coastal rainforests may yield additional populations. Collection of propagation material and translocation to botanic gardens may be the only option for protection of the species against cyclonic events.

Compiled by Raelee Kerrigan, Ian Cowie [April 2006] / **References:** Duyfjes, B.E.E. (1996). Hernandiaceae. *Flora Malesiana* (Ser.1) 12, 737 - 761.

Image courtesy of Kym Brennan

Hibiscus brennanii

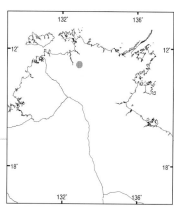

Known locations
of Hibiscus
brennanii
● = pre 1970
● = post 1970

CONSERVATION STATUS
AUSTRALIA: **VULNERABLE**
NORTHERN TERRITORY: **VULNERABLE**

DESCRIPTION

Hibiscus brennanii is an erect woody shrub to
3 m tall with pink flowers. Superficially, this
species may be difficult to distinguish from many
common *Hibiscus*. Diagnostic characters include
velvety grey/green foliage, with softly hairy leaves,
bracteoles and sepals lacking the prickly hairs
of many species. It is considered a short-lived
perennial.

Flowering: March–May

DISTRIBUTION

This species is endemic to the Northern Territory.
It is restricted to the Mt Brockman outlier of the
western Arnhem Land sandstone massif.

Conservation reserves where reported:
Kakadu National Park

ECOLOGY

Hibiscus brennanii is a putative obligate seeder and
grows on sandstone cliffs, in gullies and on broken
sandstone. Individuals are recorded growing
with *Symplectrodia lanosa*, *Pandanus basedowii*,
Micraira pungens, *Eriachne* spp., *Acacia* sp.
Baroalba and *A. scorpulorum*.

CONSERVATION ASSESSMENT

Although the Arnhem Land and Kakadu
escarpment is remote and difficult to access, this
species is considered adequately surveyed as a
relatively high proportion of herbarium collections
come from the Arnhem Land/Kakadu area.
The number of collections recorded from the
quarter degree grid cell where this taxon is found
is 4386 plant records.

This species was first collected in 1987 and
type material collected by 1990. The extent of
occurrence and likely area of occupancy of this
species is 1.5 km². The estimated total population
size for this population is 441 mature individuals
(Kerrigan 2003, 2004).

This species is classified as **Vulnerable** (under
criteria D1+2) based on:
• a population size estimated to be fewer than
  1000 individuals; and
• a restricted area of occupancy estimated to be
  approximately 2 km² (Kerrigan 2004).

THREATENING PROCESSES

Hibiscus species are often considered 'fire weeds',
regenerating strongly after wildfire. However,
Russell-Smith *et al.* (1998, 2002) suggested that
in some cases current fire regimes are affecting
obligate seeders in sandstone heath communities
and inappropriate fire regimes are a potential threat
to this species.

Unfortunately the generation time for this
species has not been assessed and the potential
for frequent fire events to kill individuals before
reproductive maturity has not been evaluated.
Similarly, seed-bank stores, seed longevity and
germination and establishment requirements are
unknown. With such a small population size and
limited distribution, the species is vulnerable to
inappropriate fire regimes and stochastic events.

CONSERVATION OBJECTIVES
AND MANAGEMENT

Research into the biology of the species is required,
to record fecundity, phenology, reproductive success,
seed-bank longevity, germination requirements and
response of seeds and adults to fire. An established
monitoring program reported that in 2004 there
were a substantial number of seedlings and juveniles
(Kerrigan 2004). Further monitoring of these
seedlings in the short term is recommended to
determine establishment rate for this species and
time to reach reproductive maturity.

Compiled by Raelee Kerrigan, Ian Cowie [April 2006] / **References:** Craven, L.A., and Fryxell, P.A. (1993). Additions to the Australian *Hibiscus* (Malvaceae): a new species and a new record. *The Beagle* 10, 1-6.
Kerrigan, R. (2003). *Kakadu Threatened Flora Report. Results of a threatened flora survey 2003.* (NT Department of Infrastructure Planning and Environment, Darwin.) / Kerrigan, R. (2004). *Kakadu Threatened Flora Report. Volume 2. Results of a threatened flora survey 2004.* (NT Department of Infrastructure Planning and Environment, Darwin.) / Russell-Smith, J., Ryan, P.G., Klessa, D., Waight, G., and Harwood, R.K. (1998). Fire regimes, fire-sensitive vegetation and fire management of the sandstone Arnhem Plateau, monsoonal northern Australia. *Journal of Applied Ecology* 35, 829-846. / Russell-Smith, J., Ryan, P.G., and Cheal, D.C. (2002). Fire regimes and the conservation of sandstone heath in monsoonal northern Australia: frequency, interval, patchiness. *Biological Conservation* 104, 91-107.

Hibiscus cravenii

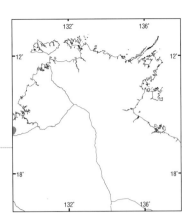

Known locations
of Hibiscus
cravenii
● = pre 1970
● = post 1970

CONSERVATION STATUS
AUSTRALIA: **VULNERABLE**
NORTHERN TERRITORY: **VULNERABLE**

DESCRIPTION
This species is a shrub to 1.5 m. Its stems are densely hairy, hairs stellate, yellowish or yellow-brown. The flower is hibiscus-like with unbranched style, petals mauve, turning blue when dry, with intense maroon spot on basal third.

This species was formerly listed as *Alyogyne cravenii*

Flowering: June, July, October and December
Fruiting: June, October and December

DISTRIBUTION
This species is endemic to the Northern Territory, where it is known only from Keep River National Park, at six localities around the base of the escarpment in the Jarnarm area and north-west of Gurrandalng.

The known extent of occurrence of this species is 17 km². Survey of known localities and survey for new populations by J. Egan in 1995 reported approximately 120 individuals from three localities associated with the Kelly's Knob sandstone within Keep River National Park. Further surveys have located three more populations and the total population size is estimated at around 500 individuals. Egan (1996) noted that the species was not found on any other geological formations in the area or on the Kelly's Knob sandstone within Hidden Valley, Western Australia.

Conservation reserves where reported:
Keep River National Park

ECOLOGY
Very little is known about the ecology of this species. It is recorded growing in sandy soils at the base of sandstone escarpments and to be scarce on sandstone scree slopes. Egan (1996) reported that no juveniles were observed in the populations she surveyed in 1995 and that the stands were even-aged and even-sized (1.5 to 2 m).

The Gurrandalng locality first collected by I. Cowie in 1998 and re-visited in 2000 had only recently been severely burnt and no individuals were observed, although burnt stems could have been overlooked. The same locality revisited in 2001 resulted in 200 to 300 individuals recorded for the area. Some adults had quite a woody base suggesting some individuals had re-sprouted after fire. Populations at Jarnarm appeared to grow in habitat that is frequently burnt (R. Kerrigan *pers. obs.*).

CONSERVATION ASSESSMENT
While it is possible that extensive targeted searches may uncover additional populations, particularly in areas inaccessible by foot, there is a high degree of confidence in the current distribution data. A summary of survey effort across the Northern Territory shows that this species is located in areas of relatively high collection effort. This taxon is classified as **Vulnerable** (under criteria D1+2) based on:

• number of mature individuals fewer than 1000 (the population is estimated to be between 200 to 500 individuals); and
• a restricted distribution of less than 10 km².

Plants in all stands were 1 to 2 m tall and evenly sized. All populations are exposed to frequent fires.

THREATENING PROCESSES
Frequent fires may threaten this species. Russell-Smith *et al.* (1998, 2002) suggested that populations of re-sprouter species may decline under too frequent burning and inappropriate fire regimes are a potential threat to this species (Egan 1996). Although some evidence exists to suggest this species may rebound from fire, the generation time for this species has not been assessed and the potential for frequent fire events to kill individuals before reproductive maturity has not been evaluated. Similarly, seed-bank stores, seed longevity and germination and establishment requirements are unknown. With such a small population size and limited distribution, the species is vulnerable to stochastic events such as inappropriate fire regimes.

CONSERVATION OBJECTIVES AND MANAGEMENT
Further research is required on the population dynamics of this species, the extent of its range, the impact of fire and other potential threatening processes. This research should be associated with an ongoing monitoring program.

Compiled by Raelee Kerrigan, Ian Cowie [April 2006] / **References:** Egan, J.L. (1996). *Assessment of "Poorly Known" (ROTAP Category K or k) Plant Taxa in the Northern Territory.* Australian Nature Conservation Agency Endangered Species Program. Project No. 490. Final Report. (Parks and Wildlife Commission of the NT, Darwin.) / Fryxell, P.A. (1987). Three new species (from Australia and Venezuela) and three new names (of Mexican plants) in the Malvaceae. *Systematic Botany* 12, 277. / Russell-Smith, J., Ryan, P.G., Klessa, D., Waight, G., and Harwood, R.K. (1998). Fire regimes, fire-sensitive vegetation and fire management of the sandstone Arnhem Plateau, monsoonal northern Australia. *Journal of Applied Ecology* 35, 829-846. / Russell-Smith, J., Ryan, P.G., and Cheal, D.C. (2002). Fire regimes and the conservation of sandstone heath in monsoonal northern Australia: frequency, interval, patchiness. *Biological Conservation* 104, 91-107.

Image courtesy of Kym Brennan

Hoya australis subsp. *oramicola*

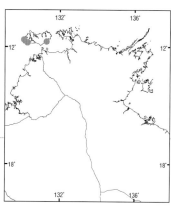

Known locations
of *Hoya australis*
subsp. *oramicola*
● = pre 1970
● = post 1970

CONSERVATION STATUS
AUSTRALIA: **VULNERABLE**
NORTHERN TERRITORY: **VULNERABLE**

DESCRIPTION

Hoya australis subsp. *oramicola* is a vine. Its leaves have sparse to dense covering of hairs and the leaf blade is succulent, less than 10 cm long, with the leaf margin strongly recurved. Glands (colleters) are absent. Latex is present. One characteristic that distinguishes this subspecies from that found on the mainland is the colour of the flowers. The mainland variety has cream flowers, whereas that of the Tiwi Islands is reddish.

Flowering: March, July
Fruiting: 3 to 4 months after flowering

DISTRIBUTION

This subspecies is endemic to the Northern Territory. It is found only on Bathurst and Melville Islands, where it is known from 11 records at seven localities (Liddle *et al.* 1994).

Conservation reserves where reported: None

ECOLOGY

This subspecies grows in coastal monsoon rainforest on dunes or red laterite.

CONSERVATION ASSESSMENT

This subspecies is considered adequately surveyed, based on extensive surveys on the Tiwi Islands and rainforest habitats across the Top End (Russell-Smith 1991; Fensham and Woinarski 1992; Woinarski *et al.* 2003). Extent of occurrence is documented at 4821 km², based on the records collated in Liddle *et al.* (1994), and the area of occupancy is 2400 ha based

on the patch size of rainforest communities where collected (Fensham and Woinarski 1992).

Very little data on abundance are available for this species. Russell-Smith (unpubl.) recorded this species as common at Lubra Point on Bathurst Island and uncommon at Conder Point on Melville Island. Targeted survey was undertaken in 2006 and four more populations were located in the south-western portion of Bathurst Island (in the same region as the prior Bathurst Island record). At these four sites, *Hoya australis* subsp. *oramicola* was considered common at two (both of them at the edge of dry rainforest behind coastal dunes). The other two populations occurred at fire-protected locations but had only a few individuals.

Targeted survey for this species in suitable habitat (dry monsoon forest around coastal dunes) was also undertaken at several other locations on both Bathurst Island and on Melville Island with no further populations found. Dunes comprise only a small proportion of the coastline of the Tiwi Islands. This subspecies has been classified as **Vulnerable** (under criteria D1+2) based on:

- an estimated population size of fewer than 1000 individuals; and
- a restricted area of occupancy estimated to be less than 20 km².

THREATENING PROCESSES

Very little is known about the threatening processes that may affect this taxon, which may be naturally rare. However, monsoon rainforests generally are

vulnerable to disturbance from cyclones, cattle, buffalo, pigs and dry season wildfires (Russell-Smith and Bowman 1992; Panton 1993; Woinarski *et al.* 2003).

The coastal rainforest communities in which this taxon occurs are unlikely to be directly affected by developing forestry activities on the Tiwi Islands (Woinarski *et al.* 2003). Nevertheless, large scale clearing of adjacent woodlands may affect local hydrology and provide opportunities for invasion by weedy species, particularly if adequate buffer zones are not instituted.

CONSERVATION OBJECTIVES AND MANAGEMENT

A recovery plan for this species, and other threatened plants on the Tiwi Islands, is due to be released in 2007, but many actions in its draft are currently being implemented through a collaborative project involving Tiwi rangers and scientists from the Department of Natural Resources, Environment and The Arts, with funding from the Natural Heritage Trust.

Research priorities are to:
- provide a more detailed assessment of its distribution, habitat requirements and population size; and
- provide an assessment of the factors limiting distribution, and/or threats to its survival.

A monitoring program should be established for at least some representative populations. Further survey may yield additional populations.

Compiled by Raelee Kerrigan, Ian Cowie, Louis Elliott [April 2007] / **References:** Fensham, R.J., and Woinarski, J.C.Z. (1992). *Yawulama: the ecology and conservation of monsoon forest on the Tiwi Islands, Northern Territory*. Report to DASET. (Conservation Commission of the Northern Territory, Darwin.) / Forster, P.I., and Liddle, D.J. (1996). Hoya. *Flora of Australia* 28, 231-237. / Liddle, D.T., Russell-Smith, J., Brock, J., Leach, G.J., and Connors, G.T. (1994) *Atlas of the vascular rainforest plants of the Northern Territory*. Flora of Australia Supplementary Series No. 3, (ABRS, Canberra.) / Russell-Smith, J. (1991). Classification, species richness, and environmental relations of monsoon rain forest in northern Australia. *Journal of Vegetation Science* 2, 259-278. / Russell-Smith, J. (1992). Plant populations and monsoon rain forest in the Northern Territory, Australia. *Biotropica* 24, 471-487. / Russell-Smith, J., and Bowman, D.M.J.S. (1992). Conservation of monsoon rainforest isolates in the Northern Territory. *Biological Conservation* 59, 51-63. / Woinarski, J., Brennan, K., Cowie, I., Kerrigan, R., and Hempel, C. (2003). *Biodiversity conservation on the Tiwi Islands, Northern Territory. Part 1. Plants and environments*. 144 pp. (Department of Infrastructure Planning and Environment, Darwin.)

Image courtesy of David Albrecht

Giant sweet potato
Ipomoea sp. Stirling

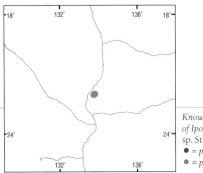

Known locations of Ipomoea sp. Stirling
● = *pre 1970*
● = *post 1970*

CONSERVATION STATUS
AUSTRALIA: **VULNERABLE**
NORTHERN TERRITORY: **VULNERABLE**

DESCRIPTION

Ipomoea sp. Stirling is a robust sprawling vine. The stems are prostrate and annual, radiating from a perennial woody root. There is at least one perennial central tuber and multiple secondary tubers. Older plants form a raised mound around the root stock with a conspicuous mat of litter from the stems of previous years. Stems are typically 1 to 3 m long but can exceed 5 m. Leaf size and shape is variable but distinct from other *Ipomoea* species in central Australia. The flowers are large and showy, typically pink with darker centre, rarely white. Flowering and fruiting are dependent on the timing of rain but typically occur in summer to autumn.

This plant has a strong place in the culture of the Anmatjirra Aboriginal people and the tubers are harvested as 'bush tucker'. Sometimes the tubers are spectacularly large (up to 2.6 kg). The Anmatjirra name for the species is 'Anjulkinha'.

The taxonomy of this plant is unresolved. It is closely related to a Queensland species, *Ipomoea polpha*, and is probably either an outlying population of *I. polpha* or a new and undescribed subspecies (L. Johnson *in litt.*). The distribution of *I. polpha* consists of several disjunct populations in central to north Queensland (Soos and Latz 1987).

DISTRIBUTION

Ipomoea sp. Stirling is known only from a small area near Ti Tree, about 200 km north-east of Alice Springs. Surveys in 2005 (Crase and Duguid *in prep.*) extended the known distribution as mapped by Soos and Latz (1987), both by increasing the size of known populations, and by preliminary mapping of an additional population. The known latitudinal range is now 19 km and the longitudinal range is 27 km.

The extent of occurrence is 39.6 km², based on polygon mapping from the 2005 survey. The known distribution can be delineated with three main polygons, which can be regarded as populations. The density of plants within these polygons varies greatly.

The 2005 surveys indicated that there are more than 50 000 individual plants, and possibly well over 100 000 (Crase and Duguid *in prep.*). This is much higher than the previous estimate of 11 000 by Soos and Latz (1987).

Conservation reserves where reported: None

ECOLOGY

Ipomoea sp. Stirling grows in *Acacia* shrublands, particularly mulga (*A. aneura*), on red earth soils, and occasionally on adjacent sandplains with spinifex (*Triodia basedowii*). All of the known populations are within a few kilometres of low rocky ranges, and experience some degree of rainfall 'run-on'.

The rainfall is strongly seasonal, with larger rain events usually occurring in the summer months. The annual stems die off in response to the low soil moisture and/or cold weather in winter.

There are anecdotal reports of cultivated plants growing through winter when irrigated. Wild plants re-sprout after even quite small rain events, including winter rains (A. Duguid, observations in 2005).

Seed production is prolific and the reasons for the very restricted distribution of this taxon are unknown. Soos and Latz (1987) speculated that relatively deep accumulations of litter may be important for successful recruitment, by conserving soil moisture. Bushfires remove litter and the overstorey which produces it and so could have a negative effect on the distribution and abundance of this taxon. It is also possible that good recruitment is restricted to years with exceptionally large rainfall events and/or good follow up rains.

THREATENING PROCESSES

Soos and Latz (1987) suggested a number of existing or potential threats, which include severe wildfire, drought and even subtle disturbance to hydrological regimes. Inappropriate road location may be a significant disturbance to local drainage patterns (Latz 1992). However, observations in 2005 indicated that the density and vigour of plants was not diminished adjacent to slightly eroding tracks, which were diverting overland flow of rainfall. Furthermore, the majority of the mapped plants were remote from the effects of the current roads.

continued.../

A winter wildfire burnt part of the known distribution in 2001. Observations in 2005 indicated that there were no substantial differences between the burnt and unburnt areas in the density and vigour of this plant. However, overstorey density was greatly affected and the 2005 survey was not able to test the importance of leaf litter to successful recruitment.

There is low to moderate levels of cattle grazing in two of the mapped populations. Some browsing damage was observed in 2005 but could not be attributed definitively to either cattle or kangaroos (*Macropus robustus* or *M. rufus*).

CONSERVATION ASSESSMENT

This taxon has been assessed as **Vulnerable**, on IUCN criterion D2, due to:

- a very restricted area of occupancy, estimated to be less than 20 km²; and
- small number of locations (three).

This status is supported by the considerable uncertainty about factors controlling distribution and abundance. However, criterion D2 includes a statement that a taxon be considered 'capable of becoming Critically Endangered ... in a very short time period'. The only foreseeable agent of such rapid demise would be an extreme disease event.

This taxon has previously been rated as vulnerable (White *et al.* 2000), based in part on a presumed decline. However, the most recent surveys provided no evidence of decline, no basis for inferring a decline and no evidence that the number of mature individuals fluctuates greatly. It is possible that fluctuations do occur with long-term variations in rainfall and fire events, but this is not evident. Given this assessment, an alternative rating of near threatened would be justifiable (Crase and Duguid *in prep.*).

CONSERVATION OBJECTIVES AND MANAGEMENT

The known area and population size were increased by the 2005 survey work relative to the 1986-1987 survey. This reduces concern about the status of this taxon, even though questions remain about why it is so restricted and whether there are active threatening processes. Further survey work on the distribution and abundance would provide some greater certainty but is unlikely to resolve ecological questions. A monitoring plot established in 1986–1987 has not yet been relocated. If relocated, it could indicate a population trend at that site. Transects established in 2005 (Crase and Duguid *in prep.*) may provide a useful baseline for ongoing monitoring. However, further work on this taxon in the next few years is only a moderate priority in the central Australian context.

Compiled by Angus Duguid, Raelee Kerrigan, David Albrecht [May 2006] / **References:** Crase, B., and Duguid, A. (in prep.) Conservation status and distribution of the rare Aboriginal food plant, *Ipomoea* sp. Stirling. Unpublished manuscript. / Latz, P.K. (1992). *Species recovery plan management phase: Ipomoea 'polpha' (ms) Johnson.* Report to the Australian National Parks and Wildlife Service, Endangered Species Program. (CCNT, Alice Springs.) / Soos, A., and Latz, P. (1987). *The status and management of the native sweet potato Ipomoea polpha in the Northern Territory.* A report to the Heritage Commission. (Conservation Commission of the Northern Territory, Alice Springs.) / White, M., Albrecht, D., Duguid, A., Latz, P., and Hamilton, M. (2000). *Plant species and sites of botanical significance in the southern bioregions of the Northern Territory. Volume 1: significant vascular plants.* A report to the Australian Heritage Commission. (Arid Lands Environment Centre, Alice Springs.)

Image courtesy of Kym Brennan

Lithomyrtus linariifolia

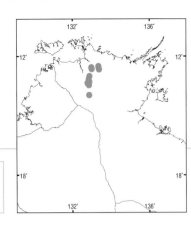

Known locations of Lithomyrtus linariifolia
● = pre 1970
● = post 1970

CONSERVATION STATUS
AUSTRALIA: **NOT LISTED**
NORTHERN TERRITORY: **VULNERABLE**

DESCRIPTION

Lithomyrtus linariifolia is usually a low spreading plant 10 to 20 cm tall, sprawling over sandstone boulders and rubble or rarely erect and up to 1 m tall. The leaves are arranged in opposite pairs and are 10 to 50 mm long by 1 to 3 mm wide and the stems are brown to orange-brown. The narrow leaves and mostly ground-hugging form distinguish this species. The flowers are pink with showy stamens and fruits are yellow-green or olive-green.

Care should be taken in identification, as the erect form can be confused with narrow leaf extremes of *L. dunlopii*. Snow and Guymer (1999) noted the dense pubescence or hairiness on the lower surface of the leaf of *L. dunlopii* as diagnostic, but this can be difficult to see. *Lithomyrtus linariifolia* has generally longer and narrower flower stalks or peduncles (R. Kerrigan *pers. obs.*).

Flowering: February–April
Fruiting: April–May

DISTRIBUTION

Lithomyrtus linariifolia is a Northern Territory endemic, known from approximately 14 localities in Kakadu National Park and Arnhem Land.

Conservation reserves where reported:
Kakadu National Park, Nitmiluk National Park

ECOLOGY

It is found in heaths or eucalypt woodlands on sandstone, in sandy or skeletal soils, often along the margins of *Allosyncarpia ternata* forest and almost always growing amongst *Triodia microstachya*. It is apparent from recent survey that this species is fire-sensitive, found only in unburnt and fire-protected pockets amongst sandstone boulders and outcrops (A. Gibbons and I. Cowie, *pers. obs.*). It appears to be an obligate seeder with no individuals observed to re-sprout.

CONSERVATION ASSESSMENT

Although the Arnhem Land and Kakadu escarpment is remote and difficult to access, this species is considered adequately surveyed as a relatively high proportion of herbarium collections come from the Arnhem Land/Kakadu area. At present 13 715 plant records are documented for the seven quarter degree grid cells where this species is known to occur.

This species was first collected in 1984 and type material was collected by Russell-Smith in 1991. Targeted surveys of this species in 2003 and 2004 (Kerrigan 2003, 2004), survey of sandstone heath communities as part of the Fire Plot programs in Nitmiluk National Park (Anon 2000) and Kakadu Anon 2001), and comprehensive survey of Nitmiluk National Park during a vegetation mapping project offer confidence in the distribution data of this species.

Lithomyrtus linariifolia is now known from 14 localities, although some localities, which are close together, may represent the same population. The extent of occurrence and population size are estimated to be 3411 km^2 and at least 200 mature individuals respectively (Kerrigan 2004).

This species was classified by Snow and Guymer (1999) as **Vulnerable** (under criterion D1), based on a small population size estimated at fewer than 1000 mature individuals.

THREATENING PROCESSES

At present, no imminent threats are identified. Russell-Smith *et al.* (1998, 2002) reported that in some cases current fire regimes are affecting obligate seeders in sandstone heath communities and inappropriate fire regimes are a potential threat to this species.

Unfortunately the generation time for this species has not been assessed and the potential for frequent fire events to kill individuals before reproductive maturity has not been evaluated. Similarly, seed-bank stores, seed longevity and germination and establishment requirements are unknown. With such a small population size, the species is vulnerable to stochastic events and inappropriate fire regimes.

CONSERVATION OBJECTIVES AND MANAGEMENT

Research into the status of the population and the role of fire in its distribution is required. Few species-specific surveys have been undertaken and further survey may yield more localities. A monitoring program for this species has been established (Kerrigan 2003, 2004).

Compiled by Raelee Kerrigan, Ian Cowie [April 2006] / **References:** Anon. (2000). *Nitmiluk National Park Fire Monitoring.* Report on Ranger Training Camp held in Nitmiluk National Park. (Parks and Wildlife Commission of the NT, Darwin.) / Anon. (2001). *Kakadu National Park, Fire Monitoring Plot, Survey and Analysis.* (eds A. Turner, B. Fodham, S. Hamann, S. Morrison, R. Muller, E.A. Pickworth, and J. Russell-Smith), Technical Report No. 72. (Kakadu National Park and the Bushfire Council of the Northern Territory, Darwin.) / Kerrigan, R. (2003). *Kakadu Threatened Flora Report. Results of a threatened flora survey 2003.* (NT Department of Infrastructure Planning and Environment, Darwin.) / Kerrigan, R. (2004). *Kakadu Threatened Flora Report. Volume 2. Results of a threatened flora survey 2004.* (NT Department of Infrastructure Planning and Environment, Darwin.) / Russell-Smith, J., Ryan, P.G., Klessa, D., Waight, G., and Harwood, R.K. (1998). Fire regimes, fire-sensitive vegetation and fire management of the sandstone Arnhem Plateau, monsoonal northern Australia. *Journal of Applied Ecology* 35, 829-846. / Russell-Smith, J., Ryan, P.G., and Cheal, D.C. (2002). Fire regimes and the conservation of sandstone heath in monsoonal northern Australia: frequency, interval, patchiness. *Biological Conservation* 104, 91-107. / Snow, N., and Guymer, G. (1999). Systematic and cladistic studies of *Myrtella* F.Muell. and *Lithomyrtus* F.Muell. (Myrtaceae). *Austrobaileya* 5, 173-207.

Image courtesy of Tourism NT

Palm Valley palm,
Red cabbage palm
Livistona mariae subsp. *mariae*

CONSERVATION STATUS
AUSTRALIA: **VULNERABLE**
NORTHERN TERRITORY: **VULNERABLE**

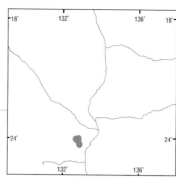

Known locations of Livistona mariae subsp. *mariae*
● = pre 1970
● = post 1970

DESCRIPTION
Livistona mariae subsp. *mariae* is a tall fan palm to 20 m high. It is an unmistakable and spectacular palm of biogeographic significance.

Flowering: May, September
Fruiting: March, May, October

DISTRIBUTION
In a recent revision, Rodd (1998) recognised three subspecies of *Livistona mariae*. The subspecies *rigida* (formerly *L. rigida*) occurs in the Top End of the Northern Territory and in Queensland, and subspecies *occidentalis* occurs in the central Kimberley region of Western Australia and western Northern Territory. The subspecies *mariae* is endemic to the MacDonnell Ranges bioregion, being restricted to a small portion of the Finke River and its tributaries. Most individuals are found in Finke Gorge National Park, with an outlying population outside the National Park, at Running Waters (White *et al.* 2000). The extent of occurrence is less than 60 km² and the actual area occupied by the existing stands is less than 50 ha. The latitudinal range is 35 km and the longitudinal range is 20 km.

Conservation reserves where reported:
Finke Gorge National Park

ECOLOGY
This species grows predominantly on the floor of gorges fed by spring waters in Hermannsburg Sandstone. The hydrology of this system and its importance for refugial processes is described by Wischusen *et al.* (2004). It also occurs in the bed and banks of sandy drainage lines but rarely reaches maturity there, probably due to occasional severe floods.

CONSERVATION ASSESSMENT
The principal IUCN criterion for rating this taxon as **Vulnerable** (under criterion D2) is its acutely restricted range.

THREATENING PROCESSES
The population at Running Waters is currently being degraded by a range of activities acting in concert, including stock and vehicle access to the wetter area of the springs. This has greatly accelerated the extent of environmental weed invasion at the site and has promoted soil disturbance and compaction.

Potential threats to individual stands include wildfire, severe flooding and the possible failure of critical springs. In the longer term, the invasion of environmental weeds such as *Cynodon dactylon* (couch grass) may inhibit the recruitment of seedlings and may contribute to the build up of fuel loads in and around palm stands increasing the risk of mortality in the event of fire.

This palm may also be affected by the development of walking tracks and tourist facilities and the associated potential for visitors to introduce soil-borne pathogens to stands.

It is possible that this distinctive palm may also be detrimentally affected by increasing aridity associated with global climate change.

CONSERVATION OBJECTIVES AND MANAGEMENT
A recovery plan for this species is being prepared (C. Nano *pers. comm.*).

Some threats are being addressed by the Parks and Wildlife Service. Monitoring of the entire population is carried out at regular intervals.

Compiled by Raelee Kerrigan, David Albrecht [February 2007] / **References:** Rodd, A.N. (1988). Revision of *Livistona* (Arecaceae) in Australia. *Telopea* 8, 49-154. / White, M., Albrecht, D., Duguid, A., Latz, P., and Hamilton, M. (2000). *Plant species and sites of botanical significance in the southern bioregions of the Northern Territory. Volume 1: significant vascular plants.* A report to the Australian Heritage Commission. (Arid Lands Environment Centre, Alice Springs.) / Wischusen, J.D.H., Fifield, L.K., and Cresswell, R.G. (2004). Hydrogeology of Palm Valley, central Australia; a Pleistocene flora refuge? *Journal of Hydrogeology* 293, 20-46.

Image courtesy of Kym Brennan

Luisia teretifolia

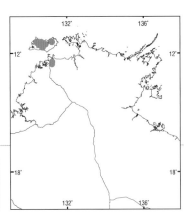

Known locations
of Luisia
teretifolia
● = pre 1970
● = post 1970

CONSERVATION STATUS
AUSTRALIA: **NOT LISTED**
NORTHERN TERRITORY: **VULNERABLE**

DESCRIPTION

Luisia teretifolia is an epiphytic orchid forming straggly clumps of slender, wiry, erect or semi-pendulous stems to 30 cm long. There are 2 to 10 leaves per stem, 15 cm x 5 mm, cylindrical in cross section. The flowers are about 10 mm across, green with a dark burgundy labellum or lip.

Flowering: February, November–December
Fruiting: November

DISTRIBUTION

This species occurs in north-east Queensland, the Northern Territory, New Guinea, Indonesia and Malaysia. In the Northern Territory, it is known from approximately 11 localities, nine from Melville Island and two on the mainland (Bankers Jungle and Crocodile Creek in Black Jungle Conservation Reserve). However no individuals were seen during surveys of both the Bankers Jungle and Crocodile Creek localities in 2003.

Conservation reserves where reported:
Black Jungle Conservation Reserve

ECOLOGY

Within the Northern Territory, this species has been collected from the margins of monsoon rainforests. In other parts of its range, it is reputedly more common in coastal and near-coastal habitats, including mangroves. It appears to prefer situations of relatively bright light and often occurs on trees that have scaly bark.

It may be associated with other epiphytes (e.g. *Dendrobium affine* and *Drynaria quercifolia*); hosts include *Sterculia quadrifida, Barringtonia acutangula, Canarium australianum* and *Vitex* spp.

CONSERVATION ASSESSMENT

There is very little information available on the abundance of this species. As an epiphyte with terete leaves, it is recorded as growing in tangled clumps and the number of individuals is difficult to assess. This species does not usually grow high up on trees and is considered easy to see (D. Jones *pers. comm.*). The readily identifiable nature of this species and the extensive rainforest survey of the mid 1980s (Russell-Smith 1991; Liddle *et al.* 1994) offer confidence that the existing collections accurately reflect the abundance and distribution of this species

It is classified as **Vulnerable** (under criteria D1+2) based on:
- a population size estimated to be fewer than 1000 mature individuals; and
- a restricted area of occupancy estimated to be less than 20 km².

THREATENING PROCESSES

Although specific threats have not been identified, orchids are often sought out by collectors. The edge-of-forest habitat seemingly preferred by this species may leave it more prone to stochastic events such as cyclones or fires.

The Tiwi Island rainforest patches where this species occurs have been excised from clearing for plantation forestry. However, the adequacy of buffers around these areas is not known – if buffers are of insufficient width, the rainforests may be more vulnerable to wind damage. Woinarski *et al.* (2003) noted that monsoon rainforest is likely to be susceptible to changes in ground water hydrology as a result of high water use by forestry plantations. There is also a risk of invasion of rainforests by grassy weeds and concomitant increased vulnerability to fire as a result of intensive development and disturbance by forestry activities.

CONSERVATION OBJECTIVES AND MANAGEMENT

A recovery plan for this species, and other threatened plants on the Tiwi Islands, is due to be released in 2007, but many actions in its draft are currently being implemented.

Research into the status of the populations and further survey are required. Live material has been lodged at George Brown Darwin Botanic Gardens. Commercial availability of this species may relieve any harvesting pressure on wild populations. A monitoring program should be established for at least some representative populations.

Compiled by Raelee Kerrigan, Ian Cowie [April 2006] / **References:** Jones, D. L. (1988). *Native Orchids of Australia.* (Reed, Sydney.) / Liddle, D.T., Russell-Smith, J., Brock, J., Leach, G.J., and Connors, G.T. (1994). *Atlas of the vascular rainforest plants of the Northern Territory.* Flora of Australia Supplementary Series No. 3, (ABRS, Canberra.) / Russell-Smith, J. (1991). Classification, species richness, and environmental relations of monsoon rain forest in northern Australia. *Journal of Vegetation Science* 2, 259-278. / Woinarski, J., Brennan, K., Cowie, I., Kerrigan, R., and Hempel, C. (2003). *Biodiversity conservation on the Tiwi Islands, Northern Territory. Part 1. Plants and environments.* 144 pp. (Department of Infrastructure Planning and Environment, Darwin.)

MacDonnell Ranges cycad
Macrozamia macdonnellii

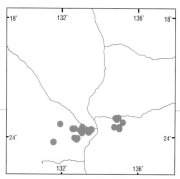

Known locations of Macrozamia macdonnellii
● = pre 1970
● = post 1970

DESCRIPTION

Macrozamia macdonnellii is a distinctive dioecious cycad, often to 2 m height, but sometimes much taller.

Fruiting: Recorded all months except February

DISTRIBUTION

Macrozamia macdonnellii is endemic to the Northern Territory. This species is scattered across the MacDonnell Ranges bioregion, to which it is almost endemic–there is one confirmed population 10 km north on Mount Hay in the Burt Plain Bioregion (White *et al.* 2000) and anecdotal reports indicate a highly disjunct population further north, on Mount Leichhardt (D. Wurst and C. Lines *pers. comm.*). Cycads were not found in a day of searching likely habitats on Mt Leichhardt in 2005 (D. Albrecht and P. Latz *pers. comm.*), so, if present, the population may be very localised.

The species is much more common in the western part of the MacDonnell Ranges bioregion than in the east, where the distribution is relatively disjunct. The confirmed latitudinal range is 140 km and the longitudinal range is 370 km.

Conservation reserves where reported:
Alice Springs Telegraph Station Historic Reserve, Arltunga Historic Reserve, Finke Gorge National Park, Ruby Gap Nature Park, Watarrka National Park, West MacDonnell National Park.

ECOLOGY

This species occurs on rocky sites, predominantly in gorges and on steep sheltered slopes but occasionally on exposed hills or mountain tops.

It mostly occurs in relatively shady locations with relatively high soil moisture (Preece 2005). Some gorges and valleys support densities greater than 100 plants per hectare and with a relatively large total population. Other locations have much smaller and sparser populations. Less than 5% of individuals recorded by Preece (2005) were seedlings.

The species is thought to be very long lived and Preece (2005) measured trunk lengths of greater than 4 m.

The pollination ecology is being studied by Mound and Terry (2001, and other publications in prep.). Pollination is by a single host-specific species of thrips.

Informal germination trials, at the Alice Springs Desert Park nursery, indicate the seeds have relatively short-lasting viability, being prone to desiccation.

Observations by David Albrecht (*pers. comm.*) indicate that recruitment is rare and probably occurs only during periods of exceptional rainfall, when soil moisture is elevated for sustained periods and when viable seed is also present or produced. The presence of the species in some exposed and elevated sites (with little shade or rainfall run-on) may be due to very exceptional wet periods of a magnitude or duration not seen during the historical record. Recruitment seems to be more frequent in areas where discharging ground water sustains prevailing high soil moisture, such as around springs.

It was previously thought that unfavourable fire regimes could be limiting the distribution of this species. However, a strong ability to re-sprout has been observed following extensive and often very intense wildfires in 2002. The study by Preece (2005)

included some testing of the influence of fire. Fire was not found to be a significant factor in the distribution of the species, but further work on this was recommended.

CONSERVATION ASSESSMENT

This species was reassessed against IUCN criteria in 2006 and its Northern Territory status changed from Vulnerable to **Near Threatened**. This was due to the reasonably large and extensive population and lack of evidence or a mechanism of decline.

THREATENING PROCESSES

The illegal collection of seed for the horticultural trade is a potential threat to accessible populations. Seed poaching is known to have occurred in the past. Recruitment could be jeopardised in accessible areas because seed production is so irregular and the seeds are viable for only a short period.

It is possible that increasing aridity could threaten the species in the future, although it is thought to have survived more arid climates in the past.

CONSERVATION OBJECTIVES AND MANAGEMENT

A recovery plan for this species is in preparation (C. Nano *pers. comm.*).

Commercial propagation using tissue culture could reduce pressure on wild populations. A monitoring program should be established for at least representative populations. Fire management programs within conservation reserves aim to reduce fire frequency in many habitats where the species occurs.

Compiled by Raelee Kerrigan, David Albrecht, Angus Duguid [February 2007] / **References:** Mound, L. A., and Terry, I. (2001). Thrips pollination of the central Australian cycad, *Macrozamia macdonnellii* (Cycadales). *International Journal of Plant Sciences* 162, 147-154. / Preece, L. D. (2005). *Distribution of the relict species Macrozamia macdonnellii in central Australia*. Honours Thesis. (University of Melbourne, Melbourne.) / White, M., Albrecht, D., Duguid, A., Latz, P., and Hamilton, M. (2000). *Plant species and sites of botanical significance in the southern bioregions of the Northern Territory. Volume 1: significant vascular plants*. A report to the Australian Heritage Commission. (Arid Lands Environment Centre, Alice Springs.)

Image courtesy of Martin Armstrong

Malaxis latifolia

CONSERVATION STATUS
AUSTRALIA: **NOT LISTED**
NORTHERN TERRITORY: **VULNERABLE**

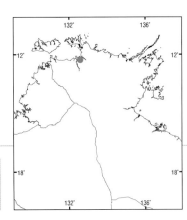

Known locations of Malaxis latifolia
● = pre 1970
● = post 1970

DESCRIPTION

Malaxis latifolia is a deciduous terrestrial orchid. Its leaves are ovate, thin textured, bright green, to 30 cm x 9 cm, sheathing at the base, with wavy margins. The flower stem grows to 30 cm tall, bearing green-brown or purplish flowers. The lower lip of the flower has three blunt apical teeth, the central one being longest and upturned. Plants are conspicuous when in flower but are very difficult to detect when dormant.

Flowering: February–May

DISTRIBUTION

This species occurs in Queensland, New Guinea, Indonesia, Malaysia and India to Japan. In the Northern Territory it is recorded from one population only, near Munmarlary.

Conservation reserves where reported:
Kakadu National Park

ECOLOGY

Jones (1988) noted that, in Queensland, the species is widespread and common in rainforests, along protected stream banks in open forest and sometimes close to low-lying swampy areas. The single Northern Territory location is in a wet (spring) rainforest.

CONSERVATION ASSESSMENT

In the Northern Territory, this species has been recorded from only one locality, and was last recorded in 1993. The 1993 record counted 27 individual plants. A specific search in 2003 failed to record any plants at this locality (Kerrigan 2003). Although these data support a category of Critically Endangered, the ephemeral nature of the above-ground parts has led us to list the species as **Vulnerable** (under criteria D1+2) based on:

• a restricted distribution estimated to be less than 20 km²; and
• a small population.

THREATENING PROCESSES

With a small population, this species is vulnerable to stochastic events. Feral pigs could detrimentally affect the population. Pressure from collectors is unlikely due to the remote locality.

CONSERVATION OBJECTIVES AND MANAGEMENT

Research into the status of the population and the extent of the species is required. A monitoring program should be established. The impact of feral pigs should be assessed, and, if necessary, exclosure fencing established.

Collection of propagation material, translocation to a botanic gardens and commercial availability of stock may protect the species from horticultural harvesting and stochastic events.

Compiled by Raelee Kerrigan, Ian Cowie [April 2006] / **References:** Jones, D. L. (1988). *Native Orchids of Australia.* (Reed, Sydney.) / Kerrigan, R. (2003). *Kakadu threatened flora report. Results of a threatened flora survey.* (NT Department of Infrastructure Planning and Environment, Darwin.)

Image courtesy of Bill Lavarack

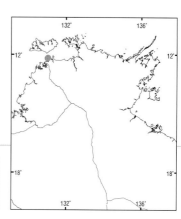

Malaxis marsupichila

Known locations
of Malaxis
marsupichila
● = pre 1970
● = post 1970

DESCRIPTION

Malaxis marsupichila is a deciduous, terrestrial orchid. Its leaves are 15 cm x 7 cm, dark green, thin-textured, shiny and stalked, with wavy margins. The flower stem grows to 50 cm tall, green and purple. The light purple to dark purple flowers are about 8 mm across with 3-lobed labellum or lower lip.

Flowering: January–April
Fruiting: May

DISTRIBUTION

This species is an Australian endemic, known from north-eastern Queensland and the Northern Territory. In the Northern Territory, it is known from only one locality, Gunn Point, where it was collected in 1984.

Conservation reserves where reported: None

ECOLOGY

This species forms colonies in sandy or clay soils rich in leaf litter. It favours protected shady locations in moist soils along the edges of patches of monsoon rainforest and also in littoral rainforest, often close to the sea (Jones 1988).

CONSERVATION ASSESSMENT

Recent attempts to relocate this population at appropriate times of the year have failed. Despite its deciduous nature (and therefore a likely negative collection bias), it is considered that this species would have been encountered during the extensive rainforest surveys, of the 1980s (Russell-Smith 1991; Liddle *et al.* 1994), if it had been more abundant or widespread. Although the above data support a category of Critically Endangered based on the size of population, it is listed instead as **Vulnerable** (under criteria D1+2) given the ephemeral nature of the above-ground parts and the limited amount of recent survey in the area.

THREATENING PROCESSES

Potential threats are highly speculative but may include illicit harvesting, possible rural or industrial development in the area, random events such as cyclones and fire, and impacts of feral pigs.

CONSERVATION OBJECTIVES AND MANAGEMENT

Further survey work is urgently required to establish the status and extent of the population, and to assess possible threats. Collection of propagation material, translocation to a botanic gardens and availability of stock commercially may protect the species from harvesting and stochastic events.

Compiled by Raelee Kerrigan, Ian Cowie [April 2006] / **References:** Jones, D. L. (1988). *Native Orchids of Australia.* (Reed, Sydney.) / Liddle, D.T., Russell-Smith, J., Brock, J., Leach, G.J., and Connors, G.T. (1994). *Atlas of the vascular rainforest plants of the Northern Territory.* Flora of Australia Supplementary Series No. 3. (ABRS, Canberra.) / Russell-Smith, J. (1991). Classification, species richness, and environmental relations of monsoon rain forest in northern Australia. *Journal of Vegetation Science 2,* 259-278.

Image courtesy of David Liddle

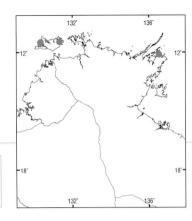

*Known locations
of Mapania
macrocephala*
● = *pre 1970*
● = *post 1970*

Mapania macrocephala

CONSERVATION STATUS
AUSTRALIA: **NOT LISTED**
NORTHERN TERRITORY: **VULNERABLE**

DESCRIPTION

Mapania macrocephala is a robust sedge to
2 m tall. The culms are 3-angled. The leaves are
up to 4 m long, the blade 3-nerved with distinct
secondary nerves and the margin spinose.
The inflorescence is terminal and globose,
4 to 7.5 cm wide. It is distinguishable from young
Pandanus by m-shaped cross-section of leaf.

Fruiting: February, June, November

DISTRIBUTION

This species occurs in Sulawesi, Maluku,
Nusa Tenggara, Philippines, New Guinea and
north Australia (Queensland and the Northern
Territory) (Simpson 1992). In the Northern
Territory, it is known from four localities; two
from Bathurst Island, one from Melville Island
and one from north-eastern Arnhem Land.
The most recent surveys (in 2006) revealed two
more populations in the vicinity of those already
known on Bathurst Island. Visits to other locations
of otherwise suitable habitat (spring-fed rainforest)
revealed no other populations.

Conservation reserves where reported: None

ECOLOGY

This sedge occurs in spring-fed wet rainforests.
Within this habitat it is generally restricted to
the wetter part of the forest, often in areas that
are subject to year-round water flow. Vigour is
markedly reduced where it occurs in drier parts of
the forest.

CONSERVATION ASSESSMENT

It is known from five populations on the Tiwi
Islands and from one in Arnhem Land. The total
number of individuals is estimated to be fewer than
250. The area of occupancy is estimated to be less
than 20 km².

There is some negative collection bias associated
with this taxon because of its similarity to
Pandanus and the remote areas in which it occurs.
More populations may exist but recent and
extensive survey efforts in both the Tiwi Islands
(Woinarski *et al.* 2003) and Arafura Swamp
area (Brennan *et al.* 2003) have yielded only one
additional population, and rainforests have been
well sampled in the Northern Territory (Russell-
Smith 1991; Liddle *et al.* 1994). The negative
collection bias associated with this taxon has led
us to list its status as **Vulnerable** (under criteria
D1+2).

THREATENING PROCESSES

There is a potential threat from pig and buffalo
activity through either grazing on juveniles or
disturbance. As a species occurring in spring-fed
rainforests, changes to hydrology could threaten
populations. *Acacia mangium* plantations are
currently being established on the Tiwi Islands,
and their effect on the water supply to spring-fed
rainforests is currently unknown.

CONSERVATION OBJECTIVES
AND MANAGEMENT

A recovery plan for this species, and other
threatened plants on the Tiwi Islands, is due
to be released in 2007, but many actions in its
draft are currently being implemented through
a collaborative project involving Tiwi rangers
and scientists from the Department of Natural
Resources, Environment and The Arts, with
funding from the Natural Heritage Trust.

Further research is required to provide a
more detailed assessment of population size,
distribution, and effects of putative threatening
processes. A monitoring program should be
established for at least representative populations.

Compiled by Raelee Kerrigan, Ian Cowie, Louis Elliott [April 2007] / **References:** Brennan, K., Woinarski, J., Hempel, C., Cowie, I., and Dunlop, C. (2003). *Biological inventory of the Arafura Swamp and catchment.* Report to Natural Heritage Trust. 255pp. (Parks and Wildlife Commission of the Northern Territory, Darwin.) / Liddle, D.T., Russell-Smith, J., Brock, J., Leach, G.J., and Connors, G.T. (1994). *Atlas of the vascular rainforest plants of the Northern Territory.* Flora of Australia Supplementary Series No. 3. (ABRS, Canberra.) / Russell-Smith, J. (1991). Classification, species richness, and environmental relations of monsoon rain forest in northern Australia. *Journal of Vegetation Science* 2, 259-278. / Simpson, D.A. (1992). *A revision of the genus Mapania.* (Royal Botanic Gardens, Kew.) / Woinarski, J., Brennan, K., Cowie, I., Kerrigan, R., and Hempel, C. (2003). *Biodiversity conservation on the Tiwi Islands, Northern Territory. Part 1. Plants and environments.* 144 pp. (Department of Infrastructure Planning and Environment, Darwin.)

Minuria tridens

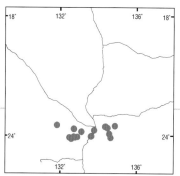

Known locations of Minuria tridens
● = pre 1970
● = post 1970

CONSERVATION STATUS
AUSTRALIA: **VULNERABLE**
NORTHERN TERRITORY: **VULNERABLE**

DESCRIPTION
Minuria tridens is a perennial sub-shrub to 30 cm high. The ray florets have lilac ligules, the disc florets yellow.

Flowering: February–March, May–October, December
Fruiting: February–March, May, July, September, December

DISTRIBUTION
Except for a single unconfirmed record from Western Australia, this species is restricted to arid areas of the Northern Territory. It is known from approximately nine locations (with 16 collections) (White *et al.* 2000).

Conservation reserves where reported:
Finke Gorge National Park, Trephina Gorge National Park, West MacDonnell National Park.

ECOLOGY
This daisy occurs on dolomite, limestone and calcrete impregnated sandstone hills, rises and ranges. It is typically found on southerly aspects in low shrublands dominated by species such as *Acacia kempeana*, *Senna artemisioides* and/or *Indigofera leucotricha*. *Triodia* species are absent from most locations. Low seed set is characteristic of most populations studied.

CONSERVATION ASSESSMENT
The species has been classified as **Vulnerable** (under criteria B2ab(iii)) based on:
• a projected decline in population size due to the effects of introduced plants;
• severely fragmented; and
• an area of occupancy estimated to be less than 2000 km².

THREATENING PROCESSES
The invasive exotic buffel grass (*Cenchrus ciliaris*) may have a negative impact through competition and altered fire regimes.

Urban and rrural subdivision on the south side of Alice Springs is likely to have some effect on the Alice Springs sub-populations of this species. Although the terrain occupied by the species is too steep for development, it is possible that the proximity of dwellings and roads will lead to increased disturbance, including accelerating invasion by buffel grass and changes to fire regimes. However, this will affect a relatively small proportion of the total known population of the species.

CONSERVATION OBJECTIVES AND MANAGEMENT
A recovery plan for this species is being prepared (C. Nano *pers. comm.*). The effect of fire and competition from buffel grass (*Cenchrus ciliaris*) and *Triodia* needs further study. A monitoring program should be established for at least representative populations.

Compiled by Raelee Kerrigan, David Albrecht [February 2007] **References:** White, M., Albrecht, D., Duguid, A., Latz, P., and Hamilton, M. (2000). *Plant species and sites of botanical significance in the southern bioregions of the Northern Territory; Volume 1: significant vascular plants*. A report to the Australian Heritage Commission. (Arid Lands Environment Centre, Alice Springs.)

Image courtesy of David Liddle

Mitrella sp. Melville Island

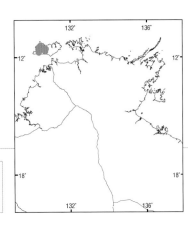

*Known locations
of Mitrella sp.
Melville Island*
● = *pre 1970*
● = *post 1970*

CONSERVATION STATUS
AUSTRALIA: **VULNERABLE**
NORTHERN TERRITORY: **VULNERABLE**

DESCRIPTION
Mitrella sp. Melville Island is a vine to 10 m, forming a semi-weeping shrub when young. The strongly aromatic leaves are lanceolate and shiny, dark-green above, bluish (glaucous) beneath. The branchlets are distinctly zig-zagged. The flowers are pinkish-orange, faintly scented. The fruit is a multi-seeded berry, pale pink/green.

Fruiting: June, September, December

DISTRIBUTION
Recorded as *Desmos* D24710 in the Rainforest Atlas (Liddle *et al*. 1994), this species is known only from the western portion of the Tiwi Islands. In the Rainforest Atlas, it was reported from approximately nine localities. Further survey by D. Liddle and L. Elliott in 2006 recorded seven additional populations.

Conservation reserves where reported: None

ECOLOGY
It is recorded as growing in monsoon rainforest in deep shade associated with perennial springs, in moist leaf litter and stagnant mulch.

CONSERVATION ASSESSMENT
This species was very difficult to code as very little data on abundance are available. This species is distinctive and as an understorey plant, juveniles are relatively visible when present.

Recent survey in 2006 suggests that where it occurs this species may be locally common, with many juveniles present in a suppressed state in the rainforest understorey. The number of large adult plants may be particularly low however, and as the species is clearly restricted to spring-fed wet rainforest on the Tiwi Islands, the available habitat is highly restricted.

Population size for this species is highly speculative and, assuming populations located in the 1980s are still extant, it has been estimated at fewer than 1000 mature individuals.

This species is considered adequately surveyed, based on extensive surveys on the Tiwi Islands and rainforest habitats across the Top End (Russell-Smith 1991; Fensham and Woinarski 1992; Woinarski *et al*. 2003.). The extent of occurrence is estimated at 960 km² and area of occupancy estimated as 180 ha based on the size of rainforest patches where collected (Fensham and Woinarski 1992).

Based on present knowledge and using the precautionary principle, this species is classified as **Vulnerable** (under criteria D1+2) based on:
- a restricted area of occupancy estimated to be less than 20 km²; and
- a small population size estimated to be fewer than 1000 individuals.

THREATENING PROCESSES
Very little is known about the threatening processes affecting this species, which may be

naturally rare. However, monsoon rainforests generally are vulnerable to disturbance from cyclones, cattle, buffalo, pigs and dry season wildfires (Panton 1993; Russell-Smith and Bowman 1992, Woinarski *et al*. 2003).

Woinarski *et al*. (2003) also noted that monsoon rainforests are likely to be most susceptible to changes in ground water hydrology as a result of high water use from *Acacia mangium* plantations being developed on the Tiwi Islands.

CONSERVATION OBJECTIVES AND MANAGEMENT
A recovery plan for this species, and other threatened plants on the Tiwi Islands, is due to be released in 2007, but many actions in its draft are currently being implemented through a collaborative project involving Tiwi rangers and scientists from the Department of Natural Resources, Environment and The Arts, with funding from the Natural Heritage Trust.

Research priorities are to:
- provide a more detailed assessment of its distribution, habitat requirements and population size; and
- provide an assessment of the factors limiting distribution, and/or threats to its survival.

Further survey may yield additional populations. A monitoring program should be established for at least representative populations.

Compiled by Raelee Kerrigan, Ian Cowie, Louis Elliott [April 2007] / **References:** Fensham, R.J., and Woinarski, J.C.Z. (1992). *Yawulama: the ecology and conservation of monsoon forest on the Tiwi Islands, Northern Territory*. Report to DASET. (Conservation Commission of the Northern Territory, Darwin.) / Liddle, D.T., Russell-Smith, J., Brock, J., Leach, G.J., and Connors, G.T. (1994). *Atlas of the vascular rainforest plants of the Northern Territory*. Flora of Australia Supplementary Series No. 3. (ABRS, Canberra.) / Panton, W.J. (1993). Changes in post World War II distribution and status of monsoon rainforests in the Darwin area. *Australian Geographer* 24, 50-59. / Russell-Smith, J. (1991). Classification, species richness, and environmental relations of monsoon rain forest in northern Australia. *Journal of Vegetation Science* 2, 259-278. / Russell-Smith, J. (1992). Plant populations and monsoon rain forest in the Northern Territory, Australia. *Biotropica* 24, 471-487. / Russell-Smith, J., and Bowman, D.M.J.S. (1992). Conservation of monsoon rainforest isolates in the Northern Territory. *Biological Conservation* 59, 51-63. / Woinarski, J., Brennan, K., Cowie, I., Kerrigan, R., and Hempel, C. (2003). *Biodiversity conservation on the Tiwi Islands, Northern Territory. Part 1. Plants and environments*. 144 pp. (Department of Infrastructure Planning and Environment, Darwin.)

Image courtesy of Ian Cowie

Monochoria hastata

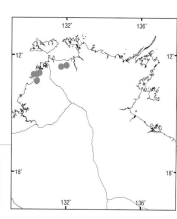

*Known locations
of Monochoria
hastata*
● = pre 1970
● = post 1970

DESCRIPTION

Monochoria hastata is an emergent aquatic herb with stems approximately 0.7 to 1.2 m long. The basal leaves are arrow shaped. The inflorescence of 25 to 60 flowers is in a dense spike, 6 to 9 cm long. The flowers are 13 to 16mm long and purple or whitish. One anther is coloured blue, about 6 mm long, the other 5 anthers are yellow and about 4 mm long. The seed capsule is 7 mm long and 5 to 6 mm diameter.

Flowering: March–June
Fruiting: April–June

DISTRIBUTION

This species occurs in India, Sri Lanka and south-east Asia, extending to New Guinea and Australia. In Australia, the only records are from the Northern Territory, on the Finniss, Reynolds and Wildman Rivers floodplains.

Conservation reserves where reported:
Kakadu National Park

ECOLOGY

This species is recorded as a component of floating mat vegetation in both the Finniss and Reynolds Rivers. It also occurs on near-permanently wet back-swamps and drainage channels, and in permanent billabongs.

CONSERVATION ASSESSMENT

Within Australia, this species has been recorded from only three floodplain localities. There is a negative collection bias associated with the swampy habitat in which this species occurs. However, extensive coverage of floodplains in the Kakadu region by Joye Maddison detected this species at only one location in that region (Wildman River). Furthermore, it is considered that the extensive surveys of the Top End floodplain communities (Wilson *et al.* 1991) during the 1990s would have detected this species more often had it been more common or widespread.

This species has been classified as **Vulnerable** (under criteria B1ab(iii,iv)+2ab(iii,iv); D2) based on:

• an inferred decline in quality of habitat and population numbers as a result of invasion by exotic weeds;
• a population estimated to be approximately 5000 (Kerrigan 2003); and
• an area of occupancy of known populations estimated to be less than 20 km² and an extent of occurrence of 3487 km².

THREATENING PROCESSES

Invasion by introduced plant species such as para grass (*Urochloa mutica*), olive hymenachne (*Hymenachne amplexicaulis*) and mimosa (*Mimosa pigra*) appears to be the most imminent threat to this species. Saltwater intrusion of wetlands resulting from rising sea levels triggered by global warming or other factors would have an adverse impact on this species. As a floodplain species, changes to hydrology would affect populations, although no such changes are envisaged in the near future.

The Wildman River population, when first discovered, had been extensively grazed by buffalo, and *Monochoria* individuals were found only in areas protected from buffalo activity. With the removal of animals from the area, the *Monochoria* population expanded and relatively large stands were observed in open water (Joye Maddison *pers. comm.*).

The same locality is now considerably congested with the native grass *Leersia hexandra*, the only open water present is beneath a small stand of *Barringtonia acutangula* and the majority of the population is now growing interspersed with *Leersia* (Kerrigan 2003). There is some concern that this population of *Monochoria hastata* may be outcompeted by *Leersia* although quite large stands persist and the species seems able to grow on dense clumps of vegetation formed by the grass.

Cowie *et al.* (2000) reported that this species is recorded overseas as being fed to cattle and used as a vegetable. As such, it may be grazed by feral animals in the area although no evidence of this was observed during recent survey.

CONSERVATION OBJECTIVES AND MANAGEMENT

Floodplain habitats are a dynamic environment, often subject to natural fluctuations in the abundance of individual species. Research into the status, population dynamics and extent of distribution of this species is required. A monitoring program has been established for the population within Kakadu National Park (Kerrigan 2003).

Compiled by Raelee Kerrigan, Ian Cowie [April 2006] / **References:** Cowie, I.D., Short, P.S., and Osterkamp Madsen, M. (2000) *Floodplain Flora.* Flora of Australia Supplementary Series No. 10. (ABRS, Canberra/PWCNT, Darwin.) / Kerrigan, R. (2003). *Kakadu Threatened Flora Report. Results of a threatened flora survey 2003.* (NT Department of Infrastructure Planning and Environment, Darwin.) / Wilson, B.A., Brocklehurst, P.S., and Whitehead, P.J. (1991). *Classification, distribution and environmental relationships of coastal floodplain vegetation, Northern Territory, Australia, March-May 1990.* Technical Report 91/2. (Conservation Commission of the Northern Territory, Darwin.)

Image courtesy of Martin Armstrong

Mukia sp. Tobermorey Station

CONSERVATION STATUS
AUSTRALIA: **NOT LISTED**
NORTHERN TERRITORY: **VULNERABLE**

Known locations of
Mukia sp. Tobermorey
Station.
● = *pre 1970*
● = *post 1970*

DESCRIPTION
Mukia sp. Tobermorey Station is a prostrate herb.
It has separate male and female flowers which are
pale yellow in colour. The fruits are ellipsoid.

Flowering: March, May
Fruiting: March, May, July, October

DISTRIBUTION
This rare species is currently known from five
locations in the central-east of the Northern
Territory. It is also known from disjunct
populations in Queensland. The apparently
disjunct distribution may be an artifact of limited
collecting effort in the intervening regions, as
there appears to be relatively uniform and suitable
habitat between these areas. The western limit
of this species' known range occurs within the
Northern Territory.

Conservation reserves where reported: None

ECOLOGY
This species occurs along creeks and in poorly
drained areas on cracking clay plains. It has been
recorded from bluebush swamps (dominated
by *Chenopodium auricomum*), gidgee (*Acacia
georginae*) shrubland and riparian woodlands
dominated by *Eucalyptus camaldulensis*.

CONSERVATION ASSESSMENT
The species is assessed as **Vulnerable** (under
criteria D1+2) based on:
• the total population estimated to be fewer than
  1000 mature individuals; and
• an area of occupancy estimated to be less
  than 20 km².

THREATENING PROCESSES
The species is unreserved. The preferred habitat of
this species is favoured by stock and feral animals
and there is no information available about its
tolerance of grazing.

CONSERVATION OBJECTIVES
AND MANAGEMENT
The preferred habitats of this species include
seasonal swamps and claypans, and intermittent
watercourses and run-on areas. Size, location and
duration of these habitats may vary markedly from
year to year and the ecology of these habitats is
poorly understood (White *et al.* 2000). Research
into the biology and potential threats to this
species is required and a monitoring program
should be established for at least representative
populations.

Compiled by Raelee Kerrigan, David Albrecht [April 2006] / **References:** White, M., Albrecht, D., Duguid, A., Latz, P., and Hamilton, M. (2000). *Plant species and sites of botanical significance in the southern bioregions of the Northern Territory. Volume 1: significant vascular plants.* A report to the Australian Heritage Commission. (Arid Lands Environment Centre, Alice Springs.)

Olearia macdonnellensis

CONSERVATION STATUS
AUSTRALIA: **VULNERABLE**
NORTHERN TERRITORY: **VULNERABLE**

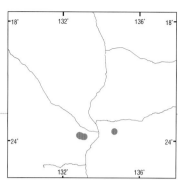

Known locations of Olearia macdonnellensis
● = *pre 1970*
● = *post 1970*

DESCRIPTION

Olearia macdonnellensis is a viscid aromatic shrub to 1.2 m high. The leaves are green and varnished. The ray florets have white ligules, the disc florets yellow (Cooke 1988).

Flowering: February, July–October
Fruiting: July, August, October

DISTRIBUTION

This species is endemic to the MacDonnell Ranges bioregion of the Northern Territory, where it is known from several disjunct populations. Most of these are in the West MacDonnell Ranges, in an area of less than 30 km by 10 km. Some work has been done to map distinct populations in this area but is incomplete (A. Schubert survey data). This group of populations was previously described as five separate locations (derived from White *et al.* 2000) based on herbarium specimen records, however there are probably more than this depending on the scale at which individual populations are defined and mapped.

A rough estimate of abundance for the largest population in the West MacDonnell Ranges is more than 1000 individuals (A. Schubert *pers. obs.*).

There is a single outlying specimen record from the East MacDonnell Ranges, but the exact location is unknown. The location indicated by the collection coordinates was searched in 2004 without success (A. Duguid *pers. obs.*). The total latitudinal range is 31 km and the longitudinal range is 187 km.

An *Olearia* specimen from Mt Edward was previously considered to be a western outlier of *O. macdonnellensis* but is now regarded as a distinct taxon.

Conservation reserves where reported:
West MacDonnell National Park.

ECOLOGY

This species occurs on a variety of aspects but consistently in areas with some natural protection from wildfires. There is typically an overstorey of trees, notably *Eucalyptus trivalvis*, but also other species including *Acacia aneura*.

The West MacDonnell's populations are centred along a single valley on the south side of the Heavitree Range. Landforms include north-facing gullies, east-facing slopes, southern slopes, northwest-facing slopes and drainage lines, but mostly with similar vegetation associations. These populations predominantly occur in areas of deeply weathered geological deposits from the Tertiary, often with areas of eroding 'break-aways' with distinctly pallid or bleached soils.

Olearia macdonnellensis appears to be very fire-sensitive. All adult plants at a site burnt by a wildfire in 2002 were observed to have died, with no recruitment in 2004 (D. Albrecht and P. Latz *pers. obs.*). In the 2005 surveys, no seedlings or re-sprouting plants were observed at sites burnt in 2002 (A. Schubert *pers. obs.*).

CONSERVATION ASSESSMENT

This species is rated as **Vulnerable** (under criteria B12ab(ii,iii,iv); D2) based on:
• extent of occurrence less than 20 000 km²;
• area of occupancy less than 20 km²;
• severely fragmented; and
• inferred decline in distribution, habitat quality and number of individuals, due to wildfire.

Although the population size is estimated to be fewer than 10 000 mature individuals, at least one population is thought to exceed 1000 and there is no quantitative evidence of declining or extremely fluctuating population.

THREATENING PROCESSES

The species is associated with fire-sensitive plant communities and fire shadow areas. Fire appears to be a threat, although further investigation of the fire ecology is required.

CONSERVATION OBJECTIVES AND MANAGEMENT

A recovery plan for this species is being prepared (C. Nano *pers. comm.*).

It is essential that extant populations are protected from hot wildfires. The 2004–05 survey work in the West MacDonnell Ranges needs to be continued to completion and a species-specific fire management plan prepared. A monitoring program should be established at representative locations. Further attempts should be made to find and map the extent of the East MacDonnells population.

Compiled by Raelee Kerrigan, David Albrecht, Angus Duguid, Andrew Schubert [February 2007] / **References:** Cooke, D.A. (1988). Two new species of *Olearia* Moench (Compositae: Astereae) from Central Australia. *Muelleria* 6, 181-184. / White, M., Albrecht, D., Duguid, A., Latz, P., and Hamilton, M. (2000). *Plant species and sites of botanical significance in the southern bioregions of the Northern Territory. Volume 1: significant vascular plants.* A report to the Australian Heritage Commission. (Arid Lands Environment Centre, Alice Springs.)

Image courtesy of Martin Armstrong

Platysace saxatilis

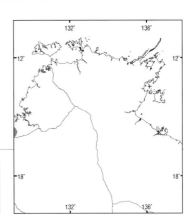

Known locations of Platysace saxatilis
● = pre 1970
● = post 1970

CONSERVATION STATUS
AUSTRALIA: **NOT LISTED**
NORTHERN TERRITORY: **VULNERABLE**

DESCRIPTION
Platysace saxatilis is a multi-stemmed shrub to 3 m height. Its leaves have a sweet spicy aroma when crushed. The flowers are white.

Flowering: April–October
Fruiting: June, October, November

DISTRIBUTION
This recently described species (Keighery 1996) is an Australian endemic. It is known from Hidden Valley, Kununurra (Western Australia) and Keep River National Park.

Conservation reserves where reported:
Keep River National Park

ECOLOGY
It occurs on sandstone cliff faces. Two collections record the species growing on sand.

CONSERVATION ASSESSMENT
In the Northern Territory, this species has a very restricted area of occupancy near the border with Western Australia. The likelihood of immigration of propagules from the Western Australian border population is unknown, but is considered low given the habitat of this species. Approximately 500 individuals were counted in a recent survey of known populations in the Northern Territory.

The species is classified as **Vulnerable** (under criteria D1+2) based on:
• an estimated population size of fewer than 1000 individuals; and
• an area of occupancy estimated to be less than 20 km².

THREATENING PROCESSES
As a cliff face species, it is susceptible to rock falls and other stochastic events. Its habitat suggests a susceptibility to fire and it is unlikely this species will colonise areas regularly burnt. Populations are difficult to assess because of their position in the landscape so it was hard to quantify the number of juveniles in the population. Recruitment is expected to be low given the limited availability of suitable crevices and low likelihood of successful dispersal to them.

CONSERVATION OBJECTIVES AND MANAGEMENT
Research into the status of the population and further survey are required. A monitoring program should be established. Access to populations to count juveniles will always be difficult. Seed has been collected by the George Brown Darwin Botanic Gardens.

Compiled by Raelee Kerrigan, Ian Cowie [April 2006] / **References:** Keighery, G.J. (1996). A new species of *Platysace* (Apiaceae) from Northern Australia. *Nordic Journal of Botany* 16, 135-137.

Image courtesy of Kym Brennan

Pternandra coerulescens

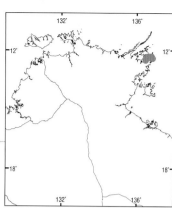

Known locations of Pternandra coerulescens
● = pre 1970
● = post 1970

DESCRIPTION

Pternandra coerulescens is a medium-sized tree to 15 m, or several-stemmed, erect, rambling shrub to 6 m tall. It has apricot-grey, smooth bark. The leaves are ovate, 3-nerved, and opposite. The flowers are blue to light purple. The fruit is subglobose, about 5 mm in diameter, yellow-green becoming black.

Flowering: February
Fruiting: February, October

DISTRIBUTION

This species is found in the Northern Territory, Queensland, south-east Asia and New Guinea (Whiffin 1990). In the Northern Territory, it is known from eight collections from four localities in north-east Arnhem Land (Liddle *et al.* 1994). As most localities were documented prior to Global Positioning System being available, the exact number of sites is difficult to determine.

Conservation reserves where reported: None

ECOLOGY

This species has been recorded from spring-fed rainforests and riparian forests.

CONSERVATION ASSESSMENT

In the Northern Territory, it is classified as **Vulnerable** (under criteria D1+2) based on:
• a restricted area of occupancy (estimated to be less than 20 km^2); and
• a small population size (estimated to be fewer than 1000 individuals).

A recent survey of riparian forests in Arnhem Land did not yield additional populations (C. Brock *pers. comm.*) and no additional populations have been recorded since 1994.

THREATENING PROCESSES

There are potential threats from cyclonic events and changes to hydrology. The impact of current fire regimes and feral animal activity is unknown.

CONSERVATION OBJECTIVES AND MANAGEMENT

Surveys are required to determine if further populations exist and to document and monitor the status of known populations.

Compiled by Raelee Kerrigan, Ian Cowie [April 2006] / **References:** Liddle, D.T., Russell-Smith, J., Brock, J., Leach, G.J., and Connors, G.T. (1994). *Atlas of the vascular rainforest plants of the Northern Territory.* Flora of Australia Supplementary Series No. 3. (ABRS, Canberra.) / Whiffin, T. (1990). Melastomataceae. *Flora of Australia* 18, 243-255.

Image courtesy of David Liddle

Darwin palm
Ptychosperma macarthurii

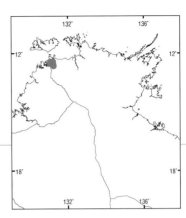

Known locations of Ptychosperma macarthurii
● = pre 1970
● = post 1970

CONSERVATION STATUS
AUSTRALIA: **ENDANGERED** (as *Ptychosperma bleeseri*)
NORTHERN TERRITORY: **ENDANGERED**

DESCRIPTION

This species is a slender clumping, feather-leaved palm with a small crown supported on a narrow trunk 3 to 6 cm in diameter.

Flowering: May, December
Fruiting: August, September, November, December

Note: There has been some debate over the taxonomic status of this palm (Shapcott 1998). It was formerly considered as a Northern Territory endemic, *Ptychosperma bleeseri*. Here, we follow Dixon *et al.* (2003) and treat *P. bleeseri* as a synonym and isolated population of *P. macarthurii*, a species more widespread in Queensland. The Northern Territory entity will be treated under this latter name in the forthcoming revision in Flora of Australia (John Dowe *pers. comm.*).

DISTRIBUTION

Ptychosperma macarthurii is known from the Northern Territory, Cape York Peninsula and New Guinea. In the Northern Territory, this species is known from eight populations with an extent of occurrence of 200 km² (Duff *et al.* 1992; Barrow *et al.* 1993; Liddle *et al.* 1996). Within this area, it is restricted to wet rainforest patches and has an area of occupancy of less than 1 km² (Anon 1998; Liddle *et al.* 2001). Population counts in 2000–01 revealed adult plants at seven locations, four of which had fewer than 20 and the smallest with only one adult plant. Of a total of

1037 adult plants, 70% occurred in one population at Crocodile Creek. These counts overstate the number of mature individuals as plants were classified as adults on the basis of size and may include individuals not capable of reproduction.

Conservation reserves where reported:
Black Jungle Conservation Reserve

ECOLOGY

This species occurs in dense rainforests associated with lowland springs near the margins of riverine floodplains. The soils typically comprise deep organic clay loams without humus development. Within the rainforest patches the species will grow in a wide range of light conditions (Duff *et al.* 1992; Barrow *et al.* 1993; Liddle *et al.* 1996).

CONSERVATION ASSESSMENT

In the Northern Territory, this species is classified as **Endangered** (under criteria A4bce; B1ab(ii,iii,iv) +2ab(ii,iii,iv); C1) based on:
- the small number of mature individuals (about 1000);
- severely fragmented populations; and
- a past observed and a projected future decline in population and quality of habitat.

THREATENING PROCESSES

Fire and feral animals have been the primary threats impinging on the populations in the 1990s (Liddle *et al.* 1992ab, 1996, 2001, 2006). There was substantial mortality following wildfires at the Whitewood Road population in 1990 and 1993, and at Black Creek in 1992. In a 1990 survey, Whitewood Road contained 42% of the known adults, however this was reduced to 5% by 2000–01. Re-survey of Bankers Jungle in 2003 showed significant impacts from grazing with the loss of juvenile and adult plants. Disturbance from feral buffalo, cattle and pigs declined in the 1990s following on from the Brucellosis and Tuberculosis Eradication Campaign, changes in land use and fencing of four of the eight populations. In the early 1990s, several populations exhibited a polarised size class structure typified by large adult and juvenile plants. In the absence of wildfire and in a period of reduced disturbance by feral animals, sufficient small juvenile plants survived and grew to infill the intermediate classes.

In addition to the above, there are increasing threats from:
- changed fire regimes due to increased fuel loads from introduced grasses around rainforest margins;
- changed land use in the catchment that could lead to a reduction in the water supply to the springs on which the rainforests depend;
- changes in surface water quantity and quality;

continued.../

- clearing proposals and any other action that could remove or damage individual rainforest patches that form an interconnected mosaic essential for the flow of genetic material; and
- hybridisation with introduced *Ptychosperma* species.

CONSERVATION OBJECTIVES AND MANAGEMENT

A recovery plan for this palm was developed in 2005 and is aimed at the long-term conservation of the species and its habitat. The plan addresses recovery of the wild populations, community involvement and education, land use planning, *ex-situ* conservation, research and monitoring (Liddle and Scott 2005).

Priority conservation actions include to:
- protect the habitat from introduced animals and fire in conjunction with ongoing monitoring to provide feedback on the population response; and
- investigate the dynamics of the water supply that maintains the spring-fed rainforests, and the requirements of those rainforests.

Compiled by Raelee Kerrigan, Ian Cowie, Dave Liddle [May 2006] / **References:** Anon. (1998). *A Management Program for Ptychosperma bleeseri Burret in the Northern Territory of Australia.* (Parks and Wildlife Commission of the Northern Territory, Palmerston.) / Barrow, P. Duff, G., Liddle, D., and Russell-Smith, J. (1993). Threats to monsoon rainforest habitat in northern Australia: the case of *Ptychosperma bleeseri* Burret (Arecaceae). *Australian Journal of Ecology* 18, 463-471. / Dixon, D., Cowie, I., and Kerrigan, R. (2003). *Ptychosperma macarthurii or P. bleeseri?* The taxonomic status of *P. bleeseri* reconsidered. *The Beagle* 19, 81-86. / Duff, G., Wightman, G., and Eamus, D. (1992). Conservation and Management of the Endangered Palm *Ptychosperma bleeseri*. In: *Conservation and Development Issues in North Australia.* (eds I. Moffatt and A. Webb). pp. 69-77. (North Australia Research Unit, Darwin.) / Liddle, D.T., and Scott, B.K. (2005). *Recovery plan for Darwin Palm in the Northern Territory of Australia, 2006 to 2010.* (NT Department of Natural Resources, Environment and the Arts, Darwin.) / Liddle, D.T., Wightman, G.M., and Taylor, S. (1992a). *Conservation Research Statement for the Palm Ptychosperma bleeseri.* Report to Australian National Parks and Wildlife Service, Endangered Species Program, Project Number 159. / Liddle, D.T., Wightman, G.M., and Taylor, S. (1992b). *Recovery Plan for the Palm Ptychosperma bleeseri.* Report to Australian National Parks and Wildlife Service, Endangered Species Program, Project Number 159. / Liddle, D.T., Taylor, S.M., and Larcombe, D.R. (1996). Population changes from 1990 to 1995 and management of the endangered rainforest palm *Ptychosperma bleeseri* Burret (Arecaceae). In: *Back from the brink; refining the threatened species recovery process.* (eds S. Stephens and S. Maxwell). pp. 110-113 (Surrey Beatty & Sons, Sydney.) / Liddle, D.T., Larcombe, D.R., and Fitzgerald P.J. (2001). From uncontrolled harvest to weeds and fire: an evolution of threats to the endangered rainforest palm, *Ptychosperma bleeseri. Palms & Cycads* 72, 18-25. / Liddle, D.T., Brook, B., Matthews, J., Taylor, S.M., and Caley, P. (2006). Threat and response: A decade of decline in a regionally endangered rainforest palm affected by fire and introduced animals. *Biological Conservation* 132, 362-375. / Shapcott, A. (1998). The genetics of *Ptychosperma bleeseri*, a rare palm from the Northern Territory, Australia. *Biological Conservation* 85, 203-209.

Glory of the centre
Ricinocarpos gloria-medii

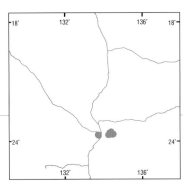

*Known locations
of Ricinocarpos
gloria-medii*
● = *pre 1970*
● = *post 1970*

CONSERVATION STATUS
AUSTRALIA: **VULNERABLE**
NORTHERN TERRITORY: **VULNERABLE**

DESCRIPTION
Ricinocarpos gloria-medii is a shrub to 2 m high, erect or spreading. The leaves are narrow, grey-green with a covering of star-shaped hairs; and the margins are strongly revolute. The flowers are white or creamy. The seed capsule is white-tomentose with star-shaped hairs (Kalotis 1981).

Flowering: May–October
Fruiting: July–October

DISTRIBUTION
This species is endemic to the Northern Territory, and confined to the MacDonnell Ranges bioregion, where it is known from five separate populations, three of which are within or overlap conservation reserves (White *et al.* 2000). Its distribution is predominantly in the East MacDonnell Ranges. However, there is one population in the West MacDonnell Ranges in the Simpsons Gap area. All populations have been mapped by Soos *et al.* (1987) who estimated the total area occupied by this species to be less than 400 ha. The latitudinal range is 20 km and the longitudinal range is 81 km.

Some more detailed mapping was undertaken by Emrys Leitch as an undergraduate student project in 2005 (Leitch 2005). The extent and up-slope edge of three populations were accurately mapped and part of a fourth was mapped.

Conservation reserves where reported:
N'Dhala Gorge Nature Park, Trephina Gorge Nature Park, West MacDonnell National Park.

ECOLOGY
Ricinocarpos gloria-medii occurs in deep gullies and well-shaded areas on south-facing slopes of quartzite or sandstone hills. Sites often contain a large amount of rock outcropping which provides protection from fire. This species has a patchy distribution within most of the identified populations. In the most favoured sites it is sometimes the dominant species over small areas, such as sheltered rock gullies and the base of steep cliffs. It also occurs as more sparsely-scattered individuals, such as on mid to lower scree slopes.

The species has been grown from cuttings but not from seeds at the Alice Springs Desert Park (Tim Collins *pers. comm.*).

This species has been regarded as fire-sensitive. However it is also known to re-sprout vigorously after fire in some circumstances. A patch of this species was burnt by a wildfire in October 2002. The fire was probably of low to moderate intensity at that location, and probably at night. Out of 13 plants completely scorched by the fire, 11 re-sprouted. Most re-sprouted from the base and a few from the stems (A. Duguid *pers. obs.*).

The survey work by Leitch (2005) found no evidence of spinifex encroachment into populations of this species.

CONSERVATION ASSESSMENT
In 2005, Leitch (2005) estimated population at three surveyed sites, as 3900 individuals.

Given known but unsampled populations, the total population is estimated to be in the order of 5000 to 15 000 plants.

Anecdotal evidence indicates the decline of *R. gloria-medii* populations at several locations.

The principal IUCN criterion for rating this species as **Vulnerable** (under criterion D2) is its acutely restricted area of occupancy (less than 400 ha).

THREATENING PROCESSES
Although it is known to re-sprout from rootstock after being burnt, hotter more frequent *Triodia*–fuelled fires may threaten the species.

CONSERVATION OBJECTIVES AND MANAGEMENT
A national recovery plan for this species, and threatened arid zone acacias, has been prepared (Nano *et al.* 2006). Recovery actions identified include to:
• implement management strategies for key threatening processes as required; and in particular to mitigate the potential threat of hot spinifex fires during summer;
• undertake research on fire, seed and reproductive biology;
• collect and store seeds from all populations in recognised seed-banks; and
• engage Indigenous ecologists to provide input into the recovery process.

Additionally, at least representative populations should be monitored to assess trends in population size and assess the impacts of threatening processes.

Compiled by Raelee Kerrigan, David Albrecht, Catherine Nano, Chris Pavey, Angus Duguid [June 2006] / **References:** Kalotis, A. (1981). Ricinocarpos. In *Flora of Central Australia*. (ed. J.Jessop), p. 190. (Reed, Sydney.) / Leitch, E. (2005). *Ricinocarpos gloria medii: a survey of populations in the East MacDonnell Ranges and Simpsons Gap*. Unpublished report to Parks and Wildlife Service of the Northern Territory. (Adelaide University, Adelaide.) / Nano, C., Harris, M., and Pavey, C. R. (2006). *Recovery plan for threatened Acacias and Ricinocarpos gloria-medii in central Australia, 2006-2011*. (NT Department of Natural Resources Environment and the Arts, Alice Springs.) / Soos, A. Latz, P.K., and Kube, P.D. (1987). *Occurrence of two rare plant populations in the eastern MacDonnell Ranges*. Technical Memorandum 87/11. (Conservation Commission of the Northern Territory, Alice Springs.) / White, M., Albrecht, D., Duguid, A., Latz, P., and Hamilton, M. (2000). *Plant species and sites of botanical significance in the southern bioregions of the Northern Territory. Volume 1: significant vascular plants*. A report to the Australian Heritage Commission. (Arid Lands Environment Centre, Alice Springs.)

Image courtesy of David Albrecht

Quandong
Santalum acuminatum

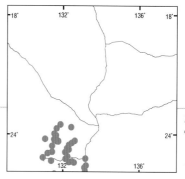

Known locations of Santalum acuminatum
● = pre 1970
● = post 1970

DESCRIPTION

Santalum acuminatum is a shrub to 6 m, with grey bark. The branchlets are often pendulous (George 1981). The flowers are small (2 to 4 mm long), partly creamy-green and partly orangish. The fruit is from 1.5 to 2.6 cm diameter and bright red. It is distinguished from other species in the genus by the smaller flowers, acute longer leaves, and bright red fruit (George 1984).

Flowering: October–December
Fruiting: September–October

DISTRIBUTION

This species is known from all Australian mainland states. It is common and widespread in Victoria, South Australia and Western Australia (George 1981, 1984). The Northern Territory population represents the northernmost extent of its range. Although there are a considerable number of records of the species in southern areas of the Northern Territory, most populations are small (typically fewer than 10 plants). A decline in abundance has been reported in the Northern Territory and in Western Australia (Murphy *et al.* 2007).

Conservation reserves where reported:
Uluru – Kata Tjuta National Park, Watarrka National Park.

ECOLOGY

The quandong occurs in dune swales, along creeks, on plains and low rises, and rarely on hills. It typically occurs in areas where the soils are sandy or loamy, sometimes with limestone or sandstone shallowly below the soil surface.

CONSERVATION ASSESSMENT

The species is assessed as **Vulnerable** (under criteria A4acde and C1) based on:
• a suspected population size reduction of at least 30% over three generations, where the cause of reduction has not ceased, based on direct observation; and
• an estimated continuing decline of at least 10% within three generations.

THREATENING PROCESSES

Many long-term residents who are familiar with the species have expressed strong concern about the decline of quandong in the Northern Territory. It is a favourite food of camels, and increasing numbers of feral camels are having a significant impact on populations. Other threats include harvesting stems and roots for carving, and the impacts of fire, rabbits, and mistletoe.

The dispersal and germination rates of quandongs have probably declined due to the widespread loss or decline of their main dispersal agents, native mammals such as bettongs and bandicoots (Murphy *et al.* 2006).

CONSERVATION OBJECTIVES AND MANAGEMENT

Further research is required into the status of this species; and particularly into the assessment of presumed threatening factors. A monitoring program should be established for at least representative populations. Based on information from this program, more targeted management is required to ameliorate the threats.

Compiled by Raelee Kerrigan, David Albrecht, Peter Latz, John Woinarski [March 2007] / **References:** George, A.S. (1981). Santalaceae. In *Flora of Central Australia*. (ed. J. Jessop) pp. 25-26. (Reed Books, Sydney.) / George, A.S. (1984). Santalaceae. In *Flora of Australia* 22 (ed. A.S. George), pp. 65-66. (Australian Government Publishing Service, Canberra.) / Murphy,M.T., Garkaklis, M.J., and Hardy, G.E.S.J. (2007). Seed caching by woylies *Bettongia penicillata* can increase sandalwood *Santalum spicatum* regeneration in Western Australia. *Austral Ecology* 32.

Image courtesy of Kym Brennan

Sauropus filicinus

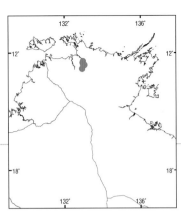

Known locations
of Sauropus
filicinus
● = pre 1970
● = post 1970

CONSERVATION STATUS
AUSTRALIA: **VULNERABLE**
NORTHERN TERRITORY: **DATA DEFICIENT**

DESCRIPTION

Sauropus filicinus is a dwarf somewhat fern-like dioecious sub-shrub, with a thickened woody base. The leaves are alternate, hairless to sparsely hairy, ovate, and arranged in two rows. Male flowers are clustered (3 to 15 per cluster) and green to pink; female flowers are solitary and red to pink.
The species may be readily confused with a similar species, *S. rimophilus*, but differs by its more stunted habit, shorter floral parts and free styles (Hunter and Bruhl 1997). Ambiguous historical records complicate the assessment of conservation status for this species.

Flowering: April–August
Fruiting: April

DISTRIBUTION

Sauropus filicinus is endemic to the Northern Territory, where it is known from seven localities– on the Mt Brockman outlier and northern outliers in Kakadu National Park, with one record from Arnhem Land.

Conservation reserves where reported:
Kakadu National Park

ECOLOGY

This species is one of more than 20 species from the area that specialise in growing from crevices in sandstone cliff faces. It is found amongst rugged sandstone pillars and outcrops that are dissected by deep gorges and crevices. It often co-occurs with the closely related *S. rimophilus*.

CONSERVATION ASSESSMENT

Hunter and Bruhl (1997) classified this species as Endangered on the basis that it was known only from the type locality. However, the number of records has increased considerably since that time. Federally the species is classified as Vulnerable.

In the Northern Territory, this species is coded as **Data Deficient** based on:
• data are considered inadequate for assessment; and
• it is known from seven localities, none of which are believed to be under threat.

Few abundance data are available for this species and it is considered not adequately surveyed. Assessments of distribution and abundance have been hampered by taxonomic uncertainty surrounding the species. Results from a 2003 survey were inconclusive as counts from permanent plots ambiguously included both *S. rimophilus* and *S. filicinus* (Kerrigan 2003). Surveys in 2004, collection of better material of the two taxa, and return of herbarium specimens on loan interstate allowed clearer differentiation between them (Kerrigan 2004; Cowie 2005).

In 2004, a total of 66 mature individuals were recorded along transects of approximately 3.5 km. It has an extent of occurrence of 229 km².

This species is both easily overlooked and difficult to collect.

It is sparsely distributed where seen; however, it grows in a relatively well protected habitat. Recruitment was not observed and successful dispersal and establishment is expected to be low as the habitat is likely to be fully stocked.

THREATENING PROCESSES

None are known. The sandstone cliff habitat of this species is naturally fire-proof and secure from disturbance. In some places, plants could be scorched by fires occurring within adjacent vegetation. Little is known about resistance of the species to fire. There are no other obvious threats. While stochastic events such as rock falls may affect localised populations, this is not thought to be a serious threat to a species with extensive, scattered populations.

CONSERVATION OBJECTIVES AND MANAGEMENT

Further counts, density and population estimates are needed at a number of places across its range. A monitoring program has recently been established (Kerrigan 2003) and should be maintained.

Compiled by Ian Cowie, Raelee Kerrigan [April 2006] / **References:** Cowie, I.D. (2005). *Kakadu Threatened Flora Report (Vol 3.). Results of a threatened flora survey.* (NT Department of Infrastructure Planning and Environment, Darwin.) / Hunter, J.T., and Bruhl, J.J. (1997). New *Sauropus* (Euphorbiaceae: Phyllantheae) taxa for the Northern Territory and Western Australia and notes on other *Sauropus* occurring in these regions. *Nuytsia* 11, 165-184. / Kerrigan, R. (2003). *Kakadu Threatened Flora Report. Results of a threatened flora survey 2003.* (NT Department of Infrastructure Planning and Environment, Darwin.) / Kerrigan, R. (2004). *Kakadu Threatened Flora Report. Volume 2. Results of a threatened flora survey 2004.* (NT Department of Infrastructure Planning and Environment, Darwin.)

Image courtesy of Ian Cowie

Schoutenia ovata

CONSERVATION STATUS
AUSTRALIA: **NOT LISTED**
NORTHERN TERRITORY: **VULNERABLE**

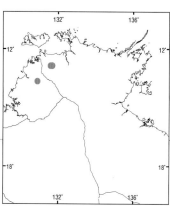

Known locations of Schoutenia ovata
● = *pre 1970*
● = *post 1970*

DESCRIPTION

Schoutenia ovata is a shrub or tree up to 10 m high. Its leaves are usually oblong or ovate, 3.5 to 10 cm long and 1.7 to 5 cm wide, with margins irregular, lobed or entire, and densely hairy. The flowers are yellowish white. The fruit is 6 mm long.

Flowering: March
Fruiting: March, May

DISTRIBUTION

This species occurs in Thailand, Indochina and Java. In Australia, it is known only from the Northern Territory, where it occurs in two disjunct populations, the Mt Bundy – Mt Goyder area and near Tipperary Station (Liddle *et al.* 1994).

Conservation reserves where reported:
Mary River National Park

ECOLOGY

This species has been collected from monsoon rainforests on granite and limestone outcrops.

CONSERVATION ASSESSMENT

This species is classified as **Vulnerable** (under criteria D1+2) based on:
• a fragmented distribution;
• a restricted area of occupancy (estimated to be less than 20km²); and
• a small estimated population size of fewer than 1000 individuals.

Anecdotal evidence suggests that the size of known populations is in the hundreds (G. Wightman and I. Cowie *pers. comm.*). The habitat in which it occurs has been sufficiently well sampled (Russell-Smith 1991; Liddle *et al.* 1994) to indicate that its apparent restriction is real.

THREATENING PROCESSES

Although this species is known from rocky outcrops that are unlikely to be affected by land clearing in the Daly Basin area, changes in fire regimes, changes to hydrology and exposure to exotic weed invasion are potential threats. Populations at Mt Bundy are vulnerable to stochastic events although no pending threats have been identified.

CONSERVATION OBJECTIVES AND MANAGEMENT

Research into the status and extent of populations, and impacts of possible threatening factors, is required. A monitoring program should be established.

Compiled by Raelee Kerrigan, Ian Cowie [April 2006] / **References:** Liddle, D.T., Russell-Smith, J., Brock, J., Leach, G.J., and Connors, G.T. (1994). *Atlas of the vascular rainforest plants of the Northern Territory.* Flora of Australia Supplementary Series No. 3. (ABRS, Canberra.) / Russell-Smith, J. (1991). Classification, species richness, and environmental relations of monsoon rain forest in northern Australia. *Journal of Vegetation Science* 2, 259-278.

Solanum carduiforme

CONSERVATION STATUS
AUSTRALIA: **VULNERABLE**
NORTHERN TERRITORY: **DATA DEFICIENT**

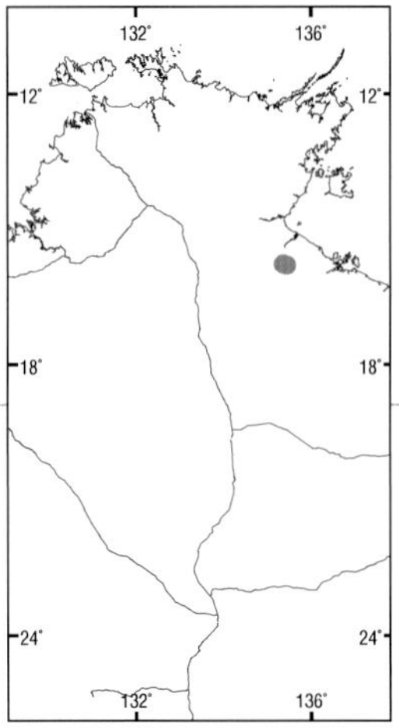

Known locations of Solanum carduiforme
● = *pre 1970*
● = *post 1970*

DESCRIPTION

Solanum carduiforme is an erect clonal herb or subshrub to 50 cm height. Its leaves are densely pubescent with stellate hairs. It has prickles to 8 mm length, abundant on all parts. The leaves are lanceolate (5 to 11 cm long x 2 to 4 cm wide), concolorous and deeply lobed. Male and female plants are separate, the male with purple many-flowered inflorescence, and the female with solitary purple flowers.

DISTRIBUTION

This species is known only from the Lawn Hill area (Queensland), Limmen Gate area (Northern Territory) and Purnululu (Bungle Bungle) National Park in the south-eastern Kimberley (Western Australia).

Conservation reserves where reported:
Limmen Gate National Park

ECOLOGY

There is remarkably little published information on this species. At Lawn Hill, it is known to occur on conglomerate rock formations (George 1982). All other locations are on sandstone.

CONSERVATION ASSESSMENT

This species was designated Vulnerable at national level when it was known only from Lawn Hill, and was considered rare there.

In the Northern Territory, there are very few records, and these provide insufficient information to assess distribution or abundance. There has been relatively little botanical collecting in the sandstone ranges of the Northern Territory Gulf hinterland. Given this lack of information, the species is coded as **Data Deficient** for the Northern Territory.

THREATENING PROCESSES

No specific threats have been demonstrated for this species, but it is possible that it would be detrimentally affected by the extensive, high intensity and frequent fires that now characterise much of the Gulf hinterland.

CONSERVATION OBJECTIVES AND MANAGEMENT

There is no existing management or recovery plan for this species.

Research and management priorities are to:

- undertake more survey to gain a better understanding of its distribution, abundance and habitat requirements;
- assess its response to factors that may threaten it; and
- establish a monitoring program for at least representative populations.

Compiled by Ian Cowie, John Woinarski [May 2006] / **References:** George, A.S. (1982). Solanaceae. *Flora of Australia* 29, 171-172.

Sticherus flabellatus var. *compactus*

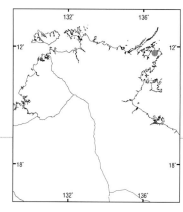

CONSERVATION STATUS
AUSTRALIA: **NOT LISTED**
NORTHERN TERRITORY: **VULNERABLE**

DESCRIPTION

Sticherus flabellatus var. *compactus* is a terrestrial fern. The plant base is 2 to 7 mm in diameter. Fronds are of 1 to 3 tiers of opposite primary branches that in turn are divided 2 to 3 times. The stipe is 7 to 96 cm long. The ultimate segments are linear, toothed along margins, and 6 to 15 mm long. The spore clusters (sporangia) are 2 to 3 mm in diameter, and located half-way between the margin and mid-rib. It can be confused with *Dicranopteris*.

DISTRIBUTION

Sticherus flabellatus is known from two varieties: var. *flabellatus* occurs in New Guinea, New Zealand, New Caledonia and the east coast of Australia; and var. *compactus* is known only from north-eastern Queensland and the Northern Territory (Short *et al.* 2003). In the Northern Territory, it is known from only one locality in north-eastern Arnhem Land.

Conservation reserves where reported: None

ECOLOGY

For the Northern Territory, it is known from "sandstone cliffs in riparian vine forests" (Short *et al.* 2003). Elsewhere, the species has been reported from along creeks and rivers on damp banks, river flats or among, or on, rocks and boulders in wet places (Chinnock and Bell 1998). It frequently forms dense colonies.

CONSERVATION ASSESSMENT

Relatively little is known about the abundance and distribution of this fern in the Northern Territory, and it could readily be considered Data Deficient. However, monsoon rainforests have been relatively well surveyed (Russell-Smith 1991; Liddle *et al.* 1994) and the taxon is sufficiently distinct to have been identified during these surveys.

Using the precautionary principle and given the knowledge we have to date, this taxon satisfies a classification of **Vulnerable** (under criteria D1+2) based on:
- an estimated population size of fewer than 1000 individuals; and
- a restricted area of occupancy estimated to be less than 20 km².

THREATENING PROCESSES

With a small population, this species is susceptible to stochastic events such as destruction of forest canopy from cyclonic events. Changes to hydrology and infestation from exotic weeds have the potential to threaten the known population but at present they are not imminent threats.

CONSERVATION OBJECTIVES AND MANAGEMENT

Further research is required to monitor the known population, to search for others, and to assess the impacts of possible threatening factors.

Compiled by Raelee Kerrigan, Ian Cowie [April 2006] / **References:** Chinnock, R.J., and Bell, G.H. (1998). Gleicheniaceae. *Flora of Australia* 48, 148-162. / Liddle, D.T., Russell-Smith, J., Brock, J., Leach, G.J., and Connors, G.T. (1994). *Atlas of the vascular rainforest plants of the Northern Territory.* Flora of Australia Supplementary Series no. 3. (Australian Biological Resources Study, Canberra.) / Russell-Smith, J. (1991). Classification, species richness, and environmental relations of monsoon rain forest in northern Australia. *Journal of Vegetation Science* 2, 259-278. / Short, P., Dixon, D., and Osterkamp Madsen, M. (2003). A review of ferns and fern allies of the Northern Territory. *The Beagle* 19, 7-80.

Image courtesy of Kym Brennan

Tarennoidea wallichii

CONSERVATION STATUS
AUSTRALIA: **NOT LISTED**
NORTHERN TERRITORY: **ENDANGERED**

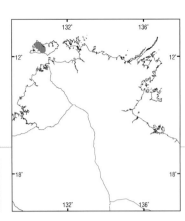

*Known locations
of Tarennoidea
wallichii*
● = *pre 1970*
● = *post 1970*

DESCRIPTION

Tarennoidea wallichii is a small tree to 5 m, with grey bark, smooth throughout. Its leaves are opposite with interpetiolar stipules, dark green, glossy. The domatia have fringing hairs. The flowers are white.

Flowering: October
Fruiting: July, October

DISTRIBUTION

This species is widespread in Malesia, extending at least as far as India. In the Northern Territory it is known only from a small set of monsoon rainforests on Melville Island.

Conservation reserves where reported: None

ECOLOGY

It occurs in drier parts of complex evergreen monsoon rainforests.

CONSERVATION ASSESSMENT

In the Northern Territory, this species is known from 13 records at a small number of sites on Melville Island (Fensham and Woinarski 1992; Liddle *et al.* 1994; Woinarski *et al.* 2003), with collections from only three separate locations there. Rainforests have been well sampled across the Northern Territory (Russell-Smith 1991), and the Tiwi Islands have also been comparatively well sampled (Woinarski *et al.* 2003), so this restriction is probably real.

This species qualifies as **Endangered** (under criterion D) based on a population size estimated to be fewer than 250 mature individuals.

THREATENING PROCESSES

The small population size makes this species susceptible to stochastic events such as cyclones and fire. The maintenance of this species depends upon the retention of the Tiwi rainforest network and control of the impact of feral animals in this environment, and moderation of the impacts of fire and intensive development in surrounding habitats.

CONSERVATION OBJECTIVES AND MANAGEMENT

A recovery plan for this species, and other threatened plants on the Tiwi Islands, is due to be released in 2007, but many actions in its draft are currently being implemented.

Research into the status of the population is required. Collection of propagation material and translocation to botanic gardens would assist in protecting this species from cyclonic events. A monitoring program should be established for at least representative populations.

Compiled by Raelee Kerrigan, Ian Cowie [April 2006] / **References:** Fensham, R.J., and Woinarski, J.C.Z. (1992). *Yawulama: the ecology and conservation of monsoon forest on the Tiwi Islands, Northern Territory.* Report to DASET. (Conservation Commission of the Northern Territory, Darwin.) / Liddle, D.T., Russell-Smith, J., Brock, J., Leach, G.J., and Connors, G.T. (1994) *Atlas of the vascular rainforest plants of the Northern Territory.* Flora of Australia Supplementary Series No. 3, (ABRS, Canberra.) / Russell-Smith, J. (1991). Classification, species richness, and environmental relations of monsoon rain forest in northern Australia. *Journal of Vegetation Science* 2, 259-278. / Woinarski, J., Brennan, K., Cowie, I., Kerrigan, R., and Hempel, C. (2003). *Biodiversity conservation on the Tiwi Islands, Northern Territory. Part 1. Plants and environments.* 144 pp. (Department of Infrastructure Planning and Environment, Darwin.)

Image courtesy of David Liddle

Thrixspermum congestum

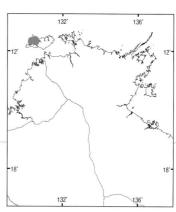

*Known locations
of Thrixspermum
congestum*
● = *pre 1970*
● = *post 1970*

CONSERVATION STATUS
AUSTRALIA: **NOT LISTED**
NORTHERN TERRITORY: **VULNERABLE**

DESCRIPTION

Thrixspermum congestum is an epiphytic orchid
forming small clumps. The stems are sparsely
branched, flattened, to 15 cm long. There are 6 to
15 leaves per plant, leathery, often yellowish-green.
The inflorescence grows to 10 cm long, and is erect
and wiry. The flowers open together, are about
15 mm across, cream or white, and fragrant.
The flowers last about one day and are produced
in sporadic groups.

Flowering: February

DISTRIBUTION

This species is known from Queensland, the
Northern Territory and New Guinea (Jones 1988).
In the Northern Territory, there are specimen
records from only two localities, on Melville Island,
with unvouchered records from a further six sites
(four from Bathurst Island and two from Melville
Island) (Liddle *et al.* 1994; Woinarski *et al.* 2003).
The grid references of the Bathurst Island sites are
unknown.

Conservation reserves where reported: None

ECOLOGY

This species grows in lowland rainforests and also
on mangroves. It is usually found in humid, airy
situations, often in exposed positions on small
branches.

CONSERVATION ASSESSMENT

There is little information available on the status
of this species. No further populations were
uncovered during extensive surveys on the Tiwi
Island between 1998–2001 (Woinarski *et al.* 2003),
and its rainforest habitat has been well sampled
(Russell-Smith 1991; Liddle *et al.* 1994), suggesting
that its apparent restriction may be real. However,
there is an element of data deficiency with this
species as flowers are recorded as lasting only
approximately 10 hours.

This species qualifies as **Vulnerable** (under
criteria D1+2) based on:
• an estimated population size of fewer than
  1000 individuals; and
• an area of occupancy estimated to be less
  than 20 km².

THREATENING PROCESSES

This species is an epiphyte and is susceptible
to cyclonic events. As a wet rainforest species,
impacts on habitat by feral animal activity or
changes in hydrology will affect population
numbers although these threats are not
considered imminent. As an orchid, pressure
from horticultural collectors may be a threat.

CONSERVATION OBJECTIVES
AND MANAGEMENT

A recovery plan for this species, and other
threatened plants on the Tiwi Islands, is due to be
released in 2007, but many actions in its draft are
currently being implemented.

Research into the status and extent of the
population, and the impacts of possible threatening
factors, is required. A monitoring program
should be established for at least representative
populations.

Living material has been collected for the George
Brown Darwin Botanic Gardens. Availability
of stock commercially may protect species from
horticultural harvesting and stochastic events.

Compiled by Raelee Kerrigan, Ian Cowie [April 2006] / **References:** Fensham, R.J., and Woinarski, J.C.Z. (1992). *Yawulama: the ecology and conservation of monsoon forest on the Tiwi Islands, Northern Territory.*
Report to DASET. (Conservation Commission of the Northern Territory, Darwin.) / Jones, D. L. (1988). *Native Orchids of Australia.* (Reed, Sydney.) / Liddle, D.T., Russell-Smith, J., Brock, J., Leach, G.J., and
Connors, G.T. (1994) *Atlas of the vascular rainforest plants of the Northern Territory.* Flora of Australia Supplementary Series No. 3. (ABRS, Canberra.) / Russell-Smith, J. (1991). Classification, species richness,
and environmental relations of monsoon rain forest in northern Australia. *Journal of Vegetation Science* 2, 259-278. / Woinarski, J., Brennan, K., Cowie, I., Kerrigan, R., and Hempel, C. (2003). *Biodiversity
conservation on the Tiwi Islands, Northern Territory. Part 1. Plants and environments.* 144 pp. (Department of Infrastructure Planning and Environment, Darwin.)

Palm Valley myrtle
Thryptomene hexandra

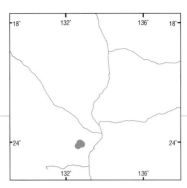

*Known locations
of Thryptomene
hexandra*
● = pre 1970
● = post 1970

CONSERVATION STATUS
AUSTRALIA: VULNERABLE
NORTHERN TERRITORY: VULNERABLE

DESCRIPTION
Thryptomene hexandra is an erect shrub to 2.5 m high. The leaves are decussate, linear-obovate, and 7 to 8 mm long. The flowers are axillary, and white.

Flowering: March, June–September

DISTRIBUTION
This species is restricted to Queensland and the Northern Territory. In the Northern Territory, it has a very restricted range, occurring only in several narrow steeply dissected valleys of Finke Gorge National Park.

Conservation reserves where reported:
Finke Gorge National Park.

ECOLOGY
This species occurs in deep sandstone 'slot gorges' and sheltered south-facing aspects of steep ranges.

CONSERVATION ASSESSMENT
This species is rated as **Vulnerable** (under criteria B2ab(iii); D2) based on:
• occurrence at fewer than 10 sites;
• a projected declining population due to increased impacts of fire and exotic invasive grasses; and
• an area of occurrence less than 20 km².

THREATENING PROCESSES
The Finke Gorge populations of *Thryptomene hexandra* occur in a very small area and are potentially threatened by the rapid invasion of the exotic invasive buffel grass (*Cenchrus ciliaris*) and, to a lesser degree, couch grass (*Cynodon dactylon*). Due to their position in the landscape, the known populations are infrequently burnt. However, the increased biomass of grassy weeds may alter this situation. The fire response of this species is unknown and it is possible that altered fire regimes could destroy populations.

CONSERVATION OBJECTIVES AND MANAGEMENT
Fire and weed management and population monitoring is ongoing at some sites within Finke Gorge National Park. Visitation to known sites should be kept to a minimum to prevent the spread of weed propagules.

Compiled by Raelee Kerrigan, David Albrecht [April 2006] / **References:** White, M., Albrecht, D., Duguid, A., Latz, P., and Hamilton, M. (2000). *Plant species and sites of botanical significance in the southern bioregions of the Northern Territory. Volume 1: significant vascular plants.* A report to the Australian Heritage Commission. (Arid Lands Environment Centre, Alice Springs.)

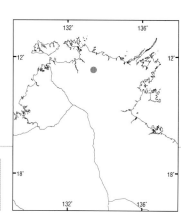

*Known locations
of Toechima* sp.
East Alligator
● = *pre 1970*
● = *post 1970*

Toechima sp. East Alligator

CONSERVATION STATUS
AUSTRALIA: **ENDANGERED**
NORTHERN TERRITORY: **ENDANGERED**

DESCRIPTION

Toechima sp. East Alligator is a small, multi-stemmed, slender-branched tree to 5 m high. It is able to regenerate from rhizomes. The bark is light grey-brown, almost smooth.

DISTRIBUTION

This species is endemic to the Northern Territory, where it is known from only one very small population in Arnhem Land near the upper East Alligator River, east of Kakadu National Park (Liddle *et al.* 1994).

Conservation reserves where reported: None

ECOLOGY

Very little is known of this unnamed taxon. It occurs in a sandstone gorge in a rainforest patch dominated by the tree *Allosyncarpia ternata*.

CONSERVATION ASSESSMENT

Although the number of individuals has not been quantified, there is strong evidence to suggest that population numbers for adult tree species in Northern Territory monsoon rainforests are typically low (Russell-Smith 1991, 1992). An estimate of approximately 250 mature individuals in this population is considered very conservative and it is likely that there are fewer then 50 individuals present.

Although the Arnhem Land escarpment is remote and difficult to access, a relatively high proportion of herbarium collections come from the Arnhem Land/Kakadu area. The quarter degree grid cell where this taxon was found has 1391 plant collection records. Consequently, despite the fact that there has been no specific survey for this species, it is felt that the comprehensive rainforest survey carried out in the 1980s (Russell-Smith 1991, 1992), and the relatively high level of collecting in the area of potential habitat generally, offers confidence that our current knowledge accurately reflects its restricted distribution and abundance.

This species qualifies as **Endangered** (under criterion D) based on a population size estimated to be fewer than 250 individuals.

THREATENING PROCESSES

It is difficult to identify imminent threats to this species, given its restriction to a remote and deep sandstone gorge in Arnhem Land. While there is evidence to indicate that monsoon rainforests are vulnerable to disturbance from cattle, buffalo, pigs and dry season wildfires (Russell-Smith and Bowman 1992), collection notes document that the population occurs in a very well protected gorge.

This species is known only from sterile or budding material and is noted as being able to regenerate as coppice from a rhizome. Although fruiting material has not been seen, species within this genus have arillate seeds (Hyland *et al.* 2002) suggesting animal dispersal vectors. Given this taxon may not be sexually reproducing or may not be able to cross with other populations, the long-term genetic viability of this taxon may be compromised.

CONSERVATION OBJECTIVES AND MANAGEMENT

Research priorities are to:

• provide a more detailed assessment of its distribution, habitat requirements and population size;
• provide an assessment of the factors limiting distribution, and/or threats to its survival, and
• establish a monitoring program.

Compiled by Raelee Kerrigan, Ian Cowie [April 2006] / **References:** Hyland, B. P. M., Whiffin, T., Christophel, D.C., Gray, B., and Elick, R.W. (2002). *Australian Tropical Rain Forest Plants. Trees, Shrubs and Vines.* (CSIRO, Melbourne.) / Liddle, D.T., Russell-Smith, J., Brock, J., Leach, G.J., and Connors, G.T. (1994). *Atlas of the vascular rainforest plants of the Northern Territory.* Flora of Australia Supplementary Series No. 3, (ABRS, Canberra.) / Russell-Smith, J. (1991). Classification, species richness, and environmental relations of monsoon rain forest in northern Australia. *Journal of Vegetation Science* 2, 259-278. Russell-Smith, J. (1992). Plant populations and monsoon rain forest in the Northern Territory, Australia. *Biotropica* 24, 471-487. / Russell-Smith, J., and Bowman, D.M.J.S. (1992). Conservation of monsoon rainforest isolates in the Northern Territory. *Biological Conservation* 59, 51-63.

Image courtesy of Martin Armstrong

Triodia fitzgeraldii

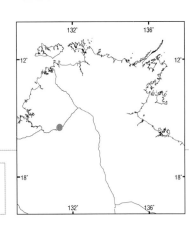

*Known locations
of Triodia
fitzgeraldii*
● = *pre 1970*
● = *post 1970*

CONSERVATION STATUS
AUSTRALIA: **NOT LISTED**
NORTHERN TERRITORY: **VULNERABLE**

DESCRIPTION
The taxonomic identity of this hummock grass
has only recently been determined – until recently
it was named as *Triodia* sp. Matt Wilson. It is
now recognised as *T. fitzgeraldii* (a rare species
previously considered restricted to the Kimberley,
Western Australia). It can be distinguished by its
fine, non-resinous and "soft" foliage and very fine,
narrow inflorescence. Spikelets are approximately
3 to 4 mm long and 2 mm wide. The inflorescence
is between 10 to 30 cm long and 5 mm wide.

Flowering: February
Fruiting: November

DISTRIBUTION
In the Northern Territory, this species is known
only from one area on the edge of a plateau 2 to 3 km
to the north of Matt Wilson lookout. Many
thousands of plants were seen in a population
extending south around the rim of an amphitheatre
for approximately 1 km. The area has not
been thoroughly surveyed and there is a strong
possibility that the population is more extensive.

In Western Australia, it is known "only from
a sandstone area south-east of Wyndham"
(Wheeler 1992).

Conservation reserves where reported:
Gregory National Park

ECOLOGY
The plant occupies the rocky cliff top at the edge
of a laterite plateau and the upper 20 metres or
so of scree slope. It was also collected from the
slope of a small gully near the top of the plateau,
on gravelly soil.

CONSERVATION ASSESSMENT
In the Northern Territory, this species has been
classified as **Vulnerable** (under criterion D2) based
on the restricted area of occupancy estimated to
be less than 20 km². Population size can be
interpreted as equivalent to more than 10 000
individuals (I. Cowie). There is no observed,
projected or inferred decline in population size,
or extreme fluctuations in area of occupancy or
population size.

THREATENING PROCESSES
With a restricted area of occupancy, this species
is susceptible to stochastic events. The species
occupies a narrow rim on rocky slopes. It is
possible the species is a poor competitor against
other *Triodia* species. The species occurs in an area
frequently exposed to fire but the role of fire
in determining its distribution is unknown.

CONSERVATION OBJECTIVES
AND MANAGEMENT
Research into the status and distribution of the
population and the impact of fire is required;
and a monitoring program should be established.

Compiled by Raelee Kerrigan, Ian Cowie [April 2006] / **References:** Wheeler, J.R. (ed.) (1992). *Flora of the Kimberley region.* (WA Herbarium, Perth.)

Typhonium jonesii

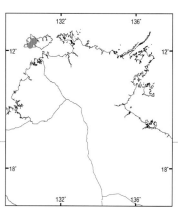

Known locations
of *Typhonium
jonesii*
● = *pre 1970*
● = *post 1970*

CONSERVATION STATUS
AUSTRALIA: **ENDANGERED**
NORTHERN TERRITORY: **ENDANGERED**

DESCRIPTION
Typhonium jonesii is a cormous perennial herb with annual aerial parts. The leaf blade is deeply tri-lobed, hastate or auriculate at base, with linear segments. The spathe or bract of the flower is pale mauve-cream. Note that the genus *Typhonium* is difficult to identify to the species level without flowering material present.

Flowering: December

DISTRIBUTION
This species is endemic to the Northern Territory. It is known only from the Tiwi Islands, with herbarium collections from one locality on Bathurst Island and two on Melville Island.

The species was first described in 1993 from material collected by D.L. Jones in 1984 (Hay 1993). Hay (1996) recorded it as locally common on the Tiwi Islands and reported three (probably sterile) non-vouchered collections – one from near Three Ways, one on the Three Ways-Snake Bay Rd on Melville Island, and one from 10 km west of Nguiu on Bathurst Island. Although taken into cultivation at Sydney Botanic Gardens, the plants did not survive and no herbarium specimens were lodged (S Goodwin, *pers. comm.*). Therefore it is not possible to verify the specific identity of these recordings.

Recent targeted survey in February and March 2007 re-located some of the previously known populations and encountered several new ones,

each of only a few individuals. Monitoring plots were set up at the two known high-density locations, with one plot recording 130 individuals with a high proportion of juveniles.

The extent of occurrence based on a minimum convex polygon of collections is estimated at 85 km² and an area of occupancy estimated at 3 ha (1 ha per population).

Conservation reserves where reported: None

ECOLOGY
Little is known of the ecology of this species. The above-ground annual shoots are seasonally dormant, emerging from an underground corm (bulb) during the wet season. It is difficult to distinguish between species of this genus without reproductive material as the leaves are commonly polymorphic. Diagnostic characters for species within the genus include the arrangement of flowers and the timing of emergent leaf parts relative to the emergent inflorescence. This species is documented as having an inflorescence emergent among new season leaves.

All three collections were located on rocky or lateritic hills, two from *Eucalyptus miniata* and *Eucalyptus tetrodonta* woodlands.

CONSERVATION ASSESSMENT
Although this species is seasonally dormant and cryptic in the landscape, it is considered adequately surveyed, based on the strong survey effort in the

area (Woinarski *et al.* 2003) and the high profile of this genus amongst collectors. While more populations may exist the paucity of collections of this species is considered to accurately reflect its very restricted distribution and abundance.

While there are no data on population size for this species, J. Egan (*pers. comm.*) reported that the species can be locally abundant. This observation has been confirmed in the field, but the density of this species is highly variable and some populations may comprise only a few individuals.

This species qualifies as **Endangered** (under criteria B1ab(iii)+2ab(iii); D) based on:
• recorded from fewer than five locations;
• an extent of occurrence less than 5000 km²;
• an area of occupancy less than 500 km²; and
• a inferred decline in the quality of habitat due to habitat clearance for the development of plantation forestry in the area.

THREATENING PROCESSES
Clearing of habitat for plantation forestry development is a potential threat for this species. Currently, extensive areas within the western half of Melville Island are being cleared and planted with the exotic *Acacia mangium*. This plantation forestry may be extended to Bathurst Island in the near future. The preferred plantation habitat and designated planting region of the western half of Melville coincide with known populations and preferred habitat of this species.

continued.../

The eucalypt forests are also affected by feral buffalo, cattle and horses; and increased clearing, road development and activity in the area around known populations may increase the invasion of exotic plants such as mission grass (*Pennisetum polystachion*) and gamba grass (*Andropogon gayanus*) (Woinarski *et al.* 2003). Although the underground corm and seasonal nature of this species offers protection from fire, the effect of perennial grass invasions on this species is unknown.

CONSERVATION OBJECTIVES AND MANAGEMENT

A recovery plan for this species, and other threatened plants on the Tiwi Islands, is due to be released in 2007, but many actions in its draft are currently being implemented.

Habitat protection at the known localities is required to maintain the status of the species. The Tiwi Islands Forestry Strategic Plan (Hadden 2000) provided the commitment that all populations of this species would be protected from clearing, with an exclusion buffer of 50 m around their perimeter.

However, it is probable that there are additional populations so far undiscovered. A high priority is for further targeted survey for this species in areas that may be subject to land clearing, including Bathurst Island. This survey needs to be undertaken in the months when the plant is likely to be visible and preferably flowering. The next opportunity for this will be December 2007 to March 2008.

Research priorities are to:
• provide a more detailed assessment of its distribution, habitat requirements and population size;
• provide an assessment of the factors limiting distribution, and/or threats to its survival; and
• provide further assessment of the taxonomy of known and new *Typhonium* populations. Potted collections have been made of these populations in 2007 in order to get flowering material by 2008 for this purpose.

A monitoring program has been established for representative populations and should be maintained.

Compiled by Raelee Kerrigan, Ian Cowie, Louis Elliot, David Liddle [April 2007] / **References:** Brock, C., Cowie, I. Harwood, B., Leach, G. Milne, D. Stirrat, S., and Woinarski J. (2000). *Plantation proposal, Melville Island: assessment of biodiversity.* Report to N.T. Department of Lands, Planning and Environment, Tiwi Land Council, and Sylvatech Australia Pty Ltd. (Parks and Wildlife Commission of the Northern Territory, Darwin.) / Hadden, K. (2000). *Tiwi Islands Plantation Forestry Strategic Plan.* (Tiwi Land Council, Darwin.) / Hay, A. (1993). The genus *Typhonium* (Araceae-Areae) in Australasia. *Blumea* 37, 345-376. / Hay, A., and S. M. Taylor (1996). A new species of *Typhonium* Schott (Araceae - Areae) from the Northern Territory, with notes on the conservation status of two Areae endemic to the Tiwi Islands. *Telopea* 6, 563-567. / Woinarski, J., Brennan, K., Cowie, I, Kerrigan, R., and Hempel, C. (2003). *Biodiversity conservation on the Tiwi Islands, Northern Territory. Part 1. Environment and Plants.* (NT Department of Infrastructure, Planning and Environment, Darwin.)

Image courtesy of Kym Brennan

Typhonium mirabile

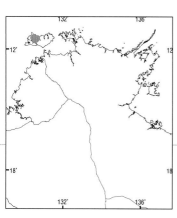

Known locations
of *Typhonium
mirabile*
● = pre 1970
● = post 1970

CONSERVATION STATUS
AUSTRALIA: **ENDANGERED**
NORTHERN TERRITORY: **ENDANGERED**

DESCRIPTION

Typhonium mirabile is a small tuberous herb with annual aerial parts. The leaves are blue-green, cordate, and held on or just above the soil surface. The spathe or bract of flower is partly buried in soil; the part below is white cream with grey mottling; the aerial part mottled grey-green; the spadix limb is smoky grey; greenish towards the base. These distinguishing features are only evident for a small part of the year when the foliage and flowers are present.

Flowering: October
Fruiting: December

DISTRIBUTION

This species is endemic to the Northern Territory. Its entire known range comprises five locations in the western half of Melville Island.

Type material for this species was taken from a specimen cultivated by D. Jones from Hanguana Jungle in 1984 (Hay 1993). Hay (1996) recorded that despite survey effort on Bathurst Island, no populations have been found there, and recent targeted survey for this species as part of a biodiversity assessment (Woinarski *et al.* 2003) located only one additional population.

The area of occupancy of these known populations is estimated at 5 to 10 ha.

Conservation reserves where reported: None

ECOLOGY

Very little is known of the ecology of this species. The above-ground annual shoots are seasonally dormant, emerging from an underground corm (bulb) during the wet season. It is difficult to distinguish between species of this genus without reproductive material as the leaves are commonly polymorphic.

It occurs very sporadically in groups in eucalypt woodland on lateritic and sandy soils, and in patches where the leaf litter is sparse or absent, mainly near the bases of young *Cycas* plants or in shade. It has been recorded from slopes and ridges.

CONSERVATION ASSESSMENT

Although this species is seasonally dormant and cryptic in the landscape it is considered adequately surveyed, based on the strong survey effort in the area (Woinarski *et al.* 2003) and the high profile nature of this species with collectors. While more populations may exist, the paucity of collections is considered to accurately reflect its very restricted distribution and abundance.

The largest known population contained around 60 individuals (Brock *et al.* 2000), suggesting the total number of mature individuals would be fewer than 250. Unfortunately, this population and another nearby one were cleared for forestry plantation in 2004.

This species qualifies as **Endangered** (under criteria B1ab(iii)+2ab(iii); D) based on:
• an extent of occurrence less than 5000 km² ;
• an area of occupancy less than 500 km²;
• a small population size (fewer than 250 mature individuals); and
• a current and projected decline in quality of habitat of this species in the near future as a result of clearing for expansion of plantation forestry.

THREATENING PROCESSES

Clearing of habitat for plantation forestry development is a threat for this species. Extensive areas within the western half of Melville Island are set aside for land clearing and plantings of *Acacia mangium*. "Soils, topography and rainfall dictate that environments suitable for plantation development are restricted largely to tall open forests dominated by *Eucalyptus tetrodonta*, *E.miniata* and/or *E. nesophila*" (Forsci 1999). The preferred plantation habitat and designated planting region of the western half of Melville coincide with known populations and preferred habitat of this species.

The eucalypt forests are also affected by feral buffalo, cattle and horses. Increased clearing, road development and activity in the area around known populations may increase the invasion of exotic plant species, particularly mission grass *Pennisetum polystachion* (Woinarski *et al.* 2003).

continued.../

Although the underground corm and seasonal nature of this species offers protection from fire, the effect of perennial grass invasions on this species is unknown.

CONSERVATION OBJECTIVES AND MANAGEMENT

A recovery plan for this species, and other threatened plants on the Tiwi Islands, is due to be released in 2007, but many actions in its draft are currently being implemented through a collaborative project involving Tiwi rangers and scientists from the Department of Natural Resources, Environment and The Arts, with funding from the Natural Heritage Trust.

Research priorities are to:
• provide a more detailed assessment of its distribution, habitat requirements and population size;
• provide an assessment of the factors limiting distribution, and/or threats to its survival.

Further survey may yield additional populations, and a monitoring program should be established for at least representative populations. Habitat protection at the known localities is required to maintain the status of the species. The Tiwi Islands Forestry Strategic Plan (Hadden 2000) provided the commitment that all populations of this species would be protected from clearing, with an exclusion buffer of 50 m around their perimeter. However, two of the few populations, including the largest known, were subsequently eliminated by land clearing for forestry plantation.

Compiled by Raelee Kerrigan, Ian Cowie, John Woinarski [January 2007] / **References:** Brock, C., Cowie, I. Harwood, B., Leach, G. Milne, D. Stirrat, S., and Woinarski J. (2000). *Plantation proposal, Melville Island: assessment of biodiversity.* Report to N.T. Department of Lands, Planning and Environment, Tiwi Land Council, and Sylvatech Australia Pty Ltd. (Parks and Wildlife Commission of the Northern Territory, Darwin.) / ForSci Pty Ltd. (1999). *Environmental Impact Assessment of fast grown plantations on the Tiwi Islands.* Report to Tiwi Land Council. (ForSci Pty Ltd.) / Hadden, K. (2000). *Tiwi Islands Plantation Forestry Strategic Plan.* (Tiwi Land Council, Darwin.) / Hay, A. (1992). A new Australian genus of Araceae, with notes on generic limits and biogeography of the Areae. *Botanical Journal of the Linnean Society* 109, 427-434. / Hay, A. (1993). The genus *Typhonium* (Araceae-Areae) in Australasia. *Blumea* 37, 345-376. / Woinarski, J., Brennan, K., Cowie, I, Kerrigan, R., and Hempel, C. (2003). *Biodiversity conservation on the Tiwi Islands, Northern Territory. Part 1. Environment and Plants.* (NT Department of Infrastructure, Planning and Environment, Darwin.)

Image courtesy of Raelee Kerrigan

Typhonium taylori

CONSERVATION STATUS
AUSTRALIA: **ENDANGERED**
NORTHERN TERRITORY: **ENDANGERED**

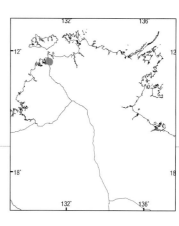

*Known locations
of Typhonium
taylori*
● = *pre 1970*
● = *post 1970*

DESCRIPTION

Typhonium taylori is a small deciduous geophytic herb. The leaf blade is subdeltoid to elliptic or narrowly lanceolate, to 45 mm long. The flower is accompanied by a leaf. The spathe is about 6.5 cm long. The spadix appendage is filiform, exceeding the spathe by about 1 cm, deflected such that it projects more or less horizontally from the spathe mouth.

It is difficult to distinguish between species of this genus without reproductive material as the leaves are commonly polymorphic. Diagnostic characters within the genus include the arrangement of flowers and the timing of emergent leaf parts relative to the emergent inflorescence. This species is documented as having an inflorescence emergent with new season leaves.

Flowering: January

DISTRIBUTION

This species is endemic to the Northern Territory, and positively known only from the type locality on the edge of the Howard River floodplain. A second collection of sterile material nearby is also likely to be *T. taylori*.

Conservation reserves where reported: None

ECOLOGY

Little is known of the ecology of this species. The above-ground annual shoots are seasonally dormant, emerging from an underground corm (bulb) during the wet season.

The species occurs in seasonally-saturated sandy soil in nutrient poor grassland or sedgeland with occasional *Melaleuca viridiflora*.

CONSERVATION ASSESSMENT

S. Taylor collected type material for this species in 1996 (Hay 1997). Recent targeted survey for this species in the Howard River floodplain as part of a biodiversity assessment survey (Cowie 2002) did not relocate or uncover any additional populations of this species.

Although this species is seasonally dormant and cryptic in the landscape it is considered adequately surveyed, based on the strong survey effort in the area and the high profile of this genus amongst collectors. While more populations may exist, the paucity of collections of this species is considered to accurately reflect its very restricted distribution and abundance.

There are no data on population size for this species. However, information based on populations of similar species in this genus would indicate population size may be between 50 and 100 individuals (Brock *et al.* 2000).

Given that a minimum convex polygon cannot be formed from two collections, the extent of occurrence for this species is based on a polygon of 2 km long by 100 m wide (50 m either side of the collection localities) and is estimated at 0.2 km². Area of occupancy is estimated at 2 ha.

Using a precautionary approach this taxon could qualify for Critically Endangered. However, in consideration of the collection bias associated with this species we have listed it as **Endangered** (under criteria B1ab(iii)+2ab(iii); D) based on:

- an estimated population size of fewer than 250 mature individuals;
- an extent of occurrence less than 5000 km²;
- an area of occupancy less than 500 km²; and
- an inferred decline in quality of habitat as a result of sand mine activity and land subdivision.

THREATENING PROCESSES

Threats to this species are potential disturbance of habitat from sand-mining, clearing for subdivision and changes to hydrology.

Sandsheets in the Howard River floodplain have been identified as an extractive mineral resource (Doyle 2003), and I. Cowie (*pers. comm.*) indicated that sandsheet communities visited during surveys in 2000 and 2001 had either shown evidence of sand-mining activity or were pegged for potential sand-mining. Although no proposed future extractive leases coincide with the two known populations of this species, there is a correlation between preferred habitat and land units already supporting extractive leases, and a very high proportion of this habitat is likely to be affected by sand-mining (Price *et al.* 2005).

continued.../

Expected population expansion in Darwin and Litchfield Shire will result in increased water demands (Haig *et al*. 2003). The impact on hydrology of the expansion of the McMinns Borefield (Haig *et al*. 2003) and inferred increase in water consumption by domestic bores is unknown. Similarly the impact of increased runoff as a result of urbanisation is unknown (Haig 2003) and needs to be investigated further.

CONSERVATION OBJECTIVES AND MANAGEMENT

Habitat protection at the known localities is required to maintain the status of the species. Research priorities are to:

• provide a more detailed assessment of its distribution, habitat requirements and population size; and

• provide an assessment of the factors limiting distribution, and/or threats to its survival.

Further survey may yield additional populations. A monitoring program should be established.

Compiled by Raelee Kerrigan, Ian Cowie [April 2006] / **References:** Brock, C., Cowie, I. Harwood, B., Leach, G. Milne, D. Stirrat, S., and Woinarski J. (2000). *Plantation proposal, Melville Island: assessment of biodiversity.* (Parks and Wildlife Commission of the Northern Territory, Darwin.) / Cowie, I. D. (2002). *Preliminary report on a survey of Utricularia (Lentibulariaceae) in the Howard River – Shoal Bay* area. (NT Department of Infrastructure Planning and Environment, Darwin.) / Doyle, N. (2003). *Extractive minerals in the outer Darwin area.* Northern Territory Geological Survey, Report 14. / Haig, T., and Townsend (2003). *An understanding of the groundwater and surface water hydrology of the Darwin Harbour Plan of Management area.* Proceedings of the Darwin Harbour Public presentations. / Hay, A. (1997). Two new species and a new combination in Australian *Typhonium* (Araceae Tribe Areae). *Edinburgh Journal of Botany* 54, 329-336. / Price, O., Milne, D., and Tynan, C. (2005). Poor recovery of woody vegetation on sand and gravel mines in the Darwin region of the Northern Territory. *Ecological Management and Restoration* 6, 118-123.

Image courtesy of Kym Brennan

Utricularia dunstaniae

CONSERVATION STATUS
AUSTRALIA: **NOT LISTED**
NORTHERN TERRITORY: **VULNERABLE**

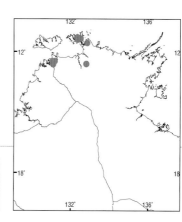

*Known locations
of Utricularia
dunstaniae*
● = pre 1970
● = post 1970

DESCRIPTION
Utricularia dunstaniae is a small, annual, terrestrial bladderwort. The inflorescence is erect, solitary, 6 to 15 cm. The flowers are apparently always solitary. The corolla is flesh-coloured, the lower lobes two with erect filiform appendages 1.5 to 4 cm long.

Flowering: March, April

DISTRIBUTION
This species is an Australian endemic, known from Western Australia (in the Mitchell Plateau) and the Northern Territory. In the Northern Territory, it is known from eight collections: these include a single collection from Jabiru (Taylor 1989), one collection from "24 miles S of Darwin" (the McMinns Lagoon area) in 1965, three collections from the Howard River floodplain (including the type collection), and one collection from the Adelaide River floodplain. The '24 mile' population has not been relocated and is apparently locally extinct. Recent populations have been recorded from Cobourg Peninsula and near Oenpelli.

Conservation reserves where reported:
Garig Gunak Barlu National Park, Kakadu National Park

ECOLOGY
The species grows in wet sand, often in shallow water, in *Melaleuca nervosa* woodland or *Verticordia* shrubland. It occurs in slightly wetter micro-habitats than other sympatric *Utricularia* species.

CONSERVATION ASSESSMENT
This species is currently known from only six localities despite extensive surveys in the Darwin rural area (Cowie 2002). Two populations are recorded to have 50 individuals each.

This species qualifies as **Vulnerable** (under criteria B2ab(iii); C2a(i), D1 + 2) based on:
• an estimated population size of fewer than 1000 mature individuals;
• area of occupancy less than 2000 km²;
• an inferred decline in area and extent and quality of habitat; and
• an inferred decline in numbers of mature individuals.

THREATENING PROCESSES
Three of the six known localities are susceptible to disturbance from sand-mining, quadbike and motorbike activity, subdivision and potential changes to hydrology (Cowie 2002).

Sandsheets in the Howard River floodplain have been identified as an extractive mineral resource and a very high proportion of this habitat is likely to be affected by sand-mining (Price *et al.* 2005).

CONSERVATION OBJECTIVES AND MANAGEMENT
Habitat protection at the known localities is required to maintain the status of the species.

Research priorities are to:
• provide a more detailed assessment of its distribution, habitat requirements and population size; and
• provide an assessment of the factors limiting distribution, and/or threats to its survival.

Further survey may yield additional populations. A monitoring program should be established.

Compiled by Raelee Kerrigan, Ian Cowie [April 2006] / **References:** Cowie, I. (2002). *Preliminary report on a survey of Utricularia (Lentibulariaceae) in the Howard River-Shoal Bay area.* Unpublished report. (Parks and Wildlife Commission of the Northern Territory, Palmerston.) / Price, O., Milne, D., and Tynan, C. (2005). Poor recovery of woody vegetation on sand and gravel mines in the Darwin region of the Northern Territory. *Ecological Management and Restoration* 6, 118-123. / Taylor, P. (1989). *The Genus Utricularia: a taxonomic monograph.* Kew Bulletin Series XIV. (Her Majesty's Stationery Office, London.)

Image courtesy of Kym Brennan

Utricularia singeriana

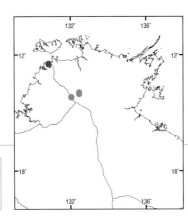

Known locations of Utricularia singeriana
● = pre 1970
● = post 1970

CONSERVATION STATUS
AUSTRALIA: **NOT LISTED**
NORTHERN TERRITORY: **VULNERABLE**

DESCRIPTION
Utricularia singeriana is a small to medium-sized, terrestrial bladderwort. The inflorescence is erect, solitary, and simple. The flower is purple, mauve or violet, the outer surface sometimes glossy-red.

Flowering: March, May
Fruiting: May

DISTRIBUTION
This species is an Australian endemic occurring in the Northern Territory and Western Australia. In the Northern Territory, it was recorded early last century from "4 miles north-east of Port Darwin" and more recently from the Edith River area and Marrawal Plateau (Upper Fergusson River area).

Conservation reserves where reported:
Nitmiluk National Park

ECOLOGY
The species occurs in wet sandy flats and swamps with short grasses and sedges (C. Michell *pers. comm.*).

CONSERVATION ASSESSMENT
This species has been recorded from three Northern Territory localities. The Port Darwin population no longer exists and anecdotal evidence from the second locality near Edith River gives a population estimate in the hundreds, with several hundred individuals counted in Nitmiluk National Park (Upper Fergusson River area). Given that the species also occurs in Western Australia, it may be more widespread than our current collections suggest. However, it was not located in a recent survey of *Utricularia*-rich areas near Darwin (Cowie 2002). In addition, a number of *Utricularia*-specific surveys have been carried out in the Northern Territory (with Darwin Herbarium staff and the world authority on the group, P. Taylor).

In the Northern Territory, the species qualifies as **Vulnerable** (under criteria D1+2) based on:
• population size fewer than 1000 individuals; and
• area of occupancy estimated to be less than 20 km².

THREATENING PROCESSES
With a small population size and restricted distribution this population is susceptible to stochastic events. The species may be affected by trampling by feral stock, or any alterations to hydrology. However, there is no information to suggest that these are current threats.

CONSERVATION OBJECTIVES AND MANAGEMENT
Habitat protection at the known localities is required to maintain the status of the species.

Research priorities are to:
• provide a more detailed assessment of its distribution, habitat requirements and population size; and
• provide an assessment of the factors limiting distribution, and/or threats to its survival.

Further survey may yield additional populations. A monitoring program should be established.

Compiled by Raelee Kerrigan, Ian Cowie [April 2006] / **References:** Cowie, I. (2002). *Preliminary report on a survey of Utricularia (Lentibulariaceae) in the Howard River-Shoal Bay area.* Unpublished report. (Parks and Wildlife Commission of the Northern Territory, Palmerston.) / Taylor, P. (1989). *The Genus Utricularia: a taxonomic monograph.* Kew Bulletin Series XIV. (Her Majesty's Stationery Office, London.)

Image courtesy of Jenni Low Choy

Wrixonia schultzii

CONSERVATION STATUS
AUSTRALIA: **VULNERABLE**
NORTHERN TERRITORY: **VULNERABLE**

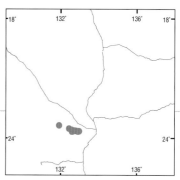

Known locations of Wrixonia schultzii
● = *pre 1970*
● = *post 1970*

DESCRIPTION

Wrixonia schultzii is a shrub to 1.5 m high. The leaves are orbicular, shaped like a ping-pong paddle, 4 to 8 mm with thickened margins. The flowers are sessile, white with purple spots and yellow patches on the centre of the lower lip. They are bilaterally symmetrical with a distinct upper and lower lip (Jessop 1981).

Flowering: April, July, September–November
Fruiting: May, September–November

DISTRIBUTION

This species is endemic to the Northern Territory, and confined to the MacDonnell Ranges bioregion, where it is restricted to the tops of the quartzite ranges in the West MacDonnell Ranges (Chewings Range, Mt Sonder) with an outlying population at Mt Edward (White *et al.* 2000). The latitudinal range is 34 km and the longitudinal range is 107 km.

Conservation reserves where reported:
West MacDonnell National Park

ECOLOGY

It occurs on shady, upper slopes and tops of quartzite mountains and ranges, particularly on southerly aspects. It grows in shallow soils.

Although it has been regarded as fire-sensitive, 65% (13 out of 20) of plants that were severely scorched by hot wildfire in 2002 were observed to have re-sprouted from the base when observed in 2003 (A. Duguid *pers. comm.*). Due to the remote location there has been no monitoring of the ongoing survival of these re-sprouts.

CONSERVATION ASSESSMENT

This species is listed as **Vulnerable** (under criteria B1ab(iii)+2ab(iii)) based on:
• a severely fragmented population;
• an extent of occurrence less than 20 000 km^2;
• an area of occupancy less than 2000 km^2; and
• an inferred decline.

THREATENING PROCESSES

This species may be intolerant of frequent and/or intense wildfire. If this is the case, fires may have played a role in determining the present distribution pattern. This should be assumed until demonstrated otherwise.

CONSERVATION OBJECTIVES AND MANAGEMENT

Population estimates and processes and/or events that may threaten this species need to be investigated as a matter of some urgency. A monitoring program should be established for at least representative populations.

Compiled by Raelee Kerrigan, David Albrecht [April 2006] / **References:** Jessop, J. (1981). *Flora of Central Australia.* (Reed Books, Sydney.) / White, M., Albrecht, D., Duguid, A., Latz, P., and Hamilton, M. (2000). *Plant species and sites of botanical significance in the southern bioregions of the Northern Territory. Volume 1: significant vascular plants.* A report to the Australian Heritage Commission. (Arid Lands Environment Centre, Alice Springs.)

Image courtesy of David Liddle

Xylopia sp. Melville Island

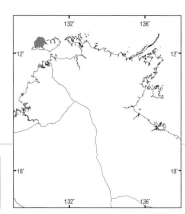

Known locations of
Xylopia sp. Melville
Island
● = *pre 1970*
● = *post 1970*

DESCRIPTION

Xylopia sp. Melville Island is an open shrub or erect small tree growing to at least 7 m, with lateral branches perpendicular to the stem. The leaves are orientated in one plane (distichous) and have distinctly wavy margins.

Very little is known of this undescribed species. It is now placed in the genus *Xylopia*, although it was formerly identified as *Miliusa* on sterile material (Fensham and Woinarski 1992). It has the currently unpublished specific name of *monosperma*.

DISTRIBUTION

This plant is thought to be endemic to the Northern Territory, where it is known only from five localities on the Tiwi Islands, two on Bathurst and three on Melville Island.

Conservation reserves where reported: None

ECOLOGY

This species grows in wet spring-fed rainforests and occurs as a small understorey tree. Little is known of its ecology, although it seems to occur generally in the outer fringe of wet rainforest in areas where the canopy is more open.

CONSERVATION ASSESSMENT

On Melville Island, this species (reported as *Miliusa* sp.) was recorded from a 25 ha rainforest patch (Hanguana Jungle), a 10 ha patch (Ilinga Jungle), a 15 ha patch (Dudwell), a 100 ha patch

(Mangkippi), and an unconfirmed patch possibly Banjo Beach Jungle (Fensham and Woinarski 1992).

Collection notes for the Hanguana Jungle specimens (in 1987) suggested that this species was common there. Four plants were relocated in 2006 with the larger individuals badly damaged by cyclone.

Where only one individual was known previously at Ilinga Jungle, more extensive survey of this jungle in 2006 revealed about 35 individuals in this population. Most individuals were immature, and there is almost no information available on its reproduction requirements and population dynamics. Fertile material has been difficult to obtain.

The total population size for this taxon is highly speculative. Applying a precautionary estimate of 50 individuals to each location, and assuming the 1987 populations are still extant, a total population size of fewer thab 250 individuals has been proposed. The extent of occurrence is approximately 470 km^2 and the area of occupancy estimated as at least 150 ha based on the size of rainforest patches where collected (Fensham and Woinarski 1992).

This species is considered adequately surveyed, based on extensive surveys on the Tiwi Islands (Woinarski *et al.* 2003) and rainforest habitats across the Top End (Russell-Smith 1991; Fensham and Woinarski 1992; Liddle *et al.* 1994). Some

specific survey was undertaken for this species during 1999, 2000 and 2001. The discovery of the Ilinga Jungle population by J. Risler was a result of those efforts, however no other populations were found or relocated.

This species is classified as **Endangered** (under criteria B1ab(iii)+2ab(iii); D) based on:
• known from five or fewer locations;
• the number of mature individuals fewer than 250;
• an extent of occurrence less than 5000 km^2;
• an area of occupancy less than 500 km^2; and
• a projected decline due to quality of habitat.

THREATENING PROCESSES

Very little is known about the processes that may threaten this species, which may be naturally rare. However, monsoon rainforests generally are vulnerable to disturbance from cyclones, cattle, buffalo, pigs and dry season wildfires (Russell-Smith and Bowman 1992, Panton 1993; Woinarski *et al.* 2003). Cyclonic frequency for the Tiwi Islands is documented at 0.8 to 1.2 cyclones per annum.

While rainforest patches where the species occurs have been excised from clearing for plantation forestry, the adequacy of buffers around these areas is not known. If buffers are of insufficient width, the rainforests may be more vulnerable to wind damage. Monsoon rainforests may also be particularly susceptible to changes in ground water hydrology as a result of high water use from

continued.../

Acacia mangium plantations developing for areas
on the Tiwi Islands. There is also a risk of invasion
of rainforests by grassy weeds and concomitant
increased vulnerability to fire as a result of
intensive development and disturbance for forestry.

CONSERVATION OBJECTIVES
AND MANAGEMENT

A recovery plan for this species, and other
threatened plants on the Tiwi Islands, is due
to be released in 2007, but many actions in its
draft are currently being implemented through
a collaborative project involving Tiwi rangers
and scientists from the Department of Natural
Resources, Environment and The Arts, with
funding from the Natural Heritage Trust.

Research priorities are to:
• provide a more detailed assessment of its
  distribution, habitat requirements and
  population size; and
• provide an assessment of the factors limiting
  distribution, and/or threats to its survival.

Further survey may yield additional populations.
A monitoring program should be established
for at least representative populations.
Habitat protection at the known localities is
required to maintain the status of the species.

Compiled by Raelee Kerrigan, Ian Cowie, Louis Elliott [April 2007] / **References:** Fensham, R.J., and Woinarski, J.C.Z. (1992). *Yawulama: the ecology and conservation of monsoon forest on the Tiwi Islands, Northern Territory.* (Consevation Commission of the Northern Territory, Darwin.) / Liddle, D.T., Russell-Smith, J., Brock, J., Leach, G.J., and Connors, G.T. (1994) *Atlas of the vascular rainforest plants of the Northern Territory.* Flora of Australia Supplementary Series No. 3. (ABRS, Canberra.) / Panton, W.J. (1993). Changes in post World War II distribution and status of monsoon rainforests in the Darwin area. *Australian Geographer* 24, 50-59. / Russell-Smith, J. (1991). Classification, species richness, and environmental relations of monsoon rain forest in northern Australia. *Journal of Vegetation Science* 2, 259-278. Russell-Smith, J. (1992). Plant populations and monsoon rain forest in the Northern Territory, Australia. *Biotropica* 24, 471-487. / Russell-Smith, J., and Bowman, D.M.J.S. (1992). Conservation of monsoon rainforest isolates in the Northern Territory. *Biological Conservation* 59, 51-63. / Woinarski, J., Brennan, K., Cowie, I., Kerrigan, R., and Hempel, C. (2003). *Biodiversity conservation on the Tiwi Islands, Northern Territory. Part 1. Plants and environments.* 144 pp. (Department of Infrastructure Planning and Environment, Darwin.)

Image courtesy of David Jones (CSIRO)

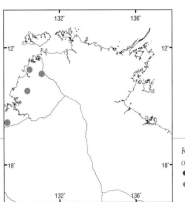

*Known locations
of Zeuxine oblonga*
● = pre 1970
● = post 1970

Zeuxine oblonga

CONSERVATION STATUS
AUSTRALIA: **NOT LISTED**
NORTHERN TERRITORY: **VULNERABLE**

DESCRIPTION
Zeuxine oblonga is a deciduous terrestrial orchid.
Its stem is fleshy, creeping, to 15 cm tall. There are
3 to 7 leaves in a loose rosette, 8 cm x 30 mm,
dark green, thin-textured with wavy margins.
The flower stem is pinkish, bearing 5 to 30 dull
green and white flowers about 4 mm across.
It is recognised by its small, dull-green and white
hairy flowers and the divided labellum or lower lip
(Jones 1988).

Flowering: September

DISTRIBUTION
This species is an Australian endemic, recorded
from the Northern Territory, Queensland and
New South Wales. In the Northern Territory, it
is known from five widely-spaced localities from
Keep River to near Adelaide River (Liddle *et al.*
1994). One of these is in the Daly River area but
specific locality information is not available.

Conservation reserves where reported:
Keep River National Park

ECOLOGY
This species occurs in dark, moist situations
on the floor of rainforests and usually grows
in colonies. It is also locally common in small
swampy areas adjacent to streams, growing in
peaty soil (Jones 1988).

CONSERVATION ASSESSMENT
Very little information is available on the status
of this species. It was recorded as uncommon
by one collector. It has not been collected since
1992, despite efforts to relocate the Keep River
population in 2000 and 2001.

As a terrestrial orchid with ephemeral above-
ground parts, there is a negative collection bias
associated with this species. In consideration
of this bias, although current data would satisfy
a classification of Endangered, it is listed as
Vulnerable (under criteria D1+2) based on:
• a population size estimated at fewer than
  1000 individuals; and
• area of occupancy estimated to be less
  than 20 km^2.

THREATENING PROCESSES
Potential threats include feral animal disturbance,
particularly by pigs. As a wet rainforest species,
changes to hydrology could affect populations
(although hydrological changes have not been
identified for any of these localities). There is a
possible threat from horticultural harvesting.

CONSERVATION OBJECTIVES
AND MANAGEMENT
Research into the status and extent of the
populations is required. Collection of propagation
material, translocation to botanic gardens and
availability of stock commercially may protect the
species from horticultural harvesting.

Compiled by Raelee Kerrigan, Ian Cowie [April 2006] / **References:** Jones, D. L. (1988). *Native Orchids of Australia.* (Reed, Sydney.) / Liddle, D.T., Russell-Smith, J., Brock, J., Leach, G.J., and Connors, G.T.
(1994) *Atlas of the vascular rainforest plants of the Northern Territory.* Flora of Australia Supplementary Series No. 3. (ABRS, Canberra.)

INVERTEBRATES

Image courtesy of MAGNT

Cognate land snail
Amphidromus cognatus

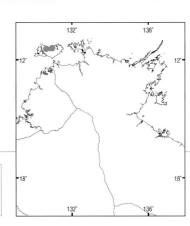

*Known locations
of Amphidromus
cognatus*
● = *pre 1970*
● = *post 1970*

CONSERVATION STATUS
AUSTRALIA: **NOT LISTED**
NORTHERN TERRITORY: **VULNERABLE**

DESCRIPTION

Amphidromus cognatus is a large (shell length: 21 to 33 mm; shell diameter: 12 to 17 mm) camaenid land snail. The colour pattern of the shell is variable; the ground colour is yellow, often with a peripheral spiral chocolate-brown band and a purplish-brown apical suffusion. The lip is white or faintly yellow. In Asia the genus is widely distributed, and avidly sought by collectors for its colouful shell, but represented in Australia only by this species (Solem 1983).

DISTRIBUTION

This snail was originally described in 1907 from three specimens apparently collected at Port Essington on Cobourg Peninsula before 1850, but it has not been found there since. The only other published records are from one site on Bathurst Island, and at least three sites on Melville Island, collected between 1976 and 1980.

Conservation reserves where reported:
Garig Gunak Barlu National Park

ECOLOGY

Most records are from collections made in trees (and the woody vine *Opilia amentacea*) in monsoon rainforest.

CONSERVATION ASSESSMENT

This species is one of a set of snail species listed here that is relatively restricted in its geographic range and is exposed to processes that may lead to its decline. This species is classified as **Vulnerable** (under criteria B1ab(i,ii,iii)+2ab(i,ii,iii)) based on:
• extent of occurrence less than 20 000 km²;
• area of occupancy less than 2000 km²;
• known to exist at fewer than 10 locations; and
• continuing decline observed, inferred or projected.

THREATENING PROCESSES

There is no direct evidence that any factors have caused a decline in the numbers or distribution of this species. However, there has been no monitoring of status. This species may be detrimentally affected by an increased frequency and intensity of fire, fuelled in part by invasive exotic grasses, by the impacts of grazing by feral animals (cattle, banteng, horses, buffalo) and potential predation by cane toads.

CONSERVATION OBJECTIVES AND MANAGEMENT

There are no existing management programs for land snail species in the Northern Territory.

Research priorities are to:
• conduct further surveys to determine whether populations occur elsewhere; and
• identify specific threats to any of the known populations.

A monitoring program should be established for at least representative populations.

Compiled by Colin Wilson, John Woinarski, Vince Kessner, Michael Braby [April 2006] / **References:** Solem, A. (1983). First record of *Amphidromus* from Australia, with anatomical notes on several species (Mollusca: Pulmonata: Camaenidae). *Records of the Australian Museum* 35, 153-166.

Land snail
Basedowena squamulosa

Image from Solem 1993

Known locations of Basedowena squamulosa
● = pre 1970
● = post 1970

DESCRIPTION
Basedowena squamulosa is a medium-sized (shell diameter: 13 to 18 mm) camaenid land snail. Distinguishing characters are listed in Solem (1993). Note that some recent treatments refer to this species as *Baccalena squamulosa*.

DISTRIBUTION
This species is restricted to the Krichauff and James Ranges west of Alice Springs, between Palm Valley and Areyonga.

Conservation reserves where reported:
Finke Gorge National Park

ECOLOGY
It is usually associated with leaf litter under fig trees in or under rocks.

CONSERVATION ASSESSMENT
This species was first collected by the Horn Expedition of 1894. Almost nothing was reported about it again for the next hundred years, until Solem (1993) reported that it was relatively common in Palm Valley.

This species is one of a set of snail species listed here that is relatively restricted in its geographic range and is exposed to processes that may lead to its decline. This species is classified as **Vulnerable** (under criteria B1ab(i,ii,iii)+2ab(i,ii,iii)) based on:
• extent of occurrence less than 20 000 km²;
• area of occupancy less than 2000 km²;
• known to exist at fewer than 10 locations; and
• continuing decline observed, inferred or projected.

THREATENING PROCESSES
There is no direct evidence that any factors have caused a decline in the numbers or distribution of this species. However, there has been no monitoring of status, and this species may be detrimentally affected by an increased frequency and intensity of fire, fuelled in part by invasive exotic grasses, particularly buffel grass (*Cenchrus ciliaris*).

CONSERVATION OBJECTIVES AND MANAGEMENT
There are no existing management programs for land snail species in the Northern Territory.

Research priorities are to:
• conduct further surveys to determine whether populations occur elsewhere; and
• identify specific threats to the known population.

A monitoring program should be established for at least representative populations. The management priority is to better safeguard the known populations through establishment of appropriate fire regimes.

Compiled by Colin Wilson, John Woinarski, Vince Kessner, Michael Braby [April 2006] / **References:** Solem, A. (1993). Camaenid land snails from Western and central Australia (Mollusca: Pulmonata: Camaenidae). VI Taxa from the red centre. *Records of the Western Australian Museum* Supplement 43, 983-1459.

Image courtesy of MAGNT

Spencer's land snail
Bothriembryon spenceri

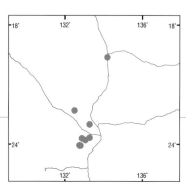

*Known locations
of Bothriembryon
spenceri*
● = *pre 1970*
● = *post 1970*

CONSERVATION STATUS
AUSTRALIA: **NOT LISTED**
NORTHERN TERRITORY: **VULNERABLE**

DESCRIPTION
Bothriembryon spenceri is a moderately-large land snail (shell diameter 16 to 20 mm).

DISTRIBUTION
This species is largely restricted to the Krichauff and Chewings Ranges west of Alice Springs, notably occurring in Palm Valley (Solem 1988). It was first collected and described in the Horn Expedition of 1894.

Conservation reserves where reported:
Finke Gorge National Park, West MacDonnell National Park.

ECOLOGY
This snail is found in leaf litter under fig trees and/or rocky areas. During unfavourable periods it buries in the soil.

CONSERVATION ASSESSMENT
This species is one of a set of snail species listed here that are all relatively restricted and presumably relictual in their geographic range and are exposed to processes that may lead to their decline. This species is classified as **Vulnerable** (under criteria B2ab(i,ii,iii)) based on:
• area of occupancy less than 2000 km^2;
• known to exist at fewer than 10 locations; and
• continuing decline observed, inferred or projected.

THREATENING PROCESSES
There is no direct evidence that any factors have caused a decline in the numbers or distribution of this species. However, there has been no monitoring of status, and this species may be detrimentally affected by an increased frequency and/or intensity of fire, fuelled in part by invasive exotic grasses, particularly buffel grass (*Cenchrus ciliaris*).

CONSERVATION OBJECTIVES AND MANAGEMENT
There are no existing management programs for land snail species in the Northern Territory.

Research priorities are to:
• conduct further surveys to determine whether populations occur elsewhere; and
• identify specific threats to any of the known populations.

A monitoring program should be established for at least representative populations. The management priority is to better safeguard the known populations through establishment of appropriate fire regimes.

Compiled by Colin Wilson, John Woinarski, Vince Kessner, Michael Braby [April 2006] / **References:** Solem, A. (1988). Non-camaenid land snails of the Kimberley and Northern Territory, Australia. I. Systematics, affinities and ranges. *Invertebrate Taxonomy* 2, 455-604.

Image from Solem 1993

Land snail
Dirutrachia sublevata

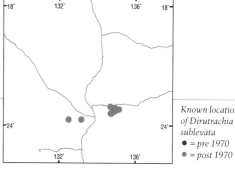

Known locations of Dirutrachia sublevata
● = pre 1970
● = post 1970

CONSERVATION STATUS
AUSTRALIA: **NOT LISTED.**
NORTHERN TERRITORY: **VULNERABLE**

DESCRIPTION
Dirutrachia sublevata is a medium-sized (shell diameter: 13 to 17 mm) camaenid land snail, with a low whorl count. Other distinguishing characters are listed in Solem (1993).

DISTRIBUTION
Solem (1993) considered that this snail is found only in the basins of Maud and Florence Creeks on the south side of the Harts Range, north east of Alice Springs. Its distribution extends for "much less than 5 km" (Solem 1993) along the range, and its known occurrence within that range is no more than several hundred square metres.

Some more recent museum collections attributed to this species extend this known range.

Conservation reserves where reported:
West MacDonnell National Park

ECOLOGY
It is found in talus, in soil under rocks or in crevices deep in rock piles (Solem 1993).

CONSERVATION ASSESSMENT
This species was first collected by the Horn Expedition of 1894. Almost nothing was reported about it again for the next hundred years. Recent surveys in central Australia have only marginally expanded its known range and provided little information on current population size.

This species is one of a set of snail species listed here that is relatively restricted in their geographic range and are exposed to processes that may lead to their decline. This species is classified as **Vulnerable** (under criteria B2ab(i,ii,iii)) based on:
• area of occupancy less than 2000 km²;
• known to exist at fewer than 10 locations; and
• continuing decline observed, inferred or projected.

THREATENING PROCESSES
There is no direct evidence that any factors have caused a decline in the numbers or distribution of this species. However, there has been no monitoring of status, and this species may be detrimentally affected by an increased frequency and intensity of fire, fuelled in part by invasive exotic grasses, particularly buffel grass (*Cenchrus ciliaris*).

CONSERVATION OBJECTIVES AND MANAGEMENT
There are no existing management programs for land snail species in the Northern Territory.

Research priorities are to:
• conduct further surveys to determine whether populations occur elsewhere; and
• identify specific threats to the known population.

A monitoring program should be established for at least representative populations. The management priority is to better safeguard the known populations through establishment of appropriate fire regimes.

Compiled by Colin Wilson, John Woinarski, Vince Kessner, Michael Braby [April 2006] / **References:** Solem, A. (1993). Camaenid land snails from Western and central Australia (Mollusca: Pulmonata: Camaenidae). VI Taxa from the red centre. *Records of the Western Australian Museum* Supplement 43, 983-1459.

Image from Solem 1993

Land snail

Divellomelon hillieri

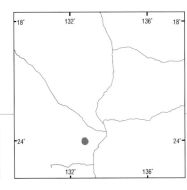

CONSERVATION STATUS
AUSTRALIA: **NOT LISTED**
NORTHERN TERRITORY: **VULNERABLE**

DESCRIPTION

Divellomelon hillieri is a relatively large (shell diameter: 16.3 to 18.6 mm) camaenid land snail, with acutely angulated periphery with thread-like keel, lack of shell microsculpture and very narrow lip. Other distinguishing characters are listed in Solem (1993).

DISTRIBUTION

This species has been recorded only along a few hundred metres of cliff face in Palm Valley in the Krichauff Ranges, west of Alice Springs.

Conservation reserves where reported:
Finke Gorge National Park

ECOLOGY

This snail is found amongst rock rubble and litter at the bottom of deep vertical rock fissures, although there have also been a few specimens reported from "under figs" nearby (Solem 1993).

CONSERVATION ASSESSMENT

This species is one of a set of snail species listed here that is relatively restricted in its geographic range and is exposed to processes that may lead to its decline. This species is classified as **Vulnerable** (under criteria B1ab(i,ii,iii)+2ab(i,ii,iii)) based on:
• extent of occurrence less than 20 000 km^2;
• area of occupancy less than 2000 km^2;
• known to exist at fewer than 10 locations; and
• continuing decline observed, inferred or projected.

THREATENING PROCESSES

There is no direct evidence that any factors have caused a decline in the numbers or distribution of this species. However, there has been no monitoring of status, and this species may be detrimentally affected by an increased frequency and intensity of fire, fuelled in part by invasive exotic grasses, particularly buffel grass (*Cenchrus ciliaris*).

CONSERVATION OBJECTIVES AND MANAGEMENT

There are no existing management programs for land snail species in the Northern Territory.

Research priorities are to:
• conduct further surveys to determine whether populations occur elsewhere; and
• identify specific threats to the known population.

A monitoring program should be established. The management priority is to better safeguard the known population through establishment of appropriate fire regimes.

Compiled by Colin Wilson, John Woinarski, Vince Kessner, Michael Braby [April 2006] / **References:** Solem, A. (1993). Camaenid land snails from Western and central Australia (Mollusca: Pulmonata: Camaenidae). VI Taxa from the red centre. *Records of the Western Australian Museum* Supplement 43, 983-1459.

Image from Solem 1993

10 mm

West MacDonnell's land snail
Granulomelon arcigerens

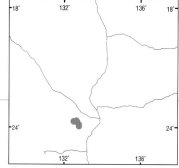

CONSERVATION STATUS
AUSTRALIA: **NOT LISTED**
NORTHERN TERRITORY: **VULNERABLE**

DESCRIPTION
Granulomelon arcigerens is a medium-sized (shell diameter: 16 to 19 mm) camaenid land snail. Distinguishing characters are listed in Solem (1993).

DISTRIBUTION
This species is known from a restricted area in the Finke River gorge, 4 to 5 km south of Glen Helen in the West MacDonnell Ranges, west of Alice Springs.

Conservation reserves where reported:
West MacDonnell National Park

ECOLOGY
This snail is found among rocks along the Finke River gorge. It is found well above the river level and hence is unlikely to be accidentally transported by floods.

CONSERVATION ASSESSMENT
This species was first collected by the Horn Expedition of 1894, when it was reported that there were "dead shells in vast abundance" (Tate 1896). Solem (1993) and V. Kessner (*pers. obs.*) reported that it had not been collected since, although some more recent museum collections attributed to this species extend its known range marginally.

This species is one of a set of snail species listed here that is relatively restricted in its geographic range and is exposed to processes that may lead to its decline. This species is classified as **Vulnerable** (under criteria B1ab(i,ii,iii)+2ab(i,ii,iii)) based on:
• extent of occurrence less than 20 000 km²;
• area of occupancy less than 2000 km²;
• known to exist at fewer than 10 locations; and
• continuing decline observed, inferred or projected.

THREATENING PROCESSES
There is no direct evidence that any factors have caused a decline in the numbers or distribution of this species. However, there has been no monitoring of status, and this species may be detrimentally affected by an increased frequency and intensity of fire, fuelled in part by invasive exotic grasses, particularly buffel grass (*Cenchrus ciliaris*).

CONSERVATION OBJECTIVES AND MANAGEMENT
There are no existing management programs for land snail species in the Northern Territory.

Research priorities are to:
• conduct further surveys to determine whether populations occur elsewhere; and
• identify specific threats to the known population.

A monitoring program should be established. The management priority is to better safeguard the known population through establishment of appropriate fire regimes.

Compiled by Colin Wilson, John Woinarski, Vince Kessner, Michael Braby [April 2006] / **References:** Solem, A. (1993). Camaenid land snails from Western and central Australia (Mollusca: Pulmonata: Camaenidae). VI Taxa from the red centre. *Records of the Western Australian Museum* Supplement 43, 983-1459. / Tate, R. (1896). Mollusca. In: *Report on the work of the Horn scientific expedition to central Australia. Part II. Zoology.* (ed. B. Spencer.) pp. 181-219. (Melville, Mullen and Slade, Melbourne.)

Image from Solem 1993

Gillen Creek land snail
Granulomelon gilleni

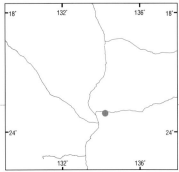

Known locations of Granulomelon gilleni
● = pre 1970
● = post 1970

CONSERVATION STATUS
AUSTRALIA: **NOT LISTED**
NORTHERN TERRITORY: **VULNERABLE**

DESCRIPTION

Granulomelon gilleni is a medium-sized (shell diameter: 14 to 17 mm) camaenid land snail, characterised by its strongly and evenly elevated apex and spire, and thick radial ribs. Other distinguishing characters are listed in Solem (1993).

DISTRIBUTION

This snail species has been recorded only from "small hills south of Southern Cross Bore, Strangways Range", near the Sandover River, central Australia (Solem 1993).

Conservation reserves where reported: None

ECOLOGY

There is no published information on the ecology of this species, although the genus is known to aestivate by sealing to rock surfaces (Solem 1993). V. Kessner (*pers. obs.*) reports that it is associated with mature spinifex.

CONSERVATION ASSESSMENT

This species was first collected in 1979, and is known only from a small area. Solem (1993) considered that this extent was about 5 km, and "undoubtedly will be extended when collecting is done in the main part of the Strangways Range". However, subsequent searching by V. Kessner suggests that the range is indeed highly localised.

This species is one of a set of snail species listed here that is relatively restricted in its geographic range and is exposed to processes that may lead to its decline. This species is classified as **Vulnerable** (under criteria B1ab(i,ii,iii)+2ab(i,ii,iii)) based on:
- extent of occurrence less than 20 000 km²;
- area of occupancy less than 2000 km²;
- known to exist at fewer than 10 locations; and
- continuing decline observed, inferred or projected.

THREATENING PROCESSES

There is no direct evidence that any external factors have caused a decline in the numbers or distribution of this species. However, there has been no monitoring of status, and this species may be detrimentally affected by an increased frequency and intensity of fire, especially so if it is associated with or dependent upon mature spinifex. The known population occurs on pastoral lands and it is not known whether pastoral activity may affect this species.

CONSERVATION OBJECTIVES AND MANAGEMENT

There are no existing management programs for land snail species in the Northern Territory.

Research priorities are to:
- conduct further surveys to determine whether populations occur elsewhere; and
- identify specific threats to the known population.

A monitoring program should be established for at least representative populations. The management priority is to better safeguard the known populations through establishment of appropriate fire regimes.

Compiled by Colin Wilson, John Woinarski, Vince Kessner, Michael Braby [April 2006] / **References:** Solem, A. (1993). Camaenid land snails from Western and central Australia (Mollusca: Pulmonata: Camaenidae). VI Taxa from the red centre. *Records of the Western Australian Museum* Supplement 43, 983-1459.

Image from Solem 1993

Land snail
Granulomelon grandituberculatum

CONSERVATION STATUS
AUSTRALIA: **NOT LISTED**
NORTHERN TERRITORY: **VULNERABLE**

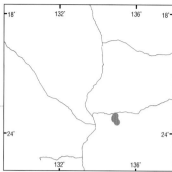

*Known locations
of Granulomelon
grandituberculatum*
● = *pre 1970*
● = *post 1970*

DESCRIPTION
Granulomelon grandituberculatum is a medium-sized (shell diameter: 14 to 17 mm) camaenid land snail, characterised by its high spire and greatly reduced radial sculpture. Other distinguishing characters are listed in Solem (1993).

DISTRIBUTION
This snail species has been recorded only in the basins of Maud and Florence Creeks on the south side of the Harts Range, north-east of Alice Springs.

Conservation reserves where reported: None

ECOLOGY
This species has very specific habitat requirements, being found in deep crevices in talus (V. Kessner *pers. obs.*).

CONSERVATION ASSESSMENT
This species was first collected by the Horn Expedition of 1894. Almost nothing was reported about it again for the next hundred years. Recent surveys in central Australia have only marginally expanded its known range and provided little information on current population size, although Solem (1993) collected it "in quantity".

This species is one of a set of snail species listed here that is relatively restricted in its geographic range and is exposed to processes that may lead to its decline. This species is classified as **Vulnerable** (under criteria B1ab(i,ii,iii)+2ab(i,ii,iii)) based on:
• extent of occurrence less than 20 000 km²;
• area of occupancy less than 2000 km²;
• known to exist at fewer than 10 locations; and
• continuing decline observed, inferred or projected.

THREATENING PROCESSES
There is no direct evidence that any external factors have caused a decline in the numbers or distribution of this species. However, there has been no monitoring of status, and this species may be detrimentally affected by an increased frequency and intensity of fire, fuelled in part by invasive exotic grasses, particularly buffel grass (*Cenchrus ciliaris*).

CONSERVATION OBJECTIVES AND MANAGEMENT
There are no existing management programs for the wild populations of any land snail species in the Northern Territory.

Research priorities are to:
• conduct further surveys to determine whether populations occur elsewhere; and
• identify specific threats to the known population.

A monitoring program should be established for at least representative populations. The management priority is to better safeguard the known populations through establishment of appropriate fire regimes.

Compiled by Colin Wilson, John Woinarski, Vince Kessner, Michael Braby [April 2006] / **References:** Solem, A. (1993). Camaenid land snails from Western and central Australia (Mollusca: Pulmonata: Camaenidae). VI Taxa from the red centre. *Records of the Western Australian Museum* Supplement 43, 983-1459.

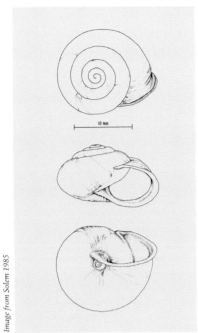

Image from Solem 1985

Desmond's land snail

Mesodontrachia desmonda

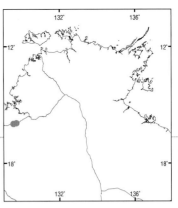

CONSERVATION STATUS
AUSTRALIA: **NOT LISTED**
NORTHERN TERRITORY: **ENDANGERED**

DESCRIPTION

Mesodontrachia desmonda is a large camaenid land snail (shell diameter: 17 to 21 mm, height: 11 to 15 mm). The shell has a light yellow horn and a white lip, and has 4.5 to 5 whorls. The apex and spire are strongly elevated, often rounded above (Solem 1985).

DISTRIBUTION

This species is endemic to the Northern Territory and is known only from a rocky ridge 8 km west of Desmond Passage, south of the Victoria Highway and south west of the Pinkerton Range. Recent records extend its known range to nearby areas of the south-east Kimberley, Western Australia.

Conservation reserves where reported: None

ECOLOGY

The species is found only under large boulders in small patches of rainforest at the base of cliffs or steep slopes amongst boab trees (*Adansonia gregorii*) (V. Kessner *pers. obs.*). Solem (1985) noted that the type locality is marked by an unusual number of large trees.

CONSERVATION ASSESSMENT

Mesodontrachia desmonda is restricted in range. There are no quantitative measures of decline but there is evidence that frequent fires degrade habitat and kill snails.

The species qualifies as **Endangered** (under criteria B2ab(iii)) based on:
• area of occupancy less than 500 km^2;
• severely fragmented; and
• continuing decline, observed, inferred or projected.

THREATENING PROCESSES

This species appears to be badly affected by the frequent fires that sweep the ridges (V. Kessner *pers. obs.*). Feral predators such as rats, mice and cane toads may have a significant impact on land snail populations (V. Kessner *pers. obs.*). It is likely that cane toads will invade these sites by about 2007, but there is no evidence of feral rats or mice at this site.

CONSERVATION OBJECTIVES AND MANAGEMENT

There are no existing management programs for land snail species in the Northern Territory.

Research priorities are to:
• conduct further surveys to determine whether populations occur elsewhere; and
• identify specific threats to the known population.

A monitoring program should be established.

Depending upon assessment of threats, management priorities may include to:
• better safeguard the known population through encouragement of appropriate fire regimes; and
• protect them from cane toads if toads are found to eat the species.

Compiled by Simon Ward, Vince Kessner, Michael Braby, John Woinarski [April 2006] / **References:** Solem, A. (1985). Camaenid land snails from Western and central Australia (Mollusca: Pulmonata: Camaenidae). V Remaining Kimberley genera and addenda to the Kimberley. *Records of the Western Australian Museum* Supplement 20, 707-981.

Image courtesy of P.Alderslade & R Willan (MAGNT)

Fitzroy land snail
Mesodontrachia fitzroyana

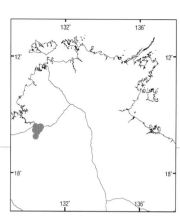

CONSERVATION STATUS
AUSTRALIA: **ENDANGERED**
NORTHERN TERRITORY: **CRITICALLY ENDANGERED**

*Known locations
of Mesodontrachia
fitzroyana*
● = pre 1970
● = post 1970

DESCRIPTION

Mesodontrachia fitzroyana is a large camaenid land snail (shell diameter: 17 to 23 mm, height 10 to 14 mm). The shell has a medium-yellow horn and a white lip, and has 5 to 6 whorls. The apex and spire are moderately elevated, somewhat rounded above (Solem 1985).

DISTRIBUTION

This species is known from a few low limestone hills that are traversed by the Victoria Highway, 24 km east of Timber Creek. The hills are about 8 km long and meet sandstone hills 1 to 2 km to the south and run out 4 to 5 km north of the highway (V. Kessner *pers. obs.*).

Conservation reserves where reported:
Gregory National Park

ECOLOGY

The species occurs under rocks in open eucalyptus woodland and small patches of rainforest within the patches of pavement limestone (V. Kessner *pers. obs.*)

CONSERVATION ASSESSMENT

Mesodontrachia fitzroyana is restricted in range, and has specific habitat requirements. There is also evidence that the population density of snails has declined. Vince Kessner collected the species in 1985 and reported being able to find thousands of snails. He made three collecting visits to the area in the late 1990s, when the snails were very difficult to find.

In the Northern Territory, this species qualifies as **Critically Endangered** (under criteria B1ab(iii,v)+2ab(iii,v)) based on:

• extent of occurrence less than 100 km²;
• area of occupancy less than 10 km²;
• severely fragmented; and
• continuing decline, observed, inferred or projected.

THREATENING PROCESSES

These snails lie dormant during the dry season, aestivating among rocks. Here they are unprotected from hot fires and are vulnerable to trampling by cattle (V. Kessner *pers. obs.*). They also become exposed when stock overgraze the covering vegetation (V. Kessner *pers. obs.*). Feral predators such as rats, mice and cane toads may have a significant impact on land snail populations (V. Kessner *pers. obs.*). Cane toads will invade these sites between 2006 and 2008, but there is no evidence to suggest presence of feral rats or mice in this location.

CONSERVATION OBJECTIVES
AND MANAGEMENT

There are no existing management programs for land snail species in the Northern Territory.

Research priorities are to:
• conduct further surveys to determine whether populations occur elsewhere; and
• identify specific threats to the known population.

A monitoring program should be established.

Depending upon assessment of threats, management priorities may include to:
• better safeguard the known population through encouragement of appropriate fire regimes and protection from heavy grazing; and.
• protect them from cane toads, if toads are found to eat the species.

Compiled by Simon Ward, Vince Kessner, Michael Braby, John Woinarski [December 2006] / **References:** Solem, A. (1985). Camaenid land snails from Western and central Australia (Mollusca: Pulmonata: Camaenidae). V Remaining Kimberley genera and addenda to the Kimberley. *Records of the Western Australian Museum* Supplement 20, 707-981.

Image from Solem 1984

Land snail
Ordtrachia australis

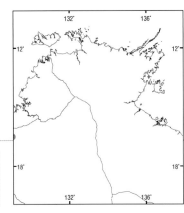

*Known locations
of Ordtrachia
australis*
● = pre 1970
● = post 1970

DESCRIPTION
Ordtrachia australis is a medium-sized
camaenid land snail (shell diameter: 12 to 16 mm;
height: 6.5 to 9 mm) with 4.5 to 5.5 normally-
coiled whorls. The apex and spire are moderately
and almost evenly elevated and there is a sharply
protruded peripheral keel (Solem 1984).

DISTRIBUTION
In the Northern Territory, this species has been
collected only on a small area of low limestone
exposures 5.4 km south of the Rosewood Station
turnoff along the Duncan Highway, adjacent to the
Western Australian border. "This is an isolated
exposure and neither topographic nor geological
maps of the region suggest possible locations
for additional colonies" (Solem 1984, p.657);
although Solem (1984) also noted that another set
of collections elsewhere on the Duncan Highway
may be attributable to this species. Recent records
extend its known range to nearby areas of the
south-east Kimberley, Western Australia.

Conservation reserves where reported: None

ECOLOGY
This species is found under limestone rocks in
open woodland and in patches of scrub.

CONSERVATION ASSESSMENT
Ordtrachia australis is very restricted in range and
habitat. There are too few collections in the area
to provide quantitative data on population trends,
however, damage to the habitat by cattle is obvious
and the population is thought to have declined
substantially in recent years under the influence of
frequent fires and overgrazing by stock (V. Kessner
pers. obs.).

In the Northern Territory, this species qualifies as
Endangered (under criteria B1ab(iii)+ B2ab(iii))
based on:
• extent of occurrence less than 5000 km²;
• area of occupancy less than 500 km² ;
• severely fragmented; and
• continuing decline, observed, inferred or
  projected.

THREATENING PROCESSES
Vince Kessner (*pers. obs.*) considers the threatening
processes for this species to be trampling by cattle
causing breakage of shell and compaction of the
soil, restricting the snail from either burrowing into
the soil or being able to climb out. He also noted
that frequent fires are changing the vegetation
structure and composition.

The arrival of predatory cane toads may contribute
further to their decline (V. Kessner *pers. obs.*):
toads are likely to arrive at this site between 2007
and 2010.

CONSERVATION OBJECTIVES
AND MANAGEMENT
There are no existing management programs for
land snail species in the Northern Territory.

Research priorities are to:
• conduct further surveys to determine whether
  populations occur elsewhere; and
• identify specific threats to the known population.

A monitoring program should be established.

Management priorities are to:
• better safeguard the known population through
  encouragement of appropriate fire regimes and
  protection from heavy grazing; and.
• protect them from cane toads, if toads are found
  to eat the species.

Compiled by Simon Ward, Vince Kessner, Michael Braby, John Woinarski [April 2006] / **References:** Solem, A. (1984). Camaenid land snails from Western and central Australia (Mollusca: Pulmonata:
Camaenidae). IV Taxa from the Kimberley, *Westraltrachia* Iredale, 1933 and related genera. *Records of the Western Australian Museum* Supplement 17, 427-705.

Image from Solem 1984

Land snail
Ordtrachia septentrionalis

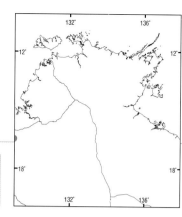

Known locations of Ordtrachia septentrionalis
● = *pre 1970*
● = *post 1970*

DESCRIPTION

Ordtrachia septentrionalis is a medium-sized camaenid land snail (shell diameter: 11 to 14 mm; height: 7 to 9 mm), with 4.5 to 5.5 normally coiled whorls. The apex and spire are moderately and evenly elevated (Solem 1984).

DISTRIBUTION

This snail is found only on a small area of low limestone exposures along 1.4 km of road south of the Rosewood Station turn off along the Duncan Highway, and in a small area of limestone 8 km to the west, in The Rock Wall on Rosewood Station (just into Western Australia) (V. Kessner *pers. obs.*).

Conservation reserves where reported: None

ECOLOGY

This snail is found among scattered limestone boulders and blocks exposed in open savanna in areas subject to heavy flooding. The snails ascend trees to survive flood events. The limestone blocks vary from a few centimetres to a couple of metres in diameter, but rarely project more than a few centimetres above ground level (V. Kessner *pers. obs.*).

CONSERVATION ASSESSMENT

Ordtrachia septentrionalis is very restricted in range and habitat. There have been only three collections of the species, by two different collectors, all during the 1980s. There are no quantitative data to assess decline, but there is evidence of damage done by cattle in the areas (churned soil and broken shells) and frequent fires (V. Kessner *pers. obs.*).

The species qualifies as **Endangered** (under criteria B1ab(iii)+ B2ab(iii)) based on:
• extent of occurrence less than 5000 km²;
• area of occupancy less than 500 km²;
• severely fragmented; and
• continuing decline, observed, inferred or projected.

THREATENING PROCESSES

Vince Kessner (*pers. obs.*) considers the threatening processes for this species to be trampling by cattle causing breakage of shell and compaction of the soil, restricting the snail from either burrowing into the soil or being able to climb out. The snail may also be affected by frequent fires, which are causing changes to the vegetation structure and composition.

The arrival of predatory cane toads may contribute to their decline (V. Kessner *pers. obs.*). Cane toads are likely to invade this area between 2007 and 2010.

CONSERVATION OBJECTIVES AND MANAGEMENT

There are no existing management programs for land snail species in the Northern Territory.

Research priorities are to:
• conduct further surveys to determine whether populations occur elsewhere; and
• identify specific threats to the known population.

A monitoring program should be established.

Management priorities are to:
• better safeguard the known populations through encouragement of appropriate fire regimes and protection from heavy grazing; and
• protect them from cane toads if toads are found to eat the species.

Compiled by Simon Ward, Vince Kessner, Michael Braby, John Woinarski [April 2006] / **References:** Solem, A. (1984). Camaenid land snails from Western and central Australia (Mollusca: Pulmonata: Camaenidae). IV Taxa from the Kimberley, *Westraltrachia* Iredale, 1933 and related genera. *Records of the Western Australian Museum* Supplement 17, 427-705.

Image from Solem 1988

Land snail

Pillomena aemula

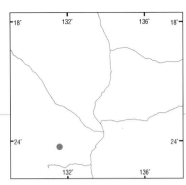

Known locations of Pillomena aemula
- = pre 1970
- = post 1970

CONSERVATION STATUS
AUSTRALIA: **NOT LISTED**
NORTHERN TERRITORY: **VULNERABLE**

DESCRIPTION

Pillomena aemula is a very small (shell diameter: 1.9 to 2.25 mm) non-camaenid landsnail, with a depressed spire, crowded radial sculpture and a thick parietal callus (Solem 1988).

DISTRIBUTION

All records of this species are from a total range of less than 1 km² around Penny Springs in the George Gill Ranges south west of Alice Springs.

Conservation reserves where reported:
Watarrka National Park

ECOLOGY

It is found in leaf litter in relatively moist areas, under patches of fig trees, cycads and scrub.

CONSERVATION ASSESSMENT

This species was recorded from the Horn Expedition to central Australia in 1894, but there were few or no other records until 1987, when Vince Kessner collected a few dead specimens around the type locality (Solem 1988).

Its known range is highly restricted. It is possible that further survey effort will extend this range. It fits the criteria for **Vulnerable** (under criterion D2) based on:
- area of occupancy less than 20 km²; and
- known to exist at fewer than five locations.

THREATENING PROCESSES

It is possible that this land snail has always been extremely restricted in range as there is no direct evidence that any external factors have yet caused a decline in their numbers or distribution.

However, in general, land snails are susceptible to the impacts of an increased frequency and intensity of fire. Invasive exotic pastures, such as buffel grass (*Cenchrus ciliaris*), create far more fuel than do the native grasses and frequently carry destructive fires.

Rare extreme events such as major floods or droughts may severely affect populations made vulnerable by the processes listed above.

CONSERVATION OBJECTIVES AND MANAGEMENT

There is no existing management program for land snail species in the Northern Territory.

Research priorities are to:
- conduct further surveys to determine whether populations occur elsewhere; and
- identify specific threats to the known population.

Management priorities are to:
- better safeguard the known populations through containing the spread of exotic grasses; and
- establish a monitoring program for the species.

Compiled by Colin Wilson, John Woinarski, Vince Kessner, Michael Braby [April 2006] / **References:** Solem, A. (1988). Non-Camaenid land snails of the Kimberley and Northern Territory, Australia. I. Systematics, affinities and ranges. *Invertebrate Taxonomy* 4, 455-605.

Image from Solem 1984

Land snail
Prototrachia sedula

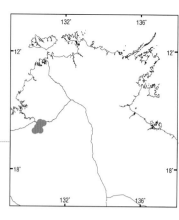

Known locations
of *Prototrachia
sedula*
● = pre 1970
● = post 1970

CONSERVATION STATUS
AUSTRALIA: **NOT LISTED**
NORTHERN TERRITORY: **VULNERABLE**

DESCRIPTION
Prototrachia sedula is a medium-sized (shell diameter: 13 to 17 mm) camaenid land snail. Distinguishing features are listed in Solem (1984).

DISTRIBUTION
Solem (1984) reported that this species was known from only one site, 24 km east of Timber Creek. Some more recent museum collections attributed to this species extend this known range marginally.

Conservation reserves where reported:
Gregory National Park

ECOLOGY
Solem (1984) reported that it occurred on the lower slopes of a low limestone cliff, under scattered boulders or rocks.

CONSERVATION ASSESSMENT
This species is apparently highly restricted, and may be exposed to processes that may lead to decline. It qualifies as **Vulnerable** (under criteria B1ab(i,ii,iii)+2ab(i,ii,iii)) based on:
• extent of occurrence less than 20 000 km^2;
• area of occupancy less than 2000 km^2;
• known to exist at fewer than 10 locations; and
• continuing decline observed, inferred or projected.

THREATENING PROCESSES
There is no direct evidence that any factors have yet caused a decline in the numbers or distribution of this snail species. However, this snail may be affected by frequent fires and the arrival of predatory cane toads (V. Kessner *pers. obs.*). Cane toads colonised this area about 2005. Cattle may directly trample this species and reduce habitat quality through soil compaction.

CONSERVATION OBJECTIVES AND MANAGEMENT
There are no existing management programs for land snail species in the Northern Territory.

Research priorities are to:
• conduct further surveys to determine whether populations occur elsewhere; and
• identify specific threats to the known population.

A monitoring program should be established.

Management priorities are to:
• better safeguard the known population through encouragement of appropriate fire regimes; and
• protect them from cane toads, if toads are found to eat the species.

Compiled by Colin Wilson, John Woinarski, Vince Kessner, Michael Braby [April 2006] / **References:** Solem, A. (1984). Camaenid land snails from Western and central Australia (Mollusca: Pulmonata: Camaenidae). IV Taxa from the Kimberley, *Westraltrachia* Iredale, 1933 and related genera. *Records of the Western Australian Museum* Supplement 17, 427-705.

Image from Solem 1993

Land snail

Semotrachia caupona

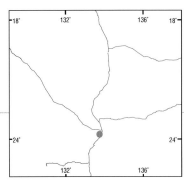

Known locations of Semotrachia caupona
● = pre 1970
● = post 1970

CONSERVATION STATUS
AUSTRALIA: **NOT LISTED**
NORTHERN TERRITORY: **VULNERABLE**

DESCRIPTION

Semotrachia caupona is a small (shell diameter: 9 to 11 mm) camaenid landsnail. Distinguishing features are listed in Solem (1993).

DISTRIBUTION

This species is known only from the south-west corner of Temple Bar, formerly known as Honeymoon Gap, in the MacDonnell Ranges west of Alice Springs.

Conservation reserves where reported:
West MacDonnell National Park

ECOLOGY

There is no published information on the ecology of this species, other than that the only collections have come from leaf litter under a large patch of fig trees.

CONSERVATION ASSESSMENT

This species is one of a set of snail species listed here that is relatively restricted in its geographic range and is exposed to processes that may lead to its decline. This species is classified as **Vulnerable** (under criteria B1ab(i,ii,iii)+2ab(i,ii,iii)) based on:
• extent of occurrence less than 20 000 km²;
• area of occupancy less than 2000 km²;
• known to exist at fewer than 10 locations; and
• continuing decline observed, inferred or projected.

THREATENING PROCESSES

There is no direct evidence that any factors have caused a decline in the numbers or distribution of this species. However, there has been no monitoring of status, and this species may be detrimentally affected by an increased frequency and intensity of fire, fuelled in part by invasive exotic grasses, particularly buffel grass (*Cenchrus ciliaris*).

CONSERVATION OBJECTIVES AND MANAGEMENT

There are no existing management programs for land snail species in the Northern Territory.

Research priorities are to:
• conduct further surveys to determine whether populations occur elsewhere; and
• identify specific threats to the known population.

A monitoring program should be established. The management priority is to better safeguard the known population through establishment of appropriate fire regimes.

Compiled by Colin Wilson, John Woinarski, Vince Kessner, Michael Braby [April 2006] / **References:** Solem, A. (1993). Camaenid land snails from Western and central Australia (Mollusca: Pulmonata: Camaenidae). VI Taxa from the red centre. *Records of the Western Australian Museum* Supplement 43, 983-1459.

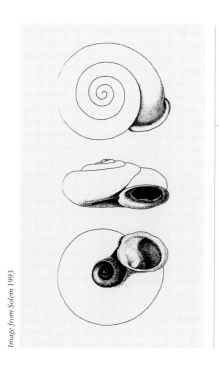

Image from Solem 1993

Ellery Gorge land snail

Semotrachia elleryi

CONSERVATION STATUS
AUSTRALIA: **NOT LISTED**
NORTHERN TERRITORY: **VULNERABLE**

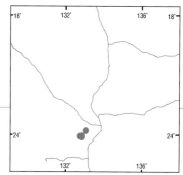

Known locations of Semotrachia elleryi
● = *pre 1970*
● = *post 1970*

DESCRIPTION

Semotrachia elleryi is a small to medium-sized (shell diameter: 10 to 13 mm) camaenid land snail. Distinguishing features are listed in Solem (1993).

DISTRIBUTION

This species has been collected at three sites in the Ellery Creek basin; at Serpentine Gorge and Ellery Creek Big Hole in the Heavitree Range west of Alice Springs, and about 40 km further south where Ellery Creek enters the Krichauff Ranges to join the Finke River.

Conservation reserves where reported:
Finke Gorge National Park, West MacDonnell National Park.

ECOLOGY

There is no published information on the ecology of this species, other than that specimens have been collected under figs and in talus at a cliff base.

CONSERVATION ASSESSMENT

This species is one of a set of snail species listed here that is relatively restricted in its geographic range and is exposed to processes that may lead to its decline. This species is classified as **Vulnerable** (under criteria B1ab(i,ii,iii)+2ab(i,ii,iii)) based on:
• extent of occurrence less than 20 000 km²;
• area of occupancy less than 2000 km²;
• known to exist at fewer than 10 locations; and
• continuing decline observed, inferred or projected.

THREATENING PROCESSES

There is no direct evidence that any factors have caused a decline in the numbers or distribution of this species. However, there has been no monitoring of status, and this species may be detrimentally affected by an increased frequency and intensity of fire, fuelled in part by invasive exotic grasses, particularly buffel grass (*Cenchrus ciliaris*).

CONSERVATION OBJECTIVES AND MANAGEMENT

There are no existing management programs for land snail species in the Northern Territory.

Research priorities are to:
• conduct further surveys to determine whether populations occur elsewhere; and
• identify specific threats to the known population.

A monitoring program should be established for at least representative populations.

The management priority is to better safeguard the known populations through establishment of appropriate fire regimes.

Compiled by Colin Wilson, John Woinarski, Vince Kessner, Michael Braby [April 2006] / **References:** Solem, A. (1993). Camaenid land snails from Western and central Australia (Mollusca: Pulmonata: Camaenidae). VI Taxa from the red centre. *Records of the Western Australian Museum* Supplement 43, 983-1459.

Image from Solem 1993

Emile's land snail
Semotrachia emilia

CONSERVATION STATUS
AUSTRALIA: **NOT LISTED**
NORTHERN TERRITORY: **VULNERABLE**

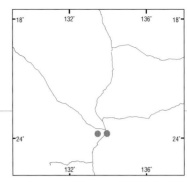

Known locations
of *Semotrachia
emilia*
● = *pre 1970*
● = *post 1970*

DESCRIPTION

Semotrachia emilia is a medium-sized (shell diameter: 11 to 13 mm) camaenid land snail, with flat or barely elevated spire. Further distinguishing features are listed in Solem (1993).

DISTRIBUTION

Solem (1993) considered that this was an extraordinarily restricted species, found only under a small group of fig trees in Emily Gap in the MacDonnell Ranges, east of Alice Springs. Some more recent museum collections attributed to this species extend this known range marginally.

Conservation reserves where reported:
Emily and Jessie Gaps Nature Park

ECOLOGY

There is no published information on the ecology of this species, other than that it aestivates attached to rock slabs in litter under a small patch of figs (Solem 1993).

CONSERVATION ASSESSMENT

This species is one of a set of snail species listed here that is relatively restricted in its geographic range and is exposed to processes that may lead to its decline. This species is classified as **Vulnerable** (under criteria B1ab(i,ii,iii)+2ab(i,ii,iii)) based on:
• extent of occurrence less than 20 000 km²;
• area of occupancy less than 2000 km²;
• known to exist at fewer than 10 locations; and
• continuing decline observed, inferred or projected.

THREATENING PROCESSES

There is no direct evidence that any factors have caused a decline in the numbers or distribution of this species. However, there has been no monitoring of status, and this species may be detrimentally affected by an increased frequency and intensity of fire, fuelled in part by invasive exotic grasses, particularly buffel grass (*Cenchrus ciliaris*).

CONSERVATION OBJECTIVES AND MANAGEMENT

There are no existing management programs for land snail species in the Northern Territory.

Research priorities are to:
• conduct further surveys to determine whether populations occur elsewhere; and
• identify specific threats to the known population.

A monitoring program should be established.

The management priority is to better safeguard the known population through establishment of appropriate fire regimes.

Compiled by Colin Wilson, John Woinarski, Vince Kessner, Michael Braby [April 2006] / **References:** Solem, A. (1993). Camaenid land snails from Western and central Australia (Mollusca: Pulmonata: Camaenidae). VI Taxa from the red centre. *Records of the Western Australian Museum* Supplement 43, 983-1459.

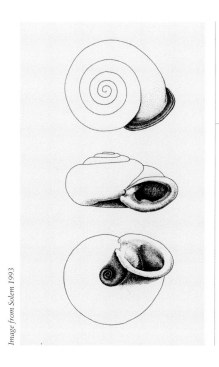

Image from Solem 1993

Land snail
Semotrachia esau

CONSERVATION STATUS
AUSTRALIA: **NOT LISTED**
NORTHERN TERRITORY: **VULNERABLE**

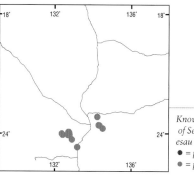

Known locations of Semotrachia esau
● = pre 1970
● = post 1970

DESCRIPTION
Semotrachia esau is a medium-sized (shell diameter: 9 to 15 mm) camaenid land snail. Distinguishing features are listed in Solem (1993).

DISTRIBUTION
Solem (1993) reported that this snail was known only from a small area along the Finke River and Palm Creek in the Krichauff Ranges west of Alice Springs, with a single isolated colony in the Palmer River drainage 78 km to the south-east. The disjunctive occurrence in the Palmer River could have resulted from accidental transport of snails during an exceptional flooding of the Finke River. Some more recent museum collections attributed to this species extend this known range.

Conservation reserves where reported:
Finke Gorge National Park

ECOLOGY
There is no published information on the ecology of this species, other than that specimens have been collected under figs (mostly) or under spinifex.

CONSERVATION ASSESSMENT
This species is one of a set of snail species listed here that is relatively restricted in its geographic range and is exposed to processes that may lead to its decline. This species is classified as **Vulnerable** (under criteria B2ab(i,ii,iii)) based on:
• area of occupancy less than 2000 km²;
• known to exist at fewer than 10 locations; and
• a continuing decline observed, inferred or projected.

THREATENING PROCESSES
There is no direct evidence that any factors have caused a decline in the numbers or distribution of this species. However, there has been no monitoring of status, and this species may be detrimentally affected by an increased frequency and intensity of fire, fuelled in part by invasive exotic grasses, particularly buffel grass (*Cenchrus ciliaris*).

CONSERVATION OBJECTIVES AND MANAGEMENT
There are no existing management programs for land snail species in the Northern Territory.

Research priorities are to:
• conduct further surveys to determine whether populations occur elsewhere; and
• identify specific threats to the known population.

A monitoring program should be established for at least representative populations.

The management priority is to better safeguard the known populations through establishment of appropriate fire regimes.

Compiled by Colin Wilson, John Woinarski, Vince Kessner, Michael Braby [April 2006] / **References:** Solem, A. (1993). Camaenid land snails from Western and central Australia (Mollusca: Pulmonata: Camaenidae). VI Taxa from the red centre. *Records of the Western Australian Museum* Supplement 43, 983-1459.

Land snail
Semotrachia euzyga

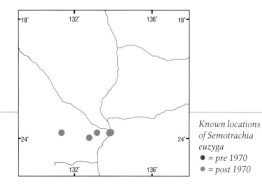

Known locations
of Semotrachia
euzyga
● = pre 1970
● = post 1970

CONSERVATION STATUS
AUSTRALIA: **ENDANGERED**
NORTHERN TERRITORY: **ENDANGERED**

DESCRIPTION
Semotrachia euzyga is a small yellow-brown camaenid land snail, about 8 mm in diameter, with a slightly elevated spire and reduced whorl count (Solem 1993).

DISTRIBUTION
This species is endemic to the Northern Territory. Although recent museum collections have extended its known range slightly, it is highly restricted, with locations including about 1 km² along the Todd River in Alice Springs, on nearby Choritza Hill, and Mt Gillen less than 8 km away (V. Kessner *pers. obs.*).

Conservation reserves where reported:
Alice Springs Telegraph Station Historical Reserve (but it has almost disappeared from the area), West MacDonnell National Park.

ECOLOGY
The species is restricted to areas around fig trees. The snails live in rocky litter under the figs and adults aestivate sealed to rocks (Solem 1993).

CONSERVATION ASSESSMENT
Semotrachia euzyga has very specific habitat requirements and has a highly restricted distribution, with most records within 10 km of the centre of Alice Springs. The species is believed to be declining (V. Kessner *pers. obs.*) but there have not been repeated counts at any location.

The species qualifies as **Endangered** (under criteria B2ab(iii,v)) based on:
- area of occupancy less than 500 km²;
- severely fragmented; and
- continuing decline, observed, inferred or projected.

THREATENING PROCESSES
This species is badly affected by fires in the exotic buffel grass (*Cenchrus ciliaris*) which is abundant in the area, and by urban development. If the associated fig trees are removed or die, the snails will disappear from the area (V. Kessner *pers. obs.*).

CONSERVATION OBJECTIVES AND MANAGEMENT
There are no existing management programs for land snail species in the Northern Territory.

Research priorities are to:
- conduct further surveys to determine whether populations occur elsewhere; and
- identify specific threats to the known population.

Management priorities are to:
- protect the habitat from urban expansion;
- better safeguard the known populations through establishment of appropriate fire regimes; and
- establish a monitoring program.

Compiled by Simon Ward, Vince Kessner, Michael Braby, John Woinarski [April 2006] / **References:** Solem, A. (1993). Camaenid land snails from Western and central Australia (Mollusca: Pulmonata: Camaenidae). VI Taxa from the red centre. *Records of the Western Australian Museum* Supplement 43, 983-1459.

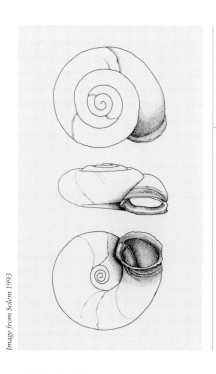

Image from Solem 1993

Land snail
Semotrachia filixiana

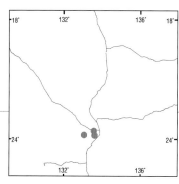

*Known locations
of Semotrachia
filixiana*
● = pre 1970
● = post 1970

DESCRIPTION
Semotrachia filixiana is a medium-sized (shell diameter: 9 to 12 mm) camaenid landsnail. Distinguishing features are listed in Solem (1993).

DISTRIBUTION
Solem (1993) reported that this species had been collected only once, at Fenn Gap West, in the MacDonnell Ranges, west of Alice Springs. Some more recent museum collections attributed to this species extend this known range marginally.

Conservation reserves where reported:
West MacDonnell National Park

ECOLOGY
There is no published information on the ecology of this species.

CONSERVATION ASSESSMENT
This species is one of a set of snail species listed here that is relatively restricted in its geographic range and is exposed to processes that may lead to its decline. This species is classified as **Vulnerable** (under criteria B1ab(i,ii,iii)+2ab(i,ii,iii)) based on:
• extent of occurrence less than 20 000 km²;
• area of occupancy less than 2000 km²;
• known to exist at fewer than 10 locations; and
• continuing decline observed, inferred or projected.

THREATENING PROCESSES
There is no direct evidence that any factors have caused a decline in the numbers or distribution of this species. However, there has been no monitoring of status, and this species may be detrimentally affected by an increased frequency and intensity of fire, fuelled in part by invasive exotic grasses, particularly buffel grass (*Cenchrus ciliaris*).

CONSERVATION OBJECTIVES AND MANAGEMENT
There are no existing management programs for land snail species in the Northern Territory.

Research priorities are to:
• conduct further surveys to determine whether populations occur elsewhere; and
• identify specific threats to the known population.

A monitoring program should be established.

The management priority is to better safeguard the known populations through establishment of appropriate fire regimes.

Compiled by Colin Wilson, John Woinarski, Vince Kessner, Michael Braby [April 2006] / **References:** Solem, A. (1993). Camaenid land snails from Western and central Australia (Mollusca: Pulmonata: Camaenidae). VI Taxa from the red centre. *Records of the Western Australian Museum* Supplement 43, 983-1459.

Image from Solem 1993

Land snail
Semotrachia huckittana

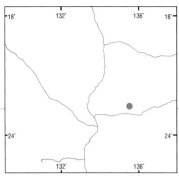

*Known locations
of Semotrachia
huckittana*
● = *pre 1970*
● = *post 1970*

DESCRIPTION
Semotrachia huckittana is a small (shell diameter: 8 to 10 mm) camaenid land snail, with low spire. Other distinguishing features are listed in Solem (1993).

DISTRIBUTION
This species has been collected only once, near Old Huckitta Homestead in the Dulcie Ranges north-east of Alice Springs.

Conservation reserves where reported:
Dulcie Ranges National Park

ECOLOGY
There is no published information on the ecology of this species, other than that the only collections have come from under moist rocks in a gorge to the north of the ruins.

CONSERVATION ASSESSMENT
This species is one of a set of snail species listed here that is relatively restricted in its geographic range and is exposed to processes that may lead to its decline. This species is classified as **Vulnerable** (under criteria B1ab(i,ii,iii)+2ab(i,ii,iii)) based on:
• extent of occurrence less than 20 000 km²;
• area of occupancy less than 2000 km²;
• known to exist at fewer than 10 locations; and
• continuing decline observed, inferred or projected.

THREATENING PROCESSES
There is no direct evidence that any factors have caused a decline in the numbers or distribution of this species. However, there has been no monitoring of status, and this species may be detrimentally affected by an increased frequency and intensity of fire, fuelled in part by invasive exotic grasses, particularly buffel grass (*Cenchrus ciliaris*).

CONSERVATION OBJECTIVES AND MANAGEMENT
There are no existing management programs for land snail species in the Northern Territory.

Research priorities are to:
• conduct further surveys to determine whether populations occur elsewhere; and
• identify specific threats to the known population.

A monitoring program should be established.

The management priority is to better safeguard the known population through establishment of appropriate fire regimes.

Compiled by Colin Wilson, John Woinarski, Vince Kessner, Michael Braby [April 2006] / **References:** Solem, A. (1993). Camaenid land snails from Western and central Australia (Mollusca: Pulmonata: Camaenidae). VI Taxa from the red centre. *Records of the Western Australian Museum* Supplement 43, 983-1459.

Image from Solem 1993

Land snail
Semotrachia illarana

CONSERVATION STATUS
AUSTRALIA: **NOT LISTED**
NORTHERN TERRITORY: **VULNERABLE**

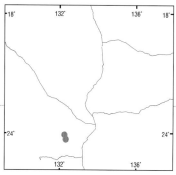

*Known locations
of Semotrachia
illarana*
● = pre 1970
● = post 1970

DESCRIPTION
Semotrachia illarana is a small (shell diameter: 7 to 8 mm) camaenid land snail. Distinguishing features are listed in Solem (1993).

DISTRIBUTION
This small snail has been reported only from Illara Waterhole south of the James Ranges on a tributary of the Palmer River, south-west of Alice Springs. Another putative location, near Areyonga (28 km to the north of Illara Waterhole) probably represents a distinct species (Solem 1993).

Conservation reserves where reported: None

ECOLOGY
There is no published information on the ecology of this species, other than that the only collections have come from leaf litter under fig trees.

CONSERVATION ASSESSMENT
This species is one of a set of snail species listed here that is relatively restricted in its geographic range and is exposed to processes that may lead to its decline. This species is classified as **Vulnerable** (under criteria B1ab(i,ii,iii)+2ab(i,ii,iii)) based on:
- extent of occurrence less than 20 000 km²;
- area of occupancy less than 2000 km²2;
- known to exist at fewer than 10 locations; and
- continuing decline observed, inferred or projected.

THREATENING PROCESSES
There is no direct evidence that any factors have caused a decline in the numbers or distribution of this species. However, there has been no monitoring of status, and this species may be detrimentally affected by an increased frequency and intensity of fire, fuelled in part by invasive exotic grasses, particularly buffel grass (*Cenchrus ciliaris*). The only known population is on a pastoral property, but there is no information available concerning the impacts upon this species of livestock grazing.

CONSERVATION OBJECTIVES AND MANAGEMENT
There are no existing management programs for land snail species in the Northern Territory.

Research priorities are to:
- conduct further surveys to determine whether populations occur elsewhere; and
- identify specific threats to the known population.

A monitoring program should be established.

The management priority is to better safeguard the known population through establishment of appropriate fire regimes.

Compiled by Colin Wilson, John Woinarski, Vince Kessner, Michael Braby [April 2006] / **References:** Solem, A. (1993). Camaenid land snails from Western and central Australia (Mollusca: Pulmonata: Camaenidae). VI Taxa from the red centre. *Records of the Western Australian Museum* Supplement 43, 983-1459.

Land snail
Semotrachia jessieana

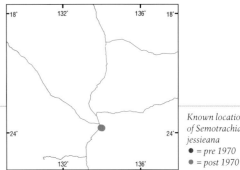

CONSERVATION STATUS
AUSTRALIA: **NOT LISTED**
NORTHERN TERRITORY: **VULNERABLE**

DESCRIPTION
Semotrachia jessieana is a small to medium-sized (shell diameter: 10 to 12 mm) camaenid land snail, with nearly flat spire. Other distinguishing features are listed in Solem (1993).

DISTRIBUTION
This snail has been found only under a single small group of fig trees, in Jessie Gap in the MacDonnell Ranges, east of Alice Springs.

Conservation reserves where reported:
Emily and Jessie Gaps Nature Park

ECOLOGY
There is no published information on the ecology of this species, other than that the collected specimens were found while aestivating on small rocks in litter under a small patch of figs. This site is in well-shaded rubble moistened by seepage at the side of a near-permanent pool (Solem 1993).

CONSERVATION ASSESSMENT
This species is one of a set of snail species listed here that is relatively restricted in its geographic range and is exposed to processes that may lead to its decline. This species is classified as **Vulnerable** (under criteria B1ab(i,ii,iii)+2ab(i,ii,iii)) based on:
• extent of occurrence less than 20 000 km²;
• area of occupancy less than 2000 km²;
• known to exist at fewer than 10 locations; and
• continuing decline observed, inferred or projected.

THREATENING PROCESSES
There is no direct evidence that any factors have caused a decline in the numbers or distribution of this species. However, there has been no monitoring of status, and this species may be detrimentally affected by an increased frequency and intensity of fire, fuelled in part by invasive exotic grasses, particularly buffel grass (*Cenchrus ciliaris*).

CONSERVATION OBJECTIVES AND MANAGEMENT
There are no existing management programs for land snail species in the Northern Territory.

Research priorities are to:
• conduct further surveys to determine whether populations occur elsewhere; and
• identify specific threats to the known population.

A monitoring program should be established.

The management priority is to better safeguard the known population through establishment of appropriate fire regimes.

Compiled by Colin Wilson, John Woinarski, Vince Kessner, Michael Braby [April 2006] / **References:** Solem, A. (1993). Camaenid land snails from Western and central Australia (Mollusca: Pulmonata: Camaenidae). VI Taxa from the red centre. *Records of the Western Australian Museum* Supplement 43, 983-1459.

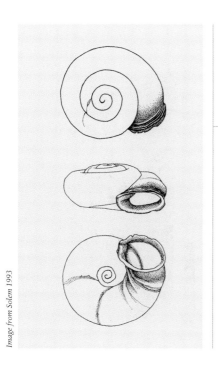

Image from Solem 1993

Land snail
Semotrachia jinkana

CONSERVATION STATUS
AUSTRALIA: **NOT LISTED**
NORTHERN TERRITORY: **VULNERABLE**

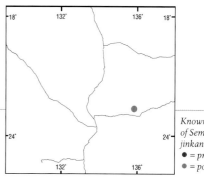

Known locations of Semotrachia jinkana
● = *pre 1970*
● = *post 1970*

DESCRIPTION
Semotrachia jinkana is a small (shell diameter: 7 to 9 mm) camaenid land snail, with moderately elevated spire. Other distinguishing features are listed in Solem (1993).

DISTRIBUTION
This species is known only from a small patch of fig trees below Jinka Spring in the Dulcie Ranges, north-east of Alice Springs.

Conservation reserves where reported: None

ECOLOGY
There is no published information on the ecology of this species, other than that the only collections have come from litter under fig trees (Solem 1993).

CONSERVATION ASSESSMENT
This species is one of a set of snail species listed here that is relatively restricted in its geographic range and is exposed to processes that may lead to its decline. This species is classified as **Vulnerable** (under criteria B1ab(i,ii,iii)+2ab(i,ii,iii)) based on:
• extent of occurrence less than 20 000 km²;
• area of occupancy less than 2000 km²;
• known to exist at fewer than 10 locations; and
• continuing decline observed, inferred or projected.

THREATENING PROCESSES
There is no direct evidence that any factors have caused a decline in the numbers or distribution of this species. However, there has been no monitoring of status, and this species may be detrimentally affected by an increased frequency and intensity of fire, fuelled in part by invasive exotic grasses, particularly buffel grass (*Cenchrus ciliaris*).

CONSERVATION OBJECTIVES AND MANAGEMENT
There are no existing management programs for land snail species in the Northern Territory.

Research priorities are to:
• conduct further surveys to determine whether populations occur elsewhere; and
• identify specific threats to the known population.

A monitoring program should be established.

The management priority is to better safeguard the known population through establishment of appropriate fire regimes.

Compiled by Colin Wilson, John Woinarski, Vince Kessner, Michael Braby [April 2006] / **References:** Solem, A. (1993). Camaenid land snails from Western and central Australia (Mollusca: Pulmonata: Camaenidae). VI Taxa from the red centre. *Records of the Western Australian Museum* Supplement 43, 983-1459.

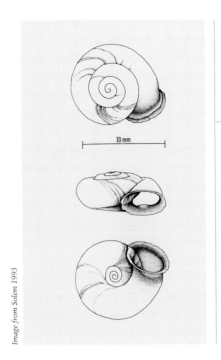

Image from Solem 1993

Land snail
Semotrachia rossana

CONSERVATION STATUS
AUSTRALIA: **NOT LISTED**
NORTHERN TERRITORY: **VULNERABLE**

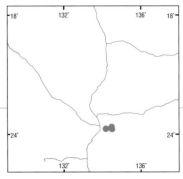

*Known locations
of Semotrachia
rossana*
● = *pre 1970*
● = *post 1970*

DESCRIPTION

Semotrachia rossana is a medium-sized (shell diameter: 11 to 12 mm) camaenid land snail, with relatively low spire. Other distinguishing features are listed in Solem (1993).

DISTRIBUTION

Solem (1993) reported that this species had been collected only from two sites along the Ross River downstream of the Ross River Resort and above N'Dhala Gorge, east of Alice Springs.
The two sites are less than 0.5 km apart. Some more recent museum collections attributed to this species extend this known range marginally.

Conservation reserves where reported:
None (the existing records are just outside N'Dhala Gorge National Park).

ECOLOGY

There is no published information on the ecology of this species.

CONSERVATION ASSESSMENT

This species is one of a set of snail species listed here that is relatively restricted in its geographic range and is exposed to processes that may lead to its decline. This species is classified as **Vulnerable** (under criteria B1ab(i,ii,iii)+2ab(i,ii,iii)) based on:
• extent of occurrence less than 20 000 km²;
• area of occupancy less than 2000 km²;
• known to exist at fewer than 10 locations; and
• continuing decline observed, inferred or projected.

THREATENING PROCESSES

There is no direct evidence that any factors have caused a decline in the numbers or distribution of this species. However, there has been no monitoring of status, and this species may be detrimentally affected by an increased frequency and intensity of fire, fuelled in part by invasive exotic grasses, particularly buffel grass (*Cenchrus ciliaris*).

CONSERVATION OBJECTIVES AND MANAGEMENT

There are no existing management programs for land snail species in the Northern Territory.

Research priorities are to:
• conduct further surveys to determine whether populations occur elsewhere; and
• identify specific threats to any of the known populations.

A monitoring program should be established for at least representative populations.

The management priority is to better safeguard the known populations through establishment of appropriate fire regimes.

Compiled by Colin Wilson, John Woinarski, Vince Kessner, Michael Braby [April 2006] / **References:** Solem, A. (1993). Camaenid land snails from Western and central Australia (Mollusca: Pulmonata: Camaenidae). VI Taxa from the red centre. *Records of the Western Australian Museum* Supplement 43, 983-1459.

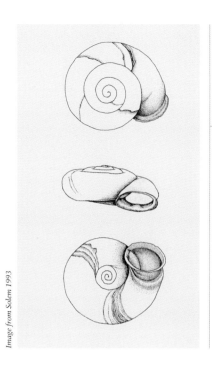

Image from Solem 1993

Runutjirbana land snail

Semotrachia runutjirbana

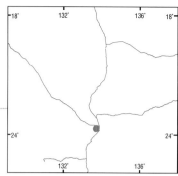

Known locations of Semotrachia runutjirbana
● = *pre 1970*
● = *post 1970*

DESCRIPTION

Semotrachia runutjirbana is a moderately small (shell diameter: 9 to 12 mm) camaenid land snail. Distinguishing features are listed in Solem (1993).

DISTRIBUTION

This species is known only from Simpsons Gap in the Runutjirba Range, west of Alice Springs.

Conservation reserves where reported:
West MacDonnell National Park

ECOLOGY

There is no published information on the ecology of this species, other than that it has been collected on rocks (Solem 1993).

CONSERVATION ASSESSMENT

This species is one of a set of snail species listed here that is relatively restricted in its geographic range and is exposed to processes that may lead to its decline. This species is classified as **Vulnerable** (under criteria B1ab(i,ii,iii)+2ab(i,ii,iii)) based on:
• extent of occurrence less than 20 000 km^2;
• area of occupancy less than 2000 km^2;
• known to exist at fewer than 10 locations; and
• continuing decline observed, inferred or projected.

THREATENING PROCESSES

There is no direct evidence that any factors have caused a decline in the numbers or distribution of this species. However, there has been no monitoring of status, and this species may be detrimentally affected by an increased frequency and intensity of fire, fuelled in part by invasive exotic grasses, particularly buffel grass (*Cenchrus ciliaris*).

CONSERVATION OBJECTIVES AND MANAGEMENT

There are no existing management programs for land snail species in the Northern Territory.

Research priorities are to:
• conduct further surveys to determine whether populations occur elsewhere; and
• identify specific threats to the known population.

A monitoring program should be established.

The management priority is to better safeguard the known population through establishment of appropriate fire regimes.

Compiled by Colin Wilson, John Woinarski, Vince Kessner, Michael Braby [April 2006] / **References:** Solem, A. (1993). Camaenid land snails from Western and central Australia (Mollusca: Pulmonata: Camaenidae). VI Taxa from the red centre. *Records of the Western Australian Museum* Supplement 43, 983-1459.

Image from Solem 1993

Winnecke land snail

Semotrachia winneckeana

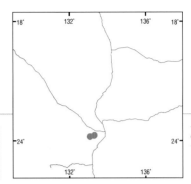

Known locations of Semotrachia winneckeana
● = pre 1970
● = post 1970

CONSERVATION STATUS
AUSTRALIA: **NOT LISTED**
NORTHERN TERRITORY: **VULNERABLE**

DESCRIPTION

Semotrachia winneckeana is a very small (shell diameter: 5.4 to 6.6 mm) camaenid land snail, with a flat to, at most, slightly elevated spire. Other distinguishing features are listed in Solem (1993).

DISTRIBUTION

This species is known from only two isolated sites in different drainage systems west of Alice Springs. One is in Spencer Gorge in the Chewings Range in the upper Hugh River catchment; the other is at Ellery Creek Big Hole in the Heavitree Range in the Finke River catchment. The two sites are 28 km apart. Solem (1993) was uncertain whether these two populations represented the same or different species, and he also noted that specimens from Standley Chasm (about 14 km east of the Spencer Gorge site) may also be referable to this species.

Conservation reserves where reported: Owen Springs Reserve, West MacDonnell National Park.

ECOLOGY

It occurs under rocks and in leaf litter under fig trees and in sheltered locations.

CONSERVATION ASSESSMENT

This species is one of a set of snail species listed here that is relatively restricted in its geographic range and is exposed to processes that may lead to its decline. This species is classified as **Vulnerable** (under criteria B1ab(i,ii,iii)+2ab(i,ii,iii)) based on:
• extent of occurrence less than 20 000 km^2;
• area of occupancy less than 2000 km^2;
• known to exist at fewer than 10 locations; and
• continuing decline observed, inferred or projected.

THREATENING PROCESSES

There is no direct evidence that any factors have caused a decline in the numbers or distribution of this species. However, there has been no monitoring of status, and this species may be detrimentally affected by an increased frequency and intensity of fire, fuelled in part by invasive exotic grasses, particularly buffel grass (*Cenchrus ciliaris*).

CONSERVATION OBJECTIVES AND MANAGEMENT

There are no existing management programs for land snail species in the Northern Territory.

Research priorities are to:
• conduct further surveys to determine whether populations occur elsewhere;
• identify specific threats to any of the known populations; and
• further refine the taxonomic position of this species.

A monitoring program should be established for at least representative populations.

The management priority is to better safeguard the known populations through establishment of appropriate fire regimes.

Compiled by Colin Wilson, John Woinarski, Vince Kessner, Michael Braby [April 2006] / **References:** Solem, A. (1993). Camaenid land snails from Western and central Australia (Mollusca: Pulmonata: Camaenidae). VI Taxa from the red centre. *Records of the Western Australian Museum* Supplement 43, 983-1459.

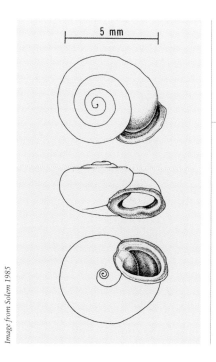

Image from Solem 1985

5 mm

Victoria's land snail

Setobaudinia victoriana

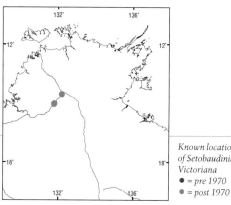

CONSERVATION STATUS
AUSTRALIA: **NOT LISTED**
NORTHERN TERRITORY: **VULNERABLE**

DESCRIPTION

Setobaudinia victoriana is a small (shell diameter: 5.2 to 6.8 mm) camaenid land snail, with a raised parietal lip, laterally compressed periphery, absence of a palatal node and small umbilicus whose last whorl decoils very rapidly (Solem 1985).

DISTRIBUTION

Solem (1985) reported that the few collections of this snail were from in and around a limestone sinkhole adjacent to the Victoria Highway, 86 km south-west of Katherine. Some more recent museum collections attributed to this species extend this known range marginally.

Conservation reserves where reported: None

ECOLOGY

The recorded specimens were in leaf litter at the base of large limestone boulders in a marshy sink, or buried in soil in open eucalyptus woodland (V. Kessner *pers. obs.*; Solem 1985).

CONSERVATION ASSESSMENT

This snail is known from an extremely restricted range. It is considered to qualify as **Vulnerable** (under criterion D2) based on:
• area of occupancy less than 20 km²; and
• known to exist at fewer than five locations.

THREATENING PROCESSES

It is possible that this land snail has always been extremely restricted in range and there is no direct evidence that any factors have caused a decline in their numbers or distribution. However, land snails are susceptible to the impacts of an increased frequency and intensity of fire. Exotic pastures, such as gamba grass (*Andropogon gayanus*) and mission grass (*Pennisetum polystachion*) create far more fuel than do the native grasses and hence frequently carry destructive fires. These exotic grasses are spreading rapidly. Overgrazing by livestock and feral animals can affect land snail habitat by trampling or disturbing aestivation sites. Cane toads, which colonised the range of this snail in about 2005, may have a significant effect, but no studies have assessed this possible impact.

CONSERVATION OBJECTIVES AND MANAGEMENT

There are no existing management programs for land snail species in the Northern Territory.

A monitoring program should be established.

Research priorities are to:
• conduct further surveys to determine whether populations occur elsewhere; and
• identify specific threats to the known population.

Compiled by Colin Wilson, John Woinarski, Vince Kessner, Michael Braby [April 2006] / **References:** Solem, A. (1985). Camaenid land snails from Western and central Australia (Mollusca: Pulmonata: Camaenidae). V Remaining Kimberley genera and addenda to the Kimberley. *Records of the Western Australian Museum* Supplement 20, 707-981.

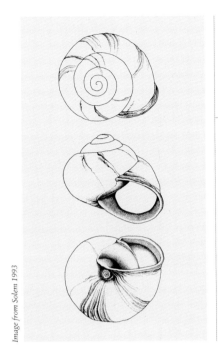

Image from Solem 1993

Bednall's land snail
Sinumelon bednalli

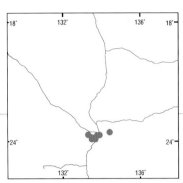

Known locations of Sinumelon bednalli
● = pre 1970
● = post 1970

DESCRIPTION

Sinumelon bednalli is a large (shell diameter: 20 to 26 mm) greenish-yellow camaenid land snail, with a weak reddish spiral colour band. The apex and spire are usually strongly and evenly elevated and there are 4 to 5 whorls (Solem 1993).

DISTRIBUTION

This species is endemic to the Northern Territory. It has been collected at only seven sites in the Macdonnell Ranges of central Australia, from Hugh Gorge 60 km west of Alice Springs to Trephina Gorge, 50 km to the east, and to a location 25 km south of Alice Springs (V. Kessner *pers. comm.*).

Conservation reserves where reported: Alice Springs Telegraph Station Historical Reserve, Owen Springs Reserve, Trephina Gorge Nature Park, West MacDonnell National Park.

ECOLOGY

The species is restricted to areas around fig trees. Adults aestivate in loose litter under the trees (V. Kessner *pers. obs.*).

CONSERVATION ASSESSMENT

Bednall's land snail has very specific habitat requirements and has been collected at a relatively small number of sites. It is a large species, yet has rarely been collected (dead or alive) and is thought to have almost disappeared from around Alice Springs.

The species qualifies as **Critically Endangered** (under criteria B2ab(iii,v)) based on:
- area of occupancy less than 10 km^2;
- severely fragmented; and
- continuing decline, observed, inferred or projected.

THREATENING PROCESSES

The species has almost disappeared from the Alice Springs area under pressure from urban expansion and fires in the exotic buffel grass. Other populations are threatened by fires and buffel grass (V. Kessner *pers. obs.*).

CONSERVATION OBJECTIVES AND MANAGEMENT

There are no existing management programs for land snail species in the Northern Territory.

Research priorities are to:
- conduct further surveys to determine whether populations occur elsewhere; and
- identify specific threats to all of the known populations.

A monitoring program should be established for at least representative populations.

Management priorities are to:
- protect the habitat from urban expansion;
- better safeguard the known populations through encouragement of appropriate fire regimes, and prevention of weed invasion.

Compiled by Simon Ward ,Vince Kessner, Michael Braby, John Woinarski [April 2006] / **References:** Solem, A. (1993). Camaenid land snails from Western and central Australia (Mollusca: Pulmonata: Camaenidae). VI Taxa from the red centre. *Records of the Western Australian Museum* Supplement 43, 983-1459.

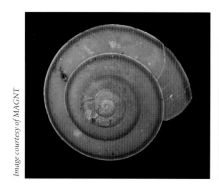

Image courtesy of MAGNT

Land snail
Trochomorpha melvillensis

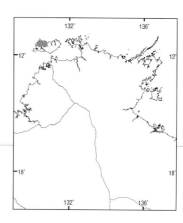

Known locations of Trochomorpha melvillensis
● = pre 1970
● = post 1970

CONSERVATION STATUS
AUSTRALIA: **NOT LISTED**
NORTHERN TERRITORY: **VULNERABLE**

DESCRIPTION
Trochomorpha melvillensis is a distinctive medium-sized (shell diameter: 9.9 to 12.4 mm) non-camaenid landsnail, with a spiral red band and sharp peripheral keel. It has a depressed spire, crowded radial sculpture and a thick parietal callus (Solem 1988).

DISTRIBUTION
The few records of this species are all from Melville Island (Garden Point, Timarambu Creek and Milakapiti).

Conservation reserves where reported: None

ECOLOGY
This species occurs under logs and tree bark in coastal monsoon rainforests.

CONSERVATION ASSESSMENT
This species appears to be restricted to Melville Island. Its known range is highly restricted and there has been sufficient survey effort in the region to suggest that it is highly localised. It fits the criteria for **Vulnerable** (under criterion D2) based on:
• area of occupancy less than 20 km²; and
• known to exist at fewer than five locations.

THREATENING PROCESSES
It is possible that this land snail has always been extremely restricted in range as there is no direct evidence that any factors have yet caused a decline in their numbers or distribution.

However, in general, land snails are susceptible to the impacts of an increased frequency and intensity of fire, a change potentially exacerbated by spread of exotic pasture grasses.

CONSERVATION OBJECTIVES AND MANAGEMENT
There is no existing management program for land snail species in the Northern Territory.

Research priorities are to:
• conduct further surveys to determine whether populations occur elsewhere; and
• identify specific threats to the known population.

Management priorities are to:
• better safeguard the known populations through containing the spread of exotic grasses; and
• establish a monitoring program for the species.

Compiled by Colin Wilson, John Woinarski, Vince Kessner, Michael Braby [April 2006] / **References:** Solem, A. (1988). Non-Camaenid land snails of the Kimberley and Northern Territory, Australia. I. Systematics, affinities and ranges. *Invertebrate Taxonomy* 4, 455-605.

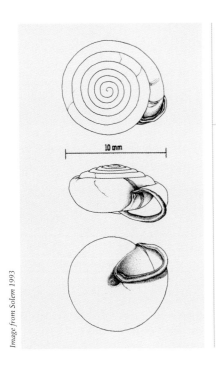

Image from Solem 1993

Watt's land snail
Vidumelon wattii

CONSERVATION STATUS
AUSTRALIA: **NOT LISTED**
NORTHERN TERRITORY: **VULNERABLE**

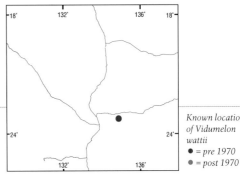

*Known locations
of Vidumelon
wattii*
● = *pre 1970*
● = *post 1970*

DESCRIPTION

Vidumelon wattii is a small to medium-sized (shell diameter: 10 to 12 mm) and distinctive camaenid land snail, with many very tightly coiled whorls. Other distinguishing features are listed in Solem (1993).

DISTRIBUTION

This snail is restricted to the basins of Maud and Florence Creeks on the south side of the Harts Range, north-east of Alice Springs. Solem (1993) considered that the total extent was 5 to 10 km.

Conservation reserves where reported: None

ECOLOGY

Whereas most of the snails listed here have specialised teeth adapted to scraping algae off rocks, this species has the teeth of a generalist feeder on dead plant matter. Within its narrow known range, it has been reported to be common in leaf litter and relatively scarce under rocks (Solem 1993). It aestivates in soil.

CONSERVATION ASSESSMENT

This species is one of a set of snail species listed here that is relatively restricted in its geographic range and exposed to processes that may lead to its decline. This species is classified as **Vulnerable** (under criteria B1ab(i,ii,iii)+2ab(i,ii,iii)) based on:
• extent of occurrence less than 20 000 km²;
• area of occupancy less than 2000 kmv;
• known to exist at fewer than 10 locations; and
• a continuing decline observed, inferred or projected.

THREATENING PROCESSES

There is no direct evidence that any factors have caused a decline in the numbers or distribution of this species. However, there has been no monitoring of status and this species may be detrimentally affected by an increased frequency and intensity of fire, fuelled in part by invasive exotic grasses, particularly buffel grass (*Cenchrus ciliaris*). Cattle may affect this species through mortality from direct trampling or through compaction of soil.

CONSERVATION OBJECTIVES AND MANAGEMENT

There are no existing management programs for land snail species in the Northern Territory.

Research priorities are to:
• conduct further surveys to determine whether populations occur elsewhere; and
• identify specific threats to any of the known populations.

A monitoring program should be established for at least representative populations.

The management priority is to better safeguard the known populations through establishment of appropriate fire regimes.

Compiled by Colin Wilson, John Woinarski, Vince Kessner, Michael Braby [April 2006] / **References:** Solem, A. (1993). Camaenid land snails from Western and central Australia (Mollusca: Pulmonata: Camaenidae). VI Taxa from the red centre. *Records of the Western Australian Museum* Supplement 43, 983-1459.

Image courtesy of Christopher Palmer

Desert sand-skipper
Croitana aestiva

CONSERVATION STATUS
AUSTRALIA: **ENDANGERED**
NORTHERN TERRITORY: **ENDANGERED**

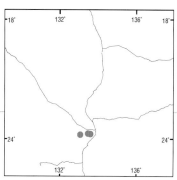

Known locations of the desert sand-skipper
● = *pre 1970*
● = *post 1970*

DESCRIPTION
The desert sand-skipper is a small brown butterfly with pale yellow markings. It has a wingspan of about 22 mm. Like other members of the skipper family, the clubs of the antennae are sharply bent near their base.

DISTRIBUTION
The desert sand-skipper is restricted to the West MacDonnell Ranges, Northern Territory (Edwards 1979; Braby 2000). It is known from four sites near Alice Springs. Six specimens were collected in February 1966: five from 25 km west-south-west (by road) of Alice Springs, and one from Standley Chasm 41 km west of Alice Springs (Edwards 1979; M.S. Upton *pers. comm.*). A further two specimens were collected from Ellery Gorge about 75 km west of Alice Springs in April 1972 (Braby 2000). After an absence of records for more than 30 years, the desert sand-skipper was re-discovered in February 2007, inhabiting gorges in the Chewings Range, west of Alice Springs.

Conservation reserves where reported:
West MacDonnell National Park

ECOLOGY
Very little is known of the ecology of the desert sand-skipper. Adults have been collected following above average rainfall. Three of the known sites are associated with moister, rocky areas that are buffered from climatic extremes, and one site lies in the more exposed sandy open plains and flats that occur between the ranges. The larval food plant and breeding habitat are unknown; however, larvae of other *Croitana* species feed on grasses in the genera *Enteropogon* and *Austrostipa* (Poaceae) (Atkins and Miller 1987; Braby 2000). Adults of these species remain close to the breeding areas and have been collected feeding at daisy flowers (Asteraceae).

CONSERVATION ASSESSMENT
The desert sand-skipper has been recorded on only few occasions. Prior to its recent re-discovery, a number of entomologists (E.D. Edwards, A.F. Atkins, C.G. Miller, M.F. Braby) searched extensively for the desert sand-skipper from the known locations and nearby areas, including the East MacDonnell Ranges, but failed to find the butterfly. Presumably the species is restricted to the MacDonnell Ranges, but it remains unclear if it has a specialised ecology, such as having an unpredictable flight period. Conservation categorisation is therefore difficult as there is a lack of information on population trends and direct threatening processes. Although there is no evidence of a decline in distribution or numbers of the desert sand-skipper, the 30-year gap in records is cause for serious concern. Moreover, there have been substantial changes to the landscape in central Australia in recent decades and a number of potential threats have been identified.

Accordingly, the species qualifies as **Endangered** (under criteria B1ab(i,ii,iii,iv)+2ab(i,ii,iii,iv)) based on:
• extent of occurrence less than 5000 km²;
• area of occupancy less than 500 km²;
• known to exist at fewer than five locations; and
• inferred or projected population decline.

THREATENING PROCESSES
Two major threats within the MacDonnell Ranges and their general vicinity have been identified. These include invasion of the introduced buffel grass and changes to the fire regime. These factors are possibly having an adverse impact on the habitat of the desert sand-skipper, in turn affecting populations of the butterfly. However, it should be emphasised that the ecological requirements of this species are poorly understood.

Buffel grass (*Cenchrus ciliaris*), was recently introduced as a pasture grass to inland central Australia. A native of southern Asia and east Africa, it is now the dominant ground cover throughout much of the arid landscape near Alice Springs, including the low-lying areas between the rocky hills of the MacDonnell Ranges. The grass forms dense monocultures and eventually displaces the native plant species, particularly other grasses (Clarke *et al.* 2005). The spread of buffel grass has been implicated in the decline of several animals and plants in central Australia. It is therefore possible that buffel grass has reduced the extent of the larval food plant of the desert sand-skipper.

continued.../

Croitana aestiva continued...

As a consequence of the invasion of buffel grass, there has been a concomitant increase in the frequency and intensity of fire. Buffel grass fuels fires that are much hotter than those generated by native grasses, but is itself resistant to fire. The greater frequency and intensity of wild fires that occur following buffel grass invasion could influence availability of larval food plants as well as have a negative impact upon survival of the early stages of the butterfly.

CONSERVATION OBJECTIVES AND MANAGEMENT

There is no existing management program for this species in the Northern Territory.

Research priorities are to:
• undertake surveys in the MacDonnell Ranges to locate additional populations and establish the distribution of the species;
• investigate the basic biology and ecology of the species to determine larval food plants and habitat requirements; and
• establish a monitoring program in an area where the species is found to persist in order to detect possible changes in range or abundance, and to measure the impacts of threatening processes.

Management priorities are to:
• control the spread of buffel grass; and
• maintain appropriate burning practices in locations where populations are found.

Compiled by Michael Braby, Colin Wilson, Chris Pavey, Chris Palmer [March 2007] / **References:** Atkins, A., and Miller, C.G. (1987). The life history of *Croitana arenaria* Edwards, 1979 (Lepidoptera: Hesperiidae: Trapezitinae). *Australian Entomological Magazine* 14, 73-75. / Braby, M.F. (2000). *Butterflies of Australia: their identification, biology and distribution.* (CSIRO, Melbourne.) Clarke, P.J., Latz, P.K., and Albrecht, D.E. (2005). Long-term changes in semi-arid vegetation: invasion of an exotic perennial grass has larger effects than rainfall variability. *Journal of Vegetation Science* 16, 237-248. / Edwards, E.D. (1979). Two new species of *Croitana* Waterhouse (Lepidoptera: Hesperiidae) from central Australia. *Australian Entomological Magazine* 6, 29-38.

Image courtesy of Michael Braby (CSIRO)

Gove crow
Euploea alcathoe enastri

CONSERVATION STATUS
AUSTRALIA: **ENDANGERED**
NORTHERN TERRITORY: **ENDANGERED**

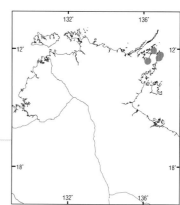

*Known locations
of the Gove crow*
● = *pre 1970*
● = *post 1970*

DESCRIPTION
The Gove crow is a large, black-brown butterfly with variable white spots near the margins of the wings. The wingspan is about 70 mm. The male is velvet-black above and dark black-brown beneath. The female is paler chocolate-brown. There are several other similar-looking crow butterflies present in the Top End: see Braby (2000) for diagnostic identification characteristics.

DISTRIBUTION
The Gove crow is restricted to the Gove Peninsula in north-eastern Arnhem Land, Northern Territory. It is currently known only from four sites. It was first discovered at Rocky Bay near Yirrkala in 1988 by G. Martin, and was subsequently recorded at three other locations, including Mosquito Creek Port Bradshaw, near Mount Bonner, and the upper Goromuru River (Fenner 1991, 1992).

Conservation reserves where reported:
Nanydjaka Indigenous Protected Area

ECOLOGY
Until a recent study (Braby 2006), little was known of the ecology of the Gove crow, although the life history, larval food plant and habitat preference had been documented for subspecies *E. a. misenus* from Torres Strait islands, north Queensland (Lambkin 2001). All specimens have been collected from patches of tropical rainforest (evergreen monsoon vine-forest) associated with permanent groundwater seepages.

Males are usually observed within small glades inside the forest or near its boundary with the surrounding savanna woodland. Females are more commonly observed in tall paperbark swampland at the edge of the rainforest (Fenner 1991; L. Wilson *pers. comm.*).

Two larval food plants (both vines) have been recorded: *Gymnanthera oblonga* and *Parsonsia alboflavescens* (Braby 2006).

CONSERVATION ASSESSMENT
Conservation categorisation is difficult because of a lack of information on population trends and direct threatening processes. The species appears to be naturally rare, with few individuals observed at each site. There is no evidence that any external factors have caused a decline in population size or distribution of the Gove crow. However, a number of potential threats have been identified on the Gove Peninsula and, if left uncontrolled, it can be reasonably inferred that these threats will reduce the extent of critical habitat and ultimately lead to decline of the Gove crow.

Accordingly, the species qualifies as **Endangered** (under criteria B1ab(i,ii,iii,iv)+B2ab(i,ii,iii,iv)) based on:
• extent of occurrence less than 2500 km^2;
• area of occupancy less than 500 km^2;
• known to exist at fewer than five locations; and
• inferred or projected population decline.

THREATENING PROCESSES
There are at least three potential factors on the Gove Peninsula that could lead to a significant decline in range and/or population size and possible extinction of the Gove crow: altered fire regimes, invasion of habitat by an aggressive exotic ant, and feral mammals.

Changes in the frequency, intensity and patchiness of fire in the landscape on the Gove Peninsula may ultimately lead to the demise of the monsoon rainforest patches, the critical habitat of the Gove crow. Such changes may be exacerbated by the fuel loads supported by exotic invasive grasses. Mission grass (*Pennisetum polystachion*) has recently become established in the town of Nhulunbuy. This grass increases the fuel load normally found in native savannas by three to five fold and, as a perennial, pushes the burning season later into the drier, windier time of the year (Panton 1993). Mission grass carries destructive hot fires into the edges of monsoon rainforest patches, leading to their shrinkage and eventual disappearance. If the rapid spread around Darwin (Kean and Price 2003) is repeated around Nhulunbuy, the resultant increase in intensity of fires on the Gove Peninsula may cause the disappearance of many wet rainforest patches, including those on which the Gove crow depends.

There is widespread concern that traditional knowledge and land management practices amongst the Yolngu Aboriginal community in north-eastern

continued.../

Arnhem Land are not being passed on from elders to the next generation.

This knowledge and management includes an understanding of traditional burning practices – the frequency and seasonal timing of patch burns. It is important that traditional land management practices are maintained on Gove Peninsula: incorrect (excessive) burning will ultimately reduce the extent of the monsoon rainforest patches.

In addition, overland access to Nhulunbuy has been recently upgraded, as has the local network of roads across the Peninsula. The more intensive land use and greater ease of access within this region has led to an increase in the frequency and extent of fires. An increase in fire associated with the road in central Arnhem Land has already been implicated in the disappearance of patches of monsoon rainforest similar to that used by the Gove crow (W.J. Panton *pers. comm.*).

The yellow crazy ant, (*Anoplolepis gracilipes*), has recently been recorded from the Gove Peninsula. This ant has a long history of environmental damage across the tropics, most recently manifested on Christmas Island where it is damaging rainforest vegetation, red land crabs and nesting sea birds. Young *et al.* (2001) concluded that the yellow crazy ant is a "serious threat to the invertebrate fauna of monsoon rainforests in northern Australia." The ant favours the permanently wet spring-fed rainforest patches used by the Gove crow.

Feral mammals, particularly water buffalo, (*Bubalus bubalis*), and, to a lesser extent, pig, (*Sus scrofa*), occur on the Gove Peninsula. These animals are known to damage or degrade monsoon rainforest patches through their effects on understorey plants, and are thus a potential threat to the integrity of the habitat of the Gove crow, especially the swamplands adjacent to the monsoon rainforest.

CONSERVATION OBJECTIVES AND MANAGEMENT

A recovery plan for this butterfly (Braby 2007) is due to be implemented in 2007, although many actions have been undertaken since 2006 collaboratively between scientists of the Department of Natural Resources, Environment and The Arts and rangers from Dhimurru Land Management Aboriginal Corporation.

Research priorities are to:
• undertake surveys in the Gove Peninsula to search for additional populations;

• investigate the basic biology and ecology of the species to determine larval food plants and breeding requirements, as well as population attributes such as longevity, movement patterns and dry season behaviour. Breeding and aggregation sites can then be identified and protected;
• establish a long-term monitoring program at one or more of the key sites in order to detect possible changes in breeding range or abundance, and to measure the impacts of threatening processes.

Management priorities are to:
• control and eradicate mission grass, and maintain vigilance against other grassy weeds that have the potential to become a serious threat on the Gove Peninsula;
• continue to implement a survey, monitoring and eradication program for the yellow crazy ant;
• maintain appropriate fire management practices; and
• develop a feral animal survey and control strategy for buffalo and pigs.

Compiled by Michael Braby, Colin Wilson [December 2006] / **References:** Braby, M.F. (2000). *Butterflies of Australia. Their identification, biology and distribution. Vol. 2.* (CSIRO Publishing, Melbourne.) Braby, M.F. (2007). National Recovery plan for the Gove crow butterfly *Euploea alcathoe enastri.* (NT Department of Natural Resources Environment, Darwin.) / Fenner, T.L. (1991). A new subspecies of *Euploea alcathoe* (Godart) (Lepidoptera: Nymphalidae) from the Northern Territory, Australia. *Australian Entomological Magazine* 18, 149-156. / Fenner, T.L. (1992). Correction and addendum. *Australian Entomological Magazine* 19, 93. / Kean, L., and Price, O. (2003). The extent of Mission grasses and Gamba grass in the Darwin region of Australia's Northern Territory. *Pacific Conservation Biology* 8, 281-290. / Lambkin, T.A. (2001). The life history of *Euploea alcathoe monilifera* (Moore) and its relationship to *E. a. eichhorni* Staudinger (Lepidoptera: Danainae). *Australian Entomologist* 28, 129-136. / Panton, W.J. (1993). Changes in post World War II distribution and status of monsoon rainforests in the Darwin area. *Australian Geographer* 24, 50-59. / Young, G. R., Bellis, G. A., Brown, G. R., and Smith, E. S. C. (2001). The crazy ant, *Anoplolepis gracilipes* (Smith) (Hymenoptera: Formicidae) in east Arnhem Land, Australia. *Australian Entomologist* 28, 97-104.

Image courtesy of Michael Braby (CSIRO)

Dodd's azure
Ogyris iphis doddi

CONSERVATION STATUS
AUSTRALIA: **NOT LISTED**
NORTHERN TERRITORY: **ENDANGERED**

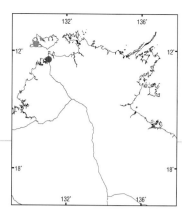

*Known locations
of Dodd's azure
● = pre 1970
● = post 1970*

DESCRIPTION

Dodd's azure is a medium-sized butterfly, with a wingspan of about 32 mm. The upperside is shining, iridescent pale blue. The underside is pale brown, with two or three broad brown-black bars edged with iridescent blue on the forewing.

DISTRIBUTION

Dodd's azure is apparently restricted to the Top End of the Northern Territory. It is known only from two sites: Darwin (Waterhouse and Lyell 1914; Dodd 1935) and Melville Island (Braby 2000). It was first discovered at Darwin in 1908-09 by F.P. Dodd and his son Walter but since that time it has not been positively recorded, although an adult resembling this species was observed hill-topping at Bens Hill Darwin in March 1992 (Meyer *et al.* 2006). Only a single specimen is known from Melville Island; it was collected from Pularumpi at light in June 1986 by P. Horner (Braby 2000; Meyer *et al.* 2006). Sands and New (2002) suggested the species may occur in the Mitchell Plateau of the Kimberley, Western Australia, based on an unconfirmed sighting.

Conservation reserves where reported: None

ECOLOGY

The general ecology of this species is well known for the nominate subspecies *O. i. iphis* from Queensland, but little has been recorded for the Northern Territory subspecies. Adults of Dodd's azure have been recorded in February, June,

September and November (Waterhouse and Lyell 1914; Braby 2000; Meyer *et al.* 2006). Dodd (1935) indicated that the larvae were feeding on mistletoe and that they were attended by ants. Specimens lodged in the Australian Museum Sydney, and the Australian National Insect Collection, Canberra, clearly indicate that Dodds' material from Darwin comprised reared specimens.

In north-eastern Queensland, the larvae of the nominate subspecies feed on foliage of mistletoes, including several species of *Amyema* and *Dendrophthoe* (Loranthaceae), and are always attended by ants, *Froggattella kirbii* (Braby 2000). The larvae shelter during the day in hollows or cracks in the haustorium of the mistletoe where the attendant ants have established a nest, and pupate in similar situations. The adults fly rapidly among the tree tops, but are rarely observed. There are at least two generations annually in Queensland, where it occurs in dry eucalypt woodland and open forest, usually on sandy soils derived from sandstone or granite (Braby 2000). The species is highly localised, but it can be seasonally abundant in places where the food plants and attendant ant occur together.

CONSERVATION ASSESSMENT

Fewer than 10 specimens of Dodd's azure are known to have been collected. Eight of these specimens were reared by the Dodds. However, it is not clear if lack of material and apparent rarity is due to insufficient survey effort or that the subspecies is in decline.

On the whole, adults of this species are rarely collected because they are relatively cryptic and difficult to sample due to their extreme localization and arboreal specialisation on mistletoe food plants, which frequently grow in the canopy of eucalypts.

For the Queensland subspecies, most collectors obtain material by rearing the immature stages. However, Meyer *et al.* (2006) noted that, despite extensive searching by several specialists in the Darwin region, they did not locate breeding colonies of *O. i. doddi*.

Conservation categorisation is therefore difficult as there is a lack of detailed information on geographic distribution and population trends. However, one threatening process has been identified that may have led to local extinction, at least in the Darwin region. Furthermore, there are currently no known extant populations.

Accordingly, the species qualifies as **Endangered** (under criteria B1ab(i,ii,iii,iv)+2ab(i,ii,iii,iv)) based on:

- extent of occurrence less than 5000 km^2;
- area of occupancy less than 500 km^2;
- known to exist at fewer than five locations; and
- inferred or projected decline.

THREATENING PROCESSES

There is no evidence that any external factors have caused a decline in numbers or distribution of Dodd's azure. However, some factors may threaten its viability.

continued.../

Darwin, and more generally throughout the Top End, has seen an increase in the frequency and intensity of burning brought about by urban and rural expansion and the uncontrolled spread of introduced perennial pasture grasses. As a result of this increased fire intensity there is anecdotal evidence to suggest that mistletoes, which readily succumb to fire, comprise a declining resource in tropical savanna woodland and other habitats on which *Ogyris iphis* and related species depend (Braby 2000; Sands and New 2002).

Within its limited range, much of its preferred eucalypt forest habitat is subject to escalating levels of land clearing, for horticulture, forestry plantation (on Tiwi Islands) or residential areas.

CONSERVATION OBJECTIVES AND MANAGEMENT

There is no existing management program for this species in the Northern Territory.

Research priorities are to:
• undertake surveys in the Tiwi Islands and the Darwin region to establish if the species is still extant, and elsewhere in the Top End to locate additional populations;
• investigate the basic biology and ecology of the subspecies to determine larval food plants and habitat requirements. Breeding sites can then be identified and protected; and

• establish a monitoring program in order to detect possible changes in range or abundance, and identify and measure impacts of threatening processes.

Management priorities are to:
• encourage appropriate fire management;
• control the spread of exotic grasses; and
• maintain adequate areas of its preferred habitat within its limited distribution.

Compiled by Michael Braby, John Woinarski [December 2006] / **References:** Braby, M.F. (2000). *Butterflies of Australia: their identification, biology and distribution.* (CSIRO Publishing, Melbourne.) / Dodd, W.D. (1935). Meanderings of a naturalist. *The North Queensland Register.* / Meyer, C.E., Weir, R.P., and Wilson, D.N. (2006). Butterfly (Lepidoptera) records from the Darwin region, Northern Territory. *Australian Entomologist* 33, 9-22. / Sands, D.P.A., and New, T.R. (2002). *The Action Plan for Australian Butterflies.* (Environment Australia, Canberra.) / Waterhouse, G.A., and Lyell, G. (1914). *The Butterflies of Australia. A monograph of the Australian Rhopalocera.* (Angus and Robertson, Sydney.)

Image courtesy of CSIRO Entomology

Atlas moth
Attacus wardi

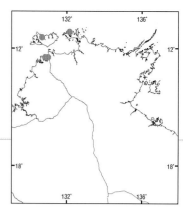

*Known locations
of the
Atlas moth*
● = *pre 1970*
● = *post 1970*

DESCRIPTION

The Atlas moth is a very large, spectacular insect, with a wingspan of about 17 cm. It is rusty-brown, with a double white band and a large, irregular white spot on each wing.

The species was originally described by L.W. Rothschild as a subspecies of *A. dohertyi* from the Oriental Region and for many years has been treated as such (e.g. Common 1990). However, Peigler (1989) treated it as a distinct species closely allied to *A. intermedius,* and this view was adopted by Edwards (1996). *Attacus wardi* is the smallest species of the genus.

DISTRIBUTION

The Atlas moth is endemic to the Top End, Northern Territory. It is known only from three localities: Darwin (Dodd 1935; Common 1990), Black Point Cobourg Peninsula (Peigler 1989.) and Melville Island (G. Martin, V. Kessner *pers. comm.*). The original specimens were reared from pupae collected from 'Port Darwin' in late 1908 and early 1909 by F.P. Dodd and one of his sons, Walter. A single specimen was collected from Cobourg Peninsula at light during rain on 28 January 1977 by E.D. Edwards (specimen in ANIC); subsequently a second specimen was collected from the same site at light in 1985 by A. Withers of Parks and Wildlife Commission of NT. The latter specimen was donated to the Museum and Art Gallery of the Northern Territory but it has not been located. More recently, a wing of the Atlas moth was collected from Milikapiti (Snake Bay)

Melville Island in March 2005 by G. Martin (specimen in private collection of D.N. Wilson). An Atlas moth was also observed near a coastal rainforest on Melville Island in the 1970s (V. Kessner *pers. comm.*).

The records from Cape York Peninsula, Queenland (Peigler 1989) are considered to be erroneous.

Conservation reserves where reported:
Garig Gunak Barlu National Park

ECOLOGY

Very little is known of the ecology of the Atlas moth. The adults are nocturnal and have been recorded during the wet season, from January to March. The Dodds collected a relatively large series of specimens, and these mostly appear to have been reared from pupae collected from the field. However, Walter Dodd noted that a few males were attracted from nearby patches of 'jungle' (monsoon rainforest) during adult emergence (Dodd 1935). Presumably these males were responding to pheromone(s) released by unmated females that had emerged in captivity. Unfortunately, the early stages, breeding biology, larval food plants and preferred habitat of the Atlas moth were not documented by the Dodds. An unpublished manuscript prepared by F.P. Dodd held at the Queensland Musuem states that some adults emerged from pupae within a few days, others up to three days, but one pupa remained dormant, emerging as an adult 14 months later in January 1910 in Kuranda, Queensland.

The species is almost certainly restricted to coastal monsoon rainforest (D.A. Lane *pers. comm.*), and adults are seasonal, probably with a single short flight period during the rainy period.

Related species of *Attacus* have large, brightly-coloured larvae with soft bristles and sparse tufts of hair over their bodies. They feed openly during the day on foliage of a wide range of food plants (Herbison-Evans and Crossley 2001). Pupation occurs in a hard, brown dense silken cocoon wrapped in leaves and suspended from, or attached to, the food plant (Holloway 1987). Paukstadt and Paukstadt (1993) described and illustrated the life history of *A. dohertyi* from western Timor and recorded cocoons from *Persea americana* (Avocado) and *Annona muricata* (Sour Sop).

CONSERVATION ASSESSMENT

Although the Dodds reared a large number of specimens during their 10 month stay in Darwin early last century, there are no further records of the Atlas moth from the Darwin region. Despite careful searching over the past 24 years (1982–2006) by G. Martin and the general willingness of the local community to donate unusually large and conspicuous insects to the Museum, the species has not been recorded from Darwin for almost 100 years. The last specimen recorded from Cobourg Peninsula (20 years ago) was the only individual observed during 11 years residence in the area (A. Withers *pers. comm.*), and none were located in targeted searches at Cobourg Peninsula during the wet season of 2006–07.

continued.../

Conservation categorisation is therefore difficult because of a lack of information on population trends and geographic distribution. However, it can be reasonably inferred that the population in the Darwin area is no longer extant, and several threatening processes may have led to its decline and local extinction.

The species qualifies as **Endangered** (under criteria B1ab(i,ii,iii)+2ab(i,ii,iii)) based on:
• extent of occurrence less than 5000 km²;
• area of occupancy less than 500 km²;
• known to exist at fewer than five locations; and
• inferred decline.

THREATENING PROCESSES

Decline of the Atlas moth in the Darwin region was probably associated with heavy use of insecticides during WWII, loss of habitat caused by Cyclone Tracey in 1974, and more recently expanding urban development (G. Martin *pers. comm.*). The patches of coastal monsoon rainforest at East Point and Lee Point, in particular, the most likely habitats of the Atlas moth, were temporarily eliminated and significantly reduced in extent by Cyclone Tracey and have taken several decades to recover. Presumably the species has not been able to re-colonise these patches from elsewhere.

CONSERVATION OBJECTIVES AND MANAGEMENT

There is no existing management program for the Atlas moth in the Northern Territory.

Research priorities are to:
• undertake surveys on the Tiwi Islands and Cobourg Peninsula to establish if the species is still extant, and elsewhere in coastal areas of the Top End to locate additional populations;
• investigate the general biology and ecology to determine larval food plants and habitat requirements. Breeding sites can then be identified and protected; and
• establish a monitoring program in an area where the species is found to persist in order to detect possible changes in range or abundance and identify threatening processes.

Compiled by Michael Braby, Colin Wilson [April 2007] / **References:** Common, I.F.B. (1990). *Moths of Australia.* (Melbourne University Press, Melbourne.) / Dodd, W.D. (1935). Meanderings of a naturalist. The North Queensland Register. / Edwards, E.D. (1996) Saturniidae. In *Checklist of the Lepidoptera of Australia. Monographs on Australian Lepidoptera. Volume 4.* (eds E.S. Nielsen, E.D. Edwards and T.V. Rangsi). pp. 264-265. (CSIRO, Melbourne.) / Herbison-Evans, D., and Crossley, S. (2001). *Saturniidae of Australia.* http://linus.socs.uts.edu.au/~don/larvae/satu/saturniidae.html / Holloway, J.D. (1987). *The moths of Borneo: Family Saturniidae.* http://www.arbec.com.my/moths/saturniidae/saturniidae.htm / Paukstadt, U. and Paukstadt, L.H. (1993). Die Präimaginalstadien von *Attacus dohertyi* W. Rothschild 1895 von Timor, Indonesien, sowie Angaben zur Biologie und Ökologie (Lepidoptera: Saturniidae). *Entomologische Zeitschrift* (Essen) 103, 281-293. / Peigler, R.S. (1989). *A Revision of the Indo-Australian genus Attacus.* (The Lepidoptera Research Foundation, Beverly Hills.)

FISH

Image courtesy of Australian Institute of Marine Science

Whale shark

Rhincodon typus

CONSERVATION STATUS
AUSTRALIA: **VULNERABLE**
NORTHERN TERRITORY: **DATA DEFICIENT**

DESCRIPTION

The whale shark is the world's largest fish, reaching a size of 20 m. It is easily distinguished by its large size, broad flattened head, large mouth and pattern of light spots and stripes on a dark background (Last and Stevens 1994). Its ventral surface is white.

DISTRIBUTION

The whale shark has a broad distribution across most tropical and warm temperate seas. The best known populations in Australia are around Ningaloo Reef, in north-western Australia. Its distribution and status in waters around the Northern Territory is poorly known, although there are at least some anecdotal records.

Conservation reserves where reported: None

ECOLOGY

The whale shark is extremely long-lived, reaching sexual maturity at about 30 years, and having a lifespan estimated at about 100 years.

It feeds primarily by suction filter feeding, and its diet includes a broad range of plankton, small crustaceans and small schooling fish. Whale sharks may aggregate in nutrient-rich waters to feed on seasonal concentrations of tropical krill and small fish.

The whale shark is highly migratory, with Western Australian populations known to disperse to waters around Christmas Island and Indonesia, perhaps extending more broadly around the Indian Ocean and towards the Philippines.

CONSERVATION ASSESSMENT

The whale shark is recognised as Vulnerable nationally, largely because of decline due to harvesting in areas outside its seasonal Australian range. There is too little information in the Northern Territory to assess its status or evaluate the significance of the Northern Territory population relative to other areas in Australia. As such, it is regarded as **Data Deficient** in the Northern Territory.

THREATENING PROCESSES

The main threat to whale sharks is targeted commercial fishing and unregulated hunting from operators outside Australian waters of populations that seasonally visit Australian waters. Within Australian waters, the main recognised threats are reduction in food resources, disturbance by tourists (Environment Australia 2005) and illegal fishing.

CONSERVATION OBJECTIVES AND MANAGEMENT

A national recovery plan for this species was established in 2005 (Environment Australia 2005). This includes actions to increase levels of international cooperation for the conservation management of the species, and to maintain and develop monitoring programs.

Compiled by John Woinarski, Helen Larson [November 2006] / **References:** Environment Australia (2005). *Whale shark (Rhincodon typus) recovery plan, 2005-2010.* (Environment Australia, Canberra.) Last, P.R., and Stevens, J.D. (1994). *Sharks and Rays of Australia.* (CSIRO, Melbourne.)

Image courtesy of Dave Watts & Lochman Transparencies

Grey nurse shark
Carcharias taurus

CONSERVATION STATUS
AUSTRALIA: **CRITICALLY ENDANGERED** *(East coast population)*
VULNERABLE *(West coast population)*
NORTHERN TERRITORY: **DATA DEFICIENT**

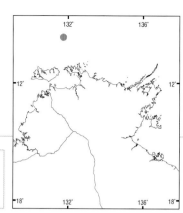

Known locations
of the grey
nurse shark
● = pre 1970
● = post 1970

DESCRIPTION

The grey nurse shark is grey-brown to bronze above and off white below. This counter-shaded, cryptic colouration is typical of species that swim in open water. Juveniles have reddish or brownish spots on the posterior half of the body. The females reach a maximum length of 3.2 m while males grow to 2.6 m (Compagno 1984; Branstetter and Musick 1994).

The grey nurse shark has a relatively short, almost conical, snout. A distinctive feature of this species is that the dorsal fins and the anal fin are of similar size.

DISTRIBUTION

The grey nurse shark is found primarily in warm-temperate (from sub-tropical to cool-temperate) inshore waters around the main continental landmasses, except in the eastern Pacific (Pollard *et al.* 1996). It occurs in habitats ranging from rocky inshore reefs down to around 200 m depth on the continental shelf (Pogonoski *et al.* 2002).

The species is rare in the Northern Territory and tends to occur further offshore than in temperate waters. The only documented Northern Territory record is from around Lynedoch Bank in the Arafura Sea.

Conservation reserves where reported: None

ECOLOGY

The grey nurse shark is a predator of a range of teleost (bony) fishes, as well as sharks, rays, squid, crabs and lobster. The species is solitary or occurs in small schools, and cooperative feeding has been observed. Large aggregations may occur around breeding time (Compagno 1984).

Females reproduce once every second year. Multiple eggs are laid in an egg sac and cannibalised until one embryo remains. Gestation is between 9 to 12 months (Gilmore *et al.* 1983).

CONSERVATION ASSESSMENT

Nationally, there have been major declines reported for this species. However, in Northern Territory waters, very little is known of grey nurse shark populations. Anecdotal evidence suggests that it is naturally rare, and the population is much smaller than in either the east or west coasts. It is also unknown whether the Northern Territory population consists of breeding individuals or comprises nomadic individuals from larger temperate zone populations.

Little is known of the size of, or trends in, the population in the Northern Territory. There are no records of the species being caught by shark fisheries and it appears that it is rarely caught as by-catch from commercial fishing operations in the Northern Territory, a factor that has contributed to dramatic population declines in other areas. The species is classified as **Data Deficient** due to lack of information on population trends in the Northern Territory and its likely natural rarity.

THREATENING PROCESSES

The most likely potential threatening process in Northern Territory waters is incidental capture by commercial fishing operations or by illegal fishers. Populations in southern waters have declined dramatically due to fishing (spear fishing, commercial fishing and recreational fishing) and beach protective shark meshing.

CONSERVATION OBJECTIVES AND MANAGEMENT

A national recovery plan for this species was established in 2002 (Environment Australia 2002). This plan includes a range of research and management measures, including habitat protection, development of monitoring programs, and ameliorative measures for fisheries management.

The managing authority for this species in the Northern Territory is the Department of Primary Industries, Fisheries and Mines. Currently there is no management program for the grey nurse shark in the Northern Territory.

The research priorities are to:
• determine the status of the population in the Northern Territory; and
• undertake an assessment of the impacts of by-catch in commercial fishing operations.

The management priorities are to:
• reduce by-catch in commercial fishing operations; and
• enhance the control and policing of illicit shark-fin fishing.

Compiled by Simon Stirrat, Helen Larson [November 2006] / **References:** Branstetter, S., and Musick, J.A. (1994). Age and growth estimates for the sand tiger in the northwestern Atlantic Ocean. *Transactions of the American Fisheries Society* 123, 242-254. / Compagno, L.J.V. (1984). FAO Species Catalogue, Vol. 4, Sharks of the World. An annotated and illustrated catalogue of sharks known to date. Part 2 – Carcharhiniformes. *FAO Fisheries Synopsis* 125, 251-655. / Environment Australia (2002). *Recovery plan for the grey nurse shark (Carcharias taurus) in Australia.* (Environment Australia, Canberra.) / Gilmore, R.G., Dodrill, J.W., and Linley, P.A. (1983). Reproduction and embryonic development of the sand tiger shark, *Odontapsis taurus* (Rafinesque). *Fishery Bulletin* 81, 201-225. / Pogonoski, J.J. Pollard, D.A., and Paxton, J.R. (2002). *Conservation Overview and Action Plan for Australian Threatened and Potentially Threatened Marine and Estuarine Fishes.* (Environment Australia, Canberra.) / Pollard, D.A., Lincoln-Smith, M.P., and Smith, A.K. (1996). The biology and conservation of the grey nurse shark (*Carcharias taurus* Rafinesque 1810) in New South Wales, Australia. *Aquatic Conservation: Marine and Freshwater Ecosystems* 6, 1-20.

Image courtesy of Richard Pillans

Speartooth shark,
Bizant River shark
Glyphis sp. A

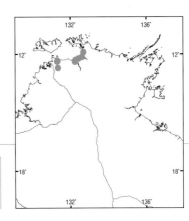

*Known locations
of the
speartooth shark*
● = *pre 1970*
● = *post 1970*

CONSERVATION STATUS
AUSTRALIA: **CRITICALLY ENDANGERED**
NORTHERN TERRITORY: **VULNERABLE**

DESCRIPTION

The speartooth shark is a medium-sized whaler shark that grows to 2 to 3 m. The dorsal surface is grey and the ventral surface paler, with an inconspicuous pale stripe on the flanks. It has a short, broadly rounded snout and small eyes. The dorsal fins are similar in size and the anal fin is about the same size as the second dorsal fin (Last and Stevens 1994).

The Wenlock River (west coast of Cape York Peninsula) population of *Glyphis* sp. A differs in pectoral fin colour from the Northern Territory specimens (H.K. Larson *pers. obs.*; S. Peverell *pers. comm.*) but the significance of this is unknown. The taxonomic status remains uncertain. Together with specimens from New Guinea this species may be synonymous with the more wide-ranging *Glyphis glyphis*.

DISTRIBUTION

The distribution of this species is not well known. It occurs in the eastern Gulf of Carpentaria and some rivers of Cape York Peninsula, Queensland, and the Alligator Rivers region across to the Adelaide River, just east of Darwin. The specimens from the Bizant River were collected in shallow, freshwater upper reaches of the river, but none have been collected there since the original discoveries in 1982. All the Northern Territory sharks have come from brackish waters, with all records from the Adelaide River being from the mouth to 100 km upstream.

Conservation reserves where reported:
Kakadu National Park

ECOLOGY

Very little is known of the biology of the speartooth shark. The small eyes and slender teeth suggest that it is primarily a fish feeder adapted to life in turbid waters (Fowler 1997). Stomach contents of specimens from the Wenlock River (Queensland) have included long-armed prawns (*Macrobrachium*), burrowing gobies (*Taenoides* or *Trypauchen*), gudgeons (*Prionobutis microps*), benthic-feeding jewfish (*Nibea squamosa*) and bony bream (*Nematalosa erebi*), indicating that the sharks hunted close to and among the soft substrate (Peverell *et al.* 2006). Species in this genus have low fecundity, small litters and breed every one or two years.

A recent acoustic tracking study (Pillans *et al.* ms) over several days showed that individual sharks move up and down stream in response to tidal cycles, traveling up to 25 km in a particular direction over one tidal cycle.

CONSERVATION ASSESSMENT

The species is listed as Critically Endangered worldwide on the 2006 IUCN Red List of Threatened Species, based on IUCN criteria C2a(i), noting that "this undescribed species is presumably very rare ... surveys targeting freshwater and estuarine elasmobranchs in northern Australia in mid to late 2002 collected no Glyphis specimens, despite sampling in

136 sites in 38 rivers. It is inferred that the population contains fewer than 250 mature individuals, further that it is presumably threatened through by-catch in commercial and recreational fishering activities and by possible habitat degradation" (http://www.flmnh.ufl.edu/fish/organizations/ssg/RLassess2006.pdf; Cavanagh *et al.* 2003). Pogonoski et al. (2002) recommended that its status in Australia should be Critically Endangered.

The speartooth shark may have a very limited distribution in the Northern Territory. The species is rare, occupies restricted habitat and is vulnerable to capture (Environment Australia 2000). However, juvenile specimens are not uncommon in the upper reaches of the Adelaide River system (T. Berra field logs, MAGNT) and at least 75 individuals have been reported from this river. In a recent study (Pillans *et al.* ms) 28 individuals were captured over a 12 day study period.

There is no evidence for decline in the known range of the species, but there are few early reports on which to base a population assessment (Environment Australia 2002). It is possible that the species has declined due to fishing pressure and other anthropogenic factors such as habitat alteration. Commercial net fishing is prohibited in the mouth of the Adelaide River to protect *Glyphis* species.

continued.../

In the Northern Territory it qualifies as
Vulnerable due to:
• small areas of extent and occupancy;
• small number of known locations; and
• uncertainty of the current population trend.

THREATENING PROCESSES
Barramundi gill netting and recreational fishing are
threatening processes in the Northern Territory,
as is the capture of juveniles for crab-pot bait.

CONSERVATION OBJECTIVES
AND MANAGEMENT
The managing authority for this species is the
Department of Primary Industry, Fisheries and
Mines. Currently there is no management program
for the speartooth shark in the Northern Territory.

Their current research priorities are to:
• determine the distribution, abundance and status
  of the species; and
• monitor and limit the impacts of commercial and
  recreational fishing operations in estuarine areas.

Compiled by Simon Ward, Helen Larson [December 2006] / **References:** Cavanagh, R.D., Kyne, P.M., Fowler, S.L., Music, J.A., and Bennett, M.B. (eds) (2003). *The conservation status of Australia Chondrichthyans*. Report to the IUCN shark specialist group Australia and Oceania Regional Red List workshop. (University of Queensland, Brisbane.) / Environment Australia (2002). *Glyphis* sp. A (Speartooth Shark). EA Threatened Species website: http://www.environment.gov.au/biodiversity/threatened/species/index.html / Fowler, S. (1997). River shark discovered in Sabah. *Shark News. Newsletter of the IUCN Shark Specialist Group* 9, 11. / Larson, H., Gribble, N., Salini, J., Pillans, R., and Peverell, S. (2004). Sharks and rays. In *Description of key species groups in the Northern Planning Area*. pp. 59-73. (National Oceans Office, Hobart.) / Last, P.R., and Stevens, J.D. (1994). *Sharks and Rays of Australia*. (CSIRO, Melbourne.) / Peverell, S.C., McPherson, G.R., Garrett, R.N., and Gribble, N.A. (2006). New records of the River Shark *Glyphis* (Carcharhinidae) reported from Cape York Peninsula, northern Australia. *Zootaxa* 1233, 53–68. / Pillans, R.D., Stevens, J.D., Kyne, P.M., and Salini, K. (ms). Acoustic tracking of *Glyphis* sp. A in the Adelaide River, Northern Territory, Australia. / Pogonoski, J.J. Pollard, D.A., and Paxton, J.R. (2002). *Conservation Overview and Action Plan for Australian Threatened and Potentially Threatened Marine and Estuarine Fishes*. (Environment Australia, Canberra.)

Image courtesy of MAGNT

Northern river shark

Glyphis sp. C.

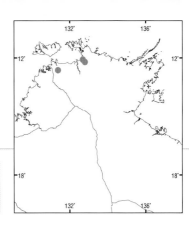

Known locations
of the northern
river shark
● = pre 1970
● = post 1970

DESCRIPTION

The northern river shark is similar to the more common bull shark that occurs in similar habitats and range. However, this species is a steely-grey colour and may be longer than 2 m. The northern river shark also has a triangular first dorsal fin, and a second dorsal fin that is two thirds the height of the first dorsal fin. Its small eye is located in the grey shaded part of the head (Last and Stevens 1994).

DISTRIBUTION

In Australia, the northern river shark is known from few records, including in the Northern Territory from the Adelaide and East and South Alligator River systems. It is also known from the Kimberley coast and King Sound in Western Australia (Thorburn and Morgan 2004). It is possible that the East Alligator population is at the easternmost limit of its Australian range. It may be the same species that occurs in the Fly River of New Guinea, where it is possibly more common.

Conservation reserves where reported:
Kakadu National Park

ECOLOGY

Little is known of the ecology of the northern river shark but it is probably restricted to shallow, brackish reaches of large rivers. This conclusion is based on the fact that it has not yet been caught in the coastal marine areas despite considerable fishing and collecting activity in these habitats (Thorburn et al. 2003; Larson *et al.* 2004).

CONSERVATION ASSESSMENT

The species is listed as Critically Endangered worldwide on the 2006 IUCN Red List of Threatened Species, based on IUCN criteria C2a(i), noting that "this undescribed species is presumably very rare ... surveys targeting freshwater and estuarine elasmobranchs in northern Australia in mid to late 2002 collected no *Glyphis* specimens, despite sampling in 136 sites in 38 rivers. It is inferred that the population contains fewer than 250 mature individuals, further that it is presumably threatened through by-catch in commercial and recreational fishing activities and by possible habitat degradation" (http://www.flmnh.ufl.edu/fish/organizations/ssg/RLassess2006.pdf; Cavanagh *et al.* 2003). Pogonoski *et al.* (2002) recommended that its status in Australia should be Endangered.

The northern river shark has a limited distribution in the Northern Territory, similar to the speartooth shark (*Glyphis* sp. A). It was only recently that these two species were recognised as both occurring in the Northern Territory. The northern river shark probably has small population sizes. The recent recognition that the species is primarily estuarine, rather than freshwater, should lead to more records.

In the Northern Territory, this species is listed as **Endangered** (under criteria B1ab(v)+2ab(v)) due to:
• extent of occurrence less than 5000 km²;
• area of occupancy less than 500 km²;

• known to occur at no more than 10 locations; and
• continuing decline (observed, inferred or projected in number of mature individuals).

THREATENING PROCESSES

Potential threatening processes in Northern Territory waters include recreational fishing and barramundi gill netting. There may be some use of juveniles as bait for crab fisheries (H. Larson *pers. comm.*).

CONSERVATION OBJECTIVES AND MANAGEMENT

The managing authority for this species is the Department of Primary Industries, Fisheries and Mines. It has prohibited commercial net fishing in the mouth of the Adelaide River to protect *Glyphis* species.

Their current research priorities are to:
• determine the distribution, abundance and status of the species across the Northern Territory.
• assess the potential impacts of fishing operations on populations.

Compiled by Simon Ward, Helen Larson [November 2006] / **References:** Larson, H., Gribble, N., Salini, J., Pillans, R., and Peverell, S. (2004). Sharks and rays. *In Description of key species groups in the Northern Planning Area.* pp. 59-73. (National Oceans Office, Hobart.) / Last, P.R., and Stevens, J.D. (1994). *Sharks and Rays of Australia.* (CSIRO, Melbourne.) / Pogonoski, J.J. Pollard, D.A., and Paxton, J.R. (2002). *Conservation Overview and Action Plan for Australian Threatened and Potentially Threatened Marine and Estuarine Fishes.* (Environment Australia, Canberra.) / Thorburn, D.C., and Morgan, D.L. (2004). The northern river shark *Glyphis* sp. C (Carcharhinae) discovered in Western Australia. Zootaxa 685, 1-8. / Thorburn, D.C., Peverell, S., Stevens, S., Last, J.D., and Rowland, A.J. (2003). *Status of freshwater and estuarine elasmobranchs in Northern Australia.* Report to Natural Heritage Trust, Canberra.

Image courtesy of Stirling Peverell

Dwarf sawfish
Pristis clavata

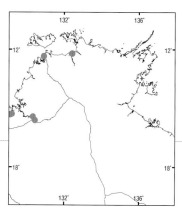

*Known locations
of the dwarf
sawfish*
● = *pre 1970*
● = *post 1970*

DESCRIPTION
The dwarf sawfish is a small, robust shark-like sawfish that grows to at least 1.4 m. The rostrum (snout) is broad and bears 18 to 22 pairs of lateral teeth starting from the base, and equally spaced. Nostrils behind the eyes are broad with large nasal flaps. The body is usually greenish-brown above and white ventrally. The pectoral fins are broadly triangular with broad bases and the dorsal fins are tall and pointed with the first dorsal fin positioned over or just forward of the pelvic fin origin. The lower lobe of the caudal fin is small and the posterior margin of the caudal fin almost straight (Last and Stevens 1994).

DISTRIBUTION
The dwarf sawfish occurs in shallow waters (2 to 3 m deep) in coastal and estuarine areas of tropical Australia, extending some distance up rivers almost into freshwater (one record from the Victoria River was about 100 km from the mouth: Thorburn *et al.* 2003). In the Northern Territory it has been recorded in several catchments, including the Keep River, Victoria River, Buffalo Creek and Rapid Creek (Darwin Harbour), and the South Alligator River (Thorburn *et al.* 2003; Peverell *et al.* 2004).

Conservation reserves where reported:
Kakadu National Park

ECOLOGY
Dwarf sawfish may move into marine waters after the wet, and during the wet season enter estuarine or fresher waters to breed (Peverell 2005). Like other sawfish it may feed on slow-moving shoaling fish, which are stunned by sideswipes of the snout, and molluscs and crustaceans that are swept out of the mud by the saw (Allen 1982). This is a long-lived species with sexual maturity attained at about 9 years and a lifespan of about 40 years (S. Peverell *unpubl.*).

CONSERVATION ASSESSMENT
The species is listed as Critically Endangered worldwide on the 2006 IUCN Red List of Threatened Species, based on IUCN criteria A2abcd+3cd+4bcd, noting that "Australian populations have declined significantly as a result of by-catch in commercial gill net and trawl fisheries throughout this limited range and this by-catch continues" (http://www.flmnh.ufl.edu/fish/organizations/ssg/RLassess2006.pdf; Cavanagh *et al.* 2003). Pogonoski *et al.* (2002) recommended that its status in Australia should be Endangered.

In the Northern Territory, the species is classified as **Vulnerable** (under criterion A2d) due to an inferred population size reduction of more than 30% over the last 10 years or three generations where the reduction may have not ceased (based on potential levels of exploitation).

Declines are inferred based on the susceptibility of the species to various fishing practices in coastal and estuarine habitats (Peverell *et al.* 2004).

THREATENING PROCESSES
Populations have been significantly reduced as a result of by-catch in commercial gill net and trawl fisheries (Pogonoski *et al.* 2002). Recreational fishing may also affect the species. Elsewhere, sawfish generally have also been affected by habitat degradation (Cavanagh *et al.* 2003).

CONSERVATION OBJECTIVES AND MANAGEMENT
The managing authority for this species is the Department of Primary Industry, Fisheries and Mines. Currently there is no management program for the dwarf sawfish in the Northern Territory.

The research priorities are to:
• investigate the distribution, status, biology and habitat requirements of the species; and
• assess the impacts (and options to ameliorate them) of fishing operations, particularly in estuarine areas.

Compiled by Helen Larson, John Woinarski, Simon Stirrat [November 2006] / **References:** Allen, G.R. (1982). *A Field Guide to Inland Fishes of Western Australia.* (Western Australian Museum, Perth.) Cavanagh, R.D., Kyne, P.M., Fowler, S.L., Music, J.A., and Bennett, M.B. (eds) (2003). *The conservation status of Australian Chondrichthyans.* Report to the IUCN shark specialist group Australia and Oceania Regional Red List workshop. (University of Queensland, Brisbane.) / Last, P.R., and Stevens, J.D. (1994). *Sharks and Rays of Australia.* (CSIRO, Melbourne.) / Peverell, S.C. (2005). Distribution of sawfishes (Pristidae) in the Queensland Gulf of Carpentaria, Australia, with notes on their ecology. *Environmental Biology of Fishes* 73, 391-402. / Peverell, S., Gribble, N., and Larson, H. (2004). Sawfish. In *Description of key species groups in the Northern Planning Area.* pp. 75-83. (National Oceans Office, Hobart.) / Pogonoski, J.J. Pollard, D.A., and Paxton, J.R. (2002). *Conservation Overview and Action Plan for Australian Threatened and Potentially Threatened Marine and Estuarine Fishes.* (Environment Australia, Canberra.) / Stobutzki, I., Miller, J.M., Heales, D.S., and Brewer, D.T. (2002). Sustainability of elasmobranchs caught as by-catch in a tropical prawn (shrimp) trawl fishery. *Fishery Bulletin* 100, 800-822. / Thorburn, D.C., Peverell, S., Stevens, S., Last, J.D., and Rowland, A.J. (2003). *Status of freshwater and estuarine elasmobranchs in Northern Australia.* Report to Natural Heritage Trust, Canberra.

Freshwater sawfish
Pristis microdon

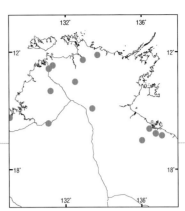

*Known locations
of the freshwater sawfish*
● = *pre 1970*
● = *post 1970*

CONSERVATION STATUS
AUSTRALIA: **VULNERABLE**
NORTHERN TERRITORY: **VULNERABLE**

DESCRIPTION

The freshwater sawfish is a medium-sized sawfish with a body length up to 3 m although reputed to reach up to 7 m. The body is yellowish, slender and shark-like with a blade-like rostrum (snout) bearing 18 to 23 pairs of lateral teeth. The teeth start near the rostrum base, and are equally spaced. Like other rays, it has gill openings (five) on the ventral surface of the head. The body is yellowish to greyish with a white ventral surface. Pectoral fins are broadly triangular with broad bases and dorsal fins tall and pointed with the first dorsal fin positioned well forward of the pelvic fin origin. The lower lobe of the caudal fin is small and the posterior margin of the caudal fin concave (Last and Stevens 1994).

DISTRIBUTION

The freshwater sawfish is known from several drainages in northern Australia from Western Australia to Queensland. In the Northern Territory, it occurs in the Keep, Victoria, Darwin, Adelaide, East and South Alligator, Daly, Goomadeer, Wearyan, McArthur and Robinson Rivers (Thorburn *et al.* 2003; Peverell *et al.* 2004).

Conservation reserves where reported:
Kakadu National Park

ECOLOGY

Freshwater sawfish prefer muddy bottoms of freshwater areas and upper reaches of estuaries. This species has been reported to be primarily a marine/estuarine species, that spends its first three to four years in freshwater. Freshwater sawfish move into marine waters after the wet season, and during the wet season enter estuarine or fresher waters to breed (Peverell 2005). They usually occur in water deeper than 1 m, but may move into shallow water to feed (Wilson 1999). Sawfishes feed on slow-moving shoaling fish, which are stunned by sideswipes of the snout, and molluscs and crustaceans that are swept out of the mud by the saw (Allen 1982).

Freshwater sawfish are viviparous and produce from one to 12 young. In Queensland, spawning occurs at the beginning of the wet season. This is a long-lived species with sexual maturity attained at about 7 years and a lifespan of about 40 years (S. Peverell *unpubl.*).

CONSERVATION ASSESSMENT

The species is listed as Critically Endangered worldwide on the 2006 IUCN Red List of Threatened Species, with extreme and continued vulnerability to fisheries (evidenced by serious declines in virtually all known populations), compounded by habitat loss and degradation over most of its range. Remaining populations are now small, fragmented and Critically Endangered globally (Cavanagh *et al.* 2003). Pogonoski *et al.*

(2002) recommended that its status in Australia should be Endangered.

The freshwater sawfish occurs in at least eight catchments in the Northern Territory and it is likely to occur in more. There is little information to determine changes in population sizes or ranges but the species is extremely vulnerable to gill-net fishing (Pogonoski *et al.* 2002; Thorburn and Morgan 2005). Serious declines are evident in overseas populations (Pogonoski *et al.* 2002) because of habitat loss and fishing impacts.

Although the freshwater sawfish is probably susceptible to gill-net fishing, there is no gill-net fishing allowed in freshwater in the Northern Territory. A few rivers are open to gill-net fishing a few kilometres upstream but not in freshwater reaches. There are no reports of by-catch of freshwater sawfish from any commercial fishery but they are caught by recreational fishers.

The species appears to be uncommon, which could be a natural consequence of being a large carnivore. There are no data to assess population trends, but relatively few individuals were recorded in recent targeted surveys. In the Northern Territory, it is classified as **Vulnerable** (under criterion A2d) based on a suspected population reduction of more than 30% over the last 10 years or three generations based on potential levels of exploitation.

continued.../

THREATENING PROCESSES

The impact of fishing practices in the Northern
Territory on freshwater sawfish is largely unknown.
Increasing development, resulting in degradation
of riverine habitat, may also threaten the species.

CONSERVATION OBJECTIVES
AND MANAGEMENT

The managing authority for this species is the
Department of Primary Industry, Fisheries and
Mines. Currently there is no management
program for the freshwater sawfish in the
Northern Territory.

The research priorities are to:
• better clarify the status of the species in the
  Northern Territory; and
• assess impacts of commercial and recreational
  fishing operations in both estuarine and
  freshwater sections of rivers where they are
  known to occur.

Compiled by Helen Larson, Simon Stirrat, John Woinarski [November 2006] / **References:** Allen, G.R. (1982). *A Field Guide to Inland Fishes of Western Australia*. (Western Australian Museum, Perth.)
Cavanagh, R.D., Kyne, P.M., Fowler, S.L., Music, J.A., and Bennett, M.B. (eds) (2003). *The conservation status of Australian Chondrichthyans*. Report to the IUCN shark specialist group Australia and Oceania
Regional Red List workshop. (University of Queensland, Brisbane.) / Last, P.R., and Stevens, J.D. (1994). *Sharks and Rays of Australia*. (CSIRO, Melbourne.) / Peverell, S.C. (2005). Distribution of sawfishes
(Pristidae) in the Queensland Gulf of Carpentaria, Australia, with notes on their ecology. *Environmental Biology of Fishes* 73, 391-402. / Peverell, S., Gribble, N., and Larson, H. (2004). Sawfish. In *Description
of key species groups in the Northern Planning Area*. pp. 75-83. (National Oceans Office, Hobart.) / Pogonoski, J.J. Pollard, D.A., and Paxton, J.R. (2002). *Conservation Overview and Action Plan for Australian
Threatened and Potentially Threatened Marine and Estuarine Fishes*. (Environment Australia, Canberra.) / Thorburn, D.C., and Morgan, D.L. (2005). Threatened fishes of the world: *Pristis microdon* Latham 1974
(Pristidae). *Environmental Biology of Fishes* 72, 465-466. / Thorburn, D.C., Peverell, S., Stevens, S., Last, J.D., and Rowland, A.J. (2003). *Status of freshwater and estuarine elasmobranchs in Northern Australia*.
Report to Natural Heritage Trust, Canberra. / Wilson, D. (1999). Freshwater sawfish *Pristis microdon*. In Australia New Guinea Fishes Associations' A-Z Notebook of Native Freshwater Fish. ANGFA Bulletin 41.

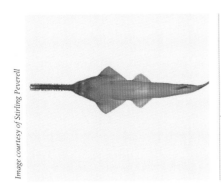

Image courtesy of Stirling Peverell

Green sawfish

Pristis zijsron

CONSERVATION STATUS
AUSTRALIA: **NOT LISTED**
NORTHERN TERRITORY: **VULNERABLE**

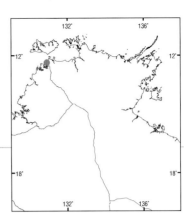

*Known location
of the green
sawfish*
● = *pre 1970*
● = *post 1970*

DESCRIPTION

The green sawfish is a large, robust shark-like sawfish growing to a length of 5 m, with some reports to 7.3 m. The rostrum (snout) is slender with 24 to 34 pairs of lateral teeth. The teeth are present on the basal quarter of the blade becoming much closer together toward the tip. The body is greenish-brown or olive above and whitish below, and the skin is rough. The pectoral fins are broadly triangular with broad bases and dorsal fins tall and pointed with the first dorsal fin positioned slightly behind the pelvic fin origin. The lower lobe of the caudal fin is small and the posterior margin of the caudal fin almost straight (Last and Stevens 1994).

DISTRIBUTION

The green sawfish is widely distributed in the northern Indian Ocean, around Indonesia and Australia. It is the sawfish species most often encountered in Australian waters (Last and Stevens 1994) and is more commonly found in Australian tropical waters. In Northern Territory waters, specimens have been collected only in Buffalo Creek in Darwin Harbour. However, there have been anecdotal sightings of the species in coastal areas of Garig Gunak Barlu National Park and literature records show its occurrence in the Arafura Sea and around Groote Eylandt.

Conservation reserves where reported:
Garig Gunak Barlu National Park

ECOLOGY

The green sawfish occurs in areas with a muddy substrate and is frequently found in shallow water (Stead 1963). Across its range, it has been reported to inhabit marine inshore waters, estuaries, lagoons and freshwater, but most records are from marine and estuarine areas (Thorburn *et al.* 2003; Peverell *et al.* 2004). Sawfish may enter estuarine or fresher waters to breed during the wet season, moving into marine waters after the wet (Peverell 2005). Sawfish generally feed on slow-moving shoaling fish, which are stunned by sideswipes of the snout, and molluscs and crustaceans that are swept out of the mud by the saw (Allen 1982). Aspects of reproduction by the green sawfish in Australian waters are not well known but anecdotal information suggests they bear up to 20 live young. This is a long-lived species with sexual maturity attained at about 6 years and the lifespan reaching about 25 years (S. Peverell *unpubl.*).

CONSERVATION ASSESSMENT

The species is listed as Critically Endangered worldwide on the 2006 IUCN Red List of Threatened Species, noting that it is extremely vulnerable to capture by target and by-catch fishing throughout its range, which has contracted significantly as a result. All populations are now seriously depleted, with records having become extremely infrequent over the last 30-40 years (Cavanagh *et al.* 2003). Pogonoski *et al.* (2002)

recommended that its status in Australia should be Endangered.

In southern waters, this once common species was regularly recorded as by-catch in commercial fisheries but it is critically endangered in New South Wales. The green sawfish regularly hinders barramundi gill-netters (Last and Stevens 1994) and so is likely to suffer from estuarine fishing operations in the Northern Territory.

The species appears to be widespread in Northern Territory waters but susceptibility to fishing practices has been demonstrated in other states. In the Northern Territory, it is classified as **Vulnerable** (under criterion A2d) due to an inferred population reduction of more than 30% over the last 10 years or three generations where the causes of the reduction have not ceased (based on potential levels of exploitation).

Declines are inferred based on susceptibility to fishing.

THREATENING PROCESSES

Incidental capture in commercial prawn and fish trawling and gill-netting are threatening processes (Last and Stevens 1994; Stobuzki *et al.* 2002). In some areas, targeted fishing may also threaten the species as the flesh is acceptable in the dried fish trade (Grant 1978). Fishing appears to have led to the decline of the species in southern states (Johnson 1999).

continued.../

Pristis zijsron continued...

CONSERVATION OBJECTIVES
AND MANAGEMENT
The managing authority for this species is the
Department of Primary Industry, Fisheries
and Mines. Currently there is no management
program for the green sawfish in the Northern
Territory. The research priorities are to:
• investigate the distribution and status of the
  species; and
• assess the impacts of fishing operations in
  estuarine areas.

Compiled by Simon Stirrat, Helen Larson, John Woinarski [May 2006] / **References:** Allen, G.R. (1982). *A Field Guide to Inland Fishes of Western Australia*. (Western Australian Museum, Perth.) Grant, E.M. (1978). *Guide to Fishes*. (Department of Harbours and Marine, Brisbane.) / Johnson, J.W. (1999) Annotated checklist of the fishes of Moreton Bay, Queensland, Australia. *Memoirs of the Queensland Museum* 43, 709-762. / Last, P.R., and Stevens, J.D. (1994). *Sharks and Rays of Australia*. (CSIRO, Melbourne.) / Peverell, S.C. (2005). Distribution of sawfishes (Pristidae) in the Queensland Gulf of Carpentaria, Australia, with notes on their ecology. *Environmental Biology of Fishes* 73, 391-402. / Peverell, S., Gribble, N., and Larson, H. (2004). Sawfish. In *Description of key species groups in the Northern Planning Area*. pp. 75-83. (National Oceans Office, Hobart.) / Stead, D.G. (1963). *Sharks and Rays of Australian seas*. (Angus and Robertson, Sydney.) / Stobutzki, I., Miller, J.M., Heales, D.S., and Brewer, D.T. (2002). Sustainability of elasmobranchs caught as by-catch in a tropical prawn (shrimp) trawl fishery. *Fishery Bulletin* 100, 800-822. / Thorburn, D.C., Peverell, S., Stevens, S., Last, J.D., and Rowland, A.J. (2003). *Status of freshwater and estuarine elasmobranchs in Northern Australia*. Report to Natural Heritage Trust, Canberra.

Image courtesy of Helen Larson (MAGNT)

Lorentz grunter

Pingalla lorentzi

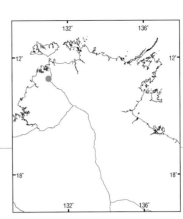

Known location of Lorentz grunter
● = pre 1970
● = post 1970

CONSERVATION STATUS
AUSTRALIA: **NOT LISTED**
NORTHERN TERRITORY: **VULNERABLE**

DESCRIPTION

Lorentz grunter is a small (maximum length of about 20 cm) perch-like fish, uniformly silver in colour with darkened scale margins dorsally. It has a white stripe from below the eye to the upper lip. The fins are mostly transparent to dusky and the anal fin has a dark grey to blackish blotch. The dorsal fin has 13 to 14 spines and 11 to 13 soft rays (Allen *et al.* 2002).

DISTRIBUTION

Lorentz grunter is rare in Australia although more widespread in New Guinea. In the Northern Territory it is known only from the Finniss River near the Rum Jungle mine site.

Conservation reserves where reported: None

ECOLOGY

Lorentz grunter occurs in small and large pools with rock and sand substrates, usually in open, unshaded sections of streams and in water temperatures between 25°C and 30°C (Allen *et al.* 2002).

The diet consists of benthic algae. The teeth of Lorentz grunter are adapted to scraping algae and other plant material from rock and wood surfaces and from sandy substrates (Allen *et al.* 2002).

Spawning appears to be in the mid wet season, from November to February.

CONSERVATION ASSESSMENT

Conservation assessment is hampered by the lack of any information on trends or threatening processes. The species can be classed as **Vulnerable** (under criterion D2) due to:
• a very restricted area of occupancy (less than 20 km^2); and
• known from only one location.

THREATENING PROCESSES

Lorentz grunter occurs relatively close to Darwin. Potential threats are degradation of waterways and riparian vegetation due to rural development, mining activity, altered fire regimes in rural areas, weed infestation and alteration of water flow and quality from erosion or pollution as a consequence of poor land management and agricultural development.

CONSERVATION OBJECTIVES AND MANAGEMENT PRIORITIES

The managing authority for this species is the Department of Primary Industry, Fisheries and Mines.

Research priorities are to:
• better define the distribution and status of this species;
• assess the impacts of a range of putative threatening processes.

Given its very limited distribution, further surveys should be carried out to determine if its occurrence is more widespread in the Finniss River and adjacent catchments.

The management priority is to establish a monitoring program at the known sites, because of the proximity of the species to developed areas.

Compiled by Simon Stirrat, John Woinarski, Helen Larson [November 2006] / **References:** Allen, G.R., Midgley, S.H., and Allen, M. (2002). *Field Guide to Freshwater Fishes of Australia.* (Western Australian Museum, Perth.)

Image courtesy of L. Corbett (MAGNT)

Angalarri grunter
Scortum neili

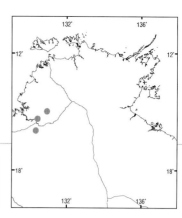

Known locations of the Angalarri grunter
● = pre 1970
● = post 1970

DESCRIPTION

The Angalarri grunter is a small (15 to 25 cm long) fish, uniformly silver-grey coloured other than a few black blotches and pale vertical barring. It is distinguished from the other three grunter species in the Timor Sea drainage by a combination of the number of transverse cheek scale rows (5 or 6), scales in a longitudinal series above the lateral line (62 to 73) and gill rakers on the first arch (34 to 40) (Corbett *et al.* 1999).

DISTRIBUTION

The Angalarri grunter has been recorded only from an upper tributary of the Angalarri River (Bradshaw station, Victoria River District) and from one individual at Limestone Gorge on the East Baines River (Midgley 1981; Allen *et al.* 1993; Corbett *et al.* 1999). These localities are part of the Victoria River system.

Conservation reserves where reported:
Gregory National Park

ECOLOGY

The species appears to be restricted to a few large (more than 5 m deep and more than 20 m wide) pools, with continuous overhanging vegetation, including rainforest elements, and a substrate comprising large rocks and crevices (Corbett *et al.* 1999).

The diet appears to be mainly vegetative matter, especially algae. It has been reported to occur in schools of up to 25 individuals, sometimes in association with other species including Jenkins grunter (*Hephaestus jenkinsi*) (Corbett *et al.* 1999).

CONSERVATION ASSESSMENT

Conservation assessment is hampered by the lack of any information on trends or threatening processes. There has been a reasonably substantial sampling of the river systems in the Victoria River District that have been sufficient to suggest that the species is highly localised.

Its status best fits **Vulnerable** (under criterion D2) based on:
• an area of occupancy less than 20 km^2; and
• known from fewer than five locations.

THREATENING PROCESSES

The main potential threats are degradation of riparian vegetation due to altered fire regimes and impacts of livestock and feral animals, and alteration of water flow and quality due to increased erosion as a consequence of poor land management. The main known site, on the Angalarri River, is zoned for limited use within the Department of Defence's Bradshaw military training area, and the other site is protected within Gregory National Park.

CONSERVATION OBJECTIVES AND MANAGEMENT PRIORITIES

The managing authority for this species is the Department of Primary Industry, Fisheries and Mines.

The main research priorities are to;
• better define the distribution and status of this species;
• assess the impacts of a range of putative threatening processes; and
• establish a monitoring program at the known sites.

This information is needed before management prescriptions can be formulated appropriately.

Compiled by John Woinarski [May 2006] / **References:** Allen, G.R., Larson, H.K., and Midgley, S.H. (1993). A new species of *Scortum* Whitley (Pisces: Terapontidae) from the Northern Territory, Australia. *The Beagle* 10, 71-74. / Corbett, L., Batterham, R., and Sewell, S. (1999). *Bradshaw field training area. Additional studies: Angalarri grunter.* Report to Department of Defence. (ERA Environmental Services Pty Ltd, Darwin.) / Midgley, S.H. (1981). *A biological resources study of the Victoria River, Fitzmaurice River, and the Keep River.* Report to the Northern Territory Department of Primary Industry and Fisheries.

Image courtesy of Neil Armstrong

Finke goby
Chlamydogobius japalpa

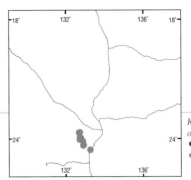

Known locations
of the Finke goby
● = *pre 1970*
● = *post 1970*

CONSERVATION STATUS
AUSTRALIA: **NOT LISTED**
NORTHERN TERRITORY: **VULNERABLE**

DESCRIPTION

The Finke goby grows to a maximum length of around 5.5 cm. It is pale yellow-brown or grey-brown, grading to a lighter belly. There are darker markings dorsally giving an appearance of fine vermiculations. The first dorsal fin has a blue median band and paler yellowish submarginal band. Breeding males display more vivid blue/white fin colouration (Allen *et al.* 2002).

DISTRIBUTION

The Finke goby has a limited distribution in the upper reaches of the Finke River system.

Conservation reserves where reported:
Finke Gorge National Park, West MacDonnell National Park.

ECOLOGY

The Finke goby is similar in ecology to the Desert goby (*Chalmydogobius eremius*) which feeds on small crustaceans, insect larvae, filamentous algae and detritus. Spawning occurs from November to March.

This species has no swim bladder. It rests on the bottom amongst detritus in shallow pools with rock, sand or gravel bottoms.

CONSERVATION ASSESSMENT

The Finke goby is restricted to the upper reaches of the Finke River but may be common within its limited range. The species is considered Vulnerable because of its restricted distribution and its potential susceptibility to decline as a result of introduction of non-native species. The species breeds well in captivity (D. Wilson *pers. comm.*).

The species is listed as **Vulnerable** in the Northern Territory (under criteria B1ab(iii)+2ab(iii)) due to:
- extent of occurrence estimated to be less than 20 000 km^2;
- area of occupancy less than 2000 km^2;
- severely fragmented or known to occur at no more than 10 locations; and
- continuing decline, observed, inferred or projected in area, extent and/or quality of habitat.

THREATENING PROCESSES

The primary threat to the Finke goby is the spread of introduced fish species, such as the mosquitofish (*Gambusia holbrooki*). This pest has been implicated in the decline of two other goby species in central Australia through competition. The mosquitofish is spreading rapidly in artificial and natural water bodies through central Australia (Wager and Unmack 2000).

CONSERVATION OBJECTIVES AND MANAGEMENT

The managing authority for this species is the Department of Primary Industry, Fisheries and Mines.

The management priority is to prevent the introduction, or manage the spread of, potentially destructive feral fishes in the Northern Territory.

Compiled by Simon Stirrat, Helen Larson [May 2006] / **References:** Allen, G.R., Midgley, S.H., and Allen, M. (2002). *Field Guide to Freshwater Fishes of Australia.* (Western Australian Museum, Perth.) Wager, R., and Unmack, P.J. (2000) *Fishes of the Lake Eyre catchment of central Australia.* (Department of Primary Industries and Queensland Fisheries Service, Brisbane.)

FROGS

Image courtesy of Ian Morris

Howard River toadlet

Uperoleia daviesae

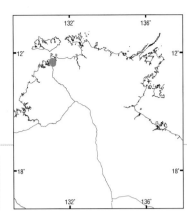

Known locations of Howard River toadlet
● = *pre 1970*
● = *post 1970*

DESCRIPTION

This is a small (17 to 23 mm snout-vent length) frog. The dorsal surface has numerous pale brown tubercles, surrounded by black, and a narrow yellow to pale red mid-vertebral stripe. The ventral surface is cream and the groin is orange-red. The toes are unfringed and have only slight basal webbing. Its short raspy call of 22 pulses distinguishes it from other sympatric species of *Uperoleia* (Young *et al.* 2005).

DISTRIBUTION

Uperoleia daviesae was discovered in 2000 and is known from only a small number of specimens and chorus recordings. It appears to be confined to sandy inundated areas in the adjacent Howard and Elizabeth River catchments, in the outer Darwin area.

Conservation reserves where reported: None

ECOLOGY

There is little information on the ecology of the species, other than that it appears to be confined to areas of sandy soils with short vegetation that is inundated in the wet season, or to adjacent melaleuca woodland areas. Typically males of the species are found calling in small numbers, amidst choruses of other, more numerous, frog species (W. Freeland *pers. comm.*).

CONSERVATION ASSESSMENT

There is little information on its population, distribution or trends in abundance. The Howard River toadlet has been classified as **Vulnerable** (under criteria B1ab(iii)+2ab(iii); D2), based on:
• the small number of locations from which it is currently known;
• threats to its habitat; and
• its very small extent of occurrence (approximately 200 km²) and area of occupancy (less than 20 km²), making it prone to the effects of human activities or stochastic events within a very short time period.

THREATENING PROCESSES

The species appears to be confined to sand sheets in the Howard and Elizabeth River catchments. These areas are in the Darwin peri-urban growth area, so are threatened by the urban expansion of Darwin; and in areas under pressure from sand mining (Price *et al.* 2005).

CONSERVATION OBJECTIVES AND MANAGEMENT

Current knowledge is insufficient to provide much guide to management. Research is required to more precisely delineate distribution, habitat preferences and ecology of the species.
This research should also provide a baseline for ongoing monitoring.

Compiled by Simon Ward [May 2006] / **References:** Price, O., Milne, D., and Tynan, C. (2005). Poor recovery of woody vegetation on sand and gravel mines in the Darwin region of the Northern Territory. *Ecological Management and Restoration* 6, 118-123. / Young, J.E., Tyler, M.J., and Kent, S.A. (2005). Diminutive new species of *Uperoleia* Grey (Anura: Myobatrachidae) from the vicinity of Darwin, Northern Territory, Australia. *Journal of Herpetology* 39, 603-609.

REPTILES

Image courtesy of EPA (Qld)

Loggerhead turtle
Caretta caretta

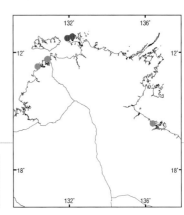

Known locations of loggerhead turtle
● = pre 1970
● = post 1970

CONSERVATION STATUS
AUSTRALIA: **ENDANGERED**
NORTHERN TERRITORY: **ENDANGERED**

DESCRIPTION

The loggerhead turtle is a marine turtle with a red-brown to brown shell (carapace) of 1 m length and a relatively large head. It usually has five pairs of large scales down each side of the shell. When ashore, this species moves with an alternating gait.

DISTRIBUTION

The species has a global distribution. In Australia, breeding is centred in the southern Great Barrier Reef and adjacent mainland, on Dirk Hartog Island (Shark Bay) and Muiron Island (North West Cape) in Western Australia. The eastern and western populations are genetically distinct. No breeding is known to occur in the Northern Territory (Chatto 1998). Loggerheads from Australia migrate to the Pacific Islands and southern Asia. The animals that feed in Northern Territory waters appear to come from both the eastern and western breeding populations. When feeding in inshore areas they inhabit sub-tidal and inter-tidal coral and rocky reefs and sea-grass meadows, as well as deeper, soft-bottomed habitats. They are "not uncommon, at least from Fog Bay around to north-east Arnhem Land" (Chatto 1998).

Conservation reserves where reported:
Garig Gunak Barlu National Park, Kakadu National Park.

ECOLOGY

Loggerhead turtles eat shellfish, crabs, sea urchins and jellyfish. Females migrate up to 2600 km from feeding areas to traditional nesting beaches.

Females lay up to six clutches of around 125 eggs each season with three to four years between breeding. Very young turtles take up a drifting existence in surface waters and feed on macro zooplankton. Immature turtles (shell length of 75 cm) then move to inshore areas. They settle in one area and do not move large distances, except to breed.

CONSERVATION ASSESSMENT

The population trends in the western stock are not known but between 1985 and 1992 the population in the southern Great Barrier Reef declined by 20%, and between 1985 and 1998 a decline of 65% occurred in the number of loggerheads nesting on Heron Island (Chaloupka and Limpus 2001). No data are available on trends in numbers feeding in Northern Territory waters.

Loggerhead turtles in the Northern Territory are non-breeding visitors from eastern or western Australia, where nesting populations are known to be in decline. Hence, the conservation status for this species in the Northern Territory should reflect that within its breeding range. Accordingly, the species qualifies as **Endangered** (under criterion A2b) due to population reduction of more than 50% over the last three generations.

THREATENING PROCESSES

Simulation models suggest that increased fox predation on eggs and mortality of pelagic juveniles from incidental capture in coastal otter trawl fisheries and oceanic long-line fisheries have led to the observed declines (Chaloupka and Limpus 2001). Loggerhead turtles have a greater propensity than other sea turtles to consume baited long-line hooks (Witzell 1998).

The main human-caused mortality factor operating within Northern Territory waters is probably capture by prawn trawlers (Poiner and Harris 1996). This fishery is under the control of the Australian Government and measures to reduce by-catch of turtles have been implemented (Environment Australia 2003). One such measure, the introduction of turtle exclusion devices into the northern prawn fishery, has probably reduced the by-catch of loggerhead turtles.

CONSERVATION OBJECTIVES AND MANAGEMENT

A national recovery plan for this species, and other marine turtles, was implemented in 2003 (Environment Australia 2003). This plan includes actions that:
- aim to reduce mortality of turtles (principally through ameliorative actions within commercial fisheries, and maintenance of sustainable harvest by Indigenous communities);
- develop and integrate monitoring programs;
- manage factors that affect reproductive success (in this case, outside Northern Territory);
- identify and protect critical habitat (including sea-grass beds); and
- enhance international actions and cooperation.

Compiled by Robert Taylor, Ray Chatto, John Woinarski [May 2006] / **References:** Chatto, R. (1998). A preliminary overview of the locations of marine turtle nesting in the Northern Territory. In *Marine turtle conservation and management in northern Australia.* (eds R. Kennett, A. Webb, G. Duff, M. Guinea and G. Hill.) pp. 33-40. (Northern Territory University, Darwin.) / Environment Australia (2003). *Recovery Plan for marine turtles in Australia.* (Environment Australia, Canberra.) / Chaloupka, M., and Limpus, C. (2001). Trends in the abundance of sea turtles resident in southern Great Barrier Reef waters. *Biological Conservation* 102, 235-249. / Poiner, I.R., and Harris, A.N.M. (1996). Incidental capture, direct mortality and delayed mortality of sea turtles in Australia's Northern Prawn Fishery. *Marine Biology* 125, 813-825. Witzell, W.N. (1998). Distribution and relative abundance of sea turtles caught incidentally by the US pelagic longline fleet in the western North Atlantic Ocean, 1992-1995. *Fishery Bulletin* 97, 200-211.

Image courtesy of EPA (Qld)

Green turtle
Chelonia mydas

CONSERVATION STATUS
AUSTRALIA: **VULNERABLE**
NORTHERN TERRITORY: **LEAST CONCERN**

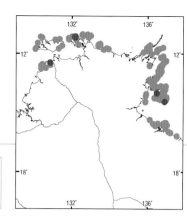

Known locations
of green turtle
● = pre 1970
● = post 1970

DESCRIPTION

The green turtle is a marine turtle with a subcircular to heart-shaped carapace up to 1 m in length. The carapace is olive-green, usually variegated with black, brown or red-brown. The carapace has four pairs of costal shields (those between the centre and outer margin of the shell).

Eggs are intermediate in size (mean diameter: 4.6 cm) compared with other marine turtles that breed in the Northern Territory. When ashore, green turtles move pairs of legs simultaneously, leaving symmetrical tracks, unlike the alternate gait of loggerhead and hawksbill turtles.

DISTRIBUTION

Green turtles occur in tropical and subtropical waters throughout the world. In Australia, the main breeding distribution includes the Great Barrier Reef, the north-west shelf of Western Australia, Wellesley Island group in the southern Gulf of Carpentaria and the Top End coast.

Many nesting sites occur in the Northern Territory, mostly from the western end of Melville Island to near the border with Queensland (Chatto 1998). Nationally significant breeding sites include Cobourg Peninsula, the mainland from Gove to the northern edge of Blue Mud Bay, the south-east of Groote Eylandt, and the northern beaches of islands in the Sir Edward Pellew group (Chatto 1998).

Conservation reserves where reported:
Barranyi National Park, Casuarina Coastal Reserve,

Garig Gunak Barlu National Park, Kakadu National Park, Nanydjaka Indigenous Protected Area.

ECOLOGY

Green turtles are primarily herbivorous, mostly eating sea-grass and algae. Juveniles are carnivorous.

Green turtles undertake long-distance dispersal around feeding areas and to and from nesting beaches. Individuals tagged in the Kimberley have been recaptured in the Top End and individuals tagged at breeding sites in the northern Great Barrier Reef have been recaptured in the southern Gulf of Carpentaria. Individuals tagged in north-eastern Arnhem Land make complex and long movements around the western shores of the Gulf of Carpentaria (Kennett *et al.* 2004)

In the Northern Territory, green turtles nest mainly on wide beaches backed by large dune systems, and may occur at high densities in such sites (Chatto 1998).

CONSERVATION ASSESSMENT

A recent assessment of trends for this species in the southern Great Barrier Reef has shown that the overall population increased by 11% per year over eight years (1985–1992), and the female nesting population increased by 3% per year between 1974 and 1998 (Chaloupka and Limpus 2001).

There are few population trend data for the Northern Territory, but some anecdotal evidence of at least localised decline of marine turtles in general

(Kennett *et al.* 2004).

Given the indications of a population at least in the thousands in both the breeding and feeding segments with no evidence of substantial decline the species is considered as **Least Concern** for the Northern Territory.

THREATENING PROCESSES

As with other marine turtles, there are a broad range of factors that threaten this species. These may include by-catch in commercial fisheries (Poiner and Harris 1996); Indigenous harvest; predation of eggs and young by dogs, pigs and goannas; marine pollution, including entanglement in ghost nets; and disturbance at main breeding sites.

CONSERVATION OBJECTIVES AND MANAGEMENT

A national recovery plan for this species, and other marine turtles, was implemented in 2003 (Environment Australia 2003).

This plan includes actions that:
• aim to reduce mortality of turtles (principally through ameliorative actions within commercial fisheries, and maintenance of sustainable harvest by Indigenous communities),
• develop and integrate monitoring programs;
• manage factors that affect reproductive success;
• identify and protect critical habitat (including sea-grass beds);
• enhance communication of information; and
• enhance international actions and cooperation.

Compiled by Robert Taylor, Ray Chatto, John Woinarski [May 2006] / **References:** Chaloupka, M., and Limpus, C. (2001). Trends in the abundance of sea turtles resident in southern Great Barrier Reef waters. *Biological Conservation* 102, 235-249. / Chatto, R. (1998). A preliminary overview of the locations of marine turtle nesting in the Northern Territory. In *Marine turtle conservation and management in northern Australia.* (eds R. Kennett, A. Webb, G. Duff, M. Guinea and G. Hill.) pp. 33-40. (Northern Territory University, Darwin.) / Environment Australia (2003). *Recovery Plan for marine turtles in Australia.* (Environment Australia, Canberra.) / Kennett, R., Robinson, C.J., Kiessling, I., Yunupingu, D., Munungurritj, N., and Yunupingu, D. (2004). Indigenous initiatives for co-management of Miyapunu/sea turtle. *Ecological Management & Restoration* 5, 159-166. / Poiner, I.R., and Harris, A.N.M. (1996). Incidental capture, direct mortality and delayed mortality of sea turtles in Australia's Northern Prawn Fishery. *Marine Biology* 125, 813-825.

Image courtesy of EPA (Qld)

Hawksbill turtle
Eretmochelys imbricata

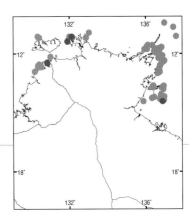

Known locations
of hawksbill turtle
● = pre 1970
● = post 1970

CONSERVATION STATUS
AUSTRALIA: **VULNERABLE**
NORTHERN TERRITORY: **DATA DEFICIENT**

DESCRIPTION

The hawksbill turtle is a marine turtle with a high domed heart-shaped carapace. The carapace is olive-green to brown with black, brown or red-brown markings. The scales of the carapace are overlapping, and there are four pairs of costal shields. The upper jaw juts forward to form a distinctive beak-shaped snout.

Eggs are small in size (mean diameter: 3.9 cm) compared with most other marine turtles that breed in the Northern Territory. Hawksbill turtles have an alternate gait, leaving an asymmetric track when ashore.

DISTRIBUTION

Hawksbill turtles occur in tropical, sub-tropical and temperate waters of all oceans of the world. In Australia, there are two main genetically isolated populations: on the western Australian coast, and in the Top End and north-eastern Queensland.

In the Northern Territory, most nesting occurs on islands rather than mainland beaches. Principal sites are concentrated around north-eastern Arnhem Land and Groote Eylandt (Chatto 1998).

Conservation reserves where reported:
Casuarina Coastal Reserve, Garig Gunak Barlu National Park, Kakadu National Park, Nanydjaka Indigenous Protected Area.

ECOLOGY

Hawksbill turtles are omnivorous, eating a wide variety of plants and animals including sponges, gastropods, sea-grass and algae. Hawksbill turtles may undertake long distance dispersal around feeding areas and to and from nesting beaches, although individuals may also be largely resident around preferred feeding areas.

In the Northern Territory, hawksbill turtles nest mainly on narrow beaches, where they frequently go under vegetation to nest, and nesting occurs mainly in the latter half of the year (Chatto 1998).

CONSERVATION ASSESSMENT

In recognition of declines at some Australian breeding grounds, world-wide trends, and a substantial array of threatening factors, the hawksbill turtle is regarded as Vulnerable nationally (Environment Australia 2003).

There are no substantial data on trends in population in the Northern Territory, although there is some anecdotal evidence of at least localised decline of marine turtles in general (Kennett *et al.* 2004). The species remains common and widespread.

Given the presence of some threats that cannot be quantified and the lack of trend data the species is best considered as **Data Deficient** in the Northern Territory.

THREATENING PROCESSES

As with other marine turtles, there are a broad range of factors that threaten this species. These may include: by-catch in commercial fisheries (Poiner and Harris 1996); Indigenous harvest; predation of eggs and young by dogs, pigs and goannas; marine pollution, including entanglement in ghost nets; and disturbance at main breeding sites.

CONSERVATION OBJECTIVES AND MANAGEMENT

A national recovery plan for this species, and other marine turtles, was implemented in 2003 (Environment Australia 2003).

This plan includes actions that:
• aim to reduce mortality of turtles (principally through ameliorative actions within commercial fisheries and maintenance of sustainable harvest by Indigenous communities);
• develop and integrate monitoring programs;
• manage factors that affect reproductive success;
• identify and protect critical habitat (including sea-grass beds);
• enhance communication of information; and
• enhance international actions and cooperation.

Compiled by Robert Taylor, Ray Chatto, John Woinarski [May 2006] / **References:** Chaloupka, M., and Limpus, C. (2001). Trends in the abundance of sea turtles resident in southern Great Barrier Reef waters. *Biological Conservation* 102, 235-249. / Chatto, R. (1998). A preliminary overview of the locations of marine turtle nesting in the Northern Territory. In *Marine turtle conservation and management in northern Australia.* (eds R. Kennett, A. Webb, G. Duff, M. Guinea and G. Hill.) pp. 33-40. (Northern Territory University, Darwin.) / Environment Australia (2003). *Recovery Plan for marine turtles in Australia.* (Environment Australia, Canberra.) / Kennett, R., Robinson, C.J., Kiessling, I., Yunupingu, D., Munungurritj, N., and Yunupingu, D. (2004). Indigenous initiatives for co-management of Miyapunu/sea turtle. *Ecological Management & Restoration* 5, 159-166. / Poiner, I.R., and Harris, A.N.M. (1996). Incidental capture, direct mortality and delayed mortality of sea turtles in Australia's Northern Prawn Fishery. *Marine Biology* 125, 813-825.

Image courtesy of EPA (Qld)

Olive ridley,
Pacific ridley
Lepidochelys olivacea

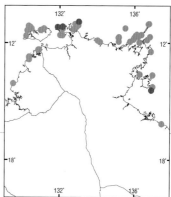

Known locations of olive ridley
● = *pre 1970*
● = *post 1970*

DESCRIPTION

The olive ridley is the smallest Australian sea turtle, with a mean curved carapace length of 70 cm. The carapace colour is olive-grey. The carapace has a diagnostic six pairs of costal scales.

Eggs are small (mean diameter: 3.6 cm) compared with other marine turtles.

DISTRIBUTION

Olive ridley turtles occur in tropical and sub-tropical waters throughout the world.

The vast majority of the nesting population in Australian waters occurs in the Northern Territory. Nesting has been recorded from Melville Island to Groote Eylandt with the highest density of nesting occurring on Melville Island, islands to the east of Croker Island and some islands off north-east Arnhem Land (Chatto 1998).

Conservation reserves where reported:
Casuarina Coastal Reserve, Garig Gunak Barlu National Park, Kakadu National Park, Nanydjaka Indigenous Protected Area.

ECOLOGY

Olive ridleys live in shallow protected waters and feed on benthic molluscs, crabs, echinoderms and gastropods. Studies elsewhere indicate some long distance dispersal between feeding and breeding grounds.

In the Northern Territory, olive ridleys breed at a wide range of sites on islands and, less commonly, mainland beaches. Olive ridleys often nest just above the high tide mark and may suffer more breeding losses through tidal inundation than do other species of marine turtle (Chatto 1998).

CONSERVATION ASSESSMENT

In recognition of world-wide trends, and a substantial array of threatening factors, the olive ridley is regarded as Vulnerable nationally (Environment Australia 2003).

In the Northern Territory, there are no accurate population estimates. The female breeding population in the Northern Territory is very roughly estimated to be between 1000 and 5000. There are no substantial data on trends in population and the species remains common and widespread. There is some anecdotal evidence of at least localised decline of marine turtles in general (Kennett *et al.* 2004).

Given the presence of some threats that cannot be quantified, and the lack of trend data, the species is best considered as **Data Deficient**.

THREATENING PROCESSES

As with other marine turtles, many factors may threaten this species. These include: by-catch in commercial fisheries (Poiner and Harris 1996); Indigenous harvest; predation of eggs and young by dogs, pigs and goannas; marine pollution, including entanglement in ghost nets; and disturbance at main breeding sites.

Mortality may occur when captured in fishing nets. The worst recorded occurrence was in Fog Bay in 1991 when an estimated 300 turtles were killed in one incident. Of 100 turtles examined from this kill, 85 were olive ridleys. However, this level of mortality is exceptional and annual by-catch is likely to be much lower.

CONSERVATION OBJECTIVES AND MANAGEMENT

A national recovery plan for this species, and other marine turtles, was implemented in 2003 (Environment Australia 2003).

This plan includes actions that:
• aim to reduce mortality of turtles (principally through ameliorative actions within commercial fisheries, and maintenance of sustainable harvest by Indigenous communities);
• develop and integrate monitoring programs;
• manage factors that affect reproductive success;
• identify and protect critical habitat (including sea-grass beds);
• enhance communication of information; and
• enhance international actions and cooperation.

Increasing numbers of wild dogs on Melville Island were thought to be causing unusually high levels of nest predation. However, since 2005, dog numbers on this island have been controlled through joint actions of Tiwi and Parks and Wildlife rangers.

Compiled by Robert Taylor, Ray Chatto, John Woinarski [May 2006] / **References:** Chatto, R. (1998). A preliminary overview of the locations of marine turtle nesting in the Northern Territory. In *Marine turtle conservation and management in northern Australia.* (eds R. Kennett, A. Webb, G. Duff, M. Guinea and G. Hill.) pp. 33-40. (Northern Territory University, Darwin.) / Environment Australia (2003). *Recovery Plan for marine turtles in Australia.* (Environment Australia, Canberra.) / Kennett, R., Robinson, C.J., Kiessling, I., Yunupingu, D., Munungurritj, N., and Yunupingu, D. (2004). Indigenous initiatives for co-management of Miyapunu/sea turtle. *Ecological Management & Restoration* 5, 159-166. / Poiner, I.R., and Harris, A.N.M. (1996). Incidental capture, direct mortality and delayed mortality of sea turtles in Australia's Northern Prawn Fishery. *Marine Biology* 125, 813-825.

Image courtesy of EPA (Qld)

Flatback turtle
Natator depressus

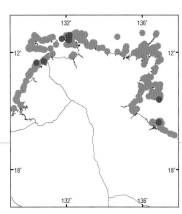

Known locations
of flatback
turtle
● = pre 1970
● = post 1970

CONSERVATION STATUS
AUSTRALIA: **VULNERABLE**
NORTHERN TERRITORY: **DATA DEFICIENT**

DESCRIPTION
The flatback turtle is a marine turtle with a low domed carapace with reflexed margins. The carapace is olive, grey or pale grey-green, with average curved length of 92 cm. There are four pairs of costal shield.

Eggs are large (mean diameter: 5.2 cm) compared with most other marine turtles that breed in the Northern Territory. When ashore, flatback turtles move pairs of legs simultaneously, leaving symmetrical tracks, unlike the alternate gait of loggerhead and hawksbill turtles.

DISTRIBUTION
Flatback turtles are restricted to tropical waters of Australia and New Guinea. They have an extensive distribution around the coastline of the Northern Territory, breeding at many mainland and island sites (Chatto 1998).

Conservation reserves where reported:
Garig Gunak Barlu National Park, Kakadu National Park, Nanydjaka Indigenous Protected Area.

ECOLOGY
Flatback turtles inhabit shallow, soft-bottomed sea beds and feed on soft corals and soft-bodied animals such as jellyfish and sea cucumbers.

They may breed during any month of the year, although this may peak in June to August (Chatto 1998).

CONSERVATION ASSESSMENT
In recognition of declines at some Australian breeding grounds and a substantial array of threatening factors, the flatback turtle is regarded as Vulnerable nationally (Environment Australia 2003).

Flatbacks probably constitute the highest breeding numbers of any sea turtle in the Northern Territory (Chatto 1998). There are no substantial data on trends in population, although there is some anecdotal evidence of localised decline of marine turtles in general (Kennett *et al.* 2004). The species remains common and widespread.

Given the presence of some threats that cannot be quantified and the lack of trend data the species is best considered as **Data Deficient**.

THREATENING PROCESSES
As with other marine turtles, many factors may threaten this species. These include: by-catch in commercial fisheries (Poiner and Harris 1996); Indigenous harvest; predation of eggs and young by dogs, pigs and goannas; marine pollution, including entanglement in ghost nets; and disturbance at main breeding sites.

CONSERVATION OBJECTIVES AND MANAGEMENT
A national recovery plan for this species, and other marine turtles, was implemented in 2003 (Environment Australia 2003).

This plan includes actions that:
• aim to reduce mortality of turtles (principally through ameliorative actions within commercial fisheries, and maintenance of sustainable harvest by Indigenous communities);
• develop and integrate monitoring programs;
• manage factors that affect reproductive success;
• identify and protect critical habitat (including sea-grass beds);
• enhance communication of information; and
• enhance international actions and cooperation.

A monitoring program for this species has been established in Kakadu National Park (Winderlich 1998).

Compiled by Robert Taylor, Ray Chatto, John Woinarski [May 2006] / **References:** Chatto, R. (1998). A preliminary overview of the locations of marine turtle nesting in the Northern Territory. In *Marine turtle conservation and management in northern Australia.* (eds R. Kennett, A. Webb, G. Duff, M. Guinea and G. Hill.) pp. 33-40. (Northern Territory University, Darwin.) / Environment Australia (2003). *Recovery Plan for marine turtles in Australia.* (Environment Australia, Canberra.) / Kennett, R., Robinson, C.J., Kiessling, I., Yunupingu, D., Munungurritj, N., and Yunupingu, D. (2004). Indigenous initiatives for co-management of Miyapunu/sea turtle. *Ecological Management & Restoration* 5, 159-166. / Poiner, I.R., and Harris, A.N.M. (1996). Incidental capture, direct mortality and delayed mortality of sea turtles in Australia's Northern Prawn Fishery. *Marine Biology* 125, 813-825. / Winderlich, S. (1998). An overview of the sea turtle research in Kakadu National Park and the surrounding area. In *Marine turtle conservation and management in northern Australia.* (eds R. Kennett, A. Webb, G. Duff, M. Guinea and G. Hill.) pp. 110-114. (Northern Territory University, Darwin.)

Leatherback turtle
Dermochelys coriacea

CONSERVATION STATUS
AUSTRALIA: **VULNERABLE**
NORTHERN TERRITORY: **VULNERABLE**

Known locations of leatherback turtle
● = *pre 1970*
● = *post 1970*

DESCRIPTION
The leatherback turtle is a massive turtle, weighing up to 500 kg and with a carapace length of 1.6 m. The shell is leathery, black with light spots and has five longitudinal ridges. Eggs are large (mean diameter: 5.3 cm). Hatchlings are black with white markings on the carapace ridges.

DISTRIBUTION
The species is distributed globally, nesting mostly in tropical areas and feeding in temperate areas. There are very few records of nesting in Australia. In the Northern Territory, the only locations where breeding has been reported are the Sir Edward Pellew Islands, near Maningrida, Danger Point on Cobourg Peninsula and Palm Bay on Croker Island. Nesting occurs in most years at Danger Point but only occasionally at other sites. No tracks of leatherbacks were found during extensive surveys of beaches across the Northern Territory coastline during the breeding season (R. Chatto *unpubl.* data).

Conservation reserves where reported:
Garig Gunak Barlu National Park

ECOLOGY
The leatherback turtle feeds within the water column and is regarded as an oceanic species. Their diet consists of macroplankton (jellyfish and salps). In Australia, they feed in sub-tropical and temperate waters of Queensland, Western Australia, New South Wales, Victoria and Tasmania. However they have also been recorded feeding off the Northern Territory coast (Cogger *et al.* 1993). Major breeding sites occur in New Guinea and Malaysia. Some animals from these areas migrate to Australian temperate waters to feed.

CONSERVATION ASSESSMENT
Population size and trends in Australia are unknown. The species has undergone significant population declines in the Indian and Pacific oceans in the last 20 or more years (Environment Australia 2003). These populations include the source of an unknown proportion of the Australian population. It is clear that the breeding population in the Northern Territory is very small compared with the other marine turtles that breed here. Threatening processes are known to be operating in Northern Territory waters.

Since population sizes and trends are unknown it is not possible to definitively assign a conservation status to the species. In such circumstances it could be considered Data Deficient. However, given the documented decline of source populations for Australian animals, the species is classified as **Vulnerable** in the Northern Territory (under criterion A2b) based on a population reduction of more than 30% over the last three generations.

THREATENING PROCESSES
Threatening processes in Northern Territory waters are by-capture from commercial fishing activity and, possibly, predation of eggs by dogs and goannas. In 1998, 18 leatherback turtles were captured by the northern prawn fishery in the northern Arnhem and western Gulf regions (Australian Fisheries Management Authority, unpublished data).

CONSERVATION OBJECTIVES AND MANAGEMENT
A national recovery plan for this species, and other marine turtles, was approved in 2003 (Environment Australia 2003).

The main anthropomorphic mortality factor operating within Northern Territory waters is probably capture of turtles by prawn trawlers. This fishery is under the control of the Australian Government and they have implemented measures to reduce by-catch of turtles (Environment Australia 2003). One such measure, the introduction of turtle exclusion devices has probably reduced the by-catch of leatherback turtles.

The management priority is to ensure that measures to reduce by-catch in fisheries are effective.

Compiled by Robert Taylor, Ray Chatto [May 2006] / **References:** Cogger, H.G., Cameron, E.E., Sadlier, R.A., and Egler, P. (1993). *The Action Plan for Australian Reptiles.* (Australian Nature Conservation Agency, Canberra.) / Environment Australia (2003). *Recovery Plan for marine turtles in Australia.* (Environment Australia, Canberra.)

Gulf snapping turtle
Elseya lavarackorum

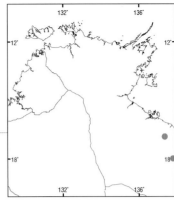

*Known locations
of Gulf snapping turtle*
● = *pre 1970*
● = *post 1970*

DESCRIPTION

The Gulf snapping turtle is a short-necked turtle, growing to 35 cm length. It is similar to the more widespread and common northern snapping turtle *E. dentata*, but can be distinguished by an undulating suture between the humeral and pectoral shields of the plastron (Wilson and Swan 2003).

Note that it was formerly listed as *Elusor lavarackorum*.

DISTRIBUTION

The Gulf snapping turtle is restricted to rivers draining into the Gulf of Queensland (Georges and Adams 1996). In the Northern Territory, this includes the Calvert to the Nicholson River systems (Cann 1998; A. Georges *pers. comm.*)

Conservation reserves where reported: None

ECOLOGY

This freshwater turtle is mainly herbivorous, taking leaves, fruits, flowers, bark and *Pandanus* roots. Juveniles may take more animal material, mostly insect larvae, and the species may be readily trapped using meat as bait (Cann 1998). Eggs are laid in soil near the water's edge.

CONSERVATION ASSESSMENT

This species is listed as Endangered nationally, largely on the basis of a presumed small range (subsequently found to be larger) (Thomson *et al.* 1997) and some presumed decline. Although there are few published records, it is known from many of the Northern Territory Gulf rivers, and there is no information on trends in abundance. Given the absence of marked threat, it is regarded as **Least Concern** in the Northern Territory.

THREATENING PROCESSES

There is some minor level of take in fisheries, nest sites may be raided by feral pigs and stock may degrade river banks (including nest sites).

CONSERVATION OBJECTIVES AND MANAGEMENT

The main research priority is to better clarify its status in the Northern Territory, including an assessment of distribution, abundance, habitat requirement and threats; and to establish a monitoring program.

Compiled by John Woinarski [May 2006] / **References:** Cann, J. (1998). *Australian freshwater turtles.* (Beaumont, Singapore.) / Georges, A., and Adams, M. (1996). Electrophoretic delineation of species boundaries within the short-necked freshwater turtles of Australia (Testudines: Chelidae). *Zoological Journal of the Linnean Society, London* 118, 241-260. / Thomson, S., White, A., and Georges, A. (1997). Re-evaluation of *Emydura lavarackorum*: identification of a living fossil. *Memoirs of the Queensland Museum* 42, 327-336. / Wilson, S., and Swann, G. (2003). *A complete guide to reptiles of Australia.* (Reed New Holland, Sydney.)

Image courtesy of Ted Johansen

Yellow-snouted gecko
Diplodactylus occultus

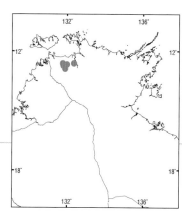

Known locations of yellow-snouted gecko
● = pre 1970
● = post 1970

CONSERVATION STATUS
AUSTRALIA: **ENDANGERED**
NORTHERN TERRITORY: **VULNERABLE**

DESCRIPTION
The yellow-snouted gecko is a small ground lizard (snout-vent length: 40 mm), dark brown above with a reddish head, four large, squarish pale brown blotches along the back, and whitish spots scattered on the flanks and limbs.

DISTRIBUTION
The yellow-snouted gecko is endemic to the Northern Territory and is known from only a few locations. Until the recent discovery of this species on Wildman Reserve (proposed Mary River National Park) and Mt Bundy Training Area (P. Horner *pers. comm.*), previous records were limited to only three specimens, all from the north-west of Kakadu National Park (King *et al.* 1982). More recent intensive targeted surveys have expanded its known range to include Annaburroo (Johansen 2006).

Conservation reserves where reported:
Kakadu National Park, Mary River National Park.

ECOLOGY
Very little is known of the ecology of this species. It is a nocturnal, ground-dwelling lizard, whose diet comprises a range of small invertebrates. Most individuals captured to date have occurred in areas with well-developed layers of leaf litter and grass (King *et al.* 1982; Johansen 2006) in open forests dominated by Darwin woollybutt (*Eucalyptus miniata*) and Darwin stringybark (*E. tetrodonta*), typically with red sandy-loam soils.

Records from Wildman Reserve include sites with sparse to moderate occurrences of introduced gamba grass (*Andropogon gayanus*) (K. Beggs *unpubl.*).

CONSERVATION ASSESSMENT
Conservation categorisation for the yellow-snouted gecko is problematic because of lack of information on its distribution and population trends at the known sites. However, it can be reasonably inferred that this species has a relatively small total population within its limited and fragmented range. Since its description, there have been remarkably few further records, despite intensive searches (Johansen 2006).

The species qualifies as **Vulnerable** (under criteria B1ab(ii,iii,iv,v)) due to:
- extent of occurrence less than 20 000 km²;
- known to exist at fewer than 10 locations; and
- continuing decline, observed, inferred or projected.

THREATENING PROCESSES
Based on meagre data, the likely threats to the yellow-snouted gecko are related to inappropriate fire regimes and spread of introduced pasture species. There have been fewer than five further records from Kakadu National Park since the capture of one individual near Kapalga in 1988, where part of its habitat was subjected to frequent, intense fire regimes. Most subsequent records (outside Kakadu) have been at sites that have not

been burned for five or more years (Johansen 2006). It is therefore likely that this species requires conservative fire management (infrequent fires or small areas burnt early in the dry season, and no extensive late dry season fires). It is also likely that this species will be disadvantaged by the spread of exotic pasture grasses, especially gamba grass, which form a denser understorey and promote more intense and extensive fires.

CONSERVATION OBJECTIVES AND MANAGEMENT
There is no existing management program for the yellow-snouted gecko in the Northern Territory.

A small captive breeding population has been maintained at the Territory Wildlife Park (G. Husband *pers. comm.*).

Research priorities are to:
- undertake further survey work and baseline ecological research aimed at establishing the distribution, abundance and ecological requirements of the yellow-snouted gecko
- establish a monitoring program for at least representative populations.

Management priorities are to:
- reduce the incidence, extent and severity of fires within its limited range; and
- reduce the extent of invasive exotic grasses in its limited known range.

Compiled by Kerry Beggs, Martin Armstrong, John Woinarski [December 2006] / **References:** Cogger, H. G. (2000). *Reptiles and Amphibians of Australia. Sixth edition.* (Reed New Holland, Sydney). / Johansen, T. (2006). The yellow-snouted gecko (*Diplodactylus occultus*), a little known endemic species of northern Australia. Report to NT Department of Natural Resources Environment and the Arts. / King, M., Braithwaite, R. W., and Wombey, J. C. (1982). A new species of *Diplodactylus* (Reptilia: Gekkonidae) from the Alligator Rivers region, Northern Territory. *Transactions of the Royal Society of South Australia* 106,15-18.

Image courtesy of Ian Morris

Bronzeback,
Bronzeback snake-lizard
Ophidiocephalus taeniatus

CONSERVATION STATUS
AUSTRALIA: **VULNERABLE**
NORTHERN TERRITORY: **DATA DEFICIENT**

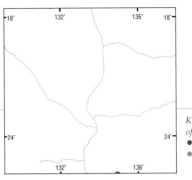

Known location
of the bronzeback
● = pre 1970
● = post 1970

DESCRIPTION
The bronzeback is a small legless lizard with a snout-vent length up to 102 mm. The tail is longer than the snout-vent length. The most striking feature of the animal is its bronze or rich fawn upper body. In contrast, the head is pale grey. It has a broad, dark brown lateral band from the snout to the tip of the tail. The underparts are grey brown. The ventral and lower lateral surfaces have a reticulated pattern formed by the white margins of the scales contrasting against the darker basal pattern (Cogger 2000).

DISTRIBUTION
The type locality is Charlotte Waters, in the extreme south of the Northern Territory. This locality probably only refers loosely to the collection site and the specimen may have come from anywhere within a 100 km radius of Charlotte Waters (Ehmann 1981).

Recent records of the bronzeback are from a series of eight sites between Abminga and Coober Pedy in the Stony Plains bioregion of northern South Australia (Ehmann and Metcalfe 1978; Ehmann 1981, 1992; Downes *et al.* 1997).

Conservation reserves where reported: None

ECOLOGY
The bronzeback is fossorial and mostly occupies areas with a dense leaf litter along temporary watercourses supporting gidgee open woodland

with a shrub understorey. In the vicinity of Arckaringa, one animal was captured under a mulga tree on an open rocky plain, 8 km from the nearest major watercourse. This observation indicates that the species' habitat preferences may be broader than previously thought.

The bronzeback is crepuscular and nocturnal. Its diet consists of various invertebrates including termites, cockroach nymphs, larvae of moths and beetles, and spiders. It appears to lay eggs rather than give birth to live young, although further observations are needed to clarify its reproductive behaviour.

CONSERVATION ASSESSMENT
The bronzeback is found only in the Stony Plains bioregion of arid Australia. The only possible Northern Territory record is the type locality, given as Charlotte Waters. Despite recent specific surveys for the species around Charlotte Waters and more general fauna surveys in the region, the species has not been reported from the Northern Territory since the type collection (more than 100 years ago). However, some areas of suitable habitat have not been surveyed. Based on this information the bronzeback is listed as **Data Deficient** in the Northern Territory.

THREATENING PROCESSES
No single factor has been identified as a major threatening process for the bronzeback. The major threat may be habitat modification resulting from overgrazing by stock (Cogger *et al.* 1993). Cattle trample and graze suitable bronzeback habitat along watercourses resulting in a loss of plant cover and leaf litter and compaction and erosion of soil. The effects of grazing by cattle, and possibly also rabbits, may exacerbate the impact of severe flooding which either washes away the leaf litter or deposits a dry sediment on top of it.

CONSERVATION OBJECTIVES AND MANAGEMENT
There is no existing management program for the species in the Northern Territory. The main management priority is to determine whether the species actually occurs in the Northern Territory.

Research priorities include to:
• conduct targeted searches (that use the method of raking and subsequent hand capture) for the species during future surveys of the Stony Plains bioregion in the Northern Territory;
• follow up (as soon as possible) any reliable potential sightings of the species; and
• encourage herpetologists carrying out surveys in northern South Australia to extend their searches into the southern Northern Territory.

Compiled by Chris Pavey [May 2006] / **References:** Cogger, H.G. (2000). *Reptiles and Amphibians of Australia*. Sixth Edition. (Reed New Holland, Sydney.) / Cogger, H., Cameron, E., Sadlier, R., and Eggler, P. (1993). *The Action Plan for Australian Reptiles*. (ANCA, Canberra.) / Downes, S., Foster, R., and Molnar, C. (1997). New insights into the distribution and habitat of the vulnerable bronzeback legless lizard *Ophidiocephalus taeniatus*. *Herpetofauna* 27, 11-13. / Ehmann, H. (1981). The natural history and conservation of the bronzeback (*Ophidiocephalus taeniatus* Lucas and Frost) (Lacertilia, Pygopodidae). In *Proceedings of the Melbourne Herpetological Symposium* (eds C.B. Brown and A.A. Martin.) pp. 7-13. (Zoological Board of Victoria, Melbourne.) / Ehmann, H. (1992). The apparent severe decline of the bronzeback legless lizard (*Ophidiocephalus taeniatus*) at Abminga. *Herpetofauna* 22, 31-33. / Ehmann, H., and Metcalfe, D. (1978). The rediscovery of *Ophidiocephalus taeniatus* Lucas and Frost (Pygopodidae, Lacertilia) the Bronzeback. *Herpetofauna* 9, 8-10.

Image courtesy of Simon Ward

Mertens water monitor
Varanus mertensi

*Known locations
of Mertens water
monitor*
● = pre 1970
● = post 1970

DESCRIPTION

Mertens water monitor is a medium to large-sized (total length to 1 m), semi-aquatic monitor (goanna), dark brown to black on the back with numerous small dark-edged cream or yellow spots. The lower lip is yellowish, speckled or barred with grey. The under surface is white to yellowish with some grey patterning on the throat and chest. The tail is very strongly compressed laterally, to provide power when swimming, has a strong two-keeled crest along the top and is about 1.5 times as long as the head and body.

DISTRIBUTION

Varanus mertensi has a broad geographic range, occupying coastal and inland waters across the far north of Australia from the Kimberley to the west side of Cape York Peninsula. In the Northern Territory, it has been recorded across most of the Top End and the Gulf region.

Conservation reserves where reported:
Black Jungle/Lambells Lagoon Conservation Reserve, Cutta Cutta Caves Nature Park, Djukbinj National Park, Elsey National Park, Flora River Nature Park, Fogg Dam Conservation Reserve, Garig Gunak Barlu National Park, Gregory National Park, Howard Springs Nature Park, Kakadu National Park, Keep River National Park, Litchfield National Park, Manton Dam, Mary River National Park, Nitmiluk National Park, Territory Wildlife Park-Berry Springs Nature Park, Umbrawara Gorge National Park.

ECOLOGY

Varanus mertensi is a semi-aquatic monitor seldom seen far from water. A strong swimmer, it mostly feeds on fish, frogs and carrion, but will also eat insects and small terrestrial vertebrates. It has an excellent sense of smell and may dig up prey when foraging, including freshwater turtle eggs (Doody *et al.* 2006). It is an accomplished climber and can be seen climbing on rocks or trees near water, often basking on branches overhanging the water or on rocks mid-stream. It lays eggs in a burrow constructed in the ground, usually in the early dry season.

CONSERVATION ASSESSMENT

Varanus mertensi is widespread in the Northern Territory, occupying all of the Top End river systems. The most important conservation issue it faces is its propensity to eat cane toads and to die from the ingested toxins.

Tests of the effects of ingesting cane toad toxins have found that *V. mertensi* is very susceptible. Comparison of the size of the mouth and the toxin load per cane toad shows that these monitors are easily able to eat a cane toad large enough to kill them (Smith and Phillips 2006).

Burnett (1997) documented anecdotal reports of declines of several species of monitors (including *V. mertensi*) on Cape York Peninsula, Queensland following the arrival of cane toads. van Dam *et al.* (2002) considered it highly likely that the population of *V. mertensi* in Kakadu National Park would be affected by cane toads.

Griffiths and McKay (2005) showed a decline in the number of sites occupied by *V. mertensi* at Manton Dam in the Northern Territory following the arrival of cane toads. The decline in site occupancy took 12 months after the arrival of cane toads to occur and when cane toad abundance increased. This suggests that *V. mertensi* may not consume cane toads as readily as other monitors (i.e. *V. panoptes*).

Smith and Phillips (2006) estimated that 86% of the Australian range of *V. mertensi* will be encompassed by the predicted range of the cane toad. Local populations will suffer crashes then slowly increase as cane toads move across the Northern Territory, but the impact on the Northern Territory-wide population will not be as severe as at individual locations.

Based on this information, *V. mertensi* is considered **Vulnerable** (under criterion A4e) due to a population size reduction of more than 30%, occurring and projected to be met within the next 10 years or three generations, due to the effects of an introduced species.

continued.../

THREATENING PROCESSES

The advance of cane toads across the Northern Territory presents the most acute threat facing this monitor. Cane toads may also deplete areas of potential prey for monitors, especially foods eaten by juveniles. This may impede the recovery of populations after the initial crash.

CONSERVATION OBJECTIVES AND MANAGEMENT

The likelihood of stopping the spread of cane toads across the Northern Territory is very small. Efforts are being made to slow their progress westwards and into Darwin and, if successful, these will ameliorate the impact on the Territory-wide population of *V. mertensi*.

Given our inability to prevent localised population crashes once cane toads arrive, conservation and management effort is best aimed at:
• trying to maintain surviving depleted populations in areas invaded by cane toads; and

• preventing cane toads from spreading to offshore islands with populations of monitors. However, *Varanus mertensi* occurs on few Northern Territory islands. It is known only from three of 60 sampled islands in the English Company and Wessel Islands group off north-east Arnhem Land, and from Groote Eylandt, Bathurst and Melville Islands (Webb 1992; Woinarski *et al.* 1999, 2003). It was not recorded on any island during a series of surveys of the Pellew Islands group (Johnson and Kerle 1991).

Compiled by Simon Ward, John Woinarski, Tony Griffiths, Lindley McKay [November 2006] / **References**: Burnett, S. (1997). Colonising cane toads cause population declines in native predators: reliable anecdotal information and management implications. *Pacific Conservation Biology* 3, 65-72. / Doody, J.S., Green, B., Sims, R, Rhind, D., West, P., and Steer, D. (2006). Indirect impacts of invasive cane toads (*Bufo marinus*) on nest predation in pig-nosed turtles (*Carettochelys insculpta*). *Wildlife Research* 33, 349–354. / Doody, J.S., Green, B., Sims, R, and Rhind, D. (in press). A preliminary assessment of the impacts of invasive cane toads (*Bufo marinus*) on three species of varanid lizards in Australia. *Mertensiella* / Griffiths, A.D. & McKay, J.L. (2005). Monitoring the freshwater goanna *Varanus mertensi* after the arrival of cane toads using site occupancy models. Report to Parks and Wildlife Service NT. (Charles Darwin University, Darwin.) / Johnson, K.A., and Kerle, J.A. (1991). *Flora and vertebrate fauna of the Sir Edward Pellew group of islands, Northern Territory*. Report to the Australian Heritage Commission. (Conservation Commission of the Northern Territory, Alice Springs.) / Smith, J.G., and Phillips, B.L. (2006). Toxic tucker: the potential impact of cane toads on Australian reptiles. *Pacific Conservation Biology* 12, 40-49. / van Dam, R.A., Walden, D.J., and Begg, G.W. (2002) *A preliminary risk assessment of cane toads in Kakadu National Park*. Scientist Report 164, Supervising Scientist, Darwin NT. / Webb, G. Pty Ltd. (1992). *Flora and fauna surveys on the western side of Groote Eylandt, N.T.* (1991-92). Report to BHP Manganese – GEMCO. / Woinarski, J., Brennan, K., Hempel, C., Armstrong, M., Milne, D., and Chatto, R. (2003). *Biodiversity conservation on the Tiwi Islands, Northern Territory. Part 2. Fauna.* 127 pp. (Department of Infrastructure Planning and Environment, Darwin.) / Woinarski, J.C.Z., Horner, P., Fisher, A., Brennan, K., Lindner, D., Gambold, N., Chatto, R., and Morris, I. (1999). Distributional patterning of terrestrial herpetofauna on the Wessel and English Company Island groups, north-eastern Arnhem Land, Northern Territory, Australia. *Australian Journal of Ecology* 24, 60-79.

Yellow-spotted monitor, Northern sand goanna, Floodplain monitor
Varanus panoptes

CONSERVATION STATUS
AUSTRALIA: **NOT LISTED**
NORTHERN TERRITORY: **VULNERABLE**

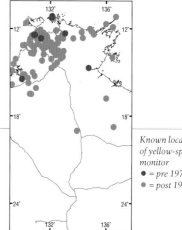

Known locations of yellow-spotted monitor
● = pre 1970
● = post 1970

DESCRIPTION

The yellow-spotted monitor is a large (total length up to 1.4 m), heavily-built terrestrial monitor, dark brown to reddish-brown on the back with alternating transverse bands of large black spots and smaller dark-edged pale yellow spots. The underside is pale but often marked with lines of spots extending from the pattern on the back. The tail is laterally compressed and the last quarter is pale with narrow dark bands.

DISTRIBUTION

Varanus panoptes has a broad geographic range across the far north of Australia from the Kimberley in Western Australia, to Cape York Peninsula, and southwards through most of Queensland. In the Northern Territory, it has been recorded across most of the Top End and the Gulf region (south to Katherine, Gregory National Park and the Gulf hinterland). A distinct subspecies occurs in the Pilbara and Gascoyne regions of Western Australia.

Conservation reserves where reported:
Black Jungle/Lambell's Lagoon Conservation Reserve, Casuarina Coastal Reserve, Charles Darwin National Park, Djukbinj National Park, Fogg Dam, Garig Gunak Barlu National Park, Gregory National Park, Kakadu National Park, Keep River National Park, Litchfield National Park, Manton Dam, Mary River National Park, Nitmiluk National Park, Umbrawara Gorge National Park.

ECOLOGY

Varanus panoptes is a robust ground-dwelling monitor occupying a variety of habitats, including coastal beaches, floodplains, grasslands and woodlands. It feeds mostly on small terrestrial vertebrates and insects. It has an excellent sense of smell and often digs up prey, especially eggs of marine and freshwater turtles (Blamires 2004, Doody *et al.* 2006). It lays a clutch of eggs in a burrow in the ground, usually in the wet season.

CONSERVATION ASSESSMENT

Varanus panoptes is widespread in the Northern Territory. The most important conservation issue it faces is its propensity to eat cane toads and to die from the ingested toxins.

Tests of the effects of ingesting cane toad toxins have found that *V. panoptes* is very susceptible. Comparison of the size of the mouth and the toxin load per cane toad shows that these monitors are easily able to eat a cane toad large enough to kill them (Smith and Phillips 2006).

Burnett (1997) documented anecdotal reports of declines of several species of monitors (including *V. panoptes*) in Queensland following the arrival of cane toads in an area, however, he also noted cases of *V. panoptes* persisting in areas, such as around Townsville, alongside cane toads, and Kutt *et al.* (2005) noted that this species had persisted following toad invasion at a site recently sampled on Cape York Peninsula.

A radio tracking study of *V. panoptes* in Kakadu National Park documented a large decline in survival immediately after the arrival of cane toads (Griffiths and Holland 2004). Larger goannas were at greater risk, but there was a large amount of variation in the population, suggesting some animals may avoid cane toads. Continued monitoring of *V. panoptes* in Kakadu showed they were still present in numerous locations three years after cane toads arrived (Griffiths and McKay 2005). Similarly, the abundance of *V. panoptes* dropped significantly (by 77% and 90%) one year after cane toads arrived at two sites on the Daly River (Doody *et al.* 2006).

A large proportion of the range of *V. panoptes* will be encompassed by the predicted range of the cane toad (Smith and Phillips 2006). As cane toads continue to spread across northern Australia, local monitor populations will suffer crashes then slowly increase.

Based on this information, *V. panoptes* is considered **Vulnerable** (under criterion A4e) due to a population size reduction of more than 30%, occurring and projected to be met within the next 10 years or three generations due to the effects of an introduced species.

continued.../

THREATENING PROCESSES

As described above, the advance of cane toads across the Northern Territory presents the most acute threat facing this monitor.

CONSERVATION OBJECTIVES AND MANAGEMENT

The likelihood of stopping the spread of cane toads across the Northern Territory is very small. Efforts are being made to slow their progress westwards and into Darwin and, if successful, these will ameliorate the impact on the Territory-wide population of *V. panoptes*.

Given our inability to prevent localised population crashes once cane toads arrive, conservation and management effort is best aimed at:
• monitoring depleted populations to examine for evidence of recovery; and
• preventing cane toads from spreading to offshore islands with populations of monitors. However, there are relatively few Northern Territory islands from which this species has been recorded.

Compiled by Simon Ward, John Woinarski, Tony Griffiths, Lindley McKay [November 2006] / **References:** Blamires, S.J. (2004) Habitat preferences of coastal goannas (*Varanus panoptes*): are they exploiters of sea turtle nests at Fog Bay, Australia? *Copeia* 2004, 370–377. / Burnett, S. (1997). Colonising cane toads cause population declines in native predators: reliable anecdotal information and management implications. *Pacific Conservation Biology* 3, 65-72. / Doody, J.S., Green, B., Sims, R, Rhind, D., West, P., and Steer, D. (2006). Indirect impacts of invasive cane toads (*Bufo marinus*) on nest predation in pig-nosed turtles (*Carettochelys insculpta*). *Wildlife Research* 33, 349–354. / Doody, J.S., Green, B., Sims, R, and Rhind, D. (in press). A preliminary assessment of the impacts of invasive cane toads (*Bufo marinus*) on three species of varanid lizards in Australia. *Mertensiella* / Greer, A.E. (1989). *The biology and evolution of Australian lizards*. (Surrey Beatty and Sons, Sydney.) / Griffiths, A.D., and Holland, D.C. (2004). Impact of the exotic cane toad (*Bufo marinus*) on the survival of lowland *Varanus* species in Kakadu National Park. Report to Kakadu National Park. (Charles Darwin University, Darwin.) / Griffiths, A.D., and McKay, J.L. (2005). Monitoring the impact of cane toads on goanna species in Kakadu National Park. Report to Kakadu National Park, Department of Environment and Heritage. (Charles Darwin University, Darwin.) / Kutt, A.S., Bolitho, E.E., Retallick, R.W.R., and Kemp, J.E. (2005). Pattern and change in the terrestrial vertebrate fauna of the Pennefather River, Gulf of Carpentaria, Cape York Peninsula. In *Gulf of Carpentaria Scientific Study Report*. pp. 261-300. Geography Monograph Series No. 10. (Royal Geographical Society of Queensland Inc., Brisbane.) / Smith, J.G., and Phillips, B.L. (2006). Toxic tucker: the potential impact of cane toads on Australian reptiles. *Pacific Conservation Biology* 12, 40-49.

Cryptoblepharus sp. New Year and Oxley Islands

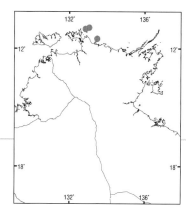

Known locations
of *Cryptoblepharus*
sp. New Year and
Oxley Islands
● = *pre 1970*
● = *post 1970*

CONSERVATION STATUS
AUSTRALIA: **NOT LISTED**
NORTHERN TERRITORY: **ENDANGERED**

DESCRIPTION
This species is a small, slender, terrestrial skink
with five digits on each foot and hand. The species
is awaiting formal description by Paul Horner
of the Museum and Art Gallery of the Northern
Territory (Horner 2006).

DISTRIBUTION
The known distribution is restricted to three
islands; North Goulburn Island (42 km²),
New Year and Oxley (the latter two are less than
2 km², and located north-east of Croker Island).
Brief searches on other islands in this area have
failed to detect this species. The North Goulburn
Island population was discovered only in 2006
(K. Brennan *pers. comm.*).

Conservation reserves where reported: None

ECOLOGY
The species is locally common in littoral habitats,
including beach sands, rocks and coral rubble, on
the three islands.

CONSERVATION ASSESSMENT
The species qualifies as **Endangered** (under
criteria B1ab(i,ii,iii,iv,v)) due to:
• extent of occurrence estimated to be less than
  5000 km²;
• severely fragmented and known to exist at no
  more than five locations; and
• projected or inferred decline.

Population decline is inferred because of storm
surge associated with cyclones, sea-level rise, or
inadvertent or deliberate introduction of exotic
predators to the two small islands.

The species was common on the two small islands
when last visited (1982: P. Horner *unpubl.*), but
there is no detailed information on population size,
trends or ecological requirements.

THREATENING PROCESSES
Threat assessment is difficult because of the lack of
ecological information. Restriction to three islands
presents a substantial risk. The coastline habitat
of these islands may be exposed to periodic storm
surges associated with cyclones (which may purge
much of the terrestrial biota) and will be reduced in
size with any rise in sea level; the highest point on
Oxley and New Year Islands is 12 m above sea level
but most is less than 5 m.

CONSERVATION OBJECTIVES
AND MANAGEMENT
The primary research priority is to better evaluate
the species' distribution and population size.

Management priorities are to:
• reduce the possibility of introduction of any new
  predators to these islands; and
• consider spreading the risk of extinction by
  translocation of some individuals to other
  suitable islands or nearby mainland.

Compiled by John Woinarski, Paul Horner [December 2006] / **References:** Horner, P. (2006). Systematics of the Snake-eyed Skinks, genus *Cryptoblepharus* Wiegmann (Squamata: Scincidae). PhD thesis, Charles Darwin University.

Image courtesy of Alaric Fisher

VRD blacksoil ctenotus

Ctenotus rimacola camptris

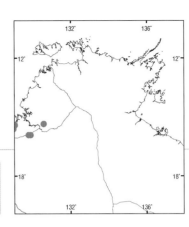

Known locations of VRD blacksoil ctenotus
● = pre 1970
● = post 1970

CONSERVATION STATUS
AUSTRALIA: **NOT LISTED**
NORTHERN TERRITORY: **VULNERABLE**

DESCRIPTION

The VRD blacksoil ctenotus is a moderately large (body length 80 mm) and robust skink, with prominent dark vertebral stripe. It is most similar to the blacksoil ctenotus *C. joanae* from the Barkly Tablelands and the more widespread robust ctenotus *C. robustus*, but distinguished from those species by a combination of scale and size characteristics (Horner and Fisher 1998). There are two subspecies of *Ctenotus rimacola*: subspecies *rimacola* has a grey ground colour while subspecies *camptris* has an olive-brown ground colour and narrower dorsal stripe.

DISTRIBUTION

Ctenotus r. camptris has a very small geographic range, restricted to the floodplains of the lower Ord and Keep Rivers (including the far north-east Kimberley, Western Australia). *Ctenotus r. rimacola* is restricted to the Victoria River District.

Conservation reserves where reported: None.

ECOLOGY

Ctenotus rimacola is restricted to grasslands, or grasslands with a sparse woodland overstorey, on cracking clay soils. It is active during the day, forages on the ground and shelters within the soil cracks. Its diet comprises a range of invertebrates.

CONSERVATION ASSESSMENT

Ctenotus rimacola was recognised as recently as 1998, so there is limited information available on parameters relevant to conservation assessment.

The total available habitat within its distribution is approximately 14 000 km^2 for subspecies *rimacola*, but less than 8000 km^2 for subspecies *camptris*, of which 370 km^2 is in the Northern Territory. While subspecies *rimacola* appears to be relatively abundant in suitable habitat, there are few records for subspecies *camptris* despite intensive biological survey in the Ord and Keep floodplains.

Fisher (2001) demonstrated that this species is sensitive to grazing pressure, and that almost all of its range is subjected to pastoralism. Based on grazing gradient studies, the population in Victoria River District may have been substantially reduced because of pastoralism. While the subspecies appears secure under current management regimes, further population decline may occur under current proposals to intensify grazing pressure.

Ctenotus rimacola camptris may face more intensive threats from recent proposals to clear around 50% of its habitat for intensive horticultural production, mostly sugar cane (Kinhill 2000). The future of this development is currently unclear, but the Keep River Plain remains a focus for potential agricultural development.

Based on this information, *C. r. camptris* is considered **Vulnerable** (under criterion A3c) due to:
• a population size reduction of more than 30%, projected or suspected, to be met within the next 10 years or three generations; and
• decline in area of occupancy, extent of occurrence and/or quality of habitat.

THREATENING PROCESSES

The most acute threat facing this lizard is potential broad scale clearing associated with conversion of native grassland to horticulture in the lower Ord and Keep River systems.

The species is also subject to a pervasive threat from grazing by livestock and feral herbivores, probably associated with a decrease in vegetation cover and changes in composition of the ground layer.

Predation by feral cats may also cause some decline in total population size. Longer-term vegetation change, notably invasion of grasslands by some woody species such as rosewood (*Terminalia volucris*), may reduce the area of suitable habitat (Sharp and Whittaker 2003).

CONSERVATION OBJECTIVES AND MANAGEMENT

The primary research priority is to more comprehensively document its abundance and distribution.

Management priorities are to:
• ensure adequate areas of suitable habitat are maintained under any scenario of increased horticultural use of the lower Ord and Keep River valleys; and
• ensure adequate areas of suitable habitat are maintained under any scenario of increased intensification of pastoralism in the Victoria River District.

Compiled by Alaric Fisher, John Woinarski [May 2006] / **References:** Fisher, A. (2001). *Biogeography and conservation of Mitchell grasslands in northern Australia.* PhD thesis. (Northern Territory University, Darwin.) / Horner, P., and Fisher, A. (1998). *Ctenotus rimacola* sp. nov. (Scincidae), a new species of lizard with two allopatric subspecies, from the Ord-Victoria region of north-western Australia. *Records of the Western Australian Museum* 19, 187-200. / Kinhill Pty. Ltd. (2000). *Ord River Irrigation Area Stage 2. Proposed development of the M2 area.* Draft Environmental Impact Statement. (Kinhill, Perth.) Sharp, B.R., and Whittaker, R.J. (2003). The irreversible cattle-driven transformation of a seasonally flooded Australian savanna. *Journal of Biogeography* 30, 783-802.

Image courtesy of Steve McAlpine

Great desert skink,
Tjakura
Egernia kintorei

CONSERVATION STATUS
AUSTRALIA: **VULNERABLE**
NORTHERN TERRITORY: **VULNERABLE**

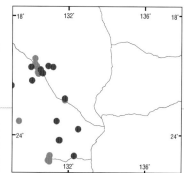

Known locations of great desert skink
● = *pre 1970*
● = *post 1970*

DESCRIPTION

The great desert skink is a large, smooth-bodied lizard with an average snout-vent length of 200 mm (maximum of 440 mm) and a body mass of up to 350 g. Males are heavier and have broader heads than females. The tail is slightly longer than the snout-vent length. The upper body varies in colour between individuals and can be bright orange-brown, dull brown or light grey. The underbody colour ranges from bright lemon-yellow to cream or grey. Adult males often have blue-grey flanks, whereas those of females and juveniles are either plain brown or vertically barred with orange and cream.

DISTRIBUTION

The great desert skink is endemic to the Australian arid zone. In the Northern Territory, most recent records (post 1980) come from the western deserts region from Uluru – Kata Tjuta National Park north to Rabbit Flat in the Tanami Desert. The Tanami Desert and Uluru populations are both global strongholds for the species.

Outside the Northern Territory, it occurs in north-west South Australia and in the Gibson Desert and southern sections of the Great Sandy Desert of Western Australia. Its former range included the Great Victoria Desert, as far west as Wiluna, and the northern Great Sandy Desert.

Conservation reserves where reported:
Uluru – Kata Tjuta National Park, Watarrka National Park, Newhaven Reserve (a large pastoral lease in the Great Sandy Desert managed for conservation by Birds Australia and the Australian Wildlife Conservancy).

ECOLOGY

The great desert skink occupies a range of vegetation types with the major habitat being sand plain and adjacent swales that support hummock grassland and scattered shrubs. In the Tanami Desert, it also occupies paleodrainage lines on lateritic soils supporting *Melaleuca* shrubs. It is an omnivore that feeds on a wide variety of invertebrates (particularly termites), small vertebrates, and the leaves, flowers and fruits of plants.

The great desert skink is a live-bearer that gives birth to between one and five young from December to February.

It is a communal species that digs complex burrow systems to a depth of more than 1 m and with a diameter (of the entire burrow system) of up to 10 m. Up to 10 individuals may share a large burrow system which can have between 5 and 10 entrances. The animals defaecate at "latrines", which are spread over an area of 1 to 3 m and located at the surface of occupied burrows.

CONSERVATION ASSESSMENT

The maximum size of each population of great desert skink in the Northern Territory has been estimated as 2250 in the Tanami Desert, 500 in Uluru – Kata Tjuta National Park and 350 in land surrounding Yulara (McAlpin 2001). This total represents about 50% of the global population of the species.

Although the species no longer occurs in eastern parts of its former range in the Northern Territory, there is a lack of information on population trends at any sites. However, it can be reasonably inferred that there is a high likelihood that remaining populations will be subjected in the near future to the same threats that have extirpated populations elsewhere. Given this premise, the species qualifies as **Vulnerable** (under criterion C2a(i)) due to:
• population fewer than 10 000 mature individuals;
• continuing decline, observed, projected or inferred, in numbers; and
• no population estimated to contain more than 1000 mature individuals.

THREATENING PROCESSES

No single factor has been demonstrated to have caused the decline of the great desert skink; however, several potential threatening processes have been identified.

Habitat homogenization as a consequence of the cessation of traditional land management practices may be a serious threat throughout much of its range.

continued.../

Large scale, intense wildfires that result from a lack of patch burning can devastate or fragment local populations. Predation by feral cats and the European fox may also be a serious threat, as could predation by native predators such as the dingo or raptors, particularly in recently burnt areas. Rabbits also have the potential to dig up burrow systems.

CONSERVATION OBJECTIVES AND MANAGEMENT

A national recovery plan for the species was adopted in 2001.

Management priorities for the species in the Northern Territory, as set out in the recovery plan, are to:
• assess causal factors in the recent decline or local extinction of the species in particular locations, and to determine critical habitat;
• manage by 2010 the population in Uluru – Kata Tjuta National Park to maintain or improve population levels (as measured by number of active burrows) against an initial baseline figure derived from five seasons of monitoring;
• improve community knowledge of the species and to improve community involvement in its recovery management;
• determine the best fire regime that leads to sustained or increased populations of great desert skink;

• reduce number, extent and impact of severe wildfires over the next decade; and
• implement feral predator control programs that result in sustained reductions in feral predator populations in Uluru – Kata Tjuta National Park over the next 10 years.

Compiled by Chris Pavey [May 2006] / **References:** Cogger, H.G. (2000). *Reptiles and Amphibians of Australia*. 6th edition. (Reed New Holland, Sydney.) / Horner, P. (1992). *Skinks of the Northen Territory*. (Northern Territory Museum of Arts and Sciences, Darwin.) / McAlpin, S. F. (2001). *A Recovery Plan for the Great Desert Skink (Egernia kintorei), 2001-2011*. (Arid Lands Environment Centre, Alice Springs). Storr, G.M. (1968). Revision of the *Egernia whitei* species-group (Lacertilia, Scincidae). *Journal of the Royal Society of Western Australia* 51, 51-62.

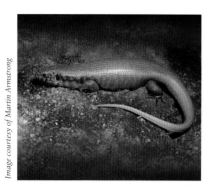

Image courtesy of Martin Armstrong

Arnhem Land egernia

Egernia obiri

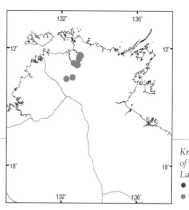

Known locations of the Arnhem Land egernia
● = pre 1970
● = post 1970

CONSERVATION STATUS
AUSTRALIA: **ENDANGERED**
NORTHERN TERRITORY: **ENDANGERED**

DESCRIPTION

Egernia obiri is a large (to at least 200 mm snout-vent length) thick-set, ground-dwelling skink, resembling a blue-tongue lizard in shape. It is grey to light brown above, with a brown longitudinal streak. The legs are short and chunky.

Until recently, the species was more widely known as *Egernia arnhemensis* (Sadlier 1990).

DISTRIBUTION

This species is restricted to the western Arnhem Land plateau and outliers, such as Jabiluka. Within this range, it has been recorded at relatively few locations, including Nawurlandja (Little Nourlangie Rock), Jabiluka, near Oenpelli, near El Sherana and Koolpin Gorge.

Conservation reserves where reported: Kakadu National Park.

ECOLOGY

This species is largely restricted to sandstone outcrops, typically with extensive fissures and cave systems. It is probably at least partly nocturnal or crepuscular (Sadlier 1990).

CONSERVATION ASSESSMENT

There is little information on its population, distribution or trends in abundance. As with other endemics of the western Arnhem Land massif, its total range spans about 34 000 km², of which about one third lies within Kakadu National Park. The limited data suggest that it is very patchily distributed with the population comprising a set of semi-isolated subpopulations. The species has been recorded at only ten locations. Each is probably less than 5 km² so the total area of occupancy is less than 50 km².

The best baseline information on status is that of many individuals caught as by-catch in mammal surveys at Nawurlandja in the late 1970s (Begg *et al.* 1981). No Arnhem Land egernias were caught there in more recent surveys that used identical procedures (Watson and Woinarski 2003). A recent trapping study of all previously known sites caught only one individual, observed one and found desiccated remains of another in a shallow cave (Armstrong and Dudley 2004). There are fewer than 10 records of the species since 1980 (Armstrong and Dudley 2004). The species qualifies as **Endangered** (under criteria A2b;B2ab(v)) on the basis of:

• its presumed decline by more than 50% in the past 15 years (three generations);
• probable total population of fewer than 2500 mature individuals; and
• limited extent of occupancy.

THREATENING PROCESSES

The ecology of this species is very poorly known. It may be affected by changes in food resources caused by altered fire regimes, or predation by cats. Cane toads may affect *E. obiri* through poisoning, but this will be difficult to determine.

CONSERVATION OBJECTIVES AND MANAGEMENT

Current knowledge is insufficient to provide much guide to management. Research is required to more precisely delineate distribution, habitat preferences, ecology and to identify threatening factors. This research should also provide a baseline for ongoing monitoring.

Compiled by Simon Ward, John Woinarski, Martin Armstrong [May 2006] / **References:** Armstrong, M., and Dudley, A. (2004). *The Arnhem Land egernia Egernia obiri in Kakadu National Park*. Report to Parks Australia North. (NT Department of Infrastructure Planning and Environment, Darwin.) Begg, R.J., Martin, K.C., and Price, N.F. (1981). The small mammals of Little Nourlangie Rock, N.T. V. The effects of fire. *Australian Wildlife Research* 8, 515-527. / Sadlier, R.A. (1990). A new species of scincid lizard from western Arnhem Land, Northern Territory. *The Beagle* 7, 29-33. / Watson, M., and Woinarski, J. (2003). *Vertebrate monitoring and resampling in Kakadu National Park, 2002*. Report to Parks Australia North. (Parks and Wildlife Commission of the Northern Territory, Darwin.)

Slater's skink
Egernia slateri

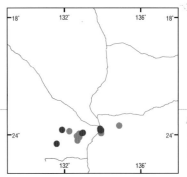

Known locations of Slater's skink
● = pre 1970
● = post 1970

CONSERVATION STATUS
AUSTRALIA: **ENDANGERED**
NORTHERN TERRITORY: **ENDANGERED**

DESCRIPTION

Slater's skink is a medium-sized, smooth-bodied lizard with an average snout-vent length of 85 mm, although large individuals grow up to 97 mm. It has a short snout and large head. The upper body is light to medium brown with each dorsal scale having a black edge. In combination these scales form a series of conspicuous black longitudinal striations on the back and on the base of the tail. The flanks may be salmon-pink and the underbody is cream to greyish-blue.

DISTRIBUTION

Two subspecies have been described; *E. s. slateri* from the southern Northern Territory and *E. s. virgata* from northern South Australia. The South Australian subspecies is known from only four specimens: three collected in 1896 from the Oodnadatta area, the other collected in 1914 between Oodnadatta and Everard Range. No other specimens of this subspecies have been located.

The Northern Territory subspecies has been collected from four locations in the Finke and MacDonnell Ranges bioregions centred on Alice Springs. In the 1960s, the subspecies appears to have been abundant around Alice Springs. Fifty-eight specimens were collected at the type locality 5 km south of Alice Springs (1964–65), another 32 specimens at the junction of Ellery Creek and Jerimah Creek, adjacent tributaries of the Finke River near Hermannsburg (1964), and a single specimen on the Palmer River on Tempe Downs Station (1965).

Since the 1960s numbers have declined dramatically at several of these sites. Surveys of the three localities listed above, plus nearby sites, failed to locate any individuals during 1995 and 1999-2000. An *Egernia* specimen obtained during a survey of Loves Creek pastoral lease, East MacDonnell Ranges, in 1989 is likely to be this species (S. McAlpin *pers.comm.*). In the same year several specimens were captured well out of range in the Bungle Bungle Range of the Kimberley region, Western Australia. However, they may represent an undescribed species (Aplin and Smith 2001).

The only records between 1989 and 2003 were seven animals captured at six locations in Finke Gorge National Park during surveys in 1995-2000. During 2004 and 2005 the species was located at five sites in the MacDonnell Ranges bioregion west of Alice Springs including new locations on Owen Springs Reserve and west of Hermannsburg.

Conservation reserves where reported: Finke Gorge National Park, West MacDonnell National Park.

ECOLOGY

Little is known about the ecology of this lizard. At most current sites, Slater's skink occurs in shrubland and open shrubland on alluvial soils close to drainage lines. However, in Finke Gorge National Park, it has been located in a range of environments including an isolated dune supporting shrubland, low rolling calcareous rises with 60% cover of spinifex and on an elevated, narrow, rocky creek line.

It is a burrowing species and digs complex burrow systems under small trees and shrubs, particularly several species of native fuschia (*Eremophilas*) including turpentine (*Eremophila sturtii*). The burrows are dug into the low pedestal of soil that usually builds up beneath these woody stems. The species is diurnal and crepuscular and feeds on arthropods. Females give birth to live young.

CONSERVATION ASSESSMENT

Based on the surveys carried out in 1995, 1999-2000 and 2005-2006, the total population of the species appears to be very low and is likely to be fewer than 1000 mature individuals. The population has also undergone a severe decline in range and has disappeared from sites where it was formerly abundant. At the type locality south of Alice Springs, 31 specimens were obtained during two days of collecting in the spring of 1964. The last specimen at the site was collected in 1975 and no individuals were seen during a survey in 1995 that involved 50 hours of active searching, 730 pitfall days and 130 Elliott trap days (Pavey 2004).

The decline in the population of Slater's skink appears to have occurred earlier than is relevant to IUCN status assignation (that is, earlier than the last 10 years or three generations).

continued.../

However, the species still qualifies as **Endangered** (under criteria B1ab(i,ii,iv,v)+2ab(i,ii,iv,v); C2(i)) due to:

- extent of occurrence less than 5000 km²;
- area of occupancy less than 500 km²;
- known to exist at fewer than five locations;
- continuing decline, observed, inferred or projected;
- population size fewer than 2500 mature individuals; and
- more than 95% of mature individuals in one subpopulation.

THREATENING PROCESSES

No threatening processes have been positively demonstrated, although degradation of its alluvial habitat as a result of invasion by the introduced buffel grass and associated changes in fire regimes appears the most likely causes of the species' decline. In particular, the decline and disappearance of Slater's skink is correlated with the introduction of buffel grass (*Cenchrus ciliaris*) into central Australia in the late 1960s. This weed has radically altered the vegetation structure and species composition of drainage systems in central Australia. Buffel grass is now the dominant ground cover at the type locality and surrounding alluvial areas.

CONSERVATION OBJECTIVES AND MANAGEMENT

A national recovery plan for the species was adopted in November 2005 (Pavey 2004). Actions within the plan include to:

- carry out targeted surveys at previous collection sites and other areas of suitable habitat;
- assess size of each population;
- assess habitat at current and former sites of occurrence to define critical habitat;
- conduct a taxonomic and phylogenetic assessment of the species using morphological and molecular characters;
- establish and maintain a captive population and develop reintroduction protocols; and
- provide community education and information.

Some of these actions are now being implemented through a project funded by the Natural Heritage Trust.

Compiled by Chris Pavey [February 2006] / **References:** Aplin, K.P., and Smith, L.A. (2001). Checklist of the frogs and reptiles of Western Australia. *Records of the Western Australian Museum Supplement* 63, 51-74. / Cogger, H.G. (2000). *Reptiles and Amphibians of Australia*. Sixth Edition. (Reed New Holland, Sydney.) / Horner, P. (1992). *Skinks of the Northern Territory*. (Northern Territory Museum of Arts and Sciences, Darwin.) / Pavey, C. (2004). *Slater's skink (Egernia slateri) recovery plan for 2005-2010.* (NT Department of Infrastructure Planning and Environment, Alice Springs.) / Storr, G.M. (1968). Revision of the *Egernia whitei* species-group (Lacertilia, Scincidae). *Journal of the Royal Society of Western Australia* 51, 51-62.

Image courtesy of Grant Husband

Oenpelli python
Morelia oenpelliensis

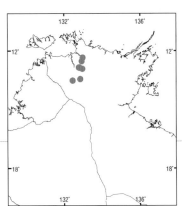

*Known locations
of the Oenpelli python*
● = pre 1970
● = post 1970

CONSERVATION STATUS
AUSTRALIA: **NOT LISTED**
NORTHERN TERRITORY: **VULNERABLE**

DESCRIPTION
The Oenpelli python is a very large (to 4 m), dark olive-brown snake, patterned with darker blotches. The underside is cream to dull yellow.

DISTRIBUTION
The Oenpelli python is restricted to the sandstone massif of western Arnhem Land. Within this area, it has been reported from the upper catchments of the Cadell, South Alligator and East Alligator River systems.

Conservation reserves where reported:
Kakadu National Park

ECOLOGY
There have been no detailed studies of this species. It is active mainly at night. During the day, it shelters in cracks, caves and crevices of rugged broken sandstone escarpments and gorges, or in large shady trees. Within this environment, it has been reported from monsoon rainforest patches, riparian areas, woodlands, open heathlands and bare rock pavements. Its diet comprises mostly medium to large mammals, particularly possums and macropods.

CONSERVATION ASSESSMENT
There have been no assessments of total population size or trends in abundance, so it is difficult to provide a detailed assessment of status.

The total area of the western Arnhem Land massif is about 34 000 km². Within this area, much of the habitat is probably unsuitable (insufficiently rocky or topographically complex). As a large solitary predator feeding on prey at relatively low abundance, its population density is probably generally low. There is some anecdotal indication of at least local decreases, possibly associated with illegal collecting in the most accessible sites. There is also some possibility of decline associated with changing fire regimes.

Accordingly, the Oenpelli python may be classified as **Vulnerable** (under criterion C2a(i)) due to:
• population size estimated at fewer than 10 000 mature individuals;
• continuing decline, observed, projected or inferred, in numbers of mature individuals; and
• no subpopulation estimated to contain more than 1000 mature individuals.

The evidence for decline is admittedly scant, circumstantial or conjectural, and there is no information available on population substructure.

THREATENING PROCESSES
This species is sought by some illicit herpetological collectors. This impact is probably minor and localised, as much of the range is almost inaccessible.

More pervasively, fire regimes across its range have changed over the last 50 or so years, to now include a far higher incidence of extensive hot, late dry season fires (Russell-Smith *et al.* 1998). It is possible that this may increase direct mortality, but, more likely, the resulting vegetation change may reduce habitat suitability either directly for this species or indirectly to its prey species.

CONSERVATION OBJECTIVES AND MANAGEMENT
Research priorities are to:
• examine the impacts of fire regimes upon the Oenpelli python directly, or its preferred prey species;
• attempt to derive some estimate of relative abundance, habitat associations and total population size; and
• collate, where appropriate, traditional ecological knowledge of this species held by Indigenous landowners in the stone country.

Management priorities are to:
• establish, collaboratively with Indigenous landowners, a monitoring program for this species, particularly with reference to its response to fire management; and
• continue to deter illicit reptile collectors.

A small captive population of this species has been maintained at the Territory Wildlife Park.

Compiled by John Woinarski [May 2006] / **References:** Russell-Smith, J., Ryan, P.G., Klessa, D., Waight, G., and Harwood, R. (1998). Fire regimes, fire-sensitive vegetation and fire management of the sandstone Arnhem Plateau, monsoonal northern Australia. *Journal of Applied Ecology* 35, 829-846.

BIRDS

Image courtesy of Kym Schwartzkopff

Emu

Dromaius novaehollandiae

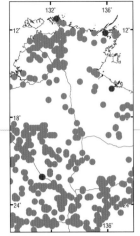

*Known locations
of the emu*
● = pre 1970
● = post 1970

DESCRIPTION

The emu is a very large flightless bird (height 1.0 to 1.9 m) with a long neck and legs. The plumage is shaggy, grey-brown and paler towards the base of the feathers. The skin of the face, throat and upper neck is almost bare and bluish. The wings are rudimentary and hang limply. The young are striped with dark brown over a buff down.

DISTRIBUTION

The emu is extremely widespread across continental Australia. It inhabits most of the Northern Territory but is scarce in the driest desert regions and most of the Top End woodlands (Marchant and Higgins 1990). It is absent from all Northern Territory islands.

Conservation reserves where reported:
Alice Springs Desert Park, Chamber's Pillar Historical Reserve, Connell's Lagoon Conservation Reserve, Dulcie Ranges National Park, Garig Gunak Barlu National Park, Gregory National Park, Illamurta Springs Conservation Reserve, Kakadu National Park, Litchfield National Park, Longreach Waterhole Protected Area, Mary River National Park, Nitmiluk National Park, Uluru – Kata Tjuta National Park, Watarrka National Park, West MacDonnell National Park.

ECOLOGY

Emus can move large distances when food or water resources decline. They are probably more sedentary in the north than they are in the south of the Northern Territory. They are omnivorous, taking seeds, fruits, insects and the growing tips of plants. They often occur in loose groups. The male incubates the eggs and broods the chicks.

CONSERVATION ASSESSMENT

Barrett *et al.* (2002, 2003) reported a significant national decline in the reporting rate for the emu between the first (1997–1981) and second (1998–2001) Australian bird atlases. The Northern Territory showed an 80% decrease (the largest of all states and territories). It is difficult to compare the results of the two surveys because different methods were used, and the second atlas covered a period with a substantially different climatic conditions to that of the first, however, there is other evidence of substantial decline from northern Australia. There are consistent anecdotal reports of broad-scale decline of emus in the Kimberley and across the Top End (Yibarbuk and Cooke 2001; Wiynjorrotj *et al.* 2005).

The species is listed as **Vulnerable** (under criterion A2b) due to an inferred reduction in population size of more than 30% over the last three generations.

THREATENING PROCESSES

In the Top End, declining numbers may be associated with the occurrence of too frequent extensive fires. These fires lead to a reduction in food supplies, particularly in the size and abundance of plants that produce fleshy fruit, and in the crop of fruit produced (Woinarski *et al.* 2004). Fires at the wrong time of year can also destroy the eggs over the long incubation period (50 to 60 days) (Marchant and Higgins 1990). In central Australia, declines may also be related to altered fire regimes or to vegetation change associated with pastoralism.

It has been suggested that the emu's decline in the Kimberley coincided with the heavy use of 1080 dingo poison in the pastoral industry (I. Morris *pers. comm.*) but this would not explain a decline in Arnhem Land where 1080 is not used.

CONSERVATION OBJECTIVES AND MANAGEMENT

The main research priorities are to assess the extent and causes of decline and to monitor populations.

Management priorities cannot be determined until factors threatening the species are more definitely determined, though a reduction in the extent and frequency of fires is likely to benefit the species.

Compiled by Rob Taylor, John Woinarski [April 2006] / **References:** Barrett, G., Silcocks, A., and Cunningham, R. (2002). Supplementary Report no. 1 - comparison of Atlas 1 (1997-1981) and Atlas 2 (1998-2001). In *The Atlas of Australian Birds (1998-2001)*. Report to the Natural Heritage Trust. (Birds Australia, Melbourne.) / Barrett, G., Silcocks, A., Barry, S., Cunningham, R., and Poulter, R. (2003). *The New Atlas of Australian Birds*. (Royal Australasian Ornithologists Union, Melbourne.) / Marchant, S., and Higgins, P.J. (1990). *Handbook of Australian, New Zealand and Antarctic Birds. Vol. 1. Ratites to Ducks.* (Oxford University Press, Melbourne). / Wiynjorrotj, P., Flora, S., Brown, N.D., Jatbula, P., Galmur, J., Katherine, M., Merlan, F., and Wightman, G. (2005). *Jawoyn Plants And Animals: Aboriginal Flora and Fauna Knowledge from Nitmiluk National Park and the Katherine area, Northern Australia.* Northern Territory Botanical Bulletin no. 29. (Northern Territory Department of Natural Resources Environment and the Arts, Darwin.) / Woinarski, J.C.Z., Risler, J., and Kean, L. (2004). The response of vegetation and vertebrate fauna to 23 years of fire exclusion in a tropical *Eucalyptus* open forest, Northern Territory, Australia. *Austral Ecology* 29, 156-176. / Yibarbuk, D., and Cooke, P. (2001). Fire, fruit and emus. In *Savanna Burning: Understanding and Using Fire in Northern Australia.* (eds R. Dyer, P. Jacklyn, I. Partridge, J. Russell-Smith and D. Williams.) p. 40. (Tropical Savannas CRC, Darwin.)

Image courtesy of Graeme Chapman

Malleefowl
Leipoa ocellata

CONSERVATION STATUS
AUSTRALIA: **VULNERABLE**
NORTHERN TERRITORY: **CRITICALLY ENDANGERED**

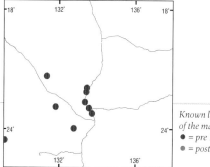

Known locations
of the malleefowl
● = pre 1970
● = post 1970

DESCRIPTION
The malleefowl is a large bird, about the size of a domestic hen with a head-body length of up to 60 cm and body mass of 1.5 to 2.5 kg. It has powerful grey legs, a short dark bill and a flattish head. The tail is long, greyish and rounded at the tip. The head, and sides and rear of the neck, are bluish-grey to grey-brown, and the chin and throat are pale chestnut. There is a broad black stripe from the throat to the upper breast. The upper body is strikingly barred and mottled grey, white, black and rufous. The rest of the underbody is creamy white (Marchant and Higgins 1993).

DISTRIBUTION
This species has a patchy distribution in semi-arid regions of southern Australia from central New South Wales to south-west and central coastal Western Australia. In the Northern Territory, it has been recorded from 12 one-degree grid cells, mostly west of the Stuart Highway and south of the Tanami Desert, with no records since the early 1960s (Benshemesh 2000). In reviewing specimen and literature reports, Storr (1977) located nine records from the south-west corner of the Northern Territory, from the Petermann Range in the extreme south-west, and north across the MacDonnell Ranges as far as Central Mount Wedge. Kimber (1985) obtained additional distributional information from Aboriginal people, including the Petermann Range, Hermannsburg, Mt Theo (Tanami Desert), Idracowra Station, Burt Well, Tea Tree, Connors Well, Aileron and Central Mount Stuart. Benshemesh (2000) noted more recent

sightings by Aboriginal inhabitants and rangers near the South Australian border.

Conservation reserves where reported: None

ECOLOGY
The malleefowl is a ground-dwelling, diurnal bird that occupies large, permanent home ranges of 1.7 to 4.6 km² in the breeding season and 0.5 to 0.75 km² in the non-breeding season (Marchant and Higgins 1993). The species is best known for its breeding system which involves the male building a large mound, up to 3 m wide and 60 cm above the ground, composed of organic material and soil. When the temperature in the chamber reaches 26 to 33° C, females begin to lay eggs that are incubated by a combination of solar radiation and heat produced by rotting organic matter in the egg chamber. The young have to dig themselves out from the mound and are self-sufficient from hatching.

The malleefowl occupies woodland, shrubland and scrub and favours areas with a shrubby understorey. It is strongly associated with mallee in most parts of its range. In arid Australia, it occupies mulga scrub, either pure stands or mixed with mallee. It feeds on the ground and roosts in the foliage of shrubs and trees at night. The diet consists mostly of seeds, although other plant material and invertebrates are also taken.

CONSERVATION ASSESSMENT
The malleefowl could be extinct in the Northern

Territory. The last definite record given by Storr (1977) was in 1931, whereas Kimber (1985) located records up to the 1950s. However, the bioregions that are most likely to support any remaining individuals, the Central Ranges and Great Sandy Desert, have never been adequately surveyed. The species may still occur in small numbers in isolated pockets in these regions. The species is classified as **Critically Endangered** (under criterion D) due to a population size estimated to number fewer than 50 mature individuals.

THREATENING PROCESSES
Threatening processes that have caused the decline of the malleefowl include predation by introduced carnivores, hunting by humans, environmental stress resulting from drought (Harlen and Priddel 1996) and changes in fire regimes (Kimber 1985). Predation by European foxes and feral cats is likely to be the major threat faced by any remaining individuals (Priddel and Wheeler 1990, 1999; Benshemesh 2000; Garnett and Crowley 2000).

CONSERVATION OBJECTIVES AND MANAGEMENT
There is a national recovery plan for malleefowl (Benshemesh 2000). In the Northern Territory management priorities include:
• searches for individuals and mounds as an integral part of biological surveys of the Central Ranges and Great Sandy Desert bioregions; and
• rapid follow-up of any potential sightings.

Compiled by Chris Pavey [April 2006] / **References:** Benshemesh, J. (2000). *National Recovery Plan for the Malleefowl.* (National Parks and Wildlife South Australia, Adelaide.) / Garnett, S.T., and Crowley, G.M. (2000). *The Action Plan for Australian Birds.* (Environment Australia, Canberra.) / Harlen, R., and Priddel, D. (1996). Potential food resources available to malleefowl *Leipoa ocellata* in marginal mallee lands during drought. *Australian Journal of Ecology* 21, 418-428. / Kimber, R. G. (1985). The history of the malleefowl in central Australia. *R.A.O.U. Newsletter* June 1985, 6-8. / Marchant, S., and Higgins, P.J. (1993). *Handbook of Australian, New Zealand and Antarctic Birds. Volume 2: Raptors to Lapwings.* (Oxford University Press, Melbourne.) / Priddel, D., and Wheeler, R. (1990). Survival of malleefowl chicks in the absence of ground-dwelling predators. *Emu* 90, 81-87. / Priddel, D., and Wheeler, R. (1999). Malleefowl conservation in New South Wales: a review. In *Proceedings of the Third International Megapode Symposium.* (eds R. Dekker, D.N. Jones and J. Benshemesh.) pp. 125-141. (Backhuys Publishers, Leiden.) / Storr, G.M. (1977). *Birds of the Northern Territory.* (Western Australian Museum, Perth.)

Christmas frigatebird,
Christmas Island frigatebird
Fregata andrewsi

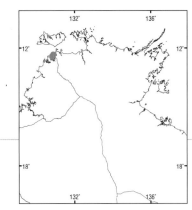

CONSERVATION STATUS
AUSTRALIA: **VULNERABLE**
NORTHERN TERRITORY: **NOT EVALUATED**

DESCRIPTION

This species is a very large, mostly black, seabird with glossy feathers on its head and back and varying white patches on its underbody. It has long slender wings and a very long, deeply-forked tail. It is larger than the more common great frigatebird *F. minor* and lesser frigatebird *F. ariel,* and has a distinctive colour pattern on its underparts (Marchant and Higgins 1990).

DISTRIBUTION

The only breeding site for this species is Christmas Island. It disperses from this site to forage in the north-east Indian Ocean, with records from off the coast of mainland south-east Asia and the islands of Indonesia and Malaysia. There are far fewer records from the coast of north-east Africa and north-west Australia. The only Northern Territory records are of one or two birds seen at Darwin on three occasions in January 1974, during a period of north-westerly gales (McKean *et al.* 1975; Storr 1977).

Conservation reserves where reported: None

ECOLOGY

As with other frigatebirds, it is a powerful flier, usually seen soaring over oceans. It eats a range of fish and squid species, with a proportion of its food derived from kleptoparasitism (forcing other birds to disgorge their prey). On Christmas Island, it nests in tall trees and has very low reproductive output.

CONSERVATION ASSESSMENT

The total population of this species is between 1000 and 2000 birds, and it is known to nest at only three sites, totaling about 170 ha, on the 135 km² Christmas Island. The Island's habitat quality is declining through clearing for a range of developments and an infestation of crazy ants (Hill and Dunn 2004). As such, a national conservation status of Vulnerable is justified. However, its occurrence in the Northern Territory is only as an extremely infrequent, non-breeding, vagrant so its conservation status is **Not Evaluated**.

THREATENING PROCESSES

On Christmas Island, its habitat quality has declined through habitat clearance for development and impacts of crazy ants. Across its non-breeding range, it may be affected by reduction in fish stocks through over-fishing and by occasional fisheries by-catch, but there is little information to suggest that these are major threats.

CONSERVATION OBJECTIVES AND MANAGEMENT

No particular conservation research or management actions are warranted for this species in the Northern Territory because of the species' vagrant status.

Compiled by John Woinarski [April 2006] / **References:** Hill, R., and Dunn, A. (2004). *National Recovery Plan for the Christmas Island Frigatebird* (Fregata andrewsi). (Department of Environment and Heritage, Canberra.) / Marchant, S., and Higgins, P.J. (1990). *Handbook of Australian, New Zealand and Antarctic birds. Vol. 1. Ratites to Ducks.* (Oxford University Press, Melbourne.) / McKean, J.L., Bartlett, M.C., and Perrins, C.M. (1975). New records from the Northern Territory. *Australian Bird Watcher* 6, 45-46.

Image courtesy of Ian Morris

Red goshawk

Erythrotriorchis radiatus

CONSERVATION STATUS
AUSTRALIA: **VULNERABLE**
NORTHERN TERRITORY: **VULNERABLE**

*Known locations
of the red goshawk*
● = *pre 1970*
● = *post 1970*

DESCRIPTION

The red goshawk is a large reddish-brown hawk, with conspicuous dark streaks from its chin to belly, conspicuously barred on the underwing and tail. The head is whitish with dark streaks. The legs and feet are strong and yellowish, with prominent red feathering known as "trousers". Its wings are longer and more pointed and the tail is shorter than the common brown goshawk.

DISTRIBUTION

The red goshawk occurs across much of northern Australia, from near Broome in the south-west Kimberley to south-east Queensland. Within this range it generally occurs in taller forests characteristic of higher rainfall areas, but there are some isolated recent records from central Australia. It appears to be unusually common on the Tiwi Islands (Bathurst and Melville).

Conservation reserves where reported:
Garig Gunak Barlu National Park, Kakadu National Park, Litchfield National Park, Nitmiluk National Park.

ECOLOGY

The red goshawk hunts mainly for medium-sized birds, generally up to the size of kookaburras and black cockatoos. Their territory size is very large (up to 200 km²: Debus and Czechura 1988; Czechura and Hobson 2000). The preferred habitat is tall, open eucalypt forest and riparian areas including paperbark forest and gallery forest. The conspicuous basket-shaped stick nest is placed in large trees typically near watercourses (Aumann and Baker-Gabb 1991).

CONSERVATION ASSESSMENT

A series of surveys across northern Australia (Debus and Czechura 1988; Aumann and Baker-Gabb 1991; Czechura and Hobson 2000) has provided generally robust information on distribution and total population. Garnett and Crowley (2000) collated these surveys to estimate the population size as 1000 breeding birds, and considered it to be Vulnerable at the national level, based on the IUCN 1994 criterion of D1 (fewer than 1000 mature individuals).

The Northern Territory population accounts for about one-third of the total population (about 330 mature individuals). An estimated 120 of these live on Melville Island (Woinarski *et al.* 2000). The Melville Island population may be reduced by about 10% due to developing forestry operations. Given these figures, the red goshawk qualifies as **Vulnerable** in the Northern Territory (under criterion C2a(i)) due to:

- a population size estimated to be fewer than 10 000 mature individuals;
- a continuing decline (observed, projected or inferred); and
- a population structure with no subpopulation containing more than 1000 mature individuals.

THREATENING PROCESSES

Nationally, the red goshawk has been threatened chiefly by clearance of preferred habitat for agriculture, with some localised problems related to illegal egg collection, shooting, and fire (Garnett and Crowley 2000). In the Northern Territory, the most immediate threat is clearing of prime habitat on Melville Island for short rotation plantations of exotic pulpwood.

CONSERVATION OBJECTIVES AND MANAGEMENT

The management priorities are to:

- minimise the impact of the developing Melville Island forestry industry, through retention of adequate habitat especially around known nest sites; and
- establish an appropriate monitoring program.

Habitat retention around nesting sites and monitoring is a required condition of forestry development (Hadden 2000; D. Baker-Gabb *pers. comm.*)

Elsewhere, across its Northern Territory range, a monitoring program should be established, and populations safeguarded from ongoing clearing of tall open forests.

Compiled by John Woinarski [April 2006] / **References:** Aumann, T., and Baker-Gabb, D.J. (1991). *The ecology and status of the red goshawk in northern Australia.* (Royal Australasian Ornithologists Union, Melbourne.) / Czechura, G.V., and Hobson, R.G. (2000). *The Red Goshawk* Erythrotriorchis radiatus *in northern Queensland: status and distribution.* Report to Queensland Parks and Wildlife Service. Debus, S.J., and Czechura, G.V. (1988). The Red Goshawk *Erythrotriorchis radiatus*: a review. *Australian Bird Watcher* 12, 175-199. / Garnett, S.T., and Crowley, G.M. (2000). *The Action Plan for Australian Birds.* 2000. (Environment Australia, Canberra.) / Hadden, K. (2000). *Tiwi Islands Plantation Forestry Strategic Plan.* (Tiwi Land Council, Darwin.) / Woinarski, J., Brennan, K., Hempel, C., Firth, R., and Watt, F. (2000). *Biodiversity Conservation on the Tiwi Islands: plants, vegetation types and terrestrial vertebrates on Melville Island.* Report to the Tiwi Land Council. (Parks and Wildlife Commission of the Northern Territory, Darwin.)

Image courtesy of Mark Ziembicki

Australian bustard

Ardeotis australis

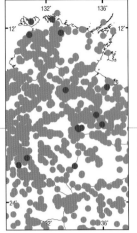

*Known locations
of the Australian
bustard*
● = *pre 1970*
● = *post 1970*

DESCRIPTION
Australia's heaviest flying bird, the Australian bustard is a large, stately bird that exhibits significant sexual size dimorphism between males and females, with males (5 to 10 kg) up to three times heavier than females (2 to 3 kg). The crown is brown-black, the neck and breast grey-white with a distinct black breast band. The bend of wing is patterned black and white. The back, wings and tail are brown with fine buff markings. Females have a narrower brown crown, less distinct or absent breast band and greyer neck and breast.

DISTRIBUTION
The Australian bustard is widespread, though generally scarce, in the Northern Territory. It is more common in the north, and tends to occur in loose aggregations, particularly during the breeding season. Its strongholds in the Northern Territory include the Barkly Tableland, Daly River region, the Victoria River District and the Tanami Desert.

Conservation reserves where reported:
Alice Springs Telegraph Station Historical Reserve, Black Jungle / Lambells Lagoon Conservation Reserve, Bullwaddy Conservation Reserve, Caranbirini Conservation Reserve, Connells Lagoon Conservation Reserve, Cutta Cutta Caves Nature Park, Davenport Range National Park, Douglas River / Daly River Esplanade Conservation Area, Elsey National Park, Flora River Nature Park, Gregory National Park, Ilparpa Swamp Wildlife Protected Area, Junction Reserve, Kakadu National Park, Keep River National Park, Kuyunba Conservation Reserve, Litchfield National Park, Longreach Waterhole Protected Area, Mary River National Park, Nitmiluk National Park, Rainbow Valley Conservation Reserve, Uluru – Kata Tjuta National Park, Watarrka National Park, West MacDonnell National Park.

Although the species has been recorded from a range of reserves, in the south of its range it is highly mobile, meaning that few reserves host permanent, let alone viable, populations of bustards year-round and many records are of single individuals. They have most commonly been recorded from Uluru – Kata Tjuta National Park, Watarrka National Park, Kakadu National Park and Gregory National Park.

ECOLOGY
The Australian bustard typically occurs in open country, preferring grasslands, low shrublands, grassy woodlands and other structurally similar but artificial habitats such as croplands and airfields (Downes and Speedie 1982). However, they respond readily to fire and are often found on recently burnt country, even in more wooded areas.

Bustards have a broad, omnivorous diet largely comprising seeds, fruit, vegetation, invertebrates and small vertebrates. They move readily, tracking rainfall, fires and food resources (e.g. grasshopper outbreaks) across the landscape opportunistically. Their movements are not well defined. However, they are believed to be nomadic or irruptive in the arid and semi-arid regions and migratory with more regular north-south movements in relation to wet/dry seasons in the north. Some populations in the Top End may also be sedentary (Ziembicki and Woinarski 2007).

The species' reproductive biology is unique in that it exhibits an "exploded" lek mating system. In lek systems, males aggregate in display arenas that are visited by females for the purpose of mating. The lek system of the bustard is referred to as "exploded" as the display arenas of the males are well spaced apart and aggregation may not be detectable until they are mapped over a larger area. Following mating, males play no further role in the breeding process and females care for young until independence.

CONSERVATION ASSESSMENT
Although still widespread in the Northern Territory, the species is relatively scarce. Localised fluctuations in numbers occur in relation to rainfall and fire events and they are locally common and possibly sedentary in several horticultural regions (e.g. Douglas-Daly Rivers region).

Outside the Northern Territory, the species' overall population size is still substantial. However, there has been a very large historical decline in abundance in southern Australia and parts of the north such that Garnett and Crowley (2000) categorised this species as Near Threatened in the *Action Plan for Australian Birds 2000*.

The widespread declines in the Northern Territory are evident from Bird Atlas reporting rates for bustards: these dropped by 70% between the first (1977–81) and second (1998–2001) atlases – a more substantial decline than for any other state or territory.

continued.../

The declines were largest in the southern regions of the Northern Territory (Barrett *et al.* 2002, 2003). These trends are consistent with anecdotal evidence from mail surveys of pastoral properties and private submissions that suggest that bustards are now absent from areas in which they were previously common. Although populations in the north are more robust, similar declining trends are evident with consistent reports of lower overall numbers (e.g. flocks of 50+ in the past to present flocks typically of fewer than 20 birds).

Assessing numbers of highly mobile birds such as bustards is inherently difficult because of their readiness to move across the landscape in response to variable climatic conditions and patchily distributed resources and naturally large population fluctuations. However, given the evidence consistently suggests an overall decline, a precautionary approach has been adopted. The species qualifies as **Vulnerable** (under criterion A2b) based on an estimated population reduction of more than 30% over the last 10 years or three generations.

THREATENING PROCESSES

The widespread decline in bustard numbers has been variously attributed to a combination of factors including predation, altered fire regimes, hunting, disturbance, habitat alteration (e.g. woody weed infestation), pesticides and grazing (Marchant and Higgins 1993; Garnett and Crowley 2000), yet there exists little information regarding the relative effects of these threats.

Another potential threatening process is hunting. Breakdown of controls on traditional hunting, compounded by access to modern weapons and vehicles, and a low reproductive rate (usually one young per year) increase the pressure on bustard populations in the Northern Territory. The conspicuousness and size of males during the breeding period may make them particularly susceptible to hunting, resulting in significant male-biased harvesting rates. Such a bias may have serious implications for the specialised lek mating system of the species.

CONSERVATION OBJECTIVES AND MANAGEMENT

Research priorities are to:
• determine population size, distribution and habitat relationships (especially in relation to fire, land use and grazing);
• assess patterns of movements;
• establish an effective monitoring program and model numbers in relation to landscape factors including rainfall and fire;
• identify key areas used for breeding and refuge sites in times of drought;
• assess factors affecting breeding success; and
• quantify the relative impact of hunting of the species, including assessment of the implications of significant male-biased harvesting.

Management priorities are to:
• develop fire management programs, with the collaboration of Indigenous landowners, that are not detrimental to this species. Particular emphasis should be placed on avoiding late dry season fires which coincide with the breeding season;
• develop harvesting protocols to minimize impacts; and
• control feral predators in key breeding habitats.

Compiled by Mark Ziembicki [April 2006] / **References:** Barrett, G., Silcocks, A., and Cunningham, R. (2002). Supplementary Report no. 1 - comparison of Atlas 1 (1977-1981) and Atlas 2 (1998-2001). In *The Atlas of Australian Birds* (1998-2001). Report to the Natural Heritage Trust. (Birds Australia, Melbourne.) / Barrett, G., Silcocks, A., Barry, S., Cunningham, R., and Poulter, R. (2003). *The new atlas of Australian birds.* (Royal Australasian Ornithologists Union, Melbourne.) / Downes, M. C., and C. Speedie (1982). *Classification of Bustard Habitat in the Northern Territory.* Report to the Conservation Commission of the Northern Territory, Darwin / Garnett, S. T., and G. M. Crowley (2000). *The Action Plan for Australian Birds.* (Environment Australia, Canberra.) / Marchant, S., and P. J. Higgins (eds) (1993). *Handbook of Australian, New Zealand and Antarctic Birds. Vol.2. Raptors to Lapwings.* (Oxford University Press, Melbourne.) / Ziembicki, M., and Woinarski, J. (2007). Monitoring continental movement patterns of the Australian Bustard through community-based surveys and remote sensing. *Pacific Conservation Biology* 13, 128-142.

Image courtesy of Bruce Mullins

Plains-wanderer
Pedionomus torquatus

CONSERVATION STATUS
AUSTRALIA: **VULNERABLE**
NORTHERN TERRITORY: **DATA DEFICIENT**

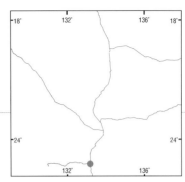

*Known locations
of the plains-
wanderer*
● = pre 1970
● = post 1970

DESCRIPTION

The plains-wanderer is a small, quail-like terrestrial bird. Compared with quail, it is more slender, has a finer bill and far longer legs. The sexes differ in plumage. The upperparts are generally mottled brown, paler on the undersides. The female has a conspicuous white-spotted black collar and rufous breast.

DISTRIBUTION

The plains-wanderer is known from sparse grasslands and open areas, mostly in south-eastern Australia (especially the Riverina), with some more isolated records in South Australia and inland Queensland. There are no confirmed records from the Northern Territory, but Bennett (1983) reported plausible records from Erldunda Station, 180 km south of Alice Springs.

Conservation reserves where reported: None

ECOLOGY

The plains-wanderer is an entirely terrestrial species. Its diet comprises seeds and invertebrates. It is usually observed walking alone, in pairs or family parties, often stopping and standing upright with neck craned. Once alarmed, they either flatten and merge with their grassland surrounds, or run away quickly: they rarely take flight (Bennett 1983). The nest is a scrape on the ground, and breeding may be aseasonal and opportunistic. The male plains-wanderer takes the major role in incubating and caring for the young.

CONSERVATION ASSESSMENT

There are no confirmed records, and few possible records, from the Northern Territory. At best the Northern Territory is marginal for the geographic range and conservation status for this species. In the Northern Territory, it is best treated as **Data Deficient.**

THREATENING PROCESSES

In its core range (outside the Northern Territory), the main threat is clearance and conversion of native grasslands to crops (Garnett and Crowley 2000). Over-grazing, particularly during droughts, may reduce habitat quality and render the species more vulnerable to predation (especially by foxes) (Baker-Gabb *et al.* 1990). Chemicals used to control plague locusts may kill plains-wanderers directly or indirectly (Garnett and Crowley 2000).

CONSERVATION OBJECTIVES AND MANAGEMENT

In the Northern Territory, the research and management priority is to more systematically assess its status, including distribution, abundance, habitat requirements and threats. However, given its probable at best marginal occurrence, actions for this species are not considered a high priority.

Compiled by John Woinarski [May 2006] / **References:** Baker-Gabb, D.J., Benshemesh, J.S., and Maher, P.N. (1990). A revision of the distribution, status and management of the plains-wanderer *Pedionomus torquatus*. *Emu* 90, 161-168. / Bennett, S. (1983). A review of the distribution, status and biology of the plains-wanderer *Pedionomus torquatus*, Gould. *Emu* 83, 1-11. / Garnett, S. T., and G. M. Crowley (2000). *The Action Plan for Australian Birds.* (Environment Australia, Canberra.)

Image courtesy of Tom Tarrant

Australian painted snipe
Rostratula australis

CONSERVATION STATUS
AUSTRALIA: **VULNERABLE**
NORTHERN TERRITORY: **VULNERABLE**

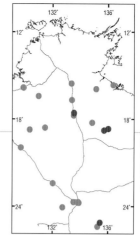

Known locations of the Australian painted snipe
● = pre 1970
● = post 1970

DESCRIPTION

The Australian painted snipe is a wader of around 220 to 250 mm in length. The head, neck and upper breast is chestnut-bronze. The back and wings are dark olive-green, finely barred black and are ornamented with bright chestnut spots and black bars. The back has a conspicuous buff-coloured V-shaped mark. A broad white band separates the neck and wings. There is a broad white horizontal band through the eye. The male is smaller and less colourful, lacking the rufous on the hind-neck. This species is generally inconspicuous, and occurs solitarily or in only small parties.

DISTRIBUTION

Until recently (Lane and Rogers 2000), the Australian painted snipe was generally considered part of a more widespread species *Rostratula benghalensis* that extended throughout Indonesia, Asia and Africa and on many Pacific Islands. As re-defined, the species is now considered restricted to Australia. Australian painted snipe are most frequently recorded in south-eastern Australia, particularly in the Murray-Darling Basin. In the Northern Territory it was recorded breeding at Tarrabool Lake on Eva Downs on the Barkly Tablelands in 1993 (Jaensch 1994), with non-breeding records from Lake Woods in 1993 and an un-named swamp on Sturt Plateau in 2001 (Jaensch 2003). It is likely that the species could occur on any shallow ephemeral wetlands in central or southern Northern Territory. It is also possible that the species could occur in northern areas of the Northern Territory.

Conservation reserves where reported: None

ECOLOGY

Australian painted snipe occur in shallow, vegetated, freshwater swamps, claypans or inundated grassland (including temporary wetlands). They feed at the water's edge and on mudflats, taking seeds and probing for invertebrates. Three to six eggs are laid in a shallow scrape nest. No sites are known where the species is resident. Its occurrence appears to be unpredictable (Rogers 2001). It is unobtrusive during the day, feeding primarily at night.

CONSERVATION ASSESSMENT

Australian painted snipe appear to have disappeared from south-western Australia (Johnstone and Storr 1998). The national reporting rate for the species has declined steadily since the 1950s (Lane and Rogers 2000) with fewer than 100 records since 1990 (Garnett and Crowley 2000). Garnett and Crowley (2000) classified the status of the species as Vulnerable at a national level because of this decline.

Assigning a status for the species in the Northern Territory is more problematic because of lack of knowledge of population size and trends. As it appears to be nomadic, the species is unlikely to have a population that is separate to that inhabiting other areas of Australia. Accordingly, it would mean the species is likely to have declined in the Northern Territory. This is supported by evidence of a decline in northern Western Australia (Johnstone and Storr 1998). Watkins (1993)

estimated that the Australian population was 1500 individuals, but provided no explanation as to how this was derived. The species qualifies as **Vulnerable** (under criteria A2b; C1) due to:

• population reduction of more than 30% over the last 10 years or three generations; and

• population size fewer than 10 000 mature individuals and continuing decline of at least 10% within 10 years or three generations.

THREATENING PROCESSES

The main process affecting the species in southern Australia is wetland drainage. Johnstone and Storr (1980) attributed the decline of painted snipe in the Kimberley to degradation of habitat by cattle. As most Northern Territory swamplands suitable for this species occur on pastoral lands, this process may also be detrimentally affecting this species in the Northern Territory, although there are no substantial data to assess this impact (Jaensch 2003).

CONSERVATION OBJECTIVES AND MANAGEMENT

Research priorities are to increase surveys of wetlands with specific searches undertaken for painted snipe. Management priorities are to ensure a range of shallow ephemeral wetlands throughout central and southern Northern Territory are managed to ensure that habitat degradation by cattle does not occur.

Compiled by Robert Taylor, Ray Chatto, John Woinarski [May 2006] / **References:** Garnett, S.T., and Crowley, G.M. (2000). *The Action Plan for Australian Birds.* (Environment Australia, Canberra.) / Jaensch, R.P. (1994). An inventory of wetlands of the sub-humid tropics of the Northern Territory. (Conservation Commission of the Northern Territory, Darwin.) / Jaensch, R.P. (2003). Recent records and breeding of painted snipe *Rostratula benghalensis* in the Mitchell Grass Downs and Sturt Plateau, Northern Territory. *Northern Territory Naturalist* 17, 31-37. / Johnstone, R.E., and Storr, G.M. (1998). *Handbook of Western Australia. Vol. 1. Non-passerines (Emu to Dollarbird).* (Western Australia Museum, Perth.) / Lane, B.A., and Rogers, D.I. (2000). The taxonomic and conservation status of the Australian Painted Snipe *Rostratula (benghalensis) australis. Stilt* 36, 26-34. / Rogers, D. (2001). Painted snipe. *Wingspan* 11 (4), 6-7. / Watkins, D. (1993). *A National Plan for shorebird conservation in Australia.* RAOU Report No. 90. (Australasian Wader Studies Group. Royal Australasian Ornithologists Union and World Wide Fund for Nature, Melbourne.)

Image courtesy of Martin Armstrong

Partridge pigeon
(eastern subspecies)
Geophaps smithii smithii

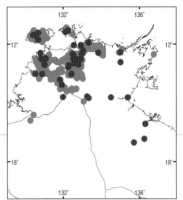

Known locations
of partridge
pigeon
● = pre 1970
● = post 1970

CONSERVATION STATUS
AUSTRALIA: **VULNERABLE**
NORTHERN TERRITORY: **VULNERABLE**

DESCRIPTION

The partridge pigeon is an unmistakable ground-dwelling pigeon. It is a medium-sized (slightly smaller than the feral pigeon *Columbia livia*), grey-brown bird with conspicuous white leading edge to the wing and red bare skin on the face. It forages entirely on the ground, and, except when flushed in alarm, rarely flies. The Kimberley subspecies, *G. smithii blauwii*, differs from the Northern Territory (eastern) subspecies *G. s. smithii*, in having yellow rather than red bare skin around the face.

DISTRIBUTION

The partridge pigeon occurs across the Top End of the Northern Territory and far east Kimberley. However it has declined or disappeared from much of the lower rainfall parts of this range over the last century. It is sparse in eastern and central Arnhem Land.

Conservation reserves where reported: Blackmore River Conservation Reserve, Butterfly Gorge Nature Park, Garig Gunak Barlu National Park, Gregory National Park, Kakadu National Park, Litchfield National Park, Mary River National Park, Nitmiluk National Park, Territory Wildlife Park/Berry Springs Nature Park, Tjuwaliyn (Douglas) Hot Springs Park, Umbrawara Gorge Nature Park.

ECOLOGY

The diet of the partridge pigeon comprises seeds, mostly of grasses but also from *Acacia* and other woody plants (Higgins and Davies 1996). It is largely sedentary, although may make local-scale movements (up to 5 to 10 km) in response to seasonal variations in water and food availability (Fraser 2001). It typically occurs singly or in small family groups, but larger aggregations may occur, especially in the late dry season, around water sources. It nests in a small scrape on the ground, mostly in the early dry season (Fraser 2001), with "nest" location preferentially in sites with relatively dense grass cover. Such sites contrast to the relatively open (typically burnt) areas preferred for feeding, and suggest that the species may be much affected by fire regimes. Small, patchy fires have been recommended for the management of this species (Fraser *et al.* 2003).

Partridge pigeons occur principally in lowland eucalypt open forests and woodlands, with grassy understoreys.

CONSERVATION ASSESSMENT

The partridge pigeon has declined substantially in the Northern Territory, and probably also in the Kimberley (Johnstone 1981; Garnett and Crowley 2000; Fraser 2001), although is still abundant in some locations (e.g. parts of Kakadu National Park, Litchfield National Park and the Tiwi Islands: Woinarski *et al.* 2003). The timing and currency of this decline is poorly resolved, but may have occurred gradually over the last century (Franklin 1999). This uncertainty renders the fit to IUCN criteria difficult to judge. The eastern subspecies of partridge pigeon most closely matches **Vulnerable** criterion C1 (population size of less than 10 000 mature individuals and estimated continuing decline of at least 10% within 10 years), although it is noted that Garnett and Crowley (2000) estimated (with low reliability) that the population was 15 000 (and decreasing).

THREATENING PROCESSES

Partridge pigeons face a number of threats, whose relative impacts have not been well established. As they forage, nest and roost on the ground, partridge pigeons are highly susceptible to predation by feral cats. Partridge pigeons are also dependent upon daily access to water for drinking, so are likely to do poorly in relatively dry years, and will be affected by any manipulation of water sources.

Probably the most important threats are the inter-related changes in grass composition and fire regimes. Across much of the Top End, exotic grasses (including mission grass *Pennisetum polystachion*, gamba grass *Andropogon gayanus* and/or other African and South American grasses) have spread rapidly over recent decades (e.g. Kean and Price 2003), and, where now present, have greatly reduced the diversity of native grasses. This will change the diversity, timing and abundance of seeds available as food to the partridge pigeon. Fire regimes have also changed appreciably over the Top End (and Tiwi Islands) over the last century, and continue to change.

continued.../

Traditional Aboriginal fire regimes were probably far more patchy and fine-scale than the regimes now prevailing. The partridge pigeon was probably greatly advantaged by a regime of frequent, patchy but localised fire, and is probably disadvantaged by the current regime of fewer but more extensive fires (Fraser *et al.* 2003). That current regime is now being made even more disadvantageous by the high fuel loads associated with exotic grasses, that make for far hotter and more extensive fire (Rossitter *et al.* 2003).

Partridge pigeons may also be affected by the change in vegetation composition and structure caused by livestock and feral animals, although the direction and magnitude of this impact is uncertain. In some cases, grazing by stock may create the more open and patchy ground layer preferred by partridge pigeons (Fraser 2001).

Partridge pigeons occur principally in tall eucalypt open forest, and their population will be reduced wherever these areas are cleared. This habitat is that currently most subjected to conversion for horticulture or forest plantation (Woinarski 2004a).

CONSERVATION OBJECTIVES AND MANAGEMENT

A national recovery plan for the eastern partridge pigeon, and other species, has recently been established (Woinarski 2004b).

The major conservation management objective is to maintain extensive areas of eucalypt open forest with intact native grass species composition, and subject to a fine-scale relatively frequent fire regime.

The basis of a monitoring program for this species has been established in Kakadu National Park (Fraser *et al.* 2003; Woinarski 2004c) and on the Tiwi Islands (D. Baker-Gabb *pers. comm.*), and maintenance or expansion of these programs will be necessary to provide a more informed measure of population trends and responses to management.

Compiled by John Woinarski [April 2006] / **References:** Franklin, D.C. (1999). Evidence of disarray amongst granivorous bird assemblages in the savannas of northern Australia, a region of sparse human settlement. *Biological Conservation* 90, 53-68. / Fraser, F.J. (2001). *The impacts of fire and grazing on the Partridge Pigeon: the ecological requirements of a declining tropical granivore.* PhD thesis. (Australian National University, Canberra.) / Fraser, F., Lawson, V., Morrison, S., Christopherson, P., McGreggor, S., and Rawlinson, M. (2003). Fire management experiment for the declining Partridge Pigeon, Kakadu National Park. *Ecological Management and Restoration* 4, 93–101. / Garnett, S.T., and Crowley, G.M. (2000). *The Action Plan for Australian Birds, 2000.* (Environment Australia, Canberra.) / Higgins, P.J., and Davies, S.J.J.F. (1996). *Handbook of Australian, New Zealand & Antarctic Birds. Volume 3. Snipe to Pigeons.* (Oxford University Press, Melbourne.) / Johnstone, R.E. (1981). Notes on the distribution, ecology and taxonomy of the partridge pigeon (*Geophaps smithii*) and spinifex pigeon (*Geophaps plumifera*) in Western Australia. *Records of the Western Australian Museum* 9, 49-63. / Kean, L., and Price, O. (2003). The extent of mission grass and gamba grass in the Darwin region of Australia's Northern Territory. *Pacific Conservation Biology* 8, 281-290. / Rossiter, N.A., Setterfield, S.A., Douglas, M.M., and Hutley, L.B. (2003). Testing the grass-fire cycle: alien grass invasion in the tropical savannas of northern Australia. *Diversity and Distributions* 9, 169-176. / Woinarski, J.C.Z. (2004a). The forest fauna of the Northern Territory: knowledge, conservation and management. In *Conservation of Australia's Forest Fauna* (second edition) (ed. D. Lunney). pp. 36-55. (Royal Zoological Society of New South Wales, Sydney.) / Woinarski, J.C.Z. (2004b). *National multi-species Recovery Plan for the Partridge Pigeon [eastern subspecies] Geophaps smithii smithii; crested shrike-tit [northern (sub)-species] Falcunculus (frontatus) whitei; masked owl [north Australian mainland subspecies] Tyto novaehollandae kimberli; and masked owl [Tiwi Islands subspecies] Tyto novaehollandiae melvillensis, 2004-2008.* (NT Department of Infrastructure Planning and Environment, Darwin.) / Woinarski, J. (2004c). *Threatened plants and animals in Kakadu National Park: a review and recommendations for management.* Report to Parks Australia North. (PWCNT, Darwin.) / Woinarski, J., Brennan, K., Hempel, C., Armstrong, M., Milne, D., and Chatto, R. (2003). *Biodiversity conservation on the Tiwi Islands, Northern Territory. Part 2. Fauna.* 127 pp. (Department of Infrastructure Planning and Environment, Darwin.)

Image courtesy of Kay Kessing

Princess parrot
Polytelis alexandrae

CONSERVATION STATUS
AUSTRALIA: **VULNERABLE**
NORTHERN TERRITORY: **VULNERABLE**

Known locations of the princess parrot.
● = pre 1970
● = post 1970

DESCRIPTION

The princess parrot is a very distinctive bird which is slim in build, beautifully plumaged and has a very long, tapering tail. It is a medium-sized parrot with total length of 40 to 45 cm and body mass of 90 to 120 g. The basic colour is dull olive-green; paler on the underparts. It has a red bill, blue-grey crown, pink chin, throat and foreneck, prominent yellow-green shoulder patches, bluish rump and back, and blue-green uppertail.

DISTRIBUTION

This species has a patchy and irregular distribution in arid Australia. In the Northern Territory, it occurs in the southern section of the Tanami Desert south to Angas Downs and Yulara and east to Alice Springs. The exact distribution within this range is not well understood and it is unclear whether the species is resident in the Northern Territory. Few locations exist in the Northern Territory where the species is regularly seen, and even then there may be long intervals (up to 20 years) between records. Most records from the MacDonnell Ranges bioregion are during dry periods.

Conservation reserves where reported:
The princess parrot is not resident in any conservation reserve in the Northern Territory but it has been observed regularly in and adjacent to Uluru – Kata Tjuta National Park, and there is at least one record from West MacDonnell National Park.

ECOLOGY

The princess parrot usually occupies swales between sand dunes and is occasionally seen on slopes and crests of dunes. This habitat consists mostly of shrubs such as *Eremophila*, *Grevillea* and *Hakea* and scattered trees. Some records are from riverine forest, woodland and shrubland. The species is highly gregarious with most sightings being of small flocks of 10 to 20 birds; however, groups of up to 100 birds occur.

Breeding takes place in hollows in large eucalypts, particularly river red gums (*Eucalyptus camaldulensis*), and also in desert oaks (*Allocasuarina decaisneana*). Breeding colonies of up to 10 pairs are sometimes recorded but solitary nesting also occurs. Four to six eggs are laid (Higgins 1999).

The princess parrot feeds on the ground and in flowering shrubs and trees. The diet consists mostly of seeds with flowers, nectar and leaves being of secondary importance.

CONSERVATION ASSESSMENT

The nomadic nature of this species combined with infrequent sightings make it very difficult to assign it a conservation status in the Northern Territory. The Australian breeding population is estimated at 5000 birds (Garnett and Crowley 2000), the majority of which occur in the Great Sandy Desert. There is some circumstantial evidence of a reduction in population size within its Northern Territory range (Garnett and Crowley 2000), although this is difficult to judge given the paucity of information on abundance.

Based on the available information, it has the status of **Vulnerable** in the Northern Territory (under criterion C2b) due to:
• population size estimated to be fewer than 10 000 mature individuals;
• continuing decline in numbers of mature individuals.

THREATENING PROCESSES

No specific threatening process has been identified for the princess parrot. Grazing by rabbits and introduced herbivores and changes in fire regimes are all likely habitat degraders. The large increase in the camel population in arid Australia may have reduced or altered the availability of favoured food plants of the princess parrot. On a local scale, illegal raiding of nests to collect eggs and capture fledglings for the overseas bird market may affect breeding colonies.

CONSERVATION OBJECTIVES AND MANAGEMENT

Research and management priorities are to:
• document any sightings of the species; and
• attempt to locate areas where the species is regularly present, particularly drought refuges, in order to undertake an assessment of threats and ecology, and provide for appropriate management.

Several princess parrots are held and displayed at the Alice Springs Desert Park, and it is a common aviary bird in Australia.

Compiled by Chris Pavey [April 2006] / **References:** Garnett, S.T., and Crowley, G.M. (2000). *The Action Plan for Australian Birds.* (Environment Australia, Canberra.) / Higgins, P.J. (ed.) (1999). *Handbook of Australian, New Zealand and Antarctic Birds. Volume 4: Parrots to Dollarbird.* (Oxford University Press, Melbourne.)

Image courtesy of WT Cooper (National Library of Australia)

Night parrot
Pezoporus occidentalis

CONSERVATION STATUS
AUSTRALIA: **ENDANGERED**
NORTHERN TERRITORY: **CRITICALLY ENDANGERED**

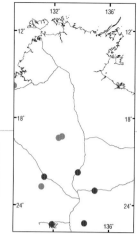

*Known locations of
the night parrot*
● = *pre 1970*
● = *post 1970*

DESCRIPTION

The night parrot is a medium-sized (22 to 25 cm head-body length) bird with a dumpy build and a short tail. The head, neck, upperbody and chest are bright green, whereas the rest of the underparts are yellow-green to yellow. The body plumage features a range of black and yellow streaks, bars and spots. The uppertail is black-brown in the centre and pale yellow on the sides. When wings are folded, the primary flight feathers are black-brown. The bill, legs and feet are blue-grey. The eyes are dark. Sexes are similar in size and appearance.

DISTRIBUTION

The distribution of the night parrot has not been well documented, but it is restricted to arid and semi-arid Australia. Twenty-two museum specimens existed prior to 1990, all but one taken in the 19th century. Of the specimens, three were collected in north-west and north-central Western Australia and the remainder in South Australia (Forshaw *et al*. 1976). F. W. Andrews collected 16 of the South Australian specimens in the vicinity of the Gawler Ranges and Lake Eyre in the 1870s. A specimen was apparently taken in south-west New South Wales in 1897 (Forshaw 1970) and a number of recent sightings, including two specimens, come from north-western Queensland in the vicinity of Boulia and Cloncurry (Boles *et al*. 1991; Garnett *et al*. 1993). Prior to the discovery of the 1990 specimen, the night parrot was widely considered to be extinct.

No specimens of the night parrot have been taken in the Northern Territory; however, sightings were made up to 1923 at the Alice Springs Telegraph Station, Horseshoe Bend Station, Idracowra Station, Henbury Station and Hermannsburg (Whitlock 1924). The notes of the Horn Expedition indicate that the species was relatively common in central Australia in the 1890s, but by the 1920s it was already scarce (Whitlock 1924). Potential sightings in the Northern Territory between 1950 and 2005 are from Harts Range, Stirling Station, Muckaty Station, Keep River National Park, Kildurk Station and the Tanami Desert. A well-publicised potential sighting of the species in the Northern Territory was in January 1996 when two individuals were reported at dusk near a stock watering point on Newhaven Station, 350 km west-north-west of Alice Springs.

Conservation reserves where reported:
There are no conservation reserves in the Northern Territory where populations of night parrot are known to be extant. The only recent (post 1930) records in reserves are of one possible sighting in Keep River National Park, and the 1996 record from Newhaven (managed by Australian Wildlife Conservancy and Birds Australia as a reserve).

ECOLOGY

Almost all our knowledge of the night parrot comes from the observations of naturalists from the late 19th century. The night parrot appears to be a nocturnal bird that forages on the ground.

During the day it rests within clumps of spinifex. It also nests within spinifex hummocks, building a rough nest in which up to four white eggs are laid. The bird becomes active during dusk and may then fly to water to drink prior to foraging. The diet consists of seeds of grasses and herbs, particularly those of spinifex (*Triodia*).

The night parrot appears to be highly nomadic, moving in response to availability of food and water. After periods of heavy rain with abundant seeding of spinifex, the species was often locally common (Wilson 1937). However, during droughts, the species would disappear from formerly suitable habitat.

The night parrot is known from spinifex grasslands in stony or sandy areas and samphire and chenopod associations on floodplains, salt lakes and clay pans. Suitable habitat is characterised by the presence of large and dense clumps of spinifex. It may prefer mature spinifex that is long unburnt (Ashby 1924).

A number of calls have been reported. The typical call when birds come into water to drink is described as a long drawn-out mournful whistle that carries for a considerable distance (Wilson 1937).

continued.../

CONSERVATION ASSESSMENT

The night parrot may be extinct in the Northern Territory. Although it was apparently not uncommon in the 19th century, numbers declined during the early part of the 20th century with no confirmed records since the mid 1920s. However, regular reports of potential sightings indicate that the species may continue to persist in low numbers.

No systematic field surveys for the species have been undertaken. In the absence of suitable surveys and following continued potential sightings, it is not appropriate to classify the night parrot as extinct. Therefore, it is classified as **Critically Endangered** (under criterion C2b) due to:

• a population size estimated to be fewer than 250 mature individuals;
• continuing decline in numbers of mature individuals; and
• extreme fluctuations in numbers of mature individuals.

THREATENING PROCESSES

Key threatening processes are likely to be habitat degradation caused by altered fire regimes and grazing by stock, and predation by introduced carnivores.

CONSERVATION OBJECTIVES AND MANAGEMENT

There is no existing management program for this species in the Northern Territory. However, any potential sightings of the species that seem feasible will be investigated.

More broadly, the conservation outlook for this species will benefit from broad-scale management of feral predators (cats and foxes), reduction in feral herbivores, and amelioration of fire regimes.

Compiled by Chris Pavey [April 2006] / **References:** Ashby, E. (1924). Notes on extinct or rare Australian birds, with suggestions as to some of the causes of their disappearance. *Emu* 23, 178-183. / Boles, W., Longmore, W., and Thompson, M. (1991). The fly-by-night parrot. *Australian Natural History* 23, 688-695. / Forshaw, J. M. (1970). Early record of the night parrot in New South Wales. *Emu* 70, 34. / Garnett, S.T., and Crowley, G.M. (2000). *The Action Plan for Australian Birds*. (Environment Australia, Canberra.) / Garnett, S., Crowley, G., Duncan, R., Baker, N., and Doherty, P. (1993). Notes on live night parrot sightings in north-western Queensland. *Emu* 93, 292-296. / Higgins, P.J. (ed.) (1999). *Handbook of Australian, New Zealand and Antarctic Birds. Volume 4: Parrots to Dollarbirds*. (Oxford University Press, Melbourne.) / Storr, G.M. (1977). *Birds of the Northern Territory*. (Western Australian Museum, Perth.) / Whitlock, F. L. (1924). Journey to central Australia in search of the night parrot. *Emu* 23, 248-281. / Wilson, H. (1937). Notes on the night parrot, with references to recent occurrences. *Emu* 37, 79-87.

Image courtesy of Ron Firth

Masked owl
(Tiwi subspecies)
Tyto novaehollandiae melvillensis

CONSERVATION STATUS
AUSTRALIA: **ENDANGERED**
NORTHERN TERRITORY: **ENDANGERED**

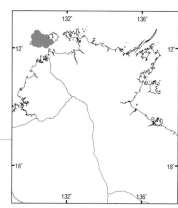

Known locations of
the Tiwi subspecies
of the masked owl
● = pre 1970
● = post 1970

DESCRIPTION

The Tiwi masked owl is a large dark owl, most likely to be confused with the barn owl *Tyto alba*, which is noticeably smaller and paler, with far weaker legs and feet and with far less feathering on the legs. It is most likely to be detected from its loud call, which comprises a highly varied set of shrieks and complex whistles.

The Tiwi subspecies is only weakly differentiated from the subspecies occurring on mainland northern Australia. Both are appreciably smaller than the two other subspecies from south-eastern and south-western Australia.

DISTRIBUTION

This subspecies of masked owl is restricted to Bathurst and Melville Islands (the Tiwi group).

Conservation reserves where reported: None

ECOLOGY

The Tiwi masked owl occurs mainly in eucalypt tall open forests especially those dominated by Darwin woollybutt (*Eucalyptus miniata*), Darwin stringybark (*E. tetrodonta*) and Melville Island bloodwood (*Corymbia nesophila*), but also roosts in monsoon rainforests, and forages in more open vegetation types, including grasslands and treeless plains (Woinarski *et al.* 2003).

Although it may roost in dense foliage, it more typically roosts, and nests, in tree hollows Mammals, up to the size of possums, constitute the bulk of its diet.

Although there is no detailed information for this subspecies, masked owls of other subspecies occupy large home ranges, estimated at 5 to 10 km² (Kavanagh and Murray 1996).

CONSERVATION ASSESSMENT

Based on extrapolation of densities and home range size from other subspecies, Garnett and Crowley (2000) estimated the total population at about 1000 breeding pairs, within a total area of about 7400 km² on the Tiwi Islands.

Although there are no data available to assess trends in this population size, the development of a major plantation forestry project centred on probably the highest quality habitat for this species, would reduce this habitat by between 300 and 1000 km², resulting in a population decline of about 5 to 15% (depending upon the actual area committed for forestry and whether the owls used the commercial plantations).

On the basis of the total population size and this projected decline, Garnett and Crowley categorised the Tiwi masked owl as **Endangered**. It qualifies (under criterion C2a) due to:
• population size estimated at fewer than 2500 mature individuals;
• an inferred or projected decline in numbers of mature individuals; and
• at least 95% of mature individuals within one subpopulation.

THREATENING PROCESSES

The most acute threatening process is conversion of large areas of its optimum habitat (eucalypt tall open forest) to short-rotation plantations of exotic timber species.

It may also be affected more pervasively by altered fire regimes, producing changed vegetation composition and then changes in the abundance of native mammals.

CONSERVATION OBJECTIVES AND MANAGEMENT

A national recovery plan for the Tiwi masked owl, and other birds, has recently been established (Woinarski 2004).

The main research priority is to derive more precise information on population size, home range and habitat requirements, and, using this information, to develop a usable population viability model.

The main management priorities are to:
• ensure the retention of adequate areas of prime habitat within a forestry management program; and
• establish a monitoring program to assess the impacts of forestry development.

Some of these research and management actions are now being implemented by Great Southern Plantations. The Tiwi Forestry Strategic Plan (Hadden 2000) commits to maintaining native forests 100 m around known roost and/or nest sites.

Compiled by John Woinarski [January 2007] / **References:** Garnett, S.T., and Crowley, G.M. (2000). *The action plan for Australian birds. 2000.* (Environment Australia, Canberra.) / Hadden, K. (2000). *Tiwi Islands Plantation Forestry Strategic Plan.* (Tiwi Land Council, Darwin.) / Kavanagh, R.P., and Murray, M. (1996). Home range, habitat and behaviour of the masked owl *Tyto novaehollandiae* near Newcastle, New South Wales. *Emu* 96, 250-257. / Woinarski, J.C.Z. (2004). *National multi-species Recovery Plan for the Partridge Pigeon [eastern subspecies] Geophaps smithii smithii; crested shrike-tit [northern (sub)-species] Falcunculus (frontatus) whitei; masked owl [north Australian mainland subspecies] Tyto novaehollandiae kimberli; and masked owl [Tiwi Islands subspecies] Tyto novaehollandiae melvillensis, 2004-2008.* (NT Department of Infrastructure Planning and Environment, Darwin.) / Woinarski, J., Brennan, K., Hempel, C., Armstrong, M., Milne, D., and Chatto, R. (2003). *Biodiversity conservation on the Tiwi Islands, Northern Territory. Part 2. Fauna.* 127 pp. (Department of Infrastructure Planning and Environment, Darwin.)

Image courtesy of D. P. Lewis

Masked owl
(north Australian mainland subspecies)
Tyto novaehollandiae kimberli

Known locations of the north Australian mainland subspecies of the masked owl
● = pre 1970
● = post 1970

DESCRIPTION

The masked owl is a large dark owl, most likely to be confused with the barn owl *Tyto alba*, which is noticeably smaller and paler, with far weaker legs and feet and with far less feathering on the legs. It is most likely to be detected from its loud call, which comprises a highly varied set of shrieks and complex whistles.

The subspecies occurring on the north Australian mainland differs from that of the subspecies *T. n. melvillensis* occurring on the Tiwi Islands in a series of minor plumage differences (described in Higgins 1999). Both subspecies are appreciably smaller than the two other subspecies from south-eastern and south-western Australia.

DISTRIBUTION

The distribution of the mainland north Australian masked owl subspecies *T. n. kimberli* is very imperfectly known, with remarkably few records across its broad range. Based on compilation of records from 1998–2002, *The New Atlas of Australian Birds* (Barrett *et al.* 2003) reported it from only one quarter degree grid cell (from a total of about 130) in northern Western Australia, two (of a total of about 320) in the Top End of the Northern Territory, one on the Barkly Tableland, and five in northern Queensland. The circumscription of this distribution is confused by (i) a number of unconfirmed records away from its main range (Higgins 1999), such as on the south-west of Cape York Peninsula and in semi-arid Northern Territory; and (ii) whether or not

the north-east Cape York Peninsula population is recognised as subspecifically distinct. Recognising the shortcomings in survey information, the current range can be considered to include the north and north-west coastal Kimberley; the Top End of the Northern Territory, including Cobourg Peninsula, extending south to around Katherine (Storr 1977), with a handful of isolated records from further south, including Jasper Gorge (the Victoria River District), McArthur River station, and Avon Downs (Barkly Tablelands) (Storr 1977; Higgins 1999; Barrett *et al.* 2003); north-eastern Queensland, including a few early records from north-eastern Cape York Peninsula (Archer-Watson Rivers) (the putative subspecies *T.n. galei*), with a broader distribution centred on Townsville.

Conservation reserves where reported: Garig Gunak Barlu National Park, Gregory National Park, Kakadu National Park, Keep River National Park, Nitmiluk National Park.

ECOLOGY

The masked owl occurs mainly in eucalypt tall open forests (especially those dominated by Darwin woollybutt *Eucalyptus miniata* and Darwin stringybark *E. tetrodonta*), but also roosts in monsoon rainforests, and forages in more open vegetation types, including grasslands. Although it may roost in dense foliage, it more typically roosts, and nests, in tree hollows. Mammals, up to the size of possums, constitute the bulk of its diet (Higgins 1999).

Although there is no detailed information for this subspecies, masked owls of other subspecies occupy large exclusive home ranges, estimated at 5 to 10 km² (Kavanagh and Murray 1996).

CONSERVATION ASSESSMENT

Too little information is known about the distribution, population size and trends in population to ascribe conservation status with any confidence. In north-eastern Queensland, the subspecies is considered to be in decline (Nielsen 1996). Given the large home ranges needed by the species, the population of mainland masked owls in the Northern Territory is probably fewer than 10,000 breeding individuals. The subspecies qualifies as **Vulnerable** under criterion C1:

• population size estimated to number fewer than 10 000 mature individuals, and
• an estimated continuing decline of at least 10% within 10 years or three generations, whichever is longer.

The assessment of trends is uncertain.

THREATENING PROCESSES

There is no reliable information on what factors may affect the status of this subspecies. It is possible that food resources may be diminishing, through broad-scale decline of small and medium-sized native mammals, possibly due to changed fire regimes (Woinarski *et al.* 2001;

continued.../

Pardon *et al.* 2003). This would lead to a subsequent decline in the masked owl population. The greatly increased cover and height of invasive exotic grasses (Rossiter *et al.* 2003) may cause a reduction in foraging efficiency for this owl.

The current regime of more intense, frequent and extensive fires may reduce the availability of large trees and hollows (Williams *et al.* 1999, 2003) required for nesting. Conversely, more extensive and less patchy fires may lead to greater foraging efficiency (Oakwood 2000). There is increasing development pressure on the optimal habitat (tall open eucalypt forest).

CONSERVATION OBJECTIVES AND MANAGEMENT

A national recovery plan for the mainland masked owl, and other birds, has recently been established (Woinarski 2004).

Recent studies on the Tiwi Islands have demonstrated that playback of calls is likely to significantly increase probability of detection of the Tiwi subspecies (Woinarski *et al.* 2003), and hence is probably a suitable detection technique for the mainland subspecies. The main research priorities are to:

• derive more precise information on population size, home range, habitat requirements, and response to putative threatening processes; and

• establish a monitoring program for at least representative populations.

Compiled by John Woinarski, Simon Ward [May 2006] / **References:** Barrett, G., Silcocks, A., Barry, S., Cunningham, R., and Poulter, R. (2003). *The new atlas of Australian birds.* (Royal Australasian Ornithologists Union, Melbourne.) / Higgins, P.J. (1999). *Handbook of Australian, New Zealand and Antarctic birds. Volume 4. Parrots to Dollarbirds.* (Oxford University Press, Melbourne.) / Kavanagh, R.P., and Murray, M. (1996). Home range, habitat and behaviour of the masked owl *Tyto novaehollandiae* near Newcastle, New South Wales. *Emu* 96, 250-257. / Nielsen, L. (1996). *Birds of Queensland's Wet Tropics and Great Barrier Reef Australia.* (Gerard Industries, Bowden.) / Oakwood, M. (2000). Reproduction and demography of the northern quoll, *Dasyurus hallucatus,* in the lowland savanna of northern Australia. *Australian Journal of Zoology* 48, 519-539. / Pardon, L.G., Brook, B.W., Griffiths, A.D., and Braithwaite, R.W. (2003). Determinants of survival for the northern brown bandicoot under a landscape-scale fire experiment. *Journal of Animal Ecology* 72, 106-115. / Rossiter, N.A., Setterfield, S.A., Douglas, M.M., and Hutley, L.B. (2003). Testing the grass-fire cycle: alien grass invasion in the tropical savannas of northern Australia. *Diversity and Distributions* 9, 169-176. / Schodde, R., and Mason, I.J. (1980). *Nocturnal birds of Australia.* (Lansdowne, Melbourne.) / Storr, G.M. (1977). *Birds of the Northern Territory.* Special Publication no. 7. (Western Australian Museum, Perth.) / Williams, R.J., Cook, G.D., Gill, A.M., and Moore, P.H.R. (1999). Fire regimes, fire intensity and tree survival in a tropical savanna in northern Australia. *Australian Journal of Ecology* 24, 50-59. / Williams, R.J., Muller, W.J., Wahren, C-H., Setterfield, S.A., and Cusack, J. (2003). Vegetation. In *Fire in tropical savannas: the Kapalga experiment.* (eds A.N. Andersen, G.D. Cook and R.J. Williams.) pp. 79-106. (Springer-Verlag, New York.) / Woinarski, J.C.Z. (2004). *National multi-species Recovery Plan for the Partridge Pigeon [eastern subspecies] Geophaps smithii smithii; crested shrike-tit [northern (sub)-species] Falcunculus (frontatus) whitei; masked owl [north Australian mainland subspecies] Tyto novaehollandiae kimberli; and masked owl [Tiwi Islands subspecies] Tyto novaehollandiae melvillensis, 2004-2008.* (NT Department of Infrastructure Planning and Environment, Darwin.) / Woinarski, J.C.Z., Milne, D.J., and Wanganeen, G. (2001). Changes in mammal populations in relatively intact landscapes of Kakadu National Park, Northern Territory, Australia. *Austral Ecology* 26, 360-370. / Woinarski, J., Brennan, K., Hempel, C., Armstrong, M., Milne, D., and Chatto, R. (2003). *Biodiversity conservation on the Tiwi Islands, Northern Territory. Part 2. Fauna.* 127 pp. (Department of Infrastructure Planning and Environment, Darwin.)

Image courtesy of Graeme Chapman

Purple-crowned fairy-wren
(western subspecies)
Malurus coronatus coronatus

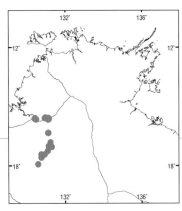

*Known locations of
the western purple-
crowned fairy-wren*
● = *pre 1970*
● = *post 1970*

CONSERVATION STATUS
AUSTRALIA: **VULNERABLE**
NORTHERN TERRITORY: **VULNERABLE**

DESCRIPTION

The purple-crowned fairy-wren is a large unmistakable fairy-wren. Males in breeding plumage have a vivid purple crown with a black centre, surrounded by a broad black band through the eyes and around the nape. The wings and back are cinnamon to sandy, the throat and breast are white, shading to rufous-buff on the flanks and belly. The tail is deep blue and all except the central pair of feathers are broadly tipped with white. Females lack the purple crown and black band, but have white eye rings and brow and broad red-brown cheek patches.

DISTRIBUTION

The purple-crowned fairy-wren is known from two subspecies, both of which occur in the Northern Territory. The eastern subspecies, *M. c. macgillivrayi* is known from north-western Queensland and the Gulf hinterland in the Northern Territory, extending as far west as the upper Roper River. The western subspecies, *M. c. coronatus*, occurs from the Victoria River catchment west to the north Kimberley (Western Australia). Within this range, purple-crowned fairy-wrens are almost entirely restricted to a narrow band around well-vegetated river channels.

Conservation reserves where reported:
Gregory National Park

ECOLOGY

Purple-crowned fairy-wrens prefer thick riparian vegetation, typically of canegrass and/or pandanus, but also sometimes occur in dense patchy shrubs up to 3 m.

Purple-crowned fairy-wrens live in small family groups, typically of two to six birds. They are territorial and sedentary, feeding in loose groups in the undergrowth or on the ground. They remain in contact using a soft chirping. They feed on a variety of insects and also eat small quantities of seeds.

If conditions are suitable they may breed throughout the year, but most breeding is during the early to mid dry season. Females typically lay three eggs in a bulky nest in the crown of a pandanus or in thick clumps of canegrass.

CONSERVATION ASSESSMENT

Recent surveys have shown that the canegrass habitat favoured by this subspecies is much more fragmented than previously thought, leading to the conclusion that there are three sub-populations in the Victoria River system.

The Northern Territory population is probably fewer than 5000 breeding individuals, with an extent of occurrence of c. 41 000 km² (Anne-Marie van Doorn *pers. comm.*). In Western Australia, the distribution has been severely reduced – the species is no longer found on the upper reaches of Pentecost River or lower reaches of the Fitzroy River and is now sparse along the middle and upper Fitzroy River, but remains in the Isdell,

Drysdale, Durack and Ord River systems (Rowley 1993; Garnett and Crowley 2000).

Some current pastoral practices and fire regimes are detrimental to the preferred habitat and are leading to decline and disappearances of fairy-wrens from known areas. However, the decline is not well documented due to the lack of good population estimates.

This subspecies is considered **Vulnerable** in the Northern Territory (under criteria B2ab and C1) due to:

- area of occupancy estimated to be less than 2000 km²;
- severely fragmented or known to occur at no more than 10 locations;
- continuing decline in area, extent and quality of habitat; and number of mature individuals;
- a population of fewer than 10 000 mature individuals;
- an expected decline of more than 10% over the next 10 years or three generations.

THREATENING PROCESSES

The greatest threat to the subspecies is degradation or loss of habitat. Livestock seeking water eat and trample riparian vegetation, and frequent and/or intense fires have also been detrimental in some places. Anne-Marie van Doorn (*pers. comm.*) reports a decrease of 50% in the adult populations at two sites where grazing and trampling was allowed around habitat patches over a two year period. The canegrass in these areas recovered

continued.../

quickly after the area was fenced, but the wren population has not yet recovered. Boekel (1979) described a similar pattern in the Victoria River area in the 1970s, with cattle grazing destroying habitat during bad droughts and exposing wrens to predation by cats, with failure to recolonise once habitat had apparently recovered. A similar pattern of decline associated with damage to riparian vegetation by livetsock was reported for the Kimberley by Smith and Johnstone (1977). Increased flood energy due to rangeland degradation has also destroyed some areas of riparian vegetation. Heavy weed invasion may also have adverse effects now and in the future. Recent studies (by Anne-Marie van Doorn) have indicated very low breeding success, largely due to nest predation. This study site is now known to have been colonized recently by the exotic black rat *Rattus rattus*, a known voracious nest predator.

CONSERVATION OBJECTIVES AND MANAGEMENT

Riparian vegetation in fairy-wren areas needs to be managed carefully. Stock should be excluded from riparian vegetation (e.g. along key large stretches of the Victoria River), and some landholders have recently established such exclosure fencing. Canegrass areas may also need to be protected from frequent fires. The impacts of black rats on the wren's reproductive success should be assessed, and a remedial program established if this predation is significant.

An existing study of purple-crowned fairy-wrens near the Victoria River crossing of the Victoria Highway would form a baseline for an ongoing monitoring program, and such monitoring should be maintained.

Compiled by Simon Ward, John Woinarski [May 2006] / **References:** Boekel, C. (1979). Notes on the status and behaviour of the Purple-crowned fairy-wren *Malurus coronatus* in the Victoria River Downs area, Northern Territory. *Australian Bird Watcher* 8, 91-97. / Garnett, S.T., and Crowley, G.M. (2000). *The Action Plan for Australian Birds 2000.* (Environment Australia, Canberra.) / Rowley, I. (1993). The purple-crowned fairy-wren *Malurus coronatus*. I. History, distribution and present status. *Emu* 93, 220-234. / Smith, G.T., and Johnstone, R.E. (1977). Status of the purple-crowned fairy-wren (*Malurus coronatus*) and buff-sided robin (*Poecilodryas superciliosa*) in Western Australia. *Western Australian Naturalist* 13, 185-188.

Image courtesy of Graeme Chapman

White-throated grass-wren
Amytornis woodwardi

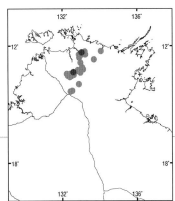

Known locations of the white-throated grass-wren
● = pre 1970
● = post 1970

CONSERVATION STATUS
AUSTRALIA: **NOT LISTED**
NORTHERN TERRITORY: **VULNERABLE**

DESCRIPTION

The white-throated grass-wren is a small shy ground-dwelling bird. It is secretive, and most observers get little more than a blurred impression of a mouse-like movement between clumps of spinifex, or a bird darting rapidly behind rocks. Its distinctive features include a long tail typically held upright or half-upright when stationary, but lowered when moving; a conspicuous white throat contrasting sharply with the head and upper parts that are black with white streaks, and a dark chestnut brown belly, rump and tail. Its presence is often revealed first by its distinctive call, a mixture of complex trills and chirps, and an alarm call characterised as a sharp "tzzzt".

DISTRIBUTION

The white-throated grass-wren is restricted to the rugged sandstone massif of western Arnhem Land, extending south-west as far as Nitmiluk National Park and north-east as far as the Mann River (Noske 1992a). Within this range of about 32 000 km², it is patchily distributed.

Conservation reserves where reported:
Kakadu National Park, Nitmiluk National Park.

ECOLOGY

The white-throated grass-wren is confined to hummock grasslands ("spinifex"), sometimes with open shrubland or woodland overstorey, mixed among dense boulder fields and sandstone pavements (Schodde 1982; Noske 1992a). The diet comprises invertebrates, seeds and other vegetable matter (Noske 1992a). Like other grass-wrens, it often occurs in

small family groups (typically of three to six birds), but also occurs singly or in pairs (Noske 1992a). Breeding occurs from December to June, and territory size is around 10 ha (Noske 1992a).

CONSERVATION ASSESSMENT

There has been some dispute about the status of this species. Based largely on an estimate of the area of potentially suitable habitat, and population density estimates at eight sites, Noske (1992a) estimated the total population at about 50 000 individuals (with a range of between 14 000 and 182 000), and considered that it was not threatened, although with the caveat that "it may be rash to assume that (it) is totally secure despite its apparent abundance". Woinarski (1992) re-analysed these and additional data, and estimated that the total population size was about 5000 to 10 000 individuals, and that the species was threatened by broad-scale habitat change associated with altered fire regimes. In response, Noske (1992b) provided a revised estimate of "in excess of 10 000" individuals. The most recent assessment is that of Garnett and Crowley (2000), who considered that the total population was 8000 breeding birds, albeit with a low reliability for this estimate.

It can be regarded as **Vulnerable** (under criteria B2ab(ii,iii) and C2a(i)) due to:
- area of occupancy less than 2000 km²;
- severely fragmented;
- continuing decline, observed, inferred or projected;
- population size fewer than 10 000 mature individuals, and

- no subpopulation estimate to contain more than 1000 mature individuals.

In all cases, the decline is presumed based on broad-scale change in habitat quality associated with altered fire regimes (Russell-Smith *et al.* 2002).

THREATENING PROCESSES

Fire regimes in the sandstone environments of western Arnhem Land have changed dramatically over the last 10 to 50 years, as traditional Aboriginal management has been disrupted or broken down. There is now a markedly increased incidence of extensive late dry season fires, leading to substantial vegetation change. The extent to which this change reduces habitat suitability for grass-wrens is uncertain, but the meagre evidence suggests that a high frequency of fires is deleterious (Woinarski 1992).

CONSERVATION OBJECTIVES AND MANAGEMENT

The principal research objectives are to:
- investigate the relationship between grass-wrens, habitat suitability and fire regimes; and
- improve the assessment of total population numbers, distribution and meta-population structure.

The main management objectives are to:
- implement a fire management program that maintains or enhances habitat quality across the range of this species; and
- establish a monitoring program for at least representative populations.

Compiled by John Woinarski [May 2006] / **References:** Garnett, S.T., and Crowley, G.M. (2000). *The Action Plan for Australian Birds. 2000.* (Environment Australia, Canberra.) / Noske, R. (1992a). The status and ecology of the white-throated grass-wren *Amytornis woodwardi. Emu* 92, 39-51. / Noske, R. (1992b). Do grasswrens have the numbers? Reply to Woinarski (1992). *Northern Territory Naturalist* 13, 5-8. / Russell-Smith, J., Ryan, P.G., and Cheal, D.C. (2002). Fire regimes and the conservation of sandstone heath in monsoonal northern Australia: frequency, interval, patchiness. *Biological Conservation* 104, 91-106. / Schodde, R. (1982). *The fairy-wrens. A monograph of the Maluridae.* (Landsdowne Editions, Melbourne.) / Woinarski, J.C.Z. (1992). The conservation status of the white-throated grass-wren *Amytornis woodwardi*, an example of problems in status designation. *Northern Territory Naturalist* 13, 1-5.

Image courtesy of Graeme Chapman

Carpentarian grass-wren
Amytornis dorotheae

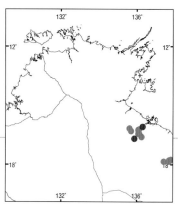

Known locations of the Carpentian grass-wren
● = pre 1970
● = post 1970

CONSERVATION STATUS
AUSTRALIA: **NOT LISTED**
NORTHERN TERRITORY: **ENDANGERED**

DESCRIPTION
The Carpentarian grass-wren is a medium-sized grass-wren with slender body and rusty-coloured back. The face is streaked black and white with a white throat in both males and females.
The crown, nape and back are streaked by white feather shafts. The tail is rusty grey and held largely upright. Adult females differ from males by having the colour of the flanks, thighs and lower belly dark chestnut rather than tawny.

DISTRIBUTION
This species is restricted to sandstone outcrops within the Carpentarian and Adelaidean systems of the Gulf of Carpentaria. Sightings are infrequent and patchy within this distribution, but the species has occurred at Nathan River Station (Northern Territory) in the north to Westmoreland Station and near Mt Isa (Queensland) in the south-east of the range (Garnett and Crowley 2000).

Conservation reserves where reported:
Caranbirini Conservation Reserve

ECOLOGY
Little information is available on the ecology of this species. It is known to live amongst mature stands of spinifex (*Triodia pungens*) on sandstone outcrops containing large boulders. The birds nest within spinifex clumps during the wet season. Clutch size is two to three eggs, and young are fed on a variety of seeds and insects.

CONSERVATION ASSESSMENT
In the Northern Territory, there have been two major surveys of the distribution of this species, by Martin and McKean (1986) and Perry (2005). In 1986, Martin and McKean found that the species was patchily distributed in sandstone ranges in the south-west of the Gulf of Carpentaria hinterland. Nearly 20 years later, Perry (2005) re-sampled eight sites where the species had previously been reported and found grass-wrens at only one of these sites. Perry (2005) also reported that prevailing fire regimes across most of the sandstone environments in the region were unsuitable for this species.

In the Northern Territory, the Carpentarian grass-wren is considered **Endangered** (under criterion B1ab) due to:
• extent of occurrence estimated to be less than 5000 km^2;
• severely fragmented; and
• continuing decline in range, habitat quality and population size.

It is likely that the population of this species in the Northern Territory is fewer than 2500 mature individuals.

THREATENING PROCESSES
Fire is currently thought to be influencing the distribution and abundance of the Carpentarian grass-wren. Results from studies elsewehere (M. Lewis *pers. obs.*) indicate lowered seed availability from *Triodia pungens* after a history of annual dry season fires. The Carpentarian grass-wren not only utilises unburnt patches of *T. pungens* as habitat and shelter but also feeds on the seeds of this species. Annual fires therefore reduce both food availability and habitat suitability.

CONSERVATION OBJECTIVES AND MANAGEMENT PRIORITIES
The primary research priorities are to monitor population numbers and make a thorough investigation of the biology of the species.

The primary management priority is to improve current burning practises by reducing the extent and incidence of late hot dry season burns, and introduce a balanced mosaic of burns.

Compiled by John Woinarski, Milton Lewis [May 2006] / **References:** Garnett, S.T., and Crowley, G.M. (2000). *The Action Plan for Australian Birds. 2000.* (Environment Australia, Canberra.) / McKean, J.L., and Martin, K.C. (1989). Distribution and status of the Carpentarian Grass-wren *Amytornis dorotheae*. *Northern Territory Naturalist* 11, 12-19. / Perry, J. (2005). *Habitat and status of the Carpentarian grasswren (Amytornis dorotheae) in the Northern Territory.* B.App.Sci. thesis. (Charles Darwin University, Darwin.)

Image courtesy of Graeme Chapman

Thick-billed grass-wren
(eastern subspecies)

Amytornis textilis modestus

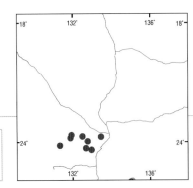

Known locations of the thick-billed grass-wren
● = pre 1970
● = post 1970

CONSERVATION STATUS
AUSTRALIA: **VULNERABLE**
NORTHERN TERRITORY: **ENDANGERED**

DESCRIPTION

This thick-billed grass-wren is a small bird (length 15 to 20 cm) with a long tail. The upperparts are dull brown in colour with the underparts being paler fawn. Feathers are streaked with white. The female has a chestnut patch on either side of the breast. The eyes are dark brown, the bill and feet are dark grey.

DISTRIBUTION

The thick-billed grass-wren occurs as three subspecies in arid and semi-arid regions of southern Australia (Higgins *et al.* 2000). The Western Australian subspecies (*A. t. textilis*) occupies inland regions of southern Western Australia; the Gawler Range subspecies (*A. t. myall*) is restricted to an area around the Gawler Ranges and upper Eyre Peninsula in South Australia; and the eastern subspecies, to which Northern Territory populations belong, occurs across north-central South Australia and into north-west New South Wales.

In the Northern Territory, the species was formerly present in the Finke River drainage basin from Mereenie Bluff and the upper Hugh River south to Lauries Creek, McMinns Creek and the lower Finke (Storr 1977). It was moderately common at one time. However, no records of the species were obtained in the Northern Territory between 1936 and 1993.

In April 1994 a small isolated population was located just south of Charlotte Waters along a drainage line. Birds have been re-sighted during subsequent surveys (Eldridge and Reid 2000; Eldridge and Pascoe 2004) and the species is now known from four locations within a 25 km² area of chenopod vegetation (S. Eldridge *pers. comm.*).

Conservation reserves where reported: None

ECOLOGY

The eastern subspecies of the thick-billed grass-wren inhabits the chenopod shrublands of inland Australia, particularly those dominated by saltbush *Atriplex* and bluebush *Maireana*. The population near Charlotte Waters is located along drainage lines in run-on areas dominated by the saltbush *Atriplex nummularia*. Other common chenopod species are *Maireana aphylla*, *Einadia nutans* ssp. *eremaea,* and *Chenopodium auricomum.*

The subspecies is sedentary and pairs usually occupy a home range of 20 to 40 ha. Birds feed on the ground, where seeds and invertebrates are obtained.

Breeding takes place in spring or summer. The nest is usually a semi-dome constructed of twigs, grasses and fibres and built within the foliage of a shrub, usually a bluebush or saltbush. Two to three eggs are laid.

CONSERVATION ASSESSMENT

The current evidence suggests that there is only one remaining population of the thick-billed grass-wren in the Northern Territory; however, more populations may be located with additional surveys. The most abrupt decline of this species in the Northern Territory occurred earlier than relevant to IUCN status assessment (generally restricted to 10 years or three generations). Based on available information, the species is considered **Endangered** in the Northern Territory (under criterion D) due to population size estimated at fewer than 250 mature individuals.

The Northern Territory population occurs very close to the South Australian border and, therefore, may be the target of immigration from sites in northern South Australia where it is widespread and locally common. Given that the subspecies has a lower global conservation status, Vulnerable, then such immigration would be justification for down-grading its Territory-wide status based on current IUCN guidelines (Gärdenfors 2001). However, immigration cannot be confirmed based on current information, therefore, the status of the thick-billed grass-wren in the Northern Territory should remain as Endangered.

THREATENING PROCESSES

The eastern subspecies of the thick-billed grass-wren has disappeared from western New South Wales since 1912 and from most of its Northern Territory range since 1936. No threatening process has yet been associated with this decline. Habitat degradation resulting from high stocking rates of livestock, and severe drought, may result in the extinction of small, isolated populations

continued.../

such as occurred in the Finke drainage of the Northern Territory (Garnet and Crowley 2000). Such a process could threaten the last remaining Territory population. However, the thick-billed grass-wren occurs on pastoral lease throughout its range and is known to survive in areas of sparse cover degraded by sheep, rabbits and drought (Garnett and Crowley 2000). Therefore, research is needed before a definite cause of decline can be established.

CONSERVATION OBJECTIVES AND MANAGEMENT

A survey and monitoring program for the thick-billed grass-wren commenced in 2002 and is ongoing. The program is carried out jointly by the Biodiversity Conservation and Biological Parks divisions of the Department of Natural Resources, Environment and The Arts.

Management priorities for the species in the Northern Territory are to:
• define the area of occupancy of the known population on New Crown Station including searches for additional subpopulations;
• assess the size of the population and effects of any possible threatening processes, and continue regular monitoring; and
• develop husbandry methods at the Alice Springs Desert Park.

Compiled by Chris Pavey [May 2006] / **References:** Eldridge, S., and Pascoe, B. (2004). Northern Territory records of the thick-billed grasswren *Amytornis textilis* and rufous fieldwren *Calamanthus campestris*. *South Australian Ornithologist* 34, 183-184. / Eldridge, S., and Reid, J. (2000). *A biological survey of the Finke floodout region, Northern Territory* (Arid Lands Environment Centre, Alice Springs.) / Gärdenfors, U. (2001). Classifying threatened species at national versus global levels. *Trends in Ecology and Evolution* 16, 511-516. / Garnett, S.T., and Crowley, G.M. (2000). *The Action Plan for Australian Birds*. (Environment Australia, Canberra.) / Higgins, P.J., Peter, J.M., and Steele, W.K. (eds) (2000). *Handbook of Australian, New Zealand and Antarctic Birds. Volume 5: Tyrant-flycatcher to chats*. (Oxford University Press, Melbourne.) / Storr, G.M. (1977). *Birds of the Northern Territory*. (Western Australian Museum, Perth.)

Image courtesy of Graeme Chapman

Slender-billed thornbill
(western subspecies)

Acanthiza iredalei iredalei

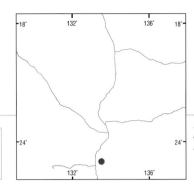

Known location
of the slender-
billed thornbill
- = pre 1970
- = post 1970

CONSERVATION STATUS
AUSTRALIA: **VULNERABLE**
NORTHERN TERRITORY: **EXTINCT**

DESCRIPTION

The slender-billed thornbill is a small bird, with head and body length of 9 to 10 cm. The upperparts are light olive-grey to dark olive-brown. The rump and base of tail are buff-yellow to yellow-olive. The forehead and cheeks are scalloped and flecked pale to deep cream. The underparts are uniformly cream-white to cream-buff. The bill is dark and the eye pale.

DISTRIBUTION

The slender-billed thornbill is endemic to Australia and occurs as three subspecies across the semi-arid regions of the southern half of the continent from the Carnarvon bioregion in Western Australia to the South Australia-Victoria border. Only one subspecies has been recorded for the Northern Territory.

In the Northern Territory, the slender-billed thornbill is known from a single specimen collected by S.A. White on the lower Finke River on Idracowra Station on 21 August 1913 (Storr 1977). There have been no records of the species in the Northern Territory since this time. A potential sighting from Barrow Creek in 1942 was assessed as "...too doubtful to be considered further" (Parker 1971).

Conservation reserves where reported: None

ECOLOGY

Across its broader range, the slender-billed thornbill occurs in shrubland, typically in areas of saltmarsh dominated by samphire, bluebush (*Maireana*) or saltbush (*Atriplex*) around salt lakes or low heath on sandplain (Schodde and Tidemann 1986; Schodde and Mason 1999). It feeds on invertebrates, mostly insects and spiders, that it captures amongst the foliage of shrubs. It rarely feeds on the ground despite the openness of its foraging habitat.

The species is usually seen in pairs or small flocks of eight to 10 birds. The breeding season runs from July to November. Pairs form between August and October and a small domed nest, constructed of grasses, bark strips and cobwebs, with a side entrance is built in a low shrub. Up to three eggs are laid.

CONSERVATION ASSESSMENT

The slender-billed thornbill is unlikely to still occur in the Northern Territory. It is known from only one record in 1913. The original label notes from the specimen indicate the species was "plentiful" there at that time (Parker 1971). The Idracowra locality was searched by Shane Parker and David Howe during May 1970 without success, although Parker (1971) noted that extensive areas of suitable habitat occur in the vicinity. Surveys in 2001 of the Finke bioregion, including Idracowra Station, did not find any evidence of the species (Pavey and Joseph 2004). Therefore, the western subspecies

of the slender-billed thornbill is classified as **Extinct** in the Northern Territory. However, given the amount of suitable habitat remaining in the southern Northern Territory, it is puzzling that the species has been located at only one site. In 2003, the specimen from Idracowra Station (now housed in the American Museum of Natural History, New York) was re-examined and found to have been correctly identified (Pavey and Joseph 2004). Therefore, the slender-billed thornbill is the only bird species considered to have become extinct in the Northern Territory since European settlement.

THREATENING PROCESSES

The western subspecies of the slender-billed thornbill, to which the Northern Territory record belongs, occupies a 400 000 km² area of southern Australia and has an estimated breeding population of 100 000 (Garnett and Crowley 2000). Indeed, Garnett and Crowley suggested that the subspecies should have a status of lower risk, Least Concern. No threatening processes have been positively identified. Habitat degradation as a result of grazing by sheep and rabbits is a potential threat in some parts of its range.

CONSERVATION OBJECTIVES AND MANAGEMENT

There is no existing management program for this species in the Northern Territory. Any reliable potential sightings of the species should be followed-up as soon as possible.

Compiled by Chris Pavey [May 2006] / **References:** Garnett, S.T., and Crowley, G.M. (2000). *The Action Plan for Australian Birds, 2000*. (Environment Australia, Canberra.) / Parker, S.A. (1971). Critical notes on the status of some central Australian birds. *Emu* 71, 99-102. / Pavey, C. R., and Joseph, L. (2004). The occurrence of the slender-billed thornbill *Acanthiza iredalei* in the Northern Territory. *South Australian Ornithologist* 34, 170-175. / Schodde, R., and Mason, I.J. (1999). *The directory of Australian birds: passerines*. (CSIRO, Melbourne.) / Schodde, R., and Tidemann, S.C. (eds) (1986). *Reader's Digest Complete Book of Australian Birds. 2nd edition*. (Reader's Digest, Sydney.) / Storr, G.M. (1977). *Birds of the Northern Territory*. (Western Australian Museum, Perth.)

Image courtesy of Martin Armstrong

Yellow chat
(Alligator Rivers subspecies)
Epthianura crocea tunneyi

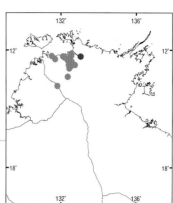

Known locations of the yellow chat
● = *pre 1970*
● = *post 1970*

CONSERVATION STATUS
AUSTRALIA: **VULNERABLE**
NORTHERN TERRITORY: **ENDANGERED**

DESCRIPTION

The yellow chat is a small bird that typically forages on the ground, in dense grass or in low shrubs. The male is a bright golden-yellow, with a prominent black chest band. The female is pale lemon-yellow, and has no chest band.

DISTRIBUTION

Yellow chats occur patchily across northern Australia, most typically in chenopod shrublands and grasslands around water sources in semi-arid areas. However, the subspecies *Epthianura crocea tunneyi* is restricted to a small geographic area encompassing the floodplains from the Adelaide River to the East Alligator River (Schodde and Mason 1999), and within this area it is known from only a small number of sites (Armstrong 2004). There have been recent (2005, 2006) records from Harrison Dam.

Conservation reserves where reported:
Harrison Dam Reserve, Kakadu National Park, Mary River National Park.

ECOLOGY

Yellow chats have been reported from tall grasslands and samphire shrublands (on coastal saltpans). Most records of the Alligator Rivers subspecies are from floodplain depressions and channels, concentrating around wetter areas at the end of the dry season (Armstrong 2004). The diet is mostly invertebrates (Higgins *et al.* 2001). Yellow chats typically occur in small groups of two to 10 individuals.

CONSERVATION ASSESSMENT

For this endemic Northern Territory subspecies, Garnett and Crowley (2000) estimated the extent of occurrence as 500 km², area of occupancy at 100 km², and the total number of breeding birds as 500. However, these estimates are of relatively low reliability. The subpopulation structure is unknown: Garnett and Crowley (2000) considered there was only one subpopulation, but it may be that there are small resident subpopulations in the floodplain system associated with each river system in the Adelaide to East Alligator area.

The most systematic assessment of the status of this subspecies (Armstrong 2004) considered that it met the criteria B1ab, B2ab and C2a for **Endangered:**

• extent of occurrence less than 5000 km²;
• severely fragmented;
• continuing decline in habitat quality;
• population fewer than 2500 mature individuals;
• continuing population decline; and
• no subpopulation estimated to contain more than 250 mature individuals.

THREATENING PROCESSES

The preferred floodplain habitats are being altered by invasion of exotic plant species (notably by *Mimosa pigra*, para grass *Brachiaria mutica* and gamba grass *Andropogon gayanus*) and vegetation change due to grazing by buffalo and cattle, by wallowing and rooting by pigs, and by altered fire regimes. Saltwater intrusion and sea-level rise,

as a consequence of global climate change, may further consume preferred habitat. Feral cats may reduce reproductive success. Of these possible threats, Armstrong (2004) considered that habitat degradation by pigs was the most serious.

CONSERVATION OBJECTIVES AND MANAGEMENT

The principal research priorities are to provide more informed estimates of population size, distribution, patterns of movement, habitat preference and response to the putative threatening processes.

Management priorities are to:
• maintain extensive areas of suitable habitat, most likely through control of exotic plants; and
• develop a monitoring program (this may be most readily based on the survey undertaken by Armstong (2004) in Kakadu National Park).

Compiled by John Woinarski, Martin Armstrong [May 2006] / **References:** Armstrong, M. (2004). *The yellow chat Epthianura crocea tunneyi in Kakadu National Park.* Report to Parks Australia (North). (NT Department of Infrastructure Planning and Environment, Darwin.) / Garnett, S.T., and Crowley, G.M. (2000). *The action plan for Australian birds. 2000.* (Environment Australia, Canberra.) / Higgins, P.J., Peter, J.M., and Steele, W.K. (eds) (2001). *Handbook of Australian, New Zealand and Antarctic birds. Volume 5. Tyrant-flycatchers to Chats.* (Oxford University Press, Melbourne.) / Schodde, R., and Mason, I.J. (1999). *The Directory of Australian Birds: Passerines.* (CSIRO, Melbourne.)

Image courtesy of Graeme Chapman

Hooded robin
(Tiwi subspecies)
Melanodryas cucullata melvillensis

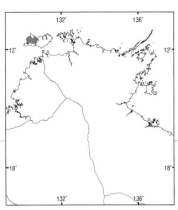

Known locations of the Tiwi hooded robin
- ● = *pre 1970*
- ● = *post 1970*

CONSERVATION STATUS
AUSTRALIA: **ENDANGERED**
NORTHERN TERRITORY: **ENDANGERED**

DESCRIPTION
The hooded robin is a small woodland bird with black head, white belly and black and white wings, tail and back.

This subspecies is not strongly differentiated in morphology from other subspecies of hooded robin on the Australian mainland (Schodde and Mason 1999), but is generally smaller in body size with a proportionally longer bill (Higgins and Peter 2002).

DISTRIBUTION
The Tiwi hooded robin is restricted to the Tiwi Islands (Bathurst and Melville). This subspecies of hooded robin was last recorded in December 1991 and January 1992 by Fensham and Woinarski (1992). The two sites at which this species was recorded then included one on Bathurst Island and one on Melville Island. These are the only records for which precise locality data are available. The only other records for this taxon (from 1911–12) were from "Melville Island" (Zietz 1914; Mathews 1914).

Conservation reserves where reported: None

ECOLOGY
On the Tiwi Islands, it has been reported from eucalypt tall open forests and treeless plains.

The most typical foraging behaviour of hooded robins is by quiet perching on tree branches or trunks and then suddenly pouncing to take invertebrate prey on the ground (Higgins and

Peter 2002). This foraging behaviour is most efficient when there is relatively little low vegetative cover (in contrast to the dense tall grasses typical of savanna woodlands in northern Australia: Woinarski and Fisher 1995).

CONSERVATION ASSESSMENT
There are extraordinarily few records of this taxon, despite recent unusually comprehensive and systematic general wildlife surveys within its range, and the generally reasonably conspicuous nature of hooded robins (Woinarski *et al.* 2003).

There are no existing data on the population size of this taxon. The entire original literature on this species comprises:
- its description by Zietz (1914), probably based on one specimen from Melville Island (measurement of only a single individual inferred in the two sentence description);
- a single word in Mathews' (1914) account of the bird fauna of Melville Island (based on a trip of unspecified duration in 1911–12). Interestingly, that single word is "common";
- two records in December 1991 and January 1992 during a survey by Fensham and Woinarski (1992). During this survey the hooded robin was recorded at one quadrat out of a total of 98 quadrats sampled, with an additional incidental (non-quadrat based) record at one of the 13 other sites sampled.
- a cumulative total of five specimens used by Schodde and Mason (1999) in considering the taxonomic status of this taxon.

A search for endemic Tiwi Island bird taxa in 1996 by Mason and Schodde (1997) failed to locate any hooded robins, and commented that "they may be local, but we doubt that they are common". No hooded robins were encountered in a major wildlife survey of the Tiwi Islands from 2000 to 2003 (Woinarski *et al.* 2003). This study included systematic bird surveys of 351 one hectare quadrats (with each quadrat sampled 10 times over three days for birds), spaced across the range of terrestrial habitats of both Bathurst and Melville Islands, and including sampling across all seasons. In addition to the systematic quadrat-based sampling, experienced zoologists spent a considerable time (total of over 400 person-days) searching more extensively for notable species, including hooded robins, beyond quadrats. No hooded robins were located in these quadrat surveys or more extensive searches.

These meagre data suggest that a decline may possibly have occurred sometime between 1912 and 1992, with this continuing until the present.

The apparent decline of the hooded robin on the Tiwi Islands is paralleled by a possible decline of another subspecies of hooded robin on the nearby Cobourg Peninsula (these two areas together comprising the Tiwi-Cobourg bioregion).

continued.../

The hooded robin was one of a small set of bird species that was recorded from the Cobourg Peninsula by John Gilbert in 1840–41 but not recorded in the only subsequent substantial survey there by Frith and Calaby (1974).

On the Tiwi Islands, decline may be exacerbated by a developing plantation forestry program that will transform 300 to 1000 km² of tall eucalypt open forest to short-rotation plantations of exotic tree species.

Based on this information, Garnett and Crowley (2000) categorised the Tiwi hooded robin as Vulnerable, under the IUCN (1994) set of criterion C2b. Using IUCN (2001) criteria, this subspecies is considered **Endangered** in the Northern Territory (under criterion C2a) due to:

- population size estimated at fewer than 2500 mature individuals;
- an inferred or projected decline in numbers of mature individuals; and
- at least 95% of mature individuals within one subpopulation.

The fit to the latter criterion assumes that there is no subpopulation structure within and between Bathurst and Melville Islands.

THREATENING PROCESSES

There is no detailed information on factors that may have contributed to the apparent decline of this taxon. The most likely is change in fire regime, from an intricate fine-scaled mosaic imposed by Aboriginal management to a more polarised regime now characterised by extensive areas burnt by larger hotter fires around more accessible areas, and a low frequency in the more remote areas (Woinarski *et al*. 2000). Low frequency of fires probably disadvantages this taxon, because the resulting dense grass cover leads to reduced foraging efficiency. A high frequency of extensive hot fires may also be disadvantageous.

The transformation of large areas of eucalypt open forest to exotic plantations is likely to detrimentally affect this taxon.

Over much of their range elsewhere, (other subspecies of) hooded robins have also declined or become locally extinct, possibly due to predation by feral cats, vegetation clearance and other change, or changes in the abundance of some invertebrate prey.

CONSERVATION OBJECTIVES AND MANAGEMENT

Research priorities are to determine population size, distribution, habitat relationships and threats (especially relationship to fire). Given the absence of records for more than a decade, a systematic and targeted search for hooded robins is highly warranted.

Management priorities are to:

- ensure that forestry developments are associated with retention of adequate areas of habitat and populations;
- develop fire management programs, with the collaboration of Indigenous landowners, that are not detrimental to this taxon.

Compiled by John Woinarski [May 2006] / **References:** Fensham, R.J., and Woinarski, J.C.Z. (1992). *Yawulama: the ecology and conservation of monsoon forest on the Tiwi Islands, Northern Territory.* Report to DASET. (Conservation Commission of the Northern Territory, Darwin.) / Frith, H.J., and Calaby, J.H. (1974). *Fauna survey of the Port Essington district, Cobourg Peninsula, Northern Territory of Australia.* Technical Paper no. 28. (CSIRO Wildlife Research, Canberra.) / Garnett, S.T., and Crowley, G.M. (2000). *The Action Plan for Australian Birds. 2000.* (Environment Australia, Canberra.) / Higgins, P.J., and Peter, J.M. (eds) (2002). *Handbook of Australian, New Zealand and Antarctic birds. Volume 6. Pardalotes to shrike-thrushes.* (Oxford University Press, Melbourne.) / Mason, I.J., and Schodde, R. (1997). *Bird survey of the Tiwi Islands, October 1996.* Report to Tiwi Land Council. (CSIRO, Canberra.) / Mathews, G.M. (1914). A list of the birds of Melville Island, Northern Territory, Australia. *Ibis* 2, 91-132. / Schodde, R. and Mason, I.J. (1999). *The Directory of Australian birds: Passerines.* (CSIRO, Melbourne.) / Woinarski, J.C.Z., and Fisher, A. (1995). Wildlife of lancewood (*Acacia shirleyi*) thickets and woodlands in northern Australia: 2. Comparisons with other environments of the region (Acacia woodlands, *Eucalyptus* savanna woodlands and monsoon rainforests). *Wildlife Research* 22, 413-443. / Woinarski, J., Brennan, K., Hempel, C., Armstrong, M., Milne, D., and Chatto, R. (2003). *Biodiversity conservation on the Tiwi Islands, Northern Territory. Part 2. Fauna.* 127 pp. (Department of Infrastructure Planning and Environment, Darwin.) / Zietz, F.R. (1914). The avifauna of Melville Island, Northern Territory. *South Australian Ornithologist* 1, 11-18.

Image courtesy of Graeme Chapman

Northern scrub-robin

Drymodes superciliaris colcloughi

CONSERVATION STATUS
AUSTRALIA: **EXTINCT**
NORTHERN TERRITORY: **DATA DEFICIENT**

DESCRIPTION

The northern scrub-robin is a thrush-sized bird that forages mostly on the ground. It is rufous-brown above and paler below, with a distinct dark vertical stripe from above the eye to the side of the throat. The wings are black with broad white tips forming a prominent double wing-bar. In the Northern Territory, it is most likely to be confused with the white-browed (or buff-sided) robin.

DISTRIBUTION

The northern scrub-robin occurs in northern Cape York Peninsula, parts of New Guinea and the Aru Islands. Its supposed presence in the Northern Territory is based solely on a set of two specimens claimed to be from the Roper River area, collected by M.J. Colclough in 1910 (Bennett 1983). This small set formed the type and only occurrences of the subspecies *D. s. colcloughi*.

Conservation reserves where reported: None

ECOLOGY

Across its broader range, the northern scrub-robin feeds mainly on invertebrates, collected by actively digging in dense leaf litter. It moves mostly by hopping. Its preferred habitat is dense vegetation, typically including rainforest.

CONSERVATION ASSESSMENT

The occurrence of this species in the Northern Territory, and indeed the existence of this subspecies, is now considered to be doubtful. Although some authorities have credited the provenance of the specimens (Parker 1970; Bennett 1983), the evidence more strongly suggests that the locality of the specimens was misattributed, and that both the putative Northern Territory specimens in fact came from Cape York Peninsula (Storr 1967; Schodde and Mason 1999): "Because doubt attaches its provenance, *colcloughi* should be struck from the Australian avian inventory until the unlikely event of its rediscovery ... (Colclough's specimens) from the Roper are probably either a case of mistaken identity or a hoax" (Schodde and Mason 1999). In their assessment of the conservation status of all Australian bird taxa, Garnett and Crowley (2000) omitted this taxon, implicitly accepting its non-existence.

It is now almost impossible to prove or disprove the locality of Colclough's specimens, which renders the assessment of status difficult. The misattribution of locality is by far the more likely possibility, in which case it should be removed from the Northern Territory fauna listing. However, in the less likely case of the provenance being correctly attributed, the taxon should be considered either Extinct or Critically Endangered, given the highly localised putative range, and the lack of any records since 1910, despite specific searches (Bennett 1983).

Given this uncertainty, **Data Deficient** seems the most parsimonious choice.

THREATENING PROCESSES

Bennett (1983) listed the degradation of its presumed habitat (riparian gallery forest, monsoon rainforest, and possibly lancewood *Acacia shirleyi* thickets) by cattle grazing and especially by changed fire regimes, as probably the major threatening processes.

CONSERVATION OBJECTIVES AND MANAGEMENT

The primary research priority is to attempt to establish its ongoing existence, through specific searches in the lower Roper River catchment and adjacent areas.

However, given its probable non-existence, such searching should be a low priority against that of other threatened taxa.

Compiled by John Woinarski [May 2006] / **References:** Bennett, S. (1983). The northern scrub-robin *Drymodes superciliaris* in the Northern Territory. *Emu* 83, 105-107. / Garnett, S.T., and Crowley, G.M. (2000). *The action plan for Australian Birds 2000.* (Environment Australia, Canberra.) / Parker, S.A. (1970). Critical notes on the status of some Northern Territory birds. *South Australian Ornithologist* 29, 115-125. / Schodde, R., and Mason, I.J. (1999). *The directory of Australian birds: passerines.* (CSIRO, Melbourne.) / Storr, G.M. (1967). *List of Northern Territory Birds.* (Western Australian Museum, Perth.)

Image courtesy of Don Franklin

Northern (crested) shrike-tit

Falcunculus (frontatus) whitei

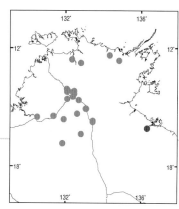

Known locations of the northern shrike-tit
- ● = pre 1970
- ● = post 1970

CONSERVATION STATUS
AUSTRALIA: **VULNERABLE**
NORTHERN TERRITORY: **VULNERABLE**

DESCRIPTION

The northern shrike-tit is a distinctive medium-sized bird. It has a dull green back and wings, yellow belly and boldly marked black and white head, with a small black crest. Its bill is unusually deep, strong and hooked.

DISTRIBUTION

This taxon forms part of a superspecies of three geographically isolated populations, in eastern and south-eastern Australia, south-western Australia and northern Australia. These taxa are variably accorded subspecific (Christidis and Boles 1994) or full specific (Schodde and Mason 1999) status.

There are remarkably few records of the northern shrike-tit (Robinson and Woinarski 1992). These are scattered widely from the south-west Kimberley east to near Borroloola. Most recent records from the Northern Territory have been in the Sturt Plateau.

Conservation reserves where reported:
Elsey National Park, Kakadu National Park, Nitmiluk National Park, (although in each case the number of records from these reserves is very few).

ECOLOGY

There have been no detailed studies on the northern shrike-tit. A review of all records (Robinson and Woinarski 1992) suggested that it occurred across a range of eucalypt forests and woodlands.

There is more information available on the two other shrike-tit taxa. Shrike-tits are insectivorous. They forage in tree canopies, seeking invertebrates on foliage or under bark. In south-eastern Australia, a high proportion of foraging is from the peeling bark of manna gum (*Eucalyptus viminalis*) and similar species; however no Northern Territory trees have this feature. The massive bill is extremely strong, and is used for chiselling and tearing bark, branches and foliage to access invertebrates sheltering within.

The other two shrike-tit taxa are known to have large home ranges, possibly extending over hundreds of hectares (Higgins and Peter 2002), and this probably also applies to the northern shrike-tit, rendering it especially susceptible to habitat fragmentaton in areas of extensive land clearing and in habitats where the main resource, invertebrates under loose bark, is uncommon (Recher 2006). Most of the few records of the northern shrike-tit refer to small parties of two to five birds.

CONSERVATION ASSESSMENT

Assessment of conservation status is hampered by the paucity of records, and lack of information on limiting factors or threatening processes. Robinson and Woinarski (1992) suggested a possible decline and a possible impact from frequent fire, but the available evidence is limited. *The New Atlas of Australian Birds* (Barrett *et al.* 2003) recorded low reporting rates for the species in northern Australia and provided evidence for a possible decline.

Garnett and Crowley (2000) considered it to meet criterion C2a for listing as Endangered (total population fewer than 2500 mature individuals, no subpopulation with more than 250 mature individuals, and declining). However, they recognised that the reliability of these estimates was low. Since the northern shrike-tit appears to be declining but is present at low densities over an extensive area and across a broad range of habitats, the species is considered **Vulnerable** in the Northern Territory.

THREATENING PROCESSES

The lack of information on the ecology of this species means that it is impossible to assess threatening processes with any degree of confidence. Most likely, habitat quality will be affected by fire regimes, as these may determine the density of large trees and the abundance of the principal food items.

CONSERVATION OBJECTIVES AND MANAGEMENT

A recovery plan for this species has been prepared recently (Woinarski 2004). Research priorities are to:
- provide a more precise estimate of total population size and trends;
- investigate the ecology of the species, with particular attention to characteristics associated with habitat suitability; and
- assess the impacts of a range of fire regimes.

Compiled by John Woinarski, Simon Ward [April 2007] / **References:** Barrett, G., Silcocks, A., Barry, S. Cunningham, R., and Poulter, R. (2003). *The New Atlas of Australian Birds.* (Birds Australia, Melbourne.) / Christidis, L., and Boles, W.E. (1994). *The Taxonomy and Species of Birds of Australia and its Territories.* Royal Australasian Ornithologists Union Monograph 2. (RAOU, Melbourne.) / Garnett, S.T., and Crowley, G.M. (2000). *The Action Plan for Australian Birds 2000.* (Environment Australia, Canberra.) / Higgins, P. J., and Peter, J. M. (eds) (2002). *Handbook of Australian, New Zealand and Antarctic Birds. Volume 6: Pardalotes to Shrike-thrushes.* (Oxford University Press, Melbourne.) / Recher, H.F. (2006). A hypothesis to explain why te south-western subspecies of the Crested Shrike-tit (*Falcunculus frontatus leucogaster*) is rare and declining. *Emu* 106, 181-186. / Robinson, D., and Woinarski, J.C.Z. (1992). A review of records of the Northern Shrike-tit *Falcunculus frontatus whitei* in northwestern Australia. *South Australian Ornithologist* 31, 111-117. / Schodde, R., and Mason, I.J. (1999). *The Directory of Australian Birds: Passerines.* (CSIRO, Melbourne.) / Woinarski, J.C.Z. (2004). *National multi-species Recovery Plan for the Partridge Pigeon [eastern subspecies] Geophaps smithii smithii; crested shrike-tit [northern (sub)-species] Falcunculus (frontatus) whitei; masked owl [north Australian mainland subspecies] Tyto novaehollandiae kimberli; and masked owl [Tiwi Islands subspecies] Tyto novaehollandiae melvillensis, 2004-2008.* (NT Department of Infrastructure Planning and Environment, Darwin.)

Image courtesy of Graeme Chapman

Grey currawong
(western subspecies)
Strepera versicolor plumbea

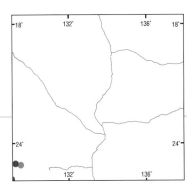

Known locations of the grey currawong
● = *pre 1970*
● = *post 1970*

CONSERVATION STATUS
AUSTRALIA: **NOT LISTED**
NORTHERN TERRITORY: **CRITICALLY ENDANGERED**

DESCRIPTION

The western subspecies of the grey currawong is a large bird (head-body length up to 50 cm). As its name suggests, it is predominantly dark in colour. Most of the upper and underbody is smoky-grey with a brownish tinge. The face and throat has a sooty wash. A large white patch is present on the wings and extends from the base of the primary flight feathers to the outer secondary flight feathers. The tips of both primary and secondary flight feathers are white. The dark tail has a broad white band at its tip. The bill and legs are black. The eye is bright yellow. Sexes are similar in size and appearance.

Five other subspecies of the grey currawong occur in Australia and these vary both in colour (from grey to brown to almost black) and size.

DISTRIBUTION

The grey currawong is endemic to Australia and occurs as six subspecies in the southern half of the continent. The distribution ranges from just north of Sydney, south through Victoria, southern South Australia and south-west Western Australia. It also occurs in eastern Tasmania. The range of subspecies *plumbea* extends from south-west Western Australia across into north-west South Australia and into the south-west corner of the Northern Territory. It has been recorded north to the Petermann Ranges and east to 35 km west of Victory Downs.

Conservation reserves where reported: None

ECOLOGY

Relatively little is known about the ecology of the grey currawong and although widespread, it is generally not common. Usually single birds or pairs are observed, although historical accounts indicate that large flocks formed. The species has a distinctive loud ringing call that draws attention to its presence. It is a carnivore that feeds mostly on insects that are obtained within the leaf litter or while foraging on tree trunks.

The species occupies a range of woodlands and forests. In the Northern Territory, it has been reported from patches of tall acacia and river red gum woodland in the foothills of the central ranges (Storr 1977).

The breeding season is from July to November. Two or three oval eggs are laid in a cup-shaped nest located on a tree branch.

CONSERVATION ASSESSMENT

Although Storr (1977) considered that the grey currawong still occurred in the Northern Territory, it appears that the last definite sightings were obtained in the 1960s (Reid and Fleming 1992). The subspecies is of conservation concern throughout its range (Schodde and Mason 1999).

Due to the absence of suitable surveys, it is not appropriate to classify the grey currawong as extinct in the Northern Territory. Therefore, it is classified as **Critically Endangered** (under criterion D) due to a population size estimated to number fewer than 50 mature individuals.

THREATENING PROCESSES

The cause(s) of the decline of the grey currawong in the Northern Territory is unknown. However, it is likely that the individuals that exist(ed) in the Territory belong to a relict population that occupies small refuges of suitable habitat. The decline of these individuals may be the result of natural processes associated with retraction of suitable habitat or alternatively, result from habitat degradation. Given that the grey currawong spends considerable time foraging on the ground, it is also possible that they suffer predation by introduced carnivores.

CONSERVATION OBJECTIVES AND MANAGEMENT

There is no existing management program for this species in the Northern Territory.

Research priorities are to:
• follow-up any potential sightings of the species; and
• when possible, to carry out a survey for the species within its range in the Northern Territory.

Compiled by Chris Pavey [May 2006] / **References:** Reid, J., and Fleming, M. (1992). The conservation status of birds in central Australia. *Rangelands Journal* 14, 65-91. / Schodde, R., and Mason, I.J. (1999). *The directory of Australian birds: passerines.* (CSIRO, Melbourne.) / Schodde, R., and Tidemann, S.C. (eds) (1986). *Reader's Digest Complete Book of Australian Birds. 2nd edition.* (Reader's Digest, Sydney.) / Storr, G.M. (1977). *Birds of the Northern Territory.* (Western Australian Museum, Perth.)

Image courtesy of M. Lewis

Gouldian finch
Erythrura gouldiae

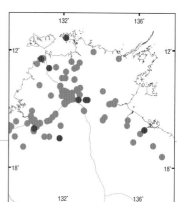

*Known locations of
the Gouldian finch*
● = *pre 1970*
● = *post 1970*

DESCRIPTION

The Gouldian finch is an easily recognised small bird: mature adults have a purple chest, yellow breast and green back, with an intensely vivid pale blue upper collar. Females are duller than males, and juveniles are completely dull green. Three colour morphs exist in the wild: black face, red face and yellow face.

DISTRIBUTION

Formerly the Gouldian finch was distributed throughout the tropical savannas of northern Australia. It is now restricted to isolated areas mostly within the Northern Territory and the Kimberley. Although the decline has occurred throughout the range, this has been most pronounced in the easternmost populations (Franklin 1999; Franklin *et al.* 2005). The largest known population is in the Yinberrie Hills (about 40 km north of Katherine).

Conservation reserves where reported:
Caranbirini Conservation Reserve, Gregory National Park, Kakadu National Park, Limmen National Park, Nitmiluk National Park.

ECOLOGY

Gouldian finches occupy two different components of the landscape on an annual cycle (Dostine *et al.* 2001). In the dry season and part of the late wet season, between February and October, they live within wooded hills that contain a group of *Eucalyptus* species commonly referred to as snappy or salmon gums.

Hollows in these trees provide nesting sites. During this period, they forage on the ground, feeding on shed seeds of native sorghum, and find water at small rocky waterholes that remain within the hills until the next wet season. During the wet season, Gouldian finches move from the hills into lowland drainages to feed upon seeds of perennial grasses, typically available from mid December. These grasses include soft spinifex, cockatoo grass and golden beard grass (Dostine and Franklin 2002).

Clutch size averages around five and fledging rate is about one to two young per pair (Tidemann *et al.* 1999). Depending on the season, pairs may raise several clutches per year. Annual survivorship is very low, with very few recoveries of banded birds from one year to the next (Woinarski and Tidemann 1992).

CONSERVATION ASSESSMENT

There is evidence of range contraction and anecdotal and quantitative evidence of past population decline for the Gouldian finch. Data from the returns of licensed finch trappers operating in the Kimberley region of Western Australia suggested a rapid decline throughout the 1970s, leading to cessation of the legal trapping industry (Franklin *et al.* 1999).

An annual monitoring program has been undertaken at the Yinberrie Hills since 1996, and this suggests that the population at this site is stable (O. Price *pers. comm.*)

In the Northern Territory, the Gouldian finch is considered **Endangered** (under criterion C2ai) due to:
• the population size estimated to number fewer than 2500 mature individuals;
• continuing decline observed in the number of mature individuals; and
• no subpopulation estimated to contain more than 250 mature individuals.

THREATENING PROCESSES

A variety of processes have been considered to have contributed to the decline of Gouldian finches (Garnett and Crowley 2000). These include the parasitic mite *Sternostoma tracheacolum* (Tidemann *et al.* 1992, Bell 1996), trapping, and pastoralism (Tidemann *et al.* 1990). However, the most important factor in the decline appears to be altered availability of food resources caused by understorey vegetation change because of pastoralism and/or changed fire regimes. Evidence suggests that large-scale late dry season fires reduce the amount of seed that the Gouldian finch relies on particularly during the early wet season (Garnett and Crowley 1994; Woinarski *et al.* 2005).

CONSERVATION OBJECTIVES AND MANAGEMENT

A series of national recovery plans have been implemented for this species. The most recent recovery plan (O'Malley 2006) was approved in 2007.

continued.../

Management priorities are to:
- maintain long-term population monitoring via waterhole counts in the late dry season in selected sites across the species' range;
- improve current burning practises through reduction of the extent of late dry season fires and with special focus on trying to protect the wet season feeding grounds; and
- improve communication for on-ground management across different landholder groups on the threatening processes affecting Gouldian finch habitat, including fire management, grazing management and feral herbivore control.

Compiled by Carol Palmer, John Woinarski [April 2007] / **References:** Bell, P.J. (1996). Survey of the nasal mite fauna (Rhinonyssidae and Kytoditidae) of the Gouldian Finch, *Erythrura gouldiae*, and some co-occurring birds in the Northern Territory. *Wildlife Research* 23, 675-686. / Dostine, P.L., and Franklin, D.C. (2002). A comparison of the diet of three finch species in the Yinberrie Hills area, Northern Territory. *Emu* 102, 159-164. / Dostine, P.L., Johnson, G.C., Franklin, D.C., Zhang, Y., and Hempel, C. (2001). Seasonal use of savanna landscapes by the Gouldian finch, *Erythrura gouldiae*, in the Yinberrie Hills area, Northern Territory. *Wildlife Research* 28, 445-458. / Franklin, D.C. (1999). Evidence of disarray amongst granivorous bird assemblages in the savannas of northern Australia: a region of sparse human settlement. *Biological Conservation* 90, 53-68. / Franklin, D.C., Burbidge A.H., and Dostine, P.L. (1999). The harvest of wild birds for aviculture: an historical perspective on finch trapping in the Kimberley with special emphasis on the Gouldian finch. *Australian Zoologist* 31, 92-109. / Franklin, D.C., Whitehead, P.J., Pardon, G., Matthews, J., McMahon, P., and McIntyre, D. (2005). Geographic patterns and correlates of the decline of granivorous birds in northern Australia. *Wildlife Research* 32, 399-408. / Garnett, S.T., and Crowley, G.M. (1994). Wet-season feeding by four species of granivorous birds in the Northern Territory. *Australian Bird-watcher* 15, 306-309. / Garnett, S.T., and Crowley, G.M. (2000). *The Action Plan for Australian Birds, 2000.* (Environment Australia, Canberra.) / O'Malley, C. (2006). *National recovery plan for the Gouldian finch (Erythrura gouldiae).* (WWF-Australia, and Parks and Wildlife Service, NT., Alice Springs.) / Tidemann, S.C. (1990). The relationship between finches and pastoral practices in northern Australia. In: *Granivorous Birds and Agriculture.* (eds J. Pinowski and J.D. Summers-Smith) pp. 305-315. (PWPN – Polish Scientific Publishers, Warsaw.) / Tidemann, S.C., Lawson, C., Elvish, R., Boyden, J., and Elvish, J. (1999). Breeding biology of the gouldian finch *Erythrura gouldiae*, an endangered finch of northern Australia. *Emu* 99, 191-199. / Tidemann, S.C., McOrist, S., Woinarski, J.C.Z., and Freeland, W.J. (1992). Parasitism of wild Gouldian Finches *Erythrura gouldiae* by the air sac mite *Sternostoma tracheacolum*. *Journal of Wildlife Diseases* 20, 80-84. / Woinarski, J.C.Z., and Tidemann, S.C. (1992). Survivorship and some population parameters for the endangered Gouldian Finch *Erythrura gouldiae* and two other finch species at two sites in tropical northern Australia. *Emu* 92, 33-38. / Woinarski, J.C.Z., Williams, R.J., Price, O., and Rankmore, B. (2005). Landscapes without boundaries: wildlife and their environments in northern Australia. *Wildlife Research* 32, 377-388.

MAMMALS

Brush-tailed mulgara, Mulgara
Dasycercus blythi

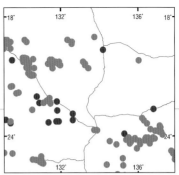

Known locations of mulgara (note that this map includes records that may be either D. blythi or D. cristicauda)
● = pre 1970
● = post 1970

CONSERVATION STATUS
AUSTRALIA: **VULNERABLE** *(as D. cristicauda)*
NORTHERN TERRITORY: **VULNERABLE**

DESCRIPTION

The brush-tailed mulgara is one of the larger carnivorous marsupials with a body mass of over 100 g, head body length of 15 cm and tail length of 9 cm. The species shows sexual dimorphism in size; males are significantly larger than females (Masters *et al.* 2003). The back is sandy brown and the belly is greyish-white. The short tail is enlarged and reddish near the body, tapering quickly to a point.

There has been considerable taxonomic confusion and re-sorting of the mulgaras. For most of the last 30 years only one species, *D. cristicauda*, was recognised. More recently, based on some genetic and morphological attributes, two species were recognised, the mulgara (*D. cristicauda*) and ampurta (*D. hillieri*) (Adams *et al.* 2000), with both occurring in the Northern Territory. However, Woolley (2005, 2006) re-considered the complex historical treatment of *Dasycercus* and re-assigned the species to the brush-tailed mulgara (*D. blythi*) and crest-tailed mulgara (*D. cristicauda*), both of which occur in the Northern Territory. Woolley (2005, 2006) distinguished these two species on the following characteristics: (i) appearance of black hairs on the distal half of the tail (a brush in *D. blythi* versus a dorsal crest in *D. cristicauda*), (ii) the number of upper pre-molar teeth (two in *D. blythi* versus three in *D. cristicauda*), and (iii) in females, the number of teats (six in *D. blythi* versus eight in *D. cristicauda*).

DISTRIBUTION

Because most previous records did not distinguish among the two species of mulgara now recognised, there is ambiguity about the distribution of both species.

The brush-tailed mulgara is known from at least the western and Simpson deserts, with confirmed records in the Northern Territory from Haast Bluff, Uluru, Papunya, Tanami Desert, Illamurta, Charlotte Waters and Crown Point (Woolley 2005, 2006).

The species was once widespread and common throughout the central deserts region of Australia. However, it began to decline in the 1930s and now has a more restricted and fragmented distribution than in the past.

Conservation reserves where reported:
Uluru – Kata Tjuta National Park

ECOLOGY

Brush-tailed mulgaras are primarily nocturnal, and shelter during the day in burrows that are about 0.5 m deep. Some animals are known to "sunbake" during the day in cold weather. The species is both insectivorous and carnivorous taking a range of insects, scorpions, centipedes, rodents, small marsupials and reptiles.

Brush-tailed mulgaras occur in a range of vegetation types; however, the principal habitat is mature hummock grasslands of spinifex, especially *Triodia basedowii* and *T. pungens*

(Masters *et al.* 2003). The location of brush-tailed mulgara colonies may be influenced by the presence of better watered areas such as palaeo-drainage systems or drainage lines in sandplain or sand dune habitats.

The species breeds once per year, mating in autumn or winter with litters of three to six young being produced between October and December. Home range size is highly variable with extremes of 1.0 to 14.4 ha recorded (Masters 2003). Home ranges of individuals overlap extensively.

CONSERVATION ASSESSMENT

Numbers fluctuate dramatically according to climatic conditions making it difficult to estimate the size of the population and, as a consequence, to determine population trends.

Assessment of the conservation status of this species is further complicated by the historical (and in some cases, current) ambiguity of records attributable to this species as distinct from those of *D. cristicauda*.

The decline in the range of the brush-tailed mulgara in the Northern Territory occurred earlier than relevant to IUCN criteria (i.e. within 10 years or three generations). However, the species qualifies as **Vulnerable** (under criterion C2a(i)) based on:
• a population estimated to be fewer than 10 000 mature individuals;
• a continuing decline observed, projected, or inferred and

continued.../

- no subpopulation estimated to contain more than 1000 mature individuals.

THREATENING PROCESSES

The cause of decline in the brush-tailed mulgara is unknown. However, it is likely that the processes of environmental degradation and habitat homogenization that have occurred throughout arid Australia following European settlement have negatively affected the mulgara. Changes in fire regimes, grazing by introduced herbivores including cattle and rabbits, and predation by introduced predators are all likely threatening processes.

CONSERVATION OBJECTIVES
AND MANAGEMENT

A national recovery plan for mulgaras is due for release in 2007.

Management priorities in the Northern Territory are to:
- better safeguard existing populations by ensuring that large areas of mature spinifex are not subjected to extensive wildfires;
- continue regular monitoring of the relatively large population(s) in Uluru – Kata Tjuta NP/ Yulara bore fields (currently being undertaken by Parks Australia and Voyages Hotels and Resorts, respectively);
- better resolve the status and distribution of the two mulgara species; and
- prevent harmful disturbances (e.g. mining operations) within lateritic areas in the north of the range.

This species is held and bred at the Alice Springs Desert Park.

Compiled by Chris Pavey, Jeff Cole, John Woinarski [December 2006] / **References:** Adams, M., Cooper, N., and Armstrong, J. (2000). Revision of *Dasycercus* systematics. A report to the South Australian Department for Environment and Heritage. / Masters, P. (2003). Movement patterns and spatial organization of the mulgara, *Dasycercus cristicauda* (Marsupialia: Dasyuridae), in central Australia. *Wildlife Research* 30, 339-344. / Masters, P., Dickman, C. R., and Crowther, M. (2003). Effects of cover reduction on mulgara *Dasycercus cristicauda* (Marsupialia: Dasyuridae), rodent and invertebrate populations in central Australia: implications for land management. *Austral Ecology* 28, 658-665. / Woolley, P.A. (2005). The species of *Dasycercus* Peters, 1875 (Marsupialia: Dasyuridae). *Memoirs of Museum Victoria* 62, 213-221. / Woolley, P.A. (2006). Studies on the crest-tailed mulgara *Dasycercus cristicauda* and the brush-tailed mulgara *D. blythi* (Marsupialia: Dasyuridae). *Australian Mammalogy* 28, 117-120.

Image courtesy of P. Canty (NPWSA)

Crest-tailed mulgara, Ampurta
Dasycercus cristicauda

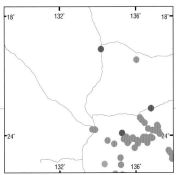

Known locations of crest-tailed mulgara (note that this map includes records that may be either D. blythi or D. cristicauda).
● = pre 1970
● = post 1970

DESCRIPTION

The crest-tailed mulgara is a robust, carnivorous marsupial with body mass up to about 190 g, and head body length to about 18 cm. The tail is short, slightly enlarged at the base and tapering to a point.

There has been considerable taxonomic confusion and re-sorting of the mulgaras. For most of the last 30 years only one species, *D. cristicauda*, was recognised. More recently, based on some genetic and morphological attributes, two species were recognised, the mulgara (*D. cristicauda*) and ampurta (*D. hillieri*) (Adams *et al.* 2000), with both occurring in the Northern Territory. However, Woolley (2005, 2006) re-considered the complex historical treatment of *Dasycercus* and re-assigned the species to the brush-tailed mulgara (*D. blythi*) and crest-tailed mulgara (*D. cristicauda*), both of which occur in the Northern Territory. Woolley (2005, 2006) distinguished these two species on the following characteristics: (i) appearance of black hairs on the distal half of the tail (a brush in *D. blythi* versus a dorsal crest in *D. cristicauda*), (ii) the number of upper pre-molar teeth (two in *D. blythi* versus three in *D. cristicauda*), and (iii) in females, the number of teats (six in *D. blythi* versus eight in *D. cristicauda*).

DISTRIBUTION

Because most previous records did not distinguish among the two species of mulgara now recognised, there is ambiguity about the distribution of both species.

Most records of this species are from the Simpson Desert and the north of South Australia, however it may occur far more widely across semi-arid and arid Australia, with (old) records from the Canning Stock Route in Western Australia and the Nullabor Plain. In the Northern Territory, there are confirmed records from Charlotte Waters and Crown Point (during the 1890s).

Conservation reserves where reported: None

ECOLOGY

The ecology of the species is poorly known; however, it is probably largely similar to the brush-tailed mulgara. Both species shelter in burrows, are primarily nocturnal, and feed on invertebrates, reptiles and small mammals (Wood Jones 1923).

The crest-tailed mulgara may prefer sand dune habitats: in the Simpson Desert, especially where these are vegetated with canegrass (*Zygochloa paradoxa*), with *Triodia basedowii* in the interdunes (Masters 1997).

CONSERVATION ASSESSMENT

Assessment of the conservation status of the crest-tailed mulgara is complicated by ambiguity of many historical records. As a consequence, information on its distribution and ecology is scarce, and very little is known about the trends in any population. The species has been recorded from a large number of sites in north-eastern South Australia and it may possibly be of less conservation concern than

currently recognised. The decline in the range of the crest-tailed mulgara in the Northern Territory occurred earlier than relevant to IUCN criteria (i.e. within the last 10 years or three generations). However, the species qualifies as **Vulnerable** (under criterion B1ab) based on:

• extent of occurrence estimated to be less than 20 000 km^2;
• severely fragmented; and
• a continuing decline.

THREATENING PROCESSES

The cause of decline in the crest-tailed mulgara is unknown. Changes in fire regimes, grazing by introduced herbivores including cattle and rabbits, and predation by introduced predators are all likely threatening processes (Maxwell *et al.* 1996).

CONSERVATION OBJECTIVES AND MANAGEMENT

A national recovery plan for mulgaras is due for release in 2007.

In the Northern Territory, there is no current specific management of this species being undertaken. Research and management priorities in the Northern Territory are to:
• better define the abundance, distribution and habitat preferences of this species; and
• establish regular monitoring programs in at least one representative population.

Compiled by Chris Pavey, Jeff Cole, John Woinarski [December 2006] / **References:** Adams, M., Cooper, N., and Armstrong, J. (2000). Revision of *Dasycercus* systematics. A report to the South Australian Department for Environment and Heritage. / Masters, P. (1997). Interim Recovery Plan for Ampurta *Dasycercus hillieri*. Report to ANCA Endangered Species Program. / Maxwell, S., Burbidge, A.A., and Morris, K. (eds) (1996). *The 1996 Action Plan for Australian marsupials and monotremes.* (Wildlife Australia, Canberra.) / Wood Jones, F. (1923). *The Mammals of South Australia. Part I.* (Government Printer, Adelaide.) Woolley, P.A. (2005). The species of *Dasycercus* Peters, 1875 (Marsupialia: Dasyuridae). *Memoirs of Museum Victoria* 62, 213-221. / Woolley, P.A. (2006). Studies on the crest-tailed mulgara *Dasycercus cristicauda* and the brush-tailed mulgara *D. blythi* (Marsupialia: Dasyuridae). *Australian Mammalogy* 28, 117-120.

Kowari
Dasyuroides byrnei

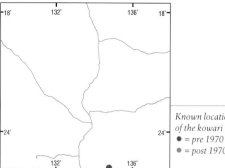

Known location of the kowari
- = pre 1970
- = post 1970

CONSERVATION STATUS
AUSTRALIA: **VULNERABLE**
NORTHERN TERRITORY: **DATA DEFICIENT**

DESCRIPTION

The kowari is a robust, grizzled-grey carnivorous marsupial up to 140 g in body mass and with a head and body length up to 180 mm. The distinguishing feature of this species is the tail, which is slightly shorter than head and body length, thick and reddish in the basal half with a large black brush encircling the distal half. The hind feet have only four toes.

DISTRIBUTION

The species occurs on the gibber plains of north-eastern South Australia and south-western Queensland, where it is patchily distributed. It is doubtful whether it still occurs in the Northern Territory. Records from the Northern Territory come from Charlotte Waters (several specimens collected by P. M. Byrne in 1895 including the lectotype), Illamurta (four specimens collected in 1895) and Barrow Creek (one specimen collected in 1901) (Mulvaney *et al*. 2000). However, suitable habitat does not occur at the last two localities, so it is highly likely that the specimens were incorrectly labelled (Parker 1973).

Conservation reserves where reported: None

ECOLOGY

The kowari is a nocturnal, terrestrial, burrowing animal that occurs on gibber patches among grasslands, sand dunes and river channels (Lim 1992). The diet consists of invertebrates and small vertebrates.

Breeding occurs between May and December with up to six to seven young per litter being born 30 to 35 days later (Aslin and Lim 1995).

CONSERVATION ASSESSMENT

In the Northern Territory, there have been no records since the few specimens collected more than 100 years ago. Although there has been a range of general wildlife surveys undertaken recently in the vicinity of those historic records, none have specifically targeted the kowari. Given the sparsity of information on this species, it is classified as **Data Deficient** in the Northern Territory.

THREATENING PROCESSES

The exact cause of the decline in the kowari is unknown (Maxwell *et al*. 1996). Introduced herbivores (cattle and rabbits) reduce cover and food for invertebrates and small vertebrates that are the prey of kowaris. Feral predators (cats and foxes) may affect the species. Roads and tracks are often located on gibber plains and the gibber is used as road base. This disturbance has the potential to have a detrimental effect on kowari habitat (Lim 1992). In its range outside the Northern Territory, an increase in traffic along roads has increased the incidence of road-killed kowaris (Lim 1992).

CONSERVATION OBJECTIVES AND MANAGEMENT

There is no existing management program for the kowari in the Northern Territory. Before any plans for management are formulated it is necessary to establish whether kowaris still occur in the Northern Territory. Targeted searches for the species should be included in any future survey of the Stony Plains bioregion in the Northern Territory and any reliable potential sightings should be followed up as soon as possible.

Compiled by Chris Pavey [May 2006] / **References:** Aslin, H.J., and Lim, L. (1995). Kowari *Dasyuroides byrnei*. In *The Mammals of Australia* (ed. R. Strahan.) pp. 59-61. (Australian Museum, Sydney.) Lim, L. (1992). *Recovery Plan for the Kowari Dasyuroides byrnei Spencer, 1896 (Marsupialia, Dasyuridea)*. (Environment Australia, Canberra.) / Maxwell, S., Burbidge, A.A., and Morris, K. (eds.) (1996). *The 1996 Action Plan for Australian Marsupials and Monotremes*. (Wildlife Australia, Canberra.) / Mulvaney, J., Petch, A., and Spencer, B. (2000). *From the Frontier: outback letters to Baldwin Spencer*. (Allen & Unwin, Sydney.) / Parker, S.A. (1973). An annotated checklist of the native land mammals of the Northern Territory. *Records of the South Australian Museum* 16, 1-57.

Image courtesy of Babs and Bert Wells

Western quoll,
Chuditch
Dasyurus geoffroii

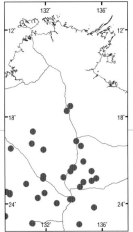

*Known locations of
the western quoll*
● = *pre 1970*
● = *post 1970*

DESCRIPTION

The western quoll is a large carnivorous marsupial (body mass of males up to 2 kg; females 1 kg) easily recognised by its body pattern of conspicuous white spots on a brown background. Its tail ends in a black bush. It is considerably larger than the northern quoll.

DISTRIBUTION

The western quoll formerly had an extensive range from western Queensland and New South Wales across central Australia to the Western Australian coast. The species now only occurs in jarrah forests, woodlands and mallee shrublands in the south-west corner of Western Australia.

In the Northern Territoy, it occurred widely across arid and semi-arid areas (Parker 1973; Burbidge *et al.* 1988).

Conservation reserves where reported:
None (although it formerly occurred in areas that are now included within Uluru – Kata Tjuta National Park and West MacDonnell National Park.)

ECOLOGY

In central Australia the western quoll occupied all types of country, whereas within its current distribution (in south-western Australia) it appears to favour climax vegetation associations (unburnt for more than 20 years).

The western quoll is active at night and is both arboreal and terrestrial, although it feeds primarily on the ground. The diet consists of mammals (including rabbits), birds, lizards, frogs, carrion, insects and crustaceans. Daytime shelter sites include hollow limbs, burrows of other species, and holes in termite mounds. The species occurs at low population densities; average male home range size is 400 ha, that of females is 55 to 120 ha. Individuals mature at 12 months and females give birth (up to six young) from May to September. Young are weaned at 22 to 24 weeks of age.

CONSERVATION ASSESSMENT

The western quoll was formerly common across large areas of central Australia (Finlayson 1961; Johnson and Roff 1982; Burbidge *et al.* 1988), but is presumed to have become extinct in the Northern Territory in the 1960s, following a broad-scale decline extending over at least the previous 50 years (Finlayson 1961; Johnson and Roff 1982; Burbidge *et al.* 1988). Several unverified reports of the species have been obtained by Parks and Wildlife over the past 20 years.

THREATENING PROCESSES

The decline of the western quoll in the Northern Territory is attributed to a range of factors including habitat alteration (mostly brought about by changes in fire regime), and competition for food and predation by cats and foxes.

CONSERVATION OBJECTIVES
AND MANAGEMENT

There are no imminent plans to re-introduce this species to the Northern Territory. A captive colony is housed in the nocturnal house of the Alice Springs Desert Park.

Compiled by Chris Pavey [May 2006] / **References:** Burbidge, A.A., Johnson, K.A., Fuller, P.F., and Southgate, R.I. (1988). Aboriginal knowledge of animals of the central deserts of Australia. *Australian Wildlife Research* 15, 9-39. / Finlayson, H.H. (1961). On central Australian mammals, Part IV. The distribution and status of central Australian species. *Records of the South Australian Museum* 41, 141-191. Johnson, K.A., and Roff, A.D. (1982). The western quoll, *Dasyurus geoffroii* (Dasyuridae, Marsupialia) in the Northern Territory: historical records from venerable sources. In *Carnivorous marsupials.* (ed. M. Archer.) pp. 221-226. (Royal Zoological Society of NSW, Sydney.) / Parker, S.A. (1973). An annotated checklist of the native land mammals of the Northern Territory. *Records of the South Australian Museum* 16, 1-57.

Image courtesy of Alan Withers

Northern quoll
Dasyurus hallucatus

CONSERVATION STATUS
AUSTRALIA: **ENDANGERED**
NORTHERN TERRITORY: **CRITICALLY ENDANGERED**

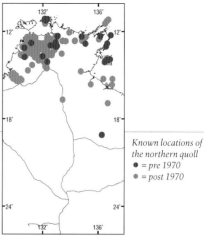

*Known locations of
the northern quoll*
● = *pre 1970*
● = *post 1970*

DESCRIPTION
The northern quoll is a distinctive carnivorous marsupial. It is the size of a small cat (weight 300 to 1100 g), with prominent white spots on a generally dark body, with a long sparsely furred tail.

DISTRIBUTION
The northern quoll occurs across much of northern Australia, from south-eastern Queensland to the south-west Kimberley, with a disjunct population in the Pilbara. It has declined across much of this range (Braithwaite and Griffiths 1994).

In the Northern Territory, it is restricted to the Top End. A 1905 record from Alexandria (Thomas 1906) marks the southern limit of its known Northern Territory distribution, now far from any recent records. It has been recorded from Groote Eylandt and the nearby North-east Island, Marchinbar Island (in the Wessel group), Inglis Island (in the English Company Islands group) and Vanderlin Island (Sir Edward Pellew group). Recently, it has also been translocated to Astell and Pobassoo islands in the English Company Island group.

Conservation reserves where reported:
Berry Springs Nature Park, Black Jungle Conservation Reserve, Charles Darwin National Park, Fogg Dam Conservation Reserve, Garig Gunak Barlu National Park, Howard Springs Nature Park, Kakadu National Park, Leaning Tree Lagoon, Limmen National Park, Litchfield National Park, Manton Dam Recreation Area, Mary River National Park, Nitmiluk National Park, Tjuwaliyn (Douglas) Hot Springs Park, Umbrawara Gorge Nature Park.

ECOLOGY
The northern quoll is a generalist predator, consuming a wide range of invertebrates and small vertebrate prey. It dens during the day in hollow logs, rock crevices and caves, and in tree hollows. Most foraging is on the ground, but it is also an adept climber.

It occurs in a wide range of habitats, but the most suitable habitats appear to be rocky areas. It is also common in many eucalypt open forests.

Northern quolls typically have an annual life cycle, with almost all males living for only one year (Oakwood 2000; Oakwood *et al.* 2002). Young are born in the mid dry season (June), and attain independence in the early wet season (November). Mating is highly synchronised, occurring in late May and early June. Males then die.

During the non-breeding season, home ranges are about 35 ha, but this increases to about 100 ha for males in the breeding season (Oakwood 2002).

CONSERVATION ASSESSMENT
Broad-scale decline of the northern quoll was described by Braithwaite and Griffiths (1994), but the extent and rate of this decline did not quite reach the relevant threshold values for IUCN threatened status.

Since that review, several studies (e.g. Watson and Woinarski 2003; Oakwood 2004) have suggested rapid collapse to local extinction of northern quoll populations in those parts of Kakadu National Park recently invaded by cane toads (*Bufo marinus*). It is likely that cane toads will occur across all of the mainland Top End within the next few years. A similar pattern of decline to that encountered in Kakadu will probably occur elsewhere as cane toads invade new areas. The exact extent of the decline is difficult to estimate and the security of island populations is uncertain.

The northern quoll has been classified as **Critically Endangered** (under criterion A3ce) based on an estimated population size reduction of more than 80% projected for the next 10 years.

THREATENING PROCESSES
Northern quolls appear to have been declining in the Northern Territory for at least several decades (Braithwaite and Griffiths 1994; Woinarski *et al.* 2001), possibly because of impacts from feral cats, disease or changed fire regimes. However, the spread of cane toads adds a far more catastrophic threat (van Dam *et al.* 2002). Quolls appear to be particularly susceptible to the poison of cane toads, and are killed when they attempt to kill or consume the toads. Major declines to regional extinction have been reported for quolls following cane toad invasion on Cape York Peninsula (Burnett 1997).

continued.../

CONSERVATION OBJECTIVES AND MANAGEMENT

There is no current recovery or management plan for this species, however a recovery plan is currently being prepared. In the short to medium term, it is unlikely that any broad-scale control mechanism can be imposed on cane toads, the primary threat to quolls. Given this outlook, the management priority is to secure the existing island populations from colonisation by cane toads. To increase the number of island populations, quolls have recently (2003) been translocated to Astell and Pobassoo Islands, where they are currently thriving.

Compiled by John Woinarski [December 2006] / **References:** Braithwaite, R.W., and Griffiths, A.D. (1994). Demographic variation and range contraction in the northern quoll, *Dasyurus hallucatus* (Marsupialia: Dasyuridae). *Wildlife Research* 21, 203-217. / Burnett, S. (1997). Colonising cane toads cause population declines in native predators: reliable anecdotal information and management implications. *Pacific Conservation Biology* 3, 65-72. / Oakwood, M. (2000). Reproduction and demography of the northern quoll, *Dasyurus hallucatus*, in the lowland savanna of northern Australia. *Australian Journal of Zoology* 48, 519-539. / Oakwood, M. (2002). Spatial and social oganization of a carnivorous marsupial *Dasyurus hallucatus* (Marsupialia: Dasyuridae). *Journal of Zoology, London* 257, 237-248. / Oakwood, M. (2004). The effect of cane toads on a marsupial carnivore, the northern quoll, *Dasyurus hallucatus*. Report to Parks Australia (Envirotek, Nana Glen). / Oakwood, M., Bradley, A.J., and Cockburn, A. (2001). Semelparity in a large marsupial. *Proceedings of the Royal Society, London* (B) 268, 407-411. / Thomas, O. (1906). On mammals from Northern Australia presented to the National Museum by Sir Wm. Ingram, Bt., and the Hon. John Forrest. *Proceedings of the Zoological Society of London* 1906, 536-543. / van Dam, R.A., Walden, D.J., and Begg, G.W. (2002). *A preliminary risk assessment of cane toads in Kakadu National Park*. Supervising Scientist Report 164. (Supervising Scientist, Darwin.) / Watson, M., and Woinarski, J. (2003). *Vertebrate monitoring and re-sampling in Kakadu National Park, 2002*. Report to Parks Australia. (Tropical Savannas Cooperative Research Centre, Darwin.) / Woinarski, J.C.Z., Milne, D.J., and Wanganeen, G. (2001). Changes in mammal populations in relatively intact landscapes of Kakadu National Park, Northern Territory, Australia. *Austral Ecology* 26, 360-370.

Image courtesy of Babs and Bert Wells

Red-tailed phascogale
Phascogale calura

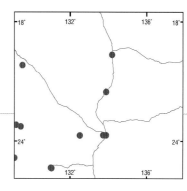

Known locations of the red-tailed phascogale
● = pre 1970
● = post 1970

CONSERVATION STATUS
AUSTRALIA: **ENDANGERED**
NORTHERN TERRITORY: **EXTINCT**

DESCRIPTION
The red-tailed phascogale is a medium-sized carnivorous marsupial (body mass of males 60 g, females 43 g) that formerly occurred in central Australia and inland southern Australia. The species has a brown body and long tail (longer than the head-body length), that is black and bushy at the tip and has a red base.

DISTRIBUTION
The red-tailed phascogale is now restricted to pockets of woodland in south-west Western Australia.

In the Northern Territory, it occurred widely across arid and semi-arid areas, extending as far north as Tennant Creek (Parker 1973; Burbidge *et al.* 1988). A recent unconfirmed report has been obtained in the vicinity of the Wallace Rockhole community.

Conservation reserves where reported:
None (although it formerly occurred in areas that are now included within Uluru – Kata Tjuta National Park and West MacDonnell National Park)

ECOLOGY
In central Australia, the red-tailed phascogale occupied sandhills and hilly country and sheltered in hollow limbs in eucalypts (especially bloodwoods) (Burbidge *et al.* 1988).

The species is strictly nocturnal and mostly arboreal, although it feeds extensively on the ground. The diet consists of insects and other invertebrates, small mammals and birds. The red-tailed phascogale had a reproductive strategy that is typical for a carnivorous marsupial in featuring a die-off of all males in spring following an intense three week mating period in July. Average male lifespan is 11.5 months and that of females is two or three years.

CONSERVATION ASSESSMENT
The red-tailed phascogale is presumed to have become extinct in the Northern Territory in the 1950s, following a broad-scale decline extending over at least the previous 50 years (Burbidge *et al.* 1988). The limited historical evidence suggests that it was probably uncommon or localised even before the advent of European settlement (Finlayson 1961; Burbidge *et al.* 1988).

THREATENING PROCESSES
The decline of the red-tailed phascogale in central Australia is attributed to predation by cats and foxes and frequent burning of suitable habitat that prevented the establishment of climax vegetation communities.

CONSERVATION OBJECTIVES AND MANAGEMENT
The species is on display in the nocturnal house of the Alice Springs Desert Park and a trial reintroduction within the Park is planned for 2007.

Compiled by Chris Pavey [May 2006] / **References:** Burbidge, A.A., Johnson, K.A., Fuller, P.F., and Southgate, R.I. (1988). Aboriginal knowledge of animals of the central deserts of Australia. *Australian Wildlife Research* 15, 9-39. / Finlayson, H.H. (1961). On central Australian mammals, Part IV. The distribution and status of central Australian species. *Records of the South Australian Museum* 41, 141-191. Parker, S.A. (1973). An annotated checklist of the native land mammals of the Northern Territory. *Records of the South Australian Museum* 16, 1-57.

Image courtesy of Kym Brennan

Northern brush-tailed phascogale
Phascogale (tapoatafa) pirata

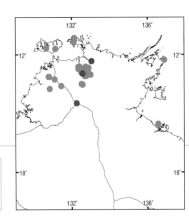

Known locations of the northern brush-tailed phascogale
● = pre 1970
● = post 1970

CONSERVATION STATUS
AUSTRALIA: **NOT LISTED**
NORTHERN TERRITORY: **VULNERABLE**

DESCRIPTION
The northern brush-tailed phascogale is a carnivorous marsupial about midway in size between the larger northern quoll and the small antechinuses and dunnarts. Its most notable feature is the long dark hairs on the tail, which form a distinctive brush. The hairs can be stiffened when alarmed, giving a bottle-brush appearance. The general body colour is dark grey, the snout is notably pointed and the eyes are large. Body weight is about 150 to 200 g.

DISTRIBUTION
Recent taxonomic studies (Rhind *et al.* 2001, Spencer *et al.* 2001) have suggested that the northern population of brush-tailed phascogale is specifically distinct from that in south-western and south-eastern Australia. As redefined, the northern brush-tailed phascogale is restricted to the Top End of the Northern Territory, and is taxonomically distinct from populations in the Kimberley and Cape York Peninsula.

There are relatively few records In the Northern Territory: the most recent (since 1980) are from the Tiwi Islands, Cobourg Peninsula, West Island, Kakadu National Park (notably around Jabiru and near Jim Jim ranger station), and Litchfield National Park. There are older records from the Gove and Katherine areas.

Conservation reserves where reported:
Garig Gunak Barlu National Park, Kakadu National Park, Litchfield National Park.

ECOLOGY
There have been no detailed studies of the northern brush-tailed phascogale, but its ecology is probably similar to that reported for its temperate relatives (Rhind 1998). The diet is predominantly invertebrates with some small vertebrates. It is a nocturnal mammal, feeding both in trees and on the ground. It shelters in tree hollows during the day. Most records are from tall open forests dominated by Darwin woollybutt (*Eucalyptus miniata*) and Darwin stringybark (*E. tetrodonta*).

CONSERVATION ASSESSMENT
Conservation assessment is hampered by the lack of precise information on range, population size and trends. Decline is evident from variation between historic statements about status and current assessments: most notably Dahl (1897) reported that "on the rivers Mary and Katherine it was frequently observed. In fact nearly everywhere inland it was very constant, and on a moonlight walk one would generally expect to see this little animal". This is certainly no longer the case. Biodiversity surveys across the Top End over the last decade have resulted in fewer than 10 captures of brush-tailed phascogales in more than 350 000 trap-nights. However this meagre tally may also partly reflect some degree of trap-shyness. Recent (2003–2005) attempts to relocate the species on West Island have been unsuccessful (Taylor *et al.* 2004; S. Ward *pers. comm.*).

It best fits the status of **Vulnerable** (under criterion C2ai) based on:
• population size estimated to number fewer than 10 000 mature individuals;
• a continuing decline, observed, projected or inferred, in numbers of mature individuals; and
• no subpopulations estimated to contain more than 1000 mature individuals.

THREATENING PROCESSES
The apparent decline to coastal areas and especially islands suggests either exotic predators (cats) or disease. Other factors potentially involved may include vegetation change due to altered fire regimes and/or pastoralism. This species may be severely disadvantaged by extensive clearing of eucalypt forests, especially those with hollow-bearing trees (Firth *et al.* 2006), for horticulture or forestry plantations. As a predator of small vertebrates, this species may be affected by the arrival of cane toads, but there is no relevant information available to assess the likelihood of this potential threat.

CONSERVATION OBJECTIVES AND MANAGEMENT PRIORITIES:
There is no existing explicit recovery plan or management program for this species.
In the interim, the major priority is to firm up knowledge of the distribution, abundance, habitat requirements and trends for this species.
This will require a detailed autecological study and a distributional survey.

Compiled by John Woinarski [January 2007] / **References:** Dahl, K. (1897). Biological notes on north-Australian mammalia. *Zoologist*, Series 4, 1, 189-216. / Firth, R.S.C., Woinarski, J.C.Z., Brennan, K.G., and Hempel, C. (2006). Environmental relationships of the brush-tailed rabbit-rat *Conilurus penicillatus* and other small mammals on the Tiwi Islands, northern Australia. *Journal of Biogeography* 33, 1820-1837. Rhind, S.G. (1998). *Ecology of the brush-tailed phascogale in jarrah forest of southwestern Australia*. PhD thesis. (Murdoch University, Perth.) / Rhind, S.G., Bradley, J.S., and Cooper, N.K. (2001). Morphometric variation and taxonomic status of brush-tailed phascogales, *Phascogale tapoatafa* (Meyer, 1793) (Marsupialia: Dasyuridae). *Australian Journal of Zoology* 49, 345-368. / Spencer, P.B.S., Rhind, S.G., and Eldridge, M.D.B. (2001). Phylogeographic structure within *Phascogale* (Marsupialia: Dasyuridae) based on partial cytochrome b sequence. *Australian Journal of Zoology* 49, 369-377. / Taylor, R., Woinarski, J., Charlie, A., Dixon, R., Pracy, D., and Rhind, S. (2004). *Report on mammal survey of the Pellew Islands, October 2003*. (NT Department of Infrastructure Planning and Environment, Darwin.)

Image courtesy of Kym Brennan

Carpentarian antechinus

Pseudantechinus mimulus

CONSERVATION STATUS
AUSTRALIA: VULNERABLE
NORTHERN TERRITORY: ENDANGERED

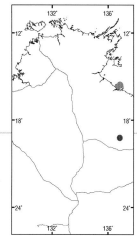

Known locations of
the Carpentarian
antechinus
● = pre 1970
● = post 1970

DESCRIPTION

The Carpentarian antechinus is a mouse-sized dasyurid marsupial, with large ears, and rufous-cinnamon fur behind the ears. When an individual is in good condition the tail is swollen to carrot-shaped. It is similar in appearance to the other *Pseudantechinus* species from the Northern Territory: *P. bilarni*, *P. ningbing* and *P. macdonnellensis*, but is typically smaller than these (less than 18 g). *Pseudantechinus mimulus* may overlap in distribution with *P. bilarni* (Fisher *et al.* 2000).

DISTRIBUTION

This species was described from one specimen collected in 1905 at "Alexandria" (a then broad geographic area including part of the Barkly Tableland). There were no further records until it was rediscovered on North Island in the Sir Edward Pellew group in 1967 (Kitchener 1991). Subsequently, it has also been reported from South-West, Centre and Vanderlin Islands in the Pellew group (Johnson and Kerle 1991; Taylor *et al.* 2004). There has also been an unconfirmed recent record from the Gulf mainland (Museum and Art Galleries of the Northern Territory). Beyond the Northern Territory, there has been a small number of recent records from near Mt Isa (Woinarski 2004).

Conservation reserves where reported:
Barranyi (North Island) National Park

ECOLOGY

The Carpentarian antechinus occurs in a range of vegetation types, but always with a high cover of rocks, boulders and crevices. The type specimen from Alexandria appears to be anomalous, in that the Barkly Tablelands does not appear to be suitable habitat. However, no detail was given of the habitat in which it was found there, and the locality may be very imprecise.

Its diet comprises mostly invertebrates, but it may also take small vertebrates. It is nocturnal, and probably shelters during the day in rock crevices or hollow logs.

CONSERVATION ASSESSMENT

In the Northern Territory, it is presently known from only four islands, with a total area of 499 km². There is no information available on its population size, but trap success has generally been low. Despite considerable survey effort, there have been no confirmed records from the Barkly region (or indeed, the Territory mainland) since 1906. Hence it appears to have declined substantially in range. However, the timing and currency of any such decline is unknown.

It fits **Endangered** (under criteria B2ab(i,ii,iii,iv,v)) based on:
- area of occupancy less than 500 km²;
- severely fragmented or known to exist at no more than five locations; and
- continuing decline, observed, inferred or projected.

THREATENING PROCESSES

There are no clear threatening processes that may have accounted for the apparent decline of this species. It may have been affected by predation from feral cats (that have recently spread to most of the large islands in the Pellew group: Taylor *et al.* 2004), although its association with rugged rocky areas would have provided some protection against this threat. Cane toads have invaded most of the large islands in the Pellew group since 2000, but their impact on this species is unknown.

The Carpentarian antechinus may also be affected by changed fire regimes, and particularly by an apparent increase in hot extensive late dry season fires.

CONSERVATION OBJECTIVES AND MANAGEMENT

A recovery plan for this species (Woinarski 2004) has recently been developed.

Research priorities are to:
- establish a monitoring program, preferably integrated with an assessment of fire management preferences, and
- sample the nearby mainland for additional populations.

Management priorities are to:
- control feral cats (and other exotic species) from islands in the Pellew group;
- evaluate options for conservation agreements with Aboriginal landowners; and
- based on monitoring results, implement a favourable fire regime.

Compiled by John Woinarski [May 2006] / **References:** Fisher, A., Woinarski, J.C.Z., Churchill, S., Trainor, C., Griffiths, A.D., Palmer, C., and Cooper, N. (2000). Distribution of the rock-dwelling dasyurids *Pseudantechinus bilarni* and *Pseudantechinus ningbing* in the Northern Territory. *Northern Territory Naturalist* 16, 1-13. / Johnson, K.A., and Kerle, J.A. (1991). *Flora and vertebrate fauna of the Sir Edward Pellew group of islands, Northern Territory.* Report to the Australian Heritage Commission. (Conservation Commission of the Northern Territory, Alice Springs.) / Kitchener, D. (1991). *Pseudantechinus mimulus* (Thomas 1906) (Marsupialia: Dasyuridae): rediscovery and redescription. *Records of the Western Australian Museum* 15, 191-202. / Taylor, R., Woinarski, J., Charlie, A., Dixon, R., Pracy, D., and Rhind, S. (2004). *Report on mammal survey of the Pellew Islands 2003.* (Lianthawirriyarra Sea Ranger Unit, Department of Infrastructure, Planning and Environment, and Tropical Savannas CRC, Darwin.) / Woinarski, J.C.Z. (2004). *National multi-species Recovery Plan for the Carpentarian Antechinus Pseudantechinus mimulus, Butler's Dunnart Sminthopsis butleri and Northern Hopping-mouse Notomys aquilo, 2004-2008.* (NT Department of Infrastructure Planning and Environment, Darwin.)

Image courtesy of Kym Brennan

Butler's dunnart
Sminthopsis butleri

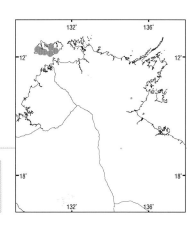

Known locations
of the Butler's
dunnart
● = *pre 1970*
● = *post 1970*

CONSERVATION STATUS
AUSTRALIA: **VULNERABLE**
NORTHERN TERRITORY: **VULNERABLE**

DESCRIPTION

Butler's dunnart is a small (about 30 g) dunnart ("marsupial mouse"), distinguished from other dunnarts of the Top End by a combination of lack of rufous markings on the face, relatively small size, and the patterning on the soles of the hind-feet (relatively hairy, with the interdigital pads fused at the base and with conspicuously enlarged unstriated apical granules) (van Dyck *et al.* 1994).

When first described (in 1979) this species was considered to extend to Cape York Peninsula and New Guinea, and hence named as the "Carpentarian dunnart". Subsequently, specimens from those areas have been split off, as *S. archeri* (the chestnut dunnart).

DISTRIBUTION

There are remarkably few records of Butler's dunnart. It was described from three specimens collected at Kalumburu (north Kimberley) between 1965 and 1966. It has not been recorded from Western Australia since, and all subsequent records have been caught from Bathurst and Melville Islands, Northern Territory. A previously-misidentified record from Melville Island in 1913 has also been re-assigned to this species (Woinarski *et al.* 1996, 2003).

Conservation reserves where reported: None

ECOLOGY

Very little is known of the ecology of this species.

The few records are associated with a range of habitats (Woinarski *et al.* 1996, 2003; Woinarski 2004), including eucalypt open forest (dominated by *Eucalyptus tetrodonta* and *E. miniata*), *Melaleuca* woodland, and "blacksoil sandplain ... heavily vegetated with eucalypt and grass" (Archer 1979). It is terrestrial and nocturnal, and shelters under logs and other cover.

As with other dunnarts, the diet of this species probably comprises invertebrates, and possibly some small vertebrates.

CONSERVATION ASSESSMENT

The status of Butler's dunnart is difficult to evaluate, given the few records and lack of any information on trends in abundance. It can be reasonably inferred that it is uncommon in its only known Northern Territory location, the Tiwi Islands. These have now been subject to a substantial biodiversity survey effort since 1991, but this sampling has produced only 15 individuals (with low captures possibly also influenced by trap-shyness). Recent (2006–07) use of deep pitfall traps has increased trap success (S. Ward, B. Hill *pers. comm.*). The Tiwi population will decline based on loss of large areas of suitable habitat (300 to 1000 km² from a total Tiwi Islands area of about 7400 km²) associated with a forestry plantation project. Consequently, Butler's dunnart fits the status of **Vulnerable** (under criterion B1ab) based on:
• extent of occurrence estimated to be less than 20 000 km²;

• severely fragmented or known to exist at no more than 10 locations; and
• continuing decline, observed, inferred or projected.

THREATENING PROCESSES

The immediate threat to the population is the loss of large areas of suitable habitat because of vegetation clearance for plantation forestry. Butler's dunnart may also be affected by predation from feral cats, and vegetation change associated with altered fire regimes, weeds and/or feral animals.

CONSERVATION OBJECTIVES AND MANAGEMENT

A recovery plan for this species (Woinarski 2004) has recently been developed, and many of the proposed actions are being implemented jointly by Tiwi rangers and scientists from the Department of Natural Resources Environment and The Arts.

Research priorities are to:
• undertake sampling to more precisely define the range and status; and
• undertake a specific study to provide more information on the ecological requirements of, and threatening factors affecting, this species.

The management priority is to ensure the retention of sufficient areas of preferred habitat on the Tiwi Islands, especially around the few sites of known occurrence.

Compiled by John Woinarski [April 2007] / **References:** Archer, M. (1979). Two new species of *Sminthopsis* Thomas (Dasyuridae: Marsupialia) from northern Australia, *S. butleri* and *S. douglasi*. *Australian Zoologist* 20, 327-345. / Van Dyck, S., Woinarski, J.C.Z., and Press, A.J. (1994). The Kakadu Dunnart, *Sminthopsis bindi* (Marsupialia: Dasyuridae), a new species from the stony woodlands of the Northern Territory. *Memoirs of the Queensland Museum* 37, 311-323. / Woinarski, J.C.Z. (2004). *National multi-species Recovery Plan for the Carpentarian Antechinus Pseudantechinus mimulus, Butler's Dunnart Sminthopsis butleri and Northern Hopping-mouse Notomys aquilo, 2004-2008.* (NT Department of Infrastructure Planning and Environment, Darwin.) / Woinarski, J.C.Z., Woolley, P.A., and Van Dyck, S. (1996). *The distribution of the dunnart Sminthopsis butleri. Australian Mammalogy* 19, 27-29. / Woinarski, J., Brennan, K., Hempel, C., Armstrong, M., Milne, D., and Chatto, R. (2003). *Biodiversity conservation on the Tiwi Islands, Northern Territory. Part 2: fauna.* (NT Department of Infrastructure, Planning and Environment, Darwin.)

Image courtesy of Mark Cowan

Long-tailed dunnart
Sminthopsis longicaudata

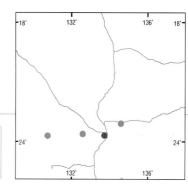

Known locations of the long-tailed dunnart
● = pre 1970
● = post 1970

DESCRIPTION

The long-tailed dunnart is a small carnivorous marsupial with a body mass of 15 to 20 g. It is immediately identifiable by its long tail, that is twice the length of the head-body. The tail ends in a tuft of long hairs. The upperbody is grey and the ventral surface is pale cream to white. The legs and feet are white and the feet have striated pads.

DISTRIBUTION

The long-tailed dunnart was first collected in the Northern Territory in 1895, although the precise locality is uncertain. The species was not recorded in the Northern Territory again until 1993 and it has been recorded since at only six sites in the West MacDonnell National Park between Serpentine Gorge and Mt Sonder (Gibson and Cole 1996). Bone material has been located in a cave at Simpson's Gap (Baynes and Johnson 1996). Outside the Northern Territory it occurs in the Pilbara, Murchison, North-eastern Goldfields, Ashburton and Gibson Desert regions of Western Australia.

Conservation reserves where reported:
West MacDonnell National Park

ECOLOGY

The long-tailed dunnart is a specialist rock-dwelling species (Freeland *et al*. 1988). All sites it is known to frequent are within rugged rocky landscapes that support a low open woodland or shrubland of acacias (especially mulga) with an understorey of spinifex hummocks, and (occasionally) also perennial grasses and cassias. The species is nocturnal and it feeds on a range of invertebrates including beetles, ants, cockroaches and spiders (Burbidge *et al*. 1995). Females in captivity give birth to up to five young between October and December (Woolley and Valente 1986).

CONSERVATION ASSESSMENT

The size of the long-tailed dunnart population in the Northern Territory is not known. However, the species has been recorded from only a small area within West MacDonnell National Park despite widespread trapping in the MacDonnell Ranges bioregion. Further, it appears to be very rare. Only six individuals have been captured in traps despite a survey effort of nearly 50 000 Elliott trap-nights and 700 pit trap-nights within its area of occurrence. Because the species is a rock-dwelling specialist, the only other region where it may occur in the arid Northern Territory is the Central Ranges bioregion.

Conservation categorisation is problematical because of a lack of information on population trends. However, the species qualifies as **Vulnerable** in the Northern Territory (under criteria D1+2) based on:

- population size estimated at fewer than 1000 mature individuals; and
- a very restricted area of occupancy such that it is prone to the effects of human activities or stochastic events.

THREATENING PROCESSES

Available information on the basic biology and distribution of the long-tailed dunnart is limited such that it is not possible to identify with certainty any threatening processes at this stage. Potential threatening processes could be inappropriate fire regimes and habitat modification as a result of the activities of introduced herbivores (especially cattle and horses), invasion by buffel grass and predation by cats and foxes.

CONSERVATION OBJECTIVES AND MANAGEMENT

There is no existing management program for the wild population of this species in the Northern Territory. Three monitoring sites, involving permanent pitfall traps, were established in the vicinity of Ormiston Gorge – Mt Sonder in late 2004. These sites were set up in locations where the species had been previously trapped. These sites will be regularly trapped by rangers based at Ormiston Gorge.

Research priorities are to:

- clarify its distribution in the western portion of the West MacDonnell National Park and map availability of suitable habitat; and
- estimate total population size in the West MacDonnell National Park.

Compiled by Chris Pavey [May 2006] / **References:** Baynes, A., and Johnson, K.A. (1996). The contributions of the Horn Expedition and cave deposits to knowledge of the original mammal fauna of central Australia. In *Exploring Central Australia: Society, the Environment and the 1894 Horn Expedition* (eds S.R. Morton and D.J. Mulvaney.) pp. 168-186. (Surrey Beatty and Sons, Sydney.) / Burbidge, A.A., McKenzie, N.L., and Fuller, P.J. (1995). Long-tailed Dunnart. In *The Mammals of Australia. 2nd Edition* (ed. R. Strahan.) pp. 146-147. (Australian Museum, Sydney.) / Freeland, W.J., Winter, J.W., and Raskin, S. (1988). Australian rock mammals: A phenomenon of the seasonally dry tropics. *Biotropica* 20, 70-79. / Gibson, D.F., and Cole, J.R. (1996). Mammals of the MacDonnell Range area. In *Exploring Central Australia: Society, the Environment and the 1894 Horn Expedition* (eds S.R. Morton and D.J. Mulvaney.) pp. 305-321. (Surrey Beatty and Sons, Sydney.) / Woolley, P.A., and Valente, A. (1986). Reproduction in *Sminthopsis longicaudata* (Marsupialia: Dasyuridae): laboratory observations. *Australian Wildlife Research* 13, 7-12

Image courtesy of P. Canty (NPWSA)

Sandhill dunnart

Sminthopsis psammophila

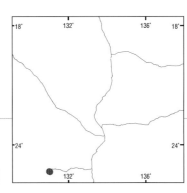

*Known locations
of the sandhill
dunnart*
● = *pre 1970*
● = *post 1970*

CONSERVATION STATUS
AUSTRALIA: **ENDANGERED**
NORTHERN TERRITORY: **DATA DEFICIENT**

DESCRIPTION

The sandhill dunnart is a medium-sized carnivorous marsupial with a body mass of 26 to 40 g. The upperparts are a plain grey to buff with darker hairs interspersed throughout. There is a dark triangle of fur on the crown and forehead. The face and flanks are buff, the eyes are dark. The underparts and feet are whitish. The tail is longer than the head-body length. The tail is grey above and darker below with a crest of short, black hairs near the tip.

DISTRIBUTION

The first specimen of the sandhill dunnart was collected by members of the Horn Expedition in 1894 near Lake Amadeus between Kurtitina Well and Uluru (Parker 1973). Since that time it has not been seen in the Territory, although remains of the species have been identified in owl pellets collected from Uluru – Kata Tjuta National Park (Baynes and Johnson 1996).

Outside the Northern Territory, the species has been recorded on the Eyre Peninsula (South Australia) and in the Great Victoria Desert (South Australia and Western Australia) (Pearson and Robinson 1990). A total of 60 individuals have been captured at all sites up to 2000 (Churchill 2001).

Conservation reserves where reported: None

ECOLOGY

The Northern Territory specimen came from sand dune country in an area covered by spinifex hummocks with groves of desert oaks in the swales. On the Eyre Peninsula, the sandhill dunnart occupies sand ridges covered by hummock grassland and mallee-broombush shrub. In the Great Victoria Desert and at Yellabinna it occurs in sandy environments, either sand plains or dunes. The vegetation occupied consists of low woodland or low open woodland with a diverse shrub understorey and a ground cover of at least 20% spinifex hummocks (Pearson and Robinson 1990). The species is insectivorous and nocturnal, and breeding takes place in spring and early summer (Pearson 1995).

CONSERVATION ASSESSMENT

The sandhill dunnart has been recorded only once in the Northern Territory and that was over 100 years ago. However, the small amount of survey work carried out in the vicinity of Lake Amadeus where the specimen was obtained means that it is premature to regard it as regionally extinct. Therefore, the status of the sandhill dunnart in the Northern Territory is **Data Deficient**.

THREATENING PROCESSES

Inappropriate fire regimes and clearance of land for agriculture are major threats faced by the sandhill dunnart in southern Australia (Churchill 2001). In particular, the species prefers large, mature spinifex clumps in which it builds a small nest chamber composed of spinifex needles. Spinifex reaches the size and structure preferred by sandhill dunnarts five to 10 years after fire and this type of spinifex constitutes only 5% of the available spinifex hummocks on sites occupied by the dunnart on the Eyre Peninsula (Churchill 2001). Therefore, fire regimes that threaten the preferred nest sites of the sandhill dunnart may represent a long term threat to the species. Predation by feral cats and foxes may also be a threat.

CONSERVATION OBJECTIVES AND MANAGEMENT

There is a national recovery plan for the sandhill dunnart (Churchill 2001), but no existing management program in the Northern Territory.

Any future survey of the Great Sandy Desert bioregion, particularly in the vicinity of Lake Amadeus, should include targeted surveys for this species.

This species is likely to benefit from fire management that maintains an adequate proportion of older-aged spinifex.

Compiled by Chris Pavey [May 2006] / **References:** Baynes, A., and Johnson, K.A. (1996). The contributions of the Horn Expedition and cave deposits to knowledge of the original mammal fauna of central Australia. In *Exploring Central Australia: Society, the Environment and the 1894 Horn Expedition* (eds S.R. Morton and D.J. Mulvaney.) pp. 168-186. (Surrey Beatty and Sons, Sydney.) / Churchill, S. (2001). *Recovery plan for the sandhill dunnart (Sminthopsis psammophila)*. (Environment Australia, Canberra.) / Parker, S.A. (1973). An annotated checklist of the native land mammals of the Northern Territory. *Records of the South Australian Museum* 16, 1-57. / Pearson, D.J. (1995). Sandhill dunnart. In *The Mammals of Australia. 2nd Edition* (ed. R. Strahan.) pp. 154-155. (Australian Museum, Sydney.) / Pearson, D.J., and Robinson, A.C. (1990). New records of the sandhill dunnart, *Sminthopsis psammophila* (Marsupialia: Dasyuridae) in South and Western Australia. *Australian Mammalogy* 13, 57-59.

Image courtesy of Babs and Bert Wells

Numbat
Myrmecobius fasciatus

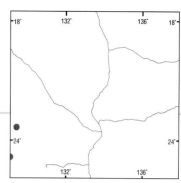

Known locations of the numbat
● = pre 1970
● = post 1970

CONSERVATION STATUS
AUSTRALIA: **VULNERABLE**
NORTHERN TERRITORY: **EXTINCT**

DESCRIPTION
The numbat is a medium-sized marsupial (body mass of 300 to 715 g) with a pointed muzzle and bushy tail, and characteristic upper body pattern consisting of a reddish back and banded hindquarters.

DISTRIBUTION
The numbat formerly occurred across southern and central Australia, but is now restricted to a few remnants of woodland in south-west Western Australia.

In the Northern Territory, it occurred in arid and semi-arid areas, mostly in the far south-west (Parker 1973; Burbidge *et al*. 1988).

Conservation reserves where reported:
None (although it formerly occurred in areas that are now included within Uluru – Kata Tjuta National Park).

ECOLOGY
In central Australia, the numbat occupied areas of mulga woodland with an understorey of spinifex or soft grasses on sand plains and lateritic plains, and was also observed on sand dunes (Burbidge *et al*. 1988).

The numbat is diurnal and terrestrial. Its diet consists only of termites. It rests at night in fallen logs and digs burrows up to 2 m deep. The species is solitary and territorial with animals defending home ranges of 25 to 30 ha. Breeding occurs only once per year.

CONSERVATION ASSESSMENT
The numbat is presumed to have become **Extinct** in the Northern Territory in the 1950s, following a broad-scale decline extending over at least the previous 50 years (Burbidge *et al*. 1988).

THREATENING PROCESSES
The reasons for the numbat's decline in central Australia are not known, but the most likely cause is predation by foxes and feral cats (Finlayson 1961), with further problems associated with vegetation change caused by exotic herbivores and by changed fire regimes.

CONSERVATION OBJECTIVES AND MANAGEMENT
There are no imminent plans to re-introduce this species to the Northern Territory. A captive colony is housed in the nocturnal house of the Alice Springs Desert Park.

Compiled by Chris Pavey [May 2006] / **References:** Burbidge, A.A., Johnson, K.A., Fuller, P.F., and Southgate, R.I. (1988). *Aboriginal knowledge of animals of the central deserts of Australia. Australian Wildlife Research* 15, 9-39. / Finlayson, H.H. (1961). *On central Australian mammals, Part IV. The distribution and status of central Australian species.* Records of the South Australian Museum 41, 141-191. / Parker, S.A. (1973). An annotated checklist of the native land mammals of the Northern Territory. *Records of the South Australian Museum* 16, 1-57.

Illustration by J.Gould (courtesy of Museum Victoria)

Pig-footed bandicoot
Chaeropus ecaudatus

CONSERVATION STATUS
AUSTRALIA: **EXTINCT**
NORTHERN TERRITORY: **EXTINCT**

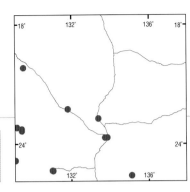

*Known locations
of the pig-footed
bandicoot*
● = *pre 1970*
● = *post 1970*

DESCRIPTION
The pig-footed bandicoot was a small bandicoot (weight about 200 g), with delicate and graceful appearance. Its ungainly name refers to its forefoot, which had only two functional toes, with hoof-like claws. It had unusually long legs for a bandicoot, and moved distinctively ("like a broken-down hack"). Its fur was orange-brown above, and lighter fawn below. Its ears were relatively long (though shorter than those of bilbies).

DISTRIBUTION
Museum records, fossil and sub-fossil evidence and information provided by elderly Aboriginal people suggest that it once occurred in a belt of country stretching from north-western Victoria, across the Nullabor Plain and the inland of South Australia into the present Western Australian wheatbelt. To the north, a specimen from Ryans Well (1891), another north-east of Charlotte Waters (1895) and one from Alice Springs (about 1916) extended its range into the southern Northern Territory. Elderly Aboriginal people recall hunting the pig-footed bandicoot in the Tanami Desert and in the country to the west of Uluru abutting and including the Gibson Desert (Johnson and Southgate 1990).

Conservation reserves where reported:
None (although it formerly occurred in areas that are now included within Uluru – Kata Tjuta National Park and West MacDonnell National Park).

ECOLOGY
From the few recorded observations of this species in the wild, the pig-footed bandicoot appears to have been a plains-dweller with a preferred habitat of open woodlands with an understorey of shrubs and grasses. It excavated a squat in which it built a nest of dried grass, leaves and twigs lined with soft fibrous grasses (Burbidge *et al.* 1988).

CONSERVATION ASSESSMENT
The pig-footed bandicoot is presumed to have become extinct in the Northern Territory in the 1950s, following a broad-scale decline extending over at least the previous 50 years (Finlayson 1961; Burbidge *et al.* 1988; Johnson and Southgate 1990). This was the last area it occupied, and it is now considered **Extinct** throughout its entire range.

THREATENING PROCESSES
The decline and extinction of the pig-footed bandicoot is attributed to a range of factors including predation by cats and foxes, and habitat alteration due to the impacts of exotic herbivores and to changed fire regimes.

CONSERVATION OBJECTIVES AND MANAGEMENT
The species is presumed extinct. No conservation management plan can offer further help.

Compiled by Chris Pavey [May 2006] / **References:** Burbidge, A.A., Johnson, K.A., Fuller, P.F., and Southgate, R.I. (1988). Aboriginal knowledge of animals of the central deserts of Australia. *Australian Wildlife Research* 15, 9-39. / Finlayson, H.H. (1961). On central Australian mammals, Part IV. The distribution and status of central Australian species. *Records of the South Australian Museum* 41, 141-191. / Johnson, K.A., and Southgate, R.I. (1990). Present and former status of bandicoots in the Northern Territory. In *Bandicoots and bilbies* (eds J.H. Seebeck, P.R. Brown, R.L. Wallis and C.M. Kemper.) pp. 85-92. (Surrey Beatty & Sons, Sydney.) / Parker, S.A. (1973). An annotated checklist of the native land mammals of the Northern Territory. *Records of the South Australian Museum* 16, 1-57.

Image courtesy of Kym Brennan

Golden bandicoot
Isoodon auratus

CONSERVATION STATUS
AUSTRALIA: **VULNERABLE**
NORTHERN TERRITORY: **ENDANGERED**

Known locations of the golden bandicoot
● = *pre 1970*
● = *post 1970*

DESCRIPTION

This species is a small bandicoot weighing up to 600 g. It is superficially similar to the more common northern brown bandicoot *Isoodon macrourus,* from which it can be distinguished in the field by its smaller size and by its hair structure.

DISTRIBUTION

In the Northern Territory, the golden bandicoot is now known from only one location, Marchinbar Island on the Wessel chain off north-eastern Arnhem Land (Fisher and Woinarski 1994). Beyond the Territory, the same subspecies *I.a. auratus* also occurs on a small portion of the mainland of the north-western Kimberley (Western Australia) and from two nearby islands, Augustus and Uwins. Another subspecies, *I.a. barrowensis* occurs on Barrow and nearby Middle Islands off the Pilbara coast (Maxwell *et al.* 1996).

The taxonomic position of these forms is currently under review. A recent study (Pope *et al.* 2001) has suggested that golden bandicoots may be conspecific with the southern brown bandicoot *I. obesulus,* with very similar genetic composition albeit some marked morphological differences. The conservation status of the taxon within the Northern Territory is unaffected by the resolution of this taxonomic issue.

The golden bandicoot formerly occurred across most of northern, central and western Australia, extending to south-western New South Wales, and across a very broad variety of habitats.

However, it declined precipitously within decades of European settlement, and disappeared from the central deserts between the 1940s and 1960s (Finlayson 1961; Parker 1973; Burbidge *et al.* 1988). The last specimen from the desert country of mainland Northern Territory was from The Granites (north-west Tanami) in 1952. There have been very few specimen records from the Northern Territory mainland north of the Tanami, but these have included the Roper River area (in 1911) and South Alligator River (around 1900) (Parker 1973; Johnson and Southgate 1990). There are also more recent records (1950s to 1980s) from mainland north-eastern Arnhem Land that are probably referable to this species (Lyne and Mort 1981; I. Morris *unpubl.).*

Conservation reserves where reported:

None; although it was formerly present in areas that have subsequently been included within at least Kakadu National Park, Watarrka National Park, West MacDonnells National Park and Uluru – Kata Tjuta National Park.

ECOLOGY

Most information on the ecology of the golden bandicoot is from a single short-term study on Marchinbar Island (Southgate *et al.* 1996). There it occurs mainly in heathland and shrubland on sandstone or sandsheets, and avoids vegetation with greater tree cover. Individuals maintain overlapping home ranges of from 12 to 35 ha. Their diet comprises a broad range of invertebrates.

CONSERVATION ASSESSMENT

In 1994–95, the total population at its single known Northern Territory site was estimated at around 1400 individuals, occurring across most of the 210 km^2 extent of Marchinbar Island (Southgate *et al.* 1996). Re-surveys of Marchinbar Island were undertaken in October 2004 and in June 2006 and the population levels appeared to be similar to the 1994–95 estimates.

The decline in the mainland population and extent generally occurred earlier than relevant to IUCN status designation criteria (i.e. within 10 years or three generations), although the status of the population, if any, on mainland north-east Arnhem Land remains unresolved.

Conservation categorisation is problematical. However, it can be reasonably inferred that there is some likelihood that this population may be exposed in the future to the same factor(s) that have so effectively extirpated populations elsewhere. Given this premise, the species qualifies as **Endangered** (under criteria B1ab+2ab; C2) based on:

- extent of occurrence less than 5000 km^2;
- known to exist at fewer than five locations;
- continuing decline, observed, inferred or projected;
- area of occupancy les than 500 km^2;
- population size fewer than 2500 mature individuals; and
- more than 95% of mature individuals in one subpopulation.

continued.../

THREATENING PROCESSES

No single factor has been demonstrated to have caused the decline of golden bandicoots, but the extent of loss on the mainland and the maintenance of some island populations suggests that it is not due to land-use factors but rather to either disease or exotic predators. The most likely causal factor is predation by feral cats.

Marchinbar Island has no feral cats, although feral dogs have been present for around 30 to 50 years, and these are known to take some bandicoots. Largely because of their impacts on golden bandicoots (and nesting marine turtles), these feral dogs were exterminated in 2004–05.

Golden bandicoots may be affected by fire regimes, and appear to prefer areas which have been burnt relatively recently (two to five years previously) and within a fine-scale mosaic. The maintenance of such a fire regime is dependent upon management by Aboriginal landowners.

The greatest threat to the Marchinbar population is the deliberate or inadvertent introduction of cats to the island, either by visiting Aboriginal landowners, by visiting fishermen or recreational sailors.

CONSERVATION OBJECTIVES AND MANAGEMENT

A national recovery plan for this species has recently been established (Palmer *et al.* 2003). Many actions in that plan are now being implemented jointly by Gumurr Marthakal rangers of north-eastern Arnhem Land and scientists from the Department of Natural Resources, Environment and The Arts, supported by Natural Heritage Trust funding.

Management priorities are to:
- better safeguard the existing population through improved communication of the need to keep the island cat-free, through encouragement of traditional Aboriginal burning practices, and through the implementation of a monitoring program;
- translocate (and thence manage) populations to at least one other nearby island through expansion of the captive population and investigation of suitability of other islands in the Wessel and English Company Islands groups; and
- investigate whether populations persist on the mainland of north-east Arnhem Land.

Compiled by Carol Palmer, John Woinarski [December 2006] / **References:** Burbidge, A.A., Johnson, K.A., Fuller, P.J., and Southgate, R.I. (1988). Aboriginal knowledge of the mammals of the central deserts of Australia. *Australian Wildlife Research* 15, 9-40. / Finlayson, H.H. (1961). On central Australian mammals, Part IV. The distribution and status of central Australian species. *Records of the South Australian Museum* 41, 141-191. / Fisher, A., and Woinarski, J. (1994). Golden Bandicoot. *Australian Natural History* 26, 20-21. / Johnson, K.A., and Southgate, R.I. (1990). Present and former status of bandicoots in the Northern Territory. In *Bandicoots and bilbies* (eds J.H. Seebeck, P.R. Brown, R.L. Wallis and C.M. Kemper.) pp. 85-92. (Surrey Beatty and Sons, Sydney.) / Lyne, A.G., and Mort, P.A. (1981). A comparison of skull morphology in the marsupial bandicoot *Isoodon*: its taxonomic implications and notes on a new species *Isoodon arnhemensis. Australian Mammalogy* 4, 107-133. / Maxwell, S., Burbidge, A.A., and Morris, K. (eds) (1996). *The 1996 Action Plan for Australian marsupials and monotremes.* (Wildlife Australia, Canberra.) / Palmer, C., Taylor, R., and Burbidge, A. (2003). Recovery plan for the Golden Bandicoot *Isoodon auratus* and golden-backed tree-rat *Mesembriomys macrurus* 2004-2009. (NT Department of Infrastructure Planning and Environment, Darwin.) / Parker, S.A. (1973). An annotated checklist of the native land mammals of the Northern Territory. *Records of the South Australian Museum* 16, 1-57. / Pope, L., Storch, D., Adams, M., Moritz, C., and Gordon, G. (2001). A phylogeny for the genus *Isoodon* and a range extension for *I. obesulus peninsulae* based on mtDNA control region and morphology. *Australian Journal of Zoology* 49, 411-434. / Southgate, R., Palmer, C., Adams, M., Masters, P., Triggs, B., and Woinarski, J. (1996). Population and habitat characteristics of the Golden Bandicoot (*Isoodon auratus*) on Marchinbar Island, Northern Territory. *Wildlife Research* 23, 647-664.

Desert bandicoot
Perameles eremiana

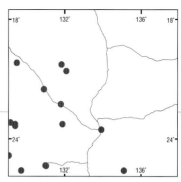

Known locations of the desert bandicoot
● = *pre 1970*
● = *post 1970*

CONSERVATION STATUS
AUSTRALIA: **EXTINCT**
NORTHERN TERRITORY: **EXTINCT**

DESCRIPTION
The desert bandicoot was a small to medium-sized (body mass about 250 g) species, similar in appearance to the barred bandicoots. It was generally orange-brown above and white below, with one or two dark bands on the hindquarters.

DISTRIBUTION
The desert bandicoot formerly occurred in south-west Northern Territory, north-west South Australia and across north-central Western Australia. In the Northern Territory, it extended as far north as the Tanami desert (Johnson and Southgate 1990).

Conservation reserves where reported:
None (although it formerly occurred in areas that are now included within Uluru – Kata Tjuta National Park and West MacDonnell National Park).

ECOLOGY
The desert bandicoot occupied sandplain and dune environments that supported either hummock or tussock grassland (Burbidge *et al.* 1988).

CONSERVATION ASSESSMENT
The last specimen was obtained in 1943 and it appears to have become **Extinct** in the Northern Territory during the 1960s, following a broad-scale decline extending over at least the previous 50 years (Finlayson 1961; Parker 1973; Burbidge *et al.* 1988; Johnson and Southgate 1990).

THREATENING PROCESSES
The decline and extinction of the desert bandicoot is attributed to a range of factors including predation by cats and foxes, and habitat alteration due to the impacts of exotic herbivores and to changed fire regimes.

CONSERVATION OBJECTIVES AND MANAGEMENT
The species is presumed extinct. No conservation management plan can offer further help.

Compiled by Chris Pavey [May 2006] / **References:** Burbidge, A.A., Johnson, K.A., Fuller, P.F., and Southgate, R.I. (1988). Aboriginal knowledge of animals of the central deserts of Australia. *Australian Wildlife Research* 15, 9-39. / Finlayson, H.H. (1961). On central Australian mammals, Part IV. The distribution and status of central Australian species. *Records of the South Australian Museum* 41, 141-191. Johnson, K.A., and Southgate, R.I. (1990). Present and former status of bandicoots in the Northern Territory. In *Bandicoots and bilbies* (eds J.H. Seebeck, P.R. Brown, R.L. Wallis and C.M. Kemper.) pp. 85-92. (Surrey Beatty & Sons, Sydney.) / Parker, S.A. (1973). An annotated checklist of the native land mammals of the Northern Territory. *Records of the South Australian Museum* 16, 1-57.

Greater bilby,
Bilby
Macrotis lagotis

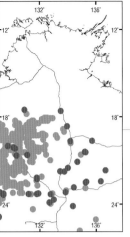

*Known locations of
the greater bilby*
● = *pre 1970*
● = *post 1970*

DESCRIPTION

The greater bilby is a large bandicoot (body mass of 800 to 2500 g for males, and 600 to 1100 g for females) with soft silky fur. The fur is ash grey over most of the body, whereas on the belly it is pure white to cream. The forelimbs are robust and equipped with three stoutly-clawed toes (and two unclawed toes) giving the animal a formidable burrowing capacity. The base of the tail is grey; the central section is black; and the tip is white. The slender hind limbs are long and resemble those of macropods. The snout is long and delicate and the ears are large and rabbit-like.

DISTRIBUTION

Within the Northern Territory, it occurs in the central and western parts of the Tanami bioregion, the southern Sturt Plateau bioregion and the northern Great Sandy Desert bioregion. The distribution is highly fragmented within this area. The most southerly recent records are in the vicinity of Kintore, the most northerly around Newcastle Waters and Wave Hill.

Historically, the greater bilby occupied a vast area of arid and semi-arid Australia. Its distribution declined dramatically in the years following European settlement and it now occupies about 20% of its former range. The species occurs in two separate geographic areas: one extending from the western deserts region of the Northern Territory and Western Australia north to the Pilbara and Kimberley regions, and the second in the Channel Country of south-west Queensland (Watts 1969; Southgate 1990a).

Conservation reserves where reported:
None (although it formerly occurred in areas that are now included within Uluru – Kata Tjuta National Park, Watarrka National Park and West MacDonnell National Park).

ECOLOGY

Habitat of the greater bilby in the Northern Territory is characterised by sandy soils dominated by hummock grasslands covered predominantly by three species of spinifex, *Triodia basedowii*, *T. pungens* and *T. schinzii*. An overstorey of low shrub cover dominated by *Acacia* and *Melaleuca* species grows over much of this country. This predominantly sandy landscape also includes rocky outcrops, laterite rises and low-lying drainage systems (Southgate 1990b). Broad-scale surveys of bilbies in the Northern Territory in the 1990s indicated that laterite and drainage-line land systems were occupied more frequently than sandplain and dune systems.

The greater bilby is omnivorous and major foods vary across seasons (Southgate 1990b). Important plant foods include seed from various grasses and sedges including button grass (*Dactyloctenium radulans*), desert flinders grass (*Yakirra australiensis*) and parakeelya (*Calandrinia* spp.) and bulbs from bush onion or yalka (*Cyperus bulbosus*) and *Wurmbea deserticola*, many of which are most abundant soon after fires (Southgate and Carthew 2006). At a site in central Australia, fruiting bodies of underground fungi were the major dietary component. Major invertebrate prey includes termites, ants, beetles, insect larvae and spiders. Most of the food of the greater bilby is excavated from the soil and holes may attain 25 cm in depth.

Bilbies dig burrows up to 2 m deep, and an individual may have over a dozen regularly used burrows within its home-range. Bilbies forage at night. Movements of 5 km during one night have been recorded for male bilbies. Males, females and juveniles may occupy overlapping home ranges. Densities of 12 to 16 individuals/km^2 are reached in optimal habitat. However, a density of 1 to 2/km^2 is more typical (Southgate 1987).

Litters, comprising one to three young, can be produced at any time of year (Southgate *et al.* 2000). Young remain in the pouch for approximately 75 days, before being cached and suckled in maternal burrows for a further two weeks prior to independence. Under ideal conditions, there is the potential to produce four litters every year. Captive animals live up to 10 years (Southgate *et al.* 2000).

continued.../

CONSERVATION ASSESSMENT

No estimates are available for the size of the Northern Territory population of the greater bilby. The range of the species in the Northern Territory is declining and contracting northwards. For example, populations located in the vicinity of Alice Springs in the late 1960s (Watts 1969) are no longer present. However, bilbies in the Northern Territory appear to be nomadic and undergo large population fluctuations in response to food availability. These characteristics result in it being difficult to accurately assess population trends for two reasons. First, no sites are known in the Northern Territory that are considered to permanently hold colonies of bilbies. Second, depending on rainfall and food availability, very few bilby records may be reported during one time period, but this can change quickly. This natural variation must be taken into account when considering the conservation status of the species.

Notwithstanding the above caveats, the greater bilby is **Vulnerable** in the Northern Territory (under criterion C2a(i)) based on:

- population size estimated to be fewer than 10 000 mature individuals;
- continuing decline in numbers of mature individuals; and
- no subpopulation estimated to contain more than 1000 mature individuals.

THREATENING PROCESSES

Predation by the introduced European fox appears to be the major threat faced by the greater bilby in the Northern Territory (Southgate 1987). Predation by other carnivores (i.e. feral cat, dingo) could also threaten bilby populations. However, there is considerable interaction between these three predators. Specifically, dingoes may protect a range of native species, including bilbies, by controlling cats and foxes either through direct predation or excluding them from carrion during droughts.

Competition with rabbits may also be an important threatening process faced by the greater bilby. However, the negative impact of rabbits has been greatly reduced following the release of rabbit calicivirus disease in the 1990s. Grazing by cattle may be a threat on some pastoral leases. Unsuitable fire regimes may restrict breeding and impede dispersal into unoccupied areas, and reduce food options and availability (Southgate and Carthew 2006).

CONSERVATION OBJECTIVES AND MANAGEMENT

A national recovery plan for the greater bilby was established in 2006 (Pavey 2006). The plan recommends the following management actions that include the Northern Territory:

- reduce fox and cat numbers at key wild populations where bilbies are in decline;
- continue husbandry and coordinated management of captive populations;
- refine monitoring methodology;
- monitor trends in occurrence at wild populations; and
- continue to manage the recovery process through a national recovery team.

The greater bilby is maintained in captivity at the Alice Springs Desert Park and is displayed in its nocturnal house. National Bilby Day takes place in September each year and the Desert Park is a focus for educational activities involving the species.

Compiled by Chris Pavey [May 2006] / **References:** Lavery, H. J., and Kirkpatrick, T. H. (1997). Field management of the bilby *Macrotis lagotis* in an area of south-western Queensland. *Biological Conservation* 79, 271-281. / Pavey, C. (2006). *Recovery Plan for the Greater Bilby, Macrotis lagotis, 2006-2011.* (NT Department of Natural Resources, Environment and the Arts, Alice Springs.) / Southgate, R.I. (1987). *Conservation of the Bilby.* Report to World Wildlife Fund. (Conservation Commission of the Northern Territory, Alice Springs.) / Southgate, R. I. (1990a). Distribution and abundance of the greater bilby *Macrotis lagotis* Reid (Marsupialia: Peramelidae). In *Bandicoots and bilbies* (eds J.H. Seebeck, P.R. Brown, R.L. Wallis and C.M. Kemper.) pp. 293-302. (Surrey Beatty & Sons, Sydney.) / Southgate, R. I. (1990b). Habitat and diet of the greater bilby *Macrotis lagotis* Reid (Marsupialia: Peramelidae). In *Bandicoots and bilbies* (eds J.H. Seebeck, P.R. Brown, R.L. Wallis and C.M. Kemper.) pp. 303-309. (Surrey Beatty & Sons, Sydney.) Southgate, R., and Carthew, S.M. (2006). Diet of the bilby (*Macrotis lagotis*) in relation to substrate, fire and rainfall characteristics in the Tanami Desert. *Wildlife Research* 33, 507-520. / Southgate, R. I., Christie, P., and Bellchambers, K. (2000). Breeding biology of captive, reintroduced and wild greater bilbies, *Macrotis lagotis* (Marsupialia: Peramelidae). *Wildlife Research* 27, 621-628. / Watts, C.H.S. (1969). Distribution and habits of the rabbit bandicoot. *Transactions of the Royal Society of South Australia* 93, 135-141.

Illustration by Frank Knight

Lesser bilby

Macrotis leucura

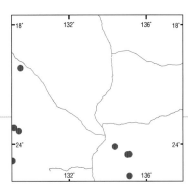

*Known locations
of the lesser bilby*
● = *pre 1970*
● = *post 1970*

DESCRIPTION

The lesser bilby was a medium-sized marsupial (body mass of 300 to 435 g) that was both smaller and less colourful than the greater bilby. The lesser bilby was grey-brown above and paler below with a white tail that was about 70% of its head-body length.

DISTRIBUTION

The species occupied spinifex and canegrass on dunes and sandy plains in two regions of arid Australia - the first in north-east South Australia and adjoining south-east Northern Territory, the other in the Gibson and Great Sandy deserts of Western Australia and adjoining regions of the Northern Territory. The western distribution was discovered only after discussions with elderly Aboriginal people (Burbidge *et al.* 1988; Johnson and Southgate 1990).

Conservation reserves where reported:
None (although it may have formerly occurred in areas that are now included within Uluru – Kata Tjuta National Park and West MacDonnell National Park).

ECOLOGY

The biology of the lesser bilby is poorly known. The species was nocturnal and sheltered during the day in a deep burrow dug amongst sand dunes. Its diet consisted of termites, ants and roots. It occurred in dunes and sandplains with spinifex, sometimes with mulga and/or tussock grass (Burbidge *et al.* 1988).

CONSERVATION ASSESSMENT

The lesser bilby is presumed to have become **Extinct** in the Northern Territory in the 1960s, following a broad-scale decline extending over at least the previous 50 years (Burbidge *et al.* 1988). It was probably extinct in the south-east of the Northern Territory by the first half of the twentieth century (Finlayson 1961).

THREATENING PROCESSES

The decline and extinction of the lesser bilby is attributed to a range of factors including predation by cats and foxes, and habitat alteration due to the impacts of exotic herbivores and to changed fire regimes.

CONSERVATION OBJECTIVES AND MANAGEMENT

The species is presumed extinct. No conservation management plan can offer further help.

Compiled by Chris Pavey [May 2006] / **References:** Burbidge, A.A., Johnson, K.A., Fuller, P.F., and Southgate, R.I. (1988). Aboriginal knowledge of animals of the central deserts of Australia. *Australian Wildlife Research* 15, 9-39. / Finlayson, H.H. (1961). On central Australian mammals, Part IV. The distribution and status of central Australian species. *Records of the South Australian Museum* 41, 141-191. Johnson, K.A., and Southgate, R.I. (1990). Present and former status of bandicoots in the Northern Territory. In *Bandicoots and bilbies* (eds J.H. Seebeck, P.R. Brown, R.L. Wallis and C.M. Kemper.) pp. 85-92. (Surrey Beatty & Sons, Sydney.) / Parker, S.A. (1973). An annotated checklist of the native land mammals of the Northern Territory. *Records of the South Australian Museum* 16, 1-57.

Southern marsupial mole, Itjaritjari
Notoryctes typhlops

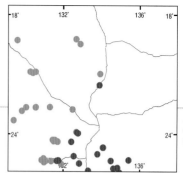

Known locations of the southern marsupial mole
- ● = pre 1970
- ● = post 1970

CONSERVATION STATUS
AUSTRALIA: **ENDANGERED**
NORTHERN TERRITORY: **VULNERABLE**

DESCRIPTION

Marsupial moles comprise their own order within the marsupials; the Notoryctemorphia (Johnson and Walton 1989). The order contains the southern marsupial mole or Itjaritjari (*N. typhlops*) and the northern marsupial mole or Kakarratul (*N. caurinus*). The southern marsupial mole consists of a southern and northern form that differ in morphology and genetics. The taxonomic implications of these differences are not fully understood.

The southern marsupial mole is a small animal (body mass 30 to 60 g, head and body length up to 140 mm) that is highly distinctive in shape and appearance (Johnson 1995). Key characteristics include a tubular body shape, lack of external ears, heavily keratinized skin on the snout, a short, cylindrical, stumpy tail and short, dense fur. Body colour ranges from almost white through pinkish-cinnamon to rich golden-red. The limbs are short and powerful. The third and fourth digits of the forefoot are greatly enlarged and bear large, triangular claws that form a cleft spade or scoop. The remaining three digits of the forefoot are small, but the first and second bear claws and are opposed to the third and fourth. The middle three digits of the hind foot also possess an enlarged claw. The female has a distinct pouch that, as in other burrowing marsupials, opens posteriorly. The eyes are vestigial, measuring only 1 mm in diameter, and are hidden under the skin. There is no lens or pupil, and the optic nerve to the brain is reduced.

DISTRIBUTION

The southern marsupial mole occurs in the sandy deserts of central Western Australia (Pearson and Turner 2000), northern South Australia (apart from records from the Fowlers Bay area near the South Australian coast) and the Northern Territory. Within the Territory, it has been recorded from locations concentrated in the south-western quarter but has been collected as far north as Barrow Creek (21° 53' S). It does not appear to occur in the Simpson Desert. The few records of marsupial moles from the north-western Tanami Desert approach the known range of the northern marsupial mole, which has not yet been confirmed from the Northern Territory (Benshemesh 2006).

Conservation reserves where reported:
Uluru – Kata Tjuta National Park, Watarrka National Park.

ECOLOGY

Southern marsupial moles are found in the sandy deserts where they occupy dunes, sandy plains, and river flats. Underground sign is most common on well-vegetated dunes (Benshemesh 2006). Aboriginal people have indicated that marsupial moles require soft sand and cannot tunnel through hard or loamy substrates that occur in swales between widely spaced dunes. This view is supported by the results of surveys of underground sign (Benshemesh 2006).

Food of marsupial moles includes various insects (adults, larvae, pupae and eggs), other invertebrates and geckoes (Winkel and Humphrey-Smith 1988).

Marsupial moles dig with the aid of flattened claws. It is not known whether they build nests or form permanent burrows (Benshemesh 2006). Although marsupial moles were previously considered to swim through the sand, recent investigations indicate that they are actually tunnellers that back-fill as they move along. Joe Benshemesh has used this behaviour to develop a survey methodology for marsupial moles; a major breakthrough in attempts to understand their distribution and patterns of occurrence. The method involves digging a steep and smooth-sided trench and then counting the sand-filled tunnels that arose from previous passage of marsupial moles, visible in cross-section. Most tunnels occur between 20 and 100 cm below the surface with some more than 2 m below the surface (Benshemesh 2006).

The marsupial mole occasionally comes to the surface and seems more inclined to do so after rain in the cooler seasons. A characteristic three furrow track in the sand is made by the mole's spade-like feet and the stumpy tail. Marsupial moles typically remain above the surface only for a short distance (usually a few metres).

Little is known about reproduction by marsupial moles, although single and twin pouch young have been reported.

continued.../

CONSERVATION ASSESSMENT

It is difficult to assign a category to *N. typhlops* because of conflicting interpretation of the available information. Some authors have interpreted anecdotal information, mainly from Aboriginal informants (Burbidge *et al.* 1988), as demonstrating that they are reasonably common but infrequently observed. Alternatively data on the rates of acquisition of specimens by museums (Johnson and Walton 1989) suggest a decline in abundance especially considering that human activities within the species' range (mining exploration, road building, tourism) have increased significantly over recent decades. The results of recent surveys carried out by Joe Benshemesh indicate that southern marsupial moles are very common in places.

The southern marsupial mole is currently classified as **Vulnerable** (under criterion C1) based on:
• population size estimated to be fewer than 10 000 mature individuals; and
• an estimated continuing decline of at least 10% within 10 years or three generations, whichever is longer.

THREATENING PROCESSES

So little is known about the southern marsupial mole's current conservation status that it is highly speculative to describe threats. Predation by feral cats, European foxes and dingoes of marsupial moles when they are above ground (Paltridge 1998), and soil compaction by stock movements or by vehicles, may be potential threats to the long-term survival of the species. Other threats that may change the abundance of ants, insect larvae and termites, such as altered fire regimes and grazing, may also be important.

CONSERVATION OBJECTIVES AND MANAGEMENT

A national recovery plan for both the southern and northern marsupial moles has been established (Benshemesh 2006). Key actions in the plan that include work in the Northern Territory are to:
• understand distribution and relative abundance;
• monitor population trends;
• assess the threats imposed by fire, grazing and predation;
• describe activity and ranging behaviour;
• prepare for captive individuals; and
• co-ordinate and manage the recovery process.

Compiled by Chris Pavey [May 2006] / **References:** Benshemesh, J. (2006). *Marsupial mole recovery plan.* (Northern Territory Department of Natural Resources, Environment and the Arts, Alice Springs.) Burbidge, A.A., Johnson, K.A., Fuller, P.F., and Southgate, R.I. (1988). Aboriginal knowledge of animals of the central deserts of *Australia. Australian Wildlife Research* 15, 9-39. / Johnson K. A. (1995). Marsupial mole, *Notoryctes typhlops.* In The Mammals of Australia (ed. R. Strahan.) pp. 409-411. (Australian Museum, Sydney.) / Johnson K. A., and Walton D.W. (1989). Notoryctidae. In *Fauna of Australia: Volume 1B Mammalia* (eds D.W. Walton and B.J. Richardson). pp 591-602. (Australian Government Publishing Service, Canberra.) / Paltridge, R. (1998). Occurrence of marsupial mole (*Notoryctes typhlops*) remains in the faecal pellets of cats, foxes and dingoes in the Tanami Desert, N.T. *Australian Mammalogy* 20, 427-429. / Pearson, D.J., and Turner, J. (2000). Marsupial mole pops up in the Great Victoria and Gibson deserts. Australian Mammalogy 22, 115-119. / Winkel, K., and Humphrey-Smith, I. (1988). Diet of the marsupial mole, *Notoryctes typhlops* (Stirling 1889) (Marsupialia: Notoryctidae). *Australian Mammalogy* 11, 159-161.

Image courtesy of Michael Barritt

Burrowing bettong,
Boodie (inland subspecies)
Bettongia lesueur graii

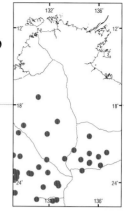

Known locations of the burrowing bettong
● = *pre 1970*
● = *post 1970*

DESCRIPTION
The burrowing bettong is a small thick-set macropod (body mass 0.9 to 1.6 kg). It is yellow-grey above and paler grey below. The ears are short and rounded, and the tail relatively robust.

DISTRIBUTION
Burrowing bettongs once lived in burrows excavated in sandy, calcareous and lateritic country over a range that encompassed nearly half of the continent, including most of Western Australia (with the exception of the north Kimberley) and South Australia, western New South Wales and the Victorian mallee. In the Northern Territory, the burrowing bettong was found extensively in the dune and sandplain deserts of the southern arid region. Early naturalists noted that it was common and, in many areas, the most abundant mammal. The mainland subspecies is now extinct; however, two subspecies occur on islands off the coast of Western Australia; one subspecies on Boodie and Barrow Islands off the Pilbara coast; the other on Bernier and Dorre Islands off Shark Bay. Both these subspecies are listed nationally as Vulnerable. The decline of this species on the mainland commenced in the nineteenth century. It disappeared from Victoria in the 1860s, but persisted in the central and western deserts until the mid twentieth century.

Old bettong warrens are still readily observed in central Australia, particularly in calcareous country where excavated stones and gravels form humps or mounds around the entrance of long abandoned warrens.

Conservation reserves where reported:
None (although it formerly occurred in areas that are now included within Finke Gorge National Park, Uluru – Kata Tjuta National Park and West MacDonnell National Park.)

ECOLOGY
In arid and semi-arid Northern Territory, the burrowing bettong occurred in a broad range of habitats, other than ranges (Burbidge *et al.* 1988). It dug extensive and distinctive warren systems, in which it would rest during the day.

CONSERVATION ASSESSMENT
The burrowing bettong is presumed to have become **Extinct** in the Northern Territory in the 1950s, following a broad-scale decline extending over at least the previous 50 years (Finlayson 1961; Burbidge *et al.* 1988).

THREATENING PROCESSES
The disappearance of the burrowing bettong from central and western Australia seems to have coincided with the establishment of the fox and the feral cat. Interestingly, bettong numbers were probably not seriously affected by rabbits, with both species sometimes sharing warrens.

CONSERVATION OBJECTIVES AND MANAGEMENT
The subspecies is presumed extinct. No conservation management plan can offer further help.

However, other subspecies persist and Parks Australia and the Mutijulu Community intend to establish a captive colony of subspecies from Western Australia within the predator-proof enclosure at Uluru – Kata Tjuta National Park that currently houses mala.

Compiled by Chris Pavey [May 2006] / **References:** Burbidge, A.A., Johnson, K.A., Fuller, P.F., and Southgate, R.I. (1988). Aboriginal knowledge of animals of the central deserts of Australia. *Australian Wildlife Research* 15, 9-39. / Finlayson, H.H. (1961). On central Australian mammals, Part IV. The distribution and status of central Australian species. *Records of the South Australian Museum* 41, 141-191. / Parker, S.A. (1973). An annotated checklist of the native land mammals of the Northern Territory. *Records of the South Australian Museum* 16, 1-57.

Illustration by J.Gould (courtesy of Museum Victoria)

Brush-tailed bettong, Woylie
Bettongia penicillata

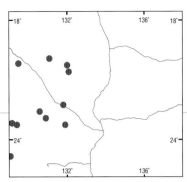

Known locations of the brush-tailed bettong
● = pre 1970
● = post 1970

CONSERVATION STATUS
AUSTRALIA: **NOT LISTED**
NORTHERN TERRITORY: **EXTINCT**

DESCRIPTION
The brush-tailed bettong is a small macropod (body mass 1.0 to 1.6 kg), yellow-grey above and paler below. The tail is well-furred, with a black crest most pronounced near the tail tip.

DISTRIBUTION
This species is now restricted to dry sclerophyll forest with a dense understorey in south-west Western Australia. Translocated populations are located in conservation reserves in Western Australia and New South Wales and on islands off the South Australian coast.

In the Northern Territory, it occurred in the Great Sandy and Tanami deserts (Finlayson 1961; Burbidge *et al.* 1988).

Conservation reserves where reported: None

ECOLOGY
Brush-tailed bettongs inhabited a wide range of habitats from desert spinifex grasslands to forests. During the day they sheltered in grass-lined nests in spinifex hummocks or grass tussocks.

In the Northern Territory, elderly Aboriginal people recall this species occurring on sandplains and dunes supporting spinifex grasslands (Burbidge *et al.* 1988). For both the burrowing and brush-tailed bettongs the fruit-bodies of underground fungi are an important dietary component, and both species are likely to have played an important role in the dispersal of fungal spores within desert ecosystems.

CONSERVATION ASSESSMENT
The brush-tailed bettong is presumed to have become **Extinct** in the Northern Territory in the 1950s, following a broad-scale decline extending over at least the previous 50 years (Burbidge *et al.* 1988).

THREATENING PROCESSES
Habitat degradation, changes to fire regimes and predation by foxes and cats are thought to account for the decline of this species from its previous extensive range.

CONSERVATION OBJECTIVE AND MANAGEMENT
There are no imminent plans to reintroduce this species to the Northern Territory. Some individuals are on display in the nocturnal house of the Alice Springs Desert Park.

Compiled by Chris Pavey [May 2006] / **References:** Burbidge, A.A., Johnson, K.A., Fuller, P.F., and Southgate, R.I. (1988). Aboriginal knowledge of animals of the central deserts of Australia. *Australian Wildlife Research* 15, 9-39. / Finlayson, H.H. (1961). On central Australian mammals, Part IV. The distribution and status of central Australian species. *Records of the South Australian Museum* 41, 141-191. Parker, S.A. (1973). An annotated checklist of the native land mammals of the Northern Territory. *Records of the South Australian Museum* 16, 1-57.

Central hare-wallaby
Lagorchestes asomatus

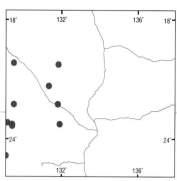

Known locations of the central hare-wallaby
● = pre 1970
● = post 1970

CONSERVATION STATUS
AUSTRALIA: **EXTINCT**
NORTHERN TERRITORY: **EXTINCT**

DESCRIPTION
The central hare-wallaby was a small hare-wallaby known to science from a single skull removed from a fresh carcass by the explorer-geologist Michael Terry between Mt Farewell and the northern end of Lake Mackay in the Northern Territory in 1932 (Parker 1973). According to Western Desert Aborigines, the species was about the size of a rabbit, with soft, grey fur, hairy feet and a short tail.

DISTRIBUTION
The former distribution of this species is known only from one collection and information supplied by elderly Aboriginal people (Burbidge *et al.* 1988). It formerly occupied parts of the central and western deserts.

Conservation reserves where reported:
None (although it may have formerly occurred in areas that are now included within Uluru – Kata Tjuta National Park and West MacDonnell National Park.)

ECOLOGY
The biology of the central hare-wallaby is known only from anecdotal information provided by elderly Aboriginal people. It sheltered in a shallow depression under spinifex clumps, but occasionally dug a short burrow (Burbidge *et al.* 1988).

CONSERVATION ASSESSMENT
The central hare-wallaby is thought to have disappeared between 1940 and 1960, following a broad-scale decline extending over at least the previous 50 years (Burbidge *et al.* 1988).

THREATENING PROCESSES
The decline and extinction of the central hare-wallaby was probably because of the impacts of predation by cats and foxes, and habitat alteration due to the impacts of exotic herbivores and to changed fire regimes.

CONSERVATION OBJECTIVES AND MANAGEMENT
The species is presumed extinct. No conservation management plan can offer further help.

Compiled by Chris Pavey [May 2006] / **References:** Burbidge, A.A., Johnson, K.A., Fuller, P.F., and Southgate, R.I. (1988). Aboriginal knowledge of animals of the central deserts of Australia. *Australian Wildlife Research* 15, 9-39. / Parker, S.A. (1973). An annotated checklist of the native land mammals of the Northern Territory. *Records of the South Australian Museum* 16, 1-57.

Mala, Rufous hare-wallaby
(central mainland form)
Lagorchestes hirsutus

CONSERVATION STATUS
AUSTRALIA: **ENDANGERED**
NORTHERN TERRITORY: **EXTINCT IN THE WILD**

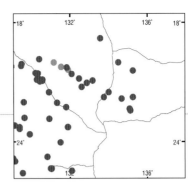

Known locations of the mala
● = *pre 1970*
● = *post 1970*

DESCRIPTION

Mala is the name given to the central Australian population (an undescribed subspecies) of the rufous hare-wallaby. The rufous hare-wallaby also has a subspecies on Bernier and Dorre Island in Shark Bay, Western Australia (Short and Turner 1992). The mala is a small wallaby with a body mass of 800 to 1600 g. The mala's scientific name, *hirsutus*, refers to the long shaggy rufous/brown hair on its back and sides. The fur on its belly and chest is pale fawn grading to white.

DISTRIBUTION

The mala is extinct in the wild on the mainland of Australia. A colony is located on Trimouille Island, Western Australia as a consequence of a translocation from the Tanami Desert to that site in 1999 (Langford and Burbidge 2001). Semi-captive populations housed in predator-proof enclosures are located at Watarrka National Park (established in 2000) and Uluru – Kata Tjuta National Park (established in 2005). Captive populations are found at the Alice Springs Desert Park, Dryandra Conservation Reserve, (south-east of Perth), François Peron National Park (central coast of Western Australia), and Scotia Sanctuary (western New South Wales).

Mala formerly occupied a broad swathe of country in woodlands and spinifex grasslands in central and western deserts and semi-deserts. Mala were still common in the Tanami Desert until the 1930s but their numbers crashed dramatically in the years following the expansion of European settlement

into the area (Bolton and Latz 1978; Burbidge *et al*. 1988). The last wild colony of mala was extinguished by a wildfire in 1992.

Conservation reserves where reported:
None (although it formerly occurred in areas that are now included within Uluru – Kata Tjuta National Park, Watarrka National Park and West MacDonnell National Park).

ECOLOGY

The ecology of the mala was studied in detail (Lundie-Jenkins 1993; Lundie-Jenkins *et al*. 1993) at Sangsters Bore in the Tanami Desert. These studies show that mala are dependent upon a specialised form of spinifex habitat. Aspects of habitat structure and diversity appear to be important in delineating between suitable and unsuitable areas. Patchiness, hummock size, food diversity and the degree of senescence, in particular, were identified as influential factors.

Mala in the Tanami Desert showed definite seasonal patterns of habitat use. Their movements between and within two adjacent vegetation systems were found to vary in response to the availability and palatability of food plants. The home ranges of individual mala were found to consist of large areas within the dense spinifex habitat and small concentrated feeding areas on saline flats adjacent to watercourses and drainage depressions.

CONSERVATION ASSESSMENT

The mala exists in the Northern Territory only in captivity. Hence it is **Extinct in the Wild.**

THREATENING PROCESSES

Most of the land where the mala lived has not been used for cattle or sheep, except in the south-west of the continent where mala habitat was severely degraded following pastoral expansion. Rabbits may have had an effect in the south but not in the north. Feral cats and European foxes have certainly had a major role in the mala's decline (Johnson 1988; Lundie-Jenkins *et al*. 1993b). Cats and foxes have been present in the desert lands for over a century. Mala and many other desert animals are easy prey for these predators and their impact on the native desert fauna is known to be significant.

The movement of Aboriginal people off their traditional country to settlements and missions is also thought to be important in the mala's decline. For thousands of years, Aboriginal people had burned the spinifex country. This involved setting fire to small patches in winter. This reduced the risk of more destructive, summer bushfires because it removed much of the flammable spinifex. However patch burning was also very helpful to animals like the mala. It produced a diverse habitat with areas of mature vegetation where the animals could shelter, and areas of succulent new growth where the animals could feed. When the Aboriginal people stopped burning the desert, the habitat changed and the

continued.../

mala and other species were affected (Bolton and Latz 1978; Loorham 1985).

Remnant and reintroduced populations were studied and managed in the Tanami Desert up to the early 1990s (Gibson *et al.* 1984; Lundie-Jenkins 1996), and the decline and loss of these populations demonstrated the major threats posed by predation by feral cats, and by inappropriate fire regimes.

CONSERVATION OBJECTIVES AND MANAGEMENT

Management of the mala in the Northern Territory presently consists of the maintenance of colonies in captivity and predator-proof enclosures (Short *et al.* 1992), including in Watarrka National Park. A revision of the national recovery plan for the rufous hare-wallaby (including the mala and the subspecies on Bernier and Dorre Island, Shark Bay) has been drafted.

Recovery actions identified for mala in the Northern Territory are to:
• maintain and enhance captive populations;
• establish a population at Uluru – Kata Tjuta National Park (underway);

• use population viability analysis to compare the viability of wild and current and potential reintroduced populations;
• co-ordinate all captive breeding populations;
• continue to enhance the involvement of the traditional owners, the Anangu, and the Mutijulu Community, in the management of the mala population in the Uluru – Kata Tjuta National Park; and
• participate in the recovery team.

Compiled by Chris Pavey [May 2006] / **References:** Bolton, B.L., and Latz, P.K. (1978). The Western Hare-Wallaby *Lagorchestes hirsutus* (Gould) (Macropodidae), in the Tanami Desert. *Australian Wildlife Research* 5, 285-293. / Burbidge, A.A., Johnson, K.A., Fuller, P.F., and Southgate, R.I. (1988). Aboriginal knowledge of animals of the central deserts of Australia. *Australian Wildlife Research* 15, 9-39. Gibson, D.F., Johnson, K.A., Langford, D.G., Cole, J.R., Clarke, D.E., and Willowra Community. (1994). The rufous hare-wallaby *Lagorchestes hirsutus*: a history of experimental reintroduction in the Tanami Desert, Northern Territory. In *Reintroduction biology of Australian and New Zealand fauna.* (ed. M. Serena.) pp. 171-176. (Surrey Beatty & Sons, Chipping Norton.) / Johnson, K.A. (1988). Rare and Endangered: Rufous Hare-wallaby. *Australian Natural History* 22, 406-407. / Langford, D.G., and Burbidge, A.A. (2001). Translocation of Mala *Lagorchestes hirsutus* from the Tanami Desert, Northern Territory to Trimouille Island, Western Australia. *Australian Mammalogy* 23, 37-46. / Loorham, C. (1985). The Warlpiri and the rufous hare-wallaby. *Habitat* 13, 8-9. / Lundie-Jenkins, G. (1993). Ecology of the rufous hare-wallaby, *Lagorchestes hirsutus* Gould (Marsupialia: Macropodidae) in the Tanami Desert, N.T. I. Patterns of habitat use. *Wildlife Research* 20, 457-476. / Lundie-Jenkins, G. (1996). Developing and implementing a recovery plan: the Mala recovery program. In *Back from the brink: refining the threatened species recovery process.* (eds S. Stephens and S. Maxwell.) pp. 162-169. (Surrey Beatty & Sons, Chipping Norton.) / Lundie-Jenkins, G., Phillips, C.M., and Jarman, P.J. (1993a). Ecology of the rufous hare-wallaby, *Lagorchestes hirsutus* Gould (Marsupialia: Macropodidae) in the Tanami Desert, N.T. II. Diet and feeding strategy. *Wildlife Research* 20, 477-494. / Lundie-Jenkins, G., Corbett, L.K., and Phillips, C.M. (1993b). Ecology of the rufous hare-wallaby, *Lagorchestes hirsutus* Gould (Marsupialia: Macropodidae) in the Tanami Desert, N.T. III. Interactions with introduced mammal species. *Wildlife Research* 20, 495-511. / Short, J., and Turner, B. (1992). The distribution and abundance of the Banded and Rufous Hare-wallabies. *Biological Conservation* 60, 157-166. / Short, J., Bradshaw, S.D., Prince, R.I.T., and Wilson, G.R. (1992). Reintroduction of macropods (Marsupialia: Macropodidae) in Australia - a review. *Biological Conservation* 62, 189-204.

Illustration by J.Gould (courtesy of Museum Victoria)

Crescent nailtail wallaby
Onychogalea lunata

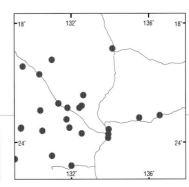

Known locations
of the crescent
nailtail wallaby
● = pre 1970
● = post 1970

CONSERVATION STATUS
AUSTRALIA: **EXTINCT**
NORTHERN TERRITORY: **EXTINCT**

DESCRIPTION

The crescent nailtail wallaby was a medium-sized macropod (body mass up to 3.5 kg), of attractive appearance. The upperparts were ash-grey with a rufous wash on the shoulders and across onto the flanks. A distinct white crescent spread from the shoulder blades down to the chest, with another white patch along the thigh.

DISTRIBUTION

The crescent nailtail wallaby formerly occupied a large area of central Australia that included the Northern Territory, South Australia and Western Australia. The species was relatively common in the late 19th century.

Conservation reserves where reported:
None (although it formerly occurred in areas that are now included within West MacDonnell National Park (Gibson and Cole 1996) and probably Watarrka and Uluru – Kata Tjuta National Parks).

ECOLOGY

The biology of the crescent nailtail wallaby is poorly known. It occupied woodland and shrublands, especially those dominated by mulga, and ate grass. During the day, it sheltered below trees and shrubs (Burbidge *et al.* 1988).

CONSERVATION ASSESSMENT

The crescent nailtail wallaby is presumed to have become **Extinct** in the Northern Territory in the 1960s, following a broad-scale decline extending over at least the previous 50 years (Finlayson 1961; Burbidge *et al.* 1988).

THREATENING PROCESSES

The decline and extinction of the crescent nailtail walaby was probably due to a range of factors including predation by cats and foxes, and habitat alteration due to the impacts of exotic herbivores and to changed fire regimes.

CONSERVATION OBJECTIVES AND MANAGEMENT

The species is presumed extinct. No conservation management plan can offer further help.

Compiled by Chris Pavey [May 2006] / **References:** Burbidge, A.A., Johnson, K.A., Fuller, P.F., and Southgate, R.I. (1988). Aboriginal knowledge of animals of the central deserts of Australia. *Australian Wildlife Research* 15, 9-39. / Finlayson, H.H. (1961). On central Australian mammals, Part IV. The distribution and status of central Australian species. *Records of the South Australian Museum* 41, 141-191. / Gibson, D.F., and Cole, J.R. (1996). Mammals of the MacDonnell Ranges area: 1894 to 1994. In *Exploring Central Australia: society, the environment and the 1894 Horn Expedition* (eds S.R. Morton and D.J. Mulvaney.) pp. 305-321. (Surrey Beatty and Sons, Sydney.) / Parker, S.A. (1973). An annotated checklist of the native land mammals of the Northern Territory. *Records of the South Australian Museum* 16, 1-57.

Black-footed rock-wallaby
Petrogale lateralis

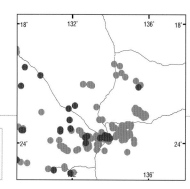

Known locations of the black-footed rock-wallaby
● = *pre 1970*
● = *post 1970*

DESCRIPTION

The black-footed rock-wallaby is a moderately-sized macropod with a body mass of 2.8 to 4.5 kg. As in other rock-wallabies, the tail (mean length of 56 cm) is longer than the head-body (mean length of 49 cm).

Northern Territory animals belong to a currently undescribed subspecies. A dense coat of dark grizzled brown fur passing to grey on the shoulders distinguishes this subspecies. The chest is grey, and the belly buff. The face is marked by a sandy cheek stripe. A dark brown to black dorsal stripe extends from between the ears to behind the shoulders. The feet are grey brown and the digits are black. The forearms are sandy dorsally and darker ventrally and the paws are dark brown to black. A distinct white stripe with wider dark brown stripe immediately ventral extends from the axillary patch to the thighs. The tail is dark grey at base and ends in a dark brown to black brush.

DISTRIBUTION

The distribution of this subspecies is centred on the MacDonnell Ranges. Its range extends north to the Davenport and Murchison Ranges, east to the Jervois Range, west to the Gibson Desert in Western Australia, and south to the Anangu-Pitjatjantjara lands of northern South Australia. (Eldrige *et al.* 1992; Pearson 1992)

Other subspecies of black-footed rock-wallabies occur in Western Australia, and islands off the coast of South Australia (Eldridge and Close 1995).

Conservation reserves where reported:
Alice Springs Telegraph Station Historical Reserve, Arltunga Historical Reserve, Davenport Range National Park, Emily and Jessie Gap Nature Park, Finke Gorge National Park, Kuyunba Conservation Reserve, Ruby Gap Nature Park, Trephina Gorge Nature Park, Watarrka National Park, West MacDonnell National Park.

ECOLOGY

Black-footed rock-wallabies occur in rocky outcrops and associated steep rocky slopes. They feed on grass, but some herbs, leaves and fruits are also eaten (Eldridge and Close 1995). Though occasionally drinking when water is present they can survive without water. Water requirements are reduced by sheltering during the day in caves and under boulders where relative humidity is higher and air temperatures cooler. They usually emerge in the late afternoon or early evening to feed. After a cold night, animals may bask in the sun during the early morning.

Breeding is potentially continuous but may be influenced by seasonal factors. Embryonic diapause is a feature of reproduction.

CONSERVATION ASSESSMENT

In southern parts of its range this wallaby has declined in density and distribution or become locally extinct. However, with the exception of recent extinctions at the Granites (Tanami Desert) and at Uluru – Kata Tjuta National Park, its population size and distribution has remained stable in the Northern Territory (Gibson 2000).

The extent of occurrence within the Northern Territory is estimated at 37 000 km² (Gibson 2000).

Although the species has disappeared from 21 of 400 sites surveyed in the Territory, most of these sites were small, isolated hills that supported small populations (Gibson 2000). Based on this information the black-footed rock-wallaby qualifies as **Near Threatened** in the Northern Territory.

THREATENING PROCESSES

Major threats faced by isolated populations in Western Australia and South Australia and parts of the Northern Territory include predation by introduced (European fox, feral cat) and native (wedge-tailed eagle) predators, and habitat degradation caused by grazing by introduced herbivores. Evidence from studies on rock-wallabies elsewhere strongly supports the contention that foxes have played a major role in the decline of the species.

CONSERVATION OBJECTIVES AND MANAGEMENT

There is no existing management program for the species in the Northern Territory. A national recovery plan for five species of rock-wallaby, including the black-footed rock-wallaby, is currently being prepared. Management priorities in the Northern Territory are to:

• continue to monitor key populations of the species; and
• protect key populations by carrying out fox and feral cat control where populations appear threatened by predation.

Compiled by Chris Pavey [May 2006] / **References:** Eldridge, M.D.B., and Close, R.L. (1995). Black-footed Rock-wallaby *Petrogale lateralis*. In *The Mammals of Australia*. 2nd Edition (ed. R. Strahan.) pp. 377-381. (Reed Books, Sydney.) / Eldridge M.D.B., Bell J.N., Pearson D.J., and Close R.L. (1992). Identification of rock-wallabies in the Warburton Region of Western Australia as *Petrogale lateralis* MacDonnell ranges race. *Australian Mammalogy* 15, 115-119. / Gibson. D.F. (2000). Distribution and conservation status of the Black-footed Rock-wallaby, *Petrogale lateralis* (MacDonnell Ranges race), in the Northern Territory. *Australian Mammalogy* 21, 213-236. / Pearson D. (1992). Distribution and abundance of the Black-footed Rock-wallaby in the Warburton region of Western Australia. *Wildlife Research* 19, 605-622.

Common brushtail possum
(central Australian population)
Trichosurus vulpecula vulpecula

Known locations of the central
Australian common brushtail
possum
● = pre 1970
● = post 1970

DESCRIPTION

The common brushtail possum is a medium-sized mammal (body mass of 1.3 to 3 kg) about the size of a domestic cat. It has large, prominent ears that have a narrowly round tip and are longer than they are broad. The bushy tail is slightly shorter than the head-body length.

DISTRIBUTION

Two subspecies of common brushtail possum occur in the Northern Territory. The subspecies *T. v. vulpecula*, occurs in isolated populations in the south of the Northern Territory. It formerly had a much more extensive distribution that included most of the Tanami and Great Sandy deserts across to the Western Australian border at Lake Mackay and Kintore, south to Charlotte Waters, east to the Todd and Hale River floodouts in the Simpson Desert, and as far north as the Murchison Ranges. Outside the Northern Territory, this subspecies occurred across much of the continent, including South Australia, Victoria, New South Wales, southern and south-western Queensland and much of Western Australia. It remains common in much of this area, including urban areas of most capital cities.

The subspecies *T. v. arnhemensis* occurs in the monsoon tropics of the Top End of the Northern Territory and in the Kimberley, Western Australia. It remains locally common (notably in some Darwin suburbs), but is generally declining (Woinarski 2005).

Other subspecies of the common brushtail possum occur in Tasmania, and north-eastern Queensland; and introduced populations abound in New Zealand.

Conservation reserves where reported:
Ruby Gap Nature Park, West MacDonnell National Park (although its status at Ruby Gap is uncertain). It formerly occurred at Uluru – Kata Tjuta National Park.

ECOLOGY

In central Australia, the common brushtail possum now occupies riverine habitat that is close to rocky outcrops and moist gullies within the ranges or rocky slopes (Kerle *et al.* 1992). This habitat occurs on various geological substrates but is characterised by a diverse association of fire-sensitive plant species. Its former habitats in central Australia included river systems supporting large eucalypts, coolibah claypans and spinifex grasslands with a shrubby overstorey (Burbidge *et al.* 1988).

A range of sites is used as day-time shelter, including caves and rock holes, tree hollows and the tops of dense trees. The diet consists of the flowers, fruits and leaves of a wide range of non-eucalypt species (Evans 1986).

CONSERVATION ASSESSMENT

In central Australia, the brushtail possum was widespread and common prior to and during the first few decades of European settlement. However, it subsequently underwent a dramatic decline in both numbers and range between the 1920s and 1950s (Finlayson 1961; Burbidge *et al.* 1988). Although the most extreme phase of the decline had occurred by the early 1940s, local extinctions continued until the last decade, with possums disappearing from Uluru – Kata Tjuta National Park, and Alcoota and The Gardens Stations during the 1980s (Kerle *et al.* 1992). Although West MacDonnell National Park is a stronghold for the species, there is no information available on actual population size. The bulk of the population may occur at rarely visited sites in the ranges with records of scats and sign at sites such as Ormiston Creek and Roma Gorge being produced by animals possibly dispersing from these core areas.

The decline in the common brushtail possum in central Australia occurred earlier than relevant to IUCN criteria (i.e. within the last 10 years or three generations). However, the subspecies *T. v. vulpecula* still qualifies as **Endangered** in the Northern Territory (under criteria B1ab(i)+2ab(i)) based on:
• extent of occurrence less than 5000 km^2;
• area of occupancy less than 500 km^2;

continued.../

- severely fragmented; and
- a continuing decline in extent of occurrence.

THREATENING PROCESSES

The decline of the common brushtail possum in central Australia has been attributed to the interaction between severe drought and a suite of potential threatening processes. These factors include habitat homogenization as a result of grazing by introduced herbivores (cattle and rabbits), increased hunting around Aboriginal settlements and (historically) for the commercial fur trade, altered fire regimes, and predation by the introduced fox and cat (Kerle *et al.* 1992; Woinarski 2004). One or more of these threatening processes is proposed to have severely reduced possum populations that had retracted to high quality refuge areas during the droughts of the 1920s and 1950s, leading to local extinctions.

CONSERVATION OBJECTIVES AND MANAGEMENT

There is no existing management program for wild populations of this species in the Northern Territory. Research priorities for the central Australian subspecies are to determine the extent of the distribution of the population in the West MacDonnell National Park.

Management priorities for the central Australian subspecies are to:
- monitor the occurrence of the species in core areas of the West MacDonnell National Park;
- undertake predator control measures if predation is shown to affect populations within conservation reserves; and
- assess the possibility of establishing a captive breeding population, and translocation options (e.g. Foulkes and Kerle 1990).

Compiled by Chris Pavey [May 2006] / **References:** Burbidge, A.A., Johnson, K.A., Fuller, P.J., and Southgate, R.I. (1988). Aboriginal knowledge of the mammals of the central deserts of Australia. *Australian Wildlife Research* 15, 9-39. / Evans, M.C. (1986). *The Diet of the Brushtail Possum in Central Australia*. Bachelor of Natural Resources thesis. (University of New England, Armidale.) / Finlayson, H.H. (1961). On central Australian mammals, Part IV. The distribution and status of central Australian species. *Records of the South Australian Museum* 41, 141-191. / Foulkes, J.N., and Kerle, J.A. (1990). *Feasibility Study for the Reintroduction of the Brushtail Possum to Uluru National Park*. Report to the Australian National Parks and Wildlife Service. / Kerle, J.A., Foulkes, J.N., Kimber, R.G., and Papenfus, D. (1992). The decline of the brushtail possum, *Trichosurus vulpecula* (Kerr 1798), in arid Australia. *Rangelands Journal* 14, 107-127. / Woinarski, J.C.Z. (2004). In a land with few possums, even the common are rare: ecology, conservation and management of possums in the Northern Territory. In *The biology of Australian possums and gliding possums* (eds R. Goldingay and S. Jackson). pp.51-62 (Surrey Beatty & Sons, Sydney.)

Bare-rumped sheathtail bat
Saccolaimus saccolaimus

CONSERVATION STATUS
AUSTRALIA: **CRITICALLY ENDANGERED**
NORTHERN TERRITORY: **DATA DEFICIENT**

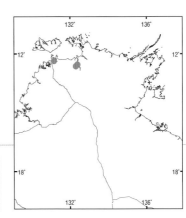

Known locations of the bare-rumped sheathtail bat
● = *pre 1970*
● = *post 1970*

DESCRIPTION

The bare-rumped sheathtail bat is a large (50 g) insectivorous bat. As with other sheathtail bats, the tip of the tail is free of the tail membrane. The fur is dark red-brown to almost black, with variably distinct white speckles, and this fur doesn't extend to the rump.

DISTRIBUTION

This species has a wide distribution from India through south-eastern Asia to the Solomon Islands, and including north-eastern Queensland and the Northern Territory. The north-eastern Australian populations are described as the subspecies *S. s. nudicluniatus*, although it is not clear whether this should be applied to the Northern Territory population (Duncan *et al.* 1999).

It was first recorded in the Northern Territory in 1979, and there have been very few records since (McKean *et al.* 1981; Thomson 1991). The confirmed records have been from the Kakadu lowlands and near Darwin (Humpty Doo and Berry Springs). McKean *et al.* (1981) asserted that it was likely to be more widespread in the Top End, but the very few records since, despite substantial survey work on microchiropteran bats (e.g. Milne *et al.* 2003, 2004), suggest that this may not be the case.

Conservation reserves where reported:
Kakadu National Park

ECOLOGY

This is a high-flying insectivorous bat. Specimens have been collected from open pandanus woodland fringing the sedgelands of the South Alligator River in Kakudu National Park (Friend and Braithwaite 1986). In the Northern Territory, it has also been recorded from eucalypt tall open forests (Churchill 1998). In Queensland, it is known mainly from coastal lowlands, including eucalypt woodlands and rainforests (Duncan *et al.* 1999). It roosts in tree hollows and caves (Duncan *et al.* 1999). More than 30 individual bats (including many non-flying young) were reported as escaping a roost in a large hollow tree following its fall, near Humpty Doo.

CONSERVATION ASSESSMENT

The national assessment of Critically Endangered was based on the apparent absence of recent records from its relatively small known historic range in north-eastern Queensland, associated with substantial vegetation clearance there.

Its status in the Northern Territory is very difficult to assign, given the remarkably few records. One problem is that there is no record of a diagnostic call assigned to this species that can be used for detection (Duncan *et al.* 1999).

In the Northern Territory, there is no information from which to consider trends in status, and no obvious threatening process. While the known range is currently very limited, this largely may reflect sampling problems. Given this lack of critical information, the taxon is best considered **Data Deficient.**

THREATENING PROCESSES

There are no obvious threatening processes. Hollow availability may be reduced by increasing levels of clearing in the Darwin – Mary River area, but this will not affect populations within Kakadu National Park.

Vegetation change associated with saltwater intrusion and/or invasion by exotic species (such as *Mimosa pigra*) may affect habitat suitability.

CONSERVATION OBJECTIVES AND MANAGEMENT

Research priorities are to:
• undertake a targeted study to better define habitat, distribution, population size, and status, and to develop more effective detection techniques; and
• resolve the taxonomic status of the Northern Territory population relative to that in north-eastern Queensland.

Compiled by Damian Milne, John Woinarski [May 2006] / **References:** Churchill, S. (1998). *Australian Bats*. (Reed New Holland, Sydney.) / Duncan, A., Baker, G.B., and Montgomery, N. (eds) (1999). *The Action Plan for Australian Bats*. (Environment Australia, Canberra.) / Friend, G.R., and Braithwaite, R.W. (1986). Bat fauna of Kakadu National Park, Northern Territory. *Australian Mammalogy* 9, 43-52. McKean, J.L., Friend, G., and Hertog, A.L. (1981). Occurrence of the sheath-tailed bat *Taphozous saccolaimus* in the Northern Territory. *Northern Territory Naturalist* 4, 20. / Milne, D.J., Reardon, T.B., and Watt, F. (2003). New records for the Arnhem sheathtail bat *Taphozous kapalgensis* (Chiroptera: Emballonuridae) from voucher specimens and Anabat recordings. *Australian Zoologist* 32, 439-445. / Milne, D.J., Armstrong, M., Fisher, A., Flores, T., and Pavey, C.R. (2004). A comparison of three survey methods for collecting bat echolocation calls and species-accumulation rates from nightly Anabat recordings. *Wildlife Research* 31, 57-63. / Thomson, B.G. (1991). *A Field Guide to Bats of the Northern Territory*. (Conservation Commission of the Northern Territory, Darwin.)

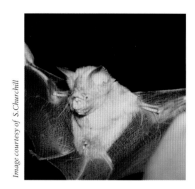
Image courtesy of S.Churchill

Arnhem leaf-nosed bat
Hipposideros (diadema) inornata

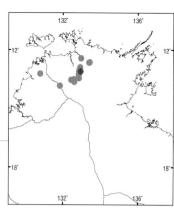

Known locations of the Arnhem leaf-nosed bat
● = pre 1970
● = post 1970

CONSERVATION STATUS
AUSTRALIA: **NOT LISTED**
NORTHERN TERRITORY: **VULNERABLE**

DESCRIPTION

The Arnhem leaf-nosed bat is a moderately large (30 g) insectivorous bat. It is pale brown above and slightly paler on the belly. It has large, acutely pointed ears and a very well-developed nose-leaf. There are no similar species in the Northern Territory.

This bat is currently considered to be a very distinctive subspecies of a variable (polymorphic) species that ranges from the Asian mainland through to the Solomon Islands, and includes a larger subspecies *H. d. reginae* from north-eastern Queensland. However, its taxonomic status is under revision and the Northern Territory population may be sufficiently distinctive to warrant elevation to species rank.

DISTRIBUTION

The Arnhem leaf-nosed bat was first reported as recently as 1969 (McKean 1970) and has been recorded only from a few locations in the western Arnhem Land sandstone massif (Deaf Adder Gorge and upper South Alligator River area) and from one site (Tolmer Falls) in Litchfield National Park (McKean and Hertog 1979).

Conservation reserves where reported:
Kakadu National Park, Litchfield National Park (however, it has not been recorded from Litchfield since 1983: Churchill 1998).

ECOLOGY

This bat roosts in caves or abandoned mine adits in cool drafty areas, close to water (Churchill 1998; Corbett and Richards 2002). Little is known of its foraging habitat or diet, but it has been reported foraging in riparian areas and in eucalypt tall open forests. Its diet includes beetles, moths, cockroaches and leaf-hoppers.

CONSERVATION ASSESSMENT

This bat appears to have a very restricted distribution (although large areas of the rugged western Arnhem Land escarpment have not been sampled), fairly narrow habitat (roost-site) requirements, is probably highly sensitive to disturbance, and has probably disappeared from one of its few known sites over the last two decades.

The species fits **Vulnerable** (under criteria B2ab(i,ii,iii,iv,v)) based on:
- an area of occupancy estimated to be less than 2000 km²;
- severely fragmented or known to exist at no more than 10 locations; and
- a continuing decline, observed, inferred or projected.

THREATENING PROCESSES

The disappearance of the population at Litchfield National Park may have been due to disturbance from humans visiting roosting caves (Corbett and Richards 2001). At this site, this threat has now been ameliorated. The known sites in western Arnhem Land are generally remote and very rarely visited.

CONSERVATION OBJECTIVES AND MANAGEMENT

Research priorities are to:
- survey to determine whether this bat still occurs within Litchfield National Park; and
- undertake a specific study that aims to better determine the species' distribution, abundance, habitat requirements and threats.

Management priorities are to:
- maintain controls over visitation to sites known to be used for roosting and breeding. Such controls are currently in place in both National Parks from which it is known; and
- establish a non-intrusive monitoring program in at least one site.

Compiled by John Woinarski, Damian Milne [May 2006] / **References:** Churchill, S. (1998). *Australian Bats.* (Reed New Holland, Sydney.) / Corbett, L., and Richards, G. (2002). *Bat survey: Gunlom land trust area.* Report to Parks Australia North. (EWL Sciences, Darwin.) / Duncan, A., Baker, G.B., and Montgomery, N. (eds) (1999). *The Action Plan for Australian Bats.* (Environment Australia, Canberra.) McKean, J.L. (1970). A new subspecies of the horseshoe bat *Hipposideros diadema* from the Northern Territory, Australia. *Western Australian Naturalist* 11, 138-140. / McKean, J.L., and Hertog, A.L. (1979). Extension of range in the horseshoe bat. *Northern Territory Naturalist* 1, 5.

Image courtesy of Kym Brennan

Brush-tailed rabbit-rat, Brush-tailed tree-rat
Conilurus penicillatus

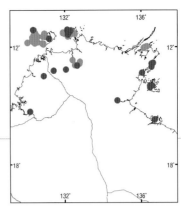

Known locations
of the brush-
tailed rabbit-rat
● = pre 1970
● = post 1970

CONSERVATION STATUS
AUSTRALIA: **NOT LISTED**
NORTHERN TERRITORY: **VULNERABLE**

DESCRIPTION

The brush-tailed rabbit-rat is a moderately large (about 150 g) partly-arboreal rat, with long brush-tipped tail (with the distal third either black or white), and long ears. The fur colour is relatively uniformly brown above, and cream below. It is distinctly smaller than the two other long-tailed tree-rats in the Northern Territory.

DISTRIBUTION

In the Northern Territory, this species has been recorded from near-coastal areas from near the mouth of the Victoria River in the west to the Pellew Islands in the east, and including Bathurst, Melville, Inglis and Centre islands and Groote Eylandt (Parker 1973; Kemper and Schmitt 1992; Woinarski 2000). There are no recent records from much of this historically recorded range, and it is currently known to persist in the Northern Territory only on Cobourg Peninsula, Bathurst, Melville, and Inglis islands, Groote Eylandt, and a small area within Kakadu National Park. Two weakly-defined subspecies are recognised from the Northern Territory: *C. p. melibius* from the Tiwi Islands, and *C. p. penicillatus* from all other Australian areas (Kemper and Schmitt 1992).

Beyond the Northern Territory, the species also occurs from a small area of higher rainfall, near-coastal north Kimberley (Western Australia), Bentinck Island (Queensland) and a small area of southern New Guinea.

Conservation reserves where reported:
Garig Gunak Barlu National Park, Kakadu National Park, Anindilyakwa Indigenous Protected Area.

ECOLOGY

The preferred habitat of the brush-tailed tree-rat is eucalypt tall open forest (Firth *et al.* 2006a). However, at least on Cobourg Peninsula, it also occurs on coastal grasslands (with scattered large *Casuarina equisetifolia* trees, beaches, and stunted eucalypt woodlands on stony slopes (Frith and Calaby 1974; PWCNT 2001).

It shelters in tree hollows, hollow logs and, less frequently, in the crowns of pandanus or sand-palms (Firth *et al.* 2006b). Most foraging is on the ground, but it is also partly arboreal. The diet comprises mainly seeds (especially of perennial grasses), with some fruits, invertebrates and leaves and grass (Firth *et al.* 2005).

CONSERVATION ASSESSMENT

Conservation assessment is hampered by lack of knowledge concerning the timing, extent and currency of geographic decline, and the lack of a comprehensive recent assessment of their status on Groote Eylandt and Centre Island. Relatively brief recent (2003-2005) surveys failed to re-locate the species on Centre Island (Taylor *et al.* 2004; S. Ward *pers. comm.*), but reported one individual on Groote Eylandt (D. Milne *pers. comm.*). Its range and population size in the Northern Territory has probably declined by well over 50% since European

settlement, but this decline cannot be dated with any assurance. Certainly, its current status no longer matches that reported more than 100 years ago: "in Arnhem Land is everywhere common in the vicinity of water" (Dahl 1897), "numerous all over Arnhem Land, and in great numbers on the rivers of the lowlands" (Collett 1897). It has declined substantially within the last 20 years at Kakadu National Park (Woinarski *et al.* 2001).

Current research will provide some assessment of the population size (or at least an index of abundance, whose assessment can be consistently repeated) on Bathurst and Melville islands, Cobourg Peninsula and Kakadu. A recent study (PWCNT 2001) found very high population density (to more than six individuals/ha) in at least two locations on Cobourg Peninsula.

Its status best fits **Vulnerable** (under the criteria B1ab(i,ii,iii,iv,v) based on:
- extent of occurrence estimated to be less than 20 000 km²;
- severely fragmented or known to exist at no more than 10 locations; and
- continuing decline, observed, inferred or projected.

Within this set, the estimate of extent is most arguable, as the islands where it is present are widely scattered. The total area of the islands known to be occupied is 11 813 km², and that of Cobourg Peninsula is 2207 km². Elsewhere on the Northern Territory mainland it is known to persist

continued.../

only in a small area (less than 20 km²) within Kakadu National Park.

The Tiwi Island subspecies *C. p. melibius* uneqivocally meets this set of criteria (with total extent of occurrence of about 8300 km²). The other subspecies *C. p. penicillatus* would meet the set of criteria B2ab(i,ii,iii,iv,v).

THREATENING PROCESSES

No single factor has been demonstrated to have caused the decline of brush-tailed tree-rats, but the extent of loss on the mainland and the maintenance of some island populations suggests that it is probably not due to land-use factors but rather to either disease or exotic predators. The most likely causal factor is predation by feral cats.

However, it is possible that broad-scale habitat change may have contributed to the apparent decline. Changed fire regimes, weeds and grazing by livestock and feral animals may have changed the availability of preferred or vital food resources (e.g. seeds or stems from particular grass species), and more frequent hot fires may have reduced the availability of hollow logs, tree hollows and the tall fruit-bearing understorey shrubs, and unfavourably changed the composition of grass species (Woinarski *et al.* 2004; Firth *et al.* 2005, 2006b).

The population on the Tiwi Islands has been substantially reduced (by an estimated 8 to 10% over the last five years) by recent clearing for forestry plantation of about 30 000 ha of its prime habitat (Firth *et al.* 2006a); and there are proposals to extend this forestry enterprise up to 100 000 ha.

CONSERVATION OBJECTIVES AND MANAGEMENT

There is no existing recovery plan or management program for this species.

In the interim, management priorities are to:
• maintain a monitoring program in at least two sites, which can also measure responses to management actions. The baseline for this monitoring has now been established, with recent studies on Cobourg Peninsula, the Tiwi Islands and in Kakadu National Park.
• work with Aboriginal landowners to maintain effective quarantine actions for island populations, most particularly relating to maintaining at least some of these islands cat-free.
• develop effective captive population breeding programs, and evaluate the possibility of establishing translocated populations (either to currently uninhabited islands or to appropriately managed conservation reserves). Such a program is currently being undertaken through the Territory Wildlife Park.
• ensure that habitat clearance for plantation forestry on the Tiwi Islands does not compromise population viability.

Compiled by John Woinarski [April 2007] / **References:** Collett, R. (1897). On a collection of mammals from North and North-west Australia. *Proceedings of the Zoological Society of London 1897*, 317-336. Dahl, K. (1897). Biological notes on north-Australian mammalia. *Zoologist,* Series 4, 1, 189-216. / Firth, R.S.C., Jefferys, E., Woinarski, J.C.Z., and Noske, R.A. (2005). The diet of the brush-tailed rabbit-rat *Conilurus penicillatus* from the monsoonal tropics of the Northern Territory, Australia. *Wildlife Research* 32, 517-524. / Firth, R.S.C., Woinarski, J.C.Z., Brennan, K.G., and Hempel, C. (2006a). Environmental relationships of the brush-tailed rabbit-rat *Conilurus penicillatus* and other small mammals on the Tiwi Islands, northern Australia. *Journal of Biogeography* 33, 1820-1837. / Firth, R.S.C., Woinarski, J.C.Z., and Noske, R.A. (2006b). Home range and den characteristics of the brush-tailed rabbit-rat *Conilurus penicillatus* in the monsoonal tropics of the Northern Territory, Australia. *Wildlife Research* 33, 397-408. / Frith, H.J., and Calaby, J.H. (1974). *Fauna survey of the Port Essington district, Cobourg Peninsula, Northern Territory of Australia.* Technical Paper no. 28. (CSIRO Wildlife Research, Canberra.) / Kemper, C.M., and Schmitt, L.H. (1992). Morphological variation between populations of the brush-tailed tree-rat (*Conilurus penicillatus*) in northern Australia and New Guinea. *Australian Journal of Zoology* 40, 437-452. / Parker, S.A. (1973). An annotated checklist of the native land mammals of the Northern Territory. *Records of the South Australian Museum* 16, 1-57. / PWCNT (2001). *Studies of the brush-tailed tree-rat* Conilurus penicillatus *in Gurig National Park.* (PWCNT, Darwin.) / Taylor, R., Woinarski, J., Charlie, A., Dixon, R., Pracy, D., and Rhind, S. (2004). *Report on mammal survey of the Pellew Islands 2003.* (Lianthawirriyarra Sea Ranger Unit, Department of Infrastructure, Planning and Environment, and Tropical Savannas CRC, Darwin.) / Woinarski, J.C.Z. (2000). The conservation status of rodents in the Top End of the Northern Territory. *Wildlife Research* 27, 421-435. / Woinarski, J.C.Z., Milne, D.J., and Wanganeen, G. (2001). Changes in mammal populations in relatively intact landscapes of Kakadu National Park, Northern Territory, Australia. *Austral Ecology* 26, 360-370. / Woinarski, J.C.Z., Armstrong, M., Price, O., McCartney, J., Griffiths, T., and Fisher, A. (2004). The terrestrial vertebrate fauna of Litchfield National Park, Northern Territory: monitoring over a 6-year period, and response to fire history. *Wildlife Research* 31, 1-10.

Illustration by J.Gould (courtesy of Museum Victoria)

Lesser stick-nest rat
Leporillus apicalis

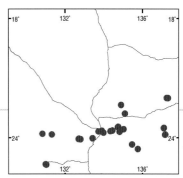

Known locations of the lesser stick-nest rat
● = pre 1970
● = post 1970

CONSERVATION STATUS
AUSTRALIA: **EXTINCT**
NORTHERN TERRITORY: **EXTINCT**

DESCRIPTION

The lesser stick-nest rat was a moderately-sized native rodent (body mass 60 g) that differed from its larger relative, the greater stick-nest rat, by the narrow brush of white hairs near the tip of its tail.

DISTRIBUTION

The last specimen of the lesser stick-nest rat was captured near Mt Crombie, south-west of the present Amata settlement, South Australia in 1933. However in the nineteenth century it occupied a broad swath of desert and semi-desert land stretching from the Riverina in New South Wales through most of inland South Australia and into the Gibson Desert, reaching the Western Australian coast in the Gascoyne region. In the Northern Territory, it occurred extensively across southern arid and semi-arid areas.

Conservation reserves where reported:
None (however it formerly occurred in areas that are now included within Uluru – Kata Tjuta National Park, Arltunga Historical Reserve, Trephina Gorge Nature Park, West MacDonnell National Park and Finke Gorge National Park: Parker 1973; Baynes and Johnson 1996).

ECOLOGY

The biology of the lesser stick-nest rat is poorly known. Its most notable feature was its construction of large, long-lasting nests of sticks, sometimes in the open, but often in caves and rock overhangs. Examination of such now-abandoned nests of this species is providing significant new information on environmental and climatic change in central Australia over a 2500-year time frame.

CONSERVATION ASSESSMENT

The lesser stick-nest rat is presumed to have become **Extinct** in the Northern Territory by the 1940s, following a broad-scale decline extending over at least the previous 30 years (Finlayson 1961; Burbidge *et al.* 1988; Cole and Woinarski 2000).

THREATENING PROCESSES

The decline and extinction of the lesser stick-nest rat was probably due to a range of factors including predation by cats and foxes, and habitat alteration due to the impacts of exotic herbivores and to changed fire regimes.

CONSERVATION OBJECTIVES AND MANAGEMENT

The species is presumed extinct. No conservation management plan can offer further help.

Compiled by Chris Pavey [May 2006] / **References:** Baynes, A., and Johnson, K.A. (1996). The contributions of the Horn Expedition and cave deposits to knowledge of the original mammal fauna of central Australia. In *Exploring Central Australia: Society, the Environment and the 1894 Horn Expedition* (eds S.R. Morton and D.J. Mulvaney.) pp. 168-186. (Surrey Beatty and Sons, Sydney.) / Burbidge, A.A., Johnson, K.A., Fuller, P.F., and Southgate, R.I. (1988). Aboriginal knowledge of animals of the central deserts of Australia. *Australian Wildlife Research* 15, 9-39. / Cole, J.R., and Woinarski, J.C.Z. (2000). Rodents of the arid Northern Territory: conservation status and distribution. *Wildlife Research* 27, 437-449. / Finlayson, H.H. (1961). On central Australian mammals, Part IV. The distribution and status of central Australian species. *Records of the South Australian Museum* 41, 141-191. / Parker, S.A. (1973). An annotated checklist of the native land mammals of the Northern Territory. *Records of the South Australian Museum* 16, 1-57.

Image courtesy of Ian Morris

Golden-backed tree-rat
Mesembriomys macrurus

CONSERVATION STATUS
AUSTRALIA: **VULNERABLE**
NORTHERN TERRITORY: **CRITICALLY ENDANGERED**

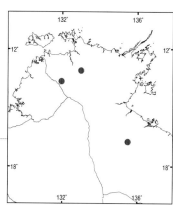

Known locations of the golden-backed tree-rat
● = pre 1970
● = post 1970

DESCRIPTION
The golden-backed tree-rat is a large rodent (about 300 g), mid-way in size between the Territory's other two semi-arboreal species, the smaller brush-tailed tree-rat and the larger black-footed tree-rat. Distinctive features include a long slightly brush-tipped tail that is white for at least the distal half, white feet, and a broad chestnut-gold stripe along the back from the crown to the base of tail.

DISTRIBUTION
In the Northern Territory, the golden-backed tree-rat is known from only three definite records (Parker 1973): at "Balanbrinni" (probably Balbarini) in the catchment of the upper McArthur River in 1901; from Nellie Creek (in the catchment of the upper Mary River) in 1903; and from Deaf Adder Gorge in 1969. The species has not been confirmed elsewhere despite many large surveys across much of the Top End over the last 30 years. These surveys have included some limited sampling at the Deaf Adder Gorge site (C. Palmer *pers. comm.*), and sampling in the general vicinity of the other two sites.

There have been several unconfirmed records based on possible sightings and hair samples (Woinarski 2000), but these remain unconfirmed and in at least some cases unlikely. Recent collation of some Indigenous knowledge of this species has indicated persistence in at least one site in the Arnhem Land plateau (M. Ziembicki *pers. comm.*).

Beyond the Northern Territory, it occurs in some coastal areas of the north Kimberley, and five offshore islands there (Abbott and Burbidge 1995; Palmer *et al.* 2003). Its range has declined substantially in Western Australia. It appears to have become regionally extinct from the Pilbara, and in at least the more arid southern margins of the Kimberley (McKenzie 1981). For example, Dahl (1897) reported that "the houses of settlers (around Broome) are always tennanted by (this species)", but it has not been reported from there subsequently.

Conservation reserves where reported:
Kakadu National Park

ECOLOGY
There is very little known of the ecology of this species. The only information from the Northern Territory is that all three records were from riverine vegetation. In the Kimberley, it has been recorded from a broad range of vegetation types, including eucalypt open forests with tussock grass understorey, rainforest patches on a variety of landforms and soils, eucalypt woodlands with hummock grass understorey, rugged sandstone screes, beaches, and blacksoil plains with pandanus. It roosts in tree hollows or, less commonly, in loosely woven nests under the spiky crown of pandanus. Its diet includes seeds, fruits, invertebrates, grass and leaves, and it forages both on the ground and in trees (Palmer *et al.* 2003).

CONSERVATION ASSESSMENT
The remarkably few records from the Northern Territory provide a poor base for assessing status. A decline can be inferred based on the lack of recent records despite substantial survey effort, but it is not possible to say when the decline occurred, or if it is ongoing. The scarcity of historic records suggests that it was already rare in the Northern Territory at the onset of European settlement, or that it declined extremely rapidly thereafter. Historic and ongoing decline in the Northern Territory population and range can be reasonably inferred from the marked decline evident in the more substantial set of records from north Western Australia.

The Northern Territory status can be considered to be **Critically Endangered** (under criteria B2ab(i,iv,v); C2a(i)) based on:

- area of occupancy estimated to be less than 10 km²;
- population size estimated to number fewer than 250 mature individuals;
- severely fragmented or known to exist at no more than five locations;
- a continuing decline, observed, projected or inferred; and
- no subpopulation estimated to contain more than 50 mature individuals.

continued.../

THREATENING PROCESSES

No single factor has been demonstrated to have caused the decline of golden-backed tree-rats, but the extent of loss on the mainland and the maintenance of some island populations (in Western Australia) suggests that it is probably not due to land-use factors but rather to either disease or exotic predators. The most likely causal factor is predation by feral cats.

However, it is possible that broad-scale habitat change may have contributed to the apparent decline. Changed fire regimes, weeds and grazing by livestock and feral animals may have changed the availability of preferred or vital food resources (e.g. seeds from particular grass species), and more frequent hot fires may have reduced the availability of hollow logs, tree hollows and the tall fruit-bearing understorey shrubs.

CONSERVATION OBJECTIVES AND MANAGEMENT

A recently developed recovery plan (Palmer *et al.* 2003) describes research and management priorities for this species across its range; and its research and management priorities in Kakadu National Park are described in Woinarski (2004).

Research priorities include to:
• sample more systematically and intensively the three known locations to determine whether any of these populations have persisted, and to attempt to confirm its presence at the few other sites with recent unconfirmed records; and
• examine the ecology of the species at any sites where populations persist, and attempt to define limiting factors.

Until more information is known about the species in the Northern Territory, it is impossible to prescribe any specific management priorities.

Compiled by John Woinarski, Carol Palmer [May 2006] / **References:** Abbott, I., and Burbidge, A.A. (1995). The occurrence of mammal species on the islands of Australia: a summary of existing knowledge. *CALMScience* 1, 259-324. / Dahl, K. (1897). Biological notes on north-Australian mammalia. *Zoologist*, Series 4, 1, 189-216. / McKenzie, N.L. (1981). Mammals of the Phanerozoic South-west Kimberley, Western Australia: biogeography and recent changes. *Journal of Biogeography* 8, 263-280. / Palmer, C., Taylor, R., and Burbidge, A. (2003). Recovery plan for the Golden Bandicoot *Isoodon auratus* and golden-backed tree-rat *Mesembriomys macrurus* 2004-2009. (NT Department of Infrastructure Planning and Environment, Darwin.) / Parker, S.A. (1973). An annotated checklist of the native land mammals of the Northern Territory. *Records of the South Australian Museum* 16, 1-57. / Woinarski, J.C.Z. (2000). The conservation status of rodents in the Top End of the Northern Territory. *Wildlife Research* 27, 421-435. Woinarski, J. (2004). *Threatened plants and animals in Kakadu National Park: a review and recommendations for management.* Report to Parks Australia North. (Parks and Wildlife Commission of the Northern Territory, Darwin.)

Illustration by Frank Knight

Short-tailed hopping-mouse
Notomys amplus

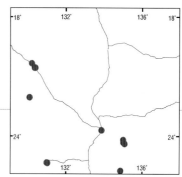

Known locations of the short-tailed hopping-mouse
● = *pre 1970*
● = *post 1970*

CONSERVATION STATUS
AUSTRALIA: **EXTINCT**
NORTHERN TERRITORY: **EXTINCT**

DESCRIPTION
The short-tailed hopping-mouse was the largest of the 10 species of hopping-mice recorded from Australia. At a mass of about 100 g, it was twice the weight of any of the species that still occur in arid Australia. This species was brown in colour with a tail length approximately the same as the head-body length.

DISTRIBUTION
The short-tailed hopping-mouse is known from two specimens collected at Charlotte Waters in the extreme south of the Northern Territory (Parker 1973) and from skeletal remains (probably several hundred years old) obtained from owl pellets at Uluru – Kata Tjuta National Park and in the Flinders Ranges, South Australia (Baynes and Johnson 1996). Information from Aboriginal residents of central Australia suggests a broader distribution in the central and western deserts.

Conservation reserves where reported:
None (although it formerly occurred in areas that are now included within Uluru – Kata Tjuta National Park).

ECOLOGY
The biology of the short-tailed hopping-mouse is unknown. It was probably a nocturnal, granivorous species.

CONSERVATION ASSESSMENT
The only specimens of the short-tailed hopping-mouse were obtained in 1896. It is presumed to have become **Extinct** not long afterwards (Finlayson 1961).

THREATENING PROCESSES
The decline and extinction of the short-tailed hopping-mouse is attributed to a range of factors including predation by cats and foxes, and habitat alteration due to the impacts of exotic herbivores and to changed fire regimes.

CONSERVATION OBJECTIVES AND MANAGEMENT
The species is presumed extinct. No conservation management plan can offer further help.

Compiled by Chris Pavey [May 2006] / **References:** Baynes, A., and Johnson, K.A. (1996). The contributions of the Horn Expedition and cave deposits to knowledge of the original mammal fauna of central Australia. In *Exploring Central Australia: Society, the Environment and the 1894 Horn Expedition* (eds S.R. Morton and D.J. Mulvaney.) pp. 168-186. (Surrey Beatty and Sons, Sydney.) / Finlayson, H.H. (1961). On central Australian mammals, Part IV. The distribution and status of central Australian species. *Records of the South Australian Museum* 41, 141-191. / Parker, S.A. (1973). An annotated checklist of the native land mammals of the Northern Territory. *Records of the South Australian Museum* 16, 1-57.

Image courtesy of S. Ward

Northern hopping-mouse
Notomys aquilo

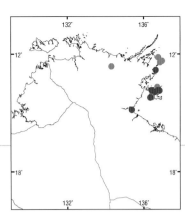

Known locations
of the northern
hopping-mouse
● = pre 1970
● = post 1970

CONSERVATION STATUS
AUSTRALIA: **VULNERABLE**
NORTHERN TERRITORY: **VULNERABLE**

DESCRIPTION

The northern hopping-mouse is a small (25 to 50 g) rodent of unmistakable appearance within its range. It has an extremely long tail (around 140 to 150% head-body length) tipped with a tuft of longer dark hairs, large ears and eyes, and very long (35 to 40 mm) narrow hind-feet. It is sandy-brown above and white below. It is the only hopping-mouse in the Top End of the Northern Territory. The spinifex hopping mouse *N. alexis* extends north to the Barkly Tableland, and is generally of similar morphology.

DISTRIBUTION

There are remarkably few documented records of the northern hopping-mouse (Woinarski *et al.* 1999; Woinarski 2004). In the Northern Territory, it is known from Groote Eylandt and coastal north-eastern Arnhem Land, with unvouchered records from a few hundred kilometres further south, west and inland; and one specimen from inland central Arnhem Land (Dixon and Huxley 1985; Woinarski *et al.* 1999). Beyond the Northern Territory, it has also been recorded from Cape York Peninsula (from only one specimen with an imprecise locality record from the last half of the nineteenth century).

Conservation reserves where reported: Anindilyakwa (Groote Eylandt) Indigenous Protected Area, Nanydjaka (Cape Arnhem) Indigenous Protected Area.

ECOLOGY

The northern hopping-mouse is largely restricted to sandy substrates, particularly those supporting floristically diverse heathlands and/or grasslands (Woinarski *et al.* 1999). It constructs elaborate communally-used burrow systems, whose vertical entrances may be obscured by a thin layer of sand (Johnson 1964; Dixon and Huxley 1985). It is active at night, and it forages entirely on the ground. Its diet comprises mainly seeds, but also some other vegetative material and invertebrates. The species appears to be trap-shy and may be most readily detected by its characteristic hopping tracks.

CONSERVATION ASSESSMENT

Conservation assessment is hampered by the lack of precise information on range, population size and trends, to such an extent that it may qualify best as Data Deficient. However, in the Northern Territory, it can be assigned the status of **Vulnerable** (under criteria B2ab) based on:
- area of occupancy estimated to be less than 2000 km²;
- severely fragmented or known to exist at no more than 10 locations; and
- continuing decline, observed, inferred or projected.

THREATENING PROCESSES

There is no detailed information on threatening processes. It is plausible that there are increased numbers of feral cats across much of its range, and that these are affecting population numbers. Fire regimes have changed across its range, notably to a higher incidence of extensive hot late dry season fires, with consequent reduction in floristic diversity. This may be to the detriment of this species, although such a link has not yet been established.

CONSERVATION OBJECTIVES AND MANAGEMENT PRIORITIES

A recovery plan for this species has been prepared recently (Woinarski 2004).

The main research priorities are to better define the distribution and status of this species and to assess the impacts of a range of putative threatening processes. Such information is needed before management prescriptions can be formulated appropriately.

A collaborative project between scientists of the Department of Natural Resources, Environment and The Arts and rangers from the Anindilyakwa Land Council commenced in 2006, supported by the Natural Heritage Trust, and aimed at improving knowledge of its status, and developing management and monitoring programs.

Compiled by John Woinarski [December 2006] / **References:** Dixon, J.M., and Huxley, L. (1985). *Donald Thomson's mammals and fishes of northern Australia.* (Nelson, Melbourne.) / Johnson, D.H. (1964). Mammals of the Arnhem Land expedition. In *Records of the American-Australian Scientific Expedition to Arnhem Land. Volume 4. Zoology.* (ed. R.L. Specht.) pp. 427-516. (Melbourne University Press, Melbourne.) / Woinarski, J.C.Z. (2004). *National multi-species Recovery Plan for the Carpentarian Antechinus Pseudantechinus mimulus, Butler's Dunnart Sminthopsis butleri and Northern Hopping-mouse Notomys aquilo, 2004-2008.* (NT Department of Infrastructure Planning and Environment, Darwin.) / Woinarski, J.C.Z., Gambold, N., Wurst, D., Flannery, T.F., Smith, A.P., Chatto, R., and Fisher, A. (1999). Distribution and habitat of the Northern Hopping Mouse *Notomys aquilo*. *Wildlife Research* 26, 495-511.

Image courtesy of P. Canty

Fawn hopping-mouse
Notomys cervinus

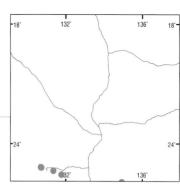

Known locations
of the fawn
hopping-mouse
● = pre 1970
● = post 1970

CONSERVATION STATUS
AUSTRALIA: **VULNERABLE**
NORTHERN TERRITORY: **ENDANGERED**

DESCRIPTION
The fawn hopping-mouse is a relatively large rodent (head-body length 95 to 120 mm, body mass 30 to 50 g). The tail (120 to 160 mm) is longer than the body and ends in a tuft of dark hairs. In contrast to the dusky hopping-mouse and spinifex hopping-mouse with which it may be confused, the fawn hopping-mouse does not have a throat pouch. Males may have a glandular area of naked or raised skin (2 to 3 mm across) on the chest between the forelimbs (Watts and Aslin 1981).

The upperbody colour varies among individuals and ranges from pale pinkish-fawn to grey. The belly is white. The ears are particularly long and the head broad and short. The eyes are very protuberant. Whiskers on the muzzle are extremely long (up to 65 mm).

DISTRIBUTION
This species is patchily distributed on gibber plains and claypans of the Lake Eyre Basin in north-east South Australia and south-west Queensland. In the Northern Territory, there are old records from gibber country near Charlotte Waters in 1895 (Baynes and Johnson 1996). More recent records are from Uluru – Kata Tjuta National Park (Great Sandy Desert bioregion) and Curtin Springs (Finke bioregion), although some authors (e.g. Reid *et al.* 1993) do not accept the Uluru records.

Conservation reserves where reported:
Uluru – Kata Tjuta National Park (unconfirmed)

ECOLOGY
The fawn hopping-mouse is a gibber-dwelling species. It lives in small family groups of two to four individuals. Burrows are up to one metre deep and have between one and three entrances.

The diet of the fawn hopping-mouse is primarily seeds, but it also eats green plant material and insects when they are seasonally available. Like other hopping mice it does not require free water, but can drink very salty water, excreting excess salt in concentrated urine and faeces.

Reproduction in this species appears to be opportunistic; breeding occurring when conditions are favourable. In captivity, gestation is between 38 and 43 days following which litters of one to five fully furred young are born (Watts 1995).

CONSERVATION ASSESSMENT
It is unclear whether the fawn hopping-mouse still occurs in the Northern Territory. No records were obtained during extensive trapping as part of the Finke bioregion survey (Neave *et al.* 2004) and intensive trapping at seven sites on Andado Station and at Mac Clark Conservation Reserve. These surveys were carried out during favourable climatic conditions that resulted in high populations of other rodents including the spinifex hopping-mouse.

Previous surveys in 1994 were located in suitable habitat for the species around Charlotte Waters (Eldridge and Reid 2000). The species is classified as **Endangered** in the Northern Territory (under criterion C2b) based on:
• population size estimated to number fewer than 2500 mature individuals;
• a continuing decline in numbers of mature individuals; and
• extreme fluctuations in number of mature individuals.

THREATENING PROCESSES
Threatening processes faced by the fawn hopping-mouse have not been identified. However, possible factors include habitat degradation, predation by introduced carnivores (cats and foxes), and competition with introduced herbivores (including cattle and rabbits).

CONSERVATION OBJECTIVES AND MANAGEMENT
There is no existing management program for the species in the Northern Territory.

Management priorities are to:
• implement targeted searches for the species in any future survey of the Stony Plains bioregion in the Northern Territory; and
• follow up any plausible sightings as soon as possible.

Compiled by Chris Pavey [May 2006] / **References:** Baynes, A., and Johnson, K.A. (1996). The contributions of the Horn Expedition and cave deposits to knowledge of the original mammal fauna of central Australia. In *Exploring Central Australia: Society, the Environment and the 1894 Horn Expedition.* (eds S.R. Morton and D.J. Mulvaney.) pp. 168-186. (Surrey Beatty and Sons, Sydney.) / Eldridge, S., and Reid, J. (2000). *A biological survey of the Finke floodout region, Northern Territory.* (Arid Lands Environment Centre, Alice Springs.) / Neave, H., Nano, C., Pavey, C., Moyses, M, Clifford, B., Cole, J., Harris, M., and Albrecht, D. (2004). *A Resource Assessment towards a Conservation Strategy for the Finke Bioregion, Northern Territory.* (NT Department of Infrastructure, Planning and Environment, Alice Springs.) / Reid, J. R. W., Kerle, J. A., and Baker, L. (1993). Mammals. *In Kowari 4: Uluru Fauna* (eds J.R.W. Reid, J.A. Kerle and S.R. Morton.) pp. 69-78. (Australian National Parks and Wildlife Service, Canberra.) / Watts, C.H.S. (1995). Fawn Hopping-mouse *Notomys cervinus.* In *The Australian Museum Complete Book of Australian Mammals.* (ed. R. Strahan.) pp. 574-575. (Angus and Robertson, Sydney.) / Watts, C.H.S., and Aslin, H.J. (1981). *The Rodents of Australia.* (Angus and Robertson, Sydney.)

Image courtesy of P.Canty

Dusky hopping-mouse
Notomys fuscus

CONSERVATION STATUS
AUSTRALIA: **VULNERABLE**
NORTHERN TERRITORY: **ENDANGERED**

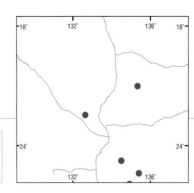

Known locations of the dusky hopping-mouse
● = *pre 1970*
● = *post 1970*

DESCRIPTION
The dusky hopping-mouse is characterised by its strong incisor teeth, long tail, large ears, dark eyes, and extremely lengthened and narrow hind-feet, which have only four pads on the sole. The head-body length is 91 to 177 mm, tail length is 125 to 225 mm, and body weight is from 20 to 50 g. Coloration of the upper parts varies from pale sandy-brown to yellowish-brown to ashy-brown or greyish. The underparts of dusky hopping-mice are white. The fur is fine, close and soft. Long hairs near the tip of the tail give the effect of a brush. The dusky hopping-mouse has a well-developed glandular area on the underside of its neck or chest. Females have four nipples.

DISTRIBUTION
The current distribution of the dusky hopping-mouse appears to be restricted to the eastern Lake Eyre Basin within the Simpson-Strzelecki Dunefields bioregion in South Australia and Queensland. An intensive survey in the 1990s located populations at eight locations in the Strzelecki Desert and adjacent Cobbler Sandhills (South Australia) and in south-west Queensland (Moseby *et al.* 1999). The species was formerly found across a much wider range that stretched as far west as Ooldea in South Australia and east to the Victoria-New South Wales border.

The species has not been recorded in the Northern Territory since 1939 when it was collected in sand dunes on Maryvale Station and on Andado Station.

Conservation reserves where reported: None

ECOLOGY
The dusky hopping-mouse occupies a variety of sandy environments that are characterised by the presence of consolidated dunes and perennial vegetation (Moseby *et al.* 1999). Most sites are close to lakes or drainage lines, and these are the only locations where relatively dense populations are known.

Little is known of the breeding biology of this species in the wild other than that it is an opportunistic breeder. In captivity, its breeding pattern is polyestrous, with no evidence of seasonality; thus it breeds throughout the year. Both sexes reach reproductive maturity at 70 days.

CONSERVATION ASSESSMENT
It is unclear whether the dusky hopping-mouse still occurs in the Northern Territory. No records were obtained during extensive trapping as part of the Finke bioregion survey (which included Maryvale Station) (Neave *et al.* 2004) and recent intensive trapping at sites on Andado Station and at Mac Clark Conservation Reserve. These surveys were carried out during favourable climatic conditions that resulted in unusually high population densities of other rodents, but did not specifically target the sandy habitat occupied by the dusky hopping-mouse. A large amount of suitable habitat in the Northern Territory in particular, the area around Charlotte Waters has not been surveyed.

Hence its continued presence in the Northern Territory remains uncertain. The species is classified as **Endangered** in the Northern Territory (under criterion C2b) based on:
- population size estimated to number fewer than 2500 mature individuals;
- a continuing decline in numbers of mature individuals; and
- extreme fluctuations in number of mature individuals.

THREATENING PROCESSES
Factors that caused the species' decline have not been positively identified but are likely to include habitat degradation and predation by introduced carnivores (cats and foxes).

CONSERVATION OBJECTIVES AND MANAGEMENT
There is no existing management program for the species in the Northern Territory.

Research priorities are to:
- undertake targeted searches for the species in the Stony Plains bioregion in the Northern Territory; and
- follow up any plausible sightings as soon as possible.

Compiled by Chris Pavey [May 2006] / **References:** Finlayson, H.M. (1939). On mammals from the Lake Eyre Basin, Part IV. The Monodelphia. *Transactions of the Royal Society of South Australia* 63, 354-364. Lee, A. K. (1995). *The Action Plan for Australian Rodents*. (ANCA, Canberra.) / Moseby, K.E., Brandle, R., and Adams, M. (1999). Distribution, habitat and conservation status of the rare dusky hopping-mouse, *Notomys fuscus* (Rodentia: Muridae). *Wildlife Research* 26, 479-494. / Neave, H., Nano, C., Pavey, C., Moyses, M, Clifford, B., Cole, J., Harris, M., and Albrecht, D. (2004). *A Resource Assessment towards a Conservation Strategy for the Finke Bioregion, Northern Territory*. (NT Department of Infrastructure, Planning and Environment, Alice Springs.) / Watts, C.H.S., and Aslin, H.J. (1981). *The Rodents of Australia*. (Angus and Robertson, Sydney.)

Illustration by J.Gould (courtesy of Museum Victoria)

Long-tailed hopping-mouse
Notomys longicaudatus

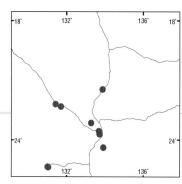

Known locations
of the long-tailed
hopping-mouse
● = *pre 1970*
● = *post 1970*

CONSERVATION STATUS
AUSTRALIA: **EXTINCT**
NORTHERN TERRITORY: **EXTINCT**

DESCRIPTION
The long-tailed hopping-mouse was a relatively large hopping-mouse (about 100 g), with an extremely long tail. It had a large neck gland (Watts and Aslin 1981).

DISTRIBUTION
The species was recorded at several sites in arid and semi-arid regions from Western Australia across into north-west New South Wales. Northern Territory records consist of specimens from the Burt Plain and Barrow Creek and skeletal remains obtained from owl pellets at the Granites (Tanami Desert) and at Uluru – Kata Tjuta National Park.

Conservation reserves where reported:
None (although it formerly occurred in areas that are now included within Uluru – Kata Tjuta National Park, Watarrka National Park and West MacDonnell National Park: Reid *et al.* 1993; Baynes and Johnson 1996).

ECOLOGY
The biology of the long-tailed hopping-mouse is largely unknown. It favoured heavier (clay) soils (Gould 1863).

CONSERVATION ASSESSMENT
The last specimen of the long-tailed hopping-mouse was obtained in 1901–02, when a large series was collected from Barrow Creek (Parker 1973). It is presumed to have become **Extinct** within a few subsequent decades.

THREATENING PROCESSES
The decline and extinction of the long-tailed hopping-mouse was probably due to a range of factors including predation by cats and foxes, and habitat alteration due to the impacts of exotic herbivores and to changed fire regimes.

CONSERVATION OBJECTIVES AND MANAGEMENT
The species is presumed extinct. No conservation management plan can offer further help.

Compiled by Chris Pavey [May 2006] / **References:** Baynes, A., and Johnson, K.A. (1996). The contributions of the Horn Expedition and cave deposits to knowledge of the original mammal fauna of central Australia. In *Exploring Central Australia: Society, the Environment and the 1894 Horn Expedition.* (eds S.R. Morton and D.J. Mulvaney.) pp. 168-186. (Surrey Beatty and Sons, Sydney.) / Gould, J. (1863). *The mammals of Australia. Vol. 3.* (The author, London.) / Parker, S.A. (1973). An annotated checklist of the native land mammals of the Northern Territory. *Records of the South Australian Museum* 16, 1-57. / Reid, J. R. W., Kerle, J. A., and Baker, L. (1993). Mammals. In *Kowari 4: Uluru Fauna* (eds J.R.W. Reid, J.A. Kerle and S.R. Morton.) pp. 69-78. (Australian National Parks and Wildlife Service, Canberra.) / Watts, C.H.S., and Aslin, H.J. (1981). *The Rodents of Australia.* (Angus and Robertson, Sydney.)

Image courtesy of P. Canty

Plains rat
Pseudomys australis

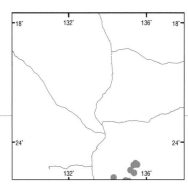

*Known locations
of the plains rat*
● = *pre 1970*
● = *post 1970*

DESCRIPTION

The plains rat is a moderately-sized rodent, with a stocky build, rounded snout and long ears. It is one of the largest rodents still present in the arid zone with a body mass up to 50 g. It has greyish upperparts, often lustrous in appearance, with paler flanks and cream or white underparts (Watts and Aslin 1981). The tail is also bi-coloured being brown or grey above and white underneath. The tail length is usually less than the head-body length.

DISTRIBUTION

The first record of the plains rat in the Northern Territory was as recently as 1974 when a specimen was collected near Bloodwood Bore on Lilla Creek Station south of Alice Springs (Corbett *et al.* 1975). Currently, it occurs in only two regions of the Territory; one in the vicinity of Charlotte Waters south to the South Australian border, the other in the eastern and southern sections of Andado Station including the Mac Clark Conservation Reserve.

Although once found throughout arid and semi-arid Australia, it is now restricted to northern South Australia and the extreme south of the Northern Territory. No specimens have been collected from New South Wales or Queensland since 1936 (Breed and Head 1991), although it was formerly widespread in both states. The current range of the species appears to be restricted to a north-south band west of Lake Eyre extending for over 700 km from Pernatty Station (northern South Australia) in the south to Mac Clark Conservation Reserve in the north.

Conservation reserves where reported:
Mac Clark Conservation Reserve (however, this reserve is only occupied during irruptions)

ECOLOGY

The plains rat lives on plains, especially stony plains (gibber), and prefers areas of cracking clay soil associated with minor drainage features. These run-on areas are generally more productive than the surrounding landscape because they receive water and nutrients even after relatively minor rainfall events (Brandle *et al.* 1999). It occurs in colonies that are usually small in size and difficult to locate. However, numbers increase dramatically following rainfall. Rainfall triggers an increase in available resources in the animal's habitat that results in high levels of reproduction. Numbers remain high while conditions are favourable and then decline rapidly. Colony size can decrease by a factor of 80 over a 29 month period (Brandle and Moseby 1999). During population irruptions, plains rats move into areas that are not occupied at other times.

The plains rat is mostly herbivorous, feeding mainly on seeds, with some green plant material; a few insects are also taken. It is nocturnal and animals live in burrows. Individuals range over areas of up to 1.6 ha (Brandle and Moseby 1999).

CONSERVATION ASSESSMENT

Conservation categorisation is problematic because of a lack of information on population trends in the Territory (although this information is currently being collected), and its relatively recent discovery in the Northern Territory. However, the species qualifies as **Endangered** in the Northern Territory (under criteria B1ac(i,ii,iv)+2ac(i,ii,iv)) based on:

- estimated extent of occurrence less than 5000 km²;
- estimated area of occupancy less than 500 km²;
- known to exist at fewer than five locations; and
- extreme fluctuations occur in extent of occurrence, area of occupancy and number of mature individuals.

The Northern Territory population in the vicinity of Charlotte Waters may be the target of immigration from sites in northern South Australia such as Abminga. Given that the species has a lower national conservation status, Vulnerable, then the occurrence of such immigration would be justification for down-grading its Territory-wide status based on current IUCN guidelines (Gärdenfors 2001). However, immigration cannot be confirmed based on current information, therefore, the status of the plains rat in the Northern Territory should remain as Endangered.

continued.../

THREATENING PROCESSES

No specific threatening process has been identified for the plains rat in the Northern Territory. However, the species is likely to be susceptible to habitat degradation, particularly of those refugial areas into which colonies retract when population size is very low. This issue may be of particular concern in the Northern Territory because all but one of the known sites occurs on pastoral leases and the one location in a reserve appears to be occupied only during population irruptions. Further, several sites of occurrence are in areas of stock concentration around bores, which are likely to suffer heavy disturbance. Predation by introduced and native predators, especially the introduced European red fox and cat, may also threaten populations by increasing the speed of declines during the bust phase of population cycles (C. Pavey unpublished data).

CONSERVATION OBJECTIVES AND MANAGEMENT

There is no existing management program for the wild population of this species in the Northern Territory. A national recovery plan is currently being drafted by the South Australian Department of Environment and Heritage.

The Alice Springs Desert Park maintains a captive colony and the species is on permanent display in the nocturnal house at the Park.

Research and management priorities are to:
- continue monitoring of populations at Mac Clark Conservation Reserve and nearby Andado Station to determine population trends and to attempt to establish locations of colonies during periods of low population size;
- assess impact of predation by introduced carnivores and predatory birds that occur in the vicinity of the plains rat colony at Mac Clark Conservation Reserve (project currently underway);
- enter into protective agreements with landowners having populations of plains rats on their properties; and
- search for additional populations.

Compiled by Chris Pavey [May 2006] / **References:** Brandle, R., and Moseby, K.E. (1999). Comparative ecology of two populations of *Pseudomys australis* in northern South Australia. Wildlife Research 26, 541-564. Brandle, R., Moseby, K.E., and Adams, M. (1999). The distribution, habitat requirements and conservation status of the plains rat, *Pseudomys australis* (Rodentia: Muridae). *Wildlife Research* 26, 463-477. / Breed, W.G., and Head, W. (1991). Conservation status of the plains rat *Pseudomys australis* (Rodentia: Muridae). Australian Mammalogy 14, 125-128. / Corbett, L.K., Newsome, A.E., and Jones, M.A. (1975). *Pseudomys australis minnie* – a new record for the Northern Territory. *Australian Mammalogy* 1, 392-393. / Eldridge, S., and Reid, J. (2000). *A biological survey of the Finke floodout region, Northern Territory.* (Arid Lands Environment Centre, Alice Springs.) / Gärdenfors, U. (2001). Classifying threatened species at national versus global levels. *Trends in Ecology and Evolution* 16, 511-516. / Watts, C.H.S., and Aslin, H.J. (1981). *The rodents of Australia.* (Angus & Robertson, Sydney.)

Image courtesy of Babs and Bert Wells

Shark Bay mouse,
Alice Springs mouse
Pseudomys fieldi

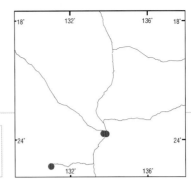

Known locations of the Shark Bay mouse
● = pre 1970
● = post 1970

CONSERVATION STATUS
AUSTRALIA: **VULNERABLE**
NORTHERN TERRITORY: **EXTINCT**

DESCRIPTION
The Shark Bay mouse is a moderately-sized rodent (body mass 30 to 50 g) with grizzled, shaggy hair (Watts and Aslin 1981). The tail is slightly longer than the head-body length.

DISTRIBUTION
This species once occurred from central Australia across central Western Australia to the coast. It is now confined to Bernier Island off Shark Bay and has recently been introduced to Doole Island (Exmouth Gulf) and Trimouille Island (Montebello Islands off the Pilbara). In central Australia, the Shark Bay mouse was recorded only from a single damaged specimen from Alice Springs in 1895, and from bones in owl pellets (probably several hundred years old) from Uluru – Kata Tjuta National Park, West MacDonnell National Park (Simpson's Gap) and the Gibson Desert (Baynes and Johnson 1996).

Conservation reserves where reported:
None (although it formerly occurred in areas that are now included within Uluru – Kata Tjuta National Park and West MacDonnell National Park).

ECOLOGY
Nothing has been recorded of the ecology of the Shark Bay mouse in central Australia. However, studies in coastal Western Australia have shown that the species uses runways and short shallow burrows; and has a broad diet including flowers, foliage, fungi and invertebrates. The litter size is three to four (Morris and Robinson 1995).

CONSERVATION ASSESSMENT
The Shark Bay mouse is presumed to have become **Extinct** in the Northern Territory in the early 20th century (Parker 1973).

THREATENING PROCESSES
The reasons for the decline and extinction of the Shark Bay mouse in central Australia are not known, but the most likely cause is predation by foxes and feral cats, with further problems associated with vegetation change caused by exotic herbivores and by changed fire regimes.

CONSERVATION OBJECTIVES AND MANAGEMENT
There are no imminent plans to re-introduce this species to the Northern Territory.

Compiled by Chris Pavey [May 2006] / **References:** Baynes, A., and Johnson, K.A. (1996). The contributions of the Horn Expedition and cave deposits to knowledge of the original mammal fauna of central Australia. In *Exploring Central Australia: Society, the Environment and the 1894 Horn Expedition.* (eds S.R. Morton and D.J. Mulvaney.) pp. 168-186. (Surrey Beatty and Sons, Sydney.)
Morris, K.D., and Robinson, A.C. (1995). Shark Bay mouse. In *The Mammals of Australia. 2nd Edition* (ed. R. Strahan.) pp. 596-597. (Reed Books, Sydney.)
Parker, S.A. (1973). An annotated checklist of the native land mammals of the Northern Territory. *Records of the South Australian Museum* 16, 1-57.
Watts, C.H.S., and Aslin, H.J. (1981). *The Rodents of Australia.* (Angus and Robertson, Sydney.)

Illustration by J.Gould (courtesy of Museum Victoria)

Canefield rat
Rattus sordidus

CONSERVATION STATUS
AUSTRALIA: **NOT LISTED**
NORTHERN TERRITORY: **VULNERABLE**

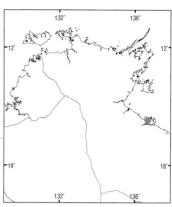

Known locations of the canefield rat
● = *pre 1970*
● = *post 1970*

DESCRIPTION

The canefield rat is a typical moderately-large rodent (up to 250 g), in the Northern Territory most like the long-haired rat (*R. villosissimus*) and the dusky rat (*R. colletti*). It has dark golden-brown coarse almost spiny fur, with long guard-hairs on the rump. The ears are light grey (cf. *R. colletti* that has dark brown ears, and *R. villosissimus* that are dark grey). *Rattus villosissimus* is also typically more grey in colour, and has even longer guard hairs distributed across more of the back.

The taxonomic status of some native *Rattus* in northern Australia is somewhat uncertain. The identity of the Northern Territory canefield rat specimens was corroborated by chromosomal analysis (Johnson and Kerle 1991).

DISTRIBUTION

In the Northern Territory, the canefield rat is known only from South-West Island in the Sir Edward Pellew group.

Elsewhere, it occurs widely in coastal areas of north-eastern Australia, as far south as far north-eastern New South Wales, and west to at least Normanton (Watts and Aslin 1981).

Conservation reserves where reported: None

ECOLOGY

The Northern Territory records are all from coastal dunes: "sandy low-lying open woodland with a grassy understorey" (Johnson and Kerle 1991).

In north-eastern Australia it occurs mostly in grasslands, typically in areas with friable soil and with a dense ground cover of grasses, sedges and herbs, and often occurs around swamps or on the grassy verges of closed forests (Watts and Aslin 1981). It is also very abundant in sugar cane crops.

It is a colonial species. It constructs extensive relatively shallow (typically less than 40 cm deep) burrows for shelter and breeding, and runways through dense vegetation. Its diet consists mainly of grass, but also includes some invertebrates and seeds.

CONSERVATION ASSESSMENT

In the Northern Territory, the species has been recorded from only one site during one field survey (in 1988). More recent surveys of several islands in the Pellew Group from 2003 to 2005 failed to trap any canefield rats (Taylor *et al.* 2004; S. Ward *pers. comm.*) and noted that the success of mammal trapping generally was lower than on two previous mammal surveys of the islands (in 1966-67 and in 1988). The trapping success was particularly low on South-West Island, and was generally low for other 'true' rat species, *Rattus tunneyi* and *Rattus villosisimus*, across the islands. In the 1988 survey canefield rats were recorded only in the dune communities of South-West Island, which cover only a small proportion of the total 95 km² area of the island, so the population of canefield rats there is probably small (fewer than 2000 individuals). The species should be classified as **Vulnerable** in

the Northern Territory (under criteria B1ab(i,ii,v) and B2ab(i,ii,v)), because of:

• extent of occurrence less than 5000 km²;
• area of occupancy less than 500 km²;
• known to exist at only one location;
• continuing decline.

THREATENING PROCESSES

Feral cats apparently reached South-West Island around 1990 (Taylor *et al.* 2004), and the highly restricted and colonial population of canefield rats there may have been susceptible to predation by these cats.

CONSERVATION OBJECTIVES AND MANAGEMENT

There is no existing recovery plan or management program for this species.

In the interim, research priorities are to:

• confirm the continued existence of this population, and establish a monitoring program, preferably integrated with an assessment of fire management preferences;
• sample the nearby mainland for additional populations; and
• further resolve the taxonomy of *Rattus* in northern Australia.

Management priorities are to:

• work with Aboriginal landowners to control feral cats (and other exotic species) on the Pellew Islands;
• evaluate options for conservation agreements with Aboriginal landowners;
• based on monitoring results, implement a favourable fire regime.

Compiled by John Woinarski [January 2007] / **References:** Johnson, K.A., and Kerle, J.A. (1991). *Flora and vertebrate fauna of the Sir Edward Pellew group of islands, Northern Territory.* Report to the Australian Heritage Commission. (Conservation Commission of the Northern Territory: Alice Springs.) / Taylor, R., Woinarski, J., Charlie, A., Dixon, R., Pracy, D., and Rhind, S. (2004) *Report on mammal survey of the Pellew Islands 2003.* (Lianthawirriyarra Sea Ranger Unit, Department of Infrastructure, Planning and Environment, and Tropical Savannas CRC, Darwin.) / Watts, C.H.S., and Aslin, H.J. (1981). *The Rodents of Australia.* (Angus and Robertson, Sydney.)

Image courtesy of Alex Dudley

False water-rat,
Water mouse
Xeromys myoides

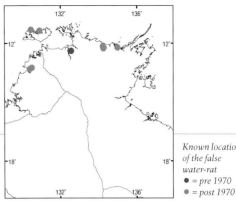

*Known locations
of the false
water-rat*
● = *pre 1970*
● = *post 1970*

CONSERVATION STATUS
AUSTRALIA: **VULNERABLE**
NORTHERN TERRITORY: **DATA DEFICIENT**

DESCRIPTION
The false water-rat is a small (35 to 50 g) rodent of unmistakable appearance. The most distinctive external features are a broad relatively short face, and very short sleek fur. Fur colour is pale grey above and white below. The eyes and ears are relatively small.

DISTRIBUTION
In the Northern Territory, it is known from only 10 records at six sites (South Alligator River in 1903, Daly River floodplain in 1972, two sites on the Tomkinson River in 1975, Melville Island in 1975 and Glyde River floodplain in 1998 and 1999) (Redhead and McKean 1975; Magnusson *et al.* 1976; Woinarski *et al.* 2000). Beyond the Northern Territory, it is also known from several sites in coastal south-eastern Queensland and one site in New Guinea.

Conservation reserves where reported:
Kakadu National Park (but this record is from 1903, well pre-dating the Park's establishment).

ECOLOGY
The ecology of the species is reasonably well known from a detailed study on North Stradbroke Island, Queensland (Van Dyck 1996). The false water-rat is a nocturnal predator eating mainly marine and freshwater invertebrates, especially including crabs, pulmonates and molluscs. It forages entirely on the ground, and is an adept swimmer. It builds and shelters in either burrows or substantial earthen mounds. Its habitats comprise mangrove forests, freshwater swamps and floodplain saline grasslands (Woinarski *et al.* 2000).

CONSERVATION ASSESSMENT
In the Northern Territory, the species can potentially be assigned the status of Vulnerable on criteria B2ab:
• area of occupancy less than 2000 km²;
• known to exist at no more than 10 locations; and
• continuing decline, observed, inferred or projected in area of occupancy, area, extent and/or quality of habitat, and number of locations or subpopulations.

However, conservation assessment is hampered by the lack of precise information on range, population size and trends, to such an extent that it may qualify best as **Data Deficient.**

It is not known what proportion of the Territory's mangroves and floodplains is suitable for (and/or occupied by) the species or what impact a range of factors (including saltwater intrusion, spread of weeds (especially *Mimosa pigra*, olive hymenachne and para grass) and grazing of the floodplains by domestic and feral water buffalo and cattle) are having on habitat quality.

THREATENING PROCESSES
There is insufficient information available to assess the impacts of possible threatening processes. There may be some predation by feral cats. However, the most plausible threatening processes relate to broad-scale habitat changes, especially those due to saltwater intrusion, spread of weeds and impacts of grazing. However, it is not clear that these changes necessarily reduce habitat quality for this species, and they are unlikely to diminish the extent of mangrove communities.

CONSERVATION OBJECTIVES
AND MANAGEMENT
The main priorities are to better define the distribution and status of this species and to assess the impacts of a range of putative threatening processes. Such information is needed before management prescriptions can be formulated appropriately.

Compiled by John Woinarski [May 2006] / **References:** Magnusson, W.E., Webb, G.J.W., and Taylor, J.A. (1976). Two new locality records, a new habitat and a nest description for *Xeromys myoides* Thomas (Rodentia: Muridae). *Australian Wildlife Research* 3, 153-157. / Redhead, T.D., and McKean, J.L. (1975). A new record of the false water-rat, *Xeromys myoides*, from the Northern Territory of Australia. *Australian Mammalogy* 1, 347-354. / Van Dyck, S. (1996). *Xeromys myoides* Thomas, 1889 (Rodentia: Muridae) in mangrove communities of North Stradbroke Island, southeast Queensland. *Memoirs of the Queensland Museum* 42, 30-37. / Woinarski, J.C.Z., Brennan, K., Dee, A., Njudumul, J., Guthayguthay, P., and Horner, P. (2000). Further records of the false water-rat *Xeromys myoides* from coastal Northern Territory. *Australian Mammalogy* 21, 245-247.

Image courtesy of Greg Miles

Arnhem rock-rat
Zyzomys maini

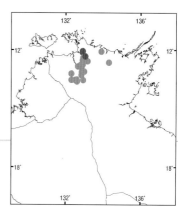

Known locations of the Arnhem rock-rat
● = pre 1970
● = post 1970

DESCRIPTION

The Arnhem rock-rat is a moderately large (100 to 150 g) rat, distinguished from most other Northern Territory rodents by its large whiskers, typically swollen tail (especially at the base), long hairs towards the tip of the tail, and the characteristic roman nose. It shares these features with the co-occurring but much smaller (30 to 70 g) common rock-rat *Z. argurus,* from which it can be separated by its larger size, colour (typically more grey than brown), and higher density of long hairs on the tail.

The rock-rats have fragile tails and fur, and many individuals may have no or greatly reduced tails, presumably as a consequence of predator attack.

DISTRIBUTION

The Arnhem rock-rat is restricted to the sandstone massif of western Arnhem Land. Until recently, it was considered conspecific with the Kimberley rock-rat *Z. woodwardi*, from the north Kimberley (Kitchener 1989).

Conservation resereves where reported:
Kakadu National Park

ECOLOGY

The ecology of the Arnhem rock-rat is relatively well-known from a series of studies in Kakadu National Park (Begg and Dunlop 1980, 1985; Begg 1981; Begg *et al.* 1981). It is an entirely terrestrial, nocturnal species, restricted to areas with large sandstone boulders or escarpment with fissures and cracks. It occurs in these areas very patchily, being restricted mostly to monsoon rainforest patches, notably in gullies and along creeklines, or in fire-protected refugia. This is a much narrower habitat than that occupied by the common rock-rat. The Arnhem rock-rat's diet comprises mainly seeds, fruit and some other vegetable matter. The seeds eaten include those from many species of rainforest tree. Large seeds may be cached, or at least moved to be eaten at relatively safe sites, resulting in distinctive piles of chewed hard seeds in rock fissures or under large overhangs (Begg and Dunlop 1980).

On the basis of its known response to a single large fire, the Arnhem rock-rat appears to be unusually fire-sensitive, with substantial decline for at least one to two years post-fire (Begg *et al.* 1981). A high frequency of fire will result in diminution of its preferred sandstone monsoon rainforests (Russell-Smith *et al.* 1993, 1998).

CONSERVATION ASSESSMENT

Conservation assessment is hampered by the lack of precise information on range and population size. Decline can be presumed on the basis of the current high frequency of fire across much of the western Arnhem Land plateau (Russell-Smith *et al.* 1998), and resultant decline in its preferred habitat, monsoon rainforests (Russell-Smith and Bowman 1992; Russell-Smith *et al.* 1993, 1998; but cf. Bowman and Dingle 2006). More directly, declines of this species have been reported from all monitoring sites in Kakadu National Park (Woinarski 2004).

It best fits the status of **Vulnerable** (under criteria B2ab(ii,ii,iv,v)) based on:
- severely fragmented or known to exist at no more than 10 locations;
- area of occupancy estimated to be less than 2000km² and
- continuing decline.

THREATENING PROCESSES

The major threatening process appears to be reduction in habitat suitability and/or extent due to increased frequency of extensive hot late dry season fires.

CONSERVATION OBJECTIVES AND MANAGEMENT PRIORITIES

There is no existing explicit recovery plan or management program for this species.

In the interim, management priorities are to:
- reduce the incidence of extensive, hot late dry season fires; and
- maintain a program for monitoring the status of at least one subpopulation, but preferably more, and preferably in association with a range of fire management practices, in order to help refine best management practice.

Compiled by John Woinarski [May 2006] / **References:** Begg, R.J. (1981). The small mammals of Little Nourlangie Rock, N.T. IV. Ecology of *Zyzomys woodwardi*, the large rock-rat, and *Z. argurus*, the common rock-rat (Rodentia: Muridae). *Australian Wildlife Research* 8, 73-85. / Begg, R.J., and Dunlop, C.R. (1980). Security eating, and diet in the large rock-rat, *Zyzomys woodwardi* (Rodentia: Muridae). *Australian Wildlife Research* 7, 63-70. / Begg, R.J., and Dunlop, C.R. (1985). Diet of the large rock-rat, *Zyzomys woodwardi*, and the common rock-rat *Z. argurus* (Rodentia: Muridae). *Australian Wildlife Research* 12, 19-24. / Begg, R.J., Martin, K.C., and Price, N.F. (1981). The small mammals of Little Nourlangie Rock, N.T. V. The effects of fire. *Australian Wildlife Research* 8, 515-527. / Bowman, D.M.J.S., and Dingle, J.K. (2006). Late 20th century landscape-wide expansion of *Allosyncarpia ternata* (Myrtaceae) forests in Kakadu National Park, northern Australia. *Australian Journal of Botany* 54, 707-715. / Kitchener, D.J. (1989). Taxonomic appraisal of *Zyzomys* (Rodentia, Muridae) with descriptions of two new species from the Northern Territory, Australia. *Records of the Western Australian Museum* 14, 331-373. / Russell-Smith, J., and Bowman, D.M.J.S. (1992). Conservation of monsoon rainforest isolates in the Northern Territory, Australia. *Biological Conservation* 59, 51-63. / Russell-Smith, J., Lucas, D.E., Brock, J., and Bowman, D.M.J.S. (1993). *Allosyncarpia*-dominated rain forest in monsoonal northern Australia. *Journal of Vegetation Science* 4, 67-82. / Russell-Smith, J., Ryan, P.G., Klessa, D., Waight, G., and Harwood, R. (1998). Fire regimes, fire-sensitive vegetation and fire management of the sandstone Arnhem Plateau, monsoonal northern Australia. *Journal of Applied Ecology* 35, 829-846. / Woinarski, J. (2004). *Threatened plants and animals in Kakadu National Park: a review and recommendations for management*. Report to Parks Australia North. (NT Department of Infrastructure Planning and Environment, Darwin.)

Image courtesy of Sean Webster

Carpentarian rock-rat
Zyzomys palatalis

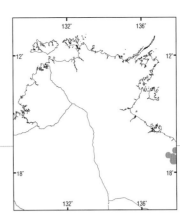

Known locations of the Carpentarian rock-rat
● = pre 1970
● = post 1970

DESCRIPTION

The Carpentarian rock-rat is a moderately-large rock-rat (average weight 120 g) with distinctly fattened tail-base. The tail is generally longer than the head-body length but is often broken off to form a stump. The fur is brown above and pale to white below. The feet are white above.

DISTRIBUTION

The Carpentarian rock-rat is known only from Wollogorang Station in the Gulf of Carpentaria hinterland where it was discovered in 1986 (Kitchener 1989). Nothing is known of its former distribution. It is known from five locations (gorges and escarpments) on Wollogorang (Banyan Gorge, Camel Creek, Moonlight Gorge, McDermott Springs and Redbank Mine), all within a radius of 35 km (Churchill 1996; Puckey 2003). Extensive surveys (including in 47 additional monsoon rainforest patches) in apparently suitable habitat in the region have not expanded its known range (Trainor *et al.* 2000).

Conservation reserves where reported: None

ECOLOGY

The species is restricted to sandstone gorges and escarpments containing a core of dry or wet rainforest vegetation, mixed with broad-leaf woodland, scree slopes and permanent water, surrounded by savanna woodlands.

Carpentarian rock-rats may breed year-round with a peak in the early to mid dry season when their dietary items of large fleshy or woody fruits and seeds are most abundant (Trainor 1996a).

Based on a radio-tracking study of 21 individuals, Puckey *et al.* (2004) calculated a mean home range size of 1.1 ha, found that individuals may move up to 2 km in one night, and showed that while most activity occurred within monsoon rainforests, at least some individuals would also forage within nearby areas of savanna woodland, although no animals moved more than 80 m away from the rainforest edge.

CONSERVATION ASSESSMENT

The population of Carpentarian rock-rats has been estimated to be 696 at Moonlight Gorge and 450 at Banyan Gorge (Trainor 1996b). No estimates for the other (probably smaller) subpopulations have been made but it is expected that the total population is fewer than 2000 individuals. Based on modeling of home range sizes, home range overlaps and availablity of putatively suitable habitat, Bowman *et al.* (2006) estimated that there may be 782 home ranges for Carpentarian rock-rats across their known sites.

The species qualifies as **Critically Endangered** (under criteria B1ab(iii)+2ab(iii)) based on:
- extent of occurrence less than 100 km²;
- area of occupancy estimated to be less than 10 km²;
- severely fragmented; and
- continuing decline, observed, inferred or projected.

Note that information relevant to the last criterion is limited and inconclusive. Until the very recent (2005) establishment of a monitoring program, there was no information available to assess trends in population. Until recently, it was considered that suitable habitat for Carpentarian rock-rats was probably declining and limited by fire (Puckey *et al.* 2001; Brook *et al.* 2002). Recent analysis of current and historic imagery instead suggests that monsoon rainforests and their margins may be increasing on this property (Bowman *et al.* 2006), however, the extent, if any, to which Carpentarian rock-rats have increased in range in association with such vegetation change remains unknown.

THREATENING PROCESSES

The major conservation problem for the Carpentarian rock-rat is its extremely limited range (and hence population), and its apparent dependence upon a core monsoon rainforest habitat.

Population modeling (Brook *et al.* 2002) has indicated that fire is a major threat, as it may degrade, diminish or alter the composition of its core monsoon rainforest patches (Trainor *et al.* 2000), a general concern for monsoon rainforest patches throughout the Northern Territory (Russell-Smith and Bowman 1992).

Cattle grazing may also detrimentally affect rainforest patches and their associated springs and creeks. However, the known sites are currently in areas of the property that are not stocked.

continued.../

Feral cats are known to occur in the areas supporting Carpentarian rock-rat populations. However their impact is unknown.

CONSERVATION OBJECTIVES AND MANAGEMENT

A management program has been developed for Carpentarian rock-rats with the aim of improving the long-term conservation status of the species and its habitat in the Northern Territory. The program has been implemented under a recently revised national recovery plan (Trainor and Woinarski 1996; Puckey *et al.* 2001).

Priorities of the current management plan are to:
• manage the known sites to eliminate threatening processes;
• continue to maintain a captive breeding colony at the Territory Wildlife Park as a safeguard against the decline of wild populations;
• carry out an experimental release program using individuals from the captive breeding colony; and
• continue scientific research to improve our understanding of the species ecology and its management.

Two trial translocation programs have been attempted recently, in apparently suitable habitat at Limmen National Park, but neither was successful. Brook *et al.* (2002) used population viability models to prioritise management actions for this species, and considered that the most effective conservation action would be to enhance fire management, with some further potential gain from strategic translocations.

Compiled by Helen Puckey, John Woinarski [May 2006] / **References:** Bowman, D.M.J.S., McIntyre, D.L., and Brook, B.W. (2006). Is the Carpentarian rock-rat (*Zyzomys palatalis*) critically endangered? *Pacific Conservation Biology* 12, 134-140. / Brook, B.W. Griffiths, A.D., and Puckey, H.L. (2002). Modelling strategies for the management of the critically endangered Carpentarian rock-rat (*Zyzomys palatalis*) of northern Australia. *Journal of Environmental Management* 65, 355-368. / Churchill, S.K. (1996). Distribution, habitat and status of the Carpentarian rock-rat, *Zyzomys palatalis*. *Wildlife Research* 23, 77-91. Kitchener, D.J. (1989). Taxonomic appraisal of *Zyzomys* (Rodentia, Muridae) with descriptions of two new species from the Northern Territory, Australia. *Records of the Western Australian Museum* 14, 331-373. Puckey, H. (2003). Additional records of the Carpentarian rock-rat *Zyzomys palatalis* at Redbank, close to the type locality. *Northern Territory Naturalist* 17, 43-45. / Puckey, H., Woinarski, J., and Trainor, C. (2001) Revised Recovery Plan for the Carpentarian Rock-rat *Zyzomys palatalis*. (Parks and Wildlife Commission of the Northern Territory, Palmerston.) / Puckey, H., Lewis, M., Hooper, D., and Michell, C. (2004). Home range, movement and habitat utilisation of the Carpentarian rock-rat (*Zyzomys palatalis*) in an isolated habitat patch. *Wildlife Research* 31, 327-337. / Russell-Smith, J., and Bowman, D.M.J.S. (1992). Conservation of monsoon rainforest isolates in the Northern Territory, Australia. *Biological Conservation* 59, 51-63. / Trainor, C. (1996a). Carpentarian Rock-rat (*Zyzomys palatalis*) survey to clarify species status. Final Report to Endangered Species Unit ANCA. / Trainor, C. (1996b). *Habitat use and demographic characteristics of the endangered Carpentarian Rock-rat Zyzomys palatalis.* M.Sc. thesis (Northern Territory University, Darwin.) / Trainor, C. R., Fisher, A., Woinarski, J., and Churchill, S. (2000). Multiscale patterns of habitat use by the Carpentarian Rock-rat (*Zyzomys palatalis*) and the Common Rock-rat (*Z. argurus*). *Wildlife Research* 27, 319-332. / Trainor, C. R., and Woinarski, J. (1996). The Carpentarian Rock-rat *Zyzomys palatalis* recovery plan. (Parks and Wildlife Commission of the Northern Territory, Palmerston.)

Central rock-rat
Zyzomys pedunculatus

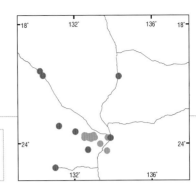

Known locations
of the central
rock-rat
● = pre 1970
● = post 1970

CONSERVATION STATUS
AUSTRALIA: **ENDANGERED**
NORTHERN TERRITORY: **ENDANGERED**

DESCRIPTION

The central rock-rat is a medium-sized rodent with a body mass between 70 and 120 g. Adults are stocky in appearance and have a distinctive 'Roman nose'. The fur is thick and soft, yellowish-brown on the upperbody and cream or white below. The tail length is equal to the head-body length. The tail is thick and well-furred.

DISTRIBUTION

The central rock-rat is endemic to the Northern Territory. Prior to 1960, specimens were taken at Illamurta (James Range) and Alice Springs during the 1890s, Hugh Creek in 1935, Napperby Hills in 1950, The Granites (Tanami Desert) in 1952, Davenport Range in 1953 and at Haast's Bluff settlement (West MacDonnell Ranges) in 1960 (Parker 1973; Wurst 1995). Cave deposits show that the species once occurred widely across central Western Australia and the Northern Territory (Baynes and Johnson 1996).

No records were obtained between 1970 and 1995 and the species was presumed to be extinct (Wurst 1990). However, it was rediscovered in the MacDonnell Ranges in 1996 and was recorded at 14 sites in the MacDonnell Ranges west of Alice Springs between 1996 and 2002. All but one of the sites is within West MacDonnell National Park; the other is on Milton Park pastoral lease. There have been no records of the species anywhere within its range since 2002. The most recent disappearance of the central rock-rat occurred at the same time as populations

of other arid rodents declined dramatically and followed massive wildfires in the MacDonnell Ranges from April to October 2002.

Conservation reserves where reported:
West MacDonnell National Park. (It also formerly occurred in what is now Uluru – Kata Tjuta National Park.)

ECOLOGY

At Ormiston Gorge, the central rock-rat occupies a range of habitats including tussock and hummock grasslands and low open woodland; and occurs on ridge-tops, cliffs, scree slopes, hills and valley floors.

The species is primarily granivorous (Nano *et al.* 2003). Seeds (1 to 10 mm in size) of shrubs, forbs and grasses are the main component of the diet, with leaf material of secondary importance. Plant stems and insects are a minor component of the diet. The majority of the plant species identified in the diet are regarded as fire-encouraged rather than fire-sensitive species. The most commonly consumed seeds were from *Sida* spp., *Glycine canescens* and *Solanum* spp. (Nano *et al.* 2003).

CONSERVATION ASSESSMENT

Conservation categorisation is difficult because the central rock-rat is similar to other arid zone rodents in undergoing dramatic population fluctuations in response to climatic conditions. For example, the species was the most frequently trapped small mammal at some sites around Ormiston Gorge in

2000 and 2001 although it was not recorded there during 1991–93 despite over 20 000 trap-nights of effort, and has not been trapped since 2002.

The species qualifies as **Endangered** (under criteria B1ac(i,ii,iii,iv)+2ac(i.ii,iii,iv), based on:
• extent of occurrence less than 5000 km²;
• area of occupancy less than 500 km²;
• severely fragmented; and
• extreme fluctuations.

THREATENING PROCESSES

No definite threatening processes have been identified for the central rock-rat (Cole 2000). However, among the potential threatening processes are predation by dingoes, foxes and cats; inappropriate fire regimes (resulting in large uncontrolled wildfires), perhaps particularly exacerbated by spread of exotic pasture grasses; and habitat degradation caused by grazing by feral herbivores.

CONSERVATION OBJECTIVES AND MANAGEMENT

A recovery plan (Cole 2000) for the central rock-rat has been partly implemented. Management priorities are to:
• locate refuge populations of the central-rock rat during periods of low population abundance;
• implement favourable fire management; and
• continue effective husbandry of the captive population. The only captive population of the species is held at the Alice Springs Desert Park.

Compiled by Chris Pavey [February 2007] / **References:** Baynes, A., and Johnson, K.A. (1996). The contributions of the Horn Expedition and cave deposits to knowledge of the original mammal fauna of central Australia. In *Exploring Central Australia: Society, the Environment and the 1894 Horn Expedition.* (eds S.R. Morton and D.J. Mulvaney.) pp. 168-186. (Surrey Beatty and Sons, Sydney.) / Cole, J. (2000). *Recovery plan for the central rock-rat (Zymoys pedunculatus).* (Parks and Wildlife Commission of the NT, Alice Springs.) / Nano, T. J., Smith, C. M., and Jeffreys, E. (2003). Investigation into the diet of the central rock-rat (*Zyzomys pedunculatus*). *Wildlife Research* 30, 513-518. / Parker, S.A. (1973). An annotated checklist of the native land mammals of the Northern Territory. *Records of the South Australian Museum* 16, 1-57. Watts, C.H.S., and Aslin, H.J. (1981). *The Rodents of Australia.* (Angus & Robertson, Sydney.) / Wurst, P.D. (1990). *Report on the survey for the central rock-rat in the Alice Springs region.* (Conservation Commission of the NT, Alice Springs.) / Wurst, D. (1995). Central rock-rat. In *The Mammals of Australia.* (ed. R. Strahan.) pp. 624-625. (Reed Books, Sydney.)

Sei whale
Balaenoptera borealis

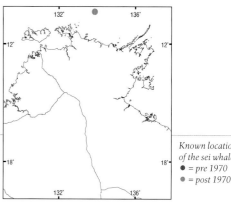

Known location of the sei whale
● = *pre 1970*
● = *post 1970*

DESCRIPTION
The sei whale is a moderately large (15 to 16 m length) baleen whale. It is dark blue-grey on the back and paler below. It has a prominent falcate dorsal fin; the baleen plates (each side of the mouth) are dark-grey or black with a fine white inner fringe (Reeves *et al.* 2002). When diving they do not arch their back as pronouncedly as other whales.

DISTRIBUTION
The sei whale has a world-wide distribution from tropical waters to near polar regions. Its distribution may be inconstant and unpredictable. Sei whales are generally deep-water animals, rarely found near the coast (Bryden *et al.* 1998). They are infrequently recorded in Australian waters.

Around the Northern Territory, there is only one record, from a trawl in Commonwealth waters in September 1989 (Chatto and Warnecke 2000).

Conservation reserves where recorded: None

ECOLOGY
Sei whales are among the fastest of all whales. They generally occur in small groups, but may form feeding aggregations. They are typically surface feeders, skimming the water with open mouths. They have a relatively broad diet including fish, krill and copepods.

CONSERVATION ASSESSMENT
Hunting pressure caused the Southern Hemisphere population of sei whales to decline from about 100 000 to 25 000 (Bryden *et al.* 1998). In the Northern Territory, there are too few records to assess its conservation status. It therefore qualifies as **Data Deficient**.

THREATENING PROCESSES
The main threat to the sei whale is the legacy of previous hunting, and current and future proposed hunting. It may also be affected by habitat degradation, including reduction in food supplies, and climate change (DEH 2005).

CONSERVATION OBJECTIVES AND MANAGEMENT
National conservation and management objectives are detailed in a national recovery plan (DEH 2005). The main Northern Territory priority is to improve knowledge of the distribution, status and habitat requirements of this species, and other whales.

Compiled by John Woinarski, Ray Chatto [May 2006] / **References:** Bryden, M., Marsh, H., and Shaughnessy, P. (1998). *Dugongs, whales, dolphins and seals: a guide to the sea mammals of Australia.* (Allen & Unwin, St Leonards.) / Chatto, R., and Warnecke, R.M. (2000). Records of cetacean strandings in the Northern Territory of Australia. *The Beagle* 16, 163-175. / DEH (2005). *Humpback whale recovery plan, 2005-2010.* (Department of Environment and Heritage, Canberra.) / Reeves, R.R., Stewart, B.S., Clapham, P.J., and Powell, J.A. (2002). *Sea mammals of the world.* (A. & C. Black, London.)

Image courtesy of Doug Coughran & Lochman Transparencies

Blue whale
Balaenoptera musculus

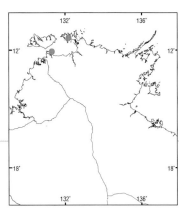

*Known locations
of the blue whale*
● = *pre 1970*
● = *post 1970*

CONSERVATION STATUS
AUSTRALIA: ENDANGERED
NORTHERN TERRITORY: DATA DEFICIENT

DESCRIPTION
The blue whale is the largest animal known, with a body length of 25 to 30 m. It is a mottled blue-grey in colour; has a very small dorsal fin, set far back in the body; and (like other baleen whales) prominent throat pleats.

DISTRIBUTION
The blue whale occurs in all oceans and inhabits coastal, shelf and oceanic waters (Reeves *et al.* 2002). In the Northern Territory, it is known from two beach-washed specimens, at Cape Hotham in 1980 (Chatto and Warnecke 2000), and at Port Essington in August 2003 (R. Chatto *pers. comm.*)

Conservation reserves where reported:
Cape Hotham Conservation Reserve, Garig Gunak Barlu National Park (but both only as single beach-washed records).

ECOLOGY
The blue whale breeds in warm waters at low latitudes, and migrates to summer in higher latitudes. Females have one calf every two to three years. Blue whales are usually solitary, but may form small short-lived groups. They feed almost exclusively on krill. Blue whales may live for 90 years or more.

CONSERVATION ASSESSMENT
Blue whales were a preferred target species for hunting, and numbers in the Southern Hemisphere are estimated to have declined from more than 300 000 to between 500 and 2300 (DEH 2005).

In the Northern Territory, there are too few records to assess status. A decline in the Northern Territory may be inferred from the world-wide decline, but Northern Territory waters may have always been marginal for this species. It therefore qualifies as **Data Deficient**.

THREATENING PROCESSES
The main threat to the blue whale is the legacy of previous hunting, and current and future proposed hunting. It may also be affected by habitat degradation, including reduction in food supplies, and climate change (DEH 2005).

CONSERVATION OBJECTIVES AND MANAGEMENT
National conservation and management objectives are detailed in a national recovery plan (DEH 2005). The main Northern Territory priority is to improve knowledge of the distribution, status and habitat requirements of this species, and other whales.

Compiled by John Woinarski, Ray Chatto [May 2006] / **References:** Chatto, R., and Warnecke, R.M. (2000). Records of cetacean strandings in the Northern Territory of Australia. *The Beagle* 16, 163-175. DEH (2005). *Blue, fin and sei whale recovery plan, 2005-2010.* (Department of Environment and Heritage, Canberra.) / Reeves, R.R., Stewart, B.S., Clapham, P.J., and Powell, J.A. (2002). *Sea mammals of the world.* (A. & C. Black, London.) /

Image courtesy of Doug Coughran & Lochman Transparencies

Humpback whale
Megaptera novaeangliae

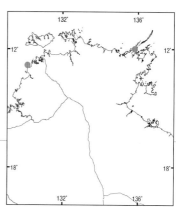

CONSERVATION STATUS
AUSTRALIA: **VULNERABLE**
NORTHERN TERRITORY: **DATA DEFICIENT**

DESCRIPTION
The humpback whale is a large (body length of 15 to 18 m) whale, with extremely long flippers and tubercles on the head and lower jaw. It is black above and white, black or mottled below. It frequently raises the flukes when it dives (Reeves *et al.* 2002).

DISTRIBUTION
The humpback whale occurs in all major oceans, mostly in coastal and continental shelf waters (Reeves *et al.* 2002). There are two main populations in Australian waters, one that migrates along the east coast and one that migrates along the west coast.

In the Northern Territory, it is known from one beach-washed specimen on the Napier Peninsula, north-eastern Arnhem Land, in 1981 (Chatto and Warnecke 2000). Recent observational records suggest a more regular southward migration each year around October along the western Northern Territory coast: this has included two individuals (mother and calf) seen off Casuarina Coastal Reserve and the Perron Islands between September and October 2002 (R. Chatto *pers. obs.*).

Conservation reserves where reported: None

ECOLOGY
The humpback whale breeds in warm waters at low latitudes, and migrates to summer in higher latitudes. Females have one calf every two to three years. Humpback whales are usually solitary, but may form small unstable groups, and males may aggregate around females. Humpback whales feed on krill and small schooling fish.

CONSERVATION ASSESSMENT
Humpback whales were a preferred target species for hunting, and numbers are estimated to have declined by 95% in the 19th and 20th century (DEH 2005). The current population is estimated at between 8000 and 14 000 on the Australian west coast and between 3000 and 4000 on the east coast (DEH 2005). These populations are reported to be now increasing (DEH 2005).

In the Northern Territory, there are too few records to assess status. A decline in the Northern Territory may be inferred from the world-wide decline, but Northern Territory waters may have always been marginal for this species. It therefore qualifies as **Data Deficient**.

THREATENING PROCESSES
The main threat to the humpback whale is the legacy of previous hunting, and current and future proposed hunting. It may also be affected by habitat degradation, including reduction in food supplies, and climate change (DEH 2005).

CONSERVATION OBJECTIVES AND MANAGEMENT
National conservation and management objectives are detailed in a national recovery plan (DEH 2005). The main Northern Territory priority is to improve knowledge of the distribution, status and habitat requirements of this species, and other whales.

Compiled by John Woinarski, Ray Chatto [May 2006] / **References:** Chatto, R., and Warnecke, R.M. (2000). Records of cetacean strandings in the Northern Territory of Australia. *The Beagle* 16, 163-175. DEH (2005). *Humpback whale recovery plan, 2005-2010.* (Department of Environment and Heritage, Canberra.) / Reeves, R.R., Stewart, B.S., Clapham, P.J., and Powell, J.A. (2002). *Sea mammals of the world.* (A. & C. Black, London.)

GLOSSARY

achene   small dry fruit with a single seed that is attached to the wall of the fruit (for example, often in daisies).

acuminate   gradually tapering to a sharp point and forming concave sides along the tip.

acute   tapering to a pointed apex with more or less straight sides.

aestivate   to become torpid or inactive during a harsh or unfavourable period (cf hibernate, which refers to inactivity during winter).

anther   the pollen bearing part of the stamen.

apex   the pointed end or tip of a structure.

apical   referring to the apex.

apical granule   a large granule at the front of an interdigital pad (typically used when describing the diagnostic characters of the feet of small mammals).

apical teeth   spine or saw-like projections from the apical portion of a leaf.

appressed   pressed close or flat against an organ, for example, hairs lying flat on the leaf surface.

auricle   a small appendage shaped like an ear.

auriculate   referring to the auricle.

axillary   usually refers to vegetative buds or inflorescences that arise from the point of attachment of the leaf with a stem.

bract   a leaf-like structure at the base of a flower or inflorescence.

bracteole   a small bract borne on the pedicel of a flower.

breakaway   the broken down edge of an elevated plateau.

buttress   with props or supports as in the flared trunks of some trees.

calcareous   chalky (a high content of calcium carbonate), or chalk-like in colour.

camaenid   a group of terrestrial snails in the family Camaenidae.

ciliate   with a fringe of hairs.

carapace   the upper shell of a turtle.

colleter   gland-like structures present on the stem between the attachment points of opposite leaves, or at the junction of a petiole and leaf blade. Common in the Asclepiadaceae and Apocynaceae families.

coppice   sprouts arising from the trunk; can arise as a response to fire.

cordate   heart shaped – usually refers to the lobing of leaf bases.

cormous   with corms (bulbs).

corolla   petals of a flower.

costal   in a turtle carapace, the plates between the outer marginals and median centrals.

crepuscular   active at dawn and/or dusk.

culm   the stem of a grass.

decussate   arranged in pairs along a stem, with each pair at right angles to the pair above and below.

deltoid   with the shape of an equilateral triangle.

dioecious   (in plants) male and female flowers borne on different plants.

disc floret   the small flower usually of a daisy inflorescence.

distal   at the far end of a structure (opposite to proximal).

distichous   leaves or leaflets arising in one plane from a stem or rachis.

diurnal   active during the day.

domatia   small gland-like structures or tufts of hairs on the undersurface of a leaf and confined to the axils of veins. Usually containing small mites.

dorsal   referring to the back (i.e. opposite to ventral, the underside).

ellipsoid   with the shape of an ellipse – three dimensional.

elliptic   with the shape of an ellipse – two dimensional.

embryonic diapause   a temporary halt to embryonic development.

emergent   individual trees that project from and are clear of the main canopy of a rainforest. Also refers to aquatic plants with parts that emerge from the water's surface.

endemic   only occurring in a specific geographic region.

ephemeral   lasting a short time.

epiphyte   growing on another plant, not parasitic.

erose   irregularly notched, toothed or indented.

eruption   (or irruption) an irregular very marked and rapid increase in population, often including a movement to new areas.

filiform   thread-like.

floret   small flower.

foliolate	referring to leaflets of a compound leaf.
geophyte, geophytic	dies back to an underground structure.
gibber	arid plains covered in small smoothed stones (or the stones themselves).
glabrous	bald, no hairs.
glaucous	with a bluish/whitish colour.
globose	spherical in shape – three dimensional.
hastate	arrow shaped, refers to the shape of leaves.
haustorium	a specialised absorbing structure of a parasitic plant, that is used to obtain food from a host plant.
humeral	in a turtle, the second pair of shields on the plastron.
inflorescence	a group of flowers.
interpetiolar stipule	a leaf-like bract that is attached to the stem between the petiole of opposite leaves.
introgression	flow of genetic material between taxa.
isobilateral	with the same structure or appearance on both sides.
keel	a longitudinal ridge.
labellum	the lip of an orchid flower.
lanceolate	lance-shaped, longer than wide, attachment at the broad end.
latex	a milky sap.
lax	loose, not compact.
lectotype	in plants refers to the selection of an individual plant specimen from one of many syntypes, that will be used to stabilise the name of the species in question.
ligule	a tongue or strap-shaped organ. The flattened part of a ray floret in daisies. The membranous appendage on the inner surface of a grass or sedge leaf at the junction of the flattened leaf blade and the leaf sheath.
lip	the edge of a structure that surrounds a hole, or the modified upper petal on an orchid flower, or the lower petals of a bilaterally symmetrical flower.
litter	accumulation of dead organic matter (typically leaves) and associated decomposing material on the surface of the ground.
lobe	a rounded division or segment of an organ, for example leaf.
Malesia	the collective term for Indonesia, Sumatra, Malaysia, Java, Lesser Sunda Islands, Borneo, Phillipines, Celebes, Moluccas, and New Guinea. Flora Malesiana is a series of publications on the flora of these countries.

mallee	a growth form of (typically eucalypt) woody plants where many trunks arise from a large underground root system; also the name of the semi-arid or arid vegetation type that is characterised by such small trees.
membranous	soft thin flexible and more or less translucent, like a membrane.
minimum convex polygon	the smallest area that contains an observed set of points.
nocturnal	active at night.
oblanceolate	lance-shaped with attachment at the narrow end.
obovate	egg-shaped with the point of attachment at the narrow end.
obtuse	blunt or rounded at the apex with the sides coming together at the apex at an angle greater than 90^0.
orbicular	approximately circular in outline.
ovate	egg-shaped with the point of attachment at the broad end.
palaeodrainage line	ancient creek lines that no longer flow. They may however still provide more moisture to plants growing along them.
pantropical	found in tropical areas throughout the world.
parietal lip	(in snails) the inner wall of the shell apperture.
pectoral	relating to the chest area; the third pair of plates in the plastron of a turtle.
peduncule	the stalk of a solitary flower or of an inflorescence.
peltate	shield-shaped. A flat structure with the stalk attached to the lower surface rather than the base or margin.
phyllode	an expanded petiole that lacks a true leaf blade – typical of some *Acacia* spp (wattles).
pinnate	a compound leaf with the leaflets arranged on either side of the rachis.
pinnule	an individual leaflet of a bipinnately (twice)-divided leaf.
plastron	the lower shell of a turtle.
polyoestrous	having multiple periods of sexual activity or receptivity each year, and hence able to produce several sets of young each year.
prostrate	lying close to the ground.
proximal	the closest point or end to a structure (opposite of distal).
pubescence	referring to hairs.
raceme	a cluster of flowers along a single stem; an inflorescence with stalked (pedillate) flowers arising along an elongated central axis.
rachis	the stalk to which the leaflets of a compound leaf are attached.

rambling	not erect. A plant that has arching stems and may use other plants for support.
ray floret	the outer ring of florets of a daisy inflorescence, each with an expanded blade similar to and resembling a petal.
reticulated	arranged in a network.
revolute	with margins rolled backwards.
rhizome	a horizontal underground root.
rhizomatous	referring to rhizomes.
rib	(in snails) an elongate sculptural element of a shell, raised above the surrounding surface.
rosette	radiating cluster of leaves or other organs usually at or near ground level.
run-on	areas in the landscape that receive (and may hold) most of their water by drainage from more elevated areas.
salps	a group of jelly-like marine invertebrate animals.
saprophyte	a plant living on dead organic matter.
sepal	the outer whorl of a flower that protects the petals. Usually green.
septate	divided into one or more partitions.
sessile	attached without a stalk, for example a sessile leaf lacks a petiole.
sorus, (Pl. sori)	a cluster of spore-bearing structures (sporangia) on a fern leaf.
spadix	a type of inflorescence with small flowers clustered on a central axis.
spathe	a large bract enclosing an inflorescence; often found in grasses and aroids.
spikelet	the ultimate cluster of flowers in a grass inflorescence.
spinose	with spines.
spinulose	with small spines.
spire	the coiled end of a snail's shell; all whorls of a spiral shell exclusive of the body whorl.
sporangia	the spore-bearing organ, commonly referred to the reproductive structures of a fern.
stellate	star-like hairs.
stipe	a stalk that supports a structure, for example a stalk attaching an ovary to the receptacle.
stochastic	happening by chance, randomly, such as cyclones, or rockfalls.
style	the stalk that connects the stigma to the ovary.

subdeltoid	almost the shape of an equilateral triangle.
subglobose	almost spherical in shape.
subsessile	almost sessile, there may be a small stalk present.
suture	the line at which two structures join.
sympatric	living in the same (or overlapping) area.
swale	the lower (valley) area between two dunes.
talus	a sloping mass of rock debris at the base of a cliff.
terete	round in cross section.
tomentose	with tomentum.
tomentum	a covering of short, soft matted woolly hairs.
tortuous	twisted or bent, usually refers to hairs.
trilobed	with three lobes.
tuberous	bearing tubers, swollen underground bulb-like structures.
umbel	a type of inflorescence with the pedicels of individual flowers originating from a common point.
umbilicus	(in snails) the hole around which the inner surface of the shell is coiled.
vagrant	only occasionally found in an area, often by accident or caprice.
ventral	referring to the front or underside (opposite of dorsal).
vermiculation	to move like a worm, or appear worm-eaten.
villous	having long soft shaggy hairs.
viscid	sticky.
water column	the open-water environment, as distinct from the sea-bed or shore.
whorl	(in plants) an arrangement of three or more leaves, petals or other organs radiating from a simple node; (in snails) a single complete turn of 360° in the spiral growth of the shell.

APPENDIX A

List of Northern Territory plant and animal species currently coded as Data Deficient

PLANTS

Acacia amentifera
Acacia aneura var. Bloods Range
Acacia aneura var. Blue Mulga
Acacia aneura var. *conifera*
Acacia aneura var. *microcarpa*
Acacia armitii
Acacia colei var. *ileocarpa*
Acacia ditricha
Acacia galioides var. *glabriflora*
Acacia helmsiana
Acacia longipedunculata
Acacia macdonnellensis subsp. *teretifolia*
Acacia manipularis
Acacia nyssophylla
Acacia olgana
Acacia oswaldii
Acacia pachyacra
Acacia pachycarpa
Acacia prainii
Acacia ramulosa var. *linophylla*
Acacia rigens
Acacia sabulosa
Acacia sp. affin. *oncinocarpa*
Acacia sp. Barklys
Acacia sp. Indiana Station
Acacia sp. Krichauff Range
Acacia sp. Kulgera
Acacia sp. Lake Mackay
Acacia sp. laterite
Acacia stellaticeps
Acacia synchronicia
Acalypha lanceolata
Acalypha pubiflora
Acalypha pubiflora subsp. *australica*
Acanthus ebracteatus
Acanthus ebracteatus subsp. *ebarbatus*
Acmella grandiflora var. *discoides*
Acrachne racemosa
Actinostachys wagneri
Adiantum atroviride
Adiantum diaphanum
Adriana tomentosa var. *tomentosa*
Aeginetia saccharicola
Alectryon kimberleyanus
Alysicarpus brownii
Amaranthus macrocarpus
Amaranthus macrocarpus var. *macrocarpus*
Amaranthus sp. Alice Springs
Amaranthus sp. Birrindudu Station
Amyema conspicua
Amyema conspicua subsp. *obscurinervis*
Amyema herbertiana
Amyema miraculosa
Amyema miraculosa subsp. *boormanii*
Aphyllodium stylosanthoides
Aponogeton queenslandicus
Arabidella trisecta
Arenga australasica
Aristida kimberleyensis
Aristida lazaridis
Aristida perniciosa

Aristida polyclados
Aristida sp. Upper Fergusson
Aristida strigosa
Asplenium sp. Litchfield
Asplenium sp. Nabarlek
Astartea intratropica
Astrebla lappacea
Atalaya sp. Elizabeth River
Atriplex angulata
Atriplex crassipes
Atriplex crassipes var. *crassipes*
Atriplex lindleyi subsp. *inflata*
Atriplex morrisii
Atriplex nummularia subsp. *omissa*
Austrodolichos sp. Arnhem
Austrostipa trichophylla
Bidens subalternans
Blumea benthamiana
Blumea lacera
Blumea pungens
Bolbitis quoyana
Bonamia alatisemina
Bonamia linearis
Boronia amplectens
Boronia decumbens
Boronia gravicocca
Boronia jucunda
Boronia wilsonii
Bothriochloa decipiens
Brachychiton sp. Wangi
Bulbostylis densa
Bulbostylis sp. Koongarra
Butomopsis latifolia
Byblis rorida
Caesia setifera
Cajanus crassicaulis
Calandrinia arenicola
Calandrinia disperma
Calandrinia polyandra
Calandrinia remota
Calandrinia sp. Yinberrie Hills
Calandrinia strophiolata
Callicarpa brevistyla
Calochilus holtzei
Calotis cuneifolia
Carex fascicularis
Cartonema sp. Goyder River
Centella asiatica
Centranthera tranquebarica
Chamaecrista deserti
Chamaecrista nomame var. *grandiflora*
Chenopodium pumilio
Chloris divaricata
Chloris pumilio
Cladium mariscus
Clausena sp. Tipperary
Cleome linophylla
Cochlospermum sp. Arnhem Land
Coelachne pulchella
Comesperma viscidulum
Commelina tricarinata
Convolvulus crispifolius
Corchorus macropetalus

Corchorus pascuorum
Corymbia pachycarpa subsp. *pachycarpa*
Corynotheca asperata
Corynotheca micrantha var. *gracilis*
Crateva religiosa
Crinum pedunculatum
Crinum venosum
Crotalaria dissitiflora subsp. *dissitiflora*
Crotalaria eremaea subsp. *eremaea*
Crotalaria montana var. *exserta*
Crotalaria novae-hollandiae subsp. *novae-hollandiae*
Crotalaria sessiliflora
Croton dockrillii
Cullen corallum
Cullen cuneatum
Cullen discolor
Cullen graveolens
Cuscuta campestris
Cyathula prostrata
Cycas maconochiei subsp. *viridis*
Cymaria dichotoma
Cymbopogon dependens
Cynanchum brachystelmoides
Cynanchum christineae
Cynanchum leibianum
Cynometra iripa
Cyperus compactus
Cyperus cracens
Cyperus cyperinus
Cyperus fucosus
Cyperus haspan subsp. *haspan*
Cyperus oxycarpus
Cyperus pilosus
Cyperus scaber
Cyperus sp. Bradshaw
Cyperus sp. Edith River
Cyperus sp. red base
Cyperus tenuiculmis
Cyperus unioloides
Cyperus viscidulus
Daucus glochidiatus var. Mulga hills
Daviesia eremaea
Dendrobium lobbii
Dendrobium trilamellatum
Dentella browniana
Dicarpidium monoicum
Dicliptera australis
Dicrastylis doranii
Didymoplexis pallens
Digitaria benthamiana
Digitaria leucostachya
Digitaria oraria
Digitaria setigera
Diodontium filifolium
Diplopeltis stuartii var. *glandulosa*
Dipteracanthus australasicus subsp. *dalyensis*
Dipteracanthus bracteatus
Distichostemon barklyanus
Dopatrium junceum
Drosera kenneallyi
Duboisia arenitensis
Echinochloa macrandra
Eclipta alatocarpa

Ectrosia lasioclada
Eleocharis acutangula
Eleocharis retroflexa
Elionurus citreus
Enneapogon intermedius
Enneapogon robustissimus
Enteropogon minutus
Eragrostis concinna
Eragrostis crateriformis
Eragrostis lanicaulis
Eragrostis petraea
Eragrostis potamophila
Eragrostis sororia
Eragrostis sp. Gibber
Eremophila hughesii
Eremophila hughesii subsp. Bloods Range
Eremophila hughesii subsp. hughesii
Eremophila sp. Lake Amadeus
Eremophila sp. Mt Edward
Eremophila tietkensii
Eriachne axillaris
Eriachne basalis
Eriachne glauca var. barbinodis
Eriachne pauciflora
Eriachne sp. Davenport Ranges
Eriachne vesiculosa
Eriocaulon carpentariae
Eriocaulon odontospermum
Eriocaulon tricornum
Eriochlamys behrii
Erodium angustilobum
Eryngium supinum
Eucalyptus gregoriensis
Eucalyptus helenae
Eucalyptus limitaris
Eucalyptus sp. Montejinni Station
Eucalyptus sparsa
Eulophia bicallosa
Euphorbia ferdinandii
Euphorbia sp. Beddome Range
Euphorbia sp. Nitmiluk large
Euphorbia sp. Nitmiluk small
Ficus tinctoria
Ficus tinctoria subsp. tinctoria
Fimbristylis arthrostyloides
Fimbristylis bisumbellata
Fimbristylis brownii
Fimbristylis corynocarya
Fimbristylis dipsacea
Fimbristylis distincta
Fimbristylis dolera
Fimbristylis dunlopii
Fimbristylis fimbristyloides
Fimbristylis insignis
Fimbristylis merrillii
Fimbristylis sp. Beverley Springs
Fimbristylis sp. Deaf Adder Gorge
Fimbristylis sp. Latz sp.F
Fimbristylis sp. minute
Fimbristylis sp. Montejinni
Fimbristylis sp. Mount Brockman
Fimbristylis sp. Mowla Bluff
Fimbristylis sp. Nitmiluk
Fimbristylis sp. Timber Creek
Fimbristylis spiralis
Fimbristylis subaristata
Fimbristylis tomentosa

Fimbristylis velata
Finlaysonia obovata
Frankenia muscosa
Frankenia stuartii
Fuirena arenosa
Fuirena nudiflora
Gardenia jabiluka
Gleichenia dicarpa
Glinus sessiliflorus
Glycine arenaria
Glycine sp. Arnhem
Gomphrena atrorubra
Gomphrena conica
Gomphrena connata
Gomphrena humilis
Gomphrena involucrata
Gomphrena lacinulata
Gomphrena leptoclada
Gomphrena leptoclada subsp. leptoclada
Gomphrena leptoclada subsp. saxosa
Gonocarpus implexus
Goodenia anfracta
Goodenia argillacea
Goodenia azurea subsp. Warburton
Goodenia chthonocephala
Goodenia cylindrocarpa
Goodenia durackiana
Goodenia halophila
Goodenia kakadu
Goodenia malvina
Goodenia minutiflora
Goodenia nigrescens
Goodenia potamica
Goodenia quadrifida
Goodenia sp. Great Sandy Desert
Goodenia sp. Spirit Hills
Goodenia subauriculata
Graptophyllum spinigerum
Grevillea dunlopii
Grevillea miniata
Grevillea pyramidalis subsp. longiloba
Grevillea refracta subsp. glandulifera
Habenaria elongata
Habenaria ferdinandi
Habenaria hymenophylla
Habenaria sp. sand flats
Habenaria triplonema
Haemodorum flaviflorum
Hakea rhombales
Halodule uninervis
Halosarcia calyptrata
Halosarcia halocnemoides subsp. tenuis
Halosarcia indica subsp. bidens
Halosarcia undulata
Hedyotis auricularia
Hedyotis auricularia var. melanesica
Heliotropium albrechtii
Heliotropium ballii
Heliotropium brachythrix
Heliotropium cupressinum
Heliotropium dichotomum
Heliotropium epacrideum
Heliotropium euodes
Heliotropium fasciculatum
Heliotropium foveolatum
Heliotropium geocharis
Heliotropium heteranthum

Heliotropium inexplicitum
Heliotropium leptaleum
Heliotropium parviantrum
Heliotropium prostratum
Heliotropium pulvinum
Heliotropium sphaericum
Heliotropium subreniforme
Heliotropium tachyglossoides
Heliotropium transforme
Heliotropium uniflorum
Hibbertia muelleri
Hibiscus aneuthe
Hibiscus arenicola
Hibiscus bacalusius
Hibiscus fryxellii
Hibiscus fryxellii var. fryxellii
Hibiscus fryxellii var. mollis
Hibiscus lobatus
Hibiscus riceae
Hibiscus setulosus
Hibiscus vitifolius
Hibiscus vitifolius subsp. vitifolius
Hoppea dichotoma
Hullsia argillicola
Hydrocotyle sp. Harts Range
Hygrochloa cravenii
Hypserpa decumbens
Hypserpa polyandra
Indigofera adenotricha
Indigofera ammobia
Indigofera polygaloides
Indigofera schultziana
Indigofera sp. Areyonga
Indigofera sp. Marrawal
Intsia bijuga
Iotasperma sessilifolium
Ipomoea brassii
Ipomoea mauritiana
Ipomoea sp. OT Station
Ipomoea sp. Ramingining
Ipomoea stolonifera
Ischaemum australe var. villosum
Ischaemum rugosum var. segetum
Iseilema calvum
Iseilema convexum
Iseilema trichopus
Isoetes cristata
Isolepis australiensis
Isotoma sp. Kakadu
Isotoma sp. Tanumbirini
Ixiochlamys nana
Jacksonia aculeata
Jacksonia sp. bifida
Jacquemontia sp. Douglas Daly
Keraudrenia hookeriana
Lawrencia sp. Glen Helen
Lawrencia sp. The Granites
Lawrencia viridi-grisea
Leiocarpa tomentosa
Lepturus geminatus
Lepturus xerophilus
Lindernia cowiei
Lindernia sp. Brennans Showy Anthers
Lindernia sp. Litchfield
Lindernia sp. long leaved
Lindernia sp. Willowra
Lindernia tectanthera

Liparis habenarina
Lipocarpha chinensis
Livistona nasmophila
Lobelia sp. Cox Peninsula
Logania centralis
Lysiana maritima
Lythrum paradoxum
Macrothelypteris torresiana
Maireana appressa
Maireana lobiflora
Maireana sedifolia
Maireana sp. Rainbow Valley
Malaccotristicha australis
Malacocera tricornis
Malaxis acuminata
Marsdenia muelleri
Marsilea costulifera
Marsilea sp. Neutral Junction
Melaleuca acacioides subsp. alsophila
Melaleuca sp. Spirit Hills
Merremia sp. Elliott
Micraira dunlopii
Micraira inserta
Micraira sp. Purnululu
Micraira spinifera
Microchloa indica
Microcorys elliptica
Microlepia speluncae
Millotia greevesii
Millotia greevesii subsp. greevesii
Millotia greevesii subsp. helmsii
Mitrasacme brachystemonea
Mitrasacme epigaea
Mitrasacme geniculosa
Mitrasacme inornata
Mitrasacme nudicaulis var. citrina
Mitrasacme patens
Mitrasacme phascoides
Mitrasacme secedens
Mitrasacme stellata
Mitrasacme troglodytica
Molineria capitulata
Muellerargia timorensis
Mukia micrantha
Mukia sp. Soudan
Murchisonia volubilis
Najas browniana
Najas foveolata
Najas pseudograminea
Nephrolepis arida
Nervilia peltata
Nervilia plicata
Nesaea repens
Nesaea striatiflora
Newcastelia cladotricha
Nicotiana debneyi
Nicotiana debneyi subsp. monoschizocarpa
Nicotiana rosulata subsp. rosulata
Nymphaea immutabilis
Nymphaea immutabilis subsp. immutabilis
Nymphoides exiliflora
Olax spartea
Oldenlandia delicata
Oldenlandia intonsa
Oldenlandia mitrasacmoides subsp. nigricans
Oldenlandia sp. Central Ranges
Oldenlandia sp. minute

Oldenlandia spathulata
Olearia arida
Olearia xerophila
Operculina sp. Cotton Island
Oplismenus hirtellus
Oryza minuta
Osteocarpum acropterum
Osteocarpum acropterum var. acropterum
Oxalis radicosa
Ozothamnus sp. Petermann Ranges
Pachystoma pubescens
Panicum latzii
Paractaenum novae-hollandiae
Paractaenum novae-hollandiae subsp. reversum
Paspalidium gracile
Paspalidium udum
Pavetta granitica
Pavetta tenella
Pennisetum basedowii
Peplidium foecundum
Peplidium sp. Marla
Peplidium sp. Tanami
Persicaria sp. Bulkine Billabong
Persicaria strigosa
Phacellothrix cladochaeta
Phaleria macrocarpa
Phoringopsis byrnesii
Phyllanthus armstrongii
Phyllanthus cauticola
Phyllanthus lacerosus
Phyllanthus lacunellus
Phyllanthus sp. broad smooth seeds
Phyllanthus sp. narrow tuberculate seed
Physalis micrantha
Pimelea penicillaris
Pityrodia byrnesii
Pityrodia chorisepala
Pityrodia loricata
Plantago cunninghamii
Plantago multiscapa
Pluchea sp. Ormiston
Polycarpaea multicaulis
Polygala gabrielae
Polygala sp. Bradshaw
Polygala sp. ciliate alae
Polymeria calycina
Polymeria pusilla
Polymeria sp. Western Tanami
Poranthera microphylla
Portulaca sp. finely echinate
Pouzolzia hirta
Proiphys alba
Prostanthera centralis
Psydrax paludosa
Psydrax saligna
Pteris comans
Pteris vittata
Pterocaulon sphaeranthoides
Ptilotus blackii
Ptilotus brachyanthus
Ptilotus capitatus
Ptilotus chippendalei
Ptilotus comatus
Ptilotus exaltatus var. glaber
Ptilotus gardneri
Ptilotus gardneri var. gardneri
Ptilotus gaudichaudii var. parviflorus

Ptilotus leucocoma
Ptilotus lophotrichus
Ptilotus obovatus var. griseus
Ptilotus robynsianus
Ptilotus rotundatus
Ptilotus royceanus
Ptilotus sp. Sandstone
Pupalia lappacea
Pycnoporus coccineus
Pycnosorus eremaeus
Remusatia vivipara
Rhodanthe gossypina
Rhynchosia filiformis
Ricinocarpos sp. Moyle
Rorippa eustylis
Rutidosis helichrysoides subsp. acutiglumis
Sarcolobus ritae
Sarcostemma brevipedicellatum
Sarcostemma esculentum
Sauropus arenosus
Sauropus filicinus
Sauropus gracilis
Sauropus sp. Austral Downs
Sauropus sp. Mann River
Sauropus thesioides
Scaevola graminea
Scaevola humilis
Scaevola obovata
Scaevola sp. Mt. Liebig
Schizachyrium dolosum
Schoenus centralis
Schoenus sp. Douglas Springs
Scleria biflora
Scleria biflora subsp. biflora
Scleria carphiformis
Scleria mikawana
Scleria pergracilis
Scleria psilorrhiza
Scleria terrestris
Sclerolaena limbata
Sclerolaena symoniana
Sedopsis sp. sandstone
Sedopsis sp. West Arnhem
Selaginella sp. Mt Howship
Senecio depressicola
Senna artemisioides subsp. James Range
Senna artemisioides subsp. Kuyunba
Senna artemisioides subsp. symonii
Senna procumbens
Sesbania erubescens
Sesbania javanica
Setaria pumila
Setaria pumila subsp. pallide-fusca
Shonia territorialis
Sida echinocarpa
Sida rohlenae subsp. occidentalis
Sida sp. Chewings Range
Sida sp. Hale River
Sida sp. Horseshoe Bend
Sida sp. Petermann Ranges
Sida sp. Watarrka
Sida subcordata
Solanum carduiforme
Solanum lasiophyllum
Solanum sp. Juicy fruit
Solanum sp. Litchfield
Solanum sp. Mt Brockman

Solanum yirrkalense
Sonchus hydrophilus
Sorghum grande
Spathoglottis paulinae
Spermacoce brachystema
Spermacoce brevidens
Spermacoce cardiophora
Spermacoce caudata
Spermacoce gibba
Spermacoce inaperta
Spermacoce juncta
Spermacoce laevigata
Spermacoce lamprosperma
Spermacoce occidentalis
Spermacoce pessima
Spermacoce phalloides
Spermacoce resinosula
Spermacoce stigmatosa
Spermacoce suprahila
Sphaerostephanos heterocarpus
Sphaerostephanos unitus
Sphaerostephanos unitus var. unitus
Sporobolus latzii
Sporobolus scabridus
Stackhousia muricata var. annual
Stackhousia sp. Lake Mackay
Stemodia grossa
Stephania japonica var. japonica
Stylidium accedens
Stylidium aquaticum
Stylidium diffusum
Stylidium divergens
Stylidium ensatum
Stylidium fluminense
Stylidium nominatum
Stylidium prophyllum
Stylidium simulans
Stylidium stenophyllum
Stylidium symonii
Stylidium tenerrimum
Swainsona acuticarinata
Swainsona cyclocarpa
Swainsona disjuncta
Swainsona laciniata
Swainsona oliveri
Swainsona purpurea
Swainsona tenuis
Symplectrodia gracilis
Synaptantha scleranthoides
Synaptantha tillaeacea var. hispidula
Synaptantha tillaeacea var. Western Tanami
Syzygium arenitense
Tacca maculata
Taenitis pinnata
Tectaria siifolia
Tephrosia crocea
Tephrosia forrestiana
Tephrosia procera
Tephrosia sp. crows foot
Tephrosia sp. Dunes
Tephrosia sp. granite
Tephrosia sp. Maud Creek
Tephrosia sp. metamorphics
Tephrosia sp. Mistake Creek
Tephrosia sp. Tee Dee Hills
Tephrosia valleculata
Thoracostachyum sumatranum

Threlkeldia inchoata
Thuarea involuta
Tietkensia corrickiae
Trachymene ceratocarpa
Trachymene umbratica
Trachymene villosa
Tragia arnhemica
Tribulopis sessilis
Tribulus ranunculiflorus
Tribulus sp. Long style
Trichanthodium skirrophorum
Trichodesma zeylanicum var. grandiflorum
Triglochin multifructum
Triglochin sp. New Haven
Triglochin sp. Tempe Downs
Triodia aristiglumis
Triodia aurita
Triodia helmsii
Triodia radonensis
Triodia roscida
Triodia triticoides
Trithuria sp. Maningrida
Triumfetta antrorsa
Triumfetta aquila
Triumfetta chaetocarpa
Triumfetta clivorum
Triumfetta clivorum subsp. brevipetala
Triumfetta deserticola
Triumfetta fissurata
Triumfetta inermis
Triumfetta litticola
Triumfetta oenpelliensis
Triumfetta prostrata
Triumfetta repens
Triumfetta ryeae
Triumfetta ryeae subsp. ryeae
Triumfetta sp. fleshy
Triumfetta triandra
Triumfetta viridis
Tropidia curculigoides
Typha orientalis
Typhonium johnsonianum
Typhonium liliifolium
Typhonium praetermissum
Typhonium russell-smithii
Typhonium sp. Berry Springs
Urochloa argentea
Urochloa atrisola
Utricularia australis
Utricularia foveolata
Utricularia sp. red
Utricularia stellaris
Utricularia tubulata
Vachellia suberosa
Vallisneria caulescens
Velleia panduriformis
Verbena macrostachya
Vernonia patula
Vigna marina
Viscum whitei
Vitex velutinifolia
Vittadinia sp. Junction Reserve
Vittadinia spechtii
Websteria confervoides
Whiteochloa multiciliata
Yakirra muelleri
Zehneria mucronata

Zornia acuta
Zornia adenophora
Zornia muelleriana subsp. muelleriana
Zornia oligantha
Zygophyllum aurantiacum subsp. simplicifolium
Zygophyllum iodocarpum
Zygophyllum rowelliae

INVERTEBRATES

Austropeplea lessoni	freshwater snail
Charon oenpelli	Oenpelli Whip-scorpion
Cristigibba wesselensis	snail
Hemisaga elongata	Northern Katydid
Hoploscapanes barbarossa	Spectacular Elephant Beetle
Panesthia tepperi	Darwin Giant Cockroach
Pupilla ficulnea	snail
Semotrachia hughana	snail
Sinumelon hullanum	snail
Torresitrachia funium	snail

Ants

Bothroponera spp. (sublaevis group) Howard Springs (1)
Bothroponera spp. (sublaevis group) Howard Springs (2)
Bothroponera spp. (sublaevis group) Melville Island
Camponotus sp. (vitreus group) Melville Island
Cerapachys sp. (longitarsus group) Berrimah
Leptogenys sp. (conigera group) Murgenella
Leptogenys spp. (clarki group) Darwin River
Leptogenys spp. (clarki group) Howard Springs
Myrmecia sp. near desertorum Marrawal Plateau
Probolomyrmex greavesi
Rhytidoponera sp. Central Arnhem Land
Rhytidoponera sp. (aurata group) Wangi Falls

Butterflies

Acrodipsas decima	Black Ant-blue
Acrodipsas myrmecophila	Small Ant-blue
Appias albina albina	White Albatross
Borbo cinnara	Common Rice Swift
Candalides cyprotus	Copper Pencil-blue
Croitana arenaria arenaria	Inland Sand Skipper
Danaus chrysippus cratippus	Lesser Wanderer
Danaus plexipus	Monarch
Deudorix diovis	Bright Cornelian
Delias aganippe	Spotted Jezabel
Hypolimnas anomala	Crow Eggfly
Junonia erigone	Northern Argus
Leptotes plinius pseudocassius	Plumbago Blue
Papilio aegeus aegeus	Orchard Swallowtail
Papilio anactus	Dainty Swallowtail
Petrelaea tombugensis	Mauve Line-blue
Protographium leosthenes geimbia	Kakadu Fourbarred Swordtail
Pseudoborbo bevani	Lesser Rice Swift
Sahulana scintillate	Glistening Line-blue
Suniana lascivia lasus	Dingy Grass-dart
Taractrocera ilia ilia	Rock Grass-dart
Telicota ancilla baudina	Green Darter
Telicota mesoptis ssp.	Narrow-brand Darter
Thechinetes albocincta	Bitter Bush-blue
Yoma sabina parva	Lurcher

FISH

Aetomylaeus vespertilio	Ornate Eagle Ray
Ammissidens hainesi	Ridged Catfish
Amniataba percoides	Barred Grunter
Antennarius commersoni	Giant Frogfish

Anyperodon leucogrammicus	White-lined Rockcod
Ariopsis pectoralis	Saw-spine Catfish
Assiculus punctatus	Blue-spotted Dottyback
Atelomycterus sp. A	Banded Catshark
Campichthys tricarinatus	Three-keel Pipefish
Caranx kleinii	Razorbelly Trevally
Carcharhinus albimarginatus	Silvertip Shark
Carcharhinus obscurus	Dusky Shark
Carcharhinus plumbeus	Sandbar Shark
Carcharias taurus	Grey Nurse Shark
Chromileptes altivelis	Barramundi Cod
Cinetodus froggatti	Froggatt's Catfish
Craterocephalus stercusmuscarum	Fly-specked Hardyhead
Dasyatis annotata	Plain Maskray
Dasyatis fluviorum	Estuary Stingray
Dasyatis leylandi	Painted Maskray
Dinematichthys megasoma	Robust Cusk
Epinephelus lanceolatus	Giant Grouper
Eucrossorhinus dasypogon	Tasselled Wobbegong
Festucalex cinctus	Girdled Pipefish
Galeus sp. A	Slender Sawtail Shark
Glaucosoma magnificum	Threadfin Pearl-perch
Glossogobius species 2	Munro's Goby
Halicampus brocki	Tasselled Pipefish
Halicampus dunckeri	Ridgenose Pipefish
Halicampus grayi	Mud Pipefish
Haliichthys taeniophora	Ribboned Pipehorse
Hemiarius insidator	Flat Catfish
Hemigaleus microstoma	Weasel Shark
Hemitaurichthys polylepis	Pyramid Butterflyfish
Heptranchias perlo	Sharpnose Sevengill Shark
Himantura chaophraya	Freshwater Whipray
Himantura granulata	Mangrove Whipray
Hippichthys cyanospilus	Blue-speckled Pipefish
Hippichthys parvicarinatus	Short-keeled Pipefish
Hippichthys penicillus	Beady Pipefish
Hippichthys spicifer	Belly-bar Pipefish
Hippocampus alatus	Winged Seahorse
Hippocampus angustus	Western Spiny Seahorse
Hippocampus dahli	Low-crowned Seahorse
Hippocampus hystrix	Thorny Seahorse
Hippocampus kuda	Spotted Seahorse
Hippocampus multispinosus	Northern Spiny Seahorse
Hippocampus planifrons	Flatface Seahorse
Hippocampus spinosissimus	Hedgehog Seahorse
Hippocampus taeniopterus	Common Seahorse
Hippocampus trimaculatus	Longnose Seahorse
Hypseleotris sp.	Katherine River Gudgeon
Iriatherina werneri	Threadfin Rainbowfish
Lophichthys boschmai	Boschma's Frogfish
Lophiocharon trisignatus	Spotted-tailed Anglerfish
Meiacanthus luteus	Yellow Fangbelly
Micrognathus micronotopterus	Tidepool Pipefish
Mogurnda mogurnda	Northern Trout Gudgeon
Mustelus sp. A	Grey Gummy Shark
Orectolobus wardi	Northern Wobbegong
Pingalla midgleyi	Midgley's Grunter
Pomacentrus littoralis	Smoky Damsel
Pomacentrus milleri	Miller's Damsel
Porochilus argenteus	Silver Catfish
Protonibea diacanthus	Black Jewfish
Psammoperca waigiensis	Sand Bass
Pseudamia nigra	Estuary Cardinalfish
Pseudanthias cooperi	Red Basslet
Pseudochromis wilsoni	Yellowfin Dottyback
Redigobius balteatus	Rhinohorn Goby
Rendahlia jaubertensis	Jaubert Sole
Rhincodon typus	Whale Shark
Rhinoprenes pentanemus	Threadfin Scat
Rhizoprionodon oligolinx	Grey Sharpnose Shark
Scortum ogilbyi	Gulf Grunter
Silhouettea hoesei	Hoese's Silhouette-goby
Solegnathus hardwickii	Pallid Pipehorse
Solegnathus lettiensis	Gunther's Pipehorse
Syngnathoides biaculeatus	Double-ended Pipehorse
Tathicarpus butleri	Blackspot Anglerfish
Tetrabrachium ocellatum	Humpback Anglerfish
Thryssa scratchleyi	Freshwater Thryssa
Trachyrhamphus bicoarctatus	Bentstick pipefish
Trachyrhamphus longirostris	Straightstick Pipefish
Urogymnus asperrimus	Porcupine Ray
Zenarchopterus buffonis	Northern River Garfish
Zenarchopterus caudovittatus	Long-jawed River Garfish
Zenarchopterus dispar	Spoonfin River Garfish
Zenarchopterus gilli	Shortnose River Garfish
Zenarchopterus rasori	Short River Garfish

FROGS

Limnodynastes depressus	Flat-headed Frog
Limnodynastes ornatus	Ornate Burrowing Frog
Litoria bicolor	Northern Dwarf Tree Frog
Uperoleia minima	
Uperoleia orientalis	Alexandria Toadlet

REPTILES

Acanthophis antarcticus	Southern Death Adder
Antaresia childreni	Children's Python
Boiga irregularis	Brown Tree Snake
Chelodina burrungandii	Sandstone Long-neck Turtle
Chelodina sp. aff *expansa*	
Cryptoblepharus litoralis	Beach Snake-eyed Skink
Cryptoblepharus sp. (Mount Borradaile)	
Cryptoblepharus sp. (Mosquito Flat)	
Cryptagama aurita	Gravel Dragon
Cryptophis pallidiceps	Northern Small-eyed Snake
Ctenophorus rufescens	Rusty Crevice Dragon
Ctenotus arnhemensis	Arnhem Land Ctenotus
Ctenotus astictus	
Ctenotus gagudju	Kakadu Ctenotus
Ctenotus kurnbudj	Alligator Rivers Ctenotus
Ctenotus lateralis	
Ctenotus stuartii	Point Stuart Ctenotus
Delma pax	
Demansia olivacea	Olive Whip Snake
Demansia papuensis	Greater Black Whip Snake
Demansia torquata	Collared Whip Snake
Demansia vestigiata	Black Whip Snake
Dendrelaphis punctulatus	Green Tree Snake
Enhydrina schistosa	Beaked Sea-snake
Enhydris polylepis	Macleay's Water Snake
Eretmochelys imbricata	Hawksbill Turtle
Gehyra koira	
Glaphyromorphus nigricaudis	Dark-tailed Skink
Hydrophis atriceps	Black-headed Sea-snake
Hydrophis czeblukovi	Fine-spined Sea-snake
Hydrophis inornatus	Plain Sea-snake
Lepidochelys olivacea	Olive Ridley
Morethia adelaidensis	
Natator depressus	Flatback Turtle
Ophidiocephalus taeniatus	Bronzeback
Oxyuranus microlepidotus	Fierce Snake
Oxyuranus scutellatus	Taipan
Pogona mitchelli	
Proablepharus naranjicaudus	
Ramphotyphlops centralis	Centralian Blind Snake
Ramphotyphlops kimberleyensis	Kimberley Shallow-soil Blind Snake
Ramphotyphlops nema	Small Darwin Blind Snake
Ramphotyphlops yirrikalae	Yirrkala Blind Snake
Simoselaps morrisi	
Strophurus robinsoni	
Suta ordensis	
Tiliqua scincoides	Common Blue-tongued Lizard
Tympanocryptis uniformis	Even-scaled Earless Dragon
Varanus glauerti	Kakadu Sandstone Goanna
Varanus scalaris	Spotted Tree Monitor
Varanus spenceri	Spencer's Monitor
Vermicella multifasciata	Northern Bandy-bandy

BIRDS

Calidris melanotos	Pectoral Sandpiper
Calonectris leucomelas	Streaked Shearwater
Conopophila whitei	Grey Honeyeater
Dacelo leachii	Blue-winged Kookaburra
Fregata minor	Greater Frigatebird
Gallinago hardwickii	Latham's Snipe
Gallinago megala	Swinhoe's Snipe
Gallinago stenura	Pin-tailed Snipe
Ixobrychus flavicollis	Black Bittern
Ixobrychus minutus	Little Bittern
Oceanites oceanicus	Wilson's Storm-petrel
Oceanodroma matsudairae	Matsudaira's Storm-petrel
Pedionomus torquatus	Plains-wanderer
Porzana fluminea	Australian Spotted Crake
Porzana pusilla	Baillon's Crake
Porzana tabuensis	Spotless Crake
Puffinus pacificus	Wedge-tailed Shearwater
Stercorarius parasiticus	Arctic Jaeger
Stercorarius pomarinus	Pomarine Jaeger
Turnix castanota	Chestnut-backed Button-quail

MAMMALS

Antechinus bellus	Fawn Antechinus
Balaenoptera borealis	Sei Whale
Balaenoptera edeni	Bryde's Whale
Balaenoptera musculus	Blue Whale
Dasyuroides byrnei	Kowari
Delphinus delphis	Common Dolphin
Globicephala macrorhynchus	Short-finned Pilot Whale
Grampus griseus	Risso's Dolphin
Kogia simus	Dwarf Sperm Whale
Macropus bernardus	Black Wallaroo
Megaptera novaeangliae	Humpback Whale
Orcinus orca	Killer Whale
Peponocephala electra	Melon-headed Whale
Physeter catodon	Sperm Whale
Planigale gilesi	Giles Planigale
Planigale tenuirostris	Narrow-nosed Planigale
Pseudantechinus bilarni	Sandstone Antechinus
Saccolaimus saccolaimus	Bare-rumped Sheathtail Bat
Sminthopsis psammophila	Sandhill Dunnart
Stenella attenuata	Spotted Dolphin
Stenella longirostris	Spinner Dolphin
Steno bredanensis	Rough-toothed Dolphin
Xeromys myoides	False Water-rat (Water-mouse)
Ziphius cavirostris	Cuvier's Beaked Whale

INDEX to Northern Territory threatened species

Z